A NEW HISTORY
OF IOWA

A NEW HISTORY OF IOWA

JEFF BREMER

University Press of Kansas

© 2023 by the University Press of Kansas
All rights reserved

Published by the University Press of Kansas (Lawrence, Kansas 66045), which was organized by the Kansas Board of Regents and is operated and funded by Emporia State University, Fort Hays State University, Kansas State University, Pittsburg State University, the University of Kansas, and Wichita State University.

Library of Congress Cataloging-in-Publication Data

Names: Bremer, Jeff, author.
Title: A new history of Iowa / Jeff Bremer.
Description: Lawrence, Kansas : University Press of Kansas, [2023] | Includes bibliographical references and index.
Identifiers: LCCN 2022061351 (print) | LCCN 2022061352 (ebook)
  ISBN 9780700635559 (cloth)
  ISBN 9780700635566 (paperback)
  ISBN 9780700635573 (ebook)
Subjects: LCSH: Iowa—History.
Classification: LCC F621 .B76 2023 (print) | LCC F621 (ebook) | DDC 977.7—dc23/eng/20221221
LC record available at https://lccn.loc.gov/2022061351.
LC ebook record available at https://lccn.loc.gov/2022061352.

British Library Cataloguing-in-Publication Data is available.

10 9 8 7 6 5 4 3

For Yana
beloved wife

and

Greg Olson
Scoutmaster

Contents

Introduction   1

Part I—Iowa to the Civil War

  1. Native Iowa: Iowa to 1833   9
  2. Iowa Territory, 1833–1846   32
  3. Frontier Iowa, 1833–1870   51
  4. Slavery, Politics, and Transportation before the Civil War   72
  5. Iowa and the Civil War, 1861–1870   90

Part II—Iowa from the Civil War to 1929

  6. Immigrants, Railroads, and Farm Protest   113
  7. Religion, Education, and Rural Life   134
  8. Cities, Industry, and Technology, 1833–1920   165
  9. Suffrage, Prohibition, and Politics, 1870–1920   185
  10. Iowa in World War I and the 1920s   207

Part III—Iowa since 1929

  11. The Great Depression and Iowa   235
  12. Iowa in World War II   256

13. Postwar Iowa, 1945–1975   276
14. Iowa and the Farm Crisis, 1975–2000   301
15. Iowa in the Twenty-First Century   322

Acknowledgments   343
Notes   349
Bibliographic Essay   437
Index   447

Introduction

Iowa has always been known for farming, growing corn, soybeans, and other crops on some of the richest soil in the world. The state is more agricultural, less urban, and less diverse than the rest of the United States. These characteristics make it a very midwestern place. When Americans think of Iowa, they think about farms and small towns. It is still a rural state. Thirty-six percent of residents live outside urban areas of twenty-five hundred people or more—double that of the nation overall. But it is no longer a state of farmers. Less than 5 percent of its population is considered "farm producers" and most residents live in towns and cities. In terms of racial diversity, at the start of the twenty-first century almost 94 percent of its population was white. As late as 2020 Iowa was the whitest state in the Midwest—a huge region stretching from Michigan and Ohio to Kansas and North Dakota—and one of the whitest states in the nation. At the same time, it has been a place of great religious diversity, with communities of Quakers, Jews, and Muslims living among Catholics and Protestants and near communal groups like the Amish. Until the 1940s, Iowa's economy was dominated by agriculture, when manufacturing displaced farming as the largest sector, more than sixty years after this occurred in Illinois. (Together, these two sectors accounted for 38 percent of the state's gross domestic product in 2018.)[1]

The historian Jon Gjerde called Iowa "the most Midwestern state." The

Midwest is the nation's agricultural heartland, as well as the region with the highest percentage of white Americans. In 2020, it grew more than 80 percent of the nation's corn and soybeans and almost half of the wheat; it also produced most of the hogs. Just as farming made the Midwest, so too it made Iowa: in the 1970s, for example, 98 percent of the state was under cultivation. The land helped make the region different from New England, the South, or the West. Vast tracts of fertile soil provided opportunities for families who pursued diversified commercial farming. A mix of migrants from the Northeast, the Great Lakes, the Upper South, and Europe settled in the area. They created a mostly egalitarian society, though racial or religious prejudice limited opportunities for many. Immigrants built towns, schools, and churches, with some places like Iowa creating a first-class public education system. "Geography, culture, and economic and political history have combined to create a distinctive Midwestern people," argued historian R. Douglas Hurt.[2]

Iowa is largely unappreciated and often misunderstood. It has a small population and sits in the middle of a huge country. Such places can be scorned by those from areas considered more important. In 1903 historian Frank I. Herriott asked, "Is Iowa's History Worth While?" It didn't have large cities, rugged mountainous regions, or the "rough and boisterous" history of western mining camps. If you needed "seismic convulsions," you had to study someplace else. But Herriott argued that all residents "declare with vehemence that Iowa is a magnificent State," criticizing a writer from the *Atlantic* who had described its "dullness and mediocrity." More than a century later, in 2010, the *New York Times* had only one reporter assigned to cover all of Iowa, Missouri, Nebraska, Kansas, and the Dakotas, who wrote about violent weather and other eccentric stories, providing local color for distant, mostly urban audiences.[3]

This book tells a new Iowa story, a vibrant, diverse one that refutes the idea that the state is dull or mediocre or that anyone should question its importance. Iowa was never a homogenous place. It has always been more complex than typically perceived, its story an untidy and messy one, full of immigrants and refugees pursuing their dreams. Nonwhite and minority populations have rarely been treated as equals, though. Its agricultural economy has often tested the fortitude of farmers. Few women enjoyed equal opportunities until the late twentieth century. This narrative chronicles how people, both ordinary and well-known, have built the state. While this is often a history of Iowa's white majority, it is also a history of Native people, African Americans, Latinas and Latinos, Asian Americans, the LGBTQ community, and Iowa's other ethnic and religious groups.

The first comprehensive history of the state, Dorothy Schwieder's *Iowa: The Middle Land*, was published in 1996. An earlier overview, *A History of Iowa*, by Leland L. Sage was published in 1974 and focused mostly on politics and white men. In contrast, Schwieder's story included those who had been left out of previous histories, from African Americans to women. Schwieder argued that Iowa was a state of moderate sensibilities, without great wealth or great poverty. It was a place of small towns and small-town values, where people valued families, communities, and education. Iowans were not known for "showiness, glitz, or hype," she noted. Her observations remain generally true long into the twenty-first century. Iowa has one of the highest high school graduation rates in the country and one of the lowest for dropouts. Economic mobility was also higher in Iowa in the late twentieth and early twenty-first centuries than most states. It has one of the highest rates of marriage and one of the lowest of divorce. The state has one of the highest labor participation rates, as well as high voter participation rates in comparison to other states. At the same time, there are stark disparities in Iowa, which reflect structural inequalities present throughout the nation. The high school dropout rate for African Americans is higher than white students and many more Black families live in poverty than white families, as median income for Black families continues to be about half that of white households.[4]

Throughout the nineteenth century, Iowa, like most of the agrarian Midwest, was more egalitarian than the rest of the country. Economic opportunity, republican government, one-room schools, and religious pluralism fostered the creation of a dense civic society. A high literacy rate encouraged and supported libraries, Chautauqua, newspapers, and reform organizations. Colleges and academies spread across Iowa. Agrarian societies, clubs, and fairs were ubiquitous in midwestern farm country. Voluntary associations and institutions were crucial to Iowa communities, promoting welfare and helping society to function. They reinforced moral values and customs. While sometimes intolerant, this was more often a democratic culture of community participation and self-improvement. This culture helps define Iowa, even if this old order has been eroded in the past century by urbanization, mass culture, and outmigration. Towns still celebrate their schools and basketball teams, even as the modern world reduces the time available for participation in church and community groups.[5]

This present volume features well-known individuals in its narrative, such as the Sauk leader Black Hawk, suffragist Carrie Chapman Catt, and President Herbert Hoover. But it also includes the stories of previously unknown farmwomen, laborers, immigrants, and refugees. This narrative adds new voices, such as those of runaway enslaved men who joined Iowa's Sixtieth Colored Regiment in the Civil War, young female pearl button factory workers, Mexican railroad workers who migrated to the state in the early twentieth century, and gay and lesbian soldiers, farmers, businesswomen, and teachers. This story also details segregation in Iowa and the struggles for equal justice by minority groups. It emphasizes the story of Iowa's women, from farm wives and suffragists to World War II army officers. It does not glorify the state, as that would distort reality and ignore those who have been left out of Iowa's story. Intolerance and injustice, as well as courage and humanity, are part of this history. There is much to celebrate in the history of Iowa, but our failures are as important to understand as our successes.[6]

Issues such as economic inequality, immigration, racial justice, and the environment have gained importance since Schwieder's book was written in the optimistic post–Cold War 1990s. This book addresses these topics while providing a broad survey of Iowa's history. It reviews familiar subjects and adds new ones to the state's story. For example, Schwieder admitted that "little scholarly work has been done on topics in Iowa history since the 1930s" and that her chapters on the period after the Great Depression were less developed than the others. *A New History of Iowa* fills in such gaps and provides an updated story for Iowa's changing population. In 2021 the state was five times as diverse as 1980, with 15 percent of its population nonwhite. Indeed, by the early 2020s, more than 130 languages were spoken in Iowa's public schools and more than one-quarter of Iowa K-12 students were nonwhite.[7]

This story is divided into three parts, each consisting of five chapters. The first section reviews Iowa history from initial settlement, about thirteen thousand years ago, until the Civil War. Part two covers the state's history from the Civil War to the 1920s, with topical chapters on subjects such as urban life and industry, as well as religion and education. The last section of the book summarizes Iowa's history from the Great Depression until the end of 2020. Each chapter can be read independently, but readers will be best served by reading them in order. This is a survey of Iowa history, not a comprehensive history. Many topics are not covered in detail.

Most chapters could easily be turned into a book and some paragraphs are summaries of entire books. See the footnotes and the bibliographic essay for further information.

Our history is always with us, though its story may be indistinct and its lessons uneasy. "The past is an inheritance, a gift, and a burden," wrote historian Jill Lepore. To understand it is to honor the living and the dead; learning from it venerates future generations.[8]

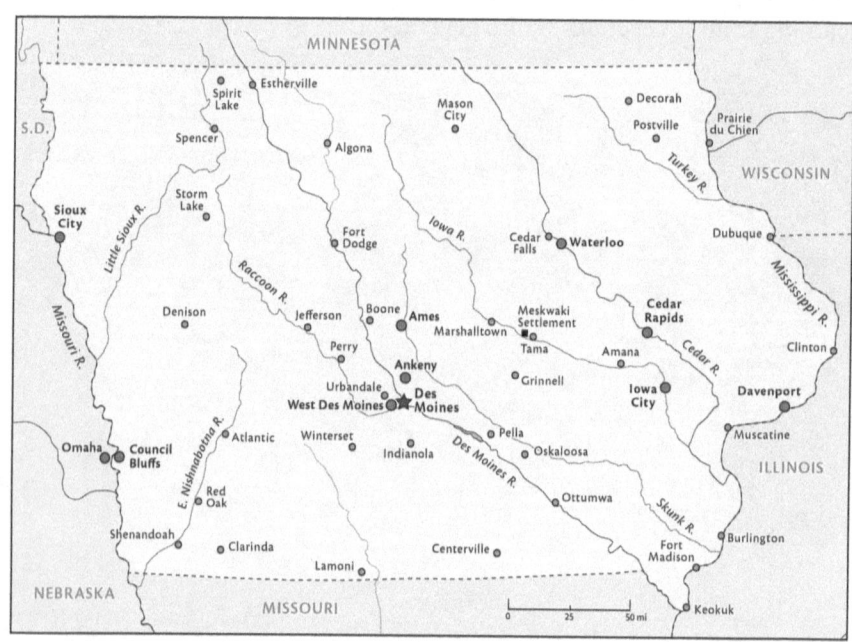

Map of Iowa cities and rivers.

PART ONE
IOWA TO THE CIVIL WAR

1
Native Iowa: Iowa to 1833

Native people lived in Iowa for thousands of years before Europeans first set foot in the territory. The state is named for the Ioway tribe, who had lived in the area since the 1600s. Later, the French forced the Sauk and Meskwaki out of the Great Lakes region in the mid-1700s—they migrated into Iowa and Illinois to escape destruction and became an important military power on the Upper Mississippi River. In June 1673, a French party, with Louis Jolliet and Jacques Marquette, entered southeast Iowa. They were the first Europeans known to have reached the state. More than one hundred years later, Julien Dubuque began mining lead near the town that would be named for him. In 1803, the United States bought the Louisiana Territory from France; the next year the American government forced the Sauk and Meskwaki to cede lands east of the Mississippi River. The Lewis and Clark expedition traveled along Iowa's western border in 1804. Fort Madison was the first American military structure in Iowa and construction began in 1808. In the 1820s, American settlers pushed across Illinois to the Mississippi River and the United States government decided finally to remove the Sauk and Meskwaki. Black Hawk, a Sauk leader, fought a short and bloody war that led to his defeat and the end of almost all Native resistance in Iowa.

Millions of years of glaciation had shaped the landscape of Iowa, long before the Black Hawk War. Giant ice sheets developed as the climate grew colder and wetter 2.5 million years ago. More snow accumulated on land than melted each year, creating vast fields of ice. Enormous glaciers thousands of feet thick expanded south from Canada in repeated waves. During the last glacial maximum, about 21,000 to 16,500 years ago, Iowa's climate was arctic, like Alaska's today. The last of these great glacial advances—a great tongue of ice stretching across the center of Iowa from the Minnesota border to the current location of Des Moines—began to melt about twelve thousand years ago. "Each advance of massive ice sheets scraped the land's surface, levelling hills and filling valleys," wrote ecologist Cornelia F. Mutel. Iowa benefited from glaciation, which blessed it with immense amounts of soil and gravel that were pushed south. Water and wind spread pulverized rock across the state, becoming the basis for Iowa's fertile soils.[1]

Iowa's prairies, forests, and wetlands have developed since the last glaciers. The state's north-central region, which was most recently covered by ice, is generally flat, with poor drainage. Before European and American settlement, it was full of lakes and wetlands, which made up one-quarter of the total state, almost nine million acres. Here there were meadows, marshes, and forested floodplains, with many lakes. It was a haven for waterfowl. The southern half of Iowa, last impacted by glaciers five hundred thousand years ago, has had time for erosion to create drainage networks. This region has hills and valleys. The northwest and northeast sections of the state, which escaped the most recent glaciation, have a gently rolling landscape. Iowa's northeast corner and the Loess Hills in western Iowa have the most topographic variation. The "Little Switzerland" region of northeast Iowa has rock outcroppings and deeply incised streams. The Loess Hills are made up of powdery soil left over by glaciers and deposited by wind. By the nineteenth century, 80 percent of Iowa was tall-grass prairie. Forests were most common in the eastern third and the south-central part of the state, especially along waterways. Northwest Iowa was the driest part of the state, receiving about twenty-five inches of rain a year, while eastern Iowa averaged thirty-three to thirty-six inches of rain a year. Southeast Iowa had a growing season as much as a month longer than northwest Iowa. Western Iowa overall was drier than the eastern half, its waters draining toward the Missouri River. Most precipitation fell in the spring and summer. Rainfall in these seasons was often the result of warmer air from the tropics colliding with air masses moving east from the Pacific and south from the Arctic. Thunderstorms were often the result.[2]

The prairies that make up most of Iowa are part of a vast grassland that extends from southern Texas to Canada. Historically, the most fertile soils in the world developed in grasslands. North American prairies, as well as those in Russia, Ukraine, and Argentina are now the most important grain-producing areas on the planet. Prairies in Canada and the United States had grasses, perennial wildflowers, and a small number of shrubs. Iowa's prairies had at least 250 species of plants; wildflowers included prairie violets, prairie phlox, purple coneflower, and sunflowers. "A carpet of grasses spread out across the plains," wrote naturalist Candace Savage, once the last glaciers retreated and the climate became warmer and drier. Grasses conserve water and are adapted to the more arid regions in the center of North America. Most of their mass is below ground, with deep roots to suck up water. They cope with drought well. Over the years, the decomposition of prairie grasses and roots enriched the topsoil, leaving dark and nutrient rich material that is some of the most productive agricultural land in the world. Even the soil in forest areas was excellent, improved by leaf litter, moss, and other plant debris. Iowa and Illinois lead the country in the amount of prime farmland, both places "blessed with such fertile soils and an agreeable climate for growing crops," wrote geologist Kathleen Woida. Iowa is part of the tall-grass-prairie region, known for the Indian grass and big bluestem that once dominated the state. Big bluestem was the most abundant tall grass and could grow ten to twelve feet high, so tall that a human could get lost in it.[3]

Iowa had an abundance of wildlife. One Indian agent, Joseph Street, described the northeastern part of Iowa as a "country so full of game" in 1833. Buffalo lived throughout Iowa as late as the mid-nineteenth century, with the largest numbers in the northwest. A herd of five thousand was reported in 1820. The territory had large numbers of elk, deer, bear, otter, and wolves. Vast flocks of passenger pigeons sometimes visited the state, which lay at the western edge of their range. One huge flock of an estimated six hundred million birds passed Dubuque about 1870. "Rich soil, abundant water, and a favorable climate produced extensive tall grass prairies, rich wetlands, and lush forests that once covered Iowa—habitats which in turn supported a surprising variety of plants and animals," wrote ecologist James J. Dinsmore. For thousands of years a relatively low human population allowed a proliferation of creatures—from waterfowl attracted to vast wetlands to black bears that preferred the forests of the eastern part of the state.[4]

Over the past two hundred years, Iowa's landscape has been transformed, as agriculture replaced the vast prairies, wetlands were drained for farming, and forests were chopped down. By the end of the nineteenth century, human settlement had eliminated animal habitats and exterminated many species in the state. These included buffalo, elk, wild turkey, white-tailed deer, beaver, wolves, passenger pigeons, and black bears. Some of these species have been reintroduced to the state, such as bison, turkey, and the white-tailed deer. Beaver came back into Iowa from the northwest. Still, it is very unlikely that bear and wolves will permanently reside in the state again, due to the lack of any large habitats for them. A small herd of bison and elk live at the Neal Smith National Wildlife Refuge, but they will probably never again roam freely in the state. On the other hand, while passenger pigeons were exterminated as a species in 1914, few would have predicted that white-tailed deer, wild turkey, and the Canada goose recovered so well that they are now sometimes considered to be a nuisance.[5]

When the first people reached Iowa about thirteen thousand years ago, they found a cold world that was recovering from an ice age. These scattered bands of migratory hunters pursued now-extinct animals such as mammoths and ground sloths. It is possible that one thousand to two thousand humans lived in Iowa about the time of first settlement. As the environment warmed in the following millennia, by 1200 BCE the climate and vegetation were like that which would be found later in the nineteenth century: "a sea of tall-grass prairie with ribbons of timbered stream valleys, slopes, and uplands," wrote Lynn M. Alex. Groups of people hunted large and small mammals, including bison. They also ate waterfowl, caught fish, consumed freshwater mollusks, and gathered wild plants and nuts. Over time, this population became less mobile, occupying semipermanent base camps. Eventually they established some small villages in eastern Iowa where there were reliable and abundant resources. They also began to grow their own food.[6]

A new cultural tradition arose in the eastern United States after about 1000 BCE, identified as the Woodland Tradition. The name refers to the forested environments of eastern North America, as well as adjacent prairies and plains. They were best known for burial mounds found in Iowa and other states. Individuals were often interred with offerings such as shell beads, carved stone pipes, tools, or food in ceramic pots. Burial mounds, as well as pottery, link Woodland communities from Iowa with those elsewhere on the continent. Native people in Iowa were part of an exchange network among settlements in eastern North America. Trade reached from the Rocky Mountains to the Gulf of Mexico and the Great Lakes. Mounds in Iowa sometimes contained obsidian from the Rocky Mountains or shells from the Atlantic and Gulf coasts. The famous effigy mounds in northeast Iowa were a custom of people who lived between 400 and 1200 CE.[7]

By 1000 CE the cultivation of corn was widespread in Iowa and many settlements had increased in size and became more permanent. Corn is native to Mexico and Central America, where it had been cultivated for more than five thousand years. Over thousands of years Native farmers developed new strains. They selected seeds from plants that performed best farther north, developing new strains that tolerated shorter growing seasons or drier conditions. They also created hybrid strains by crossing existing types. In the eastern woodlands of the United States this botanical work would have been completed by women. The Northern Flint was one of these types of corn. This variety, along with the Southern Dent, are the foundation for modern varieties of hybrid corn. "Euro-American farmers did not make similar progress in plant breeding until they developed agricultural experiment stations in the late nineteenth century," wrote historian Colin G. Calloway. Squash was one of the first domesticated plants in Mexico and South America, its cultivation moving north along with corn. Though not as nutritious as corn, it could be dried and stored. Beans, another widely grown crop, had lots of protein. They also returned nitrogen to the soil, which corn depleted. Together these three staples, often called the "three sisters" of Native American agriculture, provided a healthy diet and did not exhaust the soil.[8]

Agriculture became more important and widespread, even as hunting and foraging continued in their importance. Archaeological studies found that people grew squash, beans, and pumpkins and used storage pits for food. They utilized more tools, such as rakes and hoes for gardening and knives and scrapers made of stone that were used to process animal meat. Human burials after 1000 CE were usually in flat cemeteries as opposed to large burial mounds. A later cultural tradition in Iowa, the Oneota, was named after a geological formation along the Upper Iowa River. A distinct culture, it existed from about 900 CE to 1500 CE and was found in nearby states such as Illinois, Wisconsin, Minnesota, and Nebraska. The present-day Ioway, Omaha, Ho-chunk, and Missouri are connected linguistically, culturally, and by tribal tradition to the Oneota culture.[9]

The arrival of Europeans brought immense changes to Native peoples in

North America. Even before white settlement forced them west, European diseases devastated Indian populations. Those who lived near European settlements or in more densely settled areas were most at risk. Warfare with the English or French also hurt many tribes. Some battled each other for hunting territory so they could take part in the lucrative fur trade. This provided them with weapons, as well as manufactured goods such as blankets or pots. But Indian peoples then became more reliant on trade than on their own goods. Some groups disintegrated, their survivors adopted by neighbors. Tribes in the Northeast moved toward the Great Lakes, pushed westward by the growing European population. The impact of European colonization and expansion forced the Sauk and Meskwaki into Iowa. Meanwhile, disease, especially smallpox, weakened the Ioway.[10]

The first recorded contact between Europeans and Native people in Iowa occurred on June 25, 1673. A French exploration party, led by Louis Joliet and accompanied by Father Jacques Marquette and five others, traveled by canoe from Michilimacinac, at the very northern tip of Michigan's lower peninsula, to Green Bay, Wisconsin. The party ventured west, visiting a Miami and Kickapoo village on the way to the headwaters of the Wisconsin River, which took them to the Mississippi River. They then descended the Mississippi, looking on the forested bluffs of Iowa on June 17. They saw deer, elk, and herds of buffalo as they floated south, but no humans. On June 25 they landed on the western shore—somewhere between the Des Moines and Iowa Rivers—and found human footprints. Marquette and Joliet followed a path inland to a village of about three hundred lodges, occupied by members of the Illinois tribe. Marquette knew some of their language. The Illinois fed them a meal of corn meal, fish, and buffalo. The Frenchmen went hunting and fishing with their hosts. Six hundred tribal members escorted them back to their canoes. The French returned home after descending the Mississippi almost to the Arkansas River.[11]

Other Europeans visited Iowa and the Upper Mississippi River in the late seventeenth century. In 1682 Rene Robert Cavelier de la Salle grandly claimed the entire Mississippi River Valley for France and named it Louisiana in honor of King Louis XIV of France. Nicholas Perrot, a French fur trader, built two forts in the mid-1680s, one at the mouth of the Wisconsin River, about fifty miles northwest of present-day Dubuque. He found Native lead mines along the Mississippi and explored northeast Iowa, finding prairies and plenty of buffalo and other animals. Perrot also visited Ioway villages in 1685, probably along the Upper Iowa River. The Ioway had first encountered Europeans in April 1676, when a group traveled to Green Bay, Wisconsin. They carried buffalo hides, possibly for trade. A French priest preached to them.[12]

The Ioway are the tribe that gave the state its name. The Algonquian-speaking Illinois, Sauk, and Meskwaki called the Ioway "Ayuxba," which is pronounced "Ayuway." The French called them "Aiaouez," which eventually became the word we know today, Ioway. They are descendants of the Oneota people, as were many others who lived near the Missouri and Mississippi Rivers. From the late 1600s until the mid-1700s they lived along the Missouri River, before moving to southeast Iowa. They were one of the most powerful tribes in the area, numbering an estimated one thousand to fifteen hundred in 1760. A French explorer, Pierre Charles LeSueur, reported that they were as influential as the Sioux in the early eighteenth century. The word Sioux was a French corruption of an Ojibwe word that meant snake or enemy. The Sioux did not choose the name, but they became widely known by it. The Dakota is a general term for the eastern Sioux in Minnesota; for their part, the western Sioux that moved onto the Great Plains included the Lakota. Both divisions of the Sioux would be a constant threat to the Ioway. They were also one of many tribes that visited Iowa.[13]

The Ioway built their villages in wooded valleys near rivers. Waterways provided transportation and trade, while the valleys had fertile soil and good hunting. They lived in different types of lodges, with the largest thirty to forty feet long, twenty feet wide, and fourteen feet high. These were made of walnut or elm bark laid on a wooden frame. Other lodges had round roofs and were covered with mats made of cattail plants. The Ioway stored corn, squash, beans, and dried meat in pits. Women cooked meat and vegetables in clay pots and families ate from wooden bowls with spoons carved from wood or bison horns. They began to use metal bowls and pots, as well as metal tools and cloth, after contact with Europeans.[14]

Ioway life, especially farming and hunting, revolved around the rhythms of the seasons. Fields were close to villages. Women and older children planted corn, beans, squash, and pumpkins. Each family might tend to three to five acres, as it took about an acre of vegetables to supply one person for a year. Fields were cleared in late winter and early spring using fire and tools made from buffalo jaws. They planted corn, beans, and squash together. Women and children harvested gardens after the summer buffalo hunt. A second buffalo hunt took place in the fall and winter. French explorer Nicolas Perrot wrote that the Ioway were skilled buffalo hunters even while pursuing the large animals on foot. It would not be until about 1720 that they acquired horses, having been introduced to them by Plains tribes. Tribal members shared buffalo meat and used buffalo bones, horns, and hides to make clothing, tools, and shelter. During hunts they used buffalo-hide tipis.[15]

Disease and the threat of attack forced the tribe to migrate east, away from the Missouri River. In 1764 they lived near where the city of Omaha, Nebraska, is located today. In the middle of the 1760s a smallpox epidemic struck them, cutting their population in half. Decades later, an Iowa leader remembered that the powerful tribe had been "reduced to nothing, a mere handful of that Nation that was once masters of the land." They left the Missouri River region, probably to escape hostile neighbors such as the Sioux, who had acquired European weapons and were pushing other tribes out of the area. The Ioway migrated southeast. They were "relatively small, occupied few villages at a time, and engaged in a mixed economy of farming and hunting," wrote anthropologists Saul Schwartz and William Green. The tribe built a village on the Lower Des Moines River, called Iowaville, where they lived from about 1765 to 1820. This location placed them between Spanish-controlled Louisiana and Canada, which England had taken from France. This maximized their access to trade and autonomy from European influence. Iowaville was also away from the more numerous Sauk and Meskwaki who lived on the Mississippi River. The Ioway were skillful diplomats and traders, who, according to Schwartz and Green, "exchanged, used, repaired, recycled and modified objects following their own cultural lights."[16]

They took part in the fur trade with the British and the French in the late 1700s and early 1800s. American influence west of the Mississippi was limited until after the War of 1812, but the English government saw the fur trade as a buffer against American expansion. The English set up at least six trading posts along the Lower Des Moines River in the late eighteenth century, shipping deer, beaver, otter, and bear skins to Canada. In exchange they provided high-quality goods and weapons to tribes, far superior to the anything the Native Americans might receive from the Americans. French traders from St. Louis also visited the tribe, sometimes marrying Ioway women. Kin ties improved chances at success in the fur trade. The Ioway took advantage of the rivalry between Spain and England, stealing horses from the Spanish and flaunting ties with the British. Archaeological surveys showed that the village had brass and iron tools, stone pipes, gun parts, Euro-American ceramics, glass beads, and copper. The Ioway repaired their own weapons and manufactured lead shot on site but continued to use the bow and arrow to hunt squirrels and smaller game.[17]

The Ioway farmed, gathered wild plants, and hunted to feed themselves. Iowaville stood near the Des Moines River, with plenty of fertile land. The village was located west of the Mississippi, about a day or two of travel away from the river. They continued to cultivate corn, beans, and squash, but archaeological surveys also showed that they grew tobacco. Women and children collected fruits such as raspberry, elderberry, grapes, and strawberries. They also gathered hazelnuts, walnuts, and hickory nuts. Finally, although the village was occupied from spring to fall for agricultural purposes, many inhabitants left for hunting during the winter.[18]

The tribe faced many difficulties in the early 1800s. Hunting became more challenging in eastern Iowa as game became scarcer. Disputes over hunting territories led to conflict with the Sauk and Meskwaki. In 1807, the tribes began to raid each other. The Ioway also had to travel farther west to search for buffalo, which put them into conflict with the Osage, Omaha, and other tribes. The Omaha launched an attack in the summer of 1814; the Sioux killed twenty-two tribal members and destroyed crops in 1815. A second smallpox epidemic in the early nineteenth century killed from one-quarter to one-half of the tribe. Only eight hundred members remained afterward. The Sioux were a constant threat to their north. A lack of hunting territory reduced food and fur supplies.[19]

The vulnerable Ioways relocated to northwestern Missouri, seeking to escape the instability of Iowa. The lack of game became so bad that Ioway leader White Cloud, also known as Mahaska, complained that the Sauk and Meskwaki "eat everything." Mahaska led the Ioway in the early 1800s, trying to preserve his people in the face of American settlers in Missouri, who wanted all Indians removed. They relocated again to the northwestern corner of Missouri, relinquishing claims to the northern part of that state. They were impoverished, living in an overhunted region, and could not adequately feed themselves. In 1830 they gave up more land. Six years later, the Ioway left for Nebraska. They "were prisoners on a small reservation, that continued to be made smaller by more treaties, land speculators, and corrupt Indian agents," wrote historian Lance Foster. In less than two decades they had been uprooted at least three times. A petition to President Andrew Jackson, asking permission to return to their village on the Des

Moines River and to the "bones of their fathers," was ignored. The Ioway nation was forced across the Missouri River into Nebraska even as the United States was planning to create a new state named after them.[20]

While the Ioway unwillingly gave their name to the state, the Sauk and Meskwaki, sometimes called the Sac and Fox, are usually better known today in the historical narrative of Iowa. The two tribes became allies in 1730s and moved west toward Iowa. The Meskwaki had fled the Great Lakes region after the French and their Native allies tried to destroy them in a campaign that historian Colin G. Calloway called genocide. The tribe had opposed the French and their powerful Indian allies and demanded the return of enslaved tribal members. By 1732 only 140 Meskwaki men, women, and children survived. They found refuge with the Sauk, who were closely related through kinship, around Green Bay, Wisconsin. The French demanded the surrender of the surviving Meskwaki, but the Sauk refused. They moved west to escape future persecution and possible extermination. The two tribes settled together along the Mississippi River. In the following decades the Meskwaki rebuilt their population and formed a powerful alliance with the Sauk.[21]

The Ioways welcomed the two tribes. Meskwaki means "red-earth people." Their origin story recounts that the first humans were made of red earth or clay. But the tribe is often called the Fox. This occurred because a party of French misunderstood an explanation of who they were. The Meskwaki gave the name of their clan, which was then applied to the whole tribe. For their part, the Sauk were known by their allies as the Osakiwuk, meaning "People of the Outlet," as they had lived at the mouth of a river when the Meskwaki met them. The two tribes lived in eastern Iowa and western Illinois for almost one hundred years. In 1804 they controlled an area from the middle of Illinois to western Iowa and from southern Wisconsin to northern Missouri.[22]

The Upper Mississippi River region was a borderland between Native and European peoples in the 1700s and early 1800s. The "region became ethnically diverse," wrote historian Lucy Eldersveld Murphy, with the French, English, and Americans joining a variety of Native peoples. It was not a static world. Everyone competed for territory. The French and English fought each other in North America and Europe for many decades. Then the Americans battled the English. The Illinois fought the Meskwaki, Sauk, and Sioux for three years in the early 1750s before a peace treaty ended the violence. In the late eighteenth century, the Ioway, Sauk, and

Meskwaki drove Osage, Missouri, and Kansas hunters from Iowa. The Sioux in eastern Minnesota were still sparring with the Meskwaki in 1820, with one of their leaders, Little Raven, describing a recent attack as an assault by "a little tribe."[23]

The Sauk settled where the Rock and Mississippi Rivers met in western Illinois by the 1760s. It was called Saukenuk. A majority of the tribe lived there. Other villages were located farther south on the Mississippi River. Saukenuk's location was "an enviable one," wrote historian William T. Hagan. The rivers abounded with fish and wide meadows provided good forage for horses. Catfish that weighed more than one hundred pounds could be caught in the Mississippi River. Hundreds of acres of corn and vegetables grew on the fertile land; springs of fresh water gushed from hillsides. The forests provided an abundant variety of fruits, nuts, and berries, from plums and raspberries to crab apples. In the winter the Sauk left for buffalo hunts, returning in the spring to their lodges. Women worked in the fields, while the men met with traders to sell the year's fur and deerskin harvest, as well as tallow, maple sugar, and beeswax. They gained weapons, ammunition, tools, knives, and blankets in exchange. The Sauk warrior Black Hawk, who was born at Saukenuk in 1767, remembered, "We always had plenty—our children never cried with hunger, nor our people were never in want." Europeans and Americans who saw the area spoke of its beauty and the riches of the landscape.[24]

The Sauk flourished at Saukenuk and probably had more than one hundred lodges by 1817. That year the American Indian agent at Rock Island, Thomas Forsyth, wrote, "I have seen many Indian Villages, but I never saw such a large one or such a populous one." Each lodge was 50 or 60 feet long and as many as fifty to sixty people could live in one. Saukenuk had a large public square with a council house for ceremonies and community gatherings. Forsyth estimated that the Sauk had more than one thousand warriors, with an estimated population of forty-eight hundred in 1824. Polygamy was common in both tribes, with Sauk men sometimes marrying women from the same family. They adopted war captives and married members of other tribes, too. The Sauk were a major military power, located beyond American settlement in the early nineteenth century. It was an idyllic time, where the tribe was large and powerful. But they lived in a desirable place, with rival tribes such as the Sioux to their west and north, and with the steadily advancing line of American settlement encroaching upon their territory from the east.[25]

The Meskwaki also lived along the Mississippi River. Some lived near the Dubuque lead mines, while others lived near Saukenuk. These villages were usually located in Iowa on the western side of the Mississippi. The Meskwaki were not as numerous as the Sauk, with about sixteen hundred people in 1804. Like their neighbors, they lived in substantial lodges in villages surrounded by corn fields and gardens. Here they stayed from April to October, interrupted by a brief summer hunt. After the corn harvest, they "dispersed in small family groups for the long winter hunt," wrote Michael D. Green. Deer hunting halted once winter became severe. Families lived in wikiups made of small poles bent into a dome and covered with cattail mats. They usually lived near the headwaters of the Iowa and Des Moines Rivers, hunting bears, and trapping beaver, raccoon, and muskrat. Hunting parties traveled as far west as the Arkansas River. The Meskwaki returned to their villages in the spring, leading seasonal lives very much like their allies.[26]

Julien Dubuque convinced the Meskwaki to let him mine for lead near the town that would be named for him. Dubuque was born in 1762 in Quebec, Canada, and moved to Prairie du Chien, a French trading outpost on the Mississippi River, about 1783. He persuaded the Meskwaki to give him the sole privilege to mine the area five years later; they also used him for help in marketing the mineral. Dubuque received a huge land grant from Spain, to whom the French had given Louisiana. The Spanish granted him a tract of land twenty-one miles long and nine miles wide. He called the area the "Mines of Spain," in honor of the government that gave it to him. Dubuque married a local woman, likely Meskwaki, and was adopted into the tribe. He brought French laborers to run the mines, built a trading house, a sawmill, a smelting furnace, and grew corn. Native women labored in the mines.[27]

But his unusual position as an early Iowa business tycoon did not last. Dubuque was wealthy and influential, and the merchants in St. Louis loved him, as he bought furniture, dishes, books, and silver to supplement his lavish lifestyle. Despite a monopoly on one of the most important lead mines along the Upper Mississippi River he did not prosper. When Dubuque died in 1810 at the age of forty-five, he was bankrupt. He had been ill for years, possibly from lead poisoning, syphilis, or tuberculosis. Though he struggled in his final years, he probably established the first white settlement in Iowa.[28]

A decade later Henry Schoolcraft, a US government geologist touring the Great Lakes region, visited a Meskwaki village near Dubuque. There were large fields of corn and dozens of buildings, with a large council house. Schoolcraft reported that miners used hoes, shovels, and pickaxes to dig into hillsides. Miners, mostly women, dug horizontal shafts forty feet long. They then carried ore in baskets to the riverbanks. Traders on an island in the middle of the Mississippi River purchased and smelted the ore. The Meskwaki received credit to buy goods in return.[29]

The Meskwaki, Sauk, and Ho-chunk, often known as the Winnebago, produced more lead and fewer furs by 1820, exporting hundreds of thousands of pounds of the ore each year. Increased lead production meant more money for weapons, tools, clothing, and other goods. It also diversified Indian economies and made them less vulnerable to traders and market prices. Native and mixed-race women linked European men like Julien Dubuque to "native communities and kin networks, taught them about native culture and economics, and facilitated their participation in the exporting of lead, thus linking Indian mineral producers to an international market," wrote Lucy Eldersveld Murphy.[30]

Several other tribes lived in Iowa or hunted in the area. These included the Ho-chunk, who were forced to leave their ancestral home in Wisconsin and relocate to northern Iowa in the early 1840s. They lived in an area called the Neutral Ground, a strip of land formerly controlled by the Sioux, Sauk, and Meskwaki. About two thousand lived in northeast Iowa until forced to relocate to Minnesota in 1848. They eventually split into two groups after the US government resettled them in South Dakota. One part of the tribe returned to Wisconsin and the others moved to Nebraska. The Omaha, Ponca, Pawnee, and Otoe also hunted in western Iowa, sometimes settling in it. A small number of Potawatomie resided briefly in southwest Iowa, after removal from Michigan and before being forced into Kansas in the 1840s.[31]

The Sioux consisted of a number of related people who lived in Minnesota around 1700. Some groups expanded west, pursuing beaver for the fur trade and bison for subsistence. The Lakota and Yankton pushed onto the Plains, while the Dakota remained behind. The Dakota homeland included northern Iowa and Minnesota, where they survived by growing corn, hunting bison, deer, and elk, fishing, and gathering berries. They were the last tribe to relinquish their Iowa lands in 1851. The Sioux displaced the Omaha, Ioway, Missouri, and other tribes on the plains once they acquired guns and horses. Smallpox epidemics along the Missouri

River also reduced resistance to their expansion. By 1850 the western Sioux dominated a vast region stretching from the Platte River to Yellowstone. The Sioux often hunted in northwest Iowa. Though they did not occupy the state, they were a powerful force that weakened the Ioway and threatened the Sauk and Meskwaki for many decades.[32]

In the first years of the nineteenth century, the United States asserted its power along the Mississippi and Missouri Rivers. President Thomas Jefferson purchased the Louisiana Territory from France in 1803, the Spanish having transferred the region back to France. Jefferson dispatched an exploring party up the Missouri River in 1804—the famous Lewis and Clark expedition. He also sent army Lieutenant Zebulon Pike up the Mississippi River in 1805. Most significantly, the United States government negotiated a treaty that required Native tribes to give up land east of the Mississippi River. This laid the foundation for the Black Hawk War.[33]

The American government forced the Meskwaki and Sauk to surrender millions of acres of land in 1804. Sauk hunters killed four Americans who had trespassed on their hunting grounds and the American army, led by Indiana Territory Governor William Henry Harrison, threatened war. The governor invited Sauk chiefs to St. Louis, who thought they were negotiating a settlement for the death of the four Americans. Harrison demanded the tribes cede millions of acres. He chose old and pliable chiefs to negotiate with, supplying them with alcohol and gifts to encourage their assent. The Indian leaders were not authorized to sell any land. But Harrison convinced a few to surrender vast tracts of territory. In exchange for a small amount of money, including an annual $1,000 payment from the federal government, Native people lost land in Illinois, Missouri, and Wisconsin. The Sauk and Meskwaki gave up their claims east of the Mississippi River, an area of nearly fifteen million acres. They were allowed to remain in Saukenuk and other towns in western Illinois until the land was sold to American settlers. The two tribes earned about $60,000 a year from the fur trade. It was extremely unlikely they would have willingly sold so much land for the pittance offered by the United States. "All of our country, east of the Mississippi," Black Hawk recalled, "was ceded to the United States for *one thousand dollars* a year!" He argued that the treaty, signed by four drunk men, "has been the origin of all of our difficulties."[34]

The expedition of Lewis and Clark left St. Louis in May 1804 and ascended the Missouri River, searching for an easy route across the continent. It reached southwest Iowa in late July. William Clark noted the presence of some burial mounds near where the "Aiawuay"—Ioway—had once lived, probably in Pottawattamie County. The Americans found fish "in great plenty." Lewis and Clark visited a beautiful prairie, with groves of oak, walnut, ash, and cottonwood nearby. Turkey and prairie dogs were everywhere. They encountered Ottawa and Missouri Indians and shared food with them and a French trader. Deer, elk, and beaver thronged the prairies in almost inconceivable numbers. Coyotes barked at them from the riverbanks. "The sense of being in a Garden of Eden was strong," wrote historian Stephen Ambrose. The expedition suffered their only fatal casualty when Sergeant Charles Floyd died on August 20, probably from a ruptured or perforated appendix. Today, a monument to Floyd stands in Sioux City, Iowa. The exploring party successfully reached the Pacific Ocean and returned to St. Louis on September 22, 1806.[35]

Zebulon Pike's exploration of the Upper Mississippi River also took him through a world with little connection to the United States. Pike was a twenty-six-year-old army lieutenant who would die in the War of 1812, after further explorations into Spanish New Mexico. His instructions included reconnoitering the river, noting weather and resources, and selecting sites for forts. British fur traders were a threat to American control over the region and competed with the United States for the loyalty of tribes. Native peoples saw Americans as potential trading partners or as allies against their enemies. But they did not wish to give up their land, independence, or way of life.[36]

Pike and twenty men left St. Louis in August 1805, passing by Sauk and Meskwaki villages on their way north. Sauk men helped their boat through the rapids near the Des Moines River. The expedition passed Indian canoes frequently and met several boats of fur traders heading to St. Louis. On August 29, they had breakfast at a Meskwaki village north of Saukenuk, which Pike did not mention in his report of the voyage. They met very few Americans. The Sauk that Pike encountered were hospitable, but he did not seriously pursue any negotiations and found no diplomatic success. He had dinner with Julien Dubuque, whose attachment to the United States "ran only as deeply as the Americans' willingness to let him keep taking lead out of the ground," wrote historian Jared Orsi. Pike chose several sites for forts to strengthen the American presence along the Upper Mississippi River. Two were in Iowa. The first was in northeast Iowa across the Mississippi River from Prairie du Chien. The second was in southeast Iowa. After a tough winter in Minnesota the party returned to St. Louis in April 1806.[37]

Fort Madison was the first US military post in Iowa and the first American fort on the Upper Mississippi River. Zebulon Pike's expedition highlighted the need for a greater role for the United States in the region. In 1808, an army detachment was sent to erect a fort at the mouth of the Des Moines River, in the southeast corner of Iowa. Its commander, Lieutenant Alpha Kingsley, decided to build the structure farther north, ten miles above the rapids on the Mississippi River near the Des Moines River. Kingsley and his men arrived at the location on September 26. Construction continued for many months. Fort Madison, named for President James Madison, was in a bad location. It sat below a nearby ridge and a ravine ran alongside the fort which provided cover to any opponent. For months, the fort remained incomplete, with only five-foot walls to protect its garrison initially. Sauk, Meskwaki, and Ho-Chunk exchanged lead and fur for guns, blankets, traps, and other manufactured goods at a busy trading post outside the fort. A garrison of about sixty men lived within the fort's ten-to-twelve-foot-high stockade, which was completed in mid-1809. British posts around the Great Lakes, and their mostly French employees, proved tough competition. They had higher quality goods at lower prices and British traders were seen as less of a threat to Indian land.[38]

Fort Madison's vulnerable location made it a target for attack. The first attempt to take it occurred on April 10, 1809, led by Black Hawk and another chief. A party of warriors seized the weapons of some American soldiers but gave them back, laughing at the surprised men. American officers took the threat seriously and met with the Native leaders. Armed warriors crowded around the fort's low walls. A group went to the main gate, but they were met by soldiers and cannon. The Indians retreated. "Had our party got into the fort, all the whites would have been killed," Black Hawk wrote.[39]

The fort was besieged during the War of 1812 and eventually abandoned. Iowa saw little fighting, as the American presence was minor. The Sauks fought with the British, as they did not trust the Americans. Black Hawk explained, "*I had not discovered one good trait in the character of the Americans that had come to the country!* They made *fair promises, but never fulfilled them!*" In early September 1812, a party of Sauk and Ho-chunk quietly arrived at the fort at night. They concealed themselves and waited for a chance to get inside. A warrior fired before the gates could be stormed and eliminated any chance for a surprise attack. The two sides exchanged fire starting September 5, and the sniping went on

Makataimeshekiakiah

Black Hawk was a Sauk warrior who led Native people in the war named after him. Black Hawk, from Thomas McKenney, *History of Indian Tribes of North America*, vol. 1, 213.

for three days. The Indians tried to set the fort on fire, but "without effect, as the fire was always instantly extinguished," wrote Black Hawk. The raiding party withdrew when their ammunition ran low. Continued attacks convinced the fort's commander that its position was untenable. A lack of food, caused by the spoilage of flour and pork, forced the garrison to leave. It was evacuated and burned in November 1813.[40]

The War of 1812 had little immediate impact upon the Native peoples of Iowa. But the conflict, and the defeat of an attempt to build an Indian coalition to resist American expansion, dealt a serious blow to resistance to the United States. In the 1810s and 1820s Americans and Europeans surged westward across Illinois toward the Sauk and Meskwaki settlements along the Mississippi River. After the War of 1812 ended, the US Army built other forts in and around Iowa to keep an eye on the region's Native peoples. One of these was on Rock Island, near Saukenuk; another was located where the Des Moines River meets the Mississippi in southeast Iowa.[41]

The expansion of the United States into Ohio, Indiana, and Illinois reduced hunting territories and forced tribes to compete for diminishing resources. This led to an increase in warfare between them, as warriors intruded on hunting grounds claimed by others. The Sauk and Meskwaki hunted farther west, sometimes as far as three hundred miles, in search of pelts for the fur trade. They attacked smaller nations, such as the Omaha in Nebraska, and destroyed their main village in 1820. The Meskwaki and Sauk also continued to fight with the Dakota in Minnesota. Black Hawk recalled that when young men went west to hunt for deer and buffalo, they were prepared to kill any Sioux found on their hunting grounds. In 1822, there were more than one hundred casualties from fighting between the Sauk and Meskwaki and the Sioux. The fur trade also increased the flow of alcohol into Indian communities, which further destabilized their lives.[42]

American expansion required the acquisition of land and the replacement of its original inhabitants. This violent and relentless dispossession of Native people is known as settler colonialism. American expansion "has always been about Indian removal," wrote historian John P. Bowes. This was different from the British empire in South Asia, for example, where the colonizer told those they ruled: you work for me now. In settler colonialism, the United States forced indigenous people from their land and built a new society in the place of Native ones. This process began before the United States declared independence and continued long after American and European settlers reached the Mississippi River in the 1820s.[43]

Significant numbers of American settlers reached the Mississippi River at two important locations. In early 1830, some crossed the river and began working the lead mines near Dubuque. The Meskwaki had left because of a Dakota camp nearby. In the summer of 1830, Zachary Taylor, the American commander at Prairie du Chien, sent Lieutenant Jefferson Davis and a detachment of soldiers to drive the miners out of Iowa, which had not officially opened to American settlement. After the Black Hawk War ended in 1832, three hundred miners returned to the Dubuque lead district. Some of them had fought in the conflict and were now chased out by the army again. American settlers also moved to Saukenuk and the surrounding area. John Spencer, who was born in Vermont in 1801 and came west to join an uncle in Missouri, was one of the first to arrive as a permanent resident, in March 1829. He first saw Saukenuk on the way to mines on the Upper Mississippi River and had been "much pleased with it." There were about two dozen whites living near him in the spring of 1829. Many more came that year, destroying lodges and building fences in Indian corn fields. Spencer wrote that the Sauk were "very much displeased to find white settlers so near them." In October 1829 the US government began to sell the land around Saukenuk, from a land office in Springfield, Illinois.[44]

The American government wanted the Sauk to leave Saukenuk. In 1828 and 1829 they were ordered to move west. The governor of Illinois threatened to use force to remove them. Black Hawk did not believe that Saukenuk had been sold, only that land in Illinois south of the town had been ceded. He would not peacefully leave the lands of his ancestors. Only about one in six tribal members supported him, but this did not mean they accepted that the 1804 treaty was legitimate. The majority supported Keokuk, a military leader of the Sauk. He was willing to leave Saukenuk and move to live in Iowa. Keokuk was a gifted speaker in his forties, whose mother had been the daughter of a French man. He had traveled into the United States as far as New York and "realized the futility of resistance," wrote historian William T. Hagan. Opposing the American army would be hopeless. He also realized that a good relationship with the United States could serve the interests of his people. The Americans could help the Sauk and Meskwaki, who fought with other tribes over hunting territory. For his part, Black Hawk hated Keokuk and saw him as a self-serving man who betrayed his own people.[45]

Tensions grew worse over the next two years. Clashes between white settlers and the residents of Saukenuk increased. Whites shot Indian dogs, stole their horses, burned down lodges, and insulted Native women. They also made sure that whisky flowed into the town, against the requests of Indian leaders. White settlers attacked Native men and fought with each other over cornfields. The Sauk tore down fences built around their fields and broke the whisky barrels of whites in response. Black Hawk and sixteen hundred followers returned to Saukenuk in the spring of 1831 after a winter of hunting. Three hundred soldiers of the US Army, backed by fifteen hundred Illinois militia and a steamboat with artillery, assembled to repel this "invasion" of Illinois. They forced Black Hawk's band to retreat across the Mississippi River on June 25. The Americans had wanted conflict. Black Hawk retreated to avoid a massacre. Five days later Black Hawk and other leaders signed a document of capitulation that required them to abandon Saukenuk and accept the validity of the 1804 treaty. The Sauk "were to be banished from the center of their world, cast out and cut off from the fields of their mothers and graves of their fathers," wrote historian Kerry Trask.[46]

They moved across the Mississippi River into Iowa and found despair. The winter of 1831–1832 was severe and hunger and disease made them desperate. Food supplies dwindled and Black Hawk hoped to cross into Illinois and ascend the Rock River to join other Natives and grow corn. He also hoped to find allies to support him against the Americans.[47]

In April 1832 Black Hawk and more than one thousand of his people crossed the Mississippi and entered Illinois. Between four hundred and five hundred were warriors, but there were also many women and children. They did not go to Saukenuk but to a village up the Rock River, where they hoped to settle. Black Hawk had been told by one of his principal lieutenants, Neapope, that the British in Canada might assist him. This was untrue. No one knows if Neapope fabricated the story or if he misinterpreted what he was told when he was in Canada. A prophet from the Ho-chunk also assured Black Hawk that tribes from as far away as Texas would come to his aid if the Americans tried to take their land. In the end, no other tribe helped them. Keokuk refused to take part in any campaign, told Black Hawk to stay in Iowa, and called the prophet and Neapope liars.[48]

Black Hawk's foray into Illinois brought a quick response. More than two thousand Illinois militia mobilized for a possible conflict, as well as regular army troops that assembled on Rock Island. One of the Illinois volunteers was a twenty-three-year-old from New Salem named Abraham

Lincoln, who had been elected captain of his local militia company. Lincoln dreamed of military glory but mostly battled mosquitoes and boredom during the conflict. Another militia volunteer, John A. Wakefield, wrote about the conflict, boasting that the militia would eliminate their opponents, whom he called "demons in human shape." Black Hawk decided to retreat across the Mississippi, a sensible idea given the large number of women and children with him. Before he could get across the river, Illinois militiamen commanded by Isaiah Stillman found his encampment. Stillman's men had been drinking and were badly disciplined. They were looking for a fight.[49]

On May 14 the first skirmish of the Black Hawk War occurred, known as the Battle of Stillman's Run. Black Hawk sent men under a flag of truce to talk with the militia. The Illinois volunteers opened fire. The survivors fled, pursued by militia who lusted for more fighting. Black Hawk and about forty warriors met them with rifle fire. The poorly disciplined militia beat a hasty and panic-stricken retreat. A dozen of the Illinois volunteers were killed, and the Americans were routed by a force one-quarter their own size. Some of Stillman's men did not return for three days. Black Hawk recalled, "I was *forced* into WAR, with about *five hundred* warriors to contend against *three or four thousand!*" He had been shocked that his men had been fired on while attempting to make peace.[50]

Black Hawk feared that his band would be destroyed if they headed downriver back toward Iowa; he therefore decided to move north through Illinois toward Wisconsin. Rowdy volunteer cavalry chased after them, followed by regular troops. Black Hawk's warriors carried out raids across northern Illinois, killing and capturing some settlers. But they were short on food. Volunteer militia joined the pursuit, as did Sauk tribal enemies, who served as scouts and guides. Dakota and Ho-Chunk warriors went looking for revenge against their old opponents.[51]

By July Black Hawk and his people had made it to southern Wisconsin, desperately short of food. There was little game and poor fishing. They ate roots. Malnutrition was widespread. Black Hawk decided to move west and try to get across the Mississippi River to join the relative safety of other Sauk and Meskwaki in Iowa. This led to their discovery on July 19. The American army and militia gave chase, catching up with the exhausted band on July 21 as they crossed the Wisconsin River. More than one hundred warriors held off a much larger force and allowed most to escape. An attempt at surrender failed the next day. One large group of Meskwaki women and children attempted to flee by canoe. Many were killed, captured, or drowned.[52]

The last tragic part of the war came on August 2 at the Battle of Bad Axe, which was more of a massacre than any military clash. The steamboat *Warrior*, which had a detachment of US Army infantry onboard, discovered the retreating band near the Bad Axe River on August 1. Black Hawk raised a white flag, but the soldiers opened fire. Few of Black Hawk's people made it across the Mississippi that day. The next morning American soldiers and militia caught their opponents by the river. The remaining warriors fought stubbornly but could not halt the assault. Women and children were slaughtered, some shot while swimming across the Mississippi River. Other noncombatants were murdered onshore. The arrival of the *Warrior* doomed those in the water. The American army took about forty prisoners, mostly women and children. Fewer than one hundred escaped across the river. Black Hawk's band, which once had more than one thousand people, had been destroyed, with about five hundred killed during the campaign. Black Hawk was later captured by the Ho-chunk. When the *Warrior* steamed south after the battle, heading for Prairie du Chien, it churned through floating bodies for forty miles.[53]

The Black Hawk War ended Native resistance to American expansion in Iowa, except for the violence at Spirit Lake in 1857. The war led to the removal of the Sauk and Meskwaki from Iowa in the 1840s. The United States government forced the two tribes to cede much of eastern Iowa in the September 21, 1832, treaty that formally ended the conflict. This area, a fifty-mile-wide strip along the Mississippi River, was known as the Black Hawk Purchase. It totaled about six million acres and was to be vacated by June 1, 1833. In return, the federal government promised to pay $20,000 a year for thirty years. Four hundred square miles along the Iowa River in the southern part of the cession were set aside for Keokuk and his followers. Known as the Keokuk Reserve, it was too small to support tribal populations and lacked game. It was sold in 1836. Black Hawk was imprisoned in St. Louis with two of his sons and a few other tribal members. In the spring of 1833, he and nine others were sent to Washington. They visited President Jackson, who told them to remain at peace or face destruction. On their return trip in the summer, they stopped in Philadelphia, New York City, and Detroit. While Black Hawk lived in Iowa until his death on October 3, 1838, at age seventy-two, other tribes also paid a price for his defiance. The Ho-chunk, for example, lost their land in Wisconsin.

They were forced into northeast Iowa. By 1851 all land in Iowa that had been occupied by Native Americans had been ceded to the United States.[54]

Native people lived in Iowa for nearly thirteen thousand years before Europeans and Americans walked on its soil. The Ioway and their ancestors had resided in the region for centuries before the Sauk and Meskwaki came to live along the Mississippi River in the mid-1700s. While the first French party reached Iowa in 1673, the influence of Europeans and Americans was limited until the early 1800s. From then on, disease and the fur trade, as well as warfare, directly impacted the Indian nations in and around Iowa. By 1830 increasing numbers of Americans and Europeans reached the area, leading to the Black Hawk War. The United States government forced Native people out of Iowa, practicing Indian removal along the Upper Mississippi River just as it had elsewhere in the country. The devastating defeat in the Black Hawk War forced the Sauk and Meskwaki to cede millions of acres and eventually led to the expulsion of all tribes from the state. In June 1833, white settlers began to migrate into Iowa Territory legally.

2
Iowa Territory, 1833–1846

On June 1, 1833, Iowa officially opened to eager settlers. People rushed into the eastern portion of the territory, lured by the promise of fertile new land. Iowa was part of Michigan Territory, and then Wisconsin Territory, until July 4, 1838, at which point it was designated as Iowa Territory, a region on the west bank of the Mississippi River that stretched from Missouri to Canada. The federal government ruled territories until they became states, appointing a few officials, such as a governor and judges. It also surveyed and sold land. Iowa quickly filled up with migrants whose arrival helped spur the famous, though bloodless, "Honey War" with Missouri. While Iowa was nominally a free state, slavery was tolerated, but not widespread. The white majority strictly regulated the lives of a tiny population of African Americans. A series of treaties forced the Sauk and Meskwaki out of Iowa and opened most of the territory to settlement. After rejecting a constitution that reduced its size in 1844, Iowa voters approved a new one two years later. In December 1846 Iowa joined the United States.

Opportunities for economic gain attracted miners, traders, and fur trappers to eastern Iowa, including George Davenport. He worked as a military contractor, transporting supplies to Fort Armstrong on Rock Island after the War of 1812. Born in England, he ended up in New York in 1804 after four years as a sailor. Davenport then enlisted in the American army, serving for a decade. He became a merchant, set up trading posts in Iowa among the Sauk and Meskwaki, and served as a colonel in the Illinois militia during the Black Hawk War. After the conflict, he helped establish the town named after him. He was murdered on July 4, 1845, at his mansion on Rock Island, as part of a frontier crime wave that plagued the sparsely settled Upper Mississippi River Valley in the 1840s and 1850s. Counterfeiting and horse thievery were common; gangs of bandits fought with groups of settlers. The town of Davenport was founded in May 1836 but had fewer than one hundred residents by the end of that year. Land speculation, lumber milling, and pork processing were mainstays of its economy before the Civil War. Ferries and steamboats provided transport until the arrival of the railroad. By 1860 Davenport had more than eleven thousand residents, buoyed by Iowa's population boom in the 1850s and its position as a transport and business hub.[1]

Thousands had waited impatiently for Iowa to open for settlement on June 1, 1833. The American military, whose officers included future Confederate president Jefferson Davis, chased out those who tried to claim land early. Newcomers could settle on a strip of land about fifty miles wide adjacent to the Mississippi River—the Sauk, Meskwaki, and other tribes had not yet ceded the rest of the territory. Three ferries took people and animals across the Mississippi River to towns such as Dubuque and Burlington. Long lines of wagons waited their turn. Others crossed in boats, their horses swimming nearby. Some left before dawn, eager to explore and claim land. They were not the first to come to Iowa, however: some settlers had ventured in the early 1830s into the "Half-Breed Tract," a triangle of land between the Mississippi and Des Moines Rivers, with a racially insensitive name. About 119,000 acres in size and set aside by an 1824 treaty in which the Sauk and Meskwaki gave up land claims in northern Missouri, it was reserved for mixed-race families. White settlers moved in anyway and the US government began to survey land for sale in March 1832. The town of Keokuk was located at its very southernmost point.[2]

More than ninety-six thousand people came to the Territory of Iowa after the government opened it for settlement. One family of ten, the Duffields, arrived in March 1837. They moved from Ohio to Illinois and finally Iowa, claiming land near the Des Moines River in the southeast corner of the territory. They built a cabin with the assistance of neighbors and began farming. Another family, a newly married couple named Kitturah Penton Belknap and George Belknap, left Ohio for Iowa in October 1839. They bought a claim from a family who returned to Missouri, acquiring plows, chickens, and a small log cabin. They both worked incessantly to save money to buy their land once the government put it up for sale. Celinda Dutton moved to Iowa with her family in 1840 from New York. Her parents and five of her sisters traveled in wagons that carried household goods, as well as fruit trees, for their new home. Heading to Scott County to live near relatives, they brought a dog named Bogus with them. All three families were squatters—people who lived on government land that had not yet come up for sale.[3]

In the 1830s Iowa river towns could be rough places, teeming with miners, boatmen, and those fleeing from the government. Keokuk was a depot for the transfer of goods up the Des Moines River or over the rapids in the Mississippi River. Mining areas like Dubuque were mostly full of men chasing dreams of wealth. More than one thousand lead mining permits were issued around Dubuque in 1833 and 1834. These new towns had taverns and hotels full of male laborers or migrants heading west. Charles Augustus Murray, an English traveler, wrote that taverns were packed with loud, rough-looking blasphemers. Ferries carried wagons, animals, and people across the Mississippi River and steamboats regularly stopped by. These Mississippi River towns had residents whose "chief occupation seems to consist of drinking, fighting, and gambling," wrote Murray. They regularly shot each other, too, he noted with alarm. Alongside the thieves, fugitives, and army deserters came immigrants from Ireland, Germany, and England. Many wanted to earn the high wages in the mines near Dubuque. Their labor allowed one blast furnace to produce seventy thousand pounds of ore weekly. Annual lead production on the Upper Mississippi River eventually reached 55 million pounds by 1848, with the total value of lead double that of the fur trade and all commerce from Santa Fe. Dubuque produced 9.8 million pounds of lead in 1847.[4]

Men did not monopolize violence or daring, as the story of Louisa Massey shows. A mining claim dispute near Dubuque in the fall of 1835 led to the murder of Woodbury Massey, who was ambushed and killed by John Smith and his son William. The crime went unpunished, as the local circuit court declared that it did not have jurisdiction west of the Mississippi. The Massey family sought revenge. One of the four Massey brothers killed John Smith in Galena, Illinois, as he walked past their family store. William Smith swore vengeance and promised to kill the first Massey he could find. Seventeen-year-old Louisa Massey decided to bring an end to the feud. She disguised herself and went looking for William. A boy identified him. Louisa confronted Smith, demanding that "if you are Smith, defend yourself." He stood and she shot him. She then fled, having brought an end to the quarrel. William Smith's life was saved by a wallet in his breast pocket. He died several years later while Louisa Massey lived the rest of her life in St. Louis. Approving of her conduct, legislators seem to have named Louisa County in southeast Iowa in her honor in 1836.[5]

In May 1834 Lieutenant Colonel Stephen Kearny and three companies of United States Dragoons were ordered to establish an outpost near the mouth of the Des Moines River. (This unit consisted of soldiers on horseback and was the only mounted fighting force in the US Army in the mid-1830s.) The army wanted a stronger military presence in the area and a base for operations north of Missouri. In late September, the dragoons joined civilian contractors who had been sent from St. Louis to build the outpost. The soldiers spent weeks helping to complete work on Fort Des Moines before winter came. Life was difficult for them. Construction had been shoddy and roofs leaked. Buildings were cold and snow drifted in. Fleas and sickness plagued the soldiers—many drank too much alcohol and some deserted. The next year Kearny and his men explored northern Iowa and southern Minnesota, visiting territory mostly unknown to Americans. They traveled eleven hundred miles between June and August, passing Sauk and Meskwaki villages and encountering herds of buffalo. Kearny's officers included Captain Nathan Boone, son of the famous frontiersmen Daniel Boone, and Lieutenant Albert M. Lea. A detachment commanded by Boone clashed briefly with Sioux warriors on June 30. The dragoons mapped parts of the "Iowa District" that they saw and searched for a good location for a new fort farther west. Eight years later, the second Fort Des Moines was built where the Raccoon River flowed into the Des Moines River. The first Fort Des Moines was abandoned in June 1837, with most of its troops transferred to Fort Leavenworth in Kansas.[6]

In 1836 Albert M. Lea published a small book called *Notes on the Wisconsin Territory*. The booklet brought attention to Iowa and helped give the place its name—he referred to the region as the "Iowa District of the Wisconsin Territory." Lea reviewed the geography and recent history of the region, as well as its climate and resources. He described the landscape "as one grand rolling prairie" that was full of streams and springs. The soil was rich, the land beautiful, and the climate pleasant, he bragged, writing, "It surpasses any portion of the United States with which I am acquainted." He claimed that villages had sprung up "far in the interior" and that thirty thousand people would live in Iowa by the end of 1836. Neither of these statements were accurate and Lea's promotional pamphlet repeatedly exaggerated the development of Iowa. Lea did not have entirely wholesome motivations, as he wanted to make money selling property to immigrants. His financial speculations failed, but his pamphlet popularized the Iowa region.[7]

Those who moved across the Mississippi River into the Iowa district migrated to a region without "any regular machinery of government," wrote historian William J. Petersen. They were distant from authority and lived on land that was not even surveyed. Oddly, Iowa—as well as other parts of the northern Louisiana Purchase—had not been part of any official territory until it was added to Michigan Territory in 1834. This lack of legal clarity revealed the need for some sort of government, especially after one Iowa settler, Patrick O'Connor, murdered George O'Keaf in late spring 1834. O'Connor defied a local ad hoc Dubuque jury, arguing that he could not be punished because there were "no laws in this country." Appeals to President Andrew Jackson failed, as the federal executive had no jurisdiction over the trial. Nevertheless, O'Connor was hanged on June 20. The orphan Iowa district was added to Michigan Territory eight days later and divided into the two counties of Du Buque and De Moine. Those who lived west of the Mississippi began to plan the construction of courthouses and the enforcement of the laws of the Territory of Michigan.[8]

Iowa was part of Michigan Territory for two years, until Michigan joined the United States. In 1836 Iowa became a part of the Territory of Wisconsin, a vast area that included all territories around the Great Lakes and the northern plains that had been part of the Louisiana Purchase. Iowa Territory was created on July 4, 1838. The United States admitted new states only after they had passed through two stages of territorial government. In the first phase, officials appointed by the federal government held power. A governor, secretary, and three judges could write laws, usually adopted from other states. They also appointed other officials, such as sheriffs. Once a district had five thousand free white men, voters could elect the lower legislative branch of the local legislature, while the US Congress selected members of the upper house. Legislation required a majority of both houses, but the appointed governor could veto any laws. Territories could also send a nonvoting delegate to Congress. When the Territory of Iowa was created in 1838 it contained 22,859 people. Independent territorial status gave Iowa increased political power and its own governor.[9]

Robert Lucas was Iowa's first territorial governor. He had served as governor of Ohio and as a colonel in the army before being sent to Iowa. President Martin Van Buren appointed him for a term of three years. Lucas arrived in Burlington on August 15, 1838, adopting the town as a temporary residence until a territorial capital was chosen by the legislature. The new governor immediately called for the election of a territorial legislature, toured eastern Iowa, and asked lawmakers to eliminate gambling and drinking in the territory. Meanwhile, Van Buren appointed judges, as well as an attorney and marshal. The first territorial legislature enacted laws concerning courts, education, horses, sheriffs, and many other subjects. More than half of legislators were born in southern states, mainly Virginia and Kentucky. Most were farmers and merchants. They imposed harsh restrictions on African Americans, barring them from voting, testifying against whites in a trial, or attending white schools. Black Americans had to provide a certificate proving they were free and post a $500 bond to enter the territory. In 1840 intermarriage between Blacks and whites was made illegal. When the legislative session ended, one diarist, Theodore Parvin, noted that most of the lawmakers were "all drunk with few exceptions." Such behavior may have accounted for the governor's comment that the population of most frontier settlements was "hospitable, yet rude." However, he noted diplomatically, Iowa was comparable to any western state, and some eastern ones, in "intelligence and enterprise."[10]

A commission of three men had the task of choosing a site for the new capital, which was to become Iowa City. Their search began on May 1, 1839. Only one individual showed up; the others did not. In the afternoon, a rider was sent to collect one of two missing men so that a majority of the committee could begin the selection process. The next day the two men found a suitable location, which had plenty of stone for construction. Settlers had moved into the area in 1838, erecting cabins and a sawmill and establishing a ferry across the Iowa River. The capitol was laid out in the spring, surveyed in the summer, and the first town lots—more than one hundred—were sold in August 1839. People flooded into the new town, from tavern-keepers to doctors and lawyers—of which there were sixteen in Iowa City and nearby counties within two years. A hotel and churches were built, newspapers founded, and stagecoach lines established. The same firm that erected the Illinois capitol constructed Iowa's capitol. The cornerstone was laid on July 4, 1840. The legislature and government moved to Iowa City in 1842, where it would be located until it migrated to

Des Moines in 1857. Iowa City had nine hundred residents by 1846, with eight mail routes tying it to the rest of the territory.[11]

Families moved into Iowa hoping to acquire land, but none could be sold until it had been surveyed. The first surveys in Iowa—outside of the Half Breed Tract—began in the fall of 1836. The federal government hired surveying parties on contract to lay out the square grid of townships and sections that has segmented most of the United States. Surveyors did not get paid much—$2.75 per mile, about $85 in 2020—and worked quickly to reduce their expenses. A group led by William Burt surveyed seventy-two miles in eastern Iowa in eight days. Inspectors who audited surveyors' records found many errors. Corners were not marked and township and section lines were incorrect. The work was often hampered by cold weather, flooding, and mosquitoes, which made work difficult, but often the surveying was just shoddy, regardless of external circumstances. Surveyor Willard Barrow found armed settlers with contesting claims also provided trouble. They interfered with measurements and destroyed markers to mislead rivals. The average surveying party consisted of six to eleven men, including chainmen, an ax man, moundmen, and the deputy surveyor who led them. At least ten different groups labored in northwest Iowa in 1855. They were often in the field working for months, sometimes meeting hunters, trappers, or Sioux hunting parties. "Our work was hard, our days long," wrote Ira Cook. "We were at work in the morning as soon as we could see, worked as long as we could see at night." They lived on bread, salt pork, beans, and coffee. Hunters sometimes killed a deer, which added some variety to their diet. Despite such hardships, the enormous task of surveying the state was finished in 1858.[12]

Imperfect surveying led to the famed "Honey War" with Missouri in 1839. The dispute arose when a careless surveyor left an uncertain border between the two states. A surveyor appointed by Missouri decided that the boundary was too far south and set a new one farther north. This line gave Missouri 2,616 additional square miles of land and deprived Iowa of the southern portions of its southernmost counties. The Missouri legislature declared that this was the new border in February 1839. Farmers in Van Buren County in southeast Iowa did not appreciate their sudden annexation to a slave state. In August, Missouri Sheriff Uriah Gregory attempted to collect taxes in the disputed area. Iowans refused to pay. Gregory returned in November with several hundred men and was arrested for trespassing by the sheriff of Van Buren County. The Missouri governor then called out the militia. Some impatient Missourians cut down some "bee trees," giving the conflict its name. Iowans headed south, many armed with pitchforks and clubs, to confront the invaders. Iowan Aristarchus Cone wrote that some took shotguns, while others went armed with whiskey and broomsticks. After one very cold night many deserted. The crisis quickly passed and both sides backed down. The issue was sent to Congress to negotiate. Congress then gave the problem to the Supreme Court, which decided to accept the original border that favored Iowa.[13]

The federal government first sold land in Iowa in the autumn of 1838, but people had been scrambling to claim it since the territory had opened up. Settlers and speculators had explored eastern Iowa for years, searching for a home or for an investment opportunity. George Duffield recalled that his family had hosted many who were investigating the territory. His father had withheld information about the countryside from those with smooth manners and better clothing, while helping migrants who were plainly dressed. Squatters in Iowa, such as the Duffields, who did not yet own their land, viewed nonsettlers as a threat to their property claims. Possible speculators were viewed with suspicion—they were seen as heartless and greedy men who only sought a quick return. Settlers feared that speculators would buy the land that families lived on, depriving them of a home and any improvements, such as a cabin or fencing. Suel Foster, who bought a one-sixth interest in the town site that became Muscatine, explained the squatter ideal clearly: "The crowns of Europe handed down laws to our forefathers, but we, the 'squatters' of Iowa, handed laws up to our rulers and they acknowledged our 'sovereign power' and accommodated their laws to suit our necessity." Farmers needed to acquire land to survive and they would not let anyone steal it from them. On June 5, 1849, one farmer, Joseph Ross, killed a man who outbid him for his claim. He was later acquitted of the crime.[14]

To protect their land claims, squatters and settlers created extralegal organizations, known as claims clubs. Such organizations appeared in at least one-quarter of Iowa's counties, including Keokuk, Madison, and Boone Counties. The Johnson County Claim Association was the best known and had more than 270 members. These included Governor Robert Lucas, who was a member in 1840. Their goal was to "forestall the land speculator and claim jumper," wrote historian Allan G. Bogue. Though they were outside the normal legal system, the Iowa territorial legislature recognized and upheld squatters' claims in 1839. The territory's supreme court supported such associations too. Members pledged to assist others in protecting their claims. Clubs registered and protected land claims, mediated disputes, and helped ensure that their members were not outbid at land auctions. Hundreds of men showed up at auctions, surrounding the land office and keeping rival bidders at bay. Some clubs allowed families to make multiple claims—on up to 320 acres of land each. This helped current members but reduced the amount of land available to those who arrived later. Such associations also threatened or intimidated those who questioned the property ownership of their members or violated rules that they enforced.[15]

Mob violence was usually a last resort, but it was carried out on occasion. Claim jumping was one of the most serious frontier crimes. Death by hanging was threatened at least once, but lesser punishments were the norm. One incident known as "The Majors' War"—named after an infamous family—occurred near Oskaloosa in the mid- and late 1840s. This large household made ten land claims of 320 acres each that were viewed as legitimate. However, Jacob Majors also maintained that he owned some timber property claimed by three other men. Nearby clubs, which had members with property in the area, told him to abandon the timber land. He ignored them. Outraged neighbors destroyed some buildings on his property. In retaliation, Majors asked that those who had incited the violence be arrested. A force of five hundred armed men marched to Oskaloosa to intimidate Majors and any sheriff who might wish to defend him. Jacob Majors surrendered his deed to the disputed timberland but continued to push for the arrest of his former neighbors. He was later kidnapped, stripped naked, and coated in tar and feathers. Humiliated and defeated, he left Iowa.[16]

The first land sales in Iowa occurred in Burlington on November 19, 1838. Thousands of people filled the town. Those with more wealth stayed in hotels, while most settlers found more humble housing, often camping out. George Duffield's father, James, went to the town in November to purchase his claim. He took $200 that he had borrowed at 50 percent interest from a money lender who offered loans to squatters. James Duffield feared that he would be outbid at the land auction, but he had joined a claims club in Van Buren County and hoped this would be enough to attain his goal. At a public land auction, each quarter section, or one-quarter of a square mile, would be called out. The announcer, or crier, would then wait thirty seconds for a bid before moving on to the next quarter section. Duffield's neighbors intimidated outside speculators and ensured that he could buy his land. One man who attempted to outbid a claims club member was beaten with hickory canes, remembered Charles A. White. A club sometimes appointed a bidder who ensured that property was purchased at the minimum price. Territorial officials who ran land sales accepted such bids without question. When Duffield returned home, the family enjoyed "the joy of possession supported by title. Our claim and cabin were indeed our own," Duffield wrote. Sometime in the 1840s, Kitturah Belknap and her husband George also purchased their land. She had made butter and sold eggs and meat to earn money to buy the land; George had cut timber in winter to sell. His boots froze "as hard as bones," she wrote. The Duttons settled in the northwest corner of Scott County, rented a cabin, and set about growing crops.[17]

The receiver of the Burlington Land Office, Ver Planck Van Antwerp, recalled that when the fall auction of land concluded, "I had received over a third of a million dollars, mostly in silver." He took seven tons of coin to the Bank of the State of Missouri in St. Louis. A teller took three weeks to count the money.[18]

While the government was selling land in eastern Iowa in the late 1830s, it had not yet forced the remaining Sauk and Meskwaki from the territory. After the Black Hawk Purchase, the tribes had moved into central Iowa and away from the initial wave of settlers. They pursued a traditional cycle of hunting and agriculture, surviving in an area outside their normal hunting grounds. Their subsistence was hampered by a lack of large mammals to hunt—bison had retreated to the Great Plains and competition with settlers reduced the deer population. Scarce game forced them to hunt farther away, bringing them into conflict with the Sioux. Americans and Europeans continued to press into their land as well. Tribal divisions and recriminations over their defeat haunted the Sauk and Meskwaki. In 1836 and 1837 they were forced to sell more than a million acres of land adjacent to the Black Hawk Purchase. The ceaseless march of settlers west continually pressured the remaining tribal members. Iowa Territory had a white population of more than forty-three thousand in 1840. Thousands more came every year. Squatters took the Native Americans' land, while unscrupulous traders left them deep in debt. Disease and liquor also took their toll. The population fell by about one-half between 1833 and 1846. All of this undermined the two tribes and encouraged additional land cessions to the Americans.[19]

In 1842, the US government completed negotiations to remove the Sauk and Meskwaki from the Territory of Iowa. Initially, the government wanted them to move to southwest Minnesota, but the tribes protested, with Keokuk arguing that it was a poor and distressed area. Wapello, a leader of the Meskwaki, told the Americans that they had already been forced to sell Rock Island, Dubuque, and other places, saying, "This is all the country we have left, and we are so few now, we cannot conquer other countries. You now see me and all my nation. Have pity on us. We are but few and are fast melting away." Their options were limited. They were deep in debt to white traders and their annual annuity could not feed them. With hunting becoming increasingly difficult and whites threatening their land, the tribes sold their remaining territory in Iowa. Almost ten million acres were lost in the October 11, 1842, treaty, which mandated that all tribal members had to leave Iowa within three years. The American government planned to remove them from Iowa and send them to Kansas. The Sauk left Iowa before the deadline, but the Meskwaki did not exit the state on schedule. Only 20 percent reached Kansas before December. Meskwaki chief Poweshiek protested their removal. "Soon I will go to a new home," he said. "You will plant corn where my dead sleep. Our towns, the paths we have made, the flowers we have loved will soon be yours." The US Army rounded many up, but they disliked Kansas as it was so different from Iowa. Some Meskwaki stayed in Iowa, unwilling to leave their homeland.[20]

The removal of the original Native inhabitants of Iowa led to a frantic dash for "The New Purchase." Roads heading toward the cession were full of men, women, and children eager to take possession of it. Hundreds of restless migrants invaded the tenuous border separating Native land from areas already opened to settlement. Many drank heavily; some were violent. Incursions into Sauk and Meskwaki lands occurred so often that the US Army had to be called in to restore order and keep squatters out. Parts of central Iowa opened to settlement at midnight on April 30, 1843. Squatters with torches came in a mad dash for the best spots, which led to scenes of wild confusion and overlapping and irregular claims in the early hours of May 1. There may have been ten thousand people in the area by May 23, according to one estimate. The furious competition for new land occurred again in October when an adjacent section was opened to settlement. Nearly one hundred fifty thousand people flooded into Iowa in the 1840s, pushing settlement toward Fort Des Moines Number Two.[21]

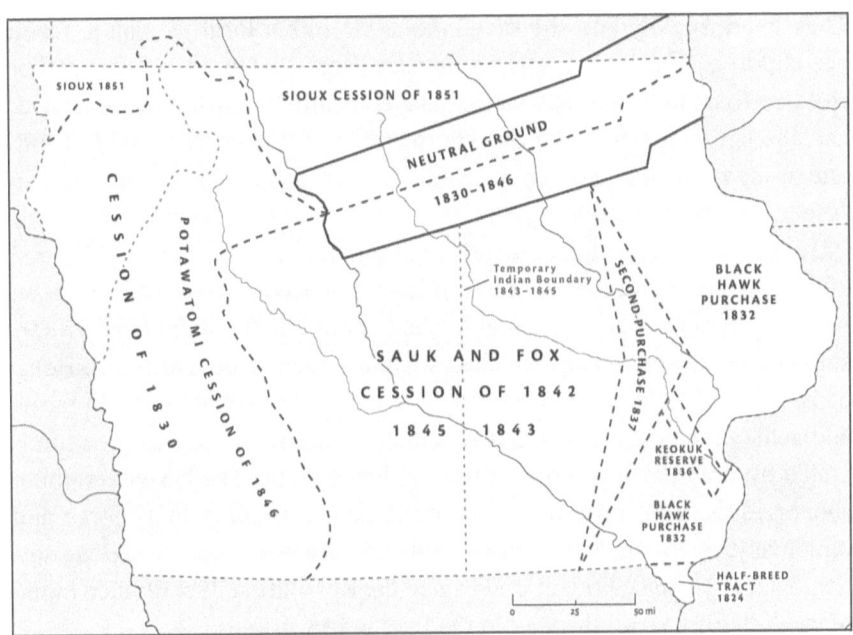

Map of Indian cessions in Iowa.

Susan Wyatt came to Iowa in 1842 with her husband, Jabe, and her daughter, named Missouri. They had married in 1838 when Susan was sixteen. The couple migrated west from Virginia and lived in Ohio, Indiana, Illinois, and Missouri before permanently settling in Jasper County, a mostly unsettled area east of Des Moines in the New Purchase. Both were far from any relatives. The family lived as squatters for several years until the land was surveyed. They built a cabin, planted a garden and fields of corn, eventually buying their land from the government. Hailstorms, early frosts, droughts, and mosquitoes made their lives challenging. Neighbors died of smallpox. Susan gave birth to seven children before her husband abandoned the family in the mid-1850s, taking most of their money. He had been caught having an affair with a nearby woman. Jabe left Susan with five children, two having died from pneumonia. Susan worked in the fields with her oldest son, Thomas, and the family gathered fruits and nuts from nearby prairies and forests. Her daughters helped with cooking and caring for chickens. Their garden, chickens, corn crop, and eggs helped feed them. Susan pickled cucumbers and tomatoes, smoked meat, made sauerkraut, and dried fruits. She sold meals to travelers who passed by.

They lived frugally and she saved money to hire a local woman to teach her children. She looked after a teenage German boy, too. Four of her children lived to be adults. One son stayed nearby to farm. She remarried, had another daughter, and moved to the town of Baxter. She died in 1908, one of the first white women to live in central Iowa. Susan Wyatt lived in Jasper County for sixty-six years.[22]

Tens of thousands of people moved into Iowa Territory in the 1830s and 1840s. Americans and Europeans quickly replaced Native tribes with an unruly, grasping, and sometimes violent society that valued land ownership and white supremacy. Restless squatters such as the Duffields, Belknaps, and Wyatts hurried into newly opened lands, seeking to build farms and achieve their dreams. Land speculators followed, their avarice moderated by irregular institutions such as claims clubs. The US government supported the westward movement of settlers through military force and diplomacy, removing Native inhabitants with little remorse. American settlement had advanced relentlessly since the Revolution. It continued in the nineteenth century all the way to the Pacific Ocean.

Debate over admission to the United States began almost as soon as Iowa Territory was established. Governor Lucas had suggested that a state constitution be written in 1839, but the legislature ignored him. When the idea was put before voters in 1840, it was defeated by a three-to-one margin. A new presidential administration replaced Lucas in 1841 with Governor John Chambers, who also endorsed statehood. Iowa voters rejected another attempt in August 1842. The United States paid the costs of territorial administration, reducing the tax burden of Iowans, which helps to explain the lack of enthusiasm for becoming a state. But, as Iowa's population increased, newcomers increasingly supported the idea. Joining the United States meant that Iowa could elect its own governor and have more influence in Washington, with its own senators and representatives. The state could also get a share of federal money to improve sections of the Mississippi River for steamboat traffic. Florida—a future slave state—needed to join the union at the same time as a free state. This would maintain equal representation in the US Senate between the two sides, an agreement that had emerged from the Missouri Compromise in 1820. If Iowa delayed its application, it might have to wait a few more years to become a state. In December 1843 Governor Chambers proposed a vote on statehood. The legislature agreed to authorize an election. Voters endorsed the idea of a constitutional convention in April 1844 and elected delegates to the convention in August.[23]

The constitutional convention began in Iowa City on October 7, 1844. Most delegates, among them former governor Robert Lucas, were farmers and nearly two-thirds had been born in northern states. More northerners than southerners came to Iowa in the 1840s and 1850s, which helped tilt the balance of constitutional delegates. Being born in a northern state did not significantly change the decisions that delegates made on race, however. Most of them were Jacksonian Democrats. Andrew Jackson was an enslaver who thought Native people were barbarians. He was also suspicious of banks. Many sections of the document echoed the United States Constitution, such as the proclamation of separation of powers and the state Bill of Rights. The constitution established a bicameral legislative branch, as well as a governor and lieutenant governor in the executive branch. A judiciary, consisting of a supreme court and a district court, made up the third part of government. The constitution also directed the legislature to create a school system. Suffrage was limited to white men over the age of twenty-one. Subjects such as banking, race, and state boundaries were major topics of debate. This constitution did not allow the incorporation of any bank or "corporation with banking privileges" unless voters approved such a charter. A serious economic depression, starting with a financial panic in 1837 and lasting until the early 1840s, had left many Americans suspicious of banks. Iowa's only chartered bank, the Miner's Bank of Dubuque, had a poor reputation due to bad loans and currency shortages. One delegate called banks "swindling machines," while another said that they were "the common enemy of mankind." The convention adjourned on November 1, 1844, and the constitution was forwarded to Congress for approval.[24]

The Iowa constitution strictly regulated the lives of the tiny population of African Americans in the territory—only 188 lived in Iowa Territory in 1840—and demonstrated the prevalent racism of white Americans of the time. Such laws were common in northern states. In the late 1830s, Black men could only vote in four states; segregated schools existed almost everywhere in the north. Ohio, Indiana, and Illinois did not allow Blacks to testify against whites in court. In its racist legislation, Iowa was very much like nearby states, such as Illinois and Michigan, where interracial marriage was banned. One committee report argued that Iowa could not be opened for Black settlement, as a flood of African Americans would endanger white Americans. This report contended that the two races could not exist together peacefully. It claimed that Black immigration would bring idleness, crime, and violence—racist falsehoods that some still repeated almost two hundred years later. The exclusion of all African Americans almost became part of the constitution. But excluding all Black Americans from the state could have endangered admission to the union, so this idea was dropped. The proposed Iowa constitution did not allow Blacks to vote or serve in the militia.[25]

Some of Iowa's first pioneers were Black. Stephen Kearny, an army officer, brought an enslaved woman to Iowa in 1834. Iowa's small African American population mostly resided in towns along the Mississippi River and worked as laborers. Many lived in Dubuque, where seventy-two Blacks resided in 1840, making up about 5 percent of the town's population. Six of the contributors to the first Methodist church in the town were African Americans. Slavery was not widespread, but it was tolerated—16 of 188 African Americans in the territory in 1840 were listed as slaves. Some owners mislabeled their human property as "free colored" in the census. The second territorial governor, John Chambers, brought a few enslaved African Americans with him. One of them, Cassius, was a servant during the legislative session. When Chambers left Iowa, Cassius and a woman named Carey Bennett claimed their freedom and refused to leave. The secretary of the territory also owned several enslaved people. Despite being tolerated, slave owning was not widely embraced by Iowans. One Keokuk slaveholder moved across the Des Moines River to Missouri to escape criticism from neighbors.[26]

In 1834 Ralph Montgomery, an enslaved man owned by Jordan Montgomery of Missouri, came to work in the Dubuque mines. Montgomery had been born about 1795 in Virginia as Rafe Nelson but forced to take the last name of his enslaver, William Montgomery. William's son, Jordan Montgomery, then enslaved Ralph in northeast Missouri. Initially, Ralph agreed to labor in Dubuque until he earned $550, plus interest, to buy his freedom. He worked for five years but was unable to pay the debt. Living costs were simply too high to save much money. In 1839 two Virginians offered to return the enslaved man to his owner for $100. Jordan Montgomery needed money and did not want to lose his investment, so he agreed. The two Virginians swore that Ralph Montgomery was a fugitive slave before a justice of the peace. A sheriff arrested him and sent him to a riverboat in handcuffs. But a merchant named Alexander Butterworth had watched the kidnapping; Butterworth had a lead mine adjacent to Ralph Montgomery. He got a writ of habeas corpus from Judge T. S. Wilson, which forced the case to be brought before a judge to determine the legal status of the arrest. Ralph was rescued just before the boat departed; he was taken before Judge Wilson, who asked that the case be transferred to the new state supreme court. Wilson happened to be a member.[27]

Ralph Montgomery's case was the second to come before the Iowa Supreme Court, but the first to be decided by the court. Montgomery had a strong argument for his freedom. American law supported the rights of an enslaved person who lived in free territory. The Missouri Supreme Court had supported at least a dozen freedom suits from enslaved people who lived in Illinois. The Missouri Compromise, which specified that territory in the Louisiana Purchase north and west of Missouri would be free, helped Ralph Montgomery's case. The Iowa court ruled that Montgomery was a free man—not a slave, nor a fugitive slave. On July 4, 1839, he was freed. The next spring, Judge Wilson found him working in the garden behind his house. The free man worked for the judge for one a day a year to express his gratitude. Ralph Montgomery died in Dubuque in 1870, having contracted smallpox while caring for someone who had the disease.[28]

While Montgomery managed to achieve his freedom, another Black man was killed by a mob in Iowa just one year later. Nathaniel Morgan and his wife Charlotte had lived in Dubuque since 1833, both working at a boardinghouse after they arrived. In 1840 Charlotte was a laundress, while Nat worked as a cook and waiter at a hotel. In early September, a group of men seized Morgan and accused him of stealing a trunk full of clothes. A mob formed, reinforced by intoxicated patrons from nearby taverns. They tied him to a post and began to whip him. He claimed innocence but then confessed, saying whatever the mob wanted. After one hundred lashes, the mob took him to where the trunk supposedly was located. They whipped him nearly forty more times when they did not find it. They took him to his house and whipped him before his wife. The mob then dragged him into the woods and killed him. A trial ended in acquittal for the accused leaders of the mob.[29]

The contradictions between the salvation of Ralph Montgomery and the death of Nathaniel Morgan were clear. Both occurred in Dubuque, but historian Robert R. Dykstra views the rescue of Montgomery to be an anomaly, given the overall racial climate of the town. Residents demonstrated an open prejudice, by specifying only whites could vote and by not hiding their ownership of slaves from census takers. While Iowa was not Dubuque, the territory was not a safe place for African Americans. The state became a much more racially progressive place in the 1860s, but it took a civil war to change racial attitudes.[30]

Iowa's admission to the United States hit a roadblock when the House of Representatives modified Iowa's borders. The state border was moved east from the Missouri River to about forty miles west of Des Moines, reducing the size of Iowa by about one-third. Northern congressmen wanted Iowa to be a smaller, so more states could be carved out of the Louisiana Purchase for admission as nonslave states. Congress approved, and President Tyler signed, this modified statehood bill, which allowed both Iowa and Florida to become states. Florida joined the United States in March 1845, but Iowa did not become a state for almost two more years. Iowans were unhappy with these new boundaries and voters rejected ratification of a constitution with altered borders in 1845. A new constitutional convention was called, and a second constitution was written in May 1846, reflecting current state boundaries. It closely resembled the document from 1844. Major changes included totally outlawing banks in the state—leading to a shortage of money and a lot of dubious currency from other places circulating in the area for years afterward. It also required a constitutional convention to amend the document, a major hurdle to any revision. In August 1846 voters ratified the new constitution with the current state boundaries.[31]

Even as Iowa struggled to join the Union, Mormon migrants sought to leave the United States. Almost twenty thousand crossed southern Iowa in the 1840s while heading to Utah to escape persecution. Their prophet, Joseph Smith, had been murdered, and they had been driven out of Illinois, where they had built a city called Nauvoo. In February 1846 Mormons began landing at Montrose, in the southeast corner of Iowa. Trailblazers headed west and built camps for those who came later. Thousands followed them across the territory in the winter. Refugees trekked through a mostly uninhabited country that had few roads, suffering from intensely cold weather and diseases ranging from malaria to scurvy. When it was above freezing, pathways turned to deep mud that slowed travel to a few miles a day. Hundreds died on their journey. Whenever possible, men worked for local farmers, clearing land or shucking corn to earn money for food. Once they arrived at the Missouri River it was too late to head to Utah. Thousands survived another winter in Iowa before departing for their new homeland in 1847. Five hundred Mormon men volunteered to fight in the Mexican War, forming the famous "Mormon Battalion." Their wages helped buy desperately needed food for others. Most people migrated to Utah in the 1840s, but thousands of Mormons continued to come west in the next decade. In 1856 and 1857 emigrant groups took the railroad line to Iowa City, then walked about thirteen hundred miles to their new homes in Utah while pushing handcarts with their possessions. In July 1856 two parties departed late and encountered blizzards while crossing the continental divide in Wyoming, losing more than two hundred people. Some Mormons stayed in southwest Iowa. Ann Binnall Butler and her husband Lorenzo lived in Woodbine, opening a store and running a sawmill. She became postmistress of the town.[32]

On December 28, 1846, Iowa joined the United States, its disorderly march to statehood finally over. Iowa elected a state governor and other representatives on October 26 without waiting for the US government to recognize its legal existence as a state. These elections may have been void, but this did not seem to trouble anyone. Iowa's first governor was Democrat Ansel Briggs, who had been a stagecoach driver and sheriff. The state also sent two congressmen to Washington, DC, and elected the first state legislature. Governor Briggs was sworn in twenty-five days before Iowa became a state. However, Iowa did not send any US senators to Washington. A political deadlock between the Whig and Democrat parties kept anyone from being elected. So, Iowa's messy political history continued until the Second General Assembly broke the stalemate and sent Democrats George W. Jones and Augustus C. Dodge to the national capitol.[33]

Dodge and Jones were good representatives of their new state and the Democratic Party—they wanted to develop the frontier by expelling Native people and subjugating African Americans. Both men had served in the Black Hawk War and staunchly supported the expansion of slavery. Dodge had been a miner and land speculator, who defended the rights of settlers who invaded the lands of Native people while serving as Iowa's territorial delegate to the US Congress in 1846. Jones, a lawyer and a businessman, enslaved four African Americans while living in Dubuque in 1840. Jones had a reputation as a "duelling character" during his own tenure as Iowa's territorial delegate. His personal corruption went unchallenged by northern representatives because he was a bully who intimidated colleagues with the threat of violence. Both Dodge and Jones voted in favor of the harsh Fugitive Slave Act of 1850—only one other free-state senator did so—as well as opening Kansas Territory to slavery in 1854. Their unyielding support of the South led to both men losing their Senate seats once Republicans became the dominant political party in Iowa in the mid- and late 1850s.[34]

Much had transpired during the brief existence of Iowa Territory. The federal government had surveyed and sold land to immigrants. It had also forced the Sauk and Meskwaki from Iowa. Almost one hundred thousand people lived in Iowa when it became a state. The tiny population of African Americans had few rights and suffered from occasional brutal violence. While slavery was dying in the state in the 1840s, the condition of Black Iowans improved little. In the fifteen years between statehood and the Civil War, Iowa gained almost one-half million people. The story of frontier Iowa is the next chapter.

3
Frontier Iowa, 1833–1870

Most immigrants to Iowa in the mid-nineteenth century were from northern states, such as Illinois, Ohio, or New York. But some were from Europe, with emigrants from Sweden and Holland among those who migrated to Iowa before the Civil War. Other immigrant groups included the Inspirationalists, who came to Iowa in the 1850s. They established a cluster of settlements known as the Amana Colonies. The Amish came to Iowa in the 1840s. People settled first in southeast Iowa, and then moved northwest following river valleys. Settlers came seeking land, which gave them economic independence. Property ownership was crucial for family security—it was their sustenance and provided land for future generations. Family farms dominated the state, with men, women, and children all working together to ensure survival and prosperity. Female labor was especially crucial to family success and women completed many important tasks. There were numerous challenges, including harsh weather, prairie fires, disease, and accidents. As farms spread across the state, villages and towns grew. They provided important transportation and market services for local communities. Americans and Europeans had settled most of the state by the time the Civil War broke out in 1861.

Immigrants went west seeking economic independence. A Wapello County history noted that older states, such as New York and Pennsylvania, were "good—to emigrate from." Migrants wanted affordable farmland so they could feed themselves and successive generations. People moved to achieve what they could not in more populated or expensive areas. Family welfare required property ownership and cheap land provided the opportunity to start a new life or to add to a family's wealth. Since most households lived in rural areas, people made their living from the soil. Inexpensive and fertile land provided unparalleled opportunities for economic gain. James Crawford wrote to his father in Vermont, extolling the virtues of Iowa, "I can raise all the provisions we shall want for one half the labor you can on the best land you have." But the ideal of the self-sufficient pioneer family was "inconsistent with the Iowa experience," argued historian Dorothy Schwieder. Most Iowa farmers also wanted to produce a surplus and make a profit to pay off debts, buy land, or improve their lives.[1]

People came to Iowa for a variety of reasons. "Push" factors were those that forced people to leave their homes, such as unemployment, hunger, or political or religious repression. "Pull" factors drew migrants to a new area, such as job prospects or positive reports from earlier migrants. There was a direct correlation between cheap land and migration in the Midwest. Inexpensive farmland was an "almost irresistible attraction to many," wrote economists Jeremy Atack and Peter Passel. Land in antebellum America provided the most obvious route to wealth accumulation and upward mobility. Property was more abundant in the West, so social mobility usually required westward migration. This drive for economic improvement was a powerful motivation for most migrants to Iowa.[2]

Most came from northern states. A. C. Sutliff left Ohio and settled in Johnson County in southeast Iowa in the early 1840s. Sutliff traveled several hundred miles searching for a good farm site in 1838. "I had not come as far as I had for chances as others. I was looking for the best and would go farther to get it," he wrote to his brother. He found a "handsome situation for a farm," with fertile land, timber, and water near a navigable river. The Sutliff family lived as squatters for a few years. He wrote that he hoped "to make enough off the land before it is offered for sale to pay for it." He planned to produce butter and cheese, as the prairies provided great pasture for cattle. "The local advantages far exceed any other country I ever saw for doing business," he boasted.[3]

Other Americans migrated from the Northeast and the Upper South. Some moved directly to Iowa, while others lived in several places before reaching the state. John Kelsey, a carpenter from Niagara County, New York, bought land near Cedar Rapids in 1848. He asked his family to come join him in November 1849, writing, "If you in tend to come atall [*sic*] the Sooner the better as real Estate is rising very fast." His parents and siblings arrived by 1851. He married Harriet Jane Rogers two years later and began farming. Sarah Welch Nossaman and her family left North Carolina in 1831, residing in Indiana and Illinois before moving to Iowa Territory. They stayed in Van Buren County until her family left for Jefferson County. Sarah married at age seventeen and went further west in 1843 with her husband and children to live south of Pella. They occupied a shanty of poles and bark, chasing snakes and skunks out of their primitive shelter.[4]

Swedes and Dutch, as well as immigrants from other nations, came to Iowa before the Civil War too. A group of Swedes established the appropriately named New Sweden in Jefferson County in 1845. They left their homes because of heavy taxes, religious discrimination, and the lack of economic opportunity. Positive reports of economic and political liberty brought many Swedes to Iowa in the nineteenth century. Some founded the town that later became Madrid, south of Boone. New Sweden had about five hundred people by the Civil War. Other Swedes, including Charles J. A. Ericson and his family, left their home country as well. They had received letters from relatives about higher wages and affordable land in the United States. In 1852 the family departed for America. None of them spoke any English. After arriving in New York City, they traveled west by steamboat and train. Ericson lived in Illinois for a few years with his brothers, working at a sawmill, a store, and a ferryboat. In 1859 he moved to Boone County, following a brother, where he opened a store at the age of twenty. He was a successful businessman and banker in Boone.[5]

Dutch immigrants also came to Iowa, settling in Marion County in 1847. Their new colony was called Pella, named for a place where Christians sought refuge after the Roman Empire destroyed Jerusalem. These immigrants left the Netherlands because of agricultural failures, religious persecution, and high taxes. Eight hundred people departed Holland and settled in southern Iowa in 1847. Other immigrants followed. Their leader, Dominee Hendrik Peter Scholte, had purchased forty-seven thousand acres with a group of associates for the colony. They wanted to live in an area that Dutch farmers would recognize as similar to their homeland and where they could grow wheat and raise cattle. Scholte also wanted the settlement to be established near navigable rivers so farmers could export surplus production and purchase necessities that they did not make themselves. The immigrants later built smaller Dutch towns in western Iowa, such as

Sioux Center. By 1860 the Dutch population in Iowa was 2,615; ten years later it was 4,513. (Iowa's many other immigrant groups will be discussed in detail in chapter 6.)[6]

The Amish were some of the first white settlers in Washington and Johnson Counties in the 1840s. They were a highly religious and distinctive community, characterized by "belief in superiority of agrarian life and desire to be isolated from influences outside their own group," wrote Elmer Schwieder and Dorothy Schwieder. A persecuted religious minority, they were descended from sixteenth century European Mennonites and their life had changed little in three hundred years. The first Amish in the American colonies settled in Pennsylvania in the early 1700s and moved west into Iowa and Missouri in the mid-nineteenth century. They rejected modernism and separated themselves from the outside world. The Old Order Amish of Iowa stressed plain clothing and agriculture, living in compact communities where they could enjoy religious freedom. Their homes had functional furniture and homemade rugs. They refused military service and any oath of loyalty. The Amish had a high level of mutual assistance and stressed frugality and self-sufficiency. Families usually farmed about one hundred acres, rotating corn, oats, and hay. Most used horses for fieldwork, even in the twentieth century, and applied animal manure to their fields rather than any artificial fertilizer.[7]

A German communal society migrated to Iowa in the 1850s, settling west of Iowa City in a collection of villages that became known as the Amana colonies. They began in Germany as the Community of True Inspiration, a religious sect that abandoned the most formal aspects of their faith and focused on simple gatherings and churches. Persecuted in Europe, they moved to New York state, then to Iowa. They sold their land in the east and bought twenty-six thousand acres in Iowa that provided lumber, clay, and rock for building and fertile soil for agriculture. They wanted their new settlement to be self-sufficient and isolated from outside influences. It was named Amana, a biblical name that meant "believe faithfully" or "remain true." Community members attended eleven church services a week, including a brief evening prayer service, often in homes. The first thirty-three members arrived in July 1855 and began to clear land and construct homes. Inspirationalists built six villages in the next seven years: Main, West, South, High, East, and Middle Amana, as well as Homestead, which was purchased for access to a nearby railroad. By the end of 1864 the community had 1,228 members. Pacifists, they did not take

Amana community members lived communal lives, sharing resources and working together. Women labored in kitchens preparing daily meals. Amana women preparing sauerkraut, ca. 1920, Homestead, Iowa. From Amana Society-People photo files, Special Collections, State Historical Society of Iowa, Iowa City.

part in the Civil War. They shared this view with Quakers and the Amish. The community paid to hire a substitute soldier in the place of those who were drafted into service.[8]

People in Amana lived communal lives wherein they shared resources and cared for each other, working "at whatever they were best qualified to do by training and experience," wrote Barbara S. Yambura in her memoir of Amana. A committee of elders in each village assigned places to live and arranged employment. Some members were farmers who worked the land, tended livestock, or produced wine from vineyards. Others were bakers, teachers, butchers, carpenters, or printers. Most villages had general stores; larger ones had watchmakers or brewers. Many men and women labored in Amana industrial enterprises, producing furniture, flour, or wool. Women mainly engaged in food processing and preparation in one of the more than fifty communal kitchens, which fed twenty to forty people a day. Such work was tedious and hot but "most appreciated the camaraderie of working with other women," wrote historian Peter Hoehnle. Children helped in kitchens and with gardening if they were not in school. Families cared for any orphans or widows. In exchange for their work, the community fed, clothed, and provided housing for its members. But whatever its members produced became the common property of everyone. Though no one received wages, the society provided credit at village stores for shoes, sugar, tobacco, or other necessary items. "Collectivism is the great leveler," wrote Millard Millburn Rice in his history of the colonies. The most talented or strongest received no more than the most humble. Amana residents donated as much as $20,000 in store credit to benevolent groups during the Civil War, reported Charles Nordhoff, who visited in 1874. (This would have been $469,000 in 2020.) Things that the colony sold allowed them to buy what they did not make themselves. The Amana villages embraced modern technologies, adopting electricity and telephones, as well as cars and trucks in the twentieth century. Much of daily life was arranged and regulated, with community elders prohibiting card playing in 1875 and bicycles in 1899. But the communal nature of Amana survived until the Great Depression.[9]

Most who came to Iowa, like those in the Amana colonies, were farmers and it took substantial resources to establish a farm. The lowest price for an acre in Iowa purchased from the United States government was $1.25. About one-third of Iowa was bought directly from the federal government with cash. Settlers also purchased another 40 percent of the state using land warrants that veterans received for military service. Veterans of the Mexican War, who had served at least one year, earned a warrant for 160 acres of land. State land grants, including those to support railroad construction, as well as property given out through the Homestead Act, made up the remainder. Of course, some land was purchased from private owners.[10]

Not all of those who wished to begin farming in Iowa could afford to buy land. These families usually rented land, hoping to accumulate enough money to buy property after a few years of work. Normally, they tried to feed themselves and produce a surplus for market sale. However, low crop prices during economic downturns reduced opportunities to earn an income. Other misfortunes, from droughts to floods, could also make it difficult to pay off debts or save money. Even a small forty-acre farm was too expensive for 40 percent of midwestern families in 1860.[11]

Family goals included accumulating property, which required earning money. In 1849, John Garnavillo wrote to a friend, Louis Trombly, arguing that good land with fine homes could be bought for less than $1,000, about

$34,900 in 2020 dollars. He suggested that Trombly move to Iowa—land had doubled in value in one year. Prices increased quickly since land was "near the market," which was accessed by a river. A friend who had visited him planned to buy a farm and leave behind rocky lands and an unhealthy country that had "nothing for their children." (He did not mention any location.) Iowa provided opportunity to purchase fertile land in a healthy place that allowed families "to provide for their children," Garnavillo contended.[12]

However, not everyone found immediate success. Mary Jane Parsons, who lived about forty miles west of Ames, noted that her family could not afford to buy coffee "all the time" and were too poor to buy shoes. They were often short on flour during their initial winter in Iowa. They built their first fences without nails because "we did not have money to buy everything and nails were expensive in a new wild country where everything had to be freighted in by oxen or horses." Near Pleasant Valley, Robert Christie wrote, "My last years farming proved a complete failure. I rented five acres of ground at six dollars an acre and did not realize ten dollars for the whole crop." Worse yet, he had discovered that his lands were to be sold by the federal government the next year. "This is a heavy blow for those that are not prepared to pay and unexpected to all." He wrote to family members and asked for money. Fortunately, his brother Lyman sent him $400 to secure their property.[13]

Most new families planted a few acres of corn and built a cabin, unless they purchased improved land that had housing. They usually brought some livestock, such as cattle, hogs, horses, or oxen to their new homes. While families were forced into a primitive existence upon arrival, few remained outside the market economy for any length of time. New migrants who couldn't get a crop in the ground often had to purchase some food their first year. Nearly everyone in rural areas consumed a large part of what they grew, especially corn and pork, as well as vegetables from a family garden. But most also wanted some items they could not produce themselves, such as sugar or coffee. These were bought from a local store, usually in exchange for surplus grain, eggs, or butter. Burlington had two stores by the end of 1833 and lumber came to Iowa from as far away as Pittsburgh.[14]

Farming was labor-intensive. All members of a family worked to feed and house themselves, often in gender-segregated tasks. The labor of men and boys usually revolved around physically demanding outdoor work.

This included the construction of buildings or fences, plowing, planting, and harvesting, as well as hunting. The work of females centered on the home and garden and encompassed a vast array of responsibilities. Their duties involved childcare, food processing and cooking, sewing and weaving, washing and cleaning, producing butter, soap, and candles, caring for chickens and cows, as well as tending to an extensive family garden. They also earned income for their family through the sale of eggs, chickens, butter, or other products from their household. And, of course, women and girls helped men and boys with fieldwork when needed.[15]

Farmwomen were "the chief laborer in the home," wrote historian Glenda Riley, often living isolated lives. They were absolutely necessary for the success of a household. But they sometimes lived miles from any other women. Marriage meant the start of a shared life, as well as the beginning of an economic partnership. This was an unequal collaboration and women lived in a male-dominated world. Susan Wyatt—mentioned in chapter 2—wed at sixteen and followed her husband Jabe to six different states. She was especially vulnerable because she had moved far away from any family members. When he abandoned his family, she was left in poverty to raise her children alone. George F. Parker recognized the burden females bore in 1940 when he wrote, "The one constant unrelieved worker in the pioneer family was the woman. To whatever class she belonged, the tale of toil was never-ending." Men could rarely successfully manage a farm without the labor of wives and children. But this meant endless days for women. Etta May Lacey Crowder wrote, "Life consisted of work and work and more work." Most of a woman's day was spent caring for children and working in a home or garden. She might only see other women once a week if the family went to church services. When Elizabeth Cammack moved to Iowa with her family in 1855, she wrote to her sister that they had "no friends near us" but one and that they had not been to church in more than a month. She mourned how "widely separated" they were. Elizabeth died at forty-six from typhoid, having given birth to eight children. Optimism for a better future helped women manage the tough realities of daily life.[16]

Food preparation was a dominant part of a woman's daily routine. Farm wives and their daughters usually spent much of their time preparing meals. People of all ages worked long and physically demanding hours and consumed thousands of calories each day. Women gathered, preserved, and produced foodstuffs, from garden vegetables to fruits, eggs, chicken, and milk products. Much of this food, such as corn or wheat, was produced by male labor. Corn could be eaten fresh or dried for later use in cornbread, mush, or corncakes. Female food production was far more varied than that of men. They cultivated a large garden, planting, weeding, and harvesting herbs and vegetables, and gathering wild and domestic fruits, including cherries, apples, and strawberries. They cared for chickens and cows. Women also had to preserve and store food for the long winters.[17]

Florence Roe Wiggins recalled that farm homes "in the early days, were veritable factories." In addition to the production of butter, women also made soap and candles, created clothing for their families, canned fruit, and cooked huge amounts of food. Women made candles using tallow, or animal fat. They dipped candlewicks in hot tallow, hanging them to dry. This was repeated until candles were large enough. Boiling lye, ash, and grease together made soap. Matilda Peitzke Paul recalled, "I used to dread to have mother call me and tell me to help with the churning. It seemed as if the butter never would come." Women cooked in an iron kettle suspended over a fireplace or in a Dutch oven—a pot with a lid set directly in coals. Strips of meat might be cooked over a fire. Bread was cooked on a board facing the fire. "And the sewing we had to do! We could get almost nothing ready-made," recalled Maria Brown. Shirts, underwear, socks, and other clothing had to be made at home. "Spinning, dyeing, weaving, knitting, beside the more routine tasks" left little time for leisure, wrote Wiggins.[18]

Women were primary caregivers to their children. They supervised, trained, and organized their offspring, their education, and their work. Elizabeth Cammack juggled childcare with washing and ironing one day while caring for her son Calvin. The boy was "verry troublesome" and climbed on furniture "in all kind of mischief." Ephraim Fairchild wrote to his parents that his children were as hardy "as pigs and as saucy as ever." He complained about tough economic times but said nothing about the perils of caring for his offspring. Matilda Peitzke Paul took pride in making all her children's clothing by hand. She also did all the washing by hand, "rubbing every garment, and often stood on one foot while rubbing and rocking the baby's cradle with the other foot to keep her from waking up." When Paul hauled water from a well, she tied the baby up in her apron.[19]

The economic production of women was crucial for a household. The family of Margaret Archer Murray migrated to Iowa in 1846 and established a farm in Jones County, in eastern Iowa. They produced much of their own food, but her mother also sent chicks and butter to market for sale. Her father took pork to Davenport to sell; he then purchased supplies for the family. Mary Lacey Crowder's mother invested in milk cows and made butter for sale. It was packed in hundred-pound crocks and stored in their cellar until taken to Algona, thirty miles away. They used this income for winter clothing and groceries. The women and children of the Crowder family helped support themselves by growing fruits and vegetables, raising chickens for food and eggs, and producing butter for exchange. Kitturah P. Belknap also made this point in a reminiscence. Belknap and her husband George had moved to Iowa in 1839 and she sold eggs, butter, pork, and wheat to earn money.[20]

Women often helped with male fieldwork. Land was plentiful, but labor was not always available or affordable. Women assisted with all aspects of supposed "men's work." Mary Ann Ferrin drove oxen for plowing when they could not hire men or boys. She met only one other white woman in fifteen months in the late 1840s. John Kenyon relied on the help of his family during harvest, writing, "Sally and the children help farm it. They are equal to two men." Sarah Kenyon took over work in her family's cornfields when their hired man quit. "I shouldered my hoe and have worked out ever since and I guess my services are just as acceptable as his," she wrote. Sarah also helped with reaping wheat. Etta Crowder wrote that women sometimes worked in the fields in her family.[21]

Male work normally occurred outside. A cabin and shelter for animals had to be built if they did not exist. Fields and gardens had to be plowed, planted, and fenced. Planting corn was done by hand, usually with the aid of family members. Tough prairie sod had to be broken, often by hired men using oxen. Harvesting corn or wheat could take weeks of taxing outdoor labor. Hay for animals was cut from wild prairies by hand with scythes. Men and boys could spend years cutting wood to provide necessary fencing, as William Porter Nutting's father did, often in the winter. Males also usually hunted for local game, while children gathered fruit or nuts. While deer could be scarce in many places, smaller game could be plentiful. George W. Clarke wrote that he successfully hunted ducks, geese, prairie chickens, and passenger pigeons near Drakeville in the 1850s. Men also butchered hogs in colder months, a bloody process often done with neighbors.[22]

Corn and pork were basic foodstuffs in frontier Iowa. It was an easy to cultivate grain, which yielded four times more food per acre than wheat. Corn pone, corn bread, grits, flapjacks, hominy, corn mush, and corn fritters were part of most meals. Hogs supplemented corn and garden vegetables and provided meat when hunting was limited or unsuccessful. They thrived in just about any area that had something to eat, so they were easy to care for. They reproduced rapidly, providing far more meat in less time than cattle. Surplus hogs could be walked to a town for sale or butchered in a time-consuming process of scalding, scraping, dressing, and curing that "brings no pleasant memories," recalled Clarke. Freshly slaughtered hogs, salted or smoked, could be preserved and sold in an era before refrigeration.[23]

Male labor was usually tied to the seasons, while most female tasks continued all year. Outdoor work increased in spring, as the ground thawed. Prairie sod was broken, and corn and wheat planted; prairie grass was then cut for hay. Crops had to be guarded against pests and weeds. Caring for lambs or shearing sheep also kept men busy in the spring. By late summer harvest came. Corn had to be stored and wheat grain separated from chaff. Wheat was then hauled to mills to grind into flour. By October the corn harvest was a major task. Husking corn or driving hogs to market often occurred in November. Once winter arrived, hog butchering started and wood cutting for heat and fencing began in earnest. Cold weather brought more leisure time for men. Livestock was usually kept in shelter in the coldest months and turned back into the fields in April.[24]

Children also provided crucial labor for farm families, helping with chores both inside and outside their homes. They were the most versatile and adaptable workers in a family and often completed chores without any adult supervision. Boys and girls helped plant and care for large family vegetable gardens, assisted with farm animals, and completed important tasks, from planting to transportation. The work of boys and girls also brought vital income from the sale of butter, eggs, and chickens to local stores. Boys completed increasingly strenuous labor as they grew older, helping with planting, plowing, and harvesting and assuming most duties of a grown man by their teenage years. Girls learned a variety of important domestic tasks from their mothers, preparing to manage their own households as adults. W. E. Sanders, who grew up southwest of Oskaloosa, called his childhood "an apprenticeship in practical living." Child work helped train younger family members for life, introducing them to the expanding commercial world of the United States and reinforcing gender roles and identity.[25]

The labor of children was as valuable as that of their parents. They could easily be employed in a variety of chores and often worked with a great deal of independence. "Every child had his or her job," wrote Florence Call Cowles, who lived near Algona. "The children worked about the farm as soon as they were old enough," remembered Celia Gullixson. Kids as young as five or six did light labor, from pulling weeds to chasing birds out of fields. As early as the age of eight, children tended livestock and chickens, hauled water, and collected eggs. Boys usually did men's work, but when needed they completed female labor, such as milking cows or cooking. Normally, girls assisted their mothers in the home and garden, but they often did tasks that normally fell to boys, including herding animals and harvesting crops.[26]

Boys' work changed according to their age. Younger boys, not yet ten or eleven, did less physically demanding tasks. These included helping to plant corn, taking care of livestock, and gathering nuts and berries. "Acquiring, increasing, and identifying domestic animals was an immense and important work," remembered George C. Duffield, who spent much of his youth locating cattle and hogs. Even the most faithful oxen, touched by an odd notion, liked to wander, he wrote. Boys protected crops from deer, racoons, and blue jays, too. Duffield's father had him spend years chopping timber for fencing and warmth. The boy grew up to live an eventful life, taking part in the California Gold Rush, serving in Iowa's Third Cavalry Regiment during the Civil War, and driving cattle north from Texas in the 1860s. He kept a diary of his adventures, which helped inspire the 1960s television series *Rawhide*, starring a young Clint Eastwood.[27]

O. J. Felton's account of his childhood in Jones County did not inspire Hollywood but it was busy, nonetheless. At the age of six or seven, Felton took cows to pasture. He spent all day with livestock, "no companions but the black shepherd dog Dash," he recalled. Henry W. Wright also watched cattle for his family in O'Brien County, accompanied by a couple of family dogs. He was six or seven, often joined by other local boys who raced horses and sometimes fought with each other. By the time boys became teenagers, most had assumed the responsibilities of adult men. J. S. Clark, whose family came to Iowa in the 1850s, harvested "great loads of pumpkins" and broke tough prairie sod with a yoke of young steers by himself. He was fifteen.[28]

Both boys and girls helped in clearing land and preparing it for planting. Older kids assisted in plowing, while younger ones broke up clumps of soil or planted kernels of corn; younger siblings brought in wood, cleaned dishes, or helped care for those too young to work. Noted Midwestern author Hamlin Garland recalled spending seventy days behind a plow all by himself at the age of eleven. "It was lonely work," he remembered. Abbie Mott Benedict gathered wild plums, berries, and crab apples; Ellison Orr collected blackberries, strawberries, and plums for his family's table. Kids also helped care for the many animals a farm family owned. Both sexes learned to drive and herd livestock at an early age, bringing cattle in from the fields for milking or taking them to pasture early in the day. "Seemingly, the only reason for being a child was that of becoming a grown-up, failing to recognize that childhood is a distinct period in the normal cycle of life," wrote C. Cruikshank about the endless toil of his youth.[29]

Women and girls were also usually responsible for caring for poultry and cows and a large garden. Girls, occasionally aided by their brothers, assisted with the routine of milking cows twice a day and in making butter. "It was up to the women to do the milking in those days, so I acquired the fine art at an early stage of life," wrote Emma Knowlton. She also helped her mother gather eggs and make soap; with her siblings she collected kindling and wood for cooking and heating. Girls, and often boys, dug potatoes, hoed vegetables, and pulled weeds. Margaret E. Archer Murray's family came to Iowa in 1846 and the labor of its children helped them survive. "We all did our share of work big and little," she wrote. Female work provided important foodstuffs for their households, which helped to diversify farm families' diets and sometimes provided income from goods sold to merchants or necessities from exchanges with neighbors.[30]

James R. Howard remembered in "Making an Iowa Farmer" that "hard work was a family necessity." When he was six years old, his family sent him to the nearest post office five miles away. He rode a horse to fetch the mail, usually bringing back "some supplies in a sack tied to the saddle." At the age of seven he planted corn; at nine he learned to plow and load hay. He completed chores every morning and night for two or three hours. "Frozen feet and faces were common," he remembered.[31]

Benjamin Gavitt fought a solitary, desperate battle against a prairie fire that threatened his family's farm at the age of ten. He saw smoke near their farm after returning from fishing in a nearby creek. Gavitt decided to try to protect the property by himself, as his mother was visiting his older sister fifteen miles away. The fire overwhelmed him, destroying a quarter mile of fencing. He retreated toward the house, using willow boughs from his fishing site to beat out any flames too close to the residence. The boy saved his home, with the help of a cleared area with minimal vegetation that could catch fire.[32]

Small family farms, like those of young Ben Gavitt, were the foundation of the US economy. Before the Civil War, most people lived in rural areas and family farms were the norm, outside of places dominated by southern planters. Westward migration pulled agriculture quickly west. Indiana joined the union in 1816, just thirty years before Iowa. Michigan became a state in 1837. Farmers in the Midwest depended on family labor for survival and upon commercial production for economic gain, such as buying land and accumulating capital. By the Civil War states like Illinois and Ohio had become breadbaskets to the nation; Iowa was to join them as a major food exporter in the 1870s. Midwestern states sold surplus farm produce to southern and northeastern states. The Northeast had a nascent manufacturing sector and growing cities that needed food. Midwestern pork, beef, and grain also went to New Orleans to be consumed in the South or exported. Many northeastern farmers quit agriculture and moved to cities or went west, unable to compete with highly productive Midwestern farms. The region was increasingly tied to the Northeast, starting with the Erie Canal in the 1820s. This economic integration accelerated once railroads linked the two regions even closer in the 1850s. By the late nineteenth century, the Midwest had become the agricultural center of the nation.[33]

Yet, before the state became part of the nation's breadbasket, Iowans had to face many challenges, ranging from blizzards and prairie fires to diseases and accidents. Cholera, malaria, and even occasional smallpox threatened lives. Snakes and mosquitoes also proved to be regular unwelcome companions and hazards. Prairie fires, both beautiful and terrifying, could quickly destroy a farm or kill those who could not escape its path. Blizzards trapped families in their homes for days, threatening livestock and the lives of those who could not find shelter.

Malaria was the most common disease among Iowans and those who lived west of the Appalachian Mountains. It was often called "ague" and afflicted anyone who lived with mosquitoes. Unfortunately, the insects were everywhere. Mary Ann Ferrin wrote that the "hum and stings of millions of musquetoes [sic]" kept her family company at night. Aristarchus Cone complained that they were "so thick you could stir them with a stick." The Midwest was an ideal breeding ground for mosquitoes, as it had lots of waterways and ponds and prairies often had poor drainage. People also lived near water sources where the insects bred. Malaria was usually not fatal in Iowa, but it made life miserable. It brought cycles of high fevers and chills that could repeat every day or two. "Almost every one in the [sic] Country had the Fever and Ague or something worse. There was hardly well enough ones to take care of the sick," wrote Cone. At one point he was too ill with malarial fevers to stand and wrote that he was so sick that he did not care if he lived or died. Malaria could be debilitating and undermined the ability of settlers to fight off additional illnesses.[34]

Other diseases, notably cholera, threatened Iowans. Cholera was a terrifying intestinal disease that could kill infected people in a day or two. Infections came from contaminated water or contact with victims, their clothing, or bedding. Outbreaks occurred in the United States in the mid-nineteenth century and came to Iowa with steamboat passengers in 1849. Caleb Forbes Davis remembered that "almost every boat put off dead or affected persons" in Keokuk, where many died in the spring of 1849. Cholera destroyed intestinal lining, leaving victims unable to absorb food or water. Victims suffered from twenty to thirty episodes of diarrhea a day, which helped spread the bacteria. Children could die in just hours. Historian Benjamin F. Gue wrote that cholera killed hundreds along the Mississippi and Des Moines Rivers, sometimes within a few hours. Measles, diphtheria, dysentery, a variety of fevers and other diseases also endangered settlers in Iowa and the Midwest.[35]

Accidents were not as common as malaria, but the cost could be high. Farm injuries impeded or ended work and life. A huge log crushed a man in Hamilton County. A wild boar killed a boy near Webster City. A broken arm that healed badly kept Daniel Brown out of the Union Army. His son William lost two toes to an accident, making walking long distances difficult. John Kenyon's hand was crushed while splitting rails—his wife gave him morphine to reduce the pain. He returned to work within weeks despite the injury. Sarah Brewer-Bonebright wrote that her brother Jack, an expert woodcutter, had to cut off the mangled toes of a neighbor boy with his ax. Winter could be as bad—if feet suffered frostbite, toes had to be amputated. Thin ice led to drowning while fishing during wintertime. Blizzards killed many. Some fell off steamboats and drowned. Others died when boats capsized or when bridges collapsed.[36]

Prairie fires terrorized Iowans. Neither roads nor creeks could prevent their advance in dry weather, wrote Sarah Brewer-Bonebright. "Sweeping with the wind, great tufts of burning grass were hurled rods ahead of the moving body of the fire," she added. Her family always prepared for fires, even if other chores may have been neglected. Families plowed up strips of land around their homes and fields to serve as barriers. They then burned off the grass between the furrows. William Porter Nutting remembered that such fires "go almost as fast as a horse could run." John and Sarah Kenyon and their family frantically battled a fire approaching their home. They employed everything they could find, from rugs and carpets to a hoe to fight it. "The flames roled higher [than] the waves on the ocean. It looked awfull [sic] to me. I was so frightened that I shook like a dog," John wrote. His wife Sarah used wet bedspreads to defend the house and livestock. "If it had not [been] for the female department everything would burn," he wrote. His beard and hair were scorched off during the four- or five-hour struggle. While the Kenyons and their neighbors saved their farms without major injury, some were not so lucky. Bonebright-Brewer knew of at least ten people killed by prairie fires in the early 1850s.[37]

Iowa weather could be harsh and unpredictable—summer storms and winter blizzards made life difficult. In 1856 Sarah Kenyon wrote to relatives, "I begin to dread the Winter. They tell such cold stories about here." Thunderstorms were usually less deadly, but no less intimidating. Mary Ann Ferrin recalled, "vivid flashes of lighting and loud peals of thunder were terrifying, and the rain poured down as if the heavens were opened." The wind blew so hard she could not keep a candle lit. Elizabeth Cammack wrote that a storm in the spring of 1855 was so strong that her husband, James, had to hold the door closed, even as "water beat in till the floor was quite wet." Sarah Bonebright-Brewer wrote of the harsh winter of 1852–1853, where snow covered the tallest fences. Her family endured a weeklong blizzard that blew snow into every crevice in their home. "Snow, snow everywhere, and the supply seemed inexhaustible. For a solid week we were confined to the cabin," she wrote. John Kenyon wrote in March 1861 of the "cold most severest weather I ever saw. The snow would blow enoughf [sic] to suffocate one to be out in it." The Reverend John Todd, who lived in Tabor, casually noted that it was so cold that water in his glass froze during dinner.[38]

Many remembered the winter of 1856–1857 as the most awful of the mid-nineteenth century. A great blizzard came on December 1, 1856, bringing three days of howling wind and snow. Many who were caught without shelter on the open prairie froze to death. Families had to tunnel out of their front door. High winds and heavy snow pummeled the state for months. Snowdrifts enveloped buildings and buried the tallest haystacks in Story County. Ropes were strung between buildings to guide people who went outside during blizzards. It was thirty degrees below zero in Charles City in December. On December 28 Reuben and David Williams were caring for cattle when a fierce storm hit them. They abandoned the livestock to find cover to save themselves. They took shelter in a grove of trees, walking or running in circles to stay warm. The two boys did this for about eight hours. Then they sought better shelter but became lost. David lay exhausted on the ground and was covered by snow. Reuben kept moving. When daylight arrived, they found themselves very close to Mason City, three miles from the grove of trees. Both survived, losing parts of their ears.[39]

There were reptilian opponents as well. Snakes, especially rattlesnakes, were a constant threat in warm weather. They were numerous and could be found in farm fields, woodlands, and prairies, as well as all sorts of unexpected places such as homes and schoolhouses. A large rattlesnake entered a school in Delaware County, sending the teacher and her students onto their benches. An adventurous boy killed the invader. Some rattlesnakes could be six to eight feet long, recalled Bonebright-Brewer. Rattlesnakes bit two of her brothers, but both survived. The usual remedy—not recommended today—was to suck the poison out of the wound and to apply a poultice. John Kenyon killed a snake in their garden—a creature that his wife Sarah described "as large round as my arm and very long." J. L. Ingalsbe, a surveyor in northwest Iowa, encountered a rattlesnake of astonishing aggressiveness while crossing the prairie on horseback. He heard a snap when something struck one of his stirrups. It was a large rattlesnake. His horse danced and snorted in terror as he repeatedly shot at the offending creature. He killed it, later dryly noting, "I have no definite idea of the size of my game but it must be quite a snake that can wrap his jaws on a horseman's stirrup."[40]

Towns grew up among a hinterland of farms, providing crucial services to the countryside. They were communication, transportation, and market hubs. Towns provided access to material goods and stagecoach, railroad, and steamboat transport. They also contained stores, artisans, post offices, and taverns, which provided a variety of goods and services. Towns arose because they served as a county seat, river port, or trade center. A land office, bank, or roads spurred growth; merchants, speculators, and lawyers offered capital and services. Settlements allowed the exchange of products

Towns provided a variety of services to the Iowa countryside, such as this Marshalltown store. Jerry Forney Fish, Fruits, and Vegetables, ca. 1870s, Marshalltown, Iowa. From Paul C. Juhl Collection, MARS_CXX_0001, Special Collections, State Historical Society of Iowa, Iowa City.

and operated as gateways for the movement of people and goods. "Villages and market towns sprang up in Iowa, almost on the heels of the first settlers," wrote historian Mildred Throne. Farm families took their surplus produce to stores in nearby towns, usually in exchange for grain, eggs, pork, or butter. In return, they received the things they could not make themselves.[41]

Ottumwa was founded in 1844 after land vacated by the Sauk and Meskwaki opened to settlement. It had ten buildings, with one store and a post office in its first year. There was no regular mail route. The postmaster sometimes carried letters in his hat. By 1848 the town received mail three times a week—much to the delight of residents and farmers who came to

Ottumwa to get their mail. Two years later there were three stores, a hotel, a courthouse, and a few homes. The courthouse also served as a primitive schoolhouse until school buildings were constructed around 1850. The town quickly gained population, with more than five hundred residents by 1850. It had a lumber mill that could not keep up with demand. That year a library was organized, as well as a literary lyceum. Three years later it also had a gunsmith, three blacksmiths, several tailors, a bakery, a newspaper, and a land office, along with eight dry good stores. It had cabinet making shops and a chair shop, too. The town was the market center for the county, as well as a transportation hub. Steamboats visited Ottumwa, sometimes bringing goods from St. Louis. During an 1851 flood, steamboats tied up to cottonwood trees on Main Street and customers visited businesses in boats. Residents also built their own craft to ship surplus produce downriver to New Orleans. The railroad came through town in 1859, tying it to Chicago and other eastern cities.[42]

Des Moines began as the location for a military fort (Fort Des Moines Number Two) in May 1843. About 140 soldiers were stationed where the Des Moines River and Raccoon River met. Soldiers patrolled central Iowa, keeping squatters at bay, and ensuring that the Sauk and Meskwaki left Iowa. By 1846 the region had been cleared of its original inhabitants and settlers surged into the middle of Iowa. The presence of the fort, which was abandoned by the military, as well as its strategic location, helped the town's growth. The name was changed to simply Des Moines after 1857. It benefited from being located on a river, which could be used by steamboats in high water. Wagon roads tied it to Oskaloosa, Iowa City, and Council Bluffs. Transportation links brought immigrants and business to the area. People came from Boone, forty miles away, to buy goods and sell their surplus. Thousands of California-bound migrants used the ferry at Des Moines to head west. By 1850 the city had regular stagecoach routes heading east and west. It also had nine dry goods stores, a baker, blacksmith shops, two hotels, two newspapers, and far more doctors than patients. Des Moines benefited from being chosen as the new state capital in 1857. A year earlier it had comprised thirty-eight hundred inhabitants; now, speculators and settlers rushed in, wrote Frank M. Mills. The "noise of the hammer and the saw waked you in the early morning and it kept you awake until midnight," he recalled. Des Moines's importance grew when telegraph lines reached the city in 1862. Railroad service arrived in 1866 and 1867, by which point the town had a population of about ten thousand.[43]

Land speculators established Sioux City in 1854. Town site promoters, led by John Cook from Council Bluffs, received help from Iowa's two US senators, who were speculators themselves. The senators, Augustus Dodge and George Jones, as well as one of Iowa's congressmen, Bernhardt Henn, each acquired a one-eighth share in the town site company. Cook was appointed deputy surveyor and bought out squatter claims in the area. Political connections brought a US land office to Sioux City, which sold millions of acres of land in northwest Iowa. The town's location on the Missouri River aided in its early growth. Steamboats regularly visited, taking fur trappers, miners, and equipment upriver. It also became the county seat. In 1856 town lots sold for as high as $1,200—more than twenty times the price from the year before.[44]

John H. Charles was one of the earliest settlers of Sioux City. He came in 1856, after working as a carpenter and a teacher in Ohio and as a miner in California. Since there was no stage route to Sioux City, Charles arrived from Fort Dodge riding in a lumber wagon. The trip took six days. On arrival, he took refuge from a blizzard in a hotel. One old man "sat by the stove with an umbrella raised over him," Charles recalled. The storm blew in so much snow that it melted near the stove and turned to rain. His companions were a "hard-looking set" who mostly talked about real estate. The land agents and speculators who filled the town could sell land for double or triple its cost in a year. Charles went to Nebraska, claimed some land, and went to work sawing logs for sale. He made enough money to buy a compass and worked as a surveyor. He was also a clerk and a justice of the peace. The town had fewer than one thousand people in 1857. Most were transients, he wrote, who came to Sioux City to buy and sell land. Like most others in the town, he became involved in the brisk real estate business of northwest Iowa. He eventually became a merchant. After the Civil War, he owned and operated steamboats with a partner. He lived in Sioux City for almost fifty years, dying in 1904. His life mirrored the economic development of his hometown.[45]

Life was more than just endless labor and toil for those who lived in frontier Iowa. People took pleasure and reward in their ability to make a living from their farms. They found fulfillment in their work and their accomplishments. Families found joy around them, as their children grew and as their neighbors became friends. They also loved their animals, which became part of their lives and could be cherished almost as much as children. Etta May Lacey Crowder recalled that her family played games, such as checkers, sang songs and hymns, and enjoyed the company of neighbors and friends whenever possible. Roger S. Galer remembered that the Iowa prairies allowed for the "realization of dreams—that the world is plastic to the touch." Life was challenging, but "all was not dreary, or commonplace or sad," he wrote. There was lots of laughter, a willingness to learn, and a "patient bending to daily tasks. If times were hard, they would soon be better." Holidays, fairs, sports competition, and church brought happiness and companionship. Families traveled twenty miles to celebrate the Fourth of July with neighbors; people loved their local county fairs. Samuel Clough wrote, "On the whole I have enjoyed my labor and been happy and believe I have done some good in the world." Clough was especially proud of his thirteen children. Albert P. Butts wrote about his wife's grandparents, who came to Iowa in 1870. Farm work gave them "something tangible to show for labor performed by their own hands," from memories of the first furrow plowed to trees that they planted. Generations found usefulness in creating lives together and in caring for each other.[46]

The pursuit of economic independence brought people to Iowa. Most migrants came from northern states, but some ventured to Iowa from countries in Western Europe such as the Netherlands and Sweden. The state's population grew tremendously after statehood, reaching 674,913 by 1860. Almost one-half million people flooded into the state in the 1850s, pushing settlement by 1860 to a rough line drawn from Mason City to Fort Dodge to Atlantic. Settlers faced a number of threats, ranging from malaria to prairie fires and weeklong blizzards. Towns sprouted in the wake of settlement, providing services to nearby residents and migrants. In the 1850s the sectional crisis dominated national politics. Iowa—the first free state resulting from the Louisiana Purchase—would be drawn into the boiling national crisis that eventually led to the Civil War.

4

Slavery, Politics, and Transportation before the Civil War

Iowa became a state on December 28, 1846, and had an important role in the events that led to the Civil War. Eight months earlier Mexican soldiers had attacked American troops in south Texas, territory claimed by both countries. This began the Mexican-American War, which ended with the American conquest of California and New Mexico. The conflict exacerbated the struggle between the North and the South over the expansion of slavery into areas such as Kansas and Nebraska. Iowans found themselves at the western edge of the sectional dispute. Some helped fugitive enslaved people escape from Missouri and Kansas. Towns such as Tabor, Salem, and Grinnell played key roles in the struggle, even if most Iowans did not support the antislavery cause until the mid-1850s or later. Once Kansas Territory opened for settlement in 1854, proslavery and antislavery settlers moved in. Iowa became a main route to the territory, supplying emigrants and weapons for the free state cause. The militant abolitionist John Brown spent months in Iowa, organizing aid for Kansas and recruiting men for his attack on a federal armory at Harpers Ferry that helped spark the Civil War. The bitter struggle over Kansas realigned state politics, driving the Democratic Party from power and aiding the rise of the Republicans, who opposed the expansion of slavery. As the dominant political party in the state, Republicans wrote a new state constitution in 1857. By the mid-1850s, railroads began to make their way into eastern Iowa, promising a transportation revolution. Steamboats, stagecoaches, and horses remained the main form of transport until after the Civil War, however.

A couple decades before railroads crisscrossed the state, the Mexican-American War worsened sectional tensions and helped bring about the eventual Civil War. The war with Mexico added 525,000 square miles of land to the United States. But southerners wanted to push slavery westward, while northerners wanted to reserve the land for free white settlers. The sectional rivalry embittered both sides and eroded bonds between them. Rapid westward expansion had made it impossible to ignore the issue of slavery for decades. The Missouri Compromise of 1820 and the Compromise of 1850, which provided a temporary solution to the issue of slavery in the West, postponed war between the North and South. In the mid-1850s conflict between proslavery and antislavery settlers in Kansas worsened tensions. John Brown's attack on Harper's Ferry in 1859 helped polarize both sides even further. Iowa played a role in both crucial events.[1]

The state sent one unit to fight in the Mexican-American War, a conflict that gave many Iowa counties their names. A full regiment of ten companies volunteered, but the government did not mobilize them. One company of 113 men joined the Fifteenth Regiment, a unit with troops from states such as Ohio and Wisconsin. They fought in 1847, from Veracruz to Mexico City. At least 40 percent died during the conflict, from disease and combat. One of the survivors was Fabian Brydolf, who took part in the campaign that captured Mexico City. He climbed the walls of the fortress of Chapultepec on September 13, 1847, a victory that broke Mexican resistance. Brydolf had been born in Sweden, worked as a painter, and came to Iowa in 1846. He later served as a colonel in the Civil War. In the 1840s and 1850s, many Iowa counties were named for battles or leaders from the Mexican war. These include Cerro Gordo, Palo Alto, and Buena Vista, all named for battles, and Butler, Clay, Guthrie, Hardin, Page, Ringgold, and Taylor, named for American military officers.[2]

Iowa was the first free state carved from the Louisiana Purchase, but its inhabitants held complex views on slavery. It shared a boundary with Missouri, which was a slave state. Many southerners moved into the counties along the Missouri border. "Most believed that slavery was the only natural condition" for African Americans, wrote historian Morton M. Rosenberg. But most Iowans also opposed the expansion of slavery into Iowa or Kansas. They feared the economic competition of slave labor, which had pushed many southerners into free states. While some Iowans saw slavery as a moral evil, few wanted to give African Americans the same rights and privileges as whites. At statehood, proslavery sentiment was common, but not widespread. For example, in 1852 L. P. Allen came to Ringgold County from North Carolina, with his family and an enslaved boy and girl. He lived in the county for a year, on property on the Missouri-Iowa border. His neighbors were mostly northerners who did not share his views on slavery. Allen sold the two enslaved children for $1,100 to an enslaver in St. Joseph, Missouri, in 1853. He left the state in the mid-1860s. Support for slavery declined in the late 1840s and 1850s, due to the immigration of more northerners and the conflict in Kansas over the expansion of the institution.[3]

White Iowans did not usually see African Americans as equals or as worthy of full citizenship. Most white Midwesterners would have agreed. Antiblack laws, as well as slavery, helped create and sustained the belief that African Americans were inferior. White migrants from the Northeast brought ideas of Black racial inferiority to the Midwest, as did migrants from the South. Black laws and racial violence existed across the region. Rioters in Cincinnati went to war against the city's Black population in 1841, firing cannons into the African American part of town. Other race riots occurred that year in Ohio. Black men were lynched in Illinois, Indiana, and Ohio in the 1830s, 1840s and 1850s. Those suspected of rape were often castrated. Iowa's territorial and state governments before the Civil War legislated white supremacy and severely constricted the rights of Blacks. These laws were designed to make them subordinate to whites and highlighted racial differences. In Iowa, African Americans could not vote, testify in court against whites, or serve in the state militia. Illinois had the same restrictions. Blacks could not practice law in Iowa, either. Schools were segregated in the state and across the North. Interracial marriage was banned in Iowa, Indiana, Illinois, and Michigan. Some Blacks were enslaved in Keokuk. All were subject to extrajudicial punishment—an African American man who was suspected of robbery in Keokuk was not arrested but was rather tied to a tree and whipped by a white man. Whites in Marion County reported an interracial couple to their constable, requesting the arrest of Rose Anne McGregor for violating the law against interracial marriage. Prosecution failed, thanks to a change of venue. While the Republican Party opposed the expansion of slavery, this did not mean that midwestern Republicans were any less racist; indeed, many within the party believed that slavery needed to be banned not because it was evil in itself but because association with any Black person degraded the white race.⁴

The strong racial bias of Iowans and Iowa legislators was shown in 1851. Lawmakers wrote an exclusionary law that prohibited the settlement of African Americans in the state. Those who came before the law passed were allowed to remain. Newcomers would be told to leave within three days or face arrest and fines. Property acquired by Blacks after the legislation passed could be confiscated to support Iowa's all-white school system. Democrats in the state strongly supported the bill, which became law. Still, this law does not appear to have been enforced but once before the Civil War, and even that unsuccessfully. In June 1857 the city marshal of Keokuk demanded that some Black residents leave town. The attempt was abandoned in the face of resistance from African Americans, though it is unclear if anyone was expelled. There is some dispute over the law's validity. It may never have been in effect: it was supposed to be published in the Mount Pleasant *True Democrat* newspaper but the paper's editor was opposed to the legislation and did not publish it. The exclusionary law also did not appear with the new 1851 state law code but was published in a separate volume of other laws passed during the 1850–1851 legislative session. Legal scholars Richard Acton and Patricia Nassif Acton wrote that all of this "added to the confusion over the law's validity." They also noted that it represented the worst of Iowa's discriminatory legislation. Most Iowans, like most northerners, did not want African Americans to live in their state.⁵

Immigrants from both the North and South pushed settlement westward across Iowa in the 1850s. People moved into the southern and western areas of the state and founded towns. Iowa's population increased from 96,088 in 1846 to 674,913 in 1860. Newcomers quickly outnumbered those from the South. Some of these migrants were antislavery and aided fugitive slaves who fled Missouri. New England settlers in the town of Denmark, ten miles southwest of Burlington, organized Iowa's first abolitionist society in 1840. Quakers founded the town of Salem in the mid-1830s. About twenty miles northwest of Denmark, it had about two hundred inhabitants by 1840. Salem was a crusading, militant antislavery outpost that was too radical for its brethren farther east. Tabor became a center of antislavery activity in southwest Iowa in the 1850s. Activists in other places in the state, including Grinnell and Iowa City, were allies in the struggle against slavery, especially in the mid- and late 1850s.⁶

In 1854 Yankees from the Northeast founded the town of Grinnell, about sixty-five miles west of Iowa City. It was named after Josiah B. Grinnell, who had been born in Vermont and educated at Auburn Theological Seminary, later becoming a minister in New York and Washington, DC. Horace Greeley, publisher of the *New York Tribune* famously told Grinnell to "Go West, young man," to improve his health. An opponent of slavery and alcohol consumption but a strong supporter of public education, Grinnell headed to Iowa. He led the committee that wrote Iowa's 1858 law that established a tax-supported public school system. Many assumed that the absence of saloons would doom the nascent village he founded. But it survived, with more than two hundred houses within two years. Grinnell was especially popular with retired preachers, earning it the name "Saints' Rest." Josiah Grinnell became a leader in the Iowa Republican party, serving as a state senator and then congressman in the mid-1860s. The town was active in the antislavery struggle, helping fugitive enslaved people escape from Missouri and Kansas.[7]

Enslaved African Americans who escaped from Missouri, and later Kansas, benefited from the accident of geography that left them near free territory, which provided greater opportunities for escape. But the risk was high, and capture could lead to severe punishment or sale away from loved ones. Enslavers pursued fugitives into free states, knowing that any successful runaway undermined the institution of slavery. They also sought to recapture their human investment. Most runaways were young men in their teens or twenties who were unmarried or did not have a family. They fled to escape punishment, sale, or the breakup of families. Sometimes they returned to try to rescue their kin. There was no set formula for success—some escaped at night, others on holidays or weekends. Some fled on horseback or in a wagon, living in woods and hiding in barns or outbuildings as they headed to freedom.[8]

In April 1848, John Walker escaped from his enslaver, Ruel Daggs, whose farm was twenty miles south of the Iowa border. He found supporters in Salem. In late May, Walker returned to Missouri to help his wife, Mary, and their four young children escape. Another family of three, Sam and Dorcas Fulcher and their daughter Julia, joined them. Several young Quaker men took the runaways north after they reached Iowa. Two men sent by Daggs intercepted the fugitives. But residents of Salem came to help and surrounded the slave catchers. The crowd, eventually up to one hundred in strength, forced the southerners to appear before a justice of the peace to prove their claim to the runaways. On the way to town, most of the fugitives escaped. The justice ruled in favor of the runaways before him. The slave catchers did not head back to Missouri empty-handed, though. They found four of the runaways outside Salem and took them back to Missouri. John and Mary Walker lost two of their children; Sam Fulcher's wife and daughter also ended up back in slavery. The five remaining runaways reportedly escaped to Canada, with the assistance of antislavery Iowans.[9]

Two days after the initial confrontation—on June 7—more than one hundred Missourians and a few supporters from Iowa rode into Salem seeking revenge and $500 in reward money from Daggs. The armed mob surrounded and searched the town but found no runaways. They identified those who had aided the fugitives and detained them in a local hotel. The next day, the county sheriff arrived, having been alerted by a Salem resident who had escaped. He ordered the release of the detainees and told the invaders to leave. They departed just before forty armed men from the town of Denmark, Iowa, arrived to liberate Salem from the proslavery terrorists. In September, Ruel Daggs filed a lawsuit against nineteen residents of Salem, seeking damages of $10,000. In 1850 a jury ruled in favor of Daggs. However, he eventually abandoned the case, after years of legal challenges and delays.[10]

While Ruel Daggs won a partial victory, recovering some of his human property, Iowa's only case determined by the 1850 Fugitive Slave Act was decided in favor of the runaway. The 1850 law sent alleged fugitives before special commissioners who determined their fate. These men earned more money if they found someone guilty. Federal marshals could also compel Americans to assist in recovering runaway slaves. In June 1855 two armed Missouri slave catchers stopped a wagon with a suspected fugitive on the east side of the Mississippi River. They all then returned to Burlington. The Missourians asked attorney George Frazee, a commissioner under the Fugitive Slave Act, to arrest the runaway they called "Dick." They believed the man, who was about fifty years old, belonged to Thomas Rutherford, a Missouri enslaver. When the dispute came before Frazee, Rutherford's son, who had arrived from Missouri, said that he did not know the Black man. "Dick" was set free and left the courtroom, accompanied by one thousand cheering supporters. The unknown fugitive crossed the Mississippi River and caught a train to Chicago. The two slave catchers fled to avoid kidnapping charges and court fees.[11]

In 1853 Charlotta and Harry Pyles, along with their sixteen children and grandchildren, escaped from enslavement in Kentucky. Harry was a fair-skinned free Black man, who had a successful leatherworking shop. His wife had the complexion and straight black hair of her Seminole mother. Her father had been African American and Charlotta was enslaved, as were all her children and grandchildren. They fled Kentucky after the death of their enslaver, Hugh Gordon, who had asked that they be freed after his death. But proslavery white relatives of the dead man kidnapped and sold one of Charlotta's children, Benjamin, to a slave trader. Frances Gordon, Hugh's daughter, inherited the Pyles family. She decided to help them escape to a free state. She was aided by a white minister from Ohio. Two sons-in-law, enslaved on other plantations, could not escape. It would be a dangerous trip—they would be watched everywhere and suspected by anyone who questioned their motives. They all left by wagon in the early fall of 1853, heading for Louisville, where they took a steamboat to St. Louis. Their destination was Minnesota and they proceeded by land in a wagon across northern Missouri. They were often stopped and interrogated by those who questioned the movement of a large group of African Americans. The presence of a white man and woman helped alleviate concerns. The refugees reached Keokuk, just as the weather turned cold. Harry and a son, Barney, found work. Harry built the family a small brick home.[12]

Charlotta wanted to gain the freedom of those who were enslaved and had been left behind. She went east and gave antislavery speeches in Philadelphia for six months, welcomed especially by Quaker families. She traveled to New York and into New England, meeting Frederick Douglass, Lucretia Mott, and Susan B. Anthony. She had never spent a day in school in her life but persuasively spoke before audiences for months. She raised $3,000 to buy the freedom of two sons-in-law, Catiline Walker and Joseph Kendricks, who were married to her daughters Julian and Emily. Her son, Benjamin, was not able to escape enslavement in Missouri. Charlotta's home became a station on Iowa's underground railroad and "Grandma Pyles" helped fugitives from Kentucky, Tennessee, and Missouri escape to Canada. She was aided by friends she had made while giving antislavery speeches, wrote her granddaughter. She lived to be seventy-four, dying in Keokuk in 1880. One daughter, Mary Ellen, worked for a Quaker family in exchange for a place to live and the chance to go to school. Mary and her husband, James Morris, lived in Iowa and raised nine children. Frances Gordon stayed with the Pyles family until she died in the early 1870s.[13]

Antislavery sentiment grew in Iowa in the 1850s, mostly due to the sectional conflict in Kansas. In May 1854, a bill to open Kansas and Nebraska to settlement became law. Settlers and speculators in Iowa and elsewhere had coveted these territories' fertile valleys and hoped for a transcontinental railroad, possibly passing through Iowa on the way to California. To obtain support for the Kansas-Nebraska Act from the South, Illinois Senator Stephen Douglass repealed the Missouri Compromise's ban on slavery north and west of Missouri. This opened Kansas Territory to slavery and brought about an undeclared shooting war between Free State settlers and those who were proslavery. By 1856 Kansas had two governments: a proslavery one, chosen in a corrupt election, and an unofficial free-soil one, which represented the majority of settlers. Violence broke out in the spring of that year when Missourians attacked the antislavery bastion of Lawrence. John Brown, who often used violence in his war against slavery, retaliated by killing five proslavery settlers. Both sides staged ambushes and massacres. As many as two hundred died in what became known as "Bleeding Kansas." News of the conflict exploded into a national debate over slavery.[14]

Iowa was the nearest free state to the struggle in Kansas and played a vital role in the battle against slavery in that territory. The state served as base to assist fugitive enslaved people and as a refuge for free state forces. It was a land route to the newly opened territory, too. Proslavery bands in Missouri turned back and disarmed northerners trying to reach Kansas in 1856 and 1857. Those heading to Kansas had to cross Iowa. It was also a source of weapons, supplies, and antislavery emigrants. Iowa sent almost as many of its own settlers to Kansas to fight against the spread of slavery, as did all of New England. Some of its citizens also volunteered to take part in John Brown's attack on Harper's Ferry.[15]

The town of Tabor, in the southwest corner of Iowa, played a key role in the struggle for Kansas. Tabor was the westernmost part of a loosely organized series of farmsteads, homes, and settlements that aided runaway slaves. Many fugitives found allies in southern Iowa, who then helped them to the next station. Ministers, merchants, farmers, and others assisted fugitives on the underground railroad. It ran generally east to the Winterset area and on to Des Moines, Grinnell, and Iowa City. Then it ran to Clinton on the Mississippi River. Sometime in the 1850s or early 1860s, Tabor residents aided runaways who had been recaptured by slave catchers get away again. They also assisted two girls in escaping from a Nebraska City enslaver. The two made it to Chicago despite being pursued by a mob of men from Nebraska. In July 1854 Tabor residents also helped six other enslaved people escape from a Mormon elder who was taking them to Utah. Within three weeks they reached Illinois and then escaped to Canada. The town was an important location on the route to Kansas. Arms and equipment often filled every storage space in the settlement.[16]

The conflict in Kansas led to the birth of a new political party in Iowa that challenged the Democratic dominance of state politics. Northern outrage over the violence led voters to punish the Democrats, who had supported opening Kansas to slavery and repealing the Missouri Compromise. All the Iowa Democrats in Congress had supported the bill. In the 1854 elections, the Whig Party—the main opposition to the Democrats since the 1830s—won the governor's election, as well as one house in the state legislature. The new governor, James W. Grimes, had become increasingly antislavery because of the Fugitive Slave law and Kansas-Nebraska Act. He was a skilled and tireless campaigner, who called the Democratic Congressmen in Iowa traitors for their support of the "Nebraska infamy." In the elections two years later, the newly organized Republican Party swept state elections, winning the governor's office with Grimes as their candidate. The party also took control of both houses of the legislature. The Republican Party absorbed smaller parties that opposed the Democrats. The political system in Iowa was realigned for decades to come. Nationally, the Republican Party replaced the Whigs as the main opposition to the Democrats.[17]

The Republican Party in Iowa did more than simply oppose the expansion of slavery—its members wanted to rewrite the state constitution. In August 1856 voters supported the idea. One of the party's main goals was to end the restriction on banks and other corporations embedded in the 1846 constitution. Iowa had been awash in depreciated currency from other states and gold and silver were scarce. A lack of trustworthy currency impaired business activity—one bank in Nebraska had only $63 to cover all its outstanding notes. Republicans also wanted to move the capital to Des Moines, which was more centrally located than Iowa City, in the belief that this would gain them political support in the western section of the state and provide a reason for railroads to build their lines west from Iowa City. Republicans in Iowa City wrote a new constitution in less than two months, between January 19 and March 5, 1857. The document authorized the creation of corporations and banks, but only if voters approved. The capital moved to Des Moines, the change balanced by a clause stipulating that a university should be permanently located in Iowa City. African Americans gained the right to a jury trial and their testimony became acceptable in state courts. However, they were still barred from voting, sitting on a jury, holding office, or serving in the militia. Each school district was left to educate nonwhites as they saw fit. White male voters ratified the new constitution by 1,630 votes of 79,000 cast. With some amendments, the 1857 Iowa constitution remains the foundation of state government.[18]

The struggle in Kansas continued, even as it changed politics in Iowa. After proslavery vigilantes closed the Missouri River route to Kansas, an overland route across Iowa became the only feasible way to reach the territory. Parties of antislavery volunteers trekked across the state beginning in the summer of 1856. Money and weapons arrived in Kansas as well. Governor Grimes played a key role in supplying guns for the struggle. He left the key to the state arsenal on his desk one day in early July. Free state forces then took fifteen hundred muskets from state storage for use in Kansas. In the fall, two hundred more muskets departed for the territory, along with a party of two hundred volunteers in twenty wagons. Antislavery migrants in 1856 and 1857 outnumbered proslavery settlers and helped tip the balance in Kansas toward their cause.[19]

The militant abolitionist John Brown found many allies in Iowa. In 1857 Brown helped transport weapons from Tabor to Kansas. In December 1858 he led a raid into Missouri that freed eleven enslaved people but ended up killing one Missouri man. The state of Missouri offered a $3,000 reward for their return. After a month in Kansas, Brown and his men returned to Tabor, having escaped a pursuing proslavery posse. They found that the town's citizens were unhappy with their violence. Brown's well-armed party left to take the fugitive slaves east, stopping at farms and towns that were part of the underground railroad. Josiah Grinnell, a longtime supporter despite Brown's notorious past, welcomed him at his home. Families in Grinnell prepared meals for the group to take east with them. News that Brown was nearby, as well as the substantial reward, led to threats of mob action or arrest. Aware of the danger, Grinnell helped obtain a boxcar to transfer the fugitives to Chicago. All reached Chicago safely. The escapees then made their way to Canada.[20]

John Brown did not just want to save Kansas, he wanted to destroy slavery. He planned to build an army of liberated slaves and conceived of an incredible scheme to invade Virginia. Brown recruited and trained men in

Iowa for his attack on a federal arsenal at Harper's Ferry, Virginia. Weapons from the arsenal would then be given to enslaved people who would spark a revolt. He planned the assault for years and spent five months in the town of Springdale, Iowa, in late 1857 and early 1858 engaging in military drills and political debate. Most of his volunteers had fought in Kansas and many had joined Brown's previous expeditions. Six were from Iowa, including two brothers, Barclay and Edwin Coppoc, who were young Quakers from Springdale. Brown planned to start his attack on October 16, 1859. Twenty-one men joined him. He did not take any rations, or scout any escape routes, or tell any enslaved people in the area that he was coming. The raid failed. Brown and most of his men were killed in the attack or hanged as traitors.[21]

Seven men survived the debacle, including Barclay Coppoc. His brother Edwin was hanged for treason, along with John Brown. But Barclay managed to escape into Pennsylvania along with three others. They traveled at night through the mountains, living on dry corn and raw potatoes, often soaked by rain. He reached Iowa, gaunt, sick, and exhausted, on December 17, 1859, one day after his brother and Brown were executed. But he was not safe yet. In late January the governor of Virginia sent a representative to Iowa and asked the state to send Coppoc to Virginia to stand trial. Samuel Kirkwood, recently sworn in as governor of Iowa, refused. Kirkwood argued that the affidavit did not have a notary's seal and that it did not charge Coppoc with any crime. A man was sent by horseback to warn Coppoc, who was guarded by friends in Springfield. On February 10, corrected paperwork reached Kirkwood, who then issued a warrant for Barclay Coppoc's arrest. By then, he had fled the state. A few months later Coppoc returned to Kansas to help runaway slaves escape from Missouri. When the Civil War broke out, he joined the Union Army, serving as a lieutenant with a Kansas regiment. He was killed in August 1861 when a train he was on plummeted off a bridge that had been sabotaged by rebel guerillas near St. Joseph, Missouri.[22]

Opposition to Black males in Grinnell schools demonstrated how difficult it was for white Iowans to fully accept African Americans. Frances Overton, a sixteen-year enslaved girl, had escaped from Missouri to Grinnell. She worked as a maid for a local family and studied at their home. After about a year in the town she enrolled in a local school. In late winter 1860, a Quaker brought four fugitive enslaved men to Grinnell. They decided to enroll in school. Resistance was immediate. Many Grinnell families did not want their children, especially daughters, in school with African American men. A vote to exclude the new students lost by a small margin. Then the meeting turned ugly. Insults flew and tempers flared. The next day, March 13, 1861, an armed mob came to the schoolhouse and blocked the young men from the school. The school district ended the term ten days early and instituted an application process that allowed nonresident students to be excluded. Even in a town known for antislavery, Black equality was still a distant prospect.[23]

Meanwhile, one group that had been driven out of Iowa returned to the state. Nearly a decade after their removal, the Meskwaki asked to purchase land in Iowa. Some tribal members had never left; others returned in the 1850s. Those who had been forced out of the state hated the drier, mostly treeless place in Kansas where they had been sent. The Iowa legislature approved their return and land purchase. The Meskwaki initially bought an eighty-acre "settlement" near Tama in central Iowa in July 1857. This was an unusual arrangement—the Meskwaki were the first tribe to buy land following removal. According to historian Eric Zimmer, they avoided assignment to a federal reservation by working with the State of Iowa, which held their land in trust, with the condition that they paid taxes and followed state laws. While most states oppressed and exploited Native peoples within their boundaries, Iowa's policies were benign, though paternalistic. The tribe survived through hunting and farming, as well as trade with non-Indians and nearby tribes. When they received federal allotment money, they purchased more land. About 250 tribal members lived in Iowa in the mid-1860s, remaining "self-sufficient and self-governing through an era infamous for the repression of Native peoples," wrote Zimmer. Ownership of land helped the Meskwaki avoid the fate of other tribes, who lost eighty million acres of land to the federal government in the late nineteenth and early twentieth centuries. The white population tolerated their Indian neighbors and lived mostly peacefully with them even after the panic brought about by attacks by the Sioux in the 1850s and 1860s.[24]

In 1857 the Spirit Lake Massacre, an incident which terrified many Iowans, occurred. This event has long been misunderstood. In 1856 overly confident white families had pushed one hundred miles north of Fort Dodge to settle in the Okoboji Lakes area. They lived in the hunting lands of the eastern Sioux, the Dakota, at the edge of white settlement. A long, harsh winter reduced the availability of game for everyone in northern Iowa. Settlers ran out of food; the Dakota ate skunk and their own horses.

Conflicts over access to food led a white militia near the town of Smithland to confiscate Dakota weapons. Their leader, Inkpaduta, was embittered and angered by the treatment of his people. The loss of hunting lands, a difficult winter, starvation, and humiliation at the hands of settlers led to the massacre. Beginning on March 8, Inkpaduta's band attacked white families around West and East Okoboji Lakes, killing thirty-two and capturing four women, two of whom later died. Some women were raped, some children brutally killed. Abbie Gardner survived to tell a horrific tale. The killings caused panic among settlers and generations of historians demonized Inkpaduta as a bloodthirsty savage who hated whites, comparing him to Satan. Historian Paul N. Beck wrote that Inkpaduta was not an evil man, but he could be impulsive and violent. The Dakota saw him as a patriot who defended his people, while whites viewed him as a villain. After the massacre, the attackers escaped and Inkpaduta was never captured or defeated in battle. He probably died in 1879. In 1862, a larger Sioux uprising in southern Minnesota led to high casualties and a savage crackdown by the American army.[25]

Decades before Iowa became a state, a transportation revolution began to transform the United States. The country was vast and settlement often sparse. People and goods moved slowly. Most roads were terrible, with mud holes, stumps, and rocks making travel hazardous. Rural and frontier communities focused on building shelter, clearing land, and growing food; they did not build decent roads. Water was the most efficient means of transport until railroads crossed the state after the Civil War. Farmers who lived near rivers built flatboats—essentially floating boxes—that made their way downstream during high water. These craft carried grain, pork, or other products. Charles A. White, who lived in Burlington in the 1830s and 1840s, wrote that farm families worked together to float surplus produce to St. Louis and New Orleans to sell. More than one hundred flatboats passed Burlington heading south down the Mississippi River in 1840. Until steamboats became widespread, most commerce flowed south with river currents; the development of steamboats, however, allowed upriver transportation and helped tie the nation together. Rapid and inexpensive steamboat transport reduced travel time and made possible the movement of all sorts of goods across the country, tying areas on the edges of settlement into the national market. But most Iowans lived away from major rivers and were isolated from the towns and commerce on the Mississippi River.[26]

Most traveled by land. Families crossed the state by wagon or horseback, wading through mud and making risky river crossings at fords. Hoyt Sherman reached Des Moines, then known as Racoon Forks or Fort Des Moines, on May 1, 1848, crossing the state in a wagon that delivered mail. There were few cabins on the prairies between Oskaloosa and Des Moines, he recalled. Residents of Des Moines talked of ague, horse thieves, and land claims. They only drank two beverages: water and whisky. In the course of his career, Sherman would serve as an attorney, banker, and third president of Equitable Life Insurance company. Rudimentary roads, like the ones on which Sherman traveled, ran along ridges, avoiding streams or swamplands. Bridges usually did not exist. Traffic left roads a maze of ruts and quagmires after rains. Primitive roads may have been passable half the year. In winter, sleighs and sleds replaced wagons. Taking surplus farm production to market often meant hauling loads of corn, wheat, or pork for more than one hundred miles. A journey to market might require weeks of difficult and lonely travel. C. L. Lucas, who lived near Boone, recalled that it could take twenty days with an ox team to reach markets in eastern Iowa. Groups traveled together, as "no teamster had any desire to make the four-hundred-mile trip alone," he wrote. Parties camped out along the way, often delayed by bad weather, illness, or injury to a horse or human. Lucas wrote that a dozen teams might camp together, which made for a "jolly time."[27]

Stagecoaches followed settlement into the interior of Iowa, moving people, freight, mail, and newspapers. The first regular stagecoach service in Iowa began on November 1, 1837, and ran south from Burlington to St. Francisville, Missouri. Service then continued south toward St. Louis. It ran twice a week and took eighteen hours to cover forty-five miles. Bad roads, as well as rain, mud, and snow delayed routes. Stagecoach lines expanded west and north, tying towns along the Mississippi River together and reaching Iowa City in 1842. Later in the 1840s routes extended west to Des Moines. The trip from Keokuk to Des Moines took fourteen days in 1849. Travel by stagecoach was a hardship, wrote Kenneth E. Colton, and should not be romanticized. Journeys could be teeth-rattling expeditions in misery, with passengers regularly helping to dig the vehicle out of the mud. Roads full of stumps and potholes flung passengers together to the floor. Passengers often walked, so horses could make it through deep mud or up a hill. Oppressive summer heat or winter blizzards made travel more hazardous. One stagecoach made it only three miles in ten hours in a blizzard. Such travel was not cheap, costing five to ten cents a mile. The trip brought together a wide variety of people, from land speculators and politicians to lawyers, clergy, and farmers. Travelers heard gossip, learned of the latest news, or had political debates. In 1858 Amelia Bloomer rode in a stagecoach from St. Joseph, Missouri, to Council Bluffs with frontiersman Kit Carson. She did not find anything remarkable about him except for his buckskin clothing. She spent two days and one night in the vehicle with her husband and six to eight other men.[28]

If people did not come to Iowa by land, they did so by steamboat. The first steamboat to travel along Iowa's eastern boundary was in 1823. Such vessels also operated on Iowa's rivers, but the state's shallow waterways usually limited their voyages. Those who lived on smaller streams and rivers had to build flatboats to move surplus goods downstream. About thirty steamboats reached Des Moines by 1860. Only one ever reached Fort Dodge. Steamboats could only travel on the Iowa and Cedar Rivers during high water. Vessels stopped regularly for wood for fuel, their crews sometimes having to cut lumber. Low water and sandbars could slow travel. Ice halted it in colder months.[29]

Passengers traveled in cabins or on the deck, in varying degrees of discomfort. Cabins were cleaner and less pungent than the crowded, dirty lower decks. Some staterooms were elegant, but most people traveled more modestly. Those with deck passage provided their own bedding and food. While this was not always comfortable, it was affordable and could cut costs by up to two-thirds. Children usually traveled at half fare. Helping the crew with other passengers or loading wood also cut expenses for those on deck. Gambling, fishing, and drinking kept deck passengers entertained. Theft was common and sanitation abysmal. Steamboats sometimes carried sick passengers from port to port and spread diseases such as cholera along their routes. Accidents and drowning took a regular and deadly toll on travelers. Captains did not change course when the cry of "man overboard" came, as the boat's large paddle wheel usually killed those in the water. Explosions, fires, and collisions provided additional dangers. Boats carried passengers' freight, as well as their livestock. A steamboat might transport hundreds of cattle, oxen, horses, or pigs. Crews disembarked animals by pushing them off the boat into the water. Livestock then swam to shore.[30]

Railroads provided many advantages over river transportation and eclipsed steamboats as the dominant form of transport after the Civil War.

Because they were not limited by the need to follow rivers or by frozen waterways, railroads could be reliable, low-cost, and operate year-round—Iowans believed they would solve their transportation problems. Once Chicago became the center of the northern rail network, any transcontinental railroad would pass through Iowa, as it was between Chicago and California. By 1855 tracks had been built across Illinois and had reached the eastern side of the Mississippi River at Dubuque, Davenport, and Burlington. Ferries provided access to Iowa until the first bridge was built across the Mississippi River at Rock Island. It was completed in April 1856. Competing steamboat companies sued to halt the construction of the bridge, as an impediment to their navigation, but failed. A month after the bridge opened a steamboat crashed into it, caught fire, and set part of the bridge ablaze. It took four months to fix the structure. The steamboat owners sued the aptly named Railroad Bridge Company, claiming that it was a hazard. Illinois lawyer Abraham Lincoln, who had won court cases for railroads before, defended the bridge owners in 1857. The jury dismissed the case.[31]

In Iowa, the building of six rail lines west in the 1850s caused a railroad mania. The opportunities for improved transportation and communication—and the chance to improve the prospects for individuals and towns—led to railroad fever in Iowa and elsewhere. Most of this support for the railways came from eastern and central Iowa, which had many more customers than the sparsely settled western parts of the state. Towns, counties, states, and the federal government provided generous financial support to railroad corporations. Towns held meetings, surveyed routes, and promised funds in attempts to gain a rail line. Many counties bought railroad bonds or provided land to companies to build track. Cities often gave property for depots or railroad yards to induce roads to pass through. The Dubuque and Pacific Railroad owned seven hundred town lots, many donated by private individuals. Private citizens also bought railroad stock, with most losing their investment due to bankruptcy and fraud. In 1856 the state legislature supported a vast subsidy that the federal government gave to the railroads—every odd numbered section within six miles of a line. This was 3,840 acres of land for every mile of track built, or about eleven percent of the entire state of Iowa.[32]

The Mississippi & Missouri Railroad built the first rail line in the state, running west from Davenport toward Iowa City. Construction began in late June 1855. The state's first locomotive floated across the Mississippi River on a flatboat on July 19. In August the company was building one-half mile of track a day. Iowa City promised $50,000 to any railroad that reached the town before the end of 1855. The company finished its route to the town in the last hours of that year in intensely cold weather, with the help of volunteers from Iowa City who laid temporary tracks and helped push the locomotive to its destination. They lit large bonfires for warmth and light.[33]

By the summer of 1859 other lines had reached Cedar Rapids and Ottumwa. Iowa had 655 miles of railroads in 1860. The longest route totaled about eighty miles, reaching from Keokuk to Eddyville, northwest of Ottumwa. A sharp economic recession in the late 1850s, as well as increasing sectional tensions, slowed down railroad construction. The Civil War interrupted the building of a line across Iowa by tying up material, capital, and labor. The first track across the entire state reached Council Bluffs in 1867. Chapter 6 will detail the completion of Iowa's railroad network, as well as the opportunities and challenges that it provided.[34]

The election of Republican Abraham Lincoln as US president in 1860 led Southern states to secede from the United States. John Brown's raid in 1859 had fueled Southern hysteria and convinced them that the North supported the violent overthrow of slavery. Iowa, and every Northern state, voted for Lincoln. Ninety percent of eligible voters in the state took part in the election. Lincoln won 55 percent of the state's votes. Before he was even inaugurated, seven states left the Union. In February 1861 they established an independent Southern government. In March, Lincoln was inaugurated but took no hostile action against the Confederacy. On April 12, 1861, Southern artillery opened fire on Fort Sumter in Charleston harbor, one of the last remaining federal outposts in the South. Three days later Lincoln called for troops to subdue the rebellion. Four more states, including Virginia, Tennessee, North Carolina, and Arkansas, had joined the Confederacy by May. The Civil War had come.[35]

Iowa had an overlooked part in the events that led to the Civil War. It played an important role in the western underground railroad, the conflict over Kansas, and John Brown's raid. Brown's suicidal attack on Harper's Ferry was a central event on the road to Civil War; more men joined him from Iowa than any other state. The decade of the 1850s saw Iowa mature, with a new political party and a new constitution. Most Iowans opposed the expansion of slavery by 1860, voting for the Republican candidate, Abraham Lincoln, even if many residents could be hostile to African Americans. Iowa's population grew by nearly five hundred thousand in the 1850s and included a small group of Meskwaki who had returned to the state. While railroads would not cross Iowa until after the Civil War, the first lines had reached eastern parts of the state by the late 1850s. Before it would be fully settled or incorporated into the national rail network, the people of Iowa had to survive the nation's greatest crisis.[36]

5
Iowa and the Civil War, 1861–1870

Iowans of all backgrounds helped the Union win the Civil War. The state provided more than fifty regiments of infantry and cavalry, as well as four artillery batteries, for the Northern army. Black Iowans, and those who had escaped enslavement in Missouri and elsewhere, made up an additional regiment of African American troops. More than 76,000 men served in the Union army; 13,001 died during the conflict. Iowa units took part in key battles and campaigns, fighting from Missouri to Georgia. They were with Grant's army at the bloody battle of Shiloh, helped pacify Missouri, served in the long campaign to capture Vicksburg, and participated in Sherman's famous March to the Sea. In Iowa, families left behind labored to continue farm production in the absence of husbands and sons. Women became farm managers, aided by their children, neighbors, or other kin. Iowans such as Alexander Clark led the struggle for civil rights in the state, while Annie Wittenmyer organized and delivered aid to Iowa soldiers. After the war, in 1868, white voters in Iowa gave Black men the right to vote in a statewide referendum—two years before the Fifteenth Amendment to the United States was ratified. In that same year, Iowa's Supreme Court ruled that the segregation of schools in the state was illegal. By the end of the 1860s, the Union had been restored and Iowa had made surprising progress toward racial equality.[1]

On April 15, 1861, three days after the Confederate attack on Fort

Sumter, President Lincoln asked for volunteers to subdue the rebellion. Iowa governor Samuel Kirkwood received a telegram from the secretary of war asking the state to provide one regiment for immediate service. Iowa congressman William Vandever took the message to Kirkwood from the end of a telegraph line in Davenport. After reading it the governor replied, "The President wants a whole regiment of men! Do you suppose, Mr. Vandever, I can raise that many?" No one even knew how many men were in a regiment. On April 18 Kirkwood called on Iowans to support the Union government, declaring, "The Nation is in peril. A fearful attempt is being made to overthrow the Constitution and dissever the Union. The aid of every loyal citizen is invoked to sustain the General Government." The call for volunteers went out, with Keokuk set as the rendezvous point for the first regiment. Thousands of men volunteered. They were to appear for service by May 20. Before that date Lincoln issued a call for eighty-two thousand more troops and the War Department ordered the state to provide two more regiments. These were the First, Second, and Third Iowa Infantry Regiments. The government extended the service of those in these last two units from ninety days to three years. There were no protests. By early June all three units were assembled in Keokuk. Most had no weapons or government uniforms. Soldiers trained using wooden sticks in the place of rifles.[2]

Seymour Dwight Thompson, who joined the Third Iowa Regiment, explained the motivations of the state's volunteers. His unit included men from almost every state and many countries. Most were from rural areas and knew hard outdoor labor. All were motivated by the goal of preserving the country. Each man "loved the Union for what it was to him," Thompson wrote. For the Irishman, America was an asylum that allowed him to escape religious oppression and find liberty that had been denied at home. German immigrants also fought for liberty and saw "in the rebellion a reactionary movement" against democracy. The rebellion represented aristocracy and injustice—the Union had to survive so that democratic institutions could endure. Men joined the Northern army to save the nation from disintegration; they volunteered to "overthrow all traitors and bring them to swift punishment," Thompson wrote. The country was "too dear an inheritance to be easily given up," he declared.[3]

While Iowa's men were organizing to fight for the Union, Missouri's commitment was in doubt. Missouri was a slave state but did not secede. Its governor refused to heed Lincoln's call for troops and tried to maneuver the state into the Confederacy. In response, Northern troops moved into Missouri to secure St. Louis and defeat a pro-Southern militia. The situation rapidly deteriorated and the state fell into its own civil war. By July all three Iowa regiments had been sent to Missouri, often equipped with weapons from the Mexican War. More than one dozen Iowa regiments would be stationed in Missouri by the end of the year. Regiments from Iowa and other Northern states spent years protecting railroads, operating as a police force, and battling guerillas. Small units, often made up of thirty to ninety men, fought irregular forces in a dangerous countryside. It was an ugly war, with few prisoners surviving capture. On July 13, 1861, John Mackley and about fifteen soldiers from the Second Iowa exchanged gunfire with rebels trying to burn a bridge near St. Joseph, Missouri. They drove off the guerillas and saved the bridge. Such skirmishes continued throughout the war. Union forces gained strategic control of the state by the spring of 1862, guarding the western flank of the Northern invasion of Tennessee. The counterinsurgency work of Iowa's soldiers played a key role in this success.[4]

Samuel H. M. Byers was the first man to join the Fifth Iowa Infantry, a fact he proudly recalled in his memoir. He volunteered at the age of twenty-two, joining the regiment in July 1861. Byers was from Oskaloosa and had just passed the Iowa bar exam. He survived four years of combat and imprisonment, finishing the war on General William T. Sherman's staff. His regiment lost 775 men from disease, death, and wounds during the war. A regiment usually had about one thousand men, so such losses represented nearly three-quarters of the original contingent. In 1861 the regiment was sent to Missouri, like many Iowa units. Byers wrote that they tramped along railroads at night, chasing guerillas all over that "unhappy" state. "Missouri was neither North nor South; she was simply hell," a place where neighbors killed each other and burned homes. "Irregular and roaming bands of villains rode everywhere" and nothing seemed too awful or too cruel, he wrote. The Fifth Infantry fought in Tennessee at the bloody battle of Iuka, losing almost half of its men to wounds or death. Byers also took part in the campaign to capture Vicksburg.[5]

More than nineteen thousand Iowans had joined the Union army by the start of 1862 and many served with General Ulysses S. Grant. After capturing two Confederate forts guarding the Tennessee and Cumberland Rivers, Grant's army moved south toward the state of Mississippi. On Sunday, April 6, an unexpected attack by forty thousand Southern troops took him by surprise. The battle that developed over the next two days—named Shiloh—involved eleven Iowa regiments. Many of the men were new to the army and some had never fired their weapons. The Union line was pushed back, with its center resting on an abandoned road. Five Iowa regiments joined other Northern units in this natural fortification, which became known as the "Hornet's Nest." Erastus B. Soper of the Twelfth Infantry recalled that the position allowed them to fire "volley after volley into the advancing foe with murderous effect." The battle, he wrote, "made a constant roar, rising and swelling and falling like the roar of some mighty tempest, interspersed with the reports of more than 100 cannon fired in rapid and constant succession. The noise was such that there could be no talking. The men could not hear one anothers' words."[6]

The Union line on either side of the Hornet's Nest was pushed back, leaving the men in it surrounded. Soper's unit fell back, under attack from all sides. "Destructive fire caused the men to fall in every direction," he wrote. They shot back as they retreated, loading their weapons as they marched. The area was "one vast slaughter pen," Soper recalled. "One could walk all over that hill on dead bodies some places two deep. Some of the wounded were praying, some cursing and others screaming with pain. It was an awful sight; once seen never to be forgotten." Surrounded and threatened with destruction, the men in the Hornet's Nest surrendered. Their stubborn defense was the "salvation of Grant's army," wrote William Preston Johnston, the son of the Confederate commander in the battle. Grant's army survived the first day of battle and went on the offensive on the second. The Union army drove their opponents from the field. Shiloh was a bloodbath, with more than ten thousand Union soldiers killed or wounded. More Americans died at Shiloh from combat wounds than had died in battle in the entire Mexican War. Iowa units suffered badly, with 1,234 killed or wounded and 1,147 captured.[7]

Victory at Shiloh, as well as the capture of New Orleans in April 1862, left the Union with control of much of the Mississippi River. After blunting a Confederate counterattack in Kentucky, Northern armies moved south to try and capture Vicksburg, the most important remaining Southern fortress on the Mississippi River. Thirty Iowa regiments and artillery batteries took part in the long campaign. It took six months of hard fighting for Grant to finally surround and besiege the city. The heat, rain, and mosquitoes left Northern soldiers miserable. "Water was scarce; food scarcer," recalled Samuel H. M. Byers. On May 16, 1863, he fought at the Battle of

Champion's Hill with his unit. His regiment advanced, then paused about one hundred yards from their opponents. "There was no charging further by our line. We halted, stood still, and for over an hour we loaded our guns and killed each other as fast as we could." He fired his musket forty times. Shot through the hand, he remembered, "the wound did not hurt; I was too excited for that." Gunpowder colored men's faces black. He continued shooting through smoke at an enemy that he could not see. "I wonder that a man on either side was left alive." Once the battle ended, he realized that Magnolia trees were in bloom, "their beautiful blossoms contrasting with the horrible scene of battle."[8]

John Myers, a member of the Twenty-Eighth Infantry Regiment, took part in the fighting around Vicksburg from April to July 1863. On May 16 he was also wounded at Champion's Hill, a Confederate defeat that forced their army to retreat to Vicksburg. He wrote, "Our Company lost nearly half" in the battle. Myers had been wounded four times, the worst injury being the loss of a big toe. He told his wife, Ceceila, who lived in Toledo, Iowa, "we hav got them surroundet so that they cant [*sic*] get away." Samuel Byers wrote that the town was bombarded "day and night for weeks." At night, shells fell like comets over Vicksburg. He recalled that Union mortar rounds tore holes big enough for a house in the ground. "Whenever a man shows himself he gets the balls sent after him like hale [*sic*]," Myers wrote. In early June deserters began to give themselves up. Civilians and soldiers ate mule meat, as well as cats and dogs. By the end of June half of the Southern army was sick, some with scurvy. By July, troops were beginning to starve. On July 4, 1863, Vicksburg surrendered. In the east, Northern troops defeated Robert E. Lee at Gettysburg. John Myers lived to see the victory, but he died of typhoid on August 14. Byers survived the war to return home to Oskaloosa.[9]

The capture of Vicksburg was a great victory, but soldiers alone did not win the war. Iowa soldiers enlisted because thousands of farmwives enabled them to do so. Women operated farms with the aid of their children, neighbors, or hired men—if such laborers were available. Sometimes they left their home and rented out their property, as Martha Turner Searle did after her husband enlisted. She found a teaching position to support herself and their child. Others moved to live with their families or in-laws. Those who stayed at home became farm managers and made significant decisions on their own. Mary Alice Vermilion confidently wrote to her husband, "I am willing to raise corn, to pay taxes, to help sustain the government, and to carry on the war." Women exchanged letters with their husbands and made choices about debts, tenants, crops, and other tasks together. They usually avoided heavy physical labor but completed all sorts of new tasks. Most shouldered additional burdens beyond those they normally completed. They were "forced to dredge up every ounce of their ingenuity in order to deal with the wartime economy," wrote historian Glenda Riley. Some increased the size of their livestock herds or sold chickens to help pay bills. One woman decided to sell corn still in the field to avoid the cost of harvesting. Another purchased nine milk cows to produce butter. In Guthrie County, a woman tended to a nine-acre cornfield to obtain an income for her family. Others paid debts or arranged for plowing, planting, and harvesting.[10]

Helen Maria Sharp managed the family farm and cared for four children under the age of twelve after her husband John enlisted in 1861. He served for a year before returning home. A younger sister helped with childcare and neighboring men assisted with cutting wood and field labor. Other farm wives gave her food. She found herself able to successfully run the farm, with the help of friends and money from John. Helen sometimes struggled to make ends meet though, especially when money sent from her husband was lost in the mail. She spent much of her time caring for livestock; church meetings helped her cope with loneliness. But Helen worried about going into debt. She planted a garden and earned money by doing washing for other women. Helen fought to hold on to hope in the face of brutal winters and a shortage of wood. "I have frosted one of my feet" while chopping wood, she wrote. She considered returning to live with her parents in Indiana. In the end, though, John Sharp returned home from the war and both he and Helen lived into the twentieth century.[11]

Marjorie Ann Rogers was left to care for her family after her husband, Dr. Samuel C. Rogers, left home. Early in the war he helped recruit and equip volunteers; he also served as a surgeon for the Union army. With her husband absent, "the whole responsibility rested with myself and the children; they were my only assistance and companions," she wrote. After Samuel joined the army, Rogers rented out the family farm and moved to the town of Toledo with her four children. They sold their livestock and lived with friends. Rogers often hauled surplus produce from the family farm to market, renting a wagon from a skeptical man who questioned her driving abilities. Marjorie took a full load to sell. She recounted, "I was not going to be laughed at because I was a woman—I would take the same as a man." When she reached town, men who were surprised by a woman driving a wagon offered to help her off. "I declined their kindness and said I would get down the same as a man if I could do a man's work." In April 1865, she was mistakenly notified of the death of her husband; nine days later she received a letter from him telling of his escape from a Confederate ambush.[12]

The Northern economy boomed during the war and many farm families benefited from increasing prices for grain and livestock. Inflation and the cost of transportation were problems, however. The North grew more wheat in 1862 and 1863 than the whole country had before the war, despite secession and the enlistment of five hundred thousand men in the army. Both mechanization, such as the introduction of reapers which cut grain, and the increased employment of women in farm fields played a role. Iowa gained 180,000 new people during the war, who began new farms and added to the state's farm output. Agricultural production increased in western states, with more corn, wheat, and oats being produced for most of the war. Food exports even went up during the conflict, as bad harvests in Europe led to increased demand for American agricultural products. Hog, cattle, and sheep raising flourished in states such as Iowa, as well. "Women by and large kept the farms, family businesses, families, and schools functioning while a major portion of male population was involved in war operations," wrote Glenda Riley.[13]

Iowa women also played an important role in aiding Union soldiers, who faced horrific living conditions in the army. Volunteer women sewed uniforms for departing soldiers and provided food, clothing, and blankets when the government could not. Open latrines, trash, and horse manure polluted army camps; inadequate clothing, equipment, and tents made soldiers' lives miserable. They often went hungry. Rations, when available, could be almost inedible. "At best soldiers would get salt pork, hardtack, bread and beans," wrote Noah Zaring, an English teacher. Malnourishment and exhaustion encouraged disease, from dysentery and typhoid to measles and mumps. Medical care was atrocious.[14]

Women banded together to provide for Union troops, joining a variety of aid societies and sanitary commissions. In Iowa there were at least forty such organizations across the state. They made clothing and bandages, prepared food, and packed boxes full of material for Iowa soldiers. Women also sent pillows, sheets, and dried fruit. Marjorie Rogers helped collect beans, dried beef, butter, pickles, and sauerkraut. Some grew food

Annie Turner Wittenmyer led relief efforts during the Civil War and was the first president of the Woman's Christian Temperance Union. Portrait of Annie Turner Wittenmyer, ca. 1890. PH5000.384, State Historical Society of Iowa, Des Moines.

for troops. They also held charity bazaars, selling items that they had produced to raise money. The Cedar Rapids Ladies Soldiers' Aid Society provided assistance to the army throughout the war, sending clothing, food, and medical supplies. This group raised more than $10,000 to assist men in the Union army. Mehitable Woods, a sanitary commission agent, took thirty-seven tons of supplies to Northern soldiers on one trip in 1864. Keokuk, at the southeastern corner of Iowa, became a departure point for soldiers and supplies. In that town lived Annie Turner Wittenmyer, a divorced woman who dedicated herself to improving the lives of soldiers during the war.[15]

Wittenmyer had moved to Keokuk in 1850 with her husband, William, who was a merchant. Three of their four children died before the war. She also divorced her husband, a rare event at the time. Despite these personal trials, she was dedicated to charitable activities, helping to establish a free school for poor children. When the war broke out three of her brothers enlisted in the Union army, so it was no surprise that she devoted herself to aiding the Northern cause. No organization such as the Red Cross existed to meet humanitarian emergencies. Wittenmyer and other women in Keokuk organized the Keokuk Soldiers' Aid Society. In April 1861 Wittenmyer visited Iowa troops and reported shortages of everything from bandages and pillows to healthy food. Aid societies outside Keokuk began to send packages for her to forward to Iowa regiments. She then began to coordinate aid campaigns across the state, even as she visited hospitals full of wounded Iowa soldiers. In January 1862 she found her sixteen-year-old brother, David, in a miserable ward, with a drunken medical director. "It was an inside view of the hospitals that made me hate war as I had never known how to hate it before," she wrote in her autobiography. Seeing that the food provided to her brother was repugnant—greasy bacon and a slice of bread—she committed herself to improving the diet of Union soldiers.[16]

David Turner and many other soldiers benefited from the efforts of Wittenmyer and the women of Iowa's home front. In September 1862 the Iowa legislature made her one of the sanitary agents for the state. In this role she "labored tirelessly to see that medical and other supplies were provided where most needed," wrote historian Robert F. Martin. She traveled widely, visiting troops from Arkansas to Tennessee and advocating on their behalf. Wittenmyer survived a train derailment and gunfire and traveled on a hospital boat at the Battle of Shiloh with two other women. "Oh, the sights and scenes I witnessed that day!" she wrote. They provided food and medical care to wounded men and prayed with the dying. In Memphis she demanded that a general send four steamboats to remove sick men from Helena, Arkansas, threatening to inform Northern newspapers if the aid was not sent. The boats arrived in one day. In May 1864 she resigned as state sanitary agent to work for the US Christian Commission. There, she was responsible for dietary kitchens in army hospitals, providing milk, fruit, vegetables, chicken, and beef to injured soldiers. She proudly wrote in her autobiography that "during the last eighteen months of the war, over two million rations were issued monthly." Praising her efforts, General Ulysses S. Grant said, "No soldier on the firing line gave more heroic service than she rendered." Wittenmyer also helped organize institutions to care for the orphans of deceased soldiers and was active in reform movements after the war.[17]

Two other Iowa women followed Annie Wittenmyer into civilian work for the Union war effort. Two sisters, Mary and Amanda Shelton, were kitchen managers. Military camps were unhealthy, and disease was widespread; civilian medical assistance was urgent. The two women were from Mount Pleasant, Iowa. Mary had been a teacher who worked for Wittenmyer beginning in August 1863, traveling to Helena, Arkansas, to care for wounded and sick soldiers. In the spring of 1864, the first kitchens opened, and Amanda began work in one. By the time the war ended there were one hundred diet kitchens, all run by women with the title "lady managers." The two young women thrived amid the challenges of wartime, grateful to be doing important work. Amanda wrote in her diary that she was *"living much."* Kitchens usually fed two hundred men and their managers were responsible for cooking and acquiring food. Mary became a regional administrator for the program, setting up new kitchens, while her sister managed one in Tennessee. After the war Mary returned to teaching, lamenting the limited economic opportunities for women. She was active in the women's suffrage movement and the first female trustee of Iowa Wesleyan College. Amanda was a bookkeeper, a school superintendent, and ran a private school in Chariton, Iowa. Both women married and lived into the twentieth century.[18]

Samuel Kirkwood served as governor for most of the war, leaving office in January 1864 after four years. He helped establish the Republican Party in Iowa, deserting the Democrats. A successful businessman and farmer with "homespun manners of talk and dress, he was the ideal candidate in frontier politics," wrote historian Leland Sage. He defeated Democrat Augustus Caesar Dodge in the gubernatorial race of 1859, showing up for a debate in a lumber wagon in contrast to Dodge, who came in an expensive coach. Kirkwood effectively managed Iowa during wartime, recruiting troops and keeping order. The governor and a few friends provided credit to equip some of Iowa's first regiments. He also supported the enlistment of African American troops, albeit only to help save the lives of white soldiers. He declined a third term as governor in 1863 and was replaced by William Milo Stone, who had been wounded at Vicksburg. Kirkwood served one more term as governor in the late 1870s and as secretary of the interior from 1881 to 1882. He died in Iowa City in 1894.[19]

Lincoln appointed five men to the Supreme Court, one of them Iowan Samuel Freeman Miller. He had been born in Kentucky, where he had earned a medical degree and practiced medicine but left the state because he opposed slavery. In the mid-1840s he began to free the enslaved people that he owned. He quietly studied law, even as he worked as a doctor, and was admitted to the Kentucky bar in 1846. Four years later he moved to Keokuk with his family. He often was involved in the complicated legal disputes tied to the "Half-Breed Tract" and regularly argued cases before the Iowa Supreme Court. Miller was an early and influential supporter of the Republican Party in the state. He was appointed to the Supreme Court in 1862, the first member who lived west of the Mississippi River, and served on the court for twenty-eight years. During the war he was the court's strongest defender of the exercise of presidential powers. As the century came to a close, he came to believe his fellow justices favored the wealthy; indeed, historian Michael A. Ross argued that Miller became a "radical anticapitalist voice on the court." Miller had a long career and is usually ranked as a "near great" justice.[20]

While most Iowans supported the Union war effort, some did not. These were usually antiwar Democrats, often called Copperheads, who gained this name in reference to the venomous snake. Union veteran Samuel H. M. Byers harshly described them in his book *Iowa in War Times* as "the great Peace Party, made up of all the bad elements of society, the haters of human liberty." Meetings and resolutions of opposition to the war occurred regularly; some loudly voiced their opposition to the federal government. Southern Iowa suffered the worst disorder and violence due to its proximity to Missouri. A provost marshal was killed near Sidney, in southwest Iowa on October 30, 1863. The courthouse in the town was blown up, too. In September 1864, two lawmen searching for deserters were murdered on the way to Oskaloosa. A month later a band of men from Missouri wearing Union blue rode through Davis County, killing men and looting their farms. They killed a Union officer, kidnapped others, and terrorized the countryside. This group of raiders escaped pursuit, riding into the chaos of Missouri. But the state mostly escaped the horrific violence that plagued its southern neighbor.[21]

Near the start of the war, Lincoln had suspended the writ of habeas corpus. This change, asserted in the wartime crisis, allowed the federal government to arrest and detain individuals indefinitely. George W. Jones, a former US senator from Iowa, was arrested in New York City in 1861 for treasonable conduct. Jones had written a letter to his lifelong friend Jefferson Davis, who had become Confederate president, expressing his hostility to the Lincoln administration and sympathy for the Southern cause. He spent sixty-four days in prison but was eventually released without a trial. The editor of the *Dubuque Herald*, D. A. Mahony, was also arrested in August 1862. He spent almost three months in jail without being charged with any crime. Those who considered Copperhead views treasonous sometimes attacked their businesses—irate soldiers threw the equipment of a Keokuk paper into the Mississippi River.[22]

The greatest threat to Iowa's support for the Union war effort—and a minor one at that—came during the "Tally War." It was also referred to as the "Skunk River War." This grandly named incident occurred in early August 1863 and resulted in only one death; still, it sparked great concern in the state. On August 1, Southern sympathizers, led by Rev. George C. Tally, drove through a Republican rally in a wagon in the strongly Unionist town of South English. Both sides were armed. A gun went off. Tally, with a revolver in hand, was killed and one other man was wounded in an exchange of gunfire. Tally's friends and allies swore revenge. Hundreds of armed men—the Skunk River Army—from nearby counties headed for South English. But many returned home in a day or two. Notified of the alleged threat, Governor Kirkwood sent troops and went to the area himself to deter any possible violence. Tally's death eliminated a charismatic critic of the war effort, even if it did not end all opposition in Iowa.[23]

Iowa recruited a regiment of men over the age of forty-five called the "graybeards," officially known as the Thirty-Seventh Iowa Infantry Regiment. They served from December 1862 until May 1865. The average age was fifty-seven, with more than one hundred of the men in their sixties. It was a unique unit, with no other like it in the Union army. The secretary of war gave permission for their enlistment, requiring that they serve only in guard and garrison duty. Many of these men were veterans of the Mexican War or other conflicts but were too old for the rigors of combat and long marches. About thirteen hundred of their sons and grandsons served in the Union army. One of its members was Charles King, who was eighty-one years old in 1863 and claimed to be the father of twenty-one children. Stephen Shellady was sixty-one years old and a former speaker of the Iowa House of Representatives. This unit completed guard duty in locations such as St. Louis, Cincinnati, Memphis, and Rock Island. They also protected trains carrying supplies to Mississippi. In Tennessee rebel guerillas attacked the train they were guarding. "Undaunted, the old frontiersmen returned shot for shot," wrote Edith Wasson McElroy, executive secretary of the Iowa Civil War Centennial Commission. Two men were killed in this incident. Less than ten of the graybeards were killed or wounded during the war; between 134 and 145 died from disease.[24]

Iowa provided a regiment of African American volunteers for the Union. When the war started Black Iowans could not vote, attend public schools, serve in the militia, or even legally settle in the state. However, by 1865 "unprecedented steps to Black equality were under way," wrote historian David Brodnax Sr., spurred, in part, by the participation of Black men in the Northern army. The African American population of Iowa was small, but it grew during the conflict. Some whites in the state helped runaways find housing and work. Wartime chaos also provided the opportunity for escape for others. John Ross Miller, an enslaved man, escaped with three others from Missouri in October 1861. They took horses and mules from their enslavers and went north, traveling at night until they reached the town of Newton. Jeff Logan also fled Missouri, leading wagons carrying twelve other enslaved people to Iowa. In Des Moines he worked at a farm and a hotel before starting his own business. Jason Green, a free Black man, reached Newton Iowa with four other runaways in 1862 or 1863. Milton Howard escaped from enslavement in Alabama and made his way to Davenport. His family had been kidnapped in Muscatine and sold into slavery in 1852. All these men joined Iowa's Black regiment. In 1862, Alexander Clark, the state's most well-known Black leader, wrote to Governor Kirkwood and offered to raise companies of African American soldiers.[25]

Clark had arrived in Muscatine in May 1842, when he was sixteen years old. Born to emancipated slaves in Pennsylvania, he learned the barbering trade from an uncle in Ohio, who also sent him to school. He married Catherine Griffin and started a family, pursuing a variety of business opportunities. Clark was a barber, but he also bought timberland and sold wood to steamboats. He invested in property and helped organize Muscatine's African Methodist Episcopal Church. He also fought to overturn the law that did not allow Blacks to enter Iowa legally and agitated for Black suffrage. Resistance to Black soldiers fell after the Emancipation Proclamation and after the courageous service of other African American units. Governor

Alexander Clark was an African American businessman who led the Black struggle for equality in nineteenth-century Iowa. He recruited Black troops to fight in the Civil War. Lithograph portrait of Alexander G. Clark. MS.ALD.4.1.13, Charles Aldrich Autograph Collection, State Historical Society of Iowa, Des Moines.

Kirkwood contrasted the sacrifice of Black soldiers with the disloyalty of Copperheads, asking "Which is the most decent man?" Once they were allowed to muster into Union service Alexander Clark helped recruit 1,153 Black soldiers from Iowa and Missouri. Clark could not join the regiment because of a leg injury.[26]

Eleven companies made up the First Iowa Volunteers (African Descent), which was renamed the Sixtieth Colored Infantry in March 1864. They finished training near St. Louis and went south to Helena, Arkansas, in

December 1863. The regiment spent most of the next fifteen months near the town in garrison duty, occasionally battling guerillas and rebel troops. Helena was a rainy, wet, and malarial place. More than three hundred soldiers from the regiment died from disease. On July 26, 1864, two companies from the regiment, along with other white and Black troops, fought a much larger Confederate force at the Battle of Wallace's Ferry. The Union soldiers were on a reconnaissance mission when fifteen hundred Southerners attacked them. Greatly outnumbered they retreated, alternately skirmishing and marching while carrying their wounded. The column dispersed a force blocking the route to Helena and the Confederate troops withdrew. An artillery officer praised Iowa's Black troops writing, "The colored men stood up to their duty like veterans." His report continued, "They marched eighteen miles at once, fought five hours, against three to one, and were as eager at the end as at the beginning for the fight. Never did men, under such circumstances, show greater pluck or daring." Many learned to read and write as soldiers. The 709 survivors mustered out of the army in October 1865.[27]

Thousands of Iowa soldiers were captured during the war and ended up in Southern prisons. Confederates often killed African American soldiers taken prisoner. For those who were captured the conditions in prisons could be appalling. The prisons were usually drastically overcrowded, with poor food, lousy sanitation, and widespread disease. Thousands of prisoners died from wounds, dysentery, pneumonia, and starvation. Men from Iowa's Twelfth Infantry Regiment were captured at the Battle of Shiloh. Charles Sumbardo spent time in a prison near Macon, Georgia. "It was not uncommon for ten or twelve deaths to occur in twenty-four hours," he wrote. Sumbardo and others were released after six months. Seth Crowhurst, also captured at Shiloh, wrote that the men he was imprisoned with suffered from scurvy and were infested with vermin. J. Warren Coates was held at Andersonville, the infamous Confederate prison. He recalled that language was powerless to explain its horrors. At one point thirty-three thousand men were held without shelter or fresh water and had little food. Men had nothing to do, wrote John H. Stibbs, "but to stand around waiting for death" at Andersonville. In August 1864, 2,992 men died there. Thousands more died in other months. The commander of the prison, Henry Wirz, was executed after the war. John Stibbs, an officer from the Twelfth Iowa, was a member of the court that found Wirz guilty.[28]

Despite Union victories at Gettysburg and Vicksburg, the war continued until April 1865. Iowa regiments were part of an incredible victory on November 25, 1863, charging uphill to take fortified ridges outside Chattanooga from the Confederates. Alonzo Abernethy was at the base of Lookout Mountain, which towered over Chattanooga. "We were ordered to advance. A more appropriate order would have been to ascend," Abernethy wrote. "The intoxication of battle carried our line steadily forward." The Union attack took the hills above the city—the Confederate line was shattered, and their army pushed back into Georgia. Samuel H. M. Byers was taken prisoner during the battle, his regiment outflanked and overwhelmed. By the spring of 1864 Sherman's campaign to take Atlanta had begun. In Virginia, Grant moved south against Robert E. Lee's troops. After a summer of fighting and maneuver, Sherman took Atlanta on September 2. This victory helped Abraham Lincoln win reelection in November 1864. Two and a half months later Sherman's army, including fifteen Iowa regiments, began its three-hundred-mile march toward Savannah, Georgia.[29]

William S. Fulz and Alexander G. Downing were both sergeants in the Eleventh Iowa and participated in this famous campaign. Much equipment was left behind, as "the privates were to be their own pack mules," wrote Fulz. The army foraged for food and mostly ate sweet potatoes, pork, beef, chicken, and turkey. "It is good country for foraging. We found plenty of fresh pork and all the sweet potatoes we could carry," noted Downing. Fulz recalled that his regiment replaced tired mules with those from nearby plantations. They took any cattle they found with them, as well. The long-distance campaign was hard on clothing and shoes, wrote Downing. "My right foot is worn through on the bottom, and my toes are wet with blood every day." Union troops destroyed railroads whenever they found them, heating rails and winding them around trees or telegraph poles so they could not be used again. They found little resistance. Sherman's army left a trail of destruction behind that did immense damage to the state and the Southern war effort. On December 20, the army captured Savannah and cut the remaining Confederacy in half. By the end of 1864, the South had lost the war, even if its leaders did not want to accept the fact.[30]

Samuel Byers spent fifteen months in Southern prisons or trying to escape from them. He survived seven months in a prison in Richmond, Virginia, before being sent to Macon, Georgia. Byers acquired a Confederate uniform by trading tobacco for it, one piece at a time. He walked out the front gate, escaped his pursuers, and hopped on a freight train. Byers ended up in Atlanta; Sherman's army was outside the city. He slept in barns and spent days wandering about the city, gathering information on rebel positions. He was captured a mile from Union lines, arrested as a spy. Documents that might have led to his execution were lost and he was taken to Columbia, South Carolina. He was held in an open field in the woods with other captured soldiers. They had no shelter. "Our food was wretched, we had almost no clothing, and the weather was very bad nearly all the time," he wrote. Those trying to escape, and there were many, were shot. Byers and another officer lived in a hole they dug for shelter. He escaped with another man while foraging for wood. They survived in the woods, receiving help from enslaved people. They were finally caught by a patrol searching for deserters and sent to a prison in Charleston. He escaped again as Sherman's army approached the city. Enslaved Southerners fed him until the Union army took Charleston in February 1865. He joined Sherman's staff for the last couple months of the war. After the war he wrote histories and memoirs of the Civil War and served as US consul to Switzerland for fifteen years. His "Song of Iowa" became the state's official song in 1911. Samuel Hawkins Marshall Byers died in 1933 in Los Angeles.[31]

Another Union officer from Iowa, Grenville Dodge, played a more prominent role in the conflict. Dodge was born in Massachusetts in 1831 and earned a degree in engineering from Norwich University. He worked as a surveyor for railroads in Illinois and Iowa and moved his family to Council Bluffs. When the Civil War broke out, he became colonel of the Fourth Iowa Infantry regiment. Dodge was wounded and had three horses shot out from under him at the Battle of Pea Ridge in Arkansas in March 1862. When his men ran out of ammunition, he ordered a bayonet charge. He was promoted to brigadier general and spent most of the rest of the war constructing railroads in southern states to support the Northern war effort. His men built 102 miles of track in forty days in 1863 using only axes, picks, and shovels. He also commanded an army corps during the Battle of Atlanta in 1864, where his soldiers held their ground against a surprise assault on the Union flank. Dodge was wounded again. The Union Pacific Railroad, which helped build the transcontinental rail line, repeatedly offered him a large salary to be their chief engineer. He refused to leave the army until the war ended. Once it did, Dodge skillfully organized the construction of the Union Pacific railroad westwards across Nebraska, Wyoming, and Utah in the late 1860s. Decades later he retired to his home in Council Bluffs, the richest man in the state.[32]

While the war ended in April 1865, its consequences for Iowa did not.

The Emancipation Proclamation helped make the Civil War a struggle to abolish slavery. The North's victory in the war brought "astonishing advances in the rights of Northern blacks," wrote historian Eric Foner. Postwar amendments to the Constitution, other federal laws, and state legislation voided laws that kept Blacks from testifying in court, voting, or entering Northern states. African Americans gained access to public education in some Northern states. Iowa also experienced radical changes that no one would have predicted a decade before.[33]

In 1868 a referendum to allow Black men to vote was approved by Iowa voters. This amendment to the Iowa constitution modified voting rights by removing the word white from relevant sections of the state constitution. Only a few states in New England, as well as Minnesota, allowed Black male suffrage. The Iowa Republican Party had supported the idea since 1865, with Governor William Stone stressing the role of African American troops in the war. Legislation to allow Black men to vote—and to reform laws regulating census, apportionment, and militia service—passed both the state house and senate. A convention of Black delegates met in Des Moines in February 1868 to press for adoption of Black male suffrage. Alexander Clark gave a rousing address reminding Iowans that "he who can be trusted with an army musket" could also "be intrusted [sic] with that boon of American liberty, the ballot." In 1868 the amendment passed with a twenty-four-thousand-vote majority. The other amendments passed as well.[34]

Postwar efforts at racial equality were not limited to referendums. Before the Civil War, Black children could not legally attend public schools in Iowa. Many African Americans did go to school with white children, but some school boards established separate schools for Black students. The town of Muscatine had a segregated school, which was located outside of town. It did not have supplies or competent teachers. Schools for white children were built in the city and were well-funded, with good teachers. On September 10, 1867, Susan Clark, Alexander Clark's daughter, was refused admittance at a grammar school in Muscatine. Clark promptly sued the school board of Muscatine, arguing that his daughter had been refused admission solely based on her race. A judge in the county ordered the school's board of directors to admit her in October 1867. The board appealed the judge's ruling to the state supreme court. The Iowa Supreme Court ruled that the school board could not require students to attend separate schools. Their opinion asserted Susan Clark's right to an education, citing the 1857 constitution's requirement that all children—regardless of religion, color, or nationality—would be provided an education. This ruling occurred more than eight decades before the United States Supreme Court struck down school segregation in the *Brown vs. Board of Education* case. It was "the first successful school desegregation case in the United States," noted historian Paul Finkelman. Other rulings by the state supreme court in the next decade supported this decision. In 1870 the legislature eliminated the words "white male" from the laws concerning legal practice. Alexander Clark Jr., who graduated from an integrated high school in Muscatine, was the first Black student to enroll in the law school at the state university in Iowa City. He received his law degree in 1879. His father also earned a law degree five years later. Alexander Clark Sr. was appointed US minister to Liberia in 1890, the highest presidential appointment offered to a Black man to that point. Clark died in Liberia the next year.[35]

Iowa made a significant contribution, and a great sacrifice in human life, to Union victory. One of every four men killed at the Battle of Shiloh was from Iowa, for example. Forty-nine percent of Iowa's white military-age population joined the Northern army or navy during the war. Catherine Desart, a widow who lived in Fayette County, had nine sons volunteer to serve in the Union Army. Three died during the war and five of the six survivors reenlisted after their initial term of service. Only four other Northern states sent a larger proportion of their military-age men to the Union forces. Iowa's population was far smaller than that of New York, Ohio, or Pennsylvania—which contributed more than one million troops combined. But more Iowa soldiers died as a percentage of those who served than any other loyal state—13,001 of 76,242 in the Union ranks. "The men and boys of Iowa regiments died from disease in a proportion unequalled by troops from any other northern state," wrote historian Robert R. Dykstra. Slightly more than 17 percent of Iowa soldiers died during the war. Only troops who fought for the Union from Arkansas, Louisiana, and Tennessee had higher mortality rates.[36]

"Iowa had two armies serving the nation—the great column, 78,000 strong, of boys in blue at the front, and that other army of men and women who furnished the muscles of war here at home," wrote Samuel H. M. Byers in *Iowa in War Times*. These people labored in the fields and gave their time and toil in non-military service, he proudly noted. "Nations are not saved by muskets alone," Byers wrote in 1888, "but in the loyal duty that lies nearest, and without visible reward."[37]

Iowans eagerly responded to Lincoln's call for volunteers to subdue the rebellion and Iowa regiments fought across the South. The state's African American regiment demonstrated its valor in Arkansas. At home, women and children ensured that family farms survived and that agricultural production kept up with wartime demands. Thousands of women in Iowa, including the indomitable Annie Wittenmyer, provided aid to Northern soldiers. Opponents of the war were a troublesome minority, but the greatest Copperhead danger, the Skunk River War, collapsed quickly. In the 1860s Iowa made great progress toward legal racial equality, even if equality of opportunity remained distant. The decades after the war brought new immigrants, increasing industrialization and urbanization, and a series of crises for the state's farmers.

PART TWO
IOWA FROM THE CIVIL WAR TO 1929

6
Immigrants, Railroads, and Farm Protest

In the decades after the Civil War, new waves of immigrants settled Iowa's empty prairies and the completion of railroad networks tied the state to the rest of the country. The railroads encouraged immigration and economic development, even as their transportation monopoly became exploitative. By 1880 the state had 1,624,615 inhabitants—almost one million more than twenty years before. Thousands took advantage of the Homestead Act to claim farms, mostly in northwest Iowa. A diverse population, many of them foreign-born, moved to the state. Czechs, Italians, Chinese, and African Americans joined previous waves of Germans, Scandinavians, Dutch, and Irish who had settled in Iowa. Northwest Iowa filled up with migrants in the late nineteenth century, its drier landscape and lack of trees, as well as distance from early settlement, making it the last section of the state to be settled. In the late nineteenth century, falling prices, grasshopper invasions, and other challenges made farming difficult and bred farm protest movements.

The first permanent white settlers of northwest Iowa had arrived in the late 1840s, but the area was not fully settled until almost 1880. For example, William Thompson came to Woodbury County from Illinois. An enterprising and eccentric man, he moved to Iowa alone. His wife had recently died, and he left his two sons with family members. Thompson planned to establish a town—named after himself of course—and sell land. But his scheme failed due to a lack of interest from other migrants, in part because the location he chose had no steamboat landing. The 1850s brought more immigrants, drawn by the establishment of Sioux City and government plans to sell land. A US land office opened in the town in 1855; the first steamboat brought supplies the next year. Sioux City was far from agricultural settlement but benefited from traffic from miners, the army, and trappers in the West. In the 1860s and 1870s tens of thousands migrated to northwest Iowa, seeking farms and fortunes on the open prairies.[1]

Settlers in northwest Iowa found an environment very different from the one they knew farther east. Endless rolling prairies dominated the landscape. Trees, other than along waterways, were rare. The climate of western Iowa was also drier and windier. This helped the spread of fires, which discouraged the growth of trees. "My first real memory of the prairie is of its vastness. One could see for miles in every direction, including up," wrote Frances Olsen Day. Her family lived near Lake City, about sixty miles northwest of Ames. Hamlin Garland called the northern Iowa prairie "wide, sunny, windy country," its horizon low and the sky vast. He lived in northeast Iowa most of his childhood, working on his family's farm. Garland left Iowa in his twenties and had a distinguished literary career, writing about farm life in the Midwest, even though he became disenchanted with the toil of agriculture. He earned a Pulitzer Prize for fiction in 1922 for *A Daughter of the Middle Border*, sequel to his autobiographical *A Son of the Middle Border*. Still, those who remained in Iowa saw opportunities in the land. The prairie soil was a rich black loam, covered with a thick layer of tangled roots. This sod was tough to plow, but the soil was full of decomposed and nutrient-rich plant material. Up to 90 percent of a prairie plant's mass was underground; roots could penetrate more than six feet below the ground. It took as many as seven yoke of oxen to break the tough prairie sod with a plow, the sort of challenging work that drove Garland to move away.[2]

Those who settled in Iowa had the chance to acquire property through the 1862 Homestead Act. This law provided up to 160 acres of land for settlers at no cost after five years of farming and improvements. It did not specify gender, so men and women could claim property. Not all land was available for homesteading in Iowa—most of the state had already passed into private hands by the time the law went into effect on January 1, 1863. "Less than five percent of Iowa land was subject to homestead," wrote historian Paul W. Gates. During the Civil War, settlers made 1,046 homestead filings in Iowa. After the war, homesteaders and speculators scrambled to secure available property. A total of 14,064 people filed for a homestead claim in Iowa—of these, 8,851 successfully owned their land after five years of residency. This was a higher rate than seen in the nation overall. Some abandoned their claims because of drought, recession, or low prices. Others migrated elsewhere. In northwest Iowa many more homesteaded than elsewhere in the state. Thousands used the law to make a claim in the 1860s and 1870s. It was a far better deal than the five or ten dollars per acre for which railroads sold their land. Private owners near Earlham, thirty miles west of Des Moines, sold property for eight to forty dollars an acre in 1871.[3]

Sod homes were a primitive type of housing often built when lumber was not available and many who took advantage of the Homestead Act lived in them. They were inexpensive to build and helped poor families start their lives. Many began life in northwest Iowa in a "soddie." Families usually moved into a normal wood-framed house as soon as they could. Abbie Mott Benedict lived in a sod home with her husband, Albert, and their three children from 1869 to 1871. She described it as desolate and windswept, but warm in the winter. Albert's brother lived with them for part of this time. Their sod shanty was fourteen by twenty feet, with heavy posts in corners to hold up a hay roof. Walls were boarded up and sod stacked like bricks outside. Strips of sod on their roof held the hay in place. It had two windows and one door. They stored potatoes in a small cellar and a year's supply of flour with them. Most sod homes began as a hole cut into a hill or prairie, with sod stacked around. Frances Olsen Day described one as "a snug shelter but rather lacking in niceties of civilized life." A soddie that she visited was very small and dim, with only two small square windows. Wood frame houses were cheaply built and not very warm. But they were "brighter and airier," Day wrote.[4]

Homesteading mostly occurred in northwest Iowa, but white settlement modified the environment of the whole state. Fields of corn replaced prairies. Domesticated animals such as hogs and cattle displaced deer, elk, and bison. Bees, butterflies, and birds lost their habitats when prairies were plowed up. Wild animals such as wolves, prairie chickens, beaver, and black bear were wiped out. So much Iowa land was turned into farms that prairies were almost exterminated in the state. Ninety-seven percent of Iowa had been converted to farmland by 1900. The Iowa countryside had been almost totally altered in a human lifetime. "The transformation has been called the most rapid and complete ecological conversion of a major biological system in Earth's history," wrote ecologist Cornelia F. Mutel.[5]

American settlement also changed Iowa's hydrology. Iowa's prairies regulated and cleaned water, slowing its movement across the landscape. Prairies operated like enormous sponges and deep roots helped soil absorb water. Streams and rivers ran clear. Water flow was steady and moderate. The destruction of prairies, the logging of forests, and the compaction of soil by livestock contributed to faster-moving water. Ditches were also dug to drain marshy areas. Buried clay pipes, known as drainage tiles, collected water below the surface and moved it to ditches or waterways. Wetlands in northern Iowa and along the Missouri and Mississippi Rivers were also drained. Millions of acres became highly productive farmland, but the state had lost about 90 percent of its wetlands by 2000. "Dewatering the Iowa landscape produced a totally new runoff-driven hydrologic regime," wrote Mutel. Water flowed faster in the state, and it was more erratic. Floods were more frequent and more severe. The soil was drier and less able to resist drought. By 1883 the Iowa River was muddy and filthy. It was no longer clear. In 1902 a Scott County farmer wrote that rain quickly ran off farms and fields did not hold moisture like they had earlier.[6]

Such environmental problems were not immediate threats to those who moved into northwest Iowa after the Civil War. In 1869 Horace C. Webb and his family left Fayette, Iowa. They went to live near Sibley, about seventy-five miles northeast of Sioux City and just south of the Minnesota border. Webb was an infant. They homesteaded on 160 acres, with several other families nearby. The family of five lived in a "little shack" of ten by twelve feet, Webb wrote. There was not a tree to be found for a few miles; men had to travel twenty-five miles to the Rock River for lumber. Winter was an endless series of blizzards and the wind "whistled through that single-boarded house like nothing on earth. Ice froze in the wash basin," he recalled. To stay warm, they twisted hay into bunches and burned it in their stoves. Some families burned buffalo chips—dried bison dung—or corncobs to stay warm. Those who could afford it purchased coal from nearby towns. The Webbs struggled to produce a good crop, battling droughts and grasshoppers their first few years. They sold their land for $1,000 and moved to Sibley by the time Horace started school.[7]

Myron Hinkley also homesteaded in 1869, moving to Cherokee County, northeast of Sioux City. "The lure of free land brought me to Iowa," he wrote. He established a nursery business that produced fruit trees and shrubs. When he arrived in Sioux City, he found one hundred men at the town's land office. He worried that he would not be able to claim the property that he wanted, but his fears were unfounded. Speculators did purchase much of the land around him, though, some of which was not improved for fifteen years. He did not have as many neighbors as he had hoped—there were only nine other farms in his township of thirty-six square miles. He grew wheat on fifty acres. After five years he gained title to his land. Hinkley proudly noted that the Homestead Act gave him independence from the whims of his father.[8]

Living on the unforgiving prairies required resilience. About 1869 Kate Emily Anderson's family moved to Dickinson County in northwest Iowa. Born in 1858 in Illinois, she married George Emerson at age nineteen and lived a few miles west of Okoboji. By 1884, she had two children, having lost a son the year before. Her husband was a carpenter and left to find work in Des Moines, Kansas City, or Minneapolis. George was gone sometimes for a year; marriage, she wrote, was a "hard place to be." It got much harder when she discovered that he had another family. She separated from him even though she was pregnant. Kate and her children lived next to her parents, who helped them. She paid off the remaining mortgage on their property, selling carpets that she made. Her hair was gray by age thirty-one. In 1892 she officially divorced George. Five years later she married Andrew Martinson, a widower with five children. Kate Emily Anderson Emerson Martinson lived until 1941.[9]

Dutch migrants moved to northwestern Iowa after the Civil War. They came from Holland, other parts of Iowa, and from states around the Great Lakes. Poor soils, high land prices, and land scarcity pushed many out of their homeland. Land around Pella, where Dutch migrants had settled before the Civil War, also became too expensive in the 1860s. Speculators, who were often not Dutch, bought up much of the land around the town. High prices limited opportunities for new farmers, with the cost per acre in some places as much as sixty dollars. Residents in the colony who decided to leave considered their options, with some moving to Kansas or Nebraska. A party sent to explore northwest Iowa came back with positive reports. In the summer of 1870, more than three hundred migrated to Sioux County from the Pella area to homestead. Many lived in sod homes, working incessantly to improve their houses and land. In October 1872 a railroad line passed through the county, tying Sioux City to St. Paul and eastern cities. Within five years, the Dutch population of the county exceeded twenty-five hundred. Other immigrants, from Norway, Sweden, Germany, and England, also came to northwest Iowa. In one township in Cherokee County, almost half the farmers came from Sweden. Another township in the county had several hundred German families. Most in Cherokee County had been born in the United States, though.[10]

Railroads built west in Iowa as the state filled up with people. The Civil War slowed construction, but Lincoln's signing of the Pacific Railroad Act on July 1, 1862, spurred work. The law gave government support to the building of a railroad across the continent, starting in Omaha. Railroads in Iowa connected Chicago to California; fortunes awaited the owners of the first lines that crossed the state since they would supply the transcontinental railway. The first railroad to do so was the Cedar Rapids and Missouri River Railroad. It had built west from the city for which it was named, passing through Marshalltown and Nevada on the way to Boone, which it reached in 1865. It completed its line to Council Bluffs on January 22, 1867. This line was the supply link for the Union Pacific Railroad, which was building west across Nebraska and Wyoming. Ferries carried material across the Missouri River, as there was no bridge. Railroad track was even laid on ice on the river in the winter.[11]

Other railroad lines also crossed Iowa in the late 1860s and early 1870s. A second road, the Rock Island, reached Council Bluffs in May 1869. Two thousand workers labored in the fall of 1866 on grading and bridging between Kellogg and Newton. By July 1868 six thousand men were building the railroad forty miles west of Des Moines. Anticipating its arrival, the town of Atlantic had been established in September 1868. In February the railroad arrived and land prices around Atlantic jumped to ten and fifteen dollars an acre. The Rock Island completed its track to Council Bluffs on May 11, 1869—one day after the transcontinental railroad was finished. A third line reached the city in November of 1869. The Des Moines Valley Railroad made it to the state capital in 1866, which was a "small, shabby frontier town, devoid of rail service and grumpy about it," according to historian Don L. Hofsommer. By 1870 a fourth line across Iowa had reached Sioux City, passing through Fort Dodge. A railroad linked St. Joseph Missouri to Council Bluffs. Railroad lines doomed other forms of transport. In the summer of 1870 the Western Stage Company, headquartered in Des Moines, sold off its horses and coaches. By 1873 the state had 3,643 miles of railroad track and railroad expansion had outrun demand for its services.[12]

Railroads altered the economic structure of the state, encouraging settlement, commerce, and industry. By 1880, Iowa had "one of the most complete railroad systems in the United States," wrote historian Joseph Frazier Wall. It had more than fifty-two hundred miles of track and was fifth among states in total mileage. No one in Iowa was more than twenty-five miles from a railroad station. Railroads did not just tie Iowa to national and international markets—they were a major consumer of coal and wood, spurring these industries in the state. Trains in Iowa carried more grain than anything else, followed by coal, livestock, and lumber. Coal mining boomed once railroads provided easy transport, ranking behind only agriculture as a major state industry from 1880 to 1930. Coal made up nearly one-quarter of all rail traffic in the state in 1886. Rail lines allowed the state's agriculture to become more diverse. In the 1880s dairy farming and cattle raising became more widespread. Railroads encouraged business to disperse across the state—the meatpacking industry grew in towns such as Ottumwa, Fort Dodge, and Waterloo. Sioux City's population increased by more than five times in the 1880s, reaching 37,893 by 1890. The city became a transportation and industrial hub. One slaughterhouse in Sioux City could process forty-five hundred animals a day. Lumber was shipped across Iowa from sawmills on the Mississippi River, providing building material for homes, farms, and businesses. Commodities from whiskey to wine came into Iowa. Ice was shipped out of the state, while salt and codfish came in. Railroads tied Iowa to the rest of the country and the world. Meanwhile, thousands of immigrants continued to come to Iowa. The state's population grew by 36 percent in the 1870s and 18 percent in the 1880s. In 1890 Iowa's population was 1,912,297, almost triple the number of 1860. Many Iowa counties experienced their greatest population increase in the decade or two after the arrival of a railroad.[13]

Railroads changed daily life. "It was the railroad that made the country," wrote Albert Butts with enthusiasm. Before railroads, he noted, "every single item of building material for houses and barns, posts and fences, and fuel for heating and cooking had to be hauled in by team and wagon," at considerable cost of time and labor. W. E. Sanders, who lived about fifteen miles south of Pella, remembered when the first railroad came through south central Iowa. He wrote that the abundance of lumber from sawmills on the Mississippi River enabled farmland to be fenced in and frame buildings to replace log cabins. Reuben Ellmaker wrote to his brother of the changes that a new railroad line brought to Jefferson County when it passed within one and a half miles of where he lived. He noted that heavy items such as iron or salt were much cheaper than before the railroad arrived. Most prices fell. "In fact, our groceries and everything we have to buy is Cheaper, generally speaking." Furthermore, improved transportation aided in reaching markets outside Iowa. "If we have anything to sell it brings the cash right at home," Ellmaker wrote. Benjamin Gavitt recalled that his mother in Harrison County had sold hogs to towns established along railways for shipment to Chicago. She also sold her butter and eggs to these places to earn money for groceries. In 1875 Plymouth County farmers shipped 443,000 bushels of wheat, 170,000 bushels of corn, 120,000 bushels of oats, and 3,600 cows and hogs to processors in Sioux City and other locations. They also bought a significant amount of consumer goods shipped in by rail.[14]

Railroads did not just bring opportunities for midwestern farmers, though. Historian David B. Danbom aptly compared railroads to modern-day airlines, arguing that "they were absolutely necessary, but their practices were detestable." Those who were initially happy to have a railroad line nearby often became discouraged quite quickly. High freight rates, political corruption, and the exploitation of farmers enraged customers.[15]

Julia Antoinette Losee Preston took a train from Altona, Illinois, to Iowa in 1869. She was to join her husband, Peter, at a new farm near Fort Dodge. Peter went by wagon with furniture. Julia traveled with her sister, her brother-in-law, and their five children. She wrote that "travel in those days was not easy." The railroad bed was far from smooth, and the cars swayed from side to side. Wheels clattered and banged against the track. "Smoke and cinders kept us dirty and dusty," she wrote in her memoir. The journey was uncomfortable and tiresome. They changed to a freight train in Iowa Falls. Everyone sat on the floor with their baggage. "We bounced and swayed about until we were bruised and sore," she wrote. The one window was nailed shut. Men played cards and "swore the air blue about their luck and the discomfort." They took the stage to Fort Dodge from Webster City. Preston mourned leaving their former home for the rough log house, the heat, and the mosquitoes. They eventually gave up farming and moved to Fort Dodge, where Peter found a job working on the railroad. Julia and Peter had two children and she found contentment in Iowa, writing "home is not in any one house, not in any one place, but always and ever, home is where loved ones live together."[16]

Railroads brought many immigrants to Iowa every year after the Civil

War. Most came from northern states, but many came from Europe. The vast majority were from Northern and Western Europe. But others who came later in the century were Italians and Czechs, members of a more diverse wave of European immigrants from southern and eastern parts of the continent. More than two hundred thousand foreign-born people lived in Iowa in 1870, about 20 percent of the total population. This number increased to 324,000 by 1890. Some newcomers included African Americans who had escaped slavery or been emancipated by the Thirteenth Amendment. A small number of Chinese also migrated to the Midwest, fleeing persecution in Western states. Trains brought children, many of them orphans, from eastern cities to live on Iowa farms.[17]

The state legislature created a board of immigration to encourage settlement and an 1870 pamphlet, *Iowa: Home for Immigrants*, attempted to lure people to the state. Representatives from the board traveled in northeastern states, lecturing about Iowa's agricultural potential. Many midwestern states distributed such handbooks—one such Minnesota guide told Norwegians that summers in Iowa were too hot for them. The state paid for sixty-five thousand copies of the Iowa booklet, which were printed in English, German, Dutch, Swedish, and Danish. Railroads and steamship lines helped to distribute them, and hundreds of copies were sent to newspapers outside the state to publicize Iowa's virtues. Unfortunately, the great Chicago fire of 1871 destroyed most copies of the booklet in Scandinavian languages. The book described Iowa's history, climate, agriculture, schools, and railroad networks; it also extolled the religious diversity of state. A section entitled "A Word to the Landless" explained how newcomers could acquire land through the Homestead Act. Corn grew with less than half of the labor required in the "worn-out soils" of eastern states. All men who were twenty-one years or older, who were residents of the state for six months, and who had committed no "infamous" crime were eligible to vote. The pamphlet was less successful than expected, with migrants leaving Iowa to escape poor crops, low prices, and a grasshopper invasion. Railroad companies helped bring in more immigrants than anything the state did.[18]

Germans first reached Iowa in the 1830s. Davenport became a destination for many, but they settled across Iowa. Towns with names such as New Vienna, Guttenberg, Avoca, and Minden showed German influences. Louisa Sophia H. Gellhorn Boylan moved with her family to Ackley in 1868. She was amazed at all the work that her mother completed, from knitting and baking to cooking, "nearly always with a baby at her breast," Sophia recalled. In Davenport, migrants established musical societies, debating clubs, and other German organizations. Many had left home to avoid required military service. Failed revolts in 1848 and 1849 against German autocrats and the Hapsburg Empire led thousands to emigrate. Many of these refugees came to Iowa. There were so many Germans that Iowa published state documents in their language. By 1860 there were 38,555 in Iowa, about one-third of the total foreign-born population and about 5 percent of the total state population. German immigrants enthusiastically supported the Union during the Civil War and were among the first to enlist once war broke out. In 1895 there were 132,347 Iowa residents who had been born in Germany, making them the largest foreign-born population at the time.[19]

Hungarians established the colony of New Buda in Decatur County, but it failed due to the limited number of settlers and economic troubles in the 1850s. Many of New Buda's settlers, usually only a couple dozen men, were intellectuals who had little experience in the hard realities of frontier life. One Hungarian aristocrat returned home to reclaim his titles and estates after the Habsburg government provided amnesty to those who had supported revolution. Most remained in Iowa, however.[20]

The Irish were one of the largest immigrant groups who came to the United States and 40,124 Iowans had been born there as of 1870. They had been coming to Iowa since 1830, when more than thirty came to work as miners in Dubuque. Many Irish migrated to Iowa in the 1850s, fleeing their homeland after the failure of the staple crop, potatoes. They often sent money home to their families to help them come to America. William and Robert Mann wrote to Joseph Brown from Washington County in July 1849. They were happy with the country, as its climate, soil, and government were preferable to Ireland. Iowa was "the best plac [sic] for a free man that I have seen," the two men wrote. Some Irish lived in urban areas such as Keokuk or Des Moines. Others farmed near Pella or Cedar Rapids. Irish laborers often worked on railroads, such as the Keokuk-Des Moines line. Settlements spread across Iowa, with groups of immigrants living in Madison, Jefferson, and Pottawattamie Counties, organizing churches, and establishing towns. By 1855 Irish families were living in Webster County and Pocahontas County in western Iowa. In 1860 the Irish made up 14 percent of Dubuque's population of 13,045 people. Most men were laborers, but twenty operated inns, boarding houses, or taverns. More than sixty were artisans, ranging from carpenters to masons; twenty-nine were merchants or grocers. Most single women worked as servants, often in boardinghouses. In 1870 Irish immigrants were concentrated in eastern Iowa, especially in counties along the Mississippi River. Significant numbers also lived around Des Moines, Fort Dodge, Iowa City, and Cedar Rapids. In 1895, 33,006 residents of Iowa had been born in Ireland.[21]

John Mulroney lived a varied life of migration and entrepreneurship that led him to northwest Iowa. Born in Ireland in 1832, he migrated to New York at the age of thirteen. He worked at a blacksmith shop in New York before farming in Connecticut. Mulroney then moved to Wisconsin and sold lumber out of a flatboat on the Mississippi River. The California Gold Rush lured him west and he worked as a miner and ran a store until 1857. Then he moved to Palo Alto County, where he was an early settler. Seven Irish families had come to Palo Alto County from Illinois in 1856; the town of Emmetsburg was named after an Irish patriot, Robert Emmet, who fought British rule. Mulroney was elected county treasurer and recorder in the first elections held after the county was organized—he won by ten votes out of forty-four that were cast. He was also a justice of the peace and the first postmaster for Soda Bar, Iowa, a tiny (now-extinct) town about seven miles south of Emmetsburg. Mulroney operated a cattle ranch in the county for eight years. He moved again to Fort Dodge, where he ran a mercantile business and did contracting work on the Mason City and Fort Dodge Railroad line.[22]

Norwegians were the first Scandinavians to come to Iowa in large numbers. Most came for economic opportunity, leaving a country where only 3 or 4 percent of the land could be cultivated. Farms were small and barely supported a family. Most laborers had no chance at advancement. Emigration increased as Norway's population grew in the nineteenth century. Norwegians began to settle in northern Illinois and southern Wisconsin in the 1840s. They came to northeast Iowa in 1846, choosing hilly and wooded land to live on. Ten years later they had moved out onto the prairies, settling in Roland and Story City in central Iowa. By 1870 twenty-five hundred Norwegians lived in Worth and Winnebago Counties in north-central Iowa. Ole Nielsen, who lived in Estherville, wrote, "From the land you can get anything you need." In Norway there were only "barren hills with no vegetation." In 1895 the state had 27,428 residents who had been born in Norway, with clusters of Norwegians near towns such as Elkader, Huxley, Decorah, and Sioux City. Luther College was established in Decorah in 1862 to train clergymen. Classes in the 1860s and 1870s were usually taught in Norwegian. For a century after its founding, its students were mostly Lutherans from the Midwest.[23]

A few immigrants from Denmark came to Iowa before the Civil War, but most arrived in the state after the conflict. One Danish poet had humorously described the United States as a place where it rained lemonade, hailed candy, and country estates were given out to immigrants. Iowa was more demanding than this whimsical portrayal, but Danes arrived by the thousands, seeking economic opportunity and landownership that had been unavailable back home. Most settled in western Iowa, a part of the state with plenty of available land. Some lived in sod homes and took advantage of the chance to acquire land through the Homestead Act. Elk Horn was a major Danish settlement in southwest Iowa, where immigrants could go for months without having to speak a language other than Danish. Substantial Danish settlements grew up around the town, which had institutions like schools and churches to preserve the culture of Denmark. By 1895 about six thousand Danish immigrants, or their children, lived in Shelby and Audubon Counties near Elk Horn.[24]

Czech migrants often settled in and around Cedar Rapids, first arriving in the 1850s. They came from a part of the Austro-Hungarian Empire known as Bohemia before Czechoslovakia became independent after World War I. They came for the same reasons that other immigrants did, looking for land or for refuge from political repression. Some fled failed revolutions against the Austrians; others did not want to serve in the Austrian army. Thomas Korab came to Iowa by wagon in 1856 with his parents, along with two other families. His uncle hunted rabbits for food as they traveled from Wisconsin. They settled near Cedar Rapids. Newcomers grew potatoes and sometimes lived three families to a cabin. Czech immigrants, some who had fled Europe to avoid military service, volunteered to fight for the Union during the Civil War. Successful migrants wrote letters home, encouraging friends to come to Iowa. They celebrated the Fourth of July, as well as Jan Hus Day (commemorating a Czech national hero) on July 6. By 1890 there were 10,928 Czech settlers in Iowa.[25]

Several thousand Italians also came to Iowa in the late nineteenth and early twentieth centuries, fleeing prolonged economic difficulties at home. Most settled in Des Moines or in the coal fields in central Iowa. They also worked on railroads in the state or in brick and tile yards. Some invested their savings in retail businesses in Des Moines. These included a tobacco store run by Marco Chiesa and a hotel and saloon near the railroad depot operated by Egidio Romano and Peter D'Appolonia. Other Italian immigrants opened up grocery stores or barbershops. Iowa's coal mines attracted single men from Italy, usually from sixteen to twenty-four years old. Earlier immigrants often sponsored new arrivals, who then brought wives or fiancées, along with children, from home. Young men often sent money back to their families in Italy. Italian immigrant families lived in small shacks, whose water wells froze in the winter. Women grew gardens and raised chickens or pigs, while caring for their kids. They often took in boarders to earn extra income. Families helped each other in tough times, adopting orphans or helping to bury the dead. Most coal camps did not have a Catholic church. Some went to a nearby town for church on occasion. Despite these difficulties, Italian men became foremen or even owned their own mines. "Life was better in America even though everyone had to work very hard," wrote historian Dorothy Schwieder about life in Iowa's coal mining districts.[26]

Chinese immigrants also moved to Iowa in small numbers in the late nineteenth century. In 1880 there were about 30 Chinese people in the state; fifteen years later there were 114. To compare, the size of the Dutch-born population was eighty times larger in 1895, when Iowa had more than two million residents. The first surge of Chinese immigrants arrived in the United States in the mid-1800s, pushed out of their homeland by external wars, internal rebellions, and rapid population growth. The California Gold Rush and railroad employment attracted thousands, even as taxes on foreign miners tried to discourage such immigration. Economic downturns fostered anti-Chinese violence in the United States. Increasingly harsh Chinese restriction and exclusion laws in the 1880s eventually halted legal Chinese immigration and created barriers to permanent residence and citizenship for those in the country. They were also victims of anti-Chinese riots and expulsions in places like Rock Springs, Wyoming, where twenty-eight miners were killed. Historian Beth Lew-Williams counted more than 170 anti-Chinese riots and expulsions in eight western states and territories as well as Alaska and Hawaii from 1885 to 1887. This violence displaced more than twenty thousand people, helped segregate the American West, spurred a migration to the eastern United States, and forced many back to China. In Iowa, "they could not entirely escape racial violence, hardship, and marginalization," wrote historian Anthony J. Miller.[27]

Chinese immigrants to Iowa rarely managed to become farmers and usually entered the laundry business, with a few becoming merchants. Chinese laborers usually worked as cooks, laundrymen, or servants—trades dominated by women that white men considered female work and did not want to do. They lived scattered across the state, usually with only a couple men living in each county. Some counties only had one Chinese person, who often ran a laundry business near a railroad depot or in a central business district. In 1900 Chinese laundries existed in fifty of Iowa's ninety-nine counties. Most Chinese in Iowa were single men, who ran a laundry because it took relatively little money to open one. An entrepreneurial immigrant could also run the business if they didn't know much English. Most laundrymen worked sixteen or eighteen hours a day, six or seven days a week. Many Iowans had the same prejudices against Chinese immigrants that other Americans had. Some refused to take their business to Chinese laundrymen. One man, Hang Lee, was chased out of Ames, falsely accused of assaulting a white woman. He lost his business and his life savings when he fled. Others suffered from vandalism, theft, or harassment. Ah Wah of Waterloo pulled out a hatchet when threatened and, along with his employee Wong Fun, chased off an attacker. Later that year, the two men fought off another assault, Ah firing a revolver in self-defense. Sam Kee found success as a laundryman in Boone, providing a comfortable life for his family before his death in 1903. Ar Shong became a prosperous merchant, owning stores in Des Moines, West Branch, and Perry. Chinese immigrants in Iowa experienced danger and isolation, suffering from hardship and discrimination in their quest for a better life in America.[28]

Iowa's African American population grew during and after the Civil War. Most came as refugees from southern states, migrating north in search of a better life. They fled enslavement during the war. Later in the century they moved north to escape lynching, segregation, and the loss of civil rights or the theft of land. Keokuk had 245 Black residents in 1860. They had their own church and a thriving school. At least 112 Blacks lived in Muscatine, working as farmers, blacksmiths, barbers, cooks, and servants. The town had churches and a school for Black students. A small colony of African Americans had moved to Fayette County from Illinois and lived in Westfield Township in an all-Black settlement. Only about one thousand lived in the state in 1860, but this population grew to 5,762 ten years later. Moses Mosely escaped from enslavement in Missouri about 1864 and lived in Mt. Pleasant, Iowa. He wrote that the "transition from slavery to freedom was beyond description." He noted that formerly enslaved people were glad to take it "in the rough" and would "make the best of it we can by improvement." In 1862 Matilda and James Busey escaped from their enslaver in Kentucky, riding in his wagon, and fled to meet the Union Army. They took nine children who lived with them; a tenth, their son Tom, could not be rescued from a nearby plantation. The family reached Davenport in 1864. Five years later Tom found them in the town. Archie Webb had escaped from a plantation in Arkansas. He reached Helena, Arkansas, found work with Iowa soldiers, and later moved to the state. Celia Curran and William Brickley also escaped to join Northern troops at Helena. William worked as a servant and Celia was a cook. They ended up in Iowa City. In 1870 Clarinda had 153 African Americans residents, where Black men worked in butter and poultry operations. Thousands of others also fled southern states for refuge in Iowa, hoping to make a better life. More than ten thousand lived in Iowa by 1890.[29]

Samuel Hall escaped from enslavement in Tennessee and eventually settled with his wife and children in Iowa. Hall had been born in North Carolina in 1818. He spent his teenage years with a "humane man," who Hall said treated enslaved people decently. But in 1855 this man died. Sam was sold away from his family, losing his wife, Margaret, and five children. His new enslaver was William Wallace. Hall was taken to southwest Tennessee, where he was enslaved for almost a decade. He saw men whipped to death and children sold away from their mothers. Hall remarried and had nine more children. During the Civil War, he provided intelligence on the Confederates to nearby Northern troops. He fled his plantation a few days after he heard about the Emancipation Proclamation and enlisted in the Union Army. A group of soldiers accompanied him on a visit to Wallace's plantation to free his family. He confronted his former enslaver, backed by Northern troops. Samuel Hall had Wallace load a wagon with food and then Hall and his family departed. He escaped enslavement at the age of forty-seven and moved north to live in Washington, Iowa, following two army officers to live in the town. Two of his children from his first marriage came to Iowa after the Civil War to live with their father. Hall worked as a farm hand, sending his children to local schools with his white neighbors. He bought a small farm, sold it, rented land, then bought another farm. He lived for almost fifty years as a free man.[30]

White Iowans had mixed feelings about the immigration of African Americans. Iowa law prohibited Black settlement in the state; it was usually ignored. Archie Webb ended up working on a farm in Des Moines, along with a few other Black men. Their presence antagonized some local whites, who had a local justice of the peace serve Webb with notice of potential arrest on January 8, 1863, for violation of the 1851 law barring Black migration. Webb refused to comply and was arrested. On February 2, 1863, Judge John Henry Gray declared the law unconstitutional as it deprived African Americans of their citizenship. Webb was freed, but some sheriffs continued to enforce the law. Legislation in 1864 repealed it. Many Iowans believed that helping escaped slaves and ending slavery was a humanitarian issue. But some whites feared that emancipated slaves would compete for jobs or reduce their own chance to get ahead. Others feared that the end of slavery might be a danger to their own status. Men in Wapello and Johnson Counties protested Black migration during the Civil War, threatening the lives of newcomers. White Iowans in Page, Muscatine, and Appanoose Counties threatened those who employed African Americans. Still, Black migration turned out to be less of a menace to whites than many feared. Samuel Hall suffered some "little humiliations" when he arrived in Iowa and there was some resistance to his children enrolling in local schools. But such problems dissipated. White Iowans learned to live with their Black neighbors, who simply wanted the same opportunities as whites. In his 1912 memoir Samuel Hall thanked Iowans for welcoming African Americans to the state. The white editor of Hall's memoir quoted his friend, "Iowa is the best state in the union toward the Negro and Iowa has always tried to help me and my people."[31]

Orphan trains also came to Iowa, bringing migrants from eastern states. The term is misleading as most children were not orphans. Many had living parents who could not care for their kids due to family breakup or poverty. Some gave up their offspring so that their children could have a better life. The Children's Aid Society and allied organizations sent about 250,000 children from eastern cities to western families from the 1850s to the 1920s. Many of these children were sent to midwestern states to join foster families. Adoptive families had to provide food, clothing, and education for any children they took in. Some benevolent groups rounded up impoverished or delinquent children, bathed and clothed them, provided them with a Bible, and sent them west. Potential parents—in Iowa and elsewhere—inspected children upon arrival like livestock. Some wanted farm laborers, while others wanted a child to love. Some siblings went to different families. On June 22 and September 15, 1892, two trains with several cars of orphans arrived in Clarinda. The local paper had advertised their arrival and some families came from thirty-five miles away in hopes of adopting a child. One fourteen-year-old boy was adopted in June. In September, the Aldrich family adopted a girl. She remembered that she had a happy life, "worshipped" by her brothers. Minnie Ketchum said of her adopted family, "I couldn't have had a better family if I'd been born into it. They took me because they wanted me."[32]

Not every orphan train migrant had a happy childhood. Paul Forch was born in New York City in 1882 and orphaned at the age of three. He believed that his parents were killed in a train accident. Forch was sent west on what his daughter called an "infamous" orphan train. A family near Blairsburg took him and immediately put the boy to work. He was "treated as a slave," he recalled. They fed him potatoes and chicken feet and worked him until his hands bled. Forch ran away at age fourteen and found employment at odd jobs, such as a cook's helper and dishwasher. He joined the army at twenty-one. After discharge from the military, he moved to Nebraska where he married and raised four children with his wife Estella. He died at the age of seventy-five, having been a farmer and a restaurant and tavern owner, but his daughter Eileen never heard him talk about his youth.[33]

People came to Iowa to farm, and farm families battled insect invasions in the 1870s. Droughts on the Great Plains pushed massive swarms of grasshoppers, formally known as the Rocky Mountain Locust, into Iowa in the mid-1870s. They plagued the state from 1873 until 1877, especially western Iowa. Some locusts arrived in the late 1860s. Few were seen east of Ames. Former Iowa governor Cyrus C. Carpenter wrote that "the reader who did not see the destruction wrought by the grasshoppers . . . would find an eye-witness story incredible." One writer compared a grasshopper invasion to an immense snowstorm—a vast cloud of specks that moved with the wind. Julia Antoinette Losee Preston wrote that the insects came like "a great rolling black cloud." Millions of buzzing grasshoppers descended on her home, with a low hiss and whine that eventually became a rumble and a roar of beating wings. Their impact stung like hail. It took a day for the swarm to pass through Fort Dodge. Preston's clothesline had been consumed and fence posts had the paint chewed off them. All plants were destroyed, too. Horace Webb remembered, "the sun was clouded as though a bad storm was coming." The insects consumed his family's garden within a few hours. "That winter all we had to pull us through was sent to us through the Government and church communities." The insects ate everything, especially living plants. They also consumed wood, paper, cotton, bark, and even the wool off of sheep. Locusts usually arrived in midsummer. They often laid eggs, which hatched in springtime and portended further agricultural calamity. Cyrus Carpenter estimated that one-quarter of the farm families in affected areas abandoned their land, selling it at "nominal prices." One banker thought that the price of property in such areas fell by 50 percent. Destruction was so widespread that the state of Iowa gave $50,000 in 1874 to help farmers buy seed. Grasshoppers last appeared in August 1876 but cold and wet weather, as well as disease, helped halt their advance in 1877 and afterward.[34]

Starting about 1870, farmers in Iowa and across the nation suffered from a perfect storm of calamities. These included falling agricultural prices, drought, and the devastating grasshopper invasion. The price of corn plummeted from 70 cents a bushel in 1864 to 24 cents a bushel in 1872. Hog and wheat prices also fell by more than half between the late 1860s and mid-1870s. In Iowa, farm surpluses only increased, as improved farm acreage more than doubled in the 1870s and the amount of corn produced increased almost 400 percent. The number of farms in the state grew by 60 percent in the decade. Low farm prices made it hard to pay back debts or purchase things that a farm family needed. An economic depression in the 1870s only worsened the situation. Railroad companies also had a near-monopoly on transportation for most of Iowa. High freight costs reduced dwindling profits among farmers. The grim situation of the 1870s contributed to political revolt in Iowa and much of rural America.[35]

The Patrons of Husbandry began as a cooperative movement among farmers who hoped to raise their living standards. It was often known as the Grange and was strongest in Iowa, Illinois, Wisconsin, and Minnesota. Open to men and women, the Grange advocated for education, cooperative purchasing, and the state regulation of transportation and grain storage. It "marked the beginning of postwar antimonopoly politics," argued historian Richard White. Grange members saw themselves as victims of powerful private corporations with monopoly power to destroy or limit competition. An employee of the US Agricultural Department named Oliver H. Kelly founded the Patrons of Husbandry in 1867. The first Grange in Iowa started in Newton in May 1868 and the organization quickly gained support in the next few years. A financial panic in 1873 helped recruit new members. Newton Ashby, an organizer for the Farmer's Alliance who lived in

Winterset, wrote, "Farmers had many grievances. Prices were very low and railroad and middleman charges were excessive." Many joined hoping that a united front of farmers could force railroads to reduce rates. In April 1872 Iowa had 317 Granges. By January of 1875 there were 1,891 in the state. The Granger program "had one of its fullest applications in Iowa," wrote historian Earle Ross. The organization had social meetings, huge picnics, debates, and parades. They met, talked, worked, and acted together for mutual advancement, wrote E. Brownell of the Madison County Grange. National and state groups also helped those hurt by the grasshopper invasion. The Grange assisted farm families with cooperative buying, banding together to purchase items at a discount from manufacturers. A Grange in Grundy County was able to offer plows and cultivators at a 30 percent discount. Efforts at cooperative sales were less successful due to competition and farmer individualism, wrote Mildred Throne.[36]

The battle against high railroad rates not only spurred the Grange but also led to the short-lived Anti-Monopoly Party in Iowa. Railroad companies charged more per mile for shipping over short distances than longer ones, arguing that expenses such as loading, labeling, and unloading were constant. Long hauls often reduced the cost per mile. However, farmers pointed out that freight rates fell when railroads faced competition from water transportation. A US Senate investigation in 1886 demonstrated that railroads charged rates far beyond actual costs. Despite farmers' demands, the state of Iowa had failed to pass legislation to control railroad rates. The Iowa Senate blocked all reform measures, hostage to its own conservatism and the railroad lobby. In mid-1873 farmers' meetings called for a new party to regulate the railroads. Members of the new Anti-Monopoly Party allied with Iowa Democrats, who had been a minority since the late 1850s. The new party elected fifty Anti-Monopoly Democrats in the state House—half of the lower house's membership—in the 1873 elections. They also elected ten candidates to the state Senate. When the legislature met in January 1874, railroad regulation could no longer be ignored. Iowa Republicans, usually allied with big business, worked with the new legislators to draft a railroad rate bill. In doing so, they preserved their long-term power in Iowa. The law went into effect on July 4, 1874. Iowa's laws set maximum passenger and freight charges, but they did not set rates in the state. Railroads attempted to undermine and overturn the law through bribery, lawsuits, and campaign contributions. Before the end of the decade regulations had been weakened, with only a commission that could investigate and report violations. The Anti-Monopoly Party collapsed in the years following its brief success, as Republicans quickly beat back the insurgent Democrats.[37]

Railroad regulation did not cure all of the ills of farmers and agrarian protest continued. Setting maximum railroad rates helped rural families, but they still suffered from the long-term decline in farm prices. The Anti-Monopoly Party was not the only third-party active in Iowa in the 1870s and 1880s. Some Iowa farmers supported the Greenback Party, which appealed to them with a program of monetary inflation and corporate regulation. The Treasury Department had been reducing the supply of paper money after the Civil War, commonly called greenbacks. The loss of paper money decreased the overall money supply in the United States. Many farmers thought this led to higher prices. The Greenback Party had some success in the late 1870s and early 1880s, electing a few members of the state legislature. With the help of the Democrats, it helped elect three men to Congress. In 1880 the Greenback candidate for president received only 32,327 votes in Iowa, despite the fact that the candidate, James B. Weaver, was a congressman from the state. (Weaver would be the Populist candidate for president in 1892.) Support for movements such as the Grange declined after its peak in 1875. It had grown too quickly and suffered from the failure of some of its enterprises. Only eight local granges existed in Iowa in 1885. But the collapse of the Grange did not lead to the end of political movements among farmers.[38]

The Farmers' Alliance, and the political movement that it bred, the Populists, continued the antimonopolist battle. Low farm prices and high railroad rates in Iowa and other states continued to hurt producers. Families found help with the Farmers' Alliance, a mutual aid society that became a social movement in the 1880s. It advocated for government control of railroads and the implementation of farmer-owned cooperatives. These cooperatives would provide credit in exchange for the storage of grain. Corn and wheat could then be sold when prices were high. The Iowa Farmers' Alliance (IFA) was organized in 1886. It helped members buy discounted machinery, flour, and coal, and organized cooperative creameries and grain storage. The election of a Democratic governor, Horace Boies, in 1889 provided the IFA with access to political power. It had allies in the state legislature from both parties. Legislation regulated some railroad charges and interest rates, achieving some IFA goals. A competitive party system in Iowa brought agrarian reformers into the political process, discouraging the creation of third parties. In Kansas and Nebraska, the political system was dominated by the Republicans who did not respond to the demands of outside reformers. The Farmers' Alliance organized the Populist Party and inflicted major defeats on the GOP in Kansas and Nebraska. In both states, the Populists took control of the state legislature and won seven of ten congressional seats. They ran as a third-party in the 1892 presidential election, attacking monopolies and economic inequality, calling for a progressive income tax and the nationalization of railroads. Their candidate, James B. Weaver, won only 8.5 percent of the nationwide vote, failing to find support east of the Mississippi River where most Americans lived. All of Iowa's thirteen electoral votes went to the GOP. The party collapsed after major election defeats in the 1890s.[39]

The decades after the Civil War transformed Iowa. Immigrants from many backgrounds came, fleeing political repression in Germany and Hungary or coming for economic opportunity from Italy or Ireland. African Americans left the South for Iowa, seeking a better life for their families. Northwest Iowa filled up with settlers despite its less hospitable environment. Railroads tied the state to the rest of the country and helped Iowa develop and diversify its economy. But their business practices bred political movements against them. By 1900 Iowa had 2,231,853 people. It had grown at a breakneck pace, its population expanding by more than twenty times since 1846, when Iowa became a state and had 96,088 inhabitants. The next chapter will review the creation of Iowa's education system, its great variety of religious denominations, as well as rural life in the late nineteenth century.[40]

7

Religion, Education, and Rural Life

People and institutions migrated west in the nineteenth century. Immigrants brought a variety of faiths to Iowa and churches and synagogues were usually among the first structures that a community built. Schools existed even before the American government officially allowed settlement, with the earliest one starting in 1830. The first public house of worship was built in Dubuque four years later. Catholicism came to Iowa with early French settlers, followed by Quakers, Methodists, Congregationalists, Jews, and many others later in the nineteenth century. Early schools were rudimentary. The one-room schoolhouse was the foundation for rural education until the mid-twentieth century. Many colleges were established in the state's early years, including those that became the University of Iowa and Iowa State University. Small towns proliferated across the state and provided services to the countryside. Cultural institutions, such as the Chautauqua movement, provided entertainment and spread knowledge. Hundreds of women's clubs served as both social outlets and champions of social reform. Other amusements, from baseball to opera houses, served as diversions from a life dominated by agricultural labor. The state fair became an important part of the state's cultural life.[1]

A house of worship was more than a religious meeting place. It was a "cultural nest," wrote historian Robert P. Swierenga, where different social classes and nationalities met. It gave members a cultural identity and brought them into a community. Churches and synagogues provided charity, educated children, and offered amusement and recreation. They took care of people, aided the grieving, buried the dead, and set moral boundaries. These institutions integrated newcomers and attracted immigrants. "Rural life truly was church centered," wrote Swierenga. Iowa congregations spoke at least a dozen languages in the mid-nineteenth century, including German, Dutch, Swedish, and Czech. The first congregations were not segregated. Churches in Dubuque, Salem, Davenport, and elsewhere had Black and white members.[2]

Many of Iowa's first non-Native inhabitants were French who brought Catholicism to the Upper Mississippi River Valley. Catholic priests from New France (eastern Canada) were some of the first Europeans to reach Iowa, coming west via the Great Lakes. Priests, usually from the Jesuit order, ministered occasionally to fur trappers and traders in the late 1700s and early 1800s. The best-known of Iowa's early priests was Father Samuel Charles Mazzuchelli, who came to Dubuque in 1835, founding the first Catholic church in the town. Other churches followed in the next few years, in Davenport, Muscatine, and Iowa City. Different Christian faiths shared a house of worship in Dubuque for at least a year, beginning in 1834. Five years later half of the town's residents were Catholic. A log house had been built by Methodists in the city, used for a church and school. It was funded by Jews, Catholics, and Protestants. In the mid-nineteenth century thousands of Catholics migrated to Iowa, including large numbers from Ireland. One priest in Fort Madison reported eighty-eight baptisms, five marriages, and five burials from 1841 to 1844. By 1851 the town had more than one hundred Catholic families. In 1849 a group of Trappist monks came to the state from Ireland and established the Trappist Abbey of New Melleray southwest of Dubuque. The abbey was in an attractive hilly area, with abundant water, but away from worldly distractions. In 1849 and 1850 forty monks came to Iowa. They grew their own food and raised enough money from selling cattle during the Civil War to build a stone, Gothic style monastery, which opened in 1875. Trappists focused their lives on manual labor, prayer, and meditation. They were vegetarians and took vows of silence. The abbey survived into the 2020s, welcoming visitors, the faithful, and new monks.[3]

The Iowa Catholic church in the mid-nineteenth century was mostly German and Irish, with some Bohemian, or Czech, members. Northeast Iowa became heavily Catholic. There were Catholic enclaves in southern and western Iowa, but the religious landscape in most of the state was Protestant. Dubuque attracted Irish immigrants, "poor enough and hungry enough to go down into the mines," wrote historian Joseph Frazier Wall. Dubuque was a Catholic and Democratic stronghold in a predominantly Republican and Protestant state. The city had the first Catholic archdiocese and was the center of Catholic life in the state. Iowa City also had a substantial Catholic population. Rural Catholics came to the town from ten miles away for Sunday Mass. Following the Civil War, Irish and German Catholics continued to move into Iowa in large numbers, but Catholics remained a minority in Iowa overall.[4]

Many Protestant denominations were established in Iowa before the Civil War, with the Methodists being the largest Protestant church in Iowa. "It was best suited in its organization and by practical experience for proselytizing on the frontier," wrote Wall. The church took its message wherever there were people. The first Methodist service in Iowa occurred at a tavern in Dubuque in November 1833. Methodism did not have trained theologians and often relied upon itinerant ministers or other faithful to spread its ideas. They often traveled around lightly settled regions—riding the circuit—to visit those in need of salvation, performing marriages, baptisms, and preaching at funerals. For example, Seymour Snyder preached in northwest Iowa in the 1860s, usually carrying a revolver or shotgun for hunting and self-defense. Camp meetings and revivals, often lasting days, brought together a temporary congregation. Methodist circuit preachers stayed with families or slept on the ground, enduring floods or blizzards to spread the gospel. They brought a hopeful message of faith, forgiveness, and eternal salvation. The church preached that everyone could be saved and that no one was too sinful. But salvation meant that people had to give up alcohol, immorality, and worldly amusements. Iowans could not always meet such demands.[5]

O. J. Felton fondly remembered the Methodist church of the 1860s and 1870s in Jones County, east of the town of Anamosa. A Methodist circuit rider had come to preach, having heard that a Congregationalist meeting took place at the schoolhouse. Then the Baptists arrived, but "the Methodists, however, kept on in the lead," wrote Felton. The community built a church, some donating money, others labor. At church, men sat on one side and women on the other. Kids often sat in front. Sunday school began at nine a.m. and continued until the arrival of the preacher. "The decorum was not very good," he remembered. Sharp whispers and some foul

Iowa was a state of great religious diversity and rural life was often centered on houses of worship. This is a Methodist church from Solon, Iowa. Congregations and clergy, ca. 1880s, Solon, Iowa. From Churches-Methodist photo files, Special Collections, State Historical Society of Iowa, Iowa City.

language interrupted the service. The preacher was sometimes laughed at. "Every man from the preacher down chewed tobacco and spit in the aisles and the floor." Revivals were held in the winter, accompanied by huge amounts of food.[6]

Frontier preachers often found converts at revivals and camp meetings, where prayers, sermons, songs, and emotional appeals helped sinners repent and find salvation. People sometimes stayed at a camp meeting for two weeks, living in tents or wagons and cooking at a campfire. "Singing could be heard a mile away," remembered Arleen Troester. In the spring of 1865 eleven-year-old Henry A. Miller was at a Methodist Church revival in Unionville. "As I listened to the preacher, I realized the imminence of my impending doom," he wrote. Hell would be the price he would pay for stealing watermelons and cussing. He feared "burning, forever and ever. And forever was a long time." Finding himself at the pulpit, he confessed his sins and promised to give up fighting, stealing chickens, and playing marbles for keeps, "for that would be gambling." He admitted in a memoir that his conversion "did improve my general conduct for some months." Despite young Henry Miller's imperfect conversion, Methodism was highly successful at finding new members in Iowa. In 1860 the church had ninety thousand followers in the state, more than double the number of any other sect.[7]

A famous group of these early Protestant migrants was "The Iowa Band," eleven Congregationalist students at Andover Theological Seminary in Massachusetts who came to Iowa to be ministers. Congregationalists were concentrated in New England and interested in expansion into the Upper Midwest as part of the antislavery struggle. They didn't have the clerical resources of Catholicism or the many untrained clergy of the Methodists and thus were at a disadvantage in the scramble for converts. Concerned also by the spread of Mormonism, the Andover students decided to go preach the gospel in Iowa. The first Congregationalist church was established in the town of Denmark in 1838. Its minister, named Asa Turner, received a letter from the theology students declaring that they wanted to come to Iowa. Turner told them to bring warm clothes and hard-working wives. The Iowa Band arrived in Denmark, in the southeast corner of the state, in November 1843. Turner was surprised but glad for the assistance. All eleven members of the Iowa band went on to establish Congregationalist churches in eastern Iowa. One of them helped found Grinnell College. All of them were antislavery and temperance supporters. In the 1850s Congregationalists helped establish the town of Tabor, in southwest Iowa, as well as Grinnell. Josiah B. Grinnell, the town's founder, had been a minister in the church. Both places were active in the antislavery struggle.[8]

The most prominent of the Iowa Band was William Salter. He had doubts about how successful their missionary work would be. "Sometimes Salter wondered if the West really wanted to be saved after all," wrote Wall. Salter wrote to his fiancée that Iowa was full of ignorant people who didn't respect the Sabbath. New settlers had much more than religion to worry about. Salter was unhappy that many skipped a Thanksgiving sermon to work on their farms. Iowa was "so new a country where so many other interests absorb the minds of men," he noted. The whole town of Bellevue hated him—or so he thought—because he had preached the truth about their sinful ways. "The wicked and the worldly and the backsliders are the main settlers of this country," he wrote in frustration in November 1845. His letters were full of stories of disease and difficult weather. But Salter did not falter and served as pastor of his church in Burlington for sixty years.[9]

The Quakers, like the Congregationalists, were involved in the antislavery struggle before the Civil War. Formally known as the Religious Society of Friends, they believed that everyone had the Inner Light of Christ, and anyone could find salvation. Most Quakers hated slavery, and many moved to Iowa to live in a free state and to contest slavery's expansion. They opposed war and dressed and lived simply and frugally, without any ordained ministers. Quakers tried to keep worldly interactions to a minimum, only marrying other Friends. They worshipped in plain meeting houses or in the homes of the faithful. "Quiet, non-resisting but persistent Friends were among the most efficient conductors" on the underground railroad, wrote historian Ruth A. Gallaher. The faith came early to Iowa, when two Quaker men, Isaac Pidgeon and Aaron Street Jr., met by chance in southeast Iowa in the fall of 1835. Pidgeon was from South Carolina; Street from Indiana. Together, they decided to found a Quaker settlement. They called it Salem, as Street had lived in Salem, Indiana, and his father had lived in Salem, Ohio.[10]

In the following years other Friends followed, from Ohio, Indiana, Tennessee, and North Carolina. Many settled in southeast Iowa. In the mid-1840s a few families moved about eighty miles north and founded the town of Oakley. By 1852 there were enough people to build a meeting house. The next year they had more than three hundred members. Others lived across the eastern part of the state. By 1860 there were forty-five Quaker settlements in eighteen counties. Six years later almost ten thousand lived in Iowa. Historian Louis Thomas Jones wrote that the social harmony of Quaker settlements meant that disputes over land titles were almost unknown.[11]

The Baptists built their first church in Iowa in 1834 near Burlington. They saw Iowa as part of the struggle to save souls and build churches. As with the Methodists, untrained laymen helped spread Baptist ideas. They preached in fields and churches and pioneer cabins and barns. Ezra Fisher, an ordained Baptist minister, lived in Iowa and western Illinois from 1839 to 1845. A graduate of Amherst College, he had been a pastor in Indiana and Illinois. In 1840 he was the only Baptist minister in Iowa Territory. He traveled 750 miles in three months in late 1841 in Iowa and Illinois, visiting homes and organizing churches and temperance groups. He helped found a Baptist church in Muscatine. In 1845 he left Iowa for Oregon Territory, where he continued to serve as a minister until his death twenty-nine years later. Baptist churches—many undoubtedly founded by Fisher—grew in number to thirteen by 1842. In 1849 the church decried the alarming violation of the Sabbath by Iowans, a problem noted by Ezra Fisher as he traveled to Oregon. In the 1850s Baptist churches were established in Cedar Falls, Des Moines, Webster City, Council Bluffs, and Centerville. In the next decade congregations were also organized in Boone, Osage, Spirit Lake, and Marshalltown. By 1860 there were an estimated twenty-eight thousand Baptists in the state, about the same number as Catholics.[12]

The Presbyterian church sent ministers to Iowa as the Congregationalists had done. The two denominations also worked together to establish churches—by combining resources they could expand their reach. No community had both a Presbyterian and a Congregationalist church. The two groups also recruited ministers for western states and supported the organization of Sunday schools. They were far more successful in gaining converts than their Congregationalist partners, though, with forty-three thousand members in 1860. One minister, Gamaliel Carter Beaman, came to Des Moines in 1846. He reportedly gave more than five thousand sermons over forty-four years. Dedicated to antislavery and temperance, he encountered mobs of opponents sixteen times. A foe of liquor consumption, he bought two saloons just to put them out of business. He then lived in one building and sold the other.[13]

Catharine Wiggins Porter was a member of the United Presbyterian church, the second largest branch of the church in Iowa. She lived with her family in Page County, near the towns of Clarinda in the 1870s and Coin in the 1880s. "We children had a strict upbringing and careful training in the Scriptures," she wrote. Tasks were completed on Saturday to prepare for the next day. She enjoyed Sunday school much more than church, but she loved to sing, "the louder the better." Sunday school occurred at ten a.m., after the family's five-mile wagon ride to church. There were two sermons each Sunday, interrupted by lunch, which was also an important social hour. Porter did not love the two long sermons, noting that "things were more lively at the Methodist church, especially when the revival season was on." After the second hour of preaching, families headed home to complete chores, eat dinner, and memorize Bible verses. Children were quizzed by adults on what they had learned. Porter was thankful for her strict childhood. "It has a tendency to stiffen one's moral backbone," she wrote.[14]

The Lutheran church came to Iowa with waves of Germans, Norwegians, Danes, and Swedes in the mid-nineteenth century. Reverend Jacob Scherer was the first Lutheran pastor in the state in 1848. The first Lutheran church was established in Iowa in Van Buren County two years later. By 1854 Lutheran pastors had preached as far west as Knoxville and possibly all the way to Council Bluffs. One church leader declared that frontier conditions for the church were "deplorable," due to challenging living conditions and the tendency of immigrants to abandon both conscience and religion in the pursuit of wealth. Many Iowa Lutherans did not speak English and "drifted gradually into other denominations," lamented A. B. Leamer. In Iowa City, some joined a Methodist church because no Lutheran pastor was available. Iowa lacked pastors because of large numbers of Lutherans in Wisconsin and Illinois. One Iowa City pastor traveled 325 miles a month on horseback to visit widely scattered congregants as far away as Fort Dodge. In 1870 Swedish immigrants founded a Lutheran congregation in the new town of Stanton, in southwest Iowa. A structure was built by Christmas of that year, with wooden planks and nail kegs serving as primitive pews. By 1883 membership comprised 994 people. The community was centered on the church, which hosted concerts, suppers, and coffee socials.[15]

Christian missionaries went to China in the late nineteenth century, tying Iowa to the world in unexpected ways. Eva and Charles Price and their two sons, originally from Des Moines, lived in Shanxi, southwest of Beijing, from 1889 to 1900. Charles was a minister, educated at Oberlin College in Ohio. Eva hoped to convert the "heathen" Chinese, who viewed the Americans with suspicion. She was the first foreign woman that most Chinese ever saw. They comforted the sick and ran a missionary school. A daughter, Florence, was born; both of Eva's sons, Stewart, and Donald, died while they were in the country. Their faith sustained Eva and Charles but could not save them from the violence of the anti-foreigner uprising known as the Boxer Rebellion: Eva, Charles, and Florence were killed about July 31, 1900.[16]

Another Iowa woman, Sarah Pike Conger, accompanied her husband, Edwin, overseas. Edwin Conger was appointed American minister to China in 1898 by President William McKinley. The couple had moved to Dexter, Iowa, from Illinois in 1868 to farm; Edwin was also a lawyer.

He was elected Iowa state treasurer and served three terms in Congress in the 1880s. In the summer of 1900, the outbreak of the Boxer Rebellion trapped the Congers and other foreigners in Beijing. They were besieged for two months, defended by US Marines and the soldiers of other nations stationed at embassies. The Congers and other personnel lived on mule and horse meat. Sarah filled sandbags, made bandages, and cared for the sick and wounded. Shells and bullets were a constant threat. "Common trials make us willing to respond to common demands," she wrote in *Letters from China*. Edwin and Sarah survived the siege. She became friends with the Chinese empress dowager, Cixi, one of the last rulers of the Qing dynasty. A feminist, Conger helped inspire the opening of schools for girls in China. While Edwin died in California in 1907, Sarah Conger lived until 1932, writing several books about her experiences in China.[17]

Iowa's Jewish population was small and lived far from the major cities that were the center of Jewish life in America. One of the first settlers in Dubuque was Alexander Levi, a French Jew who arrived in the town in 1833. He ran a grocery store. Keokuk had the largest Jewish population in the state in the mid-nineteenth century, with Iowa's first congregation organized in the city in 1855. They met in private homes and rented buildings for more than twenty years until a synagogue was built. "At its peak Keokuk's antebellum Jewish community of more than one hundred families was larger than Chicago's," wrote historian Michael J. Bell. Younker Brothers was a Jewish firm that started in the town before the Civil War and expanded into a chain of department stores. Another congregation was formally incorporated in Davenport in 1861. This community procured a Torah scroll and holiday prayer books from New York. Small clusters of Jews lived in Burlington, Ottumwa, and Muscatine, where many worked as merchants or peddlers. Many saved enough to open their own businesses. One immigrant was Moses Bloom, who settled in Iowa City in 1857 and opened a clothing store. He was elected mayor of the city in the 1870s. Bell estimated that a little more than five hundred Jews lived in Iowa at the time of the Civil War. Thirty-seven Jewish men served in Iowa regiments during the conflict. By 1877 Jewish congregations had also been established in Des Moines and Iowa City. The first synagogue was built in Keokuk in 1877. In the late nineteenth and early twentieth centuries thousands of Jewish immigrants came to Iowa, fleeing massacres in Russia and persecution in Eastern Europe. By 1918 sixteen thousand lived in the state, mostly escaping the vicious anti-Semitism in the rest of the country.

Prejudice in the state limited employment options, though, even if Jews were often integrated into society.[18]

African American churches also existed in Iowa, mainly Methodist and Baptist. They were the spiritual center of Iowa's Black communities. Iowa's Black population built their own churches when possible, which also served as locations for reunions, plays, holiday celebrations, weddings, and funerals. While the first church in Dubuque, which was Methodist, was integrated and had at least six Black members, an African Methodist Episcopal church in Muscatine may have been the first Black church in the state in 1849. Burlington and Keokuk, river towns where many fugitive enslaved people lived, also had additional African Methodist congregations. In 1868 the first African American churches were organized in Des Moines and Iowa City. Black Methodist churches were founded in Cedar Rapids, Council Bluffs, and Newton in the 1870s, 1880s, and 1890s, as were Baptist ones in Des Moines, Ottumwa, Fort Madison, and Clinton. By 1906 the state had more than seventy African American churches. The coal mining town of Buxton had eight Black churches in the early twentieth century.[19]

Churches were central to the lives of Iowans, as were schools. Iowa's first schools were usually private. An organized tax-supported state system of education took decades to create. There was little opposition to public education in the United States before the Civil War, but there was much debate over how to organize and pay for it. Until tax-supported public education became widespread in the Midwest around the Civil War, education was irregular and haphazard. In October 1830 Isaac Galland hired Berryman Jennings to teach in the Half-Breed Tract. Jennings taught seven or eight students, including Eliza, David, and Washington Galland, for three months. His pay included food and lodging, which was usually not part of teacher pay. Other schools were built in 1833 and 1834 in Keokuk, Fort Madison, and Burlington.[20]

The first one-room schoolhouse in Iowa was opened in 1839, just north of Keokuk. It was a small log building with space for only three students and a teacher. Many schools were equally rudimentary but usually more spacious. By the late 1830s there were forty to fifty schools in the state. A small sod-covered house, which had been a blacksmith's shop, served as the first school in Maquoketa in 1842. Iowa's population was scattered over thousands of square miles by the time of statehood and less than half of the school-age population was enrolled in 1854. Parents believed that education was necessary for the intellectual and moral development of children. But agricultural chores often interfered, and many families did not have extra income to send every child to school.[21]

Iowa's public school system originated in 1858 when the state government enacted major reforms. Property taxes were set aside for schools and a disorganized and patchy system was made more regular. Townships and counties held most of the authority in this system, founded on a locally controlled and mostly rural school system. Each township—a local political unit that was smaller than a county—organized its own schools. Towns with more than one thousand inhabitants could also establish their own school district. The law authorized the creation of one high school in each county, as well as the mostly advisory position of state superintendent of public instruction. Almost all decision making was left to local districts, which were usually run by an elected township board. It made decisions on the number of schools in each district, the length of their school year, what subjects would be taught, and who would be hired. "The organization and operation of Iowa's public school system reflected the prevailing belief that schools must be kept close to the people, politically as well as proximately," wrote historian Keach Johnson. Legislation in the 1860s and 1870s allowed for the creation of ever-smaller school subdistricts. By 1889 the state had more than thirteen thousand districts, townships, and independent districts.[22]

Iowans understood the importance of education for their children and wanted it to be available for them. While Iowa's educational system in the nineteenth century could be fragmented and confusing, it was usually a solid foundation for life. A basic education was practical—young people needed to know how to read religious texts or calculate profits and losses. But it was also idealistic, as schools provided opportunity and parents wanted their kids to have the chance to advance in life. Most hoped that an education would reward ability and hard work and that a poor child could become as prosperous as the richest one. An 1856 report on Iowa's schools argued that the state needed a system of public education to fully develop its agricultural wealth, as well as "the intellect and moral power of its people." A basic education prepared students to be good citizens. Americans also hoped that it could ensure good government. The native-born wanted schools to help immigrants adopt the values of their new country. Diverse Americans could "forge common ties" in schools, as Johann N. Neem wrote. Iowans of all backgrounds believed that schools were invaluable.[23]

Until 1858 Iowa schools existed in a messy private and semipublic

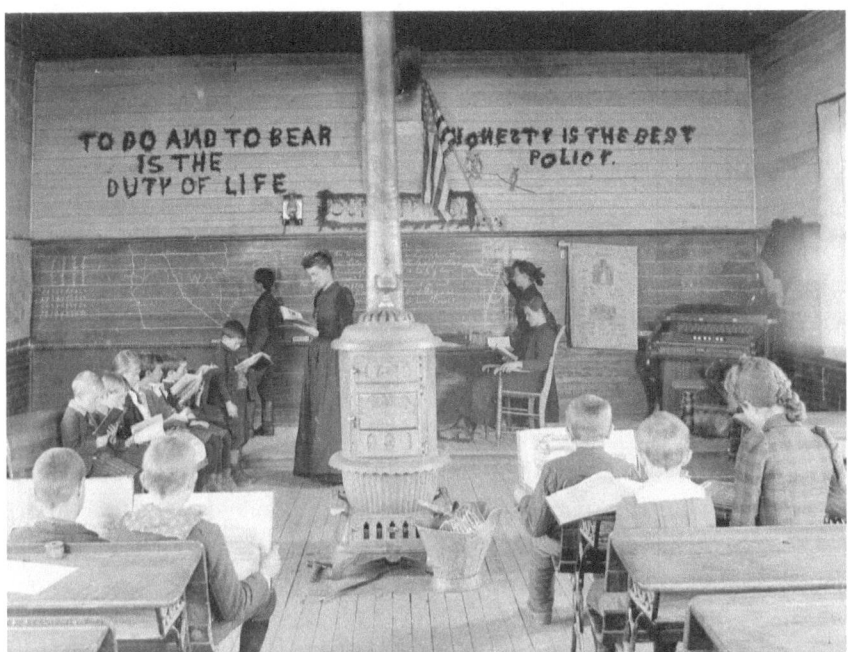

Iowa's one-room schools were the foundation of the state's public education system for more than a century. Class in session at Bear Creek Township school, Brooklyn, Iowa, ca. 1893. PH17625, State Historical Society of Iowa, Des Moines.

system, with eight hundred log schoolhouses and sixteen hundred schools in rented houses. Some lacked desks or even doors and many families sent their children to schools with books from home. Money was often scarce. Cash-poor families usually did not tax themselves for schools. Thus, many families had to pay fees, albeit a relatively small sum, to send their children to public schools. The 1858 law, combined with a fast-growing population, led to an extraordinary growth in the number of schools, districts and students. By 1900 the state had nearly fourteen thousand schoolhouses, more schools than states such as Ohio or Illinois. About one in six had fewer than ten students. Iowa did not spend a lot of money on schools or on teacher salaries, but it spent more per capita than Indiana. Iowa's school terms were longer, and the state enrolled more students. The sheer number of schools and local control may have contributed to the success of education in Iowa, wrote historian Wayne Fuller. By 1900 Iowa was tied with Nebraska as the most literate state in the nation, having ranked in the top five most literate states since 1870. By 1900, 97 percent of the state's inhabitants were literate. Iowa's literacy was demonstrated by the vast circulation of weekly county newspapers and magazines in the state, which included 838 weekly publications by 1900, with a circulation of 1,105,000. The state had a population of only 2.23 million people; many families may have subscribed to several weeklies.[24]

Across Iowa, school schedules were roughly the same, but the age and number of students, as well as their capabilities, varied greatly. Schools usually had two sessions, with a winter term beginning after harvest in the fall. It could last three or four months, or less, depending on local preferences. The spring term—sometimes called summer—usually began in March or April. The demands of farm life dictated student attendance. Male education occurred in "broken doses," wrote historian Elliott West. Boys might alternate school with labor, staying home to assist their families. Girls often outnumbered boys under twelve years old, but older students usually were boys who were trying to catch up on their education. Ages could range from five to twenty in a schoolhouse and some spoke little English. On an average day, one-third to half of students might be absent. Some boys in their teens came from homes with no books and had difficulty sounding out words, recalled Carl Hamilton. Hugh Orchard wrote that "nobody graduated from our school in those days. Students either dropped out to go to work on the farm or in the kitchen."[25]

Children rose early to complete chores before school. After breakfast they gathered books and lunch and set off. Most rural schools were located within two miles of their students. In good weather, kids met with friends to talk, sing, or play on the way to their destination. Mischievous boys might taunt bulls or dogs or cut across pastures. Kids might encounter snakes, cross swollen creeks, or walk barefoot as late as November. Sarah Gillespie Huftalen recalled that it was "more comfortable to go barefoot" since her shoes were heavy and badly made. Rain, snow, or serious cold made the trek challenging. Horse teams with a bobsled might collect students in times of deep snow. Education in the nineteenth century did not have the clocklike regularity of recent decades. Instruction normally began at nine in the morning, but reality dictated that a teacher waited for many students to appear. While the school day usually ended at 4 p.m., winter weather often led to a shorter day.[26]

A typical one-room schoolhouse was about twenty feet wide and thirty feet long, usually with several windows along each side. There was a door at the end of the building closest to the road. The schools were usually painted white and could seat up to forty students. A stove sat in the middle of the structure, with a blackboard at one end of the room. George W. Clarke remembered that schools could be frigid in the winter: "It is supposable that there were colder places on earth than that schoolhouse when winter was at its extreme but it is hard to conceive of such a place." Teachers worked as janitors and fire-starters, too. One female teacher had to chase a wolf out of a coal shed to get fuel. Lessons focused on reading, basic math, grammar, and spelling. History and geography were also covered. Students often received a strong dose of Protestant religion, including prayers or songs, along with their studies. Younger students sat in front, pupils sharing desks if they existed. Boys sat on one side of the school, with girls on the other. School days involved lots of reading aloud, spelling, and memorization. Maps or textbooks could be rare. Rosa Schreurs Jennings wrote that "teaching helps were scanty—a few old maps, no globe, a reading chart for beginners . . . a dog-eared dictionary." She painted part of a wall black to use as a blackboard. Pupils brought books from home. The one-room schoolhouse emphasized patriotism, hard work, and good manners.[27]

Carl Seashore, the son of Swedish immigrants who lived in Boone County, wrote that the main goal of teachers was to "keep students busy and working, mostly through self-help or with the aid of more advanced students." There were no lectures, but much recitation of a lesson from memory. There were no problems with discipline or motivation in his classes, as all his fellow students were the striving children of new immigrants. Seashore knew no English when he began his formal education at age seven in 1873 and estimated that he only attended six hundred days of school in eleven years. He labored for many years on his parents' eighty-acre farm, missing half the school year for most of his youth. "Out-of-door responsible activities of rich and varied interests" were a valuable substitute for formal training, he wrote. Such education—full of initiative, ingenuity, and economy—was "set in reality with necessity as a teacher." After two years at an academy—sort of a high school—Seashore went to Gustavus Adolphus University in Minnesota, then on to graduate school at Yale, where he obtained his PhD in 1895. He spent more than forty years as a psychology professor and dean at the State University of Iowa in Iowa City.[28]

Teaching could be a challenge, both in a classroom and away from it. Classes could be large and student knowledge minimal. Discipline could be a problem, especially if a young female teacher had a class full of young men. Some older boys made teachers' lives miserable. Teachers, both male and female, often quit or refused to teach another term. They resorted to physical punishment only after lesser penalties, such as forcing boys to sit on the girls' side of the classroom, failed. Celestia Lee Barker wrote in her diary that "it seems so curious to be boss of so many large boys." Barker did not record any serious problems in her diary but Sarah Gillespie Huftalen wrote that one student "took up a stick of wood & came at me," while she was disciplining a sibling. It was her first year of teaching, but she restored order and kept control of her classroom. Huftalen's career as an educator lasted more than fifty years; she was elected superintendent of schools for Page County, taking office in 1913 and serving for two years. Phoebe Sudlow was the first female city superintendent of public schools in the United States, chosen by the Davenport board of education in 1874. After four years in this position, she became an English professor at the State University of Iowa.[29]

Salaries for teachers were meager and living conditions quite imperfect. Teachers earned about thirty dollars a month in the mid- and late-nineteenth century. It was one of the few professions open to women and one of the few ways they could usually earn money working outside their homes. Some young women became teachers to help parents pay bills or send a sibling to school. The number of female teachers increased when enlistment in the Civil War reduced the ranks of male teachers. In 1862 women became a majority of teachers; in 1880 they outnumbered men two to one in Iowa. Local school boards hired educators who might only have a couple of years of high school education or less. Turnover was high and as many as one-quarter of classrooms each fall were taught by a first-year teacher. Teachers were young, with the average male being twenty-four or twenty-five years old. Women were often twenty to twenty-two. If they did not live near their school, they boarded with a local family. Living conditions could range from awful to warm and hospitable. Rosa Schreurs Jennings "taught seven years in rural one-room schools, and had a pleasant place to board." Her experience was not universal. Some teachers complained of bedbugs or poor food or pranks from children who might leave a dead lizard in their bed. Agnes Briggs Olmstead was so unhappy with the family she boarded with that she walked from her parents' farm to teach every day, sometimes returning home late at night, remembering, "I was often very, very tired and at times my feet almost refused to bear me further and wading creeks grew monotonous." She walked five miles each way.³⁰

Alice Money Lawrence moved to Iowa with her father and stepmother in 1862, settling in Grundy County. She spent most of her time in domestic labor, but she wanted to be a teacher. Lawrence spent summers working on the family farm, unable to attend school. To pay for her education she tended to five hundred sheep for her father. In November 1865, she wrote a letter to her sister in Ohio. "I've watched sheep for two months with my horse, dog, and schoolbooks, and such a time as I have had you never saw. One day I was riding through the woods reading and a limb of a big tree knocked me off!" Unhurt, she returned to studying and went off to Albion Seminary. Lawrence earned several teaching certificates and her first school was in Grundy County, where she began in 1867. She had twelve students, five who left once harvest began. She boarded with a family in a dirty and uncomfortable home, where breakfast consisted of soggy bread and eggs cooked in lard. In a letter to her sister, she wrote, "I like teaching. Oh, yes, the teaching part but not the discipline. I had to keep all of my scholars but one in at recess today, and I had to whip one boy."³¹

In summer 1869 Lawrence taught at a school in Vienna Township in Marshall County, a place with a gang of boys that had made so much trouble that at least one male teacher had resigned in the middle of a term. School directors wondered if a young woman of five feet and one inch could handle the situation. In June one boy made an "indecent" remark as she walked by. She ignored it. She caught him off guard on her return, pushing him into the aisle and spanking him with his geography book. Lawrence ordered him to go home, while the class laughed at him. There were no more problems that term. The troublesome young men swept and cleaned the schoolhouse for the summer as a sign of their respect. Her teaching career ended that year when she became engaged to a local doctor. She married Dr. Elmer Lawrence in 1870, living near Marshalltown and in Nebraska until her death in 1925.³²

Iowa's schools were not legally segregated, but the education Black students received was usually inferior to that of white pupils. The south-central Iowa town of Buxton was an exception. Its population was mostly African American, and whites and Blacks worked and lived together in the early twentieth century. Black students had a better education and greater opportunities there than elsewhere in the state. Some who had migrated from southern states could go to school for the first time. Black students had Black teachers, which was rare in Iowa. They also went to school with some white students. In much of Iowa, residential segregation led to educational segregation, especially in cities with larger Black populations like Des Moines or Waterloo. Most of Des Moines's Black population lived in the Center Street area, while most Blacks in Waterloo lived in the eastern part of the city. African American students attended schools near these areas, which ended up segregated because Black Iowans could not live in white neighborhoods.[33]

Two of Buxton's schools were mostly Black, while one was predominantly white. Dorothy Collier remembered, "We were all mixed together. I couldn't understand the prejudice when we moved to Cedar Rapids when I was nine." The mostly Black schools had all Black teachers. Many had college degrees. One of them was Murda Beason, one of two African American women who graduated from Iowa State Teachers College in 1916. The school year was eight months long and classes met for six hours a day. The curriculum included most of the same courses as other schools in the state, from reading and math to history and geography. Schools were crowded, with as many as fifty students in a class. But teachers had high expectations for their students. One former pupil remembered, "They didn't pass you just because you got too big for the seat." By fourteen, many left to go to work in the town or in nearby coal mines. Some African American students went to high school or college. Edward Carter attended the State University of Iowa and earned a BA and an MD. He returned to Buxton as the town's only Black doctor.[34]

Despite the best efforts of their teachers, children did not always appreciate school for its own sake. They enjoyed their one-hour lunch and breaks from their education more than time in class. "Readin,' 'Ritin' and 'Rithmetic were tricks one had to learn in order to propitiate teachers and get a chance for recess," wrote Harriet Connor Brown, who went on to be a teacher and a journalist. In Buxton, white and Black students played and ate together, segregated more by gender than race. Boys played marbles and baseball while girls played jump rope or hopscotch. At lunchtime farm boys might run off to search for wild plums in the countryside, invariably returning late with faces darkened by hastily eaten noontime snacks. In the warmer months, students might play ball, tag, or games such as crack-the-whip. In the winter they had snowball fights or went sledding. Children might pursue snakes or try to drown gophers with pails of water if the weather allowed. Rosa Schreurs Jennings remembered that gophers rarely emerged from their holes. "Only occasionally did one come out, wet and bedraggled, to streak across the pasture, chased by relentless, screaming boys. It would have been idle to preach mercy." Students also looked forward to Friday afternoons for weekly spelling competitions or speaking contests.[35]

The one-room country schoolhouse was the foundation for Iowa education from the 1850s until the mid-twentieth century. Most students—from 70 to 80 percent—attended rural schools from the 1850s until the 1890s. Not much changed during this time for schools in the countryside, even as Iowa's population grew by more than ten times from 1850 to 1900. The state instituted additional teacher certification requirements, which required a greater investment of time and money. Fewer men became teachers, as they had many more career options that usually paid better. By 1905, 86 percent of elementary teachers were women.[36]

High schools had been authorized as part of the 1858 school reform, but most students did not attend a secondary school until after 1911. A few towns had high schools, while more had academies—privately run secondary schools—to provide classes beyond the basic ones at one-room elementary schools. Tipton had one of the first high schools in Iowa in 1856, with thirteen students graduating two years later. Secondary schools might offer two, three, or four years of coursework, with about half offering four years of study by 1905. Courses in early high schools included algebra, history, astronomy, English, botany, and bookkeeping. Languages such as German and French were optional. The first county high school opened in Panora in Guthrie County in 1876. The state only had about 120 high schools in 1889. In 1905 only thirty-nine thousand Iowa students were enrolled at a high school. Many counties did not have one and sent their students to a nearby county. A 1911 state law made high school tuition free and stimulated the spread of education beyond elementary school. The number of high schools grew to 953 by 1934, and the number of enrolled students almost quadrupled to more than 153,000 by 1932. The curriculum broadened to include art, manual training, and agriculture. Athletic sports, debating, drama, and 4-H clubs became widespread. Elsie Boddicker Schallau attended Newhall Consolidated High School, starting in 1927. She took English or literature classes for four years, along with history, Latin, economics, physics, and geometry. Her school bus was a modified Model T truck.[37]

Rural schools could not provide the better education offered in towns and cities. Urban areas had more resources, better and more educated teachers, as well as superior buildings and equipment. They also had libraries and laboratories and offered a variety of subjects. More than 90 percent of Iowa's schools were ungraded in 1898, usually one-room schools taught by a single teacher. Schoolhouses often had a new teacher every term. Teaching was a low-paying, insecure job and its workforce was transient. Most saw teaching as a temporary occupation, with new teachers making up about one-fifth of the total each year. This resulted in a near complete replacement of Iowa's teachers every five years or so. Schoolhouses suffered from a lack of maintenance and were poorly heated. Schools might only have a handful of students at widely different grade levels. Teachers were overburdened and underpaid. Education for most rural pupils ended after elementary school since options for a secondary school were limited unless parents could afford to pay tuition for a high school or academy. Many rural children who went to high schools before World War I dropped out, unprepared for the demands of such schools or finding courses boring. Still, access to secondary education improved in 1911 as state support for high school education expanded. One-room schools dominated rural education in the state for several more decades, however.[38]

Iowa saw the founding of many public and private colleges in the nineteenth century. "Even before Iowa's public-school system had taken shape, citizens had begun to think about higher education," wrote Dorothy Schwieder. The Methodist and Catholic churches, the largest denominations in the state, established many colleges. The first college in the state was Iowa Wesleyan University, which began as Mount Pleasant Collegiate Institute. Arabella Babb Mansfield, who became the first woman in the United States admitted to the bar to practice law in 1869, graduated from Iowa Wesleyan. The Methodist church established or took control over four schools, starting with Cornell College in 1855. Other Methodist schools included Upper Iowa University and Simpson College. African American botanist George Washington Carver started college at Simpson. Morningside College in Sioux City opened in 1896. The Catholic church ran a seminary in Dubuque, which became Loras College in 1939, as well as Clarke College and Briar Cliff College, which evolved into universities in 1928 and 1930. Briar Cliff started as a women's college. The Presbyterian church also established the University of Dubuque, Coe College, and Buena Vista College. Iowa was full of private colleges, with twenty-two in existence by 1870. Most admitted women.[39]

George Washington Carver was born enslaved in Missouri in 1864. His education was limited, and he did not finish high school until his late twenties. He had always been interested in plants and animals and enrolled in Simpson College in 1890. Carver transferred to Iowa Agricultural College (now ISU), where he received a bachelor's degree in agriculture. But he was not allowed to live in the dormitory because of his race and lived in a vacant office. One of his professors, James G. Wilson, was later the secretary of agriculture. Henry A. Wallace, who would be agriculture secretary for Franklin Roosevelt, was a friend in college, as was his father, who also became an agricultural secretary. Carver joined the school's faculty as a biology teacher and earned a master's degree—he is considered the first African American faculty member at the college. In 1896 he left Ames for Alabama to lead the agriculture department at the Tuskegee Institute. Carver was especially interested in practical knowledge that would aid poor farmers. His work on soybeans and peanuts helped southerners reduce their dependence on cotton production.[40]

Other private colleges were founded in Iowa, too. Grinnell College began in Davenport as Iowa College and moved to the town of Grinnell in 1861. The school graduated its first class in the town, who were mostly female, in 1865. A tornado in 1882 badly damaged the campus, but the disaster gained attention and gifts that helped it rebuild. Drake University, founded in 1881 in Des Moines as a successor to Oskaloosa College, received its name when General Francis M. Drake left the school $20,000, about $522,000 in 2020. Decorah's Luther College, often referred to as a "preacher" college, was started by the Norwegian Evangelical Lutheran church. It only educated men until 1936. The state also had other colleges, such as Central College in Pella, a Baptist school. Its first class of thirty-seven students helped build their classroom in 1854. Wartburg College resulted from the merging of a few theological, seminary, and other schools from Illinois, Iowa, Nebraska, and Minnesota over the course of many decades.[41]

Iowa's three public universities were established in the mid-nineteenth century, with the State University of Iowa—now the University of Iowa—created first, in 1847. The state constitution of 1857 made Iowa City its permanent location. Its initial funding came from the federal government, which gave proceeds from the sale of two townships to Iowa when it became a state. The first class did not arrive until eight years later, when there were 4 faculty and 124 students. Forty-one women enrolled, their presence saving the school from closure. Only a handful of state universities admitted women by 1870, as many men believed that women could not withstand the intellectual challenges of college or that their reproductive potential would be harmed by such an education. The State University of Iowa had nine departments, including ancient and modern languages, chemistry, and history. However, most of these subjects were not taught. The school partially closed three years after opening due to low enrollment. It reopened in 1860, but the number of students remained limited. The university struggled for decades. Critics ridiculed it as "Iowa City High School," even as it added programs in moral philosophy and rhetoric and astronomy. The school also added medical, dental, and law schools but only enrolled 887 students in 1890. Women were admitted to the first class in the medical school. About half of the students at the university studied law or medicine. There were only seventy-three faculty in 1890. Things did turn around though, and in the early and mid-twentieth century the University of Iowa acquired a fine academic reputation, having survived the rough nineteenth century.[42]

The university assured Iowa City that the campus would have a "wholesome moral influence," wrote Stow Persons. Daily chapel attendance was required, as was Sunday church service. Students could choose their church from among those in town. The school required study hours and prohibited drinking, gambling, profanity, visiting a saloon, or attending a theater. Most students grew up in religious homes, so such rules were not unusual. Tuition was low, at $25 a term in 1890, about $734 in 2020. Fees for the medical school were higher, at $65 a year. No student was denied an education due to poverty; fees were waived for those who could not pay.[43]

The legislature established Iowa Agricultural College and Model Farm—now Iowa State University—in 1858, though it did not have any students until March 1869. Lawmakers did not allocate enough money or choose a location for the school. Fortunately, the federal government provided funding through the Land Grant College Act of 1862, also known as the Morrill Act, which gave each state land to sell to fund higher education. Iowa was the first state to agree to federal conditions, which included building a school within five years, and was given more than two hundred thousand acres. Proceeds from this land helped build the college. It offered "a practical education in agriculture and the mechanic arts," wrote historian Pamela Riney-Kehrberg. Iowa State was founded as a "people's college" and provided an education to those from modest backgrounds.

The freshman class had ninety-three students, including sixteen women. Strict rules set moral standards. Alcohol and tobacco use were forbidden and eventually dancing was not allowed on college grounds. Students usually lived on campus, which was a couple miles west of the small town of Ames. The campus consisted of one building, Old Main. It provided classroom space, as well as housing for most students and faculty. The cost for a year was less than $150, but students could earn $50 working on campus. A long winter break allowed them to teach a winter term in a rural school to help pay for their education. Intercollegiate athletics came in the 1890s, with fraternities and sororities in the following decade.[44]

Iowa State was one of the first land-grant schools to provide an education to both women and men. There was not complete equality on campus, however. Women could not pursue some courses and were not encouraged to take part in the same activities as men. Their education prepared them for a "separate place in the adult world," wrote Riney-Kehrberg. Meanwhile, the school became a national leader in the study of domestic economy for women. Female students learned how to be scientific farm wives, attending lectures on health care, drainage, and sewing. Some graduates used their domestic science degrees in unexpected careers. Hattie Raybourne, who graduated in 1873, worked in the state capitol as an assistant in the land office. Alice Whited was a county and state auditor. Others became homesteaders and established their own farms or went to study medicine.[45]

In 1876 the third public college in Iowa was founded. Iowa State Normal School—now the University of Northern Iowa—was established in Cedar Falls because the state owned a large brick structure built for Civil War orphans. By 1876 the orphans had all become adults and left behind an empty building. Until Iowa State Normal School opened, Iowa had no school to train its teachers, at a time when Minnesota had three such schools and Wisconsin had four. Iowa State Normal School opened in September 1876 with five faculty and twenty-seven students, who took classes in languages, natural science, mathematics, history, and geography. The school was established at the same time that new teacher certification requirements entered into force. Initially, conditions were abysmal. State funding was limited. The bill to authorize the college only passed each house with one vote to spare. There were no maps or charts and few books. Historian William J. Petersen wrote that it was "wretchedly housed and equipped." Books left at the orphanage were "soiled and dog-eared volumes, juvenile in character, and unsuited to the uses of a normal school," wrote David Sands Wright, who taught at the college and served as an administrator for fifty years. But the school survived to become a university in the twentieth century and blossomed after World War II.[46]

Eighty-eight percent of Iowa's population lived in rural areas in 1880, with at least two-thirds of all Iowans living on farms. When Iowa Agricultural College opened to students in 1869, the population of the city of Ames was 650. Mason City had only about fifteen hundred residents in 1871. In the late nineteenth century, Iowa was a rural and agricultural state, with a population spread across more than fifty thousand square miles. Even with the arrival of railroads in the state, small towns played a vital role in the economic, social, and cultural life of Iowa's people. "Little towns were built, eight to ten miles apart across the state as settlers moved westward," wrote Joseph Frazier Wall. They provided services to the rural population and served as a market center, usually with a general store, post office, a blacksmith shop, and a mill for grain. The post office might be located in a general store. Such small places often had a church or a school. Around 1880 Mason City had a bank and a bookstore, as well as one hardware business and several clothing stores.[47]

Hugh Orchard wrote that the small town of Yarmouth, about twenty-five miles northwest of Burlington, was a "mighty interesting place" in the 1870s and 1880s. A visit gave farm families a respite from working in the fields. His family picked up their mail in town, at a post office operated by a family in their home. They went to a blacksmith when needed, as well as local stores. The village had a railroad depot, too. On Saturdays the town was full of visitors from as far away as six or seven miles. There might be fifty horse teams tied up in town, he remembered. "In every store people would be sitting around on sugar sacks, nail kegs, and right on the counters—talking about the weather, and the crops, and other interesting things." Men played checkers, watched by spectators who criticized every move. Children went to buy lemonade, peanuts, and candy, listening to stories "pretty nippy for a young person to hear." Away from home and work, boys wrestled, ran races, and "worked ourselves up into a regular lather. If we had been forced to work half that hard on the farm, we would have nearly died."[48]

Rural life remained much the same in the late nineteenth century as it had been three or four decades earlier. Railroads helped tie the countryside to a wider world but the cycle of work that was governed by weather and the seasons dominated people's existence. Life was still full of manual labor, usually from first light until after dark. Children attended the local one-room schoolhouse when possible. Time was mostly spent within a few miles of home. Many farm families produced most of the foodstuffs that they consumed, but they were not subsistence farmers. Most needed to earn some income to pay taxes or a mortgage, buy land, or visit a local store. Clifford Merrill Drury wrote that corn was picked by hand around 1910. His family also made their own cider, kept two hundred chickens, and butchered their own hogs. "With the exception of such staples as sugar, flour, spices, and canned goods, we were able to raise or produce most of the food we needed," he wrote. Near the end of the 1800s the rural free delivery of mail helped reduce the isolation of farm life. The spread of telephones into the countryside allowed people to communicate with neighbors and more distant friends and families. But for most who lived in the countryside, the old rhythms of life continued into the early twentieth century.[49]

African Americans in rural Iowa usually lived separate lives from their white neighbors, even if they had greater opportunities than in southern states. Iowa was one of the most progressive states in the country in terms of Black legal equality, but discrimination was widespread. Black children went to school with their white neighbors, but hotels, theaters, and restaurants in towns were segregated. "While it appeared that blacks enjoyed a decent living on the farm in Iowa, they were expected to stay in their place," wrote historian Valerie Grim. There were about 300 Black farm families in the state in the 1880s and 1890s, with average farm size of about 120 acres. They had more economic freedom than in Southern states, where white landlords controlled commerce. White landowners did not conspire to keep Blacks from buying land in Iowa. Black farmers could make decisions for themselves and manage their farms without interference. J. P. Johnson, a Black farmer near Muscatine, sold vegetables to canneries. Another family in Clarinda raised prize-wining thoroughbred pigs. African American farmwomen raised chickens and turkeys, sold eggs, cared for cows, and marketed fruit, honey, milk, and butter. Black farmwomen operated laundry, hairdressing, and catering businesses for urban and rural customers. They also had quilting parties or women's clubs. In Algona, Blacks helped whites build schools, churches, barns, and roads. Rural African American families went to nearby towns for worship, taking lunch so they could spend time with other Black families, usually at Methodist Episcopalian services.[50]

Ada Mae Brown Brinton remembered Stuart, Iowa, which was about forty miles west of Des Moines, in the early 1900s: "Streets were either dusty or muddy. There was no solid ground of any kind. Hitching rails were along Main Street." Flies were everywhere, drawn by horse manure. Horse-drawn wagons were the main mode of transportation, but she noted that there were some bicycles in town. Trains came through the town depot at least four times a day, heading east and west. A tall stove sat in the middle of the depot building, surrounded by wooden benches. Inside, the telegraph chattered endlessly. At home her mother did "a great deal of canning of fruits and vegetables."[51]

Life in the countryside revolved around agricultural work, but amusement and recreation gave "some relief from the dull routine of securing a hard-earned living," wrote Bruce E. Mahan. Hunting and fishing helped feed a family, and corn husking combined drudgery with entertainment. Holidays like the Fourth of July and Christmas gave families and friends the opportunity to eat, socialize, and rest. A trip to the opera house also provided a chance to visit a nearby town for entertainment. Clubs provided a social outlet for women and supported social reform. The Chautauqua—sort of a traveling education and entertainment show—was popular in Iowa and the United States in the late nineteenth and early twentieth century. Sports such as baseball brought together communities in competition. Iowans also went to the state fair.[52]

Bessie C. Thompson, who was born in Webster City in 1884, recalled that "our pleasures were much simpler than they are now. There were no cars, no radios, no movies, or TV and we learned to furnish our own entertainment." She wrote that children were "more easily pleased" and always had something to do. Thompson proudly noted that her family read a lot of good books. They played checkers and dominoes, had picnics, ate apples, cooked popcorn, and went to Sunday school. She went on to become a teacher.[53]

Hunting and fishing were mostly a male sport. Men might hunt wolves with their neighbors. The hunt often came to a bloody end with dogs chasing down their quarry, which was surrounded and then clubbed to death. Other game, from deer to ducks, were also popular targets. W. F. Main recalled hunting prairie chickens. There were so many that it sounded like thunder when they took flight. Main had great success fishing for bass, pike, and "other fish by the millions." Iowans also pursued rattlesnakes, a common and sometimes dangerous problem, with cautious enthusiasm.

Though few died from their bite, most Iowans took precautions to avoid one. Whisky was supposedly a cure for a snake bite—some also considered it a preventive. One settler reported finding thirty snakes coiled up in a ball. Barefoot children learned to move quickly when they heard a rattle. Matilda Paul wrote in her memoir, "We dreaded the sound of a rattle snake any time, especially when hunting cows through long grass." A "great snake hunt" began in Madison County in April 1848 and ended on July 4. Four thousand of the creatures were reportedly eliminated. In celebration, an ox was barbequed and plenty of snakebite remedy was consumed.[54]

Corn husking and house- and barn-raising were tasks that required more labor than one family could provide. Neighbors usually gathered in a barn to husk huge piles of corn. They divided up the grain into two piles and teams tried to finish husking before their opponents. Dancing and music came afterwards. Raising a house or a barn was another task where neighbors joined together. Women prepared a large meal, while men completed the heavy labor. Females often socialized during a quilting bee. "Housewarmings" involved more dancing and fiddle-playing. Rural communities had to provide their own entertainment beyond such construction though. Often this was done at the local schoolhouse, where spelling bees and debates were a welcome break from daily routine. Debate topics ran the gamut from silly to philosophical: was fire more destructive than water or was the horse more valuable than the cow?[55]

The Fourth of July was a highly anticipated break from summer labor. The town of Bedford had a giant picnic, patriotic speeches and songs, and a huge cake in 1860. They also read the Declaration of Independence aloud for the audience. As many as twenty-five hundred attended the festivities. Thirteen-year-old Mary Van Zante—one of fourteen children—went with her family to Pella in 1889 to see fireworks and a parade. They also enjoyed a local band. W. F. Main fondly recalled the holiday in Mason City because the town provided a free barrel of lemonade. Webster City had a grand ball in 1857, which ended at sunrise. The village also staged a public reading of the Declaration of Independence, hosted speakers, and had a parade. The crowd sang patriotic songs, then went to dinner. Many toasts were given—to George Washington, to the current president of the United States, to the state governor, to a railroad, to pioneer farmers, and to "women of the age in which we live." The editor of the local paper wrote, possibly in jest, "nobody drunk." Those who did not live near a town often gathered at a convenient location shaded by trees and brought a large picnic meal. Sometimes the crowd was entertained by a speaker.[56]

Christmas celebrations varied according to national or religious background. Germans, Dutch, and Scandinavians brought the idea of St. Nicholas, or Santa Claus, to Iowa. Germans also introduced Christmas trees, with a Lutheran church in Belle Plaine placing one in front of their church in 1875. Poorer families might enjoy lots of food, popcorn, and candy, along with songs and stories. Toys that were not homemade were almost unknown in Iowa's early years, but in 1870 an Ottumwa newspaper ran an advertisement listing dolls, books, checker boards, and chess pieces for sale. Churches celebrated Christmas Eve, often providing a dinner meal. Turkey dinners were popular, as were large Christmas day breakfasts. Mary Miller remembered that her family found doughnuts in their stockings in 1842. Concerts, dances, or lectures might occur around the holiday. But such parties were not all peaceful. A Christmas dance in Tama County ended with "fights and rowdyism" in 1874. Jennie Beck remembered that her family decorated a Christmas tree with strings of popcorn and homemade molasses and sugar cookies in the early twentieth century. Stockings would be filled with oranges, apples, and nuts. Absent family members sent holiday packages for kids, with books or dolls.[57]

A visit to an opera house provided another opportunity for entertainment, as drama, lectures, musical comedies, or speeches might provide diversion. Opera houses rarely staged actual opera, though. Many of the state's larger towns erected such buildings in the 1870s and 1880s. Traveling theater companies usually visited the larger cities but also went to towns such as Fort Dodge, Ottumwa, and Marshalltown. In the early twentieth century, some opera houses converted to movie theaters. The main seating area had plush seats, while the gallery and balcony were plain. The wealthy paid a dollar for the best seats, while the gallery—full of "a motley crowd of loud-voiced, peanut-munching, feet-stamping lovers of Thespis," wrote Bruce Mahan—paid only twenty-five cents. Ushers sold candy and ice water, while boys sold gum. A theater orchestra played for productions. Shakespearean plays, such as *Twelfth Night*, *Richard III*, and *King Lear* came to Iowa, as well as obscure melodramas and tragedies. Edith Harper Ekdale wrote that Shakespeare's plays "rarely played to packed houses" at the Grand Opera in Burlington. Her family lived next to the structure, and she would sneak in to watch rehearsals on Saturdays. They often received free tickets, since stagehands borrowed props, including pet cats, from their family. Historical dramas, such as *Elizabeth, Queen of England*, *Louis XI*, and *Mary Stuart*, were popular. Mark Twain gave lectures in eastern Iowa in 1885. Belva Lockwood, a lawyer and lecturer, spoke on "Social and Political Life in Washington." Lockwood was the first women to argue a case before the Supreme Court and run for president. Less highbrow material, from minstrel shows to burlesque troupes, also came to Iowa opera houses.[58]

The first state fair was held in 1854. Since then, it has evolved into "Iowa's central cultural institution," wrote historian Chris Rasmussen. County fairs were set up to promote scientific agriculture and economic development. Fairs were vital institutions in the Midwest and provided people with a chance to exchange ideas and enjoy a break from farm work and isolation. There were dozens of county fairs in Iowa in the 1850s. The Iowa State Fair became a fall ritual, marking the end of planting and harvesting. Illinois had its first state fair in 1853. The inaugural Iowa State Fair was held in Fairfield, with exhibits of crops, machinery, crafts, and livestock. In its first twenty-five years the fair took place in ten different towns, including Muscatine, Cedar Rapids, Dubuque, and Oskaloosa. This gave more people a chance to attend. It permanently settled in Des Moines in 1879, a central location well-served by railroads. The current fairground site was selected in 1885 and more than fifty buildings were constructed that year. It was a combination of education and popular entertainment, with concerts, horse races, rides, and games. Fairs' agricultural exhibits exalted the virtuous achievements of farmers while amusements provided distractions from daily life. The fair's popularity waned in the 1890s, plagued by a long economic downturn. New events were booked to increase attendance. In 1899 entertainment included horses and riders who jumped off high platforms into ponds. The Iowa State Fair has evolved over more than 160 years, with boring lectures on soil chemistry replaced by modern amusements and a diverse variety of events, art, livestock, and deep-fried foods. It has become a cherished annual social event, attracting more than one million visitors in August 2019.[59]

Female social groups proliferated in the late nineteenth century and the first half of the twentieth century in Iowa. Men enrolled in associations like the Masons, while women joined those that worked to establish libraries, improve education, or lobbied for child welfare laws. There were 284 clubs in the state in 1903 and more than 900 in the 1930s. Some focused on sewing, art, or literature; others were associated with churches. The

The Chautauqua provided entertainment and education to rural areas in the early twentieth century. Chautauqua meeting inside tent, ca. 1910, West Branch, Iowa. From Entertainment and Amusement—Chautauqua photo files, Special Collections, State Historical Society of Iowa, Iowa City.

Shakespearean Club in Osage concentrated on literature, discussing male and female writers, ranging from Dante to the poet Elizabeth Barrett Browning. Rural women joined farm organizations attached to the Farm Bureau, while African American women joined literary and reform-minded clubs in the mining town of Buxton. Many clubwomen worked in organizations that supported suffrage, temperance, or sought to better their communities. They learned fund-raising and public speaking, funneling their energy into benevolent activities that operated within the limits that American society placed on women's activity. In the 1890s the Spencer Woman's Club, in Clay County, "became de facto public works officials," wrote historian Sara Egge. They built a public restroom for town visitors, purchased trees and seeds to beautify their town, and bought land to build Spencer's first public park. They also lobbied the state legislature for traveling libraries and supported educational activities. Another woman's club in the county sponsored a public library. The Spencer club also coordinated a suffrage campaign in 1916.[60]

The Chautauqua was a summer event, a combination of education and entertainment with concerts, debates, sermons, lectures, and other cultural activities. Traveling shows brought poetry, music, and opera to places "hungry for culture," remembered Ralph Spencer. It was also an important social event. The town of Red Oak set up a tent at the Montgomery County fairgrounds and provided camping spots to visitors for their week-long event in the summer of 1905. Churches cooked up meals for twenty-five cents or families brought food for picnics. Lectures usually occurred in the afternoon, with music at night. Orchestras or opera singers entertained the audience, while famous speakers including Jane Addams, Robert LaFollette, and William Jennings Bryan visited towns like Red Oak and Washington over the years. Bryan attracted 1,783 people to the town of Washington on June 30, 1903. The town of Le Mars had a week-long event from July 2 to 8, 1916, which included music, a play, and lectures on art and botany. Lecturers, including a history professor from the State University of Iowa, appeared annually in Washington. But it was not all high culture, as comedians also took part. The events continued until the early 1930s when radio entertainment, motion pictures, and automobile mobility brought an end to the demand for such events.[61]

Baseball was popularized by soldiers who played the game during the Civil War. In 1867 Cedar Rapids formed one of the first baseball teams in the state. It played against Vinton on June 2, who lost by twenty-three points. Other teams were established in cities like Marshalltown and Waterloo, which had six teams. A Marshalltown team traveled two days to play in Waterloo and won, 76 to 29. Many early games had more than one hundred runs. Unlike card playing or horse racing, baseball was considered respectable. It did not harm a woman's reputation to attend ball games. Gloves and mitts were considered unmanly in the 1860s and broken fingers were a badge of honor. Female baseball players were scoffed at in the late 1800s, but women from the State University of Iowa played softball before World War I. One Marshalltown player, Adrian Anson, went on to play for the Chicago White Stockings. He played with them for twenty-one years, retiring in 1897, after Chicago had won the pennant five times. Adrian Anson was a superstar of early baseball but also a staunch segregationist who ensured the sport excluded African American players.[62]

The religious diversity of Iowa and its first-rate school system helped mold the state's distinctive culture. Iowa's religious landscape was dominated by the Protestant faith, but the state was full of many different denominations. While Catholicism had been the first European religion to reach the state, it was mostly located in cities and the southeast. A wide variety of Protestant faiths, often competing to build congregations, spread across the state, with the Methodists as the largest group in the nineteenth century. The state also had a small population of Jews and African Americans, who established their own churches and synagogues. Iowa's education system became one of the most successful in the country. One-room schoolhouses could be found every couple of miles, even if Iowa's secondary system did not reach most students until the 1920s and 1930s. The state had a variety of colleges that rivaled its religious diversity, with its three public institutions finding success despite limited state aid. Its early acceptance of women in colleges was unusual and helped the state's varied institutions of higher education survive. Iowa developed a robust civic culture, supported by schools, churches and colleges, high literacy, as well as women's clubs, theater, fairs, and Chautauqua—institutions and organizations that encouraged education and social reform, provided entertainment and fellowship, and helped a frontier state mature.[63]

8
Cities, Industry, and Technology, 1833–1920

The population of Iowa tripled between the Civil War and 1920, leading to the growth of Iowa's industry and urban areas. In 1870 Des Moines had about 12,000 people; Sioux City had only 3,401; Cedar Rapids had just less than 6,000. Fifty years later Des Moines had 126,468 people, the population of Cedar Rapids was more than 45,000, and Sioux City had 71,227 inhabitants. Such rapid development brought many challenges to cities, including crime, disease, and pollution, but economic growth often made life better. Iowa's industry grew swiftly, especially once railroads tied the state to the national market. Meatpacking plants could be found in many cities, while Iowa's coal mining was the state's dominant industrial business in the late nineteenth and early twentieth centuries. In the coal town of Buxton, a majority African American population lived equally with their white neighbors for many years. A booming lumber business in towns on the Mississippi River employed thousands for decades and provided building material for the region. Muscatine had an industry that made buttons out of the shells of freshwater clams. New technology, including electricity and the telephone, improved the lives of Iowans. At the same time, dangerous working conditions and low pay made life miserable for many workers.[1]

Industrial employment attracted workers to Iowa in the late nineteenth and early twentieth centuries. Urban work drew those who did not labor in agriculture. Large businesses and corporations provided jobs in meatpacking, the lumber industry, mining, and railroads. German and Irish immigrants came to work in lumber mills in Mississippi River towns, as did those from Michigan and Wisconsin. Italians, Croatians, and African Americans worked in coal mines. The Consolidated Coal Company recruited Black workers from Virginia. Male workers in Davenport labored in flour milling or on the Rock Island Railroad, while women in the city worked as servants, clerks, or teachers. Large corporations such as J. M. Sinclair in Cedar Rapids or the Rath Packing Company in Waterloo were major employers. In Dubuque men worked in the Milwaukee Railroad repair shops while women worked in clothing factories. Workers came to Sioux City to labor for railroads, sawmills, brewers, and brickyards.[2]

Iowa's manufacturing businesses were closely tied to the dominant agricultural sector, even into the twentieth-first century. Early industry grew as farming expanded. The processing of wheat, corn, and hogs was important for a frontier economy. Mills used a water wheel to power large round stones to grind wheat, which produced flour for bread. Grinding corn provided cornmeal. Taking grain to a mill was far more efficient than grinding by hand, which was tedious and time-consuming work. Surplus hogs could be driven to a meatpacking business for slaughter, often in a town on the Mississippi River such as Dubuque or Burlington. In the late 1830s, butchers in Dubuque threw animal bones into the street to dispose of them. A town ordinance eventually changed this behavior. But small-scale packing continued until the 1870s, when railroad lines allowed the industry to move into the interior of the state and closer to beef and pork suppliers. Slaughtering was completed in the winter so that pork would not spoil. Meat was smoked or salted to preserve it and shipped downriver in the spring. The first sawmill in Iowa was built in 1829, before the state opened to white settlement. More opened up in the 1830s as migrants moved in. These early sawmills were primitive and inefficient, powered by water like grain mills. Logs had to be dragged to mills by oxen and horses or floated to mills on rivers.[3]

Iowa's sawmill business boomed from the 1850s until the 1880s. It was centered in Mississippi River towns, which had steam-powered sawmills beginning in the late 1850s. For decades, immense amounts of lumber were cut from the forests of Wisconsin and rafted down the Mississippi River to sawmills in Iowa, Illinois, and Missouri. Lumbermen were "ripsnorting individualists," wrote Stewart H. Holbrook. They fought over timber or the right to be first to send it downriver. Gunfights were common.

Iowa's river towns were centers of the nineteenth-century lumber trade. Large rafts of lumber at lumberyard on Mississippi River, ca. 1905, Clinton, Iowa. From Business and Industry—Product Production and Extraction—Lumber photo files, Special Collections, State Historical Society of Iowa, Iowa City.

Lumberjacks cut trees in the winter and rolled logs into rivers in the spring. Logs were collected near the mouths of rivers such as the Chippewa and Wisconsin where they were combined into huge rafts. One of the first reached Dubuque in 1833. By the 1850s "countless numbers of rafts were floating down the Mississippi," wrote historian William J. Petersen. Crews of about two dozen men managed the rafts, which could be three hundred feet wide and fifteen hundred feet long. Men faced death from accidents or storms. Rafts moved at the speed of the river—maybe two and a half miles per hour—and progress could be halted by upstream winds. They tied up at night and might move downstream thirty or thirty-five miles on a good day. Crewmen were often hard-drinking brawlers who terrorized river towns. For example, one hungry raft crew stole a cow from a farmer. He caught up with the raft and spotted the carcass of his cow, ready for cooking. But he abandoned the pursuit when the French raft pilot claimed that his cook had smallpox. The Civil War paralyzed the industry, as markets dried up and men joined the Union Army. But it took off again after the war. In the 1860s steamboats began to tow rafts of lumber. They moved a bit faster and began to replace the crews of log rafts.[4]

Sawmills in river towns became big businesses and cut most of the lumber in the state in the 1870s and 1880s. Larger mills replaced smaller ones; mill size increased, and numbers fell. The towns of Clinton and Lyons were the centers of the state's timber industry—in 1870 their sawmills employed 813 people. Clinton was the hub of lumber production in the country in 1877. Regular workers, "men who carried boards," might earn $1.25 or $1.45 a day (about $32 to $37 a day in 2020 dollars.) Most workers were Germans, Irish, and Swedes. In 1877 the two towns had seven sawmills with thirty-one saws. Davenport, Dubuque, and Muscatine were also important producers. Most lumber was white pine. Some mills cut wood into boards, while others planed it or produced shingles. A woodworking industry that made baskets, boxes, furniture, barrels, and coffins grew in towns along the river. Walnut, maple, and oak were popular wood for furniture. In 1859 Iowa produced 183 million board feet of lumber. Production peaked thirty years later with 608 million board feet. The industry declined quickly once the forests of Wisconsin were cut down. By 1909 Iowa sawmills produced less than one-quarter as much lumber as twenty years before. The last lumber raft reached Iowa in 1915. By then the larger corporations had moved to the Pacific Northwest, leaving behind only smaller sawmills to meet local demand.[5]

Meatpacking was another important industry in Iowa, which employed thousands, even into the twenty-first century. It has been one of the state's top manufacturing sectors and employers since the 1890s. In the 1870s meatpackers established operations near their livestock suppliers in Iowa. The state was a leading producer of hogs. Plants moved to Cedar Rapids and Ottumwa, both of which had excellent rail connections to eastern markets. The Thomas Sinclair Company built one of the largest pork processing plants in the nation in Cedar Rapids. It sat on the banks of the Cedar River, which allowed the company to harvest ice from the frozen waterway in the winter. The Sinclair Company also established a large icehouse to chill its factory in the summer. In 1890 refrigerator engines were set up, eliminating the need to use ice. Coopers, who made barrels for pork, were a large part of the workforce. In 1890 Sinclair slaughtered more than 580,000 hogs in its facility. A competitor, John Morrell and Company, established a major meatpacking plant in Ottumwa in 1877. Within two years, Ottumwa shipped out twenty million pounds of meat and lard. The city became "a leading packing center in the Midwest from the 1880s on," wrote historian Wilson J. Warren. Sioux City built stockyards to collect cattle and hogs; its economy became heavily dependent on meatpacking by the mid-twentieth century. The Rath Packing Company also built a new pork processing factory in Waterloo in 1891. By 1900 Iowa's meat packing industry ranked eighth nationally.[6]

Coal mining was a major industry in Iowa until about 1930, second only to agriculture from 1880 to 1930. Mining mostly occurred between Fort Dodge and Keokuk. The earliest mines in Iowa were in Jefferson County; wagons hauled coal to blacksmiths in towns on the Mississippi River. People used it to heat their homes. Steamboats also burned coal. In the 1840s small mines operated to meet local needs in Van Buren and Scott Counties in eastern Iowa. Mining occurred in most counties that had coal deposits, but production was limited for many years. Only 48,263 tons of coal were mined in Iowa in 1859. But this amount increased quickly, as the population grew and railroads and railroad lines provided markets and transportation. In 1875, 1,231,547 tons of coal were produced in the state. It was initially excavated from hillsides, but some mine shafts were dug into hills or deep into the ground. In some places soil was removed to reach deposits near the surface. Most Iowa mines were small and produced for local needs, but some sold significant amounts of coal to railroads. One mine supplied the Milwaukee Railroad with 375 tons of coal a day. Workers usually used a pick and an axe in the more primitive mines. Miners before the Civil War earned five cents for every bushel of coal, or about $1.25 for a ton. (Five cents in 1850 equated to about $1.71 in 2020. The price for a ton of coal was about $42.70 in 2020 dollars.) It was usually sold for about double this price.[7]

Mining expanded in the late nineteenth century, attracting investment and immigrants. The largest mine in the state in the late 1860s was in Wapello County. It shipped fifty-two thousand tons of coal in a year, especially to Keokuk. In the 1860s and 1870s mines were opened near Colfax, Ottumwa, and Newton, with ore sometimes hauled by mule to railroads. Short rail lines also carried it in some places. Many small mines in Polk County provided coal for local needs. One mine, opened in 1874, was located one mile south of the state capitol. It operated for more than twenty years. Once the railroad reached Boone County mines developed there, too. One company built a 242-foot-deep shaft three miles from Boone. It produced coal for thirty years. Six mines near Moingona in Boone County produced eight hundred to nine hundred tons of coal each day for several years, starting in 1867. Coal was sold to the Union Pacific Railroad. In the 1880s electricity was installed in some mines to aid in production. One Lucas County business employed 405 men to dig out 640 tons of coal a day. By 1884 Iowa had about five hundred coal mines. Appanoose County had more than eighty in the mid-1890s. Monroe County produced more than one million tons of coal in 1902. The state was in tenth place nationwide for coal production in 1917.[8]

Many miners were immigrants from Italy, Sweden, Croatia, or other countries. They usually lived in camps dominated by the company that employed them. Families purchased groceries at the company store and lived in rudimentary housing rented to them by their employer. A miner might earn $420 a year—equivalent to about $13,400 in 2020—and suffer from seasonal layoffs. Women helped earn money by taking in boarders, which included providing a bed, food, and laundry service. Edith Gallo Widmer Blake grew up in a coal camp near Centerville in the early 1900s. Her family of nine lived in a four-room house, with an outhouse behind it. They later moved to a farm with a larger home. Her father, Frank Gallo, worked in Mine no. 30. He went to work at seven in the morning, digging for coal underground. Her mother, Antonia, cared for their family, raised a garden, made cheese, and spent the summer filling their cellar with fruits, vegetables, meats, sausages, and sauerkraut. They also made their own wine. Her family bought shoes and coats from the Sears catalog; shoes were handed down from child to child, her father resoling them when needed. They collected their coal from a large hill of refuse ore that was too dirty for the company to use. When miners and their families had free time, the men drank wine and sang songs, women met for coffee, and kids played baseball. They visited Centerville once a year, though it was only five miles away. After coal mining camps closed in the 1920s, her family moved to Chicago. Blake married, helped her husband build their home, and raised two children.[9]

Mining was the most dangerous occupation in the United States in the late nineteenth and early twentieth centuries. In 1901 more than five thousand men were killed or seriously injured in American mines. Twenty-nine were killed in Iowa and fifty-nine injured that year. Eighteen thousand men and boys worked in Iowa mines during World War I. Explosions, falling

CITIES, INDUSTRY, TECHNOLOGY, 1833–1920

Buxton was an integrated coal-mining town that provided opportunity to African Americans in the early twentieth century. Birds-eye view of Buxton, Iowa, looking north from water tower, ca. 1909. PH5000.1024, State Historical Society of Iowa, Des Moines.

rock, and runaway coal cars could kill or injure miners. On January 24, 1902, an explosion at the Lost Creek mine near Oskaloosa killed twenty men and boys and injured fourteen more. Harry Booth, a miner and union activist in Iowa, remembered that it was "tough work." His father had a leg broken in a mine cave-in. Still, Booth recalled that "it wasn't all a dreary situation." Most mines had a union hall that had music and dances. Kids could get ice cream at such events. Families went to the circus in Oskaloosa and the company had a baseball team. Mining camps had literary societies that staged plays and poetry readings.[10]

The south-central Iowa town of Buxton became a center for coal mining—it was also an integrated town in a state almost entirely white. Dorothy Schwieder, Joseph Hraba, and Elmer Schwieder argued that it was an "atypical mining community in many respects." In the early twentieth century, a majority of its population of about five thousand was African American. Blacks and whites were paid the same for labor; the two races lived together in residential areas. Blacks and whites mingled at work and in town. For most African Americans "life in Buxton marked a golden time" in their lives, wrote the authors. Many residents had been enslaved or worked as sharecroppers and knew that Buxton was a special place. Black families owned their homes, and some sent their children to college. Prosperity in the coal industry allowed for a place like Buxton to exist. Consolidation Coal Company, which ran the mining operation, permitted independent businesses to operate and did not force employees to live in company housing. Workers could buy land and farm for additional income or retirement security. Homes were comfortable and sat on quarter acre lots. The company did not control schools and churches. Buxton flourished from 1900 to 1914 but declined in the following decade. The company abandoned it by 1923. Falling demand for coal and labor troubles undermined the economic viability of Buxton and other coal towns and camps. Mines at Buxton shut down, residents left for other mining work, and homes were moved to new towns. For years after its abandonment, former Black residents returned to hold summer reunions. They celebrated its existence but grieved the loss of what Schwieder, Hraba, and Schwieder called a "utopia" for African Americans.[11]

Coal fueled the American economy until it was replaced by other forms of power, leading to the decline of mining in Iowa. It provided the energy for industry and transportation until the 1920s, when oil, electricity, and natural gas began to replace it. Coal mining in Iowa was a short-term industry. Most demand came from railroads, which helped develop the business in the state in the late nineteenth century. But Iowa's mines were not large, and they did not produce coal as cheaply as other locations. The state only produced about 1 percent of the nation's coal. After World War I railroads purchased coal elsewhere and coal mines closed across the state. The industry was almost extinct in Iowa by the early 1950s.[12]

An unusual business developed in Muscatine, where an industry arose to make buttons from clamshells. A German immigrant, John Boepple, came to Illinois in 1887 or 1888 and found clams in the Mississippi River. He had made buttons from horns in Europe and decided to make them from the abundant freshwater mussel species in the river. Boepple's business venture in the early 1890s failed, as did the initial boom of competition that undermined his business. Hundreds had followed Boepple into the enterprise when one digger found a pearl in a clam shell that they sold to a Chicago jeweler for $2,000 ($58,700 in 2020 dollars). But the pearl button idea found success a few years later, with improved equipment that made production easier. In 1897 there were at least ten pearl button factories. The next year more than 138 million buttons were produced. In 1903 there were fifty-six such businesses—in Muscatine, Cedar Rapids, Davenport, Fort Madison—anywhere shells could be found. In 1905, 1,936 workers made their living from the industry, which was concentrated in Muscatine, where more than half of the factories were located. Huge piles of leftover clam shell pieces were used in stucco or cement. The smallest particles were added to poultry feed.[13]

Clamshells were acquired by dragging hooks in the Mississippi River. Once enough clams were collected, they were boiled. Any pearls were sold, and the cleaned shells sold to factories that cut shells into buttons. Shells were soaked to soften, then cut, and churned in a machine to produce a uniform thickness. Button cutters were men. Female employees used machines that drilled buttonholes. Fourteen- or fifteen-year-old girls arranged buttons on a moving belt to be smoothed by machinery, breathing in thick shell dust. The labor was tedious and workers sometimes lost fingers to machines. They might earn $4 to $6 a week; men usually made about twice this. (Four dollars a week equaled $127 in 2020 dollars; six dollars was $191. A male wage of $12 a week would have earned $382 in 2020 dollars.) Women also sorted, separated, and counted buttons, as well as sewing them onto cardboard pieces for retail sale. Twelve buttons sewed onto twelve pieces of cardboard earned a woman two and a half cents. In Muscatine, there were forty-three factories in 1911 that completed various stages of work. Ten large factories did all stages of production; smaller ones cut shells or completed other tasks. Workers usually labored from fifty-four to seventy-two hours a week. Attempts to organize unions in the industry were unsuccessful. A year-long strike in 1911 and 1912 failed, defeated by unified business opposition, backed by a state government and courts that brought in strikebreakers or the national guard to outlast the workers. By 1908 the local clam-fishing industry had declined, but mussels were still brought to factories on the Mississippi River. It continued until the 1930s when Japanese competition and the development of plastic buttons undermined it.[14]

Industry grew as towns gained population and railroads tied them together in the late nineteenth century. Des Moines and Sioux City became industrial centers, with smaller towns serving mostly local needs. Iowa City had pork packing, flour mills, cheese factories, and creameries. A report on Johnson County bragged that its packers shipped cured meats to Europe. It also had brewers that made thirty thousand barrels of beer a year. Sioux City emerged as a trade center for the Upper Missouri River region, linked to the east by railroads and downriver by steamboats. Its businesses produced furniture, agricultural implements, household appliances, as well as stoves, bricks, and beer. New plants made barrels, pottery, cabinets, and tools. Its sawmills provided lumber, while grain elevators and warehouses catered to storage and retail needs. The town dominated commerce north of Omaha.[15]

Dubuque was Iowa's leading industrial city until Des Moines replaced it near the end of the nineteenth century. The lumber industry supplanted lead mining in the 1850s. Meatpacking became a major enterprise by the 1880s. Railroad employment also was important, as the city was a hub of an expanding railroad network. Women worked in the clothing industry, sewing overalls for the H. B. Glover Company, or as clerks or domestic servants. Workers were not paid much and labored long hours—usually ten hours a day for six days a week. Women earned from one-half to two-thirds the salary of men. African Americans usually could only find work as waiters, servants, or cooks. Most unskilled or semiskilled workers had "a meager standard of living" in Dubuque, wrote historian Ralph Scharnau. Some skilled workers, such as tailors or printers, attempted to form small unions to protect themselves. This early unionism was unsuccessful. A seven-week streetcar worker strike that sought to improve working conditions failed. Local police and militia, supported by a business-friendly court, defeated it. Railroad workers did enjoy the benefits of unions and good wages, however. But the city stagnated from 1900 to 1940 as lumberyards closed, fires ravaged factories, and business moved to larger cities.[16]

Manufacturing was mostly an urban enterprise and most industrial workers lived in the state's larger cities. Iowa's industry was concentrated in the eastern half of the state in towns of over ten thousand people. This area was settled first and had most of the population. By 1900 corporate factories were expanding in the state, replacing smaller independent businesses and craftsmen. The number of meatpacking firms fell, as the industry consolidated. The most valuable manufactured products in 1900 included meat, butter, lumber, and flour. Iowa was the largest producer of hogs and second for cattle in 1900. Iowa also led the nation in the production of creamery butter from 1879 to 1899. The state had 816 creameries that produced 18 percent of the nation's butter in 1900. Many dairies, owned by farmer cooperatives, existed in the state's northeast. Even though Iowa's lumber business declined in the early twentieth century, woodworking industries in the state benefitted from timber brought by railroads from western states.

Favorable eastbound shipping rates ensured that companies which made doors or window frames could find a supply of wood. Flour milling continued but was a declining industry like lumber. Other smaller manufacturers in the state produced engines, machine tools, stoves, vehicles, farm implements, pumps, and wagons. Railroads were major employers, consuming large amounts of wood, coal, and iron. Iowa railroad shops repaired tens of thousands of locomotives and passenger and freight cars every year.[17]

Working conditions in Iowa's manufacturing sector could be appalling. Men, women, and children often labored in dangerous and filthy conditions. A report by the Iowa Commissioner of Labor estimated that two-thirds to three-quarters of factories in the state were hazardous to the health and safety of employees. Thousands were injured at work every year in the early 1900s. In 1910 one writer estimated that as many as ten thousand workers may have been injured in Iowa. Historian Ezekiel Downey called such losses a "blood tax" inflicted on workers. Hundreds of multistory businesses had no fire escapes or used dangerous equipment that could kill or maim employees. Workers were exposed to revolving shafts, saws, and unguarded wheels; grinding machines or saws produced dust, sparks, and splinters. A board thrown by a circular saw killed a laborer in a factory. Another man in a flour mill was killed when his clothing was caught in machinery and his arm torn off. Only 7 percent of factories had fire escapes and many stairways were locked, leaving workers with no way to escape from a fire except by jumping out of windows. Factories were often unheated and unventilated. Smoke in one foundry was so thick that a visitor could not see across the room. Dirt and filth covered floors, sometimes an inch deep. More than five thousand children worked in Iowa factories in 1902, many who had never attended school. Some were only ten years old, noted one horrified factory inspector. Children usually worked the same long hours as adults. The Commissioner of the Iowa Bureau of Labor Statistics, Edward D. Brigham, wrote that the abuse of children in industrial enterprises was "practically a criminal conspiracy" and that the state of Iowa needed to immediately reform its laws on child labor.[18]

Iowa developed a strong labor movement in the late nineteenth and early twentieth centuries, as the state's industries grew. Mining and meatpacking were important businesses, but railroads and farm equipment manufacturers were also major employers. Rail lines crisscrossed the state and employed a small army of workers. The farm sector demanded manufactured equipment, which was often built in Iowa. Rivers towns such as Dubuque,

Davenport, and Burlington built up a substantial industrial base. As industry grew, the state's economy diversified. The service sector expanded, as did construction. Iowa's working class began to look more like the rest of the country. The state had a history of farm protest and anti-monopoly sentiment, and workers resisted their mistreatment.[19]

The most successful early union in Iowa was the United Mine Workers (UMW). It substantially improved the lives of its members long before other unions flourished in the state. Miners normally worked ten- or twelve-hour days. Hundreds were fired when they tried to join the UMW in the early 1890s. The economic depression of the mid-1890s led to the closing of mines and wage cuts. Once the economy recovered, the UMW negotiated an eight-hour workday for miners in 1898. The union also won higher pay, improved medical care, safer working conditions, and better housing for its members. Protests to the state legislature brought improved schools to mining camps as well. "The UMW was an immensely constructive force in the lives of Iowa's coal mining families," wrote Dorothy Schwieder.[20]

Workers in Iowa's other industries were less successful in fighting for their rights. Some skilled crafts, such as printers, machinists, and railroad employees, built unions to protect their workers. But these organizations only aided a small number of people. Most were not part of a union. The meatpacking and farm equipment industries defeated most attempts to organize, firing union leaders and replacing striking workers during walkouts. Only butchers and machinists formed small craft unions in these industries. Still, the strong demand for labor in World War I aided the creation of unions. Wages increased and many employees benefited from an eight-hour workday. However, the end of the war and an economic downturn undermined the labor movement. Strikes by meatpacking, railroad, and mining workers failed in Iowa and across the country in the early 1920s. It would not be until 1935 that federal laws protected the right of employees to form unions.[21]

While working conditions were often awful, Iowa provided more opportunity to women than many other states. In 1884 Dr. Jennie McCowen wrote that Iowa had a "progressive and liberal attitude" toward women. McGowen had earned a medical degree from the State University of Iowa and worked as a doctor in Davenport starting in 1880. She wrote a newspaper column for a national suffrage paper, edited two state medical journals, and was active in state reform movements. She noted that the 1880

Iowa census had found more than eighty thousand women who worked for wages in a variety of occupations, most in professional and personal services. A large number, she wrote, worked with a husband, father, or male relative in agriculture and were not reported in these census figures. Women managed hotels, general stores, drug stores, and bookstores, and earned an income as shoemakers, pharmacists, barbers, and editors. They were farmers, florists, bookkeepers, blacksmiths, printers, and telegraph operators, too. Two women were bank presidents; the state librarian was female. Women teachers were paid $30 a month, about 80 percent as much as men. (This would be about $816 in 2020 dollars.) They made up about two-thirds of all teachers and more than 20 percent of superintendents and principals. Female county superintendents and court reporters made salaries equal to men. Girls and women, she wrote with pride, were admitted on equal terms to elementary and secondary schools, as well as universities and medical and law schools. The exceptions were Catholic and Episcopal schools. The first woman elected to be a full professor in the country was Miss H. J. Cook at Cornell College. Women had equal property rights and controlled their own wages; they could sue to protect their property and personal rights. They had first gained limited property rights in Iowa in the mid-1840s. These had been expanded by the end of the Civil War. They did not have the right to vote though, a topic explored in the next chapter.[22]

Des Moines was the largest city in the state by 1880, as well as its manufacturing leader. Mary Turner was secretary and treasurer of the Street Railway Company in the city. She was also a major stockholder. The state capital would have also had female teachers, nurses, clerks, students, and merchants. It was a "walking city," an urban area with mixed commercial, industrial, and residential areas in the late 1800s. There were no tall buildings and some homes had horse stables behind them. Theaters thrived, with the Bijou known for burlesque. There were canoe races on weekends on the Des Moines River and good fishing continued until about 1890, wrote T. I. Stoner. Residents lived near their jobs and walked to work. Des Moines was geographically small, densely populated, and congested. It "grew from a pioneer settlement into a modern city" in the late nineteenth century, wrote William C. Page and Leah D. Rogers. About twenty people lived per acre. Dwellings crowded each other, with little space for yards or privacy. The use of coal and wood contributed to fire danger, aggravated by a lack of fire hydrants and water mains. Streets were unpaved—choking with dust when dry and rutted, muddy swamps in the rain. Odors from industry and animals were prevalent. Irish immigrants lived in town, able to walk to the City Brewery to fill a small pail with beer for five cents, about $1.47 in 2020.[23]

Despite the dirt and the danger, Iowa's working- and middle-class urban residents often benefited from the nation's economic development between the Civil War and the World War I. Overall working hours fell and most people earned more money. Mass production provided cheaper goods and a greater variety of them. Canned goods, dried fruits, noodles, and processed cheese and meat diversified diets. Coca-Cola, Corn Flakes cereal, Cracker Jack snacks, and Jell-O were widely available by the early twentieth century. Ice boxes and refrigerated railroad cars allowed fresh vegetables to reach customers during the winter. The benefits of mass production were not evenly distributed though, and the poor suffered from inadequate nutrition, disease, and difficult physical labor. The average height of Americans fell in the mid- and late-nineteenth century. Contaminated foods increased infant mortality. For urban dwellers who were better off, department stores sold almost everything a family could need, while mail-order catalogs helped rural customers buy the things they needed. Women found work as clerks, buyers, and managers.[24]

Urbanization brought serious public health challenges. The Des Moines and Cedar Rivers were used as trash dumps. Filth and waste covered the streets of cities. Horses in Des Moines deposited thirty tons of manure and fifteen hundred gallons of urine on its streets every eight hours in 1870. Dead animals had to be removed. Factories that produced fertilizer or glue claimed many horse carcasses, but smaller animals often lay where they died. Des Moines had laws that required the removal of garbage, but they were usually ignored. Trash was often left in streets, attracting flies and rats that carried disease. Piles of rubbish made it difficult for wagons to navigate roads. In 1880 no Iowa city had a public sewer system. Most people in cities depended on outhouses and privies. They often overflowed, contaminating streets and waterways. Licensed scavengers cleaned them out, working only between 11 p.m. and 4 a.m. The waste was usually thrown into the Des Moines River. Epidemic disease was a constant threat. Cholera, typhoid, and tuberculosis killed many urban residents, especially children. In this, Iowa's cities were not unusual: almost one in four newborns died within a year of birth in American cities in 1890. "While decaying filth and noxious odors represented one of the most unpleasant aspects of life in the Gilded Age, most people took the situation for granted," wrote historian Lawrence Larsen about Des Moines.[25]

Every Iowa city except Council Bluffs had a system of water delivery in 1880. The availability of clean water is usually taken for granted today. However, waterworks cost a lot of money and many city services were provided by private businesses. No Iowa city had a public water system—all of them were operated by private organizations that were given a monopoly by city governments. In Davenport, engines pumped water from the Mississippi River directly into twenty-two miles of water mains. The water that reached customers was a milky color. Those who got their water from such private sources usually boiled it.[26]

While public health may have been abysmal in Des Moines and other cities in Iowa, urban areas often took fire and police protection more seriously. Burlington had major fires in 1871 and 1873. The entire upper part of Council Bluffs was destroyed in fires during the winter of 1854–1855. Some Iowa cities had professional fire departments, but many urban residents used buckets of water to fight fires. Des Moines had twenty-six firemen, a steam fire engine, two hook-and-ladder trucks, and a half-dozen horse carriages in the 1880s. Boone, Iowa City, and Marshalltown also bought improved equipment to fight fires. Firemen had lanterns, rope, hose carts, and some vehicles by 1890. Iowa cities contained most blazes and kept losses down, even with basic equipment. Uniformed police in Des Moines worked twelve-hour shifts, often walking a few miles every day. They were armed with clubs and revolvers. Most arrests were for drunkenness, larceny, assault and battery, or for "keeping houses of ill-fame," wrote Larsen. By 1900 the Des Moines police had eighty-seven officers, with sixty-one on foot patrol. In the 1910s they began to patrol the city in automobiles, vigorously pursuing bootleggers and illegal liquor sales. In the 1930s bank robberies skyrocketed and the Depression bred crime, especially larceny.[27]

The construction of streetcar routes in the 1870s began to change Des Moines's geography. In January 1868 the city's first streetcars, pulled by horses, began service. They took residents from the Polk County courthouse to the capitol. The system was privately owned. Cattle that wandered about city streets sometimes halted traffic. Electric streetcars, powered by a local station, were introduced in 1878. By 1890 Des Moines had nearly fifty miles of track. In the 1870s and 1880s the walking city began to spread out and it became less dense. Streetcars allowed wealthier residents to move to early suburbs. They had fences, private yards, trees, and wide streets. Homes were separate from each other and families enjoyed more privacy. Des Moines doubled in size in the 1880s, growing to 50,093 people by 1890. Its growth slowed in the 1890s, but the city expanded to 86,368 by 1910. Its population doubled by 1950 but then grew much slower for the rest of the twentieth century as residents moved into suburbs.[28]

Sioux City's rapid growth allowed saloons, gambling halls, and prostitution to flourish in the late nineteenth and early twentieth centuries. The town's red-light district was concentrated close to the railroad tracks near an African American neighborhood. Prostitution was tolerated by city officials as long as it was separated from the wealthier parts of town and not too visible. They also allowed it because sex workers brought customers to local businesses, from restaurants and breweries to hotels, saloons, and doctors. As long as lawbreakers such as gambling halls and madams paid a regular fine and kept order, they were allowed to operate. Such fines operated as an informal business license and helped fund city services. Most prostitutes were under twenty-five years old and lived in abysmal conditions. They became sex workers because there were few jobs and little economic opportunity. Violence and abuse were common; they lost most of their money to madams, pimps, and rent. Alcoholism and drug abuse plagued their lives. Suicide was a common way to retire from this awful labor. Houses of prostitution in Sioux City were segregated, with two bordellos for Black customers. Some women worked for madams at brothels. There were seventeen major ones in the town in 1900. They also operated out of saloons and dance halls. Some worked from small one or two-room shacks, soliciting customers who passed by. Reformers who sought to eradicate prostitution succeeded in only pushing the business to south Sioux City.[29]

Davenport was a crossroads of trade in the late nineteenth century, its businesses ranging from lumber and flour milling to meatpacking and prostitution. The city had plenty of steamboat traffic and railroads that tied it to the rest of the country. Davenport attracted migrants who sought to make a living. It was a shopping and entertainment center, full of saloons and stores, along with bordellos. Women worked in hotels, department stores, and in food processing and light industry, usually for low pay that could not support a family. They, and their children, were dependent on men. There were exceptions, though: one nurse with nine children and a drunken husband worked to support everyone. Sex work was part of the daily life of the city. Poverty, divorce, and desperation pushed girls and women into it. Men saw women on the city's streets, or in its jails, as sexually available and they exploited girls as young as ten or twelve for sex. Prostitution was seen as a social threat and regulated through a licensing system that brought monthly fines. Delinquent and problem girls were sent to Catholic reformatories, where their lives were strictly regulated. Brothels were abruptly closed in 1909, sending women to look for a new way to support themselves. Female sexuality was controlled by men who ignored the obvious fact that prostitution was the result of male predation and female poverty.[30]

Iowa's Mississippi River towns were centers of its African American population. Many Blacks were formerly enslaved people who settled in Keokuk, Davenport, and Muscatine. Keokuk had the state's largest Black population in the nineteenth century. Some became barbers or tailors; others opened laundries or restaurants. Austin A. Bland moved to Keokuk in 1861 and worked as a stretcher bearer on hospital boats during the war. Bland brought his mother and three sisters with him. He opened a store and a saloon, as well as a sign and poster business that he operated for forty years. In the early 1900s he ran the Bland Hotel, with a restaurant and pool hall. The city had about two thousand Black citizens at the time. Other Bland family members ran a blacksmith shop that served white and Black customers and a carpet-laying business. Davenport had Black-owned saloons and beauty parlors; Clinton had Black-owned restaurants and candy and ice-cream stores. One sold as much as 120 gallons of ice cream a day.[31]

Iowa's urban areas quickly adopted new technologies, including the telephone. A few were installed in towns such as Des Moines, Iowa City, and Dubuque by 1880. The first switchboard appeared in Keokuk in 1878. The first central exchange, with individual lines connected to a main one that ran to an office, was created in Iowa City over the winter of 1880–1881. Many homes or businesses shared the same line. By the spring of 1881, seventy-three subscribers in Iowa City were making about one thousand calls a day. Early adopters included grocers, drug stores, mills, and homes. A band played over a shared line for entertainment until the novelty wore out. Business benefited from this new system, with one grocery store receiving five orders in one morning. A grocer advertised that it would gladly take telephone orders from thirsty customers who wanted to take advantage of a shipment of fifty cases of beer.[32]

Telephone service relied more on people than technology in its early years. It wasn't until the mid-twentieth century that automated switching and direct dialing became widespread. In Bennett, Iowa, such technology did not arrive until 1972. Telephone operators were almost always women—in World War I, 99 percent of operators were female. Managers saw them as superior to young men, as women were thought to have better temperament, shown by their supposed greater courtesy and patience. Operators, both in urban and rural areas, tied a community together. They provided news of births, illnesses, or emergencies. One operator in Cedar County provided weather updates. Most employees were young, from sixteen to twenty-one, and worked eleven-hour shifts. Operators were expected to be polite and proper, but to also work with machine-like efficiency. Employers viewed their staff as almost temporary help, who were expected to resign upon marriage. Despite its drawbacks, the job was one of the few occupations considered acceptable for middle-class white women.[33]

The state was a national leader in adopting the new technology in the late nineteenth and early twentieth centuries. Fayette County in northeast Iowa got its first telephones in 1878. More than 86 percent of rural Iowa homes had a telephone in 1917, even if they did not have electricity. Farmers often had to string their own telephone wire—sometimes a half-mile—to reach the trunk line, which usually ran along roads. Most homes shared the same party line and could thus listen to their neighbors' conversations. This could be useful, if an operator did not know if a family was home, as someone might chime in that they were away from home. People often heard gossip about friends. Nellie Knight Carpenter operated the Randalia telephone office about forty-five miles northeast of Waterloo from 1920 to 1942. She lived in a small house that served as the telephone switchboard along with her four children. Her husband died in the flu epidemic after World War I. To support her family, Nellie took a job making $40 a month, about $517 in 2020 dollars. Her hours were technically 6 a.m. to 9:30 p.m. but she had to answer emergency calls at all hours. The family rarely left the house together, but her son Vern Carpenter wrote that the job provided "the security we needed." The position also ensured that the family was aware of who had sexually transmitted diseases and who was involved in extramarital affairs or spousal abuse. Vern recalled that overheard phone calls revealed that two married couples traded partners. Nellie, who often served as an on-call counselor to her neighbors, made sure that her children kept such information to themselves.[34]

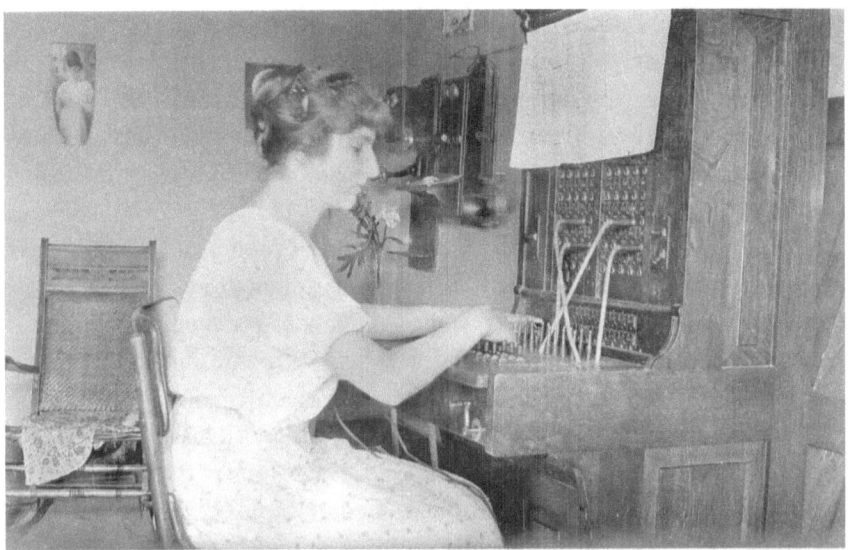

Telephone service spread quickly across Iowa in the late nineteenth and early twentieth centuries. Work as a telephone operator was demanding and one of the few jobs deemed acceptable for middle-class white women. Miss Ethel Howe, operator, ca. 1918, Nemaha, Iowa. From Communication—Telephone photo files, Special Collections, State Historical Society of Iowa, Iowa City.

Electricity was a novelty in Iowa cities in the early and mid-1880s. Early lamps produced a very bright and hot light and weren't too popular. Des Moines saw its first lights in 1884 and Cedar Rapids had its first power plant three years later. With improved lighting and greater demand, electrical use spread. By 1900 parts of southeast Iowa began to receive electricity. Perry had part-time electrical power starting in 1892. Power plants were built in Iowa City, Davenport, and Des Moines and power service extended to urban areas. Some plants ran on coal, others on water power. But Cedar Rapids did not receive twenty-four-hour lighting until 1912. Five years later most of the city's seventeen thousand buildings had electricity. Some power plants shut down during the day due to low demand. In small towns the new lighting system replaced kerosene oil lamps that had to be individually lit each night. Early power systems were inefficient and could not take substantial increases in power demand. In the town of Marion, the electrical company debated whether to let a woman use an electric iron because it might overload the system. In Red Oak, one-half of the town could use an iron on Tuesday. The other half of town could use it on Wednesday. It usually cost 20 to 25 cents for each kilowatt hour around 1900. This would be roughly $6.40 to $8.00, priced in 2020 dollars. In some parts of Iowa in the 2010s the average cost per kilowatt hour was about ten cents, an extraordinary bargain compared to a 1900 price that was sixty-four to eighty times a much.[35]

Electricity changed daily life, lighting up the evening and powering everything from streetcars and movies to department stores and factories. It powered radios and pumped water. Appliances reduced the burden of laundry and kept food from spoiling. By the 1890s "most of Iowa's larger towns had replaced the horse-drawn cars with electrical ones," wrote Alan Axelrod. Electricity also drove rail lines between cities in Iowa, such as the one from Cedar Rapids to Iowa City. Such transport survived until automobiles and buses replaced them. Cedar Rapids even had an electric truck in 1910. Almost everyone in Iowa's cities had electricity by the 1930s, but few Iowa farmers did. Building power lines into the countryside was expensive and profits were limited for rural service. Electricity would not be available to most rural Iowans until after the 1930s, thanks to a New Deal program that encouraged the building of electrical lines in the countryside.[36]

Iowa changed greatly between the Civil War and World War I. Immigration more than tripled the state's population during these five decades and many thousands moved into Iowa's cities or worked in its industrial enterprises. While agriculture dominated the state's economy, coal and meatpacking were increasingly important industries in the late nineteenth and early twentieth centuries, eclipsing the milling and lumber business. Manufacturing work was dangerous and difficult and urban life was often crowded and polluted. Electricity improved the lives of urban residents and telephones helped ease the isolation of rural areas. But the challenges of mass immigration, rapid urbanization, and industrialization sparked reform movements in Iowa and the United States. Issues such as temperance and women's suffrage dominated political debates between the two wars. These will be the subjects of the next chapter.

9

Suffrage, Prohibition, and Politics, 1870–1920

Two main issues eclipsed most others in Iowa politics from the Civil War to the 1920s, namely, the crusade for temperance—the war against alcohol consumption—and the long struggle for women's suffrage. National leaders of the suffrage battle included Carrie Chapman Catt, who grew up in Iowa. Both campaigns culminated during the Progressive Era of the early twentieth century, which was characterized by a national, state, and local movement to address the negative consequences of industrialization. While Iowa was not a center of the progressive movement, the state saw greater government regulation of business and political reforms that reduced the power of corporations, especially railroads, in the state. This period also saw the establishment of the university-based extension program, as well as conservation efforts, the spread of public libraries, and other reform movements. The years before World War I were a boom time for American agriculture and Iowa farmers benefited from a growing demand for foodstuffs following an economic depression in the 1890s. Rural free delivery of the mail and high prices improved the lives of farm families, even if urban amenities such as electricity and automobiles did not become widespread in rural areas until after the war.

The fight against alcohol consumption, which culminated with national prohibition in the 1920s, played out in Iowa for many decades. Prohibition was "the most emotional, politically significant, and tenacious of all issues in nineteenth and twentieth-century Iowa," noted historian Dorothy Schwieder. It was sometimes the defining issue for elections in the state, especially in the 1880s and 1890s, and legislators tried almost every way of controlling the traffic of liquor in Iowa through legislation. The Republican Party, which dominated Iowa politics from the Civil War onward, led the fight against alcohol consumption most of the time. The Democratic Party, usually supported by immigrants from places such as Ireland and Germany where alcohol was culturally important, fought against the regulation of the trade. Prohibition supporters wanted a "dry state" without alcohol, while "wets" opposed efforts to ban it.[1]

Prohibition opponents saw the regulation of alcohol as an attack on their cultural values and personal liberty. The German and Irish inhabitants of Iowa had a tradition of liquor consumption. Saloons and beer gardens were social hubs, places where people gathered, listened to music, and ate meals. This often happened on Sundays, when many Protestant Americans spent their days in church or at home. Germans and Irish, who were often Catholic or Lutheran, staunchly opposed prohibition. Methodists and Baptists usually supported it. The clash over alcohol consumption was a political, cultural, and religious issue that lasted for decades.[2]

Liquor consumption was part of daily life before the Civil War. Most people drank it, from farmers who produced their own cider to urban workers who consumed it throughout the day. Social occasions, from weddings and funerals to elections and corn huskings, included liquor. Many drank alcohol because fresh water was not available. Settlers in early Iowa drank it during harvests or to cure malaria or snakebites. By 1830 Americans guzzled seven gallons of pure alcohol each year, equivalent to 1.7 bottles of 80-proof liquor each week, per person. The regular consumption of such vast amounts of liquor wrecked families. Those who suffered most, especially women, fought to eliminate drunkenness. Major temperance campaigns began in the United States in the 1830s and 1840s. One of Iowa's first temperance conventions occurred in Burlington in 1839. It included the territorial governor, Robert Lucas, and the chief justice of the Iowa Supreme Court, Charles Mason.[3]

Iowa's temperance movement found success early. Legislation passed in 1847 allowed each county to grant licenses to sell alcohol, an idea that is known as the local option. Every county except Keokuk prohibited liquor sales. Shops selling alcohol were supposed to close, but many continued their business. Two years later, a new law allowed counties to grant liquor licenses to anyone who applied and paid at least fifty dollars. Legislation in the next few years was a confusing mess of regulation that satisfied no one but managed to spur a grass-roots temperance campaign that flooded the legislature with petitions in favor of prohibition in the 1850s. Temperance lecturers traveled the state and newspapers supported the cause. An Iowa temperance convention declared that it would not support any candidate who did not fully back prohibition. The public campaign worked. The legislature passed a prohibition law, the governor signed it, and the state's voters approved it by 2,910 votes out of 48,200 cast. On July 1, 1855, Iowa completely forbid the sale or manufacture of alcohol, with the exception of homemade cider or wine. The law also allowed the importation of liquor in original packaging. The state was technically "dry," less than ten years after it joined the union.[4]

The 1855 prohibition law did not eliminate the liquor industry in the state. "Women played an active part in keeping some sections of Iowa dry," wrote M. M. Morris and E. E. Jack. Sometime after the Civil War one man attempted to set up a saloon in Newton. A wagon full of alcohol was hauled into town, only to be ambushed by women from local churches known as the "Black Apron Hatchet Brigade." They were armed with hatchets, hidden beneath their aprons. In one afternoon they knocked open every container. A few bystanders laid on the ground to drink the liquor as it ran to the street. The helpless owner abandoned the town but set up a new establishment in the woods north of Newton. The local constable chased him out of the area.[5]

The temperance crusade faded during the Civil War but revived shortly afterward. Enforcement of the 1855 law had been lenient and subsequent laws weakened it. "An unofficial local-option prevailed—in which each town set its own standards for liquor control—and bootlegging became common," wrote Julie E. Nelson. Bootlegging included the illegal production and distribution of liquor. This system did not satisfy those who wanted alcohol outlawed and the antiliquor forces mobilized again. Forty thousand people signed a petition calling for absolute prohibition. In the 1870s lecturers traveled across the state and asked Iowans to take a temperance pledge and wear a blue ribbon to demonstrate their commitment. In Manchester, every saloon but one closed as customers took pledges not to drink. In Mitchellville a partially built saloon was torn down by locals. Fifteen thousand people marched in Marshalltown in June 1878 at a Blue Ribbon celebration. Temperance groups staged all-day prayer meetings in 1882, as the battle came to a climax. That year Iowa voters approved a strict prohibition amendment to the state constitution.[6]

Prohibitionists found their celebration to be short-lived. The Iowa Supreme Court struck down the amendment on a technicality in January 1883. Constitutional amendments had to be approved by two subsequent legislative assemblies before they were submitted for a statewide vote. The 1882 amendment was slightly different. Four words were omitted in the resolution passed by the legislature the second time. The court ruled that the amendment had not been legally adopted.[7]

The anti-liquor forces and their opponents returned to their struggle. It continued for fifty more years, until the end of national prohibition in 1933. Historian Ruth A. Gallaher aptly described the century-long contest between wet and dry forces in Iowa as one where the two sides went "round and round, apparently getting no farther than a squirrel in a cage." This battle continued in the 1880s, with the Republicans promising to pass new prohibition legislation. They rallied their supporters with the pledge "a school on every hill and no saloon in the valley." The GOP won the election in 1884, as usual, and passed the strongest antiliquor laws in Iowa history.[8]

An important ally in the temperance fight was Judith Ellen Foster, one of the first female lawyers in Iowa. Raised by religious parents in the Northeast, she taught school and devoted herself to missionary work among the poor. In Chicago she met E. C. Foster, a lawyer whom she married in 1869. They moved to Clinton, Iowa, that year. She studied law and was admitted to the bar in 1872, aiding her husband in trial cases. Foster was the fourth woman to practice before the Iowa Supreme Court. She joined the temperance crusade in Clinton and gave one of her first antiliquor lectures in June 1874. She was such an effective and eloquent orator that her house was destroyed by an arsonist in September. Local newspapers blamed saloon keepers who despised those who tried to close their shops. Foster was elected the corresponding secretary of the state's Women's Christian Temperance Union in November 1874 and spent the next few years organizing local branches across the state. She devoted her life to the prohibition cause and helped lead the push for a constitutional amendment in Iowa to ban alcohol. She gave hundreds of temperance speeches across the state and nation in the 1880s. After her husband moved to Washington, DC, to work for the Treasury Department, she was appointed to a variety of government positions. These included serving as a sanitary inspector during the Spanish-American War and an appointment as a special agent of the Department of Justice in 1908. There she inspected the condition of women inmates in state and federal prisons.[9]

In 1884 the Iowa legislature enacted a new state-wide prohibition law with the help of advocates like Foster, which brought much resistance and some political unrest. While the law went into effect on July 4, beer and wine continued to be openly sold in many places. Riots against enforcement of the law broke out in Iowa City, Fort Dodge, Muscatine, Sioux City, and Marshalltown. In Iowa City, a brewery celebrated July Fourth with an illegal beer party. Law enforcement closed it and brought charges against two local brewers. On August 13 the "Iowa City Beer Riots of 1884" took place, with drunken mobs roaming the streets, attacking law enforcement officers, and leaving at least one city lawyer covered in tar. Iowa struggled to enforce the ordinance. Sheriffs counted almost four hundred saloons in the state in 1887, with many more unreported or operating covertly. However, many places forced out saloons and liquor became harder to find in ninety Iowa counties. Those who wanted a drink could get a "prescription" from a doctor that could be filled at a local "pharmacy." Some ordered cases of liquor by mail, which was legal if it came in its original package. Others went to a nearby city or crossed state lines in search of alcohol.[10]

Resistance to the 1884 law was so great that it helped to elect a Democratic governor—an almost unthinkable event—in 1889. The Republicans split over full prohibition and ran a weak candidate. Horace Boies, the victor in 1889, had been a Whig and a Republican and ran as a conservative Democrat in opposition to absolute prohibition. He served four years as governor. Boies did not consume alcohol but opposed prohibition because it infringed upon individual rights. He was the only Democrat elected as Iowa governor between 1854 and 1932 and was a contender for the Democratic presidential nomination in 1892 and 1896. The Democrats also "performed the miracle of Iowa history," noted Leland Sage, by winning six of the state's eleven seats in the United States House of Representatives in 1890. These were surprising Democratic successes from a party that normally existed as token opposition. The state was so Republican that Iowa US senator John Dolliver proclaimed in 1883, "Iowa will go Democratic when Hell goes Methodist." Dolliver said this six years before Boies was elected, but the statement was usually correct even in the twentieth century. The Democratic wave was temporary, with only one Democratic Congressman being reelected in 1892, and Iowa returned to GOP control by the mid-1890s.[11]

In 1874 the Women's Christian Temperance Union (WCTU) was organized to support the temperance crusade. Iowan Annie Wittenmyer was president of the national organization that year and ran it for five years. The largest women's organization in the country at the time, the WCTU was populated by women who sought to reduce the destructive effects of alcohol abuse and protect their families from the desertion, violence, immorality, and financial irresponsibility brought on by drunkenness. Men could not join the organization. It was established and run by women who sought to reform American society and achieve full female citizenship. Members were mostly white and native-born and unable to transcend the biases of their time. They could be hostile to the poor, immigrants, or African Americans. The WCTU gave local chapters autonomy to pursue any issue of concern, from temperance to prison reform. Frances Willard, president of the WCTU from 1879 to 1899, argued that if women had even a limited right to vote—the "Home Protection Ballot"—they could help defend their families from the dangers of saloons.[12]

In Iowa the WCTU pursued the battle against liquor county by county, as local option laws led to shifting alcohol regulations across the state. The WCTU helped enact temperance legislation in Clay County in the northwest part of the state. They also lobbied voters to elect a series of pro-temperance mayors. Local newspapers published their message and editors recounted their meetings for readers. Martha Janes, president of the Spencer Iowa WCTU, had her own front-page weekly column in the county newspaper, the *Clay County News*, in 1884. She argued that women deserved the right to vote since they had shown their civic virtue and community service fighting for temperance. They also paid taxes and had to obey the same laws as men. Janes was a fearless and stalwart temperance and suffrage activist, as well as the mother of three children. She was also the first female ordained minister in the Free Baptist conference, a more liberal branch of the church. Janes was a powerful orator, with unshakable convictions, who accused men of robbing women of their God-given liberty and freedom in her columns.[13]

An equally outspoken temperance advocate moved to Sioux City in 1885. It was a boomtown full of immigrant workers from Germany and Ireland who valued their neighborhood saloons and access to liquor. The city's saloon and brewery businesses ignored the state's prohibition law. Prostitution and gambling flourished. In October 1885 a fiery Methodist minister, George Haddock, made Sioux City his new home. He was determined to enforce Iowa's new prohibition laws and shut down illegal bars. Haddock believed that he was fighting the devil and that success would lead to sober workers and empty jails. But the minister and his supporters also wanted a homogenous state without the cultural and ethnic diversity that new immigrants brought. He gathered evidence to use in court against illegal saloons. His self-righteous zeal earned him enemies among brewers and saloon owners, whose businesses were threatened. Haddock was shot while walking home on August 3, 1886. Two men were indicted for the murder, which received national attention. One was acquitted, the other found guilty of manslaughter. Haddock's death led to a backlash against the liquor trade. Victories by prohibition forces occurred in Sioux City, even as the state's laws began to trend away from an unwavering hostility to liquor.[14]

In 1894 the state revised the strict prohibition law from a decade earlier. It was impossible to enforce and as many as three hundred drinking establishments existed in Des Moines. In an attempt to deal with this situation, new legislation, called the Mulct law, was enacted. It was "a political mongrel, neither prohibition, license, not local option, but a mixture of all three," wrote Ruth A. Gallaher. Prohibition was not repealed but the new law allowed the return of the local option in the state. The Mulct law continued until it was repealed, with some additional revisions. The state passed a bewildering amount of prohibition legislation from the 1890s until the passage of the Eighteenth Amendment. One of these was the Moon Law of 1909, which limited the number of saloons to one for every thousand inhabitants if communities consented. Saloons in operation in 1909 were exempt from this law. Twenty-five bills to restrict liquor were introduced in 1911. The prohibition "merry-go-round" continued in the early twentieth century, noted Gallaher.[15]

On the first day of 1916 the Mulct law was repealed and the 1884 prohibition law went back into effect. The next year a prohibition amendment to the Iowa constitution was defeated. In January 1919 Iowa ratified the Eighteenth Amendment to the United States Constitution, which instituted nationwide prohibition on the manufacture, sale, or transportation of intoxicating liquor. Prohibition existed in Iowa until 1933, with the state allowing beer with a low alcohol content to still be sold. Later that year, Congress repealed the Eighteenth Amendment and the state's long and complex history of liquor prohibition came to a sudden end.[16]

The struggle for female suffrage did not absorb the energies of Iowa legislators or ministers like prohibition did. The long campaign for suffrage began in 1848 when more than two hundred women, and about forty men, met at a woman's-rights convention in Seneca Falls, New York. Women had fought for fairer treatment by arguing for greater property rights in states like New York; they had also boycotted tea and made clothing for the Revolutionary army decades before. But in 1848 they advocated for more radical ideas. The Seneca Falls convention argued that women were the equals of men and challenged the subordinate status of females in the United States.[17]

The suffrage movement began in Iowa before the Civil War. Amelia Bloomer, from Council Bluffs, and Frances Dana Gage of Ohio, gave a series of lectures in 1854 and 1855 on the subject. Bloomer had attended the Seneca Falls convention but would play a relatively minor role in Iowa's suffrage contest. It found more support after the war, spurred by the debate over providing voting rights to African American men. Suffrage supporters argued that women paid taxes just like men and that females were just as literate as men. They made up almost half the population of the state, with "one-half of its stability, intelligence, and virtue," as a suffrage petition to the Iowa House of Representatives argued in 1866. The push to give women the right to vote at the same time Black men received it failed. In 1868 the state constitution was amended to give African American men voting rights but not women.[18]

In 1869 the first state suffrage association was established in Dubuque and other such organizations quickly proliferated. A year later the Iowa Woman Suffrage Association (IWSA) was formed. It became one of the main organizations advocating for the female vote in the state and "worked diligently to cultivate grassroots support while pressuring the Iowa legislature to put a woman suffrage amendment to the voters," wrote historian Sara Egge. The IWSA sent petitions to the legislature with thousands of signatures and introduced many suffrage bills in the late 1800s. It held local meetings across the state to discuss and debate the topic, some attendees coming from many miles away. Supporters formed "Political Equality Clubs" and organized "Woman's Day" events at fairs. Newspapers published accounts of meetings and some suffragists, such as Martha Janes, wrote regular columns in papers. Suffrage lecturers traveled across Iowa, spreading their message from county to county. Some in the WCTU, like Janes, argued for both temperance and women's suffrage.[19]

In 1870 a resolution that authorized a suffrage amendment to the state constitution was introduced. It passed both houses of the state legislature with strong support. No state had granted women the right to vote, but "things looked promising for would-be female voters in Iowa in the winter of 1871/72," wrote historian Diana Pounds. The Iowa campaign to persuade the public and lawmakers to support the cause brought in Susan B. Anthony and Elizabeth Cady Stanton, who spent three days in Des Moines in the summer of 1871 while on a cross-country speaking tour. The IWSA had its first state convention in Des Moines in October. Newspapers in the state covered the debates about suffrage, with the *Des Moines Register* providing positive coverage of the convention. However constitutional amendments had to be approved by two consecutive meetings of the state assembly. In 1872 the resolution failed in the state senate, with five senators who had voted for the proposal in the previous session now voting against it. The campaign for suffrage was damaged by traditional ideas on the subordinate status of women, as well as the association of the suffrage movement with the potential sexual license of liberated women.[20]

Opponents of suffrage sometimes associated political equality with sexual immorality, or "free love." This was a damning accusation against any woman, who had to live in a world that considered her inferior and told her to obey her husband. Women were assumed to be physically and mentally subordinate to men. Too much education might damage a woman's reproductive organs. A woman's place in nineteenth-century America was at home, where her main tasks were to be a good mother and wife. The idealized American woman was pure, feminine, and submissive, untainted by the wicked world outside her home. Church and popular culture reinforced this ideal. Suffragists had to refute a society that confined them to the "woman's sphere" and deprived them of basic rights without violating their allegiance to home and family. Women had to convince men that they could satisfactorily meet the demands of home and civic life. Unfortunately, a public battle over sexual morality, and the place of women in American society, undermined the suffrage campaign in Iowa. Victoria Woodhull, a New York journalist, stockbroker, and suffrage ally, advocated unpopular ideas such as socialism and sexual freedom that tainted the national suffrage movement. Woodhull's scandalous ideas grabbed headlines and the controversy helped tie the suffrage movement to free love, damaging its reputation. In March 1872 the Iowa Senate voted 24–22 against a proposed suffrage amendment. Although Woodhull did not destroy the

Iowa suffrage movement alone, she did help reinforce opposition to giving women the right to vote.[21]

In the 1870s and 1880s the suffrage campaign continued. Equal suffrage petitions were submitted to the legislature almost every session from 1870 until 1918. Lawmakers usually passed a resolution in one house and rejected it in the other, or passed it in one session but not the next. A suffrage amendment passed both houses of the General Assembly in 1874 but did not survive the next session of the legislature. In 1876 a suffrage resolution passed the state house but failed by two votes in the senate. In 1882 a suffrage law passed the Nineteenth General Assembly; in the Twentieth Assembly it passed the senate but failed to get a vote in the house. Many legislators supported female suffrage, but few saw it as important for their political campaigns. The Republican Party had adopted a bold stance on prohibition in the 1880s, alienating some of its supporters in the process. To advocate another major policy—suffrage—might antagonize other constituents. Remaining in power meant sacrificing the potential votes of women.[22]

In 1894 the efforts of the Iowa suffrage movement gained a partial victory when women won the right to vote in municipal and school elections. Suffrage forces focused on gaining limited voting rights, abandoning more ambitious efforts to pass a franchise amendment to the state constitution. The Iowa suffrage movement was inspired by Wyoming, a new state that had joined the union in 1890 with full female voting rights. By 1894 the Iowa legislature was flooded with petitions—as many as fifty presented to the senate in one day—supporting it. That year the Iowa legislature granted women the right to vote in municipal and school elections involving taxes, borrowing money, and issuing bonds. Females voted in favor of public libraries, often voting to increase taxes to support the construction of Iowa's many Carnegie libraries.[23]

By the early 1910s some states had given women the right to vote and there was increasing support for extending the franchise to women in Iowa and elsewhere. By 1900 more newspapers in Iowa began to support women's rights and men were beginning to realize that political equality was inevitable, even if the march toward it was uneven. Washington, California, Kansas, Oregon, and Utah gave women the right to vote between 1910 and 1912, but state referenda failed in midwestern states such as Wisconsin, Ohio, and Michigan. In 1913 and 1915 suffrage legislation passed both houses in the Iowa legislature and was approved by the governor. An amendment to the Iowa constitution that would give women the right to vote was set for a June 5, 1916, vote. Opponents argued that women could best serve Iowa by staying at home and that their interests were already represented by their husbands. Voters failed to approve the amendment which was defeated by 10,141 votes of 335,839 cast.[24]

The suffrage movement in Iowa and the United States highlighted the efforts of many outstanding women. Among them was Amelia Bloomer, who moved to Council Bluffs, Iowa, with her husband, Dexter, in 1855. She had been a teacher, deputy postmaster, and wrote for Dexter's newspaper in New York. Bloomer established her own paper, the *Lily*, in which she published an article supporting a new style of clothing that ended up named after her. It included a loose skirt to replace the tight corsets and heavy clothing that restricted movement. She continued to publish her paper in Iowa, encouraging women to buy land in the state. "Women can own and hold property, both real and personal, and I am happy to know that many women are availing themselves of these provisions," she wrote in a May 1855 letter. One female typesetter was saving her wages to buy land near Council Bluffs. She also told readers to send their daughters to the university in Iowa City, which welcomed women. Bloomer lectured on temperance in Iowa, working with the WCTU, but was not as active in the women's rights movement as others in Iowa, such as Annie Savery or Carrie Chapman Catt, due to her dedication to the temperance cause.[25]

Annie Savery was involved, though briefly, in the suffrage movement in Iowa. She had been born in London and lived in New York before coming to Des Moines in 1854 with her husband, James Savery, who owned a hotel that Annie managed. They eventually amassed a real estate fortune, donating to the Des Moines Library and Grinnell College. Annie Savery was mostly self-educated and acquired an outstanding library of books. She had a deep interest in Shakespeare and literature. She taught herself to speak and read French and graduated from the law school of the State University of Iowa in 1875. Savery was also involved in reforming the appalling Polk County jail and improving medical care in Des Moines. In the late 1860s she began to give suffrage speeches and helped establish the first Polk County suffrage organization. She emerged as the leader of the Iowa women's rights movement in the early 1870s. But she refused to condemn Woodhull, who had been a strong supporter of suffrage. Savery's reputation was tarred by association with the free love controversy. The failure of the suffrage bill in 1872 led to the end of her active involvement in the movement. She died in New York City in 1891, having moved there with her husband to manage business interests.[26]

Carrie Chapman Catt was the most famous of the suffragists with ties to Iowa. Though born in Wisconsin in 1859, she spent most of her childhood in Charles City, Iowa. In 1872 her father voted in the presidential election, along with a hired man who worked for her family. Carrie asked her father why her mother could not vote. He replied that since he owned the farm, he had the right to vote. She argued that her mother's labor had helped pay for it, too. He said that men knew more than women. In response she countered that "their hired man didn't known half as much as her mother," wrote Louise R. Noun. That year the thirteen-year-old girl became a suffragist. She graduated from Iowa State Agricultural College in 1880, the only women in her class. She paid her way through college working in the library, washing dishes, and teaching. After graduation she was a teacher, principal, and superintendent of schools in Mason City. She also wrote columns for the local newspaper called "Woman's World." Her columns were stirring and eloquent calls to equality. She noted that more than 1,000 Iowa farms were owned by women and that the state had 125 female physicians in 1885.[27]

In 1885 she married Leo Chapman, editor of the *Mason City Republican*, who later died of typhoid in California, not long after the couple moved there. She lived in that state for two years and worked as a reporter until returning to Charles City. She then married George Catt and joined the Iowa Woman Suffrage Association as a writer and lecturer. Full-time involvement with the suffrage movement began in 1889 when she traveled across the state and began organizing political equality clubs. The financial support of her husband allowed her to become active in the National Woman Suffrage Association, where she quickly earned a reputation as an effective and vocal suffrage leader. She worked in Iowa in the early 1890s and campaigned for women's rights in Colorado, Idaho, and California later in the decade. Success was mixed, as Colorado and Idaho approved suffrage but California did not. Catt succeeded Susan B. Anthony as president of the National Woman Suffrage Association in 1900 and helped lead state and national suffrage campaigns until the Nineteenth Amendment gave most women the right to vote in 1920.[28]

The patriotism that women demonstrated during World War I greatly aided the drive for suffrage in Iowa and the United States. "Women were ubiquitous in wartime activities," wrote historian Sara Egge, taking part

Carrie Chapman Catt was a teacher, principal, journalist, and suffrage leader. She was president of the National Woman Suffrage Association in the early 1900s. Portrait of Carrie Chapman Catt, 1909. MS 71.20, Iowa Women's Suffrage Collection, State Historical Society of Iowa, Des Moines.

in wartime bond drives, Red Cross chapters, and promoting food conservation and rationing. Such activity helped prove that women deserved the right to vote, since they had demonstrated they were devoted and loyal citizens. Female suffrage, designed to uplift democracy and inspire the world, became part of the war effort. In 1917 both houses of the Iowa legislature passed a suffrage amendment without opposition. The bill only needed approval in the next session before it went back to the voters. Victory seemed assured. But a procedural error in the secretary of state's office nullified the legislation. A small error wasted two years of work. In the spring of 1919 the United States House and Senate passed a federal suffrage amendment. Individual states began to ratify it and suffragists mobilized to support the cause again. Iowa was the tenth to state ratify the Nineteenth Amendment. In August 1920 the amendment became part of the United States Constitution after ratification by thirty-six states.[29]

Iowa saw significant regulation of its economy and political system in the early twentieth century, led by a mostly forgotten progressive governor named Albert Baird Cummins. Wealthy individuals and corporations wielded great power in the United States, influencing elections and ignoring widespread poverty and deep inequality. Cummins was a Republican who challenged his party's business-friendly conservatism, running an antimonopoly campaign. He was elected governor in 1901 and served until 1908, when he was appointed to the US Senate. Cummins was senator until 1926, usually supporting progressive causes. One of the great reform successes was the establishment of a primary for elected offices in the state, which undermined corporate power in elections. An editor in Knoxville wrote that the best argument for such a law was the opposition of railroads to the proposal. Other new laws also regulated food and drug production in the state, which almost eliminated deaths from food poisoning. A 1907 law prohibited corporations from providing any financial or other aid to candidates running for office. The state also regulated railroad rates; big businesses were forced to pay taxes on property they owned in the state. Reforms to the state's education law mandated school attendance from age seven to sixteen or until students completed the equivalent of eighth grade. Changes to child labor laws made it illegal for those under the age of sixteen to work in any job that might injure their health or morals and limited working hours for those younger than fourteen. Bills to allow ballot initiatives and referendums failed to become law though.[30]

In the 1890s and early 1900s Iowa produced a number of national political figures, who ended up in Congress or the presidential cabinet. David B. Henderson was speaker of the House of Representatives from 1899–1903, the first from west of the Mississippi River. Henderson was an anti-imperialist who had lost a foot in the Civil War. Jonathan Dolliver was a progressive US senator for a decade at the start of the twentieth century. Like Cummins, he was a staunch supporter of Theodore Roosevelt. William Boyd Allison served in the Senate for thirty-five years, his long service giving him great power on financial matters. William Hepburn, a member of the House for more than twenty years, helped pass the Pure Food and Drug Act. James Wilson, usually known as "Tama Jim," was secretary of agriculture for three presidents. Wilson acquired his nickname to distinguish him from Iowa senator James F. Wilson, called "Jefferson Jim." Tama Jim Wilson had been a congressman and was a professor of agriculture at Iowa Agricultural College when President McKinley asked him to join his cabinet. He served William McKinley, Theodore Roosevelt, and William Howard Taft over a period of sixteen years and is usually seen as one of the most important agriculture secretaries. Theodore Roosevelt also chose another Iowan, former governor Leslie Shaw, as his treasury secretary. These men were imperfect creatures of their time. Hepburn, for example, was an imperialist who favored a racist Chinese exclusion policy. The start of the 1900s, wrote historian Loren N. Horton, was the point that probably "marked Iowa's greatest moment in terms of national political power."[31]

The Progressive era saw substantial conservation victories in Iowa and the United States. An Iowa congressman from Oskaloosa, John F. Lacey, helped write the 1906 Antiquities Act and other laws protecting wildlife and forests across the country. The 1906 law preserved land that became parts of many national parks and monuments. In the Southwest these included Grand Canyon National Park, Zion, Arches, and Bryce Canyon National Parks in Utah, and Death Valley in California. The law was also used to help create Grand Teton National Park in Wyoming and Denali National Park in Alaska. Iowa also experienced its own conservation movement that led to the creation of Iowa state parks and other protected areas. Iowa clubwomen were strong supporters of conservation and state parks. They planted trees, lobbied for legislation in letter-writing campaigns and wrote newspaper editorials. Their work also helped establish Effigy Mounds National Monument in northeast Iowa. The State Park Act became law in 1917 and authorized the creation of public parks with historic or scientific interest or scenic beauty. Three years later the first state park, Backbone State Park, was established in Delaware County. By 1931 there were forty Iowa state parks. Public demand grew with the spread of automobiles, which encouraged visits. In the 1930s New Deal programs such as the Civilian Conservation Corps helped build at least one thousand structures in the parks, especially campgrounds, of which only a few had existed in the 1920s. Between 1931 and 1941 about fifty parks were added to the system, often with federal aid. At its centennial in 2020 the park, conservation, and recreation system in Iowa totaled nearly 383,000 acres and had 15 million annual day-use visitors.[32]

The early twentieth century also saw the birth of agricultural extension in the United States. Seaman Knapp, who had been an agriculture professor in Ames, pioneered the idea of disseminating farm knowledge to rural communities when working for the US Department of Agriculture in Texas. Knapp worked for Tama Jim Wilson, the secretary of agriculture, who had been his successor in Ames. (Iowa Agricultural College and Model Farm became Iowa State College of Agriculture and Mechanic Arts in 1898). Knapp emphasized practical education, such as improving crop strains or modifying growing practices to improve yields or fight insect infestations. In 1914 federal legislation that funded county extension personnel became law. It provided money to support county agents, as extension employees were called, as well as female home agents, who worked with rural women. The federal government provided one-third of the funding, matched by states and counties that each provided an additional third. Programs were based at the land-grant college in each state. In 1906 Iowa had created its own state extension program, but it had only a handful of staff. Iowa State College professor Perry G. Holden organized a traveling exhibit, the Seed Corn Gospel Train, to spread knowledge of the science of corn culture. It ran from 1904 to 1906. Historian Dorothy Schwieder wrote that Holden "might be called the father of Iowa Extension." The Iowa Extension Service helped increase farm production during both world wars, improved the health and lives of rural people, helped organize relief during the Great Depression, and served the people of Iowa into the twenty-first century.[33]

The spread of the settlement house idea also helped to improve the lives of Iowans starting in the 1890s. Chicago's Hull House, founded by Nobel Peace Prize winner Jane Addams, was the most famous of these institutions. Often staffed by young, educated women, they provided immigrants and the poor with health care, training, and education. The Roadside Settlement in Des Moines had its origins in the late 1880s in female church groups that gave food, clothing, and other aid to the needy. By 1896 it was based in a rented apartment, staffed by volunteers. Eight years later Flora Dunlap, a graduate of Cincinnati Wesleyan College who had worked at Hull House, became the head resident. A new building was built in one of the poorest sections of the city, the South Bottoms, which was southeast of the capitol. It had a library, dining room, bathing and laundry facilities, and provided classes and training for boys and girls. There were social clubs and basketball teams. It also provided day care for working women. Nurses lived at the building in the early 1910s to provide medical care. It was open to African Americans, though adults and older children usually met separately from whites. Dunlap served as the organization's director for two decades and was an active community leader. In 1912 she was the first woman elected to the Des Moines school board. She did not run for reelection, calling her term futile as none of the men on the board would speak to her or listen to her. She was the first president of the Iowa League of Women Voters, serving in 1919 and 1920, and led government relief

Flora Dunlap was head resident at the Roadside Settlement House in Des Moines in the early twentieth century. She was also the first woman elected to the Des Moines School Board. Flora Dunlap. MS71.7.23, Iowa Women's Suffrage Collection, State Historical Society of Iowa, Des Moines.

programs during the Great Depression. Flora Dunlap Elementary School in Des Moines was named for her.[34]

There were other settlement houses in Iowa, including the Negro Community Center and the Jewish Community Center in Des Moines, as well as those in Sioux City and Cedar Rapids. The Roadside Settlement organized evening English classes for immigrants at a local school in 1907. More than one hundred people showed up. Many were Jews and a Jewish branch of the settlement was established. It hosted night courses, a sewing school, and had a gym. The organization moved to West Eighth Street and Forest Avenue and was named the Jewish Community Center. It had an auditorium, library, and a gym, with classes in music, crafts, and drama. The center was open to everyone and most visitors were not Jewish. The Negro Community Center of Des Moines grew out of services provided to African American soldiers during the First World War. The center, which had operated out of an old school and then a large house, gained its official name in 1933. It had a library, provided health care, recreation, and hosted Black clubs, fraternal organizations, and church groups. Boy Scout troops and Camp Fire Girls met there. A community house began in Sioux City, on the second floor of a building at a lumber yard on the east side of town. It provided games and clubs for children, classes to prepare immigrants for citizenship exams, and taught people to read. Russians, Italians, Danes, Armenians, and Mexicans studied together at night. A "Women of All Nations Club" exchanged recipes and listened to music. In 1934 a permanent structure was built. It survived floods and provided food, shelter, medical care, preschool education, and vocational training during the Great Depression. A Cedar Rapids community house aided the poor and immigrants like the institutions in Sioux City and Des Moines.[35]

Iowa also benefited from the construction of public libraries and the opportunities for education, enlightenment, and informed citizenship they made available. The Carnegie Corporation, funded by industrialist Andrew Carnegie, provided money to build 101 libraries in 99 Iowa towns between 1892 and 1917. Few public libraries existed in the Midwest before the 1870s, but Carnegie helped change this. Iowa only had fifteen public libraries in 1891, supported by local taxes. Almost one-half of 1,679 Carnegie libraries that were built were in the Midwest. Most towns could not afford an expensive building that could cost as much as $50,000 or the annual burden of library maintenance, which could run $5,000. To attract a Carnegie library, towns had to supply a construction site and help maintain it. The first such library in Iowa, and the first outside Pennsylvania, was opened in Fairfield in 1893. Fairfield's public library began in 1853 in a rented room with 525 books, so the modern brick building of 1893 was a huge improvement. In the 1890s and early 1900s Iowa towns from Davenport to Council Bluffs added public libraries thanks to the program. Mason City's opened in 1904. Some in the town saw the library—which had a series of temporary homes before burning down—as an alternative to saloons. Residents, often female, advocated for libraries for their communities. Iowa clubwomen were especially strong advocates for libraries. They founded and staffed them, sometimes applying for Carnegie library grants. Young H. E. Wilkinson went to high school in Mason City, starting in 1904, and would have visited the new library. Endless bookshelves provided a feast for his mind. He wrote of spending an hour or two each time reading books by Horatio Alger or Hamlin Garland. "One hardly knew what to enjoy first," he wrote. He often followed a visit to the library with two banana splits at nearby Skondras' Olympia Candy Kitchen.[36]

Iowa and the nation suffered from an economic depression in the 1890s. In 1893 one of the largest corporations in the country, the National Cordage

Company, failed. This triggered a stock market collapse, bank failures, and widespread bankruptcies. The times were worse than any in memory, with at least 20 percent of factory workers out of work in the country. Desperate unemployed men left home looking for a job, banding together in small tramp armies. Some groups headed to Washington, DC, to demand aid. One unemployed band, known as Kelly's Army, traveled across Iowa in the spring of 1894, heading for the national capitol. Among them was the writer Jack London, who walked barefoot into the town of Underwood near Council Bluffs. They camped at the fairgrounds at Atlantic, were often fed by local farmers, and marched across the state, sometimes in pelting rain. About one thousand men reached Des Moines on April 29. They were encouraged to move east by citizens concerned about their presence. Kelly's Army built rafts to float down the Des Moines River to the Mississippi. In July they reached Washington. Congress did nothing. Local and state governments sent the men home by railroad.[37]

Iowa experienced difficult economic times, with a severe downturn made worse by years of dry weather. No rain fell for two months in the summer of 1894 and a long-running drought hit its nadir that year. It withered corn and hay crops and cut yields by almost half. Wells, creeks, and ponds went dry. Livestock were killed because there was not enough grain to feed them. Orchards were wiped out by the drought. The next year saw bountiful harvests but very low prices and no farm profits. Historian Benjamin F. Gue lamented that everyone around him suffered except those who loaned money. Agricultural prices fell in the mid-1890s; debts went up and farm foreclosures increased. The number of those who rented their land in Iowa grew by almost 50 percent between 1880 and 1900. Schoolteachers found homeless men sleeping in their classrooms. People were "glad to eke out an existence," wrote historian Cyrenus Cole about the 1890s.[38]

Agricultural prosperity returned by 1900 and the first two decades of the twentieth century were golden times for American agriculture, which saw a sustained period of income gains for farm families, a stark change from the low prices of the late nineteenth century. Iowans benefited from strong demand and high prices for agricultural goods. Farm income doubled and the value of farm property tripled nationwide, as the increase in farm acreage dramatically slowed. In Iowa the value of land grew by 127 percent from 1900 to 1910 alone, from $36.35 an acre to $82.58 per acre. From 1870 to 1900 the amount of farmland in the country had more than doubled. In the first twenty years of the 1900s, it grew by only 12 percent. The population of the country, and demand for farm goods, grew faster than production. The agricultural economy improved as prices increased and farm families grew wealthier. They made their homes more convenient, with more furnishings and improved kitchens and toilets. A few bought automobiles in the countryside. Sarah Jane Kimball, from Jones County, saw her first automobile in July 1906. She took her first ride in one six years later. Many also purchased corn harvesting machinery. A feeling of optimism spread across the Midwest as the economy and the quality of life improved. One orator claimed in 1899 that "there is nothing but corn, cattle, and contentment," from Indiana to Nebraska.[39]

The free delivery of mail to rural areas further bettered the lives of Iowans. It brought the outside world to the farmhouse gate. The lives of rural families improved economically with higher incomes in the early 1900s; the arrival of rural mail, as well as telephones, also made their lives easier. Rural free delivery began in West Virginia in 1896 and spread across the country. Iowa had twenty-three rural mail routes three years later. Farm families and newspaper editors agitated for additional routes, as mail provided access to news, market reports, weather forecasts, and political developments. Rural free delivery helped farmers "be more up-to-date and to overcome the time disadvantages associated with their geographic isolation," wrote journalism professor Roy Alden Atwood. Such information reduced the knowledge deficit of farmers, as they could access all of the literature, information, and entertainment available in urban areas. Until 1901 Sarah Jane Kimball's family had to visit the post office in the small town of Wyoming to pick up letters, newspapers, magazines, seeds, and packages they had ordered by mail. After that year they only had to travel to town for heavy packages from retailers like Sears Roebuck and Company. Rural free delivery came to Cerro Gordo County in 1902. H. E. Wilkinson recalled that his family proudly placed a metal mailbox on a sturdy post, with his father's name written on it in red paint.[40]

Rural free delivery had positive and negative consequences. It led an to increase in personal correspondence, as families had a more reliable and faster way to communicate with friends and relatives. Women especially exchanged letters thanks to the ease of sending and receiving mail. Families subscribed to newspapers outside their local area; new magazines targeted to rural readers appeared. The advantages of rural mail delivery were reflected in land prices along rural routes, which increased by two to five dollars per acre. At the same time, direct mail service eliminated

The free delivery of mail to rural areas brought the world to Iowa's farms. But roads were often awful, and vehicles sometimes had to be pulled out of the mud by horses. Mail carrier Joe Guter stuck in mud, ca. 1930s, Bremer County, Iowa. From Postal Service—Rural—Free Delivery photo files, Special Collections, State Historical Society of Iowa, Iowa City.

the necessity for smaller post offices in villages and small towns, with 207 Iowa post offices closing in 1909. Many stores that had housed these minor post branches also disappeared. Local merchants, who had benefited from the business of farm families who came to town, also suffered. While mail-order business boomed, local retailers lost their customers. Those in rural Iowa had access to a huge variety of mass-produced commodities, often at lower prices than local merchants. Competition quickly drove merchants to offer the same prices as catalog retailers. Rural mail delivery also "citified the country" by undermining the social and cultural autonomy of smaller towns. Families no longer went to their local general store to gather, shop, and talk. As the early twentieth century wore on, the countryside began to look more like urban America. But there were fewer people living in the state in 1910 than ten years earlier. Iowa was the only state to lose population in the first decade of the century.[41]

Iowa had struggled with the issues of prohibition and women's suffrage for many decades. Prohibition had taken most of the energy of Iowa's politicians and suffrage had been sacrificed in the endless battle against liquor consumption. But by 1920 both issues had been addressed by amendments to the United States Constitution. World War I brought an end to progressive reforms, as the nation's energies were focused on the conflict in Europe. But new libraries, state parks, and a stronger government improved the lives of Iowans. In the early 1900s rural areas recovered from the economic misery of the late-nineteenth century. Farm families enjoyed rising living standards and the regular delivery of the mail, as well as the telephone, which tied them closer to the world outside their homes. World War I and the 1920s would accelerate this process and bring new challenges to the state.

10
Iowa in World War I and the 1920s

World War I brought prosperity to Iowa, as high farm prices and increased employment boosted the fortunes of its inhabitants. The war affected every family in Iowa: men served in the military, while their families bought war bonds or volunteered for the Red Cross. The conflict heightened social tensions across the country, as patriotic zeal trampled over individual rights. In Iowa, excessive nationalism led to extralegal punishment for those seen as lacking sufficient wartime patriotism. The state also experienced a resurgent Ku Klux Klan and national Prohibition. Meanwhile, new forms of communication and transportation began to transform Iowa, as radio, improved roads, automobiles, and movies reshaped daily life. After the war ended, commodity prices crashed, and the state fell into a prolonged agricultural recession. By the time the Great Depression hit Iowa, it had already suffered a decade of distress.

The United States avoided involvement in World War I for almost three years. Allied nations—Russia, France, England, and others—faced the Central Powers, including the Austro-Hungarians, the Ottoman Empire, and Germany. The war ground to a stalemate by late 1914 and millions of soldiers were killed. Americans watched the conflict in horror and determined to stay out of the bloodbath, despite submarine attacks that killed Americans. At the same time, the United States became the "most important factory, banker, and food supplier" for the Allies during the war, wrote historian Michael S. Neiberg. American exports to Allied countries boosted the US economy and the demand for corn, wheat, and pork helped farmers in Iowa and elsewhere by raising agricultural prices. In April 1917 the United States was pulled into the war. Unrestricted submarine warfare, along with a German promise to return territory Mexico had lost in its war with the United States in the 1840s, helped push the country into the conflict. The United States declared war on Germany on April 6. A total of 114,224 men and women from Iowa eventually served in the US Army, Marine Corps, or Navy.[1]

The American government faced a huge task—it needed to train, equip, and deploy an army and navy of millions of men. It also needed to raise vast sums of money to pay for the war and encourage the production of everything from ships to shoes. New bureaucracies were created to manage the war effort and gain the support of the population. Controversial legislation, notably the Espionage Act, punished anyone obstructing the war effort or engaging in spying or sabotage.[2]

The Red Cross served a vital function during the conflict, both overseas and at home. Hundreds of thousands of Iowa women supported the war by completing millions of hours of volunteer work for the organization. Clubwomen enthusiastically joined the Red Cross in large numbers. Iowa had only nine Red Cross chapters in early 1917, but its volunteer ranks swelled quickly after the war began in April. The organization had more than one million members and 164 chapters in the state by the time the conflict ended. A greater percentage of Iowa's population joined the Red Cross than from Illinois, Nebraska, or Wisconsin. A vast amount of labor went into producing supplies for military and humanitarian uses, ranging from surgical dressings to sweaters and socks knitted by volunteers. Much of this material was made in workrooms set up in city halls, schools, courthouses, and private homes. One mother of three soldiers said, "It is for me military duty. It gives me a chance to be a soldier with my sons." In April 1918 volunteers across the country produced more than 25 million dressings and four hundred thousand pieces of clothing. Women in Sioux City made 50,000 surgical dressings and knitted 9,611 items. One woman—identified only as Mrs. William E. Wilson—volunteered more than five thousand hours to the Red Cross in Iowa in 1917 and 1918.[3]

The Red Cross supplied all nurses for the American military during the war and aided civilian medical care. Eight hundred and sixty-two Iowa women volunteered for the Red Cross, with about half serving overseas.

Thirteen nurses from Scott County served in Europe, while twenty-one more were posted around the country or to Puerto Rico. Four died while in military service, largely due to the flu epidemic. Nurses in Europe worked in hospital trains, convalescent hospitals, and near combat zones. Many labored in surgical units immediately behind the front lines, sometimes for forty-eight hours at a time. Conditions were often horrific and exhausting, as large numbers of badly wounded men required care. Hospital trains came at night, injured men stumbling through the dark, wrote Lois Orr Preach. She worked at a hospital twenty-five miles behind the front lines that cared for one thousand men. Preach cleaned up the wounded and dressed burns; men were then sent for medical care farther back behind the lines. Merle Wright volunteered to serve as a nurse in France and arrived in March 1918. She toiled in a hospital about fifty miles behind the front lines. Nursing was quite different from the United States, she recalled, as "we did not have the satisfaction of watching our patients recover." Wounded men went back to the front or left for other hospitals after a few days.[4]

Much of the Red Cross's time was spent raising money to assist in caring for troops and suffering Europeans. Iowa chapters were asked to raise one million dollars in the first war fund drive. Much of this money was earned through auctions of antiques, jewelry, or even horses. One boy gave his puppy for auction, and it earned ten dollars for the organization. The dog was returned to its young owner. A mock court gave "fines" of one to four dollars to those who violated laws that did not exist to help raise money. Iowans gave far more than their state quota in the fund drives for the Red Cross, usually exceeding requirements by 30 percent. There was public pressure to join the Red Cross or to give it money. Contributions and memberships were solicited by private and public employers, at businesses, banks, and clubs. The Iowa Red Cross did its part to solicit the $400 million that the organization raised during the war.[5]

Iowa women also volunteered for canteen work, providing refreshments to traveling soldiers, as well as the sick and wounded. Fifty-seven Iowa cities had canteen stations where local chapters sent volunteers to meet servicemen at railroad stations. They handed out cigarettes, candy, coffee, fruit, or other items such as newspapers and magazines. At some places soldiers could have lunch, while a few had showers, including Boone, Cedar Rapids, and Council Bluffs. Some canteens provided easy chairs where soldiers could relax and read or listen to music. Chapters paid for these services out of the funds they raised locally. These services continued for some time after the war ended. In the first six months of 1919, Iowa canteens helped 311,396 men who were heading home after the conflict. At the Des Moines canteen, the Red Cross served 1,844 gallons of coffee and 33,345 sandwiches in the first five months of 1919. The Sioux City canteen gave out 94,000 doughnuts and more than 559,000 cigarettes around the same time.[6]

The federal government asked Americans to conserve food during the war, so more could be used for military purposes or for European relief efforts. The Food Administration, headed by Iowan Herbert Hoover, also encouraged the increased production of foodstuffs. This agency achieved its goals through public campaigns, which asked American families to consume less wheat and sugar, eliminate waste, grow gardens, and use homemade soap. The government urged people to eat potatoes instead of grains and avoid a "fourth meal" at social functions hosted by clubs or fraternal organizations. Iowa's hotels and restaurants took part in the food conservation campaign by not serving meat or wheat on some days. Sugar was provided only on request and limited to one teaspoon per person. Hotels and restaurants limited customers to two ounces of wheat bread, a half-ounce of butter, and a half-ounce of cheddar cheese. Businesses that used too much sugar could lose their access to this rationed commodity. Serious violations of federal rules led to temporary closures of merchants, with a contribution to the Red Cross paid in lieu of a fine.[7]

The northern Iowa town of Estherville provides an example of American support for the war effort. Fifty-three men from the town volunteered for duty within a week of the country's entry into the conflict. A total of 612 men from Estherville served, with 1,284 registering for the draft. Local civilians tried to make the war more bearable for those in the military by giving time and money to the Red Cross. Women knitted 87 sweaters and sewed 678 handkerchiefs and 225 shirts in four months, while the YMCA in the town raised $10,000 for the Red Cross in one campaign. The citizens of Emmet County, where Estherville was located, bought $2,650,000 in war bonds. Some borrowed money from local banks to buy bonds. These bonds often paid less in interest than banks charged to make loans. But individuals and businesses bought them anyway. Farmers plowed up meadows and pastures to bring more acreage into production.[8]

The war was financed through new taxes and by the sale of war bonds. The conflict cost $35.5 billion, with Liberty Loans (war bonds) raising $21.4 billion. Increased taxes paid for the remainder. The Woodrow

Wilson administration consistently promoted bonds to small investors, desiring the enthusiastic participation of most Americans in the war effort. Newspaper advertising encouraged bond sales with catchy phrases such as "If you can't enlist—invest!" Americans were urged to buy bonds "till you feel the pinch of buying." Iowa's population was largely rural and spread across the countryside, isolated by poor transportation and communication networks. The government worried that a dispersed agricultural population would not be interested in such purchases. Fortunately, high prices left the state's farm families better off than before the war. Bonds sold in amounts as low as $50, with interest rates of 3.5 percent at the start of the war; rates increased as the war continued. Interest was exempt from all taxes except the inheritance tax, which affected only the wealthiest. Nationwide drives to buy bonds featured religious and political leaders, as well as movie stars. In another effort to boost sales, information about the bonds was provided in thirty-three foreign languages.[9]

The Federal Reserve set quotas for the sale of Liberty Loans for states, counties, and cities. Those who invested too little faced hostility from their neighbors. Iowans responded with enthusiasm to loan drives later in the war, being the first state in the country to reach its quota in the third and fourth campaigns. The first two loan drives fell short of mandated goals, though, with Story County only meeting one-third of its quota. Businesses, government, media, and neighbors pressured people to buy. Local committees, usually made up of bankers, helped decide how much each family needed to purchase. This was based upon income, investments, and savings. In Linn County, families were asked to purchase an amount equal to 2 percent of the value of their real estate. Those who did not quickly buy their allotment of bonds were called before a "loyalty" or "slacker" court, a group of local men who asserted jurisdiction over such matters and forced compliance with quotas. Such "courts" had no legal authority. But they collected information from banks and neighbors to determine who was not buying enough bonds. The Pottawatomie County court "redeemed" 447 "slackers" and those judged as pro-German. The Scott County "Liberty Loan Court" interviewed more than one thousand men and gained an additional $600,000 in bond sales. Individuals judged as insufficiently patriotic could have their names posted in towns. A yellow "slacker board" stood in the main square in Estherville with the names of those who had bought smaller amounts of bonds than demanded. Occasionally, threats such as arson or the loss of a job motivated some to invest in the war effort.[10]

Wartime propaganda pushed the need for national unity and patriotism. The federal Committee on Public Information (CPI) was responsible for mobilizing American support for the war. It used films, literature, and "Four Minute Men" to help secure popular support for the conflict. Publications from the CPI included pamphlets such as "German Plots and Intrigues" and "Why America Fights Germany." The federal government sponsored lectures by "Four Minute Men," who briefly spoke about the need to buy war bonds, conserve food, or register for the draft. They often talked to audiences watching movies—it took about four minutes to change movie reels, which gave this group their name. Speakers gave a presentation in Ottumwa between wrestling matches. The woman's division sent female speakers to women's groups and churches. In Scott County, about sixty "dependable" men, such as ministers and lawyers, made up the ranks of the organization. They also wrote articles supporting the war for local newspapers. In Maquoketa, the chairman of the local Four Minute Men organization provided material for newspapers to publish. Nationwide at least 75,000 speakers talked to 314 million people.[11]

Overzealous patriotism and the intolerance of foreigners undermined civil liberties in Iowa. Wartime hysteria demanded 100 percent Americanism. Immigrants and those who spoke German, or who espoused any sympathy for the Central Powers, were forced to demonstrate their patriotism. Some German Americans, suspected of disloyalty, were forced to kiss the American flag, or kneel before it. Intimidation and physical violence were used to enforce bond purchases or draft registration. Those who did not quickly register with their local draft board might find their names published in their local paper as a draft dodger. Students at Davenport High School burned all the German books in their school library. Noncitizens had to turn in all weapons to police. The "American Protective League" investigated thousands suspected of disloyalty in Iowa, searching for spies, slackers, or the unpatriotic without success. Iowa governor William L. Harding issued a proclamation—known as the "Babel Proclamation"—on May 23, 1918, banning the use of any foreign language in all public spaces, including churches, schools, or even funerals. Danish, Dutch, and Norwegian communities were outraged to be seen as a danger, even while speaking languages of nations allied to the United States. Of all the states, only Iowa had such a strict ban, which led to the closure of many private schools, churches, and newspapers, some permanently. Condemnation of the governor's edict did not stop enforcement. Five German-speaking women were fined $225 (about $3,870 in 2020) for talking in a foreign language on a shared telephone line. One Iowan was convicted of violating the Espionage Act. Reverend William Schumann of Pomeroy was jailed for two years for criticizing the war and liberty bond campaigns.[12]

The anti-German frenzy had a devastating effect on German cultural institutions in Iowa and the United States. It led to the closing of German newspapers across the country. In Iowa fifteen of twenty-six German papers shut down. German American organizations disbanded or changed their names. Anything German had to be renamed. German measles became liberty measles and sauerkraut became liberty cabbage. The town of Germania, Iowa, changed its name to Lakota. The German Savings Bank in Davenport named itself the American Commercial and Savings bank. Many families changed their last names to sound less foreign, as well. Schmidt became Smith and Koch was changed to Cook, for example. The German language was not taught in elementary schools in Scott County after the war.[13]

The nation faced many challenges in building an army to fight in Europe. The military built training facilities from scratch and found that most of its soldiers knew little about weapons. Equipment shortages left many soldiers without a rifle until they departed for France. Some trained with broomsticks in the place of weapons. Many new soldiers wore their civilian clothes for the first weeks of training due to uniform shortages. Almost one-third of recruits were illiterate. The typical recruit weighed 142 pounds and stood five feet and seven inches tall. Despite insufficient training, a lack of weapons and equipment, and poor leadership, American troops generally fought well. The American role in the war was limited, but it was still bloody. More American troops died in combat in World War I than in the conflicts in Korea or Vietnam.[14]

Iowa hosted training camps for white and Black soldiers, as well as African American officers. Camp Dodge, north of Des Moines, trained tens of thousands of Black and white soldiers during the war. Black officers received training at Fort Des Moines—the only such facility in the country. In October 1917 the first class of 639 officers graduated. They served with the Ninety-Second Division in France. One of them was James B. Morris Sr., who grew up in Atlanta and had a close friend lynched when he was a boy. Morris went to Hampton University in Virginia and earned a law degree at Howard University before coming to Iowa. He passed the Iowa bar exam eight days before he joined the US Army. In France, he wrote, "black

African American army officers received training at Fort Des Moines, the only such facility in the United States. They served with the 92nd Division in France in World War I. Group of Black officers at Camp Dodge, Iowa, 1918. PH1993.31.47, State Historical Society of Iowa, Des Moines.

soldiers were fighting another man's war for the freedom we might never experience." He was badly wounded in November 1918. Morris returned to Des Moines after the war and became a lawyer; he found a resurgent Ku Klux Klan in the state. In 1922 Morris purchased the most important Black newspaper in the state, the *Bystander*. The KKK demanded that he sell it. Armed with shotguns, Morris and his brother chased them off his lawn and threatened to kill anyone who returned. The KKK did not visit him again. He published the paper for almost fifty years, advocating for Black rights for decades, all while keeping his full-time job as a lawyer.[15]

James B. Morris was also a member of the National Association for the Advancement of Colored People (NAACP), one of the most effective organizations fighting discrimination and racism. Morris was president of the Des Moines branch from 1920 to 1923. It led the drive for equality in the state, with legal activism, protests, and education campaigns. The group defended a Black woman who refused to sit in the segregated section of a theater and helped defeat a bill that would have forbidden interracial marriages. Segregation was widespread in Des Moines, like most large northern cities. Blacks and whites rarely mingled and economic opportunities were limited for African Americans. The NAACP challenged housing and employment discrimination. The Des Moines chapter started in 1915, with whites and Blacks as members, including Republican governor George Clarke. Supporters included the editor of the *Des Moines Register*, Harvey Ingham, who criticized the resurgent Klan of the 1920s. Additional branches of the NAACP were established in the 1920s in Council Bluffs, Waterloo, Cedar Rapids, and Davenport.[16]

Between ten thousand and fifteen thousand African American men, mostly from Alabama, trained at Camp Dodge along with many more white troops. The military set up a training base for them in Iowa because the state was more racially tolerant than the South. The NAACP and Black newspapers also pressed the government to open such a facility. Despite this reputation, segregation was common in restaurants, hotels, and theaters in Des Moines. Black conscripts were kept in southern parts of the camp, segregated from white troops. Discipline was swift and harsh. When three Black men were suspected of raping a white woman, they were quickly hanged before the forty-three thousand soldiers at the camp. The event horrified soldiers of both races. Iowa's Black soldiers eventually joined the Ninety-Second Division in France, which was mostly used for work behind the lines. Some men experienced combat, where they fought well, despite inadequate training and a lack of equipment.[17]

The first American units began to arrive in France in the summer of 1917, but significant numbers of troops did not appear until the next year. In between, the military situation deteriorated for the Allies. In November 1917 Vladimir Lenin seized power in Russia and signed a peace treaty with the Central Powers, removing Russia from the war. This allowed more than one million German troops from the eastern front to move west. Germany hoped to win the war with a submarine assault on shipping, as well as a massive spring offensive in 1918.[18]

Merle Hay, from Glidden, was one of the first Americans killed during the war. He was also the first Iowan to die in the conflict. Hay was born in 1896 and the eldest of three children. He quit his job repairing farm equipment in Coon Rapids and enlisted a month after the United States entered the war. Eight Glidden men, including Hay, enlisted in May 1917. His unit joined the front lines that fall. In the early morning of November 3, 1917, Hay and two other American soldiers were killed during a German raid. He posthumously won the French Croix de Guerre. His body was returned to the United States in 1921. Only two of the eight men who joined the military with him returned alive from the war. A granite monument in his honor sits in his hometown, about sixty miles west of Ames.[19]

One unit, full of Iowans, experienced sustained combat in 1918 in France. The 168th Infantry Regiment was an Iowa National Guard detachment that became part of the "Rainbow Division." The division received

Merle Hay was one of the first Americans killed in World War I. A monument in his honor sits in his hometown of Glidden. Merle Hay. PH.WWI. CarrollCo.19, World War One Casualties Collection, State Historical Society of Iowa, Des Moines.

its name because it was made up of soldiers from more than twenty-five states. They arrived in France in late 1917; elements joined the front lines in early 1918. It was one of the first major American units in combat. They lived in trenches that resembled "a badly drained irrigation ditch," wrote Colonel John Taber, and took shelter from artillery barrages in gloomy, damp dugouts. Soldiers were often infested with lice. Tangled masses of rusted barbed wire separated them from a barren no-man's land that existed between German and Allied troops. Snipers and heavy shelling provided a constant threat. Everyone feared a gas attack. Hours of intense artillery bombardment sent them into shelters sixty feet underground. Men crowded together in darkness, unable to even turn around. Some fainted, while the wounded gasped for air. Above ground there was little rest. "A nervous burst of machine gun fire, the boom of a grenade down the line, the crack of a rifle"—such sounds accompanied life in trenches between raids and artillery barrages. The German spring offensive was halted, thanks in part to American soldiers such as those in the Rainbow Division.[20]

The second half of the year would be far bloodier. The 168th and the Rainbow Division took part in an allied counterattack in 1918 after the failure of the German offensive. In July three days of fighting killed or wounded half of the regiment. "Men were torn and blown to atoms before the eyes of their comrades," Taber wrote. Soldiers spent cold nights in foxholes filled by rain, kept awake by the crackle of machine guns and the boom of artillery. "When we had completed the heartbreaking task of conquering one hill, there was always another one in front of it," he wrote. The regiment lost 1,175 men in October, as allied lines moved forward. Corporal Fred H. Takes, a soldier in the Eighty-Second Division, recorded in his diary that his company only had 16 of its original 220 men left by early November. Iowan Arthur Zelle penned a letter to a cousin three days before the war ended saying he had "some awful experiences. I had thought quite often that the Germans would get me, but I got out of it every time. I called on our good Lord many a time and He sure was with me for my comrades were falling on both sides of me." By November, the German retreat had turned into a rout. Some days the 168th advanced mostly unopposed. Fred Takes recalled that church bells were ringing shortly after eleven a.m. on the day the war ended. Some French men celebrated, throwing their caps in the air. "We knew the war was over and we expected to see home again," he wrote in weary gratitude. Iowa soldier Ernest F. Merkles, serving with the 168th, did not survive the war, however. The son of German immigrants, he was killed in July 1918 at the age of nineteen.[21]

Even before the war ended a new enemy was attacking humans around the world—an influenza outbreak killed between fifty and one hundred million people worldwide. It took the lives of about 675,000 Americans, including 7,700 in Iowa. This epidemic, which probably originated in pigs in western Kansas, spread across the world in 1918 and 1919. This particular influenza virus mutated sometime in 1918 after being transmitted to Europe—it came roaring back to the United States that autumn. The disease was devastatingly lethal. "In the U.S. at least a quarter of the population was infected, and, in the military, an even higher proportion became ill," wrote historian Gerald N. Grob. Dorothy Unmack's whole family fell ill—her brother Roy with a 105-degree temperature. She remembered her father kneeling by her brother's bed and praying for him. "We all survived that winter," she wrote in her memoir. Young people were hit the hardest and almost as many military personnel died from the virus as had died in battle. At Camp Dodge almost half of the men were sick in the fall. In some towns, city councils ordered all schools, churches, and movie theaters shut. Businesses reduced their hours, and the football season was delayed; schools were turned into temporary hospitals in Des Moines. People wore "flu masks" made of gauze to try and prevent infection. Beulah Marie Lucas wrote in her diary that people avoided gathering in large groups. In December 1918 she caught the flu. She was in bed for eight days, too weak to "stay on my feet for any length of time." Lucas was fortunate—she lived in Pocahontas until she died at age ninety-one. Doctors could do little but ask patients to stay in bed, keep warm, and hope. Some Iowans were skeptical of the death toll. Business and labor groups protested public health measures and people refused to wear masks. By the summer of 1919 the third wave of the contagion had subsided. Americans became weary of the emergency. Few took precautions when a new variant emerged in 1920, which was "lethal enough that it should have counted as a fourth wave," argued historian John M. Barry. Fortunately, the virus mutated into a seasonal influenza and deaths fell to prepandemic levels by 1921.[22]

The Red Cross gave whatever assistance it could to combat the influenza outbreak. It sent out 140 nurses in October and November 1918 to help stricken Iowans, both military and civilian. In Waterloo, 36 women provided 860 hours of service as drivers, ferrying people to and from hospitals and homes. At Camp Dodge, thirty cars driven by female Red Cross volunteers carried five thousand to six thousand people a day to hospitals, often working sixteen hours a day. When a patient died, female volunteers opened their homes to bereaved families, often cooking them meals, as well as arranging for the transfer of remains. The motor pool helped many parents see their son before he died, ferrying them from hotels to barracks. Volunteers also made phone calls on behalf of the sick. Female drivers made thousands of trips in Iowa, bringing blankets, meals, and supplies to suffering men and taking doctors and nurses to patients, even while they were sick themselves.[23]

By the end of the war, Iowa native Herbert Hoover had gained renown nationwide for his administrative and humanitarian efforts during the war and after. Hoover was born in West Branch in 1874. He was orphaned as a young boy and often hungry. A keen student despite his poverty and lack of education, he was admitted to the first class of Stanford students. He earned a degree in geology and became an engineer. Intelligence and relentless determination, along with a bit of luck, led him to become a mining engineer for a company in Australia, even though he was only twenty-two with little work experience. The previously poor orphan thrived over the following decades, his obsession with work and cold demeanor serving him well in business. He became a talented manager, extracting efficiency from his employees by firing those who went on strike. Hoover traveled endlessly, living in China and England and inspecting mines from Burma to Egypt. By the time World War I erupted, he was worth at least $4 million, equivalent to more than $100 million in 2020. As already mentioned, he led the Food Administration during the war and organized food relief for Europe, helping to save millions of lives. When the Republicans won the presidency in 1920, he became secretary of commerce. In 1928 he was elected president, the only Iowan to ever hold the highest office in the country.[24]

But even the genius of Herbert Hoover could not help the American farmer after the war ended. The collapse of farm prices after the conflict brought an end to the booming agricultural sector in Iowa. Demand for corn, wheat, and pork during the war had kept prices high. Money flowed into the wallets of farm families. They brought marginal land into production to meet wartime needs or bought additional property. "This boom was soon felt in the prices of farm products and ultimately in the price of farmlands," wrote Lonzo Jones. Farm income doubled in six years, but mortgage debt doubled as well. Land increased in value in some places in Iowa from $82 an acre to $400. But the wartime boom collapsed.[25]

Iowa and other farming areas fell into a prolonged economic recession that lasted throughout the 1920s. The federal government kept wheat prices artificially high for eighteen months after the war ended in November 1918. Surplus grain went overseas to feed the hungry recovering from the conflict. But in early 1920 the government removed price supports and commodity prices plummeted by two-thirds by mid-1921. Export markets dwindled, as the world slowly recovered from the Great War. Prohibition undermined the demand for barley. Farm prices fell further, pushed down by bumper crops in the early 1920s. Land prices plummeted, too. Farmers could not pay the debts that they had incurred during wartime. By 1921 farm journals carried bankruptcy guides. Almost one million families across the country lost their land. "As far as I was concerned, the twenties were hard times. The thirties were many times worse," wrote Allen Gregory, who lived near Harlan.[26]

The instability of the war years contributed to the brief success of the Socialist Party in Iowa. In April 1920 Davenport elected a socialist mayor and a socialist city council majority. Surprisingly, this came in the aftermath of the Russian Revolution and amid an anticommunist hysteria. This was no radical departure from American politics in the early twentieth century.

The labor leader Eugene V. Debs ran as the Socialist Party candidate and received almost one million votes in the 1912 presidential election. The socialists successfully fielded candidates in twelve hundred elections nationwide. Campaigning on a local platform of increased teacher pay, free textbooks, and lower streetcar fares, the socialists of Davenport benefited from the votes of Germans, who were driven away from the usual political parties by wartime intolerance and anti-immigrant frenzy. Their mayoral candidate was also a popular doctor. A postwar recession forced the socialists to raise taxes and cut infrastructure spending; their ambitious agenda of the nationalization of private resources was never enacted at the local, state, or national level. Charges of waste and corruption also hurt their chances at reelection in Davenport. In 1922 they lost power, never to regain it in the state.[27]

The 1920s brought major changes to daily life, especially in rural areas. While Iowa escaped widespread industrial strikes and the terrible racial violence that plagued other parts of the country, it did experience profound upheaval. Iowans eagerly bought automobiles and the new form of transportation began to reshape their lives. People in towns and on farms went to movies for entertainment and eagerly listened to their new radios. The struggle over Prohibition and the Klan threatened Iowa, as well.[28]

William Ashley "Billy" Sunday was a representative of the rural and small-town order that seemed threatened by a modernizing America. He was a highly successful, flamboyant, and controversial preacher who became a national sensation in the early twentieth century. Sunday preached to anywhere between eighty to one hundred million Americans over his career. He had been born near Ames in 1862 to a poor family; his father was killed in the Civil War and his mother placed him in an orphanage. Sunday worked as a farmhand and at a furniture store, joining a local baseball team where his exceptional athletic skills gained attention. He was recruited by Adrian Anson, captain of the Chicago White Stockings, and played major league baseball for eight years. A religious conversion led him to Christian evangelism, which became his life's work. His charisma and vigor drew audiences, as did he plain-spoken, folksy manner. He "shouted, laughed, stormed, sweated," wrote Robert F. Martin, and preached against the evils of drinking, gambling, greed, and laziness, which he viewed as threats to the family, church, and community. Sunday spoke to millions in the 1910s, arguing that older and traditional values still mattered, even as a rapidly changing culture and society seemed to leave many behind. In the 1920s his crowds grew smaller, and his message seemed less relevant, as Americans became more comfortable with a more urban and mobile society of mass entertainment and improved transportation. He died in 1935.[29]

Prohibition was the not the success that its supporters had hoped for. The production, transport, and sale of alcohol were banned by the Eighteenth Amendment, but all its ingredients were widely available. Home consumption was still legal. Americans could easily brew their own beer or make their own gin. Whiskey could be made with a few pieces of equipment, as well as grain, yeast, water, and sugar. In the Iowa town of Templeton, almost every family was involved in producing the famous rye whiskey named for the place. Elsewhere, men sold half-pint bottles at dances, recalled Gerald Goodwin. He was afraid to drink it though, as homemade liquor "was made in the most unsanitary conditions." In eastern Iowa, illegal alcohol producers and distributors known as bootleggers provided their product to customers in milk cans painted white. In Estherville, suppliers left booze near designated fence posts; locations were revealed to customers after payment. Alcohol could also be easily found at local speakeasies or underground bars. And because other countries did not ban alcohol, organized crime made vast sums of money from the smuggling or production of liquor. The amount of money provided to enforce Prohibition was meager and enforcement usually a failure. Repeal came in 1933.[30]

The KKK experienced a revival in the United States and Iowa in the 1920s. The Klan had been created after the Civil War to enforce white supremacy in the South. In Iowa, its rebirth stemmed from white resistance to immigration and cultural change. Members may have also feared the loss of economic status due to the long recession of the decade. The "second Klan" of the 1920s organized as opponents of foreigners, African Americans, Catholics, and Jews. Members swore allegiance to "100 percent Americanism" and promised to fight immigration and uphold prohibition. The Klan was popular and had millions of members. Newspaper editor James B. Morris Sr. estimated that the Klan had one hundred thousand members in Iowa, but forty thousand was probably closer to the actual number. Their targets in Iowa included Catholics, who were thought to support bootlegging, as well as immigrants. The KKK burned crosses, staged marches, and intimidated and terrorized many. Three thousand members marched in Des Moines in June 1926. Fifteen thousand rallied in the town of Perry in 1924. They managed to divide communities, but their influence in Iowa was fortunately brief and, as far as we know, nonfatal.

The Klan dominated the town of Argyle in southeast Iowa, controlling local businesses and influencing local politics. Farmers who refused to join were beaten, as were local Catholics. One member in central Iowa wrote to his girlfriend, complaining of squabbling and disorganization among his klavern (local unit). The second Klan collapsed in the late 1920s after a series of scandals involving its leaders, including rape and murder.[31]

The Klan did not focus its attention upon Iowa's African Americans, whose numbers were small. Indeed, they comprised less than 1 percent of the total state population until 1970. In 1900 Iowa only had about ten thousand Black residents. This number almost doubled by 1920, as increased employment opportunities, as well as the demand for wartime workers, drew migrants. Most African Americans in Iowa had to work in low-paying jobs, with women laboring as maids and cooks and men working as porters or janitors. But railroads, manufacturers, and meatpacking plants accepted more Black workers in the early twentieth century. Some came to Iowa to work for the Illinois Central Railroad, following the railroad route from Mississippi to the Midwest. In Sioux City, African Americans made up almost half of the employees in meatpacking plants in the mid-1920s. Men worked the killing floor in these places in hot, bloody, and nauseating conditions. Almost one thousand workers at the Rock Island Arsenal in 1918 were Black. A John Deere factory in Waterloo employed African Americans. Women were custodians, while men had the most hazardous and exhausting jobs in the foundry. Generally, while Iowa was not a racial paradise, it was better than the South.[32]

Iowa also attracted other immigrant groups, who began to move to the state in increasing numbers in the 1910s and 1920s, drawn by employment opportunities and pushed out of their homeland by a civil war. A tiny population of Mexicans lived in Iowa in the late 1800s—the census only counted twenty-nine in 1900—but their numbers increased in the early twentieth century. They came to Iowa to work on farms and railroads, fleeing the bloodshed of the Mexican Revolution and limited economic opportunities. A labor shortage during World War I helped draw Mexican immigrants to Iowa and the United States; families followed men to the state. David Macias left Zacatecas, Mexico, and came to live in Bettendorf in 1914. His brother Manuel Macias followed, as did other Mexican workers. Many Mexican migrants to Iowa had lived in Texas and suffered from the ugly racial repression and segregation of that state. They did not escape such discrimination in Iowa, but their small numbers and recent arrival provoked less backlash from the white population than they experienced in Texas. By 1920 Iowa had more than twenty-five hundred Mexican inhabitants.[33]

Mexican immigrants lived in difficult circumstances and usually worked the toughest jobs. Laborers often came to Iowa on work contracts and could be deported if they quit their jobs. The US Department of Labor often restricted them to agricultural employment and ensured that they could not become American citizens. In such circumstances, they could be easily exploited by the businesses that hired them. Mexicans lived in towns and cities, usually in areas with other immigrants. Men worked as farm laborers, completed railroad maintenance, or toiled in meatpacking or brick factories. David Macias came to work for a factory in Bettendorf, losing his left arm in a near-fatal accident. Magdaleno and Maria Cano came to Iowa in 1927 with their three children, having left Guanajuato, Mexico, to work in the United States. They lived with another Mexican family until Magdaleno found employment with the Rock Island Railroad. The Canos lived in a boxcar by the railroad tracks until the family moved to Iowa City; they had trouble finding a place to live, as whites discriminated against them. Magdaleno and Maria had six more children, became American citizens, and bought a home. Maria worked as a seamstress. Other Mexican immigrants worked in sugar beet fields in northern Iowa or southern Minnesota. They also worked as day laborers, hoping for temporary employment.[34]

Mexican families lived in shacks, cottages, and railroad boxcars in the neighborhoods of Holy City in Bettendorf and Cook's Point in Davenport. Other Mexican immigrant communities developed in other towns, mostly in eastern Iowa. The Bettendorf Company, which supplied manufactured goods for railroads, provided primitive housing for some of its workers. The neighborhood of Holy City grew in Bettendorf, where Ernest Rodriquez wrote that living conditions were "austere," which was a polite way of noting the difficult circumstances that Mexican immigrants confronted. Rodriquez and his sister Patricia were born in a boxcar converted into housing. Bathing was done in the river and toilets consisted of community outhouses, he recalled. There was no electricity or running water—coal for stoves was often taken from freight trains. The first homes in Cook's Point were built about 1916 on an empty two-acre lot bordering the Mississippi River. By 1927 about 100 people lived there; this number increased to about 270 by 1949. A community faucet provided water;

residents chipped ice from it in the winter. Families usually did not have access to electricity or running water at Cook's Point. They used kerosene lamps for lighting and stoves for heating. There were no paved streets or sidewalks. Women and children spent much of their time hauling water for cooking and bathing. Limited to domestic labor by racial and gender discrimination, women usually worked in the informal economy. They supplemented family income by taking in boarders or by doing laundry or sewing; some also raised chickens and pigs, grew gardens, and sold eggs for extra income. Farm work paid little and wages fell during the 1920s. Unlike earlier waves of immigrants, few Mexican families could accumulate capital to buy their own land. They lived in some of the worst and most challenging circumstances in the state. Still, despite being denied opportunity and equality, scores of men from Cook's Point and Holy City fought for the United States in World War II.[35]

Immigrants also came from the Middle East. An orphaned boy in Syria, Salom Rizk, discovered that his mother had been an American citizen and spent years trying to come to Iowa to join family members. He lived in Syria with his grandmother after the death of his mother. Then his grandmother also died and Salom was left a "ragged half-starved orphan," with no shoes and no kin in a war-torn country. He learned from a teacher that he was an American citizen, as his mother had been one. Rizk spent five years trying to get documents to prove his citizenship, working at a hotel for three dollars a month. In 1927 he made it to Sioux City, where he stayed with his brother and labored in a meatpacking plant, as a peddler, and as a dishwasher. The young man was amazed at the bounty and wealth of the United States. Rizk followed a friend to Ames and began fourth grade at the age of twenty; he was astonished that his education was free. A semester later he had advanced to the ninth grade and later opened a shoe store. By the mid-1930s he was giving lectures about his immigrant experience in Iowa. He eventually toured around the country, giving patriotic speeches about his beloved United States. *Reader's Digest* magazine hired him to give lectures in American schools in the 1940s and he eventually gave speeches before about one million schoolchildren in nearly fifteen hundred schools. While emphasizing the virtues of his new home, he warned that racial arrogance, national pride, and militarism could endanger the United States.[36]

Muslim immigrants from Syria, Jordan, Lebanon, and other countries in the Middle East built a mosque in Cedar Rapids. The first immigrant

Muslims may have come to the city as early as 1885. But it is more likely they first arrived at the start of the twentieth century. Some were grocers, others were farmers. Many such early immigrants were single men who came to the United States seeking economic opportunity. They often worked as peddlers in the Midwest. Others came to the region from South Asia or Bosnia. Arab Christians had also come to Iowa and their Muslim friends and family followed. Many Muslim communities did not have enough money to establish a mosque and met in private homes, restaurants, or rented buildings. Some of the first known mosques in the United States were in North Dakota, Indiana, and Michigan in the 1920s. Funds to build the Cedar Rapids structure were raised from Muslim communities across the country and from community dinners. Muslims helped build the St. George Orthodox Church in Cedar Rapids and Christians helped build the mosque in return. Construction finished in 1935. It is commonly known today known as the Mother Mosque. Tradition claims that it was the first structure built specifically as a mosque in the United States, but Muslims in North Dakota built one several years earlier. The faithful worshipped at the mosque in Cedar Rapids for decades until they moved to the new Islamic Center in Cedar Rapids. It was renovated in the early 1990s and became a cultural center and offered services once more.[37]

Automobiles brought greatly increased mobility for Iowans who could afford them, but early cars provided many challenges for their owners. The first autos were primitive, often unreliable, and open to the weather. Such vehicles could only be "used when road conditions were good," wrote Kenneth Hassebrock, who was a child living near Lakota, in north-central Iowa, in the 1920s. Travel could be unpleasant, with gravel roads developing a washboard surface that "induces a maximum impact on the rear end," he added. Clouds of dust and small stones kicked up by passing cars rained down on passengers. Windshields could shatter when hit by larger rocks. A 1904 rural speed limit was set at twenty miles per hour—driving over forty-five miles per hour was not recommended. Long trips required advance planning, as restaurants and gas stations could be rare. Drivers often had to ask for directions to the next town, as road signs did not exist, wrote Keith Graham. H. E. Wilkinson recalled that roads were so bad that a rainstorm could strand travelers away from home overnight until roads dried out. "The natural course of human events dictated that the act of getting stuck to be reserved for those trips where all passengers were dressed in their Sunday clothes," noted Hassebrock. For example, traveling with a friend named Herndon, George B. Hippee suffered from deep mud, flat tires, and breakdowns on a trip from Des Moines to Spirit Lake in 1905, which took four days. "If I had not sworn so much, I would not have been so tired. I would swear awhile and then Herndon would swear awhile, but we were both justified in it." Enterprising farmers charged one dollar, or more, to help retrieve vehicles stuck in the mud, often with the help of horses.[38]

When they weren't stuck in the mud, autos reduced the obstacle of time and distance for rural folk. They were quite useful for a dispersed rural population, which often lived ten or more miles from the nearest town. In 1905 there were 1,573 registered cars in the state. But car ownership spread quickly. In Greene County, about one in five families owned an auto in 1920. Farm families found that autos allowed them to easily market crops, visit doctors or neighbors, or travel to nearby towns for entertainment, shopping, or school. Elizabeth R. Miller wrote that her family could reach the nearest town, which was seven miles away, in only twenty minutes by car. Driving a horse took ninety minutes. Farmers used vehicles to take commodities to market. Cars might tow a trailer full of goods to town. One eleven-year-old boy used the family auto to deliver milk in Jefferson. Many grocery stores delivered to their customers who lived in town. This was usually not an option for those who lived away from cities and towns. With a car, families had greater access to foods not produced on their farm, often at lower prices.[39]

The famous Model T, produced by Ford Motor Company, helped make car ownership available to millions of families. More than half the cars sold in the United States in 1923 were Model Ts. It was a sturdy, generally reliable, and affordable vehicle for Americans. It was easy to service, and parts could be purchased through mail order catalogs. Ford dealers and service stations were found in hundreds of locations, many of them in small towns. By 1926 93 percent of farm families in Iowa had cars, a higher percentage than in urban areas. Keith Graham's father bought an early Model T for less than $400 in 1913. (A $350 expense that year was equal to about $9,440 in 2020 dollars.) While the vehicle made their lives much easier, its peculiar design made for some occasional odd driving. The car's gas tank fed the engine by gravity—on steep hills the fuel could not reach the carburetor. Drivers sometimes had to back up a hill to ensure that fuel reached the engine.[40]

In 1924 eight Iowa women drove across the American West, traveling more than nine thousand miles in nine weeks. This group, mostly teachers

Des Moines was a thriving city of 142,559 people in 1930 and had not yet suffered the worst of the Great Depression. View of downtown Des Moines near Grand Avenue and Highway 65, 1930. PH1988.23.2107, Des Moines Pioneer Club Collection, State Historical Society of Iowa, Des Moines.

who had grown up on farms, bought two Model Ts and packed them with tents, cots, fishing gear, and other equipment. They took turns driving, fixed flat tires, and stayed in campgrounds in about a dozen states. Gas was ten cents a gallon. In Wyoming, they found "sagebrush and more sagebrush." But they marveled at Yosemite National Park and the deep indigo blue of Crater Lake in Oregon. The group took dusty roads past lumber camps in the Pacific Northwest, hiking to a glacier at Mount Rainier National Park. They headed home in August, passing through Yellowstone, where bears stalked through their campsite. Of all the roads they encountered on their trip, the roads were the worst in Iowa, where summer rains turned dirt into sticky troughs of mud. They encountered no problems on their adventure. The love of travel stuck with one woman in the group, Marie, who lived in Mexico, toured Europe, and lived in Egypt for three years. She also earned an MA from Columbia University and taught at the teacher's college in Cedar Falls.[41]

Cars did more than move much faster than horses—they began to reshape the commercial and social landscape of Iowa. (They also did not leave manure behind.) Vehicles freed urban residents from the tyranny of set travel schedules of streetcars or trains. Cars allowed rural families to venture away from their nearby communities or their local general store. Businesses in small towns and at crossroads began to decline as autos encouraged journeys farther from home. Improved highways allowed families to travel to Des Moines for shopping. New businesses appeared in cities, including auto repair shops, auto parts stores, and car dealerships. Rural institutions, such as one-room schoolhouses, suffered when students left for larger schools with more resources. Fewer people went to church when families went on Sunday drives. The automobile helped to transform daily life in Iowa and other rural states throughout the twentieth century.[42]

More cars meant a demand for better roads, which were quite terrible during this time period. They were usually dirt and passable only in good weather. Iowa had more than 102,000 miles of roads in 1904, with less than 2 percent improved with gravel or other rock. A road trip from Clinton to Chicago took nine hours in 1904. The journey included 101 miles of near-death experiences on rocky roads, which were often interrupted by herds of cattle. A passenger noted, "A succession of hair-breadth escapes forces on you the conviction that you were not born to die so soon." Ruth Wenger wrote that it took her family a whole day to travel 130 miles from Winterset to Waterloo. Eula Van Meter's family took a trip from Iowa to California in 1915. Directions west from Iowa City included following a trolley line and turning right at a gymnasium. Iowa state law delegated road maintenance to the most local level in some places until the 1920s. Townships and counties built and maintained roads, with rural residents paying a road tax. This levy was often paid when people completed road work, usually close to their own property. Men might haul gravel or level a stretch of a dirt road. Such local institutions could not handle increasing traffic and maintenance costs.[43]

The American government began to spend money to deal with the growing problem of inadequate road networks. The Federal Highway Act of 1916 provided federal money to match state spending—it spent $75 million in its first five years. States spent an equal amount. Iowa received $146,200 in the first year and $731,000 in 1920. Concerns about national defense after World War I brought new spending. In 1919 an army convoy, which included an unknown officer named Dwight D. Eisenhower, took two months to travel across the country. The convoy spent a week in late

July in Iowa, visiting towns from Clinton to Denison. It made a detour to visit Merle Hay's hometown of Glidden. Dry weather sped their progress, even if it left men covered in dust. This trip highlighted the poor condition of American roads. New taxes on gasoline—sometimes as high as three cents a gallon—paid for improved roads. Iowa paved fifty-nine hundred miles of road and placed gravel on a similar distance of dirt roads. By 1930 a vehicle could travel from Des Moines to all ninety-nine county seats on paved roads.[44]

The Lincoln Highway, which runs across Iowa from the Mississippi River to the Missouri River, was a segment of a transcontinental highway that stretched from New York City to San Francisco. In 1913 the road was named after Abraham Lincoln, to help gain support for its creation. Supporters debated routes, raised money, and got states to promise aid. But the Lincoln highway consisted of barely linked dirt and gravel roads. While World War I interrupted any grand plans for a transcontinental road, in the 1920s construction on the Lincoln Highway took off as the country fell into a road-building frenzy. The highway ran from Clinton on the Mississippi River to Council Bluffs in the west, passing through Cedar Rapids, Marshalltown, Ames, Jefferson, and other towns. At first, the highway was mostly mud, dirt, and gravel, with limited sections that were paved. Still, by the late 1920s the Lincoln Highway was mostly paved and well-marked across Iowa.[45]

If the introduction of cars and paved roads revolutionized transportation, radio was a revolution in entertainment, even if it did not radically reshape life like automobiles. It brought music, news, sports, drama, comedy, and politics directly into people's homes far quicker than newspapers could. Americans learned more about the world and could immediately follow sporting events or listen to concerts. By 1922 more than five hundred stations were on the air. Iowa farmers gathered around a radio at a local gas station to listen to boxing matches or baseball games, wrote Robert Stech. Margaret Ott Onerheim remembered her family's first radio, which they bought in 1928. It filled a corner of their living room, and its battery was as large as the one found in their car. The battery ran low regularly and had to be taken to town to be recharged. Her family listened to music from station WOI in Ames in the morning; in the afternoons they caught a station from South Dakota, which played "the music of a little-known band led by Lawrence Welk," she recalled. In the evenings the family sat around a table with a kerosene lamp and read the newspaper, finished homework, or wrote letters. By 1930 more than twelve million families owned radios, out of the thirty million families in the country.[46]

While families often listened to the radio for news and entertainment, they began to visit movie theaters more often. Films became longer and more complex in the 1910s, with comedies and cowboy films being staples of the early industry. Everett Ludley, who lived in Manchester, remembered a serial called the *Hooded Terror*, where a villain tried to kidnap an unsuspecting heroine, who was rescued by a dashing hero. The Keystone Cops or Fatty Arbuckle, staples of early silent films, usually followed. Half of the theaters in the country were in small towns. The movie theater was often the most impressive building in such places. Virgil Lagomarcino fondly wrote of the one movie theater in Waverly as an "exciting place even before the day dawned when actor's voices could be heard." Dialogue appeared between scenes on screen; the climax of a movie was heightened by live organ music from a local musician. Lagomarcino recalled that films were mostly silent in small town Iowa in the 1920s. Iowans flocked to movies, which provided a cheap escape. Mexicans and African Americans in Iowa sat in segregated balconies in movie theaters in Des Moines, recalled John Ortega.[47]

Daily life on Iowa's many farms did not change as quickly as entertainment did. Work routines had altered little from the mid-nineteenth century, despite the arrival of radio and autos. Ruth Perkins Messenger and her family lived on an eighty-acre farm in Harrison County. She was born in 1899 and was a teacher for three years before her marriage to Franklin Messenger in 1920. A wood-burning stove heated their home and they cut ice from a nearby river to keep perishables cold during the summer. They chopped their wood by hand. Ruth and her husband, Frank, picked their own corn, stacking it up around their children in their horse-drawn wagon. She churned butter and baked bread for the family, caring for two hundred chickens and selling eggs and butter. Ruth canned strawberries and raspberries and tended to a large garden. The family used an outdoor privy. She gave birth to three sons, the first, Donald, weighing ten and a half pounds. In 1942 their farm received electrical power. Ruth Perkins Messenger died in 2000, having lived throughout the twentieth century.[48]

Iowa looked more like the world that we live in today by the end of the 1920s, with paved roads full of automobiles and urban areas with movie theaters. World War I had brought general prosperity but unleashed a war hysteria and shameful intolerance. The state suffered from an extended agricultural downturn after the end of the conflict, even as new technology radically reshaped daily life. Opportunities for entertainment had expanded with radio and movies. The arrival of the automobile heralded great social dislocations in the future, while providing improved transport. The temporary rebirth of the Klan had brought crime and violence to the state, as had the prohibition on alcohol. The stock market crash of late 1929 ended fifteen years of tremendous social and economic change and ushered in a decade that tested all Americans.

PART THREE
IOWA SINCE 1929

11
The Great Depression and Iowa

Iowans suffered terribly during the Great Depression, which followed almost a decade of economic misery in the state. The stock market crash of 1929 did not solely bring about the depression, but it helped undermine an already fragile economy. The Great Depression had many causes, ranging from a slowing economy to weak manufacturing and financial sectors. Iowa was hit hard by the economic calamity—the banking system in the state collapsed, as did farm prices. Foreclosures and unemployment destroyed lives and bred despair, leading to desperate rural protests. Franklin Roosevelt's election brought the New Deal, stabilized the financial and agricultural sectors, employed tens of thousands of Iowans, and helped bring electricity to many parts of the state. While the New Deal was an incomplete success, it had a profound impact on the lives of most Iowans.

The famous speculative mania of Wall Street in the late 1920s, as well as the long agricultural recession that afflicted rural America in the decade, contributed to the Great Depression. On the surface, the postwar years seemed to be a prosperous, booming time. But income growth had been limited to the wealthiest and millions of families lived near subsistence levels. Late in the decade, the American economy had begun to slow; meanwhile, parts of Europe and Asia fell into recession. In October 1929 the stock market plummeted, after having doubled in value since early 1928. The crash did not create the depression, but it contributed to the economic downturn already in the making. By 1926 auto manufacturing had slowed, as did housing construction. Business inventories rose and consumer demand fell. Even as business slowed, the stock market boomed, fed by easy credit and greed for greater gains. Wall Street's decline in 1929 presaged an overall economic deterioration. Commodity prices crashed. Corn prices fell almost 80 percent in three years. In 1930 the economy contracted by 12.6 percent and unemployment increased.[1]

The nation did not immediately fall into the horrific "hard times" that we associate with the period. Only a couple of million Americans—about 2 percent—had invested in the stock market, so the economic pain was initially limited. But business confidence was damaged and banks reduced credit to cover their losses. The shaky American financial system contributed greatly to this brewing disaster. It had always been unstable. Hundreds of banks had failed each year during the 1920s, wiping out their customers' deposits. Over thirteen hundred banks collapsed in 1930, with more than two thousand failing in 1931. Panicked mobs of depositors besieged banks. As the crisis accelerated in 1930, employers reduced spending and began to lay off workers. Within fifteen months of the October crash, almost three million workers lost their jobs and unemployment approached 9 percent. By late 1931 the economic crisis had turned into the Great Depression. International commerce collapsed, as nations erected trade barriers to stimulate their own economies, interrupting capital flows. Investors began to withdraw gold from the United States. Attempting to halt the flow of capital out of the country, the Federal Reserve increased interest rates—exactly the opposite of the financial stimulus that the nation needed. The American economy, beset by a myriad of crises, shed millions of workers. More than half of Americans who had jobs worked part time. By March 1933 the financial system had collapsed across most of the country and thirty-four states had closed their banks. Unemployment reached nearly 25 percent in 1933.[2]

President Herbert Hoover struggled unsuccessfully to handle the growing crisis throughout most of his presidency. His conservative political ideology limited his ability to combat the calamity. Hoover's emphasis upon individual effort and his belief that America provided boundless economic opportunity restricted his response. He believed that cooperative endeavor and charitable aid could fight the crisis. He also feared that too much federal aid would undermine the work ethic of Americans. Hoover spent more money on federal construction programs than previous presidents and established the Reconstruction Finance Corporation to assist large businesses and financial institutions. But these measures were not enough. In New York City scores of people starved to death. As the economy contracted and the nation suffered, Hoover gained a reputation as a heartless figure who refused to help millions of Americans in misery.[3]

For many, life had been difficult even before the Depression. One-third of the population of the United States lived in chronic poverty, including almost all nonwhites, most elderly, and millions of rural people. Slim Collier, a bartender from Waterloo, did not live in a house with running water until he was eleven. In the late 1930s Collier and others who were desperate for work gathered at four a.m. in the hopes of being chosen by farmers to labor for fifteen cents an hour. When he joined the army in 1941, he was one of two recruits in his company who had completed the eighth grade. John R. Ortega wrote that his grandmother had died in childbirth in 1927, leaving behind eight children. His family lived in a "drafty shed" in Buffalo Center, where his infant sister Josephine died from pneumonia. Ortega's father did not have the money to buy a casket, so he built one for his daughter. Men at the stockyards in Sioux City worked seven days a week in conditions so cold that their lunches froze solid. Collier told historian Studs Terkel that the once the Depression hit, the "dominant thing was helpless despair and submission. There was anger and rebellion among a few, but, by and large, that quiet desperation and submission."[4]

Neal Smith's family were tenant farmers in Keokuk County in the 1920s and 1930s. His parents had been seriously ill, which left them deep in debt. Almost everyone who lived around him was poor so "we didn't really know how poor we were," he wrote. Fortunately, they lived on a farm, which allowed them to live off their garden, hunt game, and gather berries and walnuts. Tramps visited his family, as there was a railroad nearby. They shared what little they had with these visitors, as did their neighbors. Despite the wandering homeless men, they never locked their doors. Tramps were poor, but they wouldn't steal, he wrote. Smith hunted fox, crows, and gophers for the money the county paid for killing pests. He also hunted rabbits to help feed his family. He didn't shoot every creature though—he had several pet raccoons.[5]

As the economy contracted, the prices of almost everything declined, even as income to purchase them evaporated. Falling commodity prices for farm goods such as corn, pork, and eggs cut family income. In late 1932 a bushel of corn earned a farmer ten cents. Property prices tumbled, leaving many with debts that exceeded the value of their land. The collapsing banking system destroyed savings, eliminated credit for people and businesses, and left the United States with a cash shortage. In some Iowa counties lenders owned almost 30 percent of the farmland, the original owners having lost it after falling behind on payments. Arthur Leaf lost his home, land, livestock, and almost all his possessions in 1930. His church also expelled him. To survive he sold magazine and newspaper subscriptions, tools, groceries, and nursery stock, traveling by car from town to town. His wife, Marie, cared for their children in his absence. He worked on a farm they rented on weekends. Forty years after the Depression, Oscar Heline bitterly remembered the foreclosure process: "First they'd take your farm, then they took your livestock, then your farm machinery. Even your household goods. And they'd move you off." Property prices had been falling since the early 1920s, down almost 70 percent in eastern Johnson County by the middle of the 1930s. In one township in the county, the average sale price fell below one hundred dollars an acre in 1936.[6]

Iowa led the nation in bank failures from 1921 to 1931, with an average of eighty-seven banks failing each year. Almost half of the banks in the state in 1921 had closed or had their assets liquidated by 1933. The state's economy had suffered from low commodity prices since the early 1920s and the depressed agricultural economy strained not only family budgets but also jeopardized the survival of local banks that served the small towns and rural population of the state. Iowa had the largest total mortgage debt in the country—more than twice any other state. This was, in part, due to the increasing cost of land during and immediately after World War I. Land prices had doubled between 1914 and 1920 and the total of mortgage loans had increased by almost as much. A combination of low prices and high debt left Iowans in a precarious economic situation.[7]

Bank deposits fell in Iowa in the 1920s, even as they increased across the country. The failure of Iowa banks cost its citizens $201 million from 1920 to 1930, as depositors were unprotected by any insurance on their accounts. (In 2020 this would be nearly $3 billion.) As the financial system collapsed in the United States generally and in Iowa specifically, people hoarded cash or withdrew their savings. This further undermined the stability of banks. In the first six months of 1932 deposits fell by 17 percent in Iowa. "These were good hard-working people whose entire savings disappeared like smoke," wrote James Hearst. One of Hearst's neighbors killed himself so his family could live off the insurance proceeds. Forty Iowa banks failed in just two days in January 1933. By early 1933 the banking system in Iowa was "essentially bankrupt," wrote historian Calvin W. Coquillette. The state legislature passed, and the governor signed, emergency legislation to slow the banking panic in Iowa. This law allowed banks to restrict withdrawals. By the time Franklin Roosevelt was inaugurated in March 1933, the economy of Iowa had ground to a halt.[8]

In the 1930s the environment seemed to conspire with the Depression to spread misery. The winter of 1935–1936 was the coldest in Iowa in more than a century. Snow fell throughout January and February and high winds piled up snowdrifts. Otto W. Knauth wrote that wild animals, such as skunks, were found frozen to death while standing in open areas. Faye Elsie Tomilinson Wookey recalled that the temperature in February did not rise above zero and that it could fall to twenty-five degrees below zero at night. The town of Red Oak got forty-three inches of snow in January and February. Wookey and her family slept next to their stove. A scorching summer followed the brutal winter. In the summer they slept outside on cots to try and stay cool. It was often more than one hundred degrees during the day. There was no rain and wells went dry. Strong winds brought red dirt from the central plains that covered them while they slept at night. Irma J. Long remembered the hellish summer: "Heat, heat, heat. We have been literally buried in it." The high temperature "stifles and burns and saturates everything." The blistering summer killed more than four hundred Iowans, she wrote. One day the temperature reached 116 degrees.[9]

At this time, most people in Iowa still lived in rural areas. Diaries and letters from the early 1930s revealed how the Depression undermined the ability of Iowa's farm families to make an adequate living. Elmer Powers, who lived in Boone County, expressed the fulfillment that came from farming, writing in his diary, "the farm is by far the best place of all." It was more than a business or a way to accumulate wealth, he noted. A farm was "life itself," and to "be close and work with nature is one of life's greatest opportunities." James Hearst wrote that a farm was "part of our life, like our own flesh and blood."[10]

James Hearst grew up on a farm near Cedar Falls and became a distinguished writer and poet, despite a devastating accident at age nineteen that left him a paraplegic. He dropped out of college and underwent almost two years of physical therapy. Hearst then pursued a rigorous study of self-education—he read every book he could find in one county and then read all those in the next one. He began to write poems and stories in the winter when not working on his family's farm. In 1941 he became an English professor at Iowa State Teacher's College (now UNI), where he taught until 1974. Hearst published a dozen books of poetry, as well as an autobiography before he died in 1982. His poetry and prose expressed a deep love of rural life and the people of Iowa.[11]

Farm life was threatened by debt and low prices. Elmer Powers wrote in October 1931 that such prices for crops were "hard, cruel, bitter facts" and that "the scars of these days are going to show on the farms of this community for years to come." Martie Ward noted in her diary that some families desperately sold land for as little as twenty or forty dollars an acre. This would have equaled $310 to $620 an acre in 2020 dollars. James and Ruby Howorth recalled in an interview that their family had eaten raccoon and rabbit as children when food was scarce in the 1930s. Clara Ackerman wrote in December 1932 that "there has been a terrible calamity in this county in the last week—five banks have closed—with only 3 left in the county. People have lost thousands of dollars. We only have $11.00 at this time." Ackerman wrote that people dreaded what might come next. "A good many are reading the Book of Revelation trying to connect the prophecy with the present times." There was "no branch of farming or stock raising" that offered any profit over production cost, she lamented. All but two or three of the banks in Cedar Rapids had failed, recalled Ruth Mumford. People stood in lines outside open banks, hoping to get their money. Gladys Moeller Lage's family burned corn to stay warm, as they could not sell it at a profit and could not afford to buy coal.[12]

Farmwomen such as Ackerman had critical roles in maintaining a family farm and helping it survive. The importance of their work increased during the Depression. They completed an endless variety of tasks and helped earn money. James Hearst wrote about his mother that it seemed "a kind of miracle that she could accomplish all she did." Much of what a family consumed was produced under the direction of women. They prepared and cooked a huge amount of food, cared for chickens and large gardens and orchards, while tending to children, doing laundry, and sewing. One woman reported to anthropologist Deborah Fink that she managed three hundred chickens; another woman harvested one hundred bushels of potatoes one year. Many milked cows and churned butter, butchered chickens, and collected eggs. In the typical farm family of moderate means, female production totaled almost half of net family income in the mid-1930s. Chickens or eggs might pay for doctor visits or store debts, while baking, cooking, churning or nursing assistance might go toward other costs. Income from their work helped to feed their families, too. Fay Goodman recalled that money earned from eggs and cream "was what you spent for groceries that week." Inez Frick Henze Badger wrote that her family of thirteen survived off the money earned by her mother. "We lived on the egg and cream checks," Badger recalled. Women also earned cash through sewing and mending, babysitting, selling tomato plants or quilts.[13]

Women were also behind a remarkable effort to provide food to the unemployed in Des Moines in late 1931 and early 1932. Nine women, including a welfare worker, a teacher, a journalist, and housewives, organized a massive food drive to feed the hungry. They started with nine dollars. "We have stopped whining about a depression that scarcely exists for us," one said. They established the Des Moines Women's Relief Association, collecting leftover vegetables, bread, and meat trimmings before they were thrown out. The group set up food stations and acquired secondhand stoves, tables, and equipment. Unemployed men helped paint buildings and connect stoves; they also dug ditches for water lines and built shelves from donated lumber. Women staffed the kitchens and prepared meals. An unemployed mother of five ran one of the stations. An unemployed truck driver collected food from packinghouses and markets. Within a week of starting work, one kitchen was serving six hundred meals a day. Meals came with bread and usually included a soup or stew with ingredients such as noodles, carrots, rice, beans, or cabbage. The association bought fresh ham for two or three cents a pound, often adding ham or potatoes to soup. The organization helped thousands of people in need of food and hope.[14]

The Depression was especially difficult for African Americans. Like all Iowans, they lost their jobs and the income from employment. Hard times hurt Black workers worst, as they were usually the first to be fired. Almost every Black worker at Waterloo's John Deere plant was laid off in the 1930s. The handful who remained had their wages and hours cut. Black families relied on federal relief programs, female income, odd jobs, and help from the African American community. When possible Black workers found employment in cities, especially in meatpacking plants. "Black women held the family together during the lean years," wrote historian Valerie Grim, especially when men could not find work. They grew extra produce for sale or barter and sold eggs or chickens to pay bills, like white women. Rural families planted gardens to help feed themselves. Black

The Farm Holiday Association staged protests to try and halt the sale of farm goods to increase prices during the Great Depression. Martial law was declared, and the movement collapsed. Roadblock organized by Farmer's Holiday Association members near Sioux City, Iowa, 1932. PH14814, State Historical Society of Iowa, Des Moines.

women cooked, sewed, and cared for the children of middle-class white families.[15]

The 1932 presidential election that ushered Franklin Roosevelt into office brought little immediate change to the United States. The crisis only worsened as the country awaited the decisions of its new leader. By 1933 the nation's economy had shrunk by half and farm income was down by two-thirds from the low levels of 1929. In North Dakota almost every farmer had been bankrupted by a combination of drought, grasshoppers, low prices, and hail. In nearby South Dakota, mothers fed tumbleweed soup to their children. Urban areas suffered too. Chicago could not pay its teachers throughout the winter of 1932 and 1933. Iowa teachers did not receive regular paychecks either, remembered Hearst. Across the nation, half of families were behind on mortgage payments. By 1933 millions had lost their housing to foreclosures. Marriage and divorce rates declined—they were too expensive—as did birthrates.[16]

The situation in Iowa was equally difficult. In November 1932, Powers lamented, "many people think that they do not have anything to be thankful for." A local banker attempted suicide two days after Powers wrote this entry. As Christmas neared, he noted, "not many farm folks are talking about Christmas gifts." Desperate unemployed women in Des Moines turned to prostitution to survive, charging from one to three dollars for sex. This would have been about $19–$57 in 2020 dollars. Robert Boland collected coal that had fallen off railcars to help heat his family's house in Dubuque. A barter economy dominated rural parts of the state, as people exchanged food and clothing to survive. Families raised large gardens and chickens to feed themselves, taking eggs and poultry to local stores in trade. They shared houses to save expenses and grew potatoes in their backyards. "In those last trying months under Hoover, a chaotic situation came frightfully close to anarchy," wrote John M. Wilkinson.[17]

Harsh economic circumstances led to a series of protests in Iowa. In 1929 the state had mandated that farmers test cattle for bovine tuberculosis, resulting in a violent farm protest known as the Cow War, centered in eastern Iowa in Cedar and Muscatine Counties. While Iowa farmers had usually supported high standards for the testing and grading of livestock and grain, this new requirement was badly timed and implemented. The state recruited veterinarians who visited counties, searching for, and eradicating tubercular livestock. Then they moved on to another county. Such a group of outsiders, who arrived and confiscated diseased cattle when farmers were economically vulnerable, proved highly unpopular. Farmers argued that the payments that they received were below the value of their livestock. Families lost an average of $130 for each animal killed, a huge blow to family finances in the midst of the Depression. Furthermore, farmers did not believe that the TB test was fully reliable.[18]

By 1931 resistance to the program was widespread, especially after some lost entire herds to the disease. Farmers armed themselves and barred state veterinarians from visiting their farms to test their animals. In March, mobs of hundreds of farmers blocked veterinarians from giving tests. Farmers flooded into Des Moines to protest the law later that month, but legislation supporting voluntary testing failed. The conflict flared up again when the state veterinarian was stopped from giving tests in August by another armed mob. In September, 450 farmers with clubs battled deputies in a fog of tear gas. Several people were injured and law enforcement was forced to retreat. In response, Governor Dan Turner sent two thousand men from the Iowa National Guard into five counties in southeast Iowa to enforce the tests. Troops stayed for two months. Several years later the program was modified to use local vets to carry out the tests. There were no further incidents of resistance to the program and bovine tuberculosis, which could spread to children, was eliminated in Iowa.[19]

As the Depression deepened, other desperate rural insurgencies sprang up, inspired, in part, by the Cow War. The most important of these was the Farmer's Holiday Association, whose protests peaked in 1932 and 1933, just as the Great Depression was at its worst and farm prices at their lowest. This group was active across parts of the Midwest, from the Dakotas to Iowa. Milo Reno led the movement and was elected president of the state association in 1932. Born in southern Iowa, and reared in the populist tradition of fiery, idealistic rhetoric, he had opposed the compulsory testing of cattle for TB. Reno was the most vocal advocate in the state on behalf of struggling farm families, arguing that farmers deserved to earn their cost of production, with a guaranteed profit. The Farmer's Holiday Association planned strikes, attempted to halt the movement of farm goods to market, and tried to halt foreclosures. In Iowa, its actions occurred in the northwest section of the state near Sioux City, often attracting hundreds of men but never more than a small percentage of local farmers.[20]

The protest began in the summer of 1932, when farmers attempted to block highways and withhold farm products from market. They stopped vehicles and dumped milk into ditches, in a vain effort to reduce supply and increase prices. This mostly occurred in Plymouth County in northwest Iowa. Mass arrests and jail time helped clear the roads and disrupt protests, but the relatively small number of those involved did not influence milk prices in the state. In the second phase of the protest, which occurred in early 1933, farmers attempted to halt foreclosures. Women often joined, swelling the size of crowds. In one confrontation with sheriff deputies a fight broke out, leaving at least one protestor injured. On April 27, 1933, the most serious violence occurred when about 250 men seized Judge Charles C. Bradley and threatened to hang him if he refused to halt foreclosures. A rope was tied around Bradley's neck, who did not agree to the mob's demands. The judge promised to "do the fair thing to all men" and the crowd dispersed, unwilling to lynch a brave man. That same day a mob of six hundred farmers trying to halt a foreclosure fought with twenty-five deputies at a courthouse. The governor of Iowa called out the National Guard and declared martial law in five Iowa counties, effectively crushing the protest. A few went to jail for their actions. The Farmers'

Holiday movement collapsed in the state in the mid-1930s. Many members lost their farms and their motivation for struggle; New Deal programs also provided financial assistance to those who had supported the association.[21]

When Franklin Roosevelt was inaugurated as president on March 4, 1933—the last such event before the date was moved to January—every sector of the American economy seemed to be failing. Roosevelt had promised the American people a "new deal," a phrase that he had used in accepting the Democratic nomination for president. His administration cobbled together a set of programs to address the crises facing the country. The New Deal was a mix of plans to reform some sectors of the economy, such as banking, and provide work to the millions of unemployed. While it failed to end the Great Depression, the New Deal did much to reduce the misery of Americans and helped build the infrastructure that supported American prosperity in the 1940s and afterward. Some of these programs were the messy result of political compromise, while others were hastily thrown together during a vast emergency. It was an imperfect solution to an unprecedented crisis. Government spending more than doubled in the 1930s, but the New Deal did not bring socialism to the United States, as its worst critics cried. It helped Americans and it helped Iowans. It provided crucial relief to millions of people and helped save capitalism from its own failures.[22]

In early March 1933 the new president called Congress into emergency session. Addressing the collapse of the American banking system was the most important task. Credit was "the lubricant of capitalism," wrote historian Michael E. Parrish, and it had dried up, as banks failed, and states declared banking holidays. Roosevelt officially announced a nationwide banking holiday two days after taking office. On March 9 the Emergency Banking Act became law. It gave the federal government sweeping new powers to reorganize any bank and provide funding to improve its balance sheets by buying stock or assuming debts. Federal officials inspected banks, allowing solvent ones to reopen, while placing troubled ones under supervision. On March 14 Roosevelt explained what the government was doing to assist the financial sector in his first "fireside chat" over the radio. He reassured Americans that any bank that opened for business the next day would be solvent. Americans believed him. Deposits flooded back into the financial system and the banking crisis passed. Reforms later that year provided government insurance for deposits, administered by the Federal Deposit Insurance Corporation (FDIC), with costs shared by the government and banks.[23]

One of Franklin Roosevelt's most trusted aides during the Depression and World War II was Harry Hopkins, who was born in Sioux City in 1890. He contracted typhoid when he was ten years old and suffered from poor health for the rest of his life. But his physical challenges helped him bond with Franklin D. Roosevelt, who had contracted polio at age thirty-nine and was disabled. Roosevelt spent the last twenty-four years of his life in a wheelchair, only able to stand with heavy steel braces on his legs. Hopkins graduated from Grinnell College in 1912 with degrees in history and political science and became a social worker in New York. He followed FDR to Washington, DC, after Roosevelt's election. Hopkins became head of the Civil Works Administration and the Works Progress Administration, two New Deal agencies that employed millions of Americans in the 1930s. He was a pragmatic reformer and humanitarian who supported Social Security, public housing, and unemployment insurance. "Compassion suffused his nature," wrote historian David M. Kennedy. Hopkins was secretary of commerce at the end of FDR's second term. He was then Roosevelt's closest advisor, living in the White House for three years during World War II. His health worsened after cancer surgery removed most of his stomach. Hopkins died in 1946 at the age of fifty-five and his ashes were later interred at the Grinnell city cemetery.[24]

Jay Norwood "Ding" Darling was not a personal advisor to the president, but he was the most influential political cartoonist in the country in the mid-twentieth century and an important conservationist. Darling moved from Michigan to Iowa in 1886 at the age of ten. The boy loved the unspoiled prairies and wildlife near his home in Sioux City. He started drawing for the *Sioux City Journal* before moving to the *Des Moines Register and Leader* in 1906, where he spent most of his career. He won two Pulitzer Prizes. In 1931 Darling was appointed to the Iowa State Fish and Game Commission. Three years later he became head of the federal government's Biological Survey and greatly expanded the National Wildlife Refuge system. The refuge system preserved millions of acres of habitats for waterfowl and other animals. Roosevelt appointed him to the position despite Darling's attacks on FDR in his political cartoons. Ding Darling also helped found the National Wildlife Federation. He died in 1962. A wildlife refuge in Florida, which he helped save from development, is named for him.[25]

Another Iowan who played a key role in the Roosevelt Administration was Henry A. Wallace, editor of the Iowa newspaper *Wallace's Farmer*, who became secretary of agriculture in 1933. Wallace's father, Henry C., had been agriculture secretary in the 1920s and both men had been longtime advocates for struggling farmers. The younger Wallace was a progressive Republican, who experimented with hybrid corn and had started a seed business in the 1920s. This company, Pioneer Hi-Bred, was funded by an inheritance his wife had received and was worth nearly $10 billion in 1999. Wallace's articles, essays, and leaflets discussed topics that impacted agriculture, ranging from monetary policy to tariffs to the evils of big business. The ongoing crisis of American agriculture had helped convince him that the government needed to help farmers find markets overseas or reduce surpluses and raise prices. As agriculture secretary, Henry A. Wallace helped manage and usher in a revolution in policy that changed the relationship between farmers and their government. He was a practical idealist, committed to social justice and the preservation of American agriculture. Wallace is usually regarded as the nation's greatest agricultural secretary.[26]

One of the first tasks of Wallace and the new administration was to find a way to help American farmers. The biggest problem was low prices. One of the first pieces of New Deal legislation was the Agricultural Adjustment Act (AAA). In part, it tried to increase farm prices by reducing livestock numbers and the amount of acreage planted. The government asked cotton growers to plow up their crop and paid farmers to slaughter millions of pigs to avoid a future pork surplus. Iowan Slim Collier recalled, "We went out and bought 'em and killed 'em. This is how desperate it was. It was the only way to raise the price of pigs." One hundred million pounds of pork and lard from the slaughter was given to families in need. The AAA also paid wheat farmers to reduce their production for 1934. These measures helped increase the price of many crops. Iowa's corn farms did not need to destroy any part of their crop, since a severe drought helped to reduce production in the mid-1930s. The government paid corn farmers thirty cents a bushel, based on average yields in earlier years, to avoid planting corn. Oscar Heline, a lifelong farmer, remembered how families felt as lives slowly improved. "It was Wallace who saved us, put us back on our feet. He understood our problems." Farm income in Iowa more than doubled by 1935, when more than 85 percent of Iowa land was enrolled in AAA programs. More than two million acres of Iowa farmland went purposefully unplanted in 1934. Farmers signed 175,765 contracts for benefits totaling $73 million, worth about $1.4 billion in 2020.[27]

While the financial system began to recover and farm prices started to rise in 1933, millions still suffered from hunger and unemployment. A variety of New Deal programs attempted to reduce unemployment. The Civilian Conservation Corps (CCC) provided government jobs to five hundred thousand young men nationwide in its first two years. The CCC operated forty-six camps across Iowa during the Depression, starting in 1933. It hired men between the ages of seventeen and twenty-five to complete conservation work overseen by the army, ranging from planting trees to building campgrounds, roads, trails, cabins, and bridges. In Iowa, the CCC built state parks, state preserves, and wildlife refuges. Nearly forty-six thousand had worked for the program by the time it ended. "The average enrollee was said to be twenty years old with an eighth-grade education. He came from a family of six children," one report noted. Because of regular meals and physical labor, workers gained, on average, ten pounds. They received $30 a month, with $22 to $25 automatically sent home. (Thirty dollars in 1935 equaled about $566 in 2020.) The money that Wilbur Putnam sent to his family in Dubuque helped his parents to pay back taxes on their home.[28]

CCC camps were located across the state and employed white, Latino, and Native men. African American males usually lived in segregated camps, several of which existed in Minnesota. It does not seem that such segregated camps existed in Iowa. But Black CCC workers lived in separate barracks in one camp built at Lake View. Each location had about two hundred enrollees. Camps began with tents but were upgraded to wooden barracks; they also had dining and recreation halls, which might have a pool table, checkers, and card games. Every camp had a library. One of the first camps opened near Ledges State Park, south of Boone. Men planted 350,000 trees and completed projects to combat erosion. The CCC constructed dams, trails, fences, and parking lots around Eldora and Chariton. Crews from the Lenox camp built 701 structures by 1935, including dams and diversion ditches.[29]

In 1934 there were about four hundred Meskwaki living on their land near Tama. The tribe had purchased land whenever they could, using federal annuities. In 1915 they owned 3,253 acres. They remained under state jurisdiction until it was transferred to the federal government in 1908. Families lived in small homes without electricity or running water. They cut wood by hand and pumped water from nearby faucets. Some carried water a mile to their homes. The Meskwaki lived lives that were very much culturally and physically separate from their white neighbors. There was little intermarriage with whites and English was a second language for many children. Some elders did not speak English at all. Before the Depression many Meskwaki had worked in Tama. The CCC's Indian Division employed more than one hundred Meskwaki. A camp in Tama enrolled about twenty men from the tribe, where they built a community and cultural center, constructed roads, and planted trees. The Works Progress Administration (WPA) erected a cannery to aid the tribe with food preservation. Government employment provided much-needed income, as the Depression had eliminated job opportunities nearby. There was so much demand for work among the Meskwaki that it was rotated among men, so as many as possible could earn an income.[30]

Sebastian Alvarez joined the CCC in 1934 after graduating from high school. He worked at a camp near Maquoketa. Much of the labor that he did reduced soil erosion—he helped build dams and ditches and planted sod. He spent three years with the CCC, some of that time as a supervisor. Alvarez had been born in Leon, Mexico, and his family had migrated to the United States in 1917, fleeing violence and poverty. Alvarez's father, Santiago, found work with the Santa Fe Railroad and the family lived in abandoned railroad boxcars in Fort Madison. To survive they raised chickens and pigs and grew potatoes and vegetables. They dug their own wells for water. By the late 1920s his family had built their own home and had electricity. Mexicans encountered persistent racism in Iowa. "We were really discriminated in public places," such as restaurants and theaters, he said in an interview. They had to sit in the back of their church, too. Only the railroads would hire Mexicans, he said. He was drafted in World War II, later working for the railroads for fifteen years and retiring from the post office after twenty-three more years.[31]

The CCC also provided education to its workers. Young men from Ledges State Park studied at Boone High School to earn high school credits, taking classes from fourteen teachers at night. A CCC district history reported that "every evening several truck loads of CCC boys" went to the town. A majority of teachers in Boone volunteered their services to the CCC. The Chariton camp offered courses in truck driving, auto mechanics, surveying, and mathematics, while men at the Lenox site could take English, reading, and journalism. When they were not working or studying, men entertained themselves, playing basketball, baseball, football, or competing in boxing tournaments. Card games, ping-pong, and pool were also popular.[32]

Other New Deal programs, such as the WPA also provided employment to Iowans. It completed work in every Iowa county, building baseball parks, schools, roads, and other infrastructure. The WPA was launched in 1935 and employed millions, mostly men, in construction. It also provided jobs for skilled workers, women, African Americans, and the young. John Ortega's father worked for the WPA for $16 a week to help feed his family during winters when fieldwork was not available. An engineer earned about $100 a month, while an unskilled laborer might make $60. The WPA helped with flood control in Sioux City and assisted in digging a new channel for the Floyd River. In Dubuque the WPA built the airport, a municipal swimming pool, and a recreation center. In Keokuk and Pella it dug swimming pools, while constructing a golf course in Ames. The program also raised city halls in towns such as Mount Pleasant. The WPA constructed libraries, cataloged their contents, and surveyed historical records. It built schools and provided other educational services, ranging from adult education to after-school programs. It employed more than eight million people by 1943.[33]

In 1938 the WPA hired more than 41,000 people in Iowa, including 4,326 women. Only one person per household could work for the WPA and men received preference. If the husband of a married woman was ill or disabled, this rule was waived. Most of those in the WPA women's programs in Iowa were divorced or widowed, however. They often engaged in sewing, so clothing could be given to those in need. But women also labored in clerical, education, and library classifications. Domestic aides helped with the sick and disabled; library workers set up the first WPA bookmobile in Lucas County. Cooks and servers helped provide almost four million hot lunches to students in Iowa, a program that continued at many schools even after the WPA ended in the middle of World War II. Sixty-eight Iowa counties had nursery schools sponsored by the program.[34]

The WPA was an innovative and sometimes controversial program that also supported creative efforts in the arts, theater, and music. Detractors argued that it wasted money on arts programs and produced material critical of American society. Yet WPA projects also created lasting treasures in Iowa and across the country. Forty thousand unemployed writers worked for the Federal Writer's Project, producing regional and state guidebooks, as well as collecting the stories of formerly enslaved people. More than one hundred WPA workers helped write the Iowa state guide, called *Iowa: A Guide to the Hawkeye State*. Actors and playwrights working for the

Grant Wood was Iowa's most famous artist. Grant Wood at work in his "Kare No More" studio at Clear Lake, Iowa, ca. 1941. PH17386, State Historical Society of Iowa, Des Moines.

WPA's Federal Theater Project performed plays across the country, while musicians gave concerts or taught students to play instruments. The Iowa Federal Theater Project presented more than twenty plays in Des Moines in the spring of 1937. In 1935 and 1936 the WPA's Federal Music Project sponsored more than one hundred concerts in Des Moines at parks, schools, and other public places. Iowa artists on the WPA payroll produced more than one hundred original paintings that were given to schools and libraries, as well as murals in public buildings still visible today.[35]

The Iowa artist Grant Wood, now famous for his *American Gothic* painting, completed work for the New Deal during the 1930s. Wood was born near Anamosa in 1891. A quiet and shy boy, he began to manifest artistic talents in high school. He took drawing classes at the State University of Iowa while working as a teacher at a one-room schoolhouse. Wood then enlisted in the army during World War I, but the conflict ended before he was deployed overseas. In the 1920s he visited Europe several times, living in Paris and traveling to Italy to live with fellow painters.

After his return to Cedar Rapids in 1924, he set up a studio and home in a large spare room in a building owned by a friend. He was extraordinarily productive over the next eleven years at this location and most of his best-known work was produced during this time. In 1930 *American Gothic* won him immediate fame. He was briefly employed as the director of Iowa's Public Works of Art Project in 1934. The artists that Wood hired, including Christian Petersen, painted murals at Iowa State College depicting Iowa's cultural history—from farming to engineering. Later that year, he was appointed an associate professor of fine arts at the State University of Iowa. He spent the rest of his career at the school, struggling to be accepted by his colleagues because of his homosexuality, lack of a college degree, and a style that was seen as outdated. Grant Wood died in 1942 at the age of fifty. His reputation as an artist grew in the decades after his death.[36]

Another program, the National Youth Administration (NYA), helped young people between the ages of sixteen and twenty-five. It allowed students to attend college by providing work-study jobs. It also provided part-time employment to millions of high school students. In Sioux City the NYA funded recreation and training for youth, including classes in carpentry and office work. Its young workers in Iowa also repaired buildings, landscaped highways, developed parks, and built more than one hundred playgrounds. NYA employees helped establish new branch libraries, as well as traveling libraries, especially in rural areas. Women worked in hospitals and food preparation through the program, which employed more than eight thousand Iowans in February 1940.[37]

The National Labor Relations Act of 1935 changed the relationship between workers and employers, defending the rights of wage earners to organize and banning unfair labor practices. The law made it illegal to discourage union membership or fire employees who tried to set up a union. Historian David M. Kennedy argued that such laws "rearranged the balance of power between capital and labor" and helped more evenly distribute income to workers. Additional New Deal laws in 1938 set minimum wages and a forty-hour work week. This aided industrial employees, though minimum wage legislation left out millions of agricultural and domestic service workers who were often nonwhite or female. These laws, as well as others such as Social Security (which established modest old age pensions), helped produce a more stable, less volatile American economy that distributed its benefits more evenly. Iowa's industrial sector grew rapidly during World War II and in the postwar decades. New Deal labor reforms ensured that Iowans had higher wages and better lives.[38]

The New Deal also helped bring electricity to rural Iowans. In the 1910s and 1920s, electrical companies focused on providing power to more populated and wealthier urban areas. It was unprofitable to build the necessary infrastructure for scattered homes in the countryside. Only about 10 percent of farms in the Midwest had electricity in the 1930s, while 85 percent of households in urban and suburban areas did. In Iowa less than 15 percent of farms had power. Without electricity, rural homes lacked the comforts and conveniences that people in cities had. Women had to scrub laundry by hand in an outdoor tub; irons were heated on a fire. Food preservation was difficult without ice. Lanterns provided lighting in the absence of electricity. Private companies charged new rural customers up to a $1,000 deposit to extend service to country homes. (This would be $15,500 in 2020.) It also cost twice as much per kilowatt-hour to provide electricity to such homes.[39]

The Roosevelt Administration proposed that the federal government provide long-term and low-cost loans to local cooperatives that provided electrical service to areas without it. This would solve the problem of high costs in rural areas. The Rural Electrification Administration (REA) was created to manage this vast undertaking. Farmers and other residents combined to form a cooperative and recruit members, select officers, and apply for a loan to build distribution lines. Electricity was purchased from private companies. In Linn County, one cooperative's application to the REA in 1937 showed that 569 farms desired power. The organization received a grant for $228,000 to build two hundred miles of lines. By July 1939 the infrastructure had been built and farms began to be illuminated. The number of farms with power more than doubled by 1939 nationwide. By 1945 one-half of farmers had electricity.[40]

Farm families were eager for electrical power. Clara Saride Winkie recalled that a team of men were building electrical lines near her house. A supervisor told her that the workers could run a line to her home that evening if she would provide dinner for his men. Her family would have electricity before nightfall. She immediately set to work putting together a meal. Winkie cooked up mashed potatoes and homemade biscuits, serving them with butter and honey, as well as a salad. Her family got power that night.[41]

Electricity changed life for rural people forever. James Hearst remembered that nothing transformed the rural world like the coming of electricity. "The break with the past gave us an entrance to the modern world," he wrote. Bright lights replaced the "dim glow of smoky lanterns" and electricity ended much of the "hard arm and back work" of farming. Families could store food in a refrigerator, avoiding the need for an icebox. Electricity helped keep the home warm and powered a radio. "Everyone could play table games or read at any time of the day or night," wrote Robert Seltz. An electric heater also helped keep sows and newborn piglets alive during the winter and kept water for animals from freezing. Hens produced more eggs with light. Electric water pumps eliminated the need to carry water to the home; they also brought indoor plumbing and an end to outdoor latrines. Mary Hagen recalled that electricity made water always available. "Wash water was no longer heated in a copper boiler over a two burner kerosene stove," she wrote. Drinking water did not have to be carried from the well either, she gladly noted. Livestock required lots of water and pumps saved an average of one-half hour of work each day. Rural schools brightened with new lights, too.[42]

The New Deal poured more than a billion dollars into Iowa during the Depression, about eighteen or nineteen billion in 2020 dollars. The state received more money per capita than any other state in the Midwest, except for North and South Dakota, with the federal government spending $467 per person in Iowa, about $8,500 to $9,000 in 2020. New Deal programs employed tens of thousands of people in the state, helped the farm economy recover, and began to bring electrical power to Iowa's rural majority. While the New Deal did not end the Depression—it took enormous spending during World War II to achieve this goal—it brought some relief and some recovery to Iowans. The financial system in the state stabilized and money from the government flowed into Iowa beginning in 1933. Iowa started to recover faster than anyone could have imagined, with car sales in 1935 increasing by 149 percent from their low point two years earlier. The WPA had almost 23,000 workers on its rolls that year and the CCC had 8,338 in August 1935 in 46 camps. Unemployment remained high, though. The economic recovery continued into the late 1930s, interrupted by another economic downturn in 1937. Despite the recovery from the depths of the Depression, corporations, banks, and insurance companies owned 19 percent of Iowa farmland by 1937. But thirty thousand farms in the state received electrical power in 1936. Sales tax revenue reached a new high in that year. Beer and cigarette sales increased that year, as well.[43]

The Great Depression left permanent scars on Americans. James Hearst recalled how the crisis affected his family: "We just dug in and faced what had to be faced and survived. But no one who weathered the depression ever escaped without a kind of obsession for security." Arthur Leaf, the traveling salesman, eventually found success. Art and Marie lived frugally, fearing hard times. They never bought a new car, but they found a new church. Marie taught in a rural school and their kids went to college. They purchased a farm in Hamilton County and paid it off long before they died.[44]

As the decade came to a close, the spread of fascism in Europe and Asia began to threaten the unsteady peace that had existed since World War I. Even as Iowans struggled to rebuild their lives after the Depression, new challenges faced the United States. Americans wanted to avoid the brutality of a new war, especially those in Iowa who had suffered from tough economic times for almost twenty years. But the bitter reality of a world at war would drag the nation into its greatest conflict.

12
Iowa in World War II

World War II brought an end to the Great Depression and created an economic boom driven by extraordinary government spending during the conflict. Iowa and the rest of the country were spared the devastation that afflicted Europe and Asia, but more than eight thousand Iowans died during the war. Men and women from the state served around the world and civilians labored long hours in factories and on farms. Iowa had a major training center for the Women's Army Corps, which prepared them for noncombat military duty. Like Americans everywhere, families in the state grew victory gardens, collected scrap metal, bought war bonds, and lived with the rationing of staple goods. The state hosted thousands of prisoners of war while Iowa State College (now ISU) produced uranium for atomic weapons. By 1945 the state had been transformed by the war, as cities grew, people departed rural areas, and full employment and high farm prices led to widespread prosperity.

The end of World War I had left Europe with a fragile peace. The victors, England and France, had been scarred by the terrible bloodshed and feared another war. The Germans felt humiliated in their defeat and were burdened with a weak democracy that collapsed in the early Depression years. Adolf Hitler consolidated his power after becoming chancellor in 1933, using fear and emergency decrees to eliminate any opposition. He then sought vengeance against Germany's enemies. Italy and Japan believed that they had been cheated by the Allies, who denied them territorial gains after the war. In 1937 Japan invaded China. In 1938 Germany annexed Austria. The next year Hitler invaded Czechoslovakia. He then made territorial demands on Poland. France and England promised to aid the country if it was attacked. Hitler invaded anyway and France and England declared war.[1]

The United States avoided the conflict and remained strongly isolationist until 1941. A Gallup poll in the spring of 1939 showed that 70 percent of Americans thought that involvement in World War I had been a mistake. But the new war went badly for the Allied powers and Germany conquered France, Belgium, and the Netherlands in a swift invasion in the spring of 1940. Nazi Germany then dominated Western Europe and England faced Hitler alone. The United States was still officially neutral, but President Roosevelt signaled support for Britain by providing fifty destroyers in exchange for bases in the Western Hemisphere. He then pushed for a "Lend-Lease" bill, where America provided military equipment to the beleaguered, nearly bankrupt British. In Europe, Germany conquered Yugoslavia and Greece and sent troops to North Africa. Hitler's armies invaded the Soviet Union in June 1941 and advanced toward Moscow. The Nazi juggernaut seemed unstoppable.[2]

Before the Nazis conquered the Netherlands two Iowa girls from Danville exchanged letters with pen pals in Amsterdam, including with one named Anne Frank. Their teacher, Birdie Matthews, had visited Amsterdam and provided the two girls, Betty and Juanita Wagner, some names of possible pen pals. Juanita randomly picked Anne's name. They wrote to each other about school, friends, and their families. Anne's sister Margot also sent a letter. The last was dated April 29, 1940, just twelve days before the German invasion of the Netherlands. The Wagner family learned of the fate of the Frank family after the war ended.[3]

Still, some Jews escaped the Nazis and reached safety in Iowa. Twenty families from Germany came to Sioux City, including Helena and Richard Oster, who arrived in 1939. Their savings had been confiscated by the Nazis. A relative sent them thousands of dollars to help them escape. Richard's mother was not allowed to leave Germany and was killed in the Holocaust. The Osters followed one of Helena's brothers to Sioux City, where Richard eventually set up a livestock business. The town had a Jewish population of at least twenty-five hundred in the mid-1920s. Anti-Semitism was common. The Klan had been popular in the area, staging regular rallies and parades against immigrants and religious minorities. Local country clubs refused to admit Jews; banks, large companies, and some stores also would not hire them. It was difficult for Jewish teachers or clerks to find jobs. Many lived in the western part of town, along West Seventh Street, an area full of Jewish delis, groceries, bakeries, and markets. Jewish soldiers from Iowa fought the Nazis in World War II. Paul Delman flew seventy-five missions over Europe. Joseph Goldstein was a medic with the Fourth Infantry Division, who landed in Normandy on D-Day. He was twice wounded and won a Silver Star for bravery, refusing medical treatment until all other casualties were cared for.[4]

The Scattergood Hostel in West Branch, near Iowa City, provided a temporary home for some who escaped the war in Europe. It provided housing for European refugees from 1939 to 1943. The hostel was located at the former Scattergood Friends School. Named after a Philadelphia philanthropist, it provided a home to 185 people over four years. Most guests were Austrian and German, with a few others from Russia, Poland, France, Hungary, Czechoslovakia, and Latvia. Some were Jews, while others had been political opponents of the Nazis, journalists, artists, or academics. The mostly Quaker staff of recent college graduates and local farmers taught English to the newcomers, as well as American culture, and tried to integrate them into the United States. The staff also fed and housed the refugees and helped them find jobs in the country. Some took classes at the nearby State University of Iowa, while others learned how to drive a car. Many had harrowing stories—one Jewish woman, Grete Baeck, escaped Germany right before Hitler ordered its borders closed. She eventually reached New York with three dollars. Baeck knew five languages, but English was not one of them. One couple escaped Germany after most of their neighbors had been arrested, arriving in New York City the day before the war began. After 1943 the number of guests fell—few were able to escape Europe by then. Controversy over sending Japanese internees to the hostel also helped lead to its closure. It has been a Quaker school since 1944.[5]

When the Japanese attacked Pearl Harbor on December 7, 1941, a sailor from Iowa, Vincent DeCook, was stationed on the cruiser *Minneapolis* about twenty miles offshore. DeCook had been born in Long Grove, a small town just north of Davenport, and served as a yeoman second class. About eight in the morning anti-aircraft bursts filled the sky over Pearl Harbor and DeCook saw many planes over the island. The *Minneapolis* went to general quarters. At 2:20 p.m. word arrived that Japan had declared war. The attack interrupted another Iowan, Robert Boland, who was on the way to church. He saw the battleship *Arizona* hit by the bomb that destroyed the ship. Three days later the undamaged *Minneapolis* entered Pearl Harbor. DeCook wrote that he witnessed "a sight of death and destruction." Ships, planes, and buildings had been wrecked and boats were still hauling dead men to shore. Eighteen ships, including eight battleships, had been sunk or capsized and twenty-four hundred Americans killed. The attack on Hawaii brought the United States into World War II.[6]

Radio announcements of the attack shocked, and then enraged, a population that had hoped to avoid another war. The *Cedar Rapids Gazette* wrote, "Yesterday, there were interventionists, and isolationists, republicans and democrats, new dealers, and anti-new dealers. Today there are only Americans." Men rushed to volunteer for the military. On December 8 more than one hundred Navy volunteers kept the Davenport recruiting office open until long past midnight. Jerry Twedt, an elementary-age boy living in Roland during the early 1940s, wrote that the outbreak of war brought "abrupt and wrenching changes to central Iowa." Couples either quickly married or postponed it. Families lay awake at night worrying about their husbands or sons. Across the Midwest men joined long lines in front of court houses or recruiting stations. Six months after Pearl Harbor, on June 7, 1942, 325 men across the state took their military oath, swearing to seek vengeance for the attack. Pearl Harbor left some Iowans angry and intolerant of outsiders. In April 1942, Japanese men who were recent Iowa State College graduates, were assaulted by a mob and chased out of Shenandoah. On the west coast 120,000 people of Japanese origin, most of them American citizens, were sent by presidential order to internment camps, deprived of their liberty for years and losing most of their hard-earned wealth.[7]

Iowa would play its part by sending its men and women to war and marshaling its agricultural and industrial resources for victory. World War II required an incredible effort at production that mobilized all sectors of American society. Defense spending had already increased before the war began, with almost $900 million spent each month by mid-1941. Halfway through 1942 government expenditures equaled the size of the entire economy of the year before. New cities were created during the war, such as Los Alamos, where scientists lived to work on the atomic bomb. More than fifteen million people entered the armed forces or the civilian labor force, with millions leaving the countryside for work in urban areas. In Iowa, people went to work in industrial jobs in towns and cities, such as Des Moines, Davenport, and Burlington. Away from factories and battlefields, civilians in Iowa rushed to support the war effort in a variety of ways.[8]

The government sought to channel civilian energies to help with war production. Families collected tin cans and other materials, with salvage committees established across the state. Women were encouraged to conserve, substitute, and economize, as well as collect metal, tin cans, and rubber. One less can per week for each family saved enough steel to build five thousand tanks. Children participated by combing through junk piles and ditches looking for scrap metal and rubber. Jerry Twedt recalled that the kids at his elementary school accumulated so much that "the entire school was bulging with scrap metal." Children in Winterset gathered twenty-one tons of scrap iron in two days, while Boy Scouts in Burlington collected nineteen tons of tin cans. The fire station in the town of Red Oak donated its 2,550-pound bell for recycling. Women across the state gave up aluminum cookware or utensils. The government also rationed rubber, as the Japanese had conquered a vital source of this commodity in Southeast Asia. Americans collected old rubber for wartime use, ranging from floor mats in cars to old tires.[9]

Rationing of many foodstuffs was introduced in the summer of 1942, disrupting daily life for the next three years. As most people wanted to contribute to the war effort, they accepted this system's necessity. Wartime demands led to a shortage of important commodities, to which the federal government limited civilian access. Sugar, coffee, butter, meat, and canned vegetables were rationed, as well as shoes. Everyone in the country received a book of ration stamps that could be used to purchase scarce items. Cooks used corn syrup to replace sugar in cookies or added yellow dye to white margarine, so it looked like butter. The burden of conservation fell on women and children, who grew food, collected scrap, canned and preserved garden produce and saved, sorted, and recycled everything from paper to household grease. John R. Ortega, who lived in Des Moines, recalled that his schoolmates bought war stamps and collected newspapers and scrap metal for the war.[10]

Tires and gasoline were also rationed, leading to many changes in daily life. The sale of new tires had halted after Japan invaded rubber-rich Southeast Asia in December 1941, while gasoline rationing began five months later in May. Fuel was not in short supply, but it was rationed to reduce the consumption of rubber. Most families received an allotment of five gallons of gasoline a week. Some, such as doctors or war workers, received more. To conserve fuel, the speed limit was reduced to thirty-five miles per hour. Americans took the right to travel—and the independence it gave—for granted. But they learned to take public transportation to work or to walk more. Those in rural areas found ways around government regulations. Vernon Sietmann, of Marshall County, recalled that farmers removed tires from their tractors or combines and illegally used them on their cars. Auto fatalities plummeted nationwide, as Americans drove less. Entertainment became simpler during the war, as people read books or completed crossword puzzles. Publishers marketed cheap paperback books that sold for twenty-five cents. Social lives improved, as Americans got to know their neighbors better. Families found a new interest in cooking or sewing. Tens of millions still went to movies, though.[11]

Families also turned to growing their own gardens to help feed themselves and to free up foodstuffs for the war effort. This saved money, as well as rationing points. Americans grew twenty million victory gardens, raising vegetables everywhere—from big rural fields to small backyard plots. Ten million gardens appeared in urban areas. Des Moines had two thousand such plots. Amateur gardeners grew a variety of vegetables, with the most popular being corn, tomatoes, squash, beans, peas, carrots, and lettuce. In Council Bluffs, more than 2,000 children grew gardens, harvesting more than 11,500 bushels of food. Iowa City provided plots of land for use by its citizens. The city plowed, harrowed, and staked out each plot for $1.50 each year. By the end of 1943, Iowans had planted 455,000 victory gardens, totaling over 70,000 acres. About two-thirds of Iowa families took part in 1944. Professors at Iowa State College had a common garden, with more than two hundred academics working in it. Factory workers in Des Moines tended crops after their shifts ended. Schools and prisons also grew gardens. Victory gardens grew about one-third of all vegetables consumed during the war.[12]

People across the country also bought war bonds, providing billions for the war effort, while saving money for the future. Bonds could be sold in modest amounts, such as $25, which would be about $370 in 2020. This encouraged ordinary people to invest in the war effort. The $25 bonds were purchased at a cost of $18.75 and would be paid out in ten years, averaging about 3 percent interest each year. The federal government conducted a series of war bond drives to help pay the cost of the conflict and keep the national debt down. Investing in bonds also kept wartime inflation in check, as it reduced the demand for scarce goods. Young Jerry Twedt saved a dime a week to buy ten-cent war stamps, which could buy larger bond amounts. "We all had relatives who were soldiers, and spending the money on ourselves was like stealing from them," he wrote.[13]

Bonds were sold by appealing to the patriotism of Americans, as well as their fears of fascism. In July 1942 Des Moines hosted a two-mile long parade, with ten thousand marchers who included World War One veterans and the Drake University band. Civilian air patrol planes flew overhead, dropping leaflets encouraging Iowans to buy war bonds. Army jeeps visited towns and cities, offering rides to those who invested in a war bond. Buying a $25 bond could earn a movie ticket. Merchants in Des Moines contributed proceeds from one day's sales—$760,403—to invest in bonds. Their money helped finance two B-17 bombers through the "Buy Bombers With Bonds" project. By the time the war had ended, Iowans had purchased $2.4 billion in war bonds.[14]

The small northern Iowa town of Estherville, and the surrounding Emmet County, sacrificed much for the war effort, as they had in World War I. Two of its citizens were at Hickam Field in Hawaii when the Japanese air raid started the war. More than fourteen hundred men from Emmet County joined the military during the conflict. Fifty-five men from the county lost their lives, a rate about double that of the state overall. Deemer Lee, editor of the local paper, proudly noted that county citizens bought more war bonds than their quota in each of the eight bond drives during the war. "Sales resulted largely because of a deep sense of responsibility to support the war and particularly the local men engaged in military action," he wrote. Residents gathered scrap iron and tin cans and gave many thousands of dollars to the Red Cross. "Businessmen helped farmers harvest their crops," he recalled fondly, and people gathered surplus clothing for their Russian allies. The town surgeon volunteered and was sent to Europe. Throughout the war, manpower shortages plagued the area. Lee employed Dorothy Story to work in his newsroom. She impressed him so much that she continued as an employee after the war.[15]

Iowans volunteered for the armed forces or were drafted, with 286,600 men serving during the war. The town of Odebolt sent nine men from the Patten family to the military. The father joined eight sons in the Navy. All the Patten men survived the war. Virginia Reyes of Des Moines, a Mexican immigrant, had six sons serving in the armed forces. The Defosse family from Mediapolis also sent six sons to join the military and all returned safely. Many families were not so fortunate. Of the total enlistment from the state, 8,398 died during the conflict. Iowans served across the globe, in all theaters of war. Both men and women served, with females in noncombat duties. The first Iowan to die was nineteen-year-old Melvin Laskowski from Sheffield, who was killed while on duty at Pearl Harbor.[16]

Frank Sanache, a Meskwaki from Tama, served as a code talker in the Army in North Africa. Henry Langrehr parachuted into Normandy on D-Day with the Eighty-Second Airborne Division. William Quinones, the son of Mexican immigrants in Mason City, was a corporal in the army in Europe. Luther Smith served with the Army Air Force as one of the famed Tuskegee airmen. Harold Hayes, an Iowa army medic, survived a plane crash and a two-month ordeal in Albania, while Darlene Diebler Rose endured years in a Japanese prisoner of war camp. Ted Allenby, from Dubuque, was a gay man who volunteered for the Marines and fought at Iwo Jima.

Sanache, along with twenty-six other Meskwaki, enlisted in the Iowa National Guard in January 1941—eleven months before the attack on Pearl Harbor. Frank's brother Willard also joined the guard. Of these twenty-seven Meskwaki men, eight became army code talkers. More than fifty of the tribe's men joined the US armed forces during the war. The American military used Native languages to encode sensitive battlefield information during the war. The Navajo, who provided more than four hundred men for this effort, are most identified with what became known as the "code talkers." The Meskwaki soldiers served in the Thirty-Fourth Infantry Division in North Africa and Italy. Frank Sanache helped direct artillery fire against German positions, often deploying far ahead of his unit with a walkie-talkie, sometimes for twenty-four hours at a time. He was captured in Tunisia and sent to a prisoner-of-war camp in Poland, where his daily ration included two potatoes, a slice of bread, and a cup of soup. He survived the war and returned to Iowa to work for nearly four decades in a paper mill. Other Meskwaki soldiers suffered even more, their bodies ravaged by years in prisoner of war camps. Dewey Youngbear had escaped German POW camps three times but been recaptured. He died in 1948 from tuberculosis that he caught while a prisoner. The contributions of Native code talkers went without recognition for decades, as the code and their work were classified until 1968. Sanache passed away in 2004, the last survivor of the Meskwaki code talkers.[17]

Henry Langrehr, who lived in the Mississippi River town of Clinton, joined the army in April 1943 while a senior in high school. He came from a family of ten children. Langrehr volunteered to be a paratrooper, in part because they were paid extra, and ended up in the Eighty-Second Airborne. His fiancé, Arlene, worked twelve-hour shifts in a factory at home, sometimes seven days a week. Paratroopers were dropped behind the landing beaches at night on D-Day. Before Lengrehr jumped out of the cargo aircraft the two men behind him were killed. Once he had landed, he killed a German soldier whose trench he stumbled into and disabled a German tank, shooting its crew as they climbed out. He was injured and taken prisoner after twenty-three days of fighting in Normandy. His injuries made surgery necessary; he spent a month in a Paris hospital. Langrehr was then sent to a prisoner of war camp, where he was beaten and forced to work in a coal mine. His clothes, soaked with sweat, froze in the winter. In March 1945 he escaped with a friend named Jim. He killed a soldier who saw them, but Jim was gunned down. Langrehr moved westward at night toward Allied armies, taking cover in forests and stealing food. Sometimes he had to kill German soldiers he stumbled upon. In early April he made contact with infantry pursuing the retreating German army. By the end of the ordeal he weighed only ninety pounds, having lost sixty pounds since D-Day. Langrehr returned home and married Arlene on July 1. His memoir was published in 2020.[18]

William Quinones joined the army the same month he graduated from Mason City High School. His father had immigrated from Mexico, working for railroads and in farm fields; his mother did not speak English. All five of their sons served in the American military, in either World War II or the Korean War. William's artillery battery was sent to France in September 1944, and he spent much of the fall in a foxhole, often in the rain. Some nights he slept with two phones, so he could keep in touch with soldiers at the front. He wrote dozens of letters to his family, thanking them in one for eight letters he received in one day. Quinones reassured them that he was safe. They sent him cookies and candy for Christmas. On December 26, 1944, he was killed in Germany by enemy fire.[19]

An African American man from Des Moines, Luther Smith Jr., fought with one of the most storied units of the war. Smith was a graduate of Roosevelt High School and a student at the State University of Iowa when the war began. He graduated from flight school in Tuskegee, Alabama, in May 1943, and joined the segregated Army Air Force as part of the 332nd Fighter Group. This unit and the Ninety-Ninth Pursuit Squadron are popularly known today as the "Tuskegee Airmen." Smith was one of thirteen Iowans who served in these units, fighting discrimination in the military while battling the Axis overseas. He flew 133 combat missions over Germany, Austria, Hungary, and other countries before his P-51 Mustang was damaged in an attack on an ammunition dump in October 1944. Smith broke his hip after ejecting from his aircraft and spent six months as a prisoner-of-war, mostly in hospitals. He lost part of his right leg to his injuries and bone infections. Smith won a Distinguished Flying Cross for his service and earned an engineering degree at the State University of Iowa after the war. He spent a year looking for work after graduation. Employers didn't want to hire a Black engineer, with General Electric turning him down for a job. Later they contacted him for an interview, after his wife, Lois, had reprimanded the company for their racist hiring practices. Smith worked for GE for thirty-seven years as an aerospace engineer, often on projects classified even in the twenty-first century.[20]

Harold Hayes and Darlene Diebler Rose survived harrowing trials. Hayes graduated from Indianola High School before he was drafted. He was one of thirty noncombatants—mostly nurses and medics—who survived a plane crash in Albania in November 1943. Emerging from the wreckage, Hayes and the other survivors found themselves in a country occupied by Nazi troops. Helped by anti-German partisans, they trekked through bitterly cold weather, dodging Nazi patrols and feuding guerilla bands. Sick and near starving they stumbled, often lost, across rugged terrain. Dysentery, parasites, and blizzards tormented them. A rescue attempt using transport planes failed. After two months of peril, they reached the Albanian coast, and the British Royal Navy evacuated them to Italy. Hayes became an aeronautical engineer and lived until 2017. Iowan Darlene Deibler Rose and her husband Russell were missionaries in New Guinea. Once Japan conquered the island they were imprisoned in horrific conditions. Darlene survived starvation and abuse, in large part due to her Christian faith, narrowly avoiding execution. Her husband, Russell, died in the war. She returned to the United States emaciated and weighing only eighty pounds after years of forced labor. Darlene remarried and returned with her second husband to continue her missionary work in New Guinea for almost thirty years. She lived until 2004.[21]

Ted Allenby was seventeen when he heard of the attack at Pearl Harbor. Born in Dubuque, he enlisted in the US Marines because they were the toughest outfit in the military. Allenby was as patriotic as his fellow

Marines, but he was a gay man who could not reveal his sexual identity. He recalled that he thought being gay was a "dirty little secret" that could be compared to a disease. Of course, there was nothing wrong with him, but American society did not then tolerate or understand homosexuality. He was not the only gay man in the Marine Corps. But they were all "frightened and furtive," and he drank and got in fights to deflect any suspicion. "I had a lot of hostility and fear," he told historian Studs Terkel. Allenby and his fellow marines of the Fourth Division landed on the beaches of Iwo Jima on February 19, 1945. His unit took enormous casualties, but he survived. He wept as the bodies of his comrades were buried in huge pits on the island. After the war he went to college and worked as a journalist before returning to the marines as a chaplain. In 1963 his identity was discovered, and he was dishonorably discharged. Seventeen years later a legal case restored his benefits and an honorable discharge. Sometime in the early 1980s he told Terkel, "I'm out of the closet and I don't care who knows . . . I'm not hiding any more."[22]

Wartime casualties dealt the towns of Waterloo and Red Oak heavy blows. One family in Waterloo lost five sons when the cruiser *Juneau* was sunk in the fighting around Guadalcanal in November 1942. After Pearl Harbor, all five sons of Thomas and Alleta Sullivan volunteered for the Navy—Frank, Joseph, Matt, and Albert died when the ship sank or soon afterward. George lived for three or four days in the ocean, searching for his brothers amid the wreckage of their ship, before dying himself. Only ten men from the *Juneau* survived their injuries or shark attacks. The five Sullivan brothers became national heroes. Their parents paid a price greater than any other American family, having lost all five of their sons in the war. A patriotic 1944 film called *The Fighting Sullivans* told the tragic story of their death.[23]

Three-and-a-half months after the death of the Sullivan brothers, an attack in North Africa routed inexperienced American GIs in one of the first major land battles fought by the United States in the European theater. The Thirty-Fourth Infantry Division, filled with troops from National Guard units from Iowa, had been decimated. Veteran German soldiers took thousands of prisoners. On the evening of March 6, 1943, telegrams began to arrive, notifying families that their loved ones were missing in action. Twenty-seven of these messages reached families in Red Oak. Telegrams informing families of killed and wounded never stopped coming during the war. Men from the town were killed in Italy, southern France, Germany, and the Philippines. They died in POW camps or crossing the Atlantic Ocean. Fifty men from Red Oak, a town of fifty-six hundred, lost their lives during the war and more than one hundred were wounded. Howard Koenemann, who had played basketball in local schools, was killed in Italy in December 1943. Deacon Clifford Powell of the town's First Congregational Church spoke about Koenemann—and all who gave their lives for their country. "We have in our midst those who complain of the little inconveniences to which they are subjected; those who blindly use the war to play partisan politics; those who ignorantly urge the elimination of various races and minority groups. In the name of Howard Koenemann, I indict all these as un-American, unpatriotic, and un-Christian."[24]

While men fought overseas, women also provided crucial support to the war effort as workers. Before millions of men left for military service, there was resistance to female workers. However, as the male labor force fell drastically, such resistance crumbled. Employers needed workers regardless of their gender or race. Almost five million women joined the labor force during the war. At the peak of their employment, women made up 36 percent of the work force. Married women, who had normally stayed home to raise children, joined the labor market in large numbers, eventually surpassing the number of working single women for the first time. Women held almost one-third of manufacturing jobs and found employment as steelworkers, welders, riveters, and miners. The Chicago and North Western Railroad hired women to service locomotives in states such as Iowa and Illinois. They worked in Boone, Council Bluffs, and Clinton. But women were usually relegated the lowest-paying jobs that had the least opportunity for advancement. Men could make three to five times the salary of women in shipyards. Most women made less than five dollars a day—about $75 in 2020 wages—while men could earn a maximum of $22 a day in these jobs, approximately $329 in 2020 dollars.[25]

In Iowa the Des Moines Ordnance Plant, near Ankeny, produced billions of rounds of .30 and .50 caliber ammunition. It was a huge factory, with almost twenty thousand workers at one point. Sixty percent of its workers were female, reflecting national trends, as women made up half of the staff at plants making bullets nationwide. Such factories were usually located in rural areas because of the threat of accidental explosions. The work was tedious and difficult, with the same tasks repeated hundreds or thousands of times a day. Women workers helped assemble bullets and cartridges for small arms, weighing and pouring powder. Lillie Cordes Landolt, the

Almost five million women took jobs during World War II and worked in industry, like those here at the Des Moines ordnance factory. Women inspecting 50-caliber ammunition at Des Moines ordnance plant during World War II. PH1987.44.43, US Rubber Company Collection, State Historical Society of Iowa, Des Moines.

mother of five children, labored at the plant in Des Moines. She recalled, "Making bullets was interesting. I had a huge machine. The ammunition is made in many parts, and the part we worked on was the bullet, which started out as brass." The bullet was shaped like a tiny cup about one-half inch across.[26]

Fern McCarthy worked at the ordnance plant in Burlington. It opened in the summer of 1941 and employed more than twelve thousand people making artillery and mortar shells, as well as bombs. Employees went through two security checks to enter and had to change into khaki overalls and shoes without metal parts, to avoid any risk of a spark that could ignite ammunition at the plant. McCarthy found constant danger and the threat of injuries at her job. An explosion in December 1941 killed thirteen men. Another explosion in March 1942 killed or wounded more than sixty. McCarthy was not hurt, but she had much difficulty finding housing in Burlington. New residents had overwhelmed the town. At one point she was offered a chicken coop to live in. She worked a different shift from her mother, so she could help care for her younger sister.[27]

One example of an Iowa woman employed outside the war industry was Ethel Jarred. She worked at a meatpacking plant in Ottumwa on the killing and cutting line. Her husband served in the military, and she wanted to work to help pay off their house. She earned fifty-nine cents an hour, loading meat into boxes with a pitchfork. She recalled, "I don't think I weighed much over 118 pounds then. By the end of the day I don't think I could even lift a fork to feed myself." When she got home that first night, she was covered in blood. "I'd never been that dirty before." Women encountered formidable resistance to their employment. As Jarred remembered, "It was up to we women to prove to the men we could be just as respectable as the wives that was at home." They did.[28]

Women served important noncombat duties for the military during the war. They could volunteer to serve in the US Army, Navy, Marines, Coast Guard, and Army Air Force. The American military realized that women could complete many tasks that supported frontline units; female personnel would free up men for other duties. Opposition in Congress and elsewhere led to criticism that seems ridiculous from the vantage point of the twenty-first century. But wartime necessities helped to break down resistance. The bill that allowed the creation of the Women's Army Auxiliary Corps (WAAC) passed in May 1942. (WAAC was later shortened to WAC, or Women's Army Corps, in 1943.) In the Army Air Force, women worked as radio operators, air traffic controllers, and mechanics. In the Army, they were weather forecasters, photographers, lab technicians, and clerks. They worked as cryptologists, too. Women also served in the Navy and Coast Guard, in communications and clerical work and other duties, doing tasks from decoding and training to navigation. Women Airforce Service Pilots (WASPs) flew more than sixty million miles, flying planes from factories to military bases. Thirty-nine of them died during the war. More than two hundred job categories were open to women in the Marines. Female military personnel set an extraordinary example during the war that defied stereotypes and prejudice.[29]

One of the major training bases for WAACs was at Fort Des Moines, where women of all races—a vast majority of them white—received military instruction. During World War II more than sixty-five thousand women were trained there. In July 1942 the first group of WAACs arrived. Only 440 women were admitted from a pool of 30,000 who applied to serve. Almost all of those in the first class were professionals, such as teachers and lawyers, and 99 percent of them had college degrees. The *Des Moines Evening Tribune* wrote that the WAAC base would be a "West Point for Women." Rachel Prager demonstrated the unusual abilities of many female volunteers. She was born in Poland before World War I and fled to Russia before emigrating to the United States in 1918. She served as a translator, as she was fluent in five languages, including Russian, German, and French.[30]

One of those who trained at the base was Mary Elizabeth Osen, born in 1913 near Cumberland, Iowa. Osen taught elementary school for eleven years before she joined the WACs. She began her training at Fort Des Moines in March 1943, learning military regulations, Army history, and administration. She also experienced drill, kitchen duty, and physical training. After additional training in Georgia she was assigned to New Guinea, then to the Philippines, completing signal office and clerical duties. Occasional air raids and snipers posed threats, while rain and mud made life difficult. WAC facilities were primitive, and the women slept in tents. Osen encountered little sustained danger but did write to her family about a plane crash that killed ten WACs. One of those lost had been a friend. After her return home, she was a librarian for thirty years in Illinois.[31]

Rosemary Tharp joined the Navy during the war. After graduating from Iowa State Teacher's College, she worked at a company manufacturing cartridge belts in Waterloo. "Working conditions were bad—hot and noisy and dangerous." Tharp taught social studies for one year before joining the female branch of the Navy, the WAVES, at twenty-two. She received training at Smith College and Mount Holyoke College. Tharp became a communications officer and was assigned to a naval station in Minneapolis. She was head of the base's communications department, though a male officer was technically her superior on paper, as women were not supposed to command men. Tharp coded intelligence information about Japan for the Army. She wrote that she learned things about herself that she would not have learned as a teacher—organizing an office, leading people, and enjoying wartime challenges. She married Herman Tharp in 1944 and lived in Iowa City, working at the University of Iowa Hospitals, after the war.[32]

Ortha Neff served as a Red Cross nurse in Hawaii and Okinawa during the war. Neff had been a teacher in Charter Oak and Knoxville before joining the Red Cross in 1944. She worked in a small mobile hospital. The "days long, hot, and wearing," she wrote—nurses were on their feet most of the time. A Japanese shell destroyed her tent in Okinawa. She wrote that a voice had told her to go to a supply tent, saving her life. She returned home safely to Iowa in late 1945 and had a long career as a staff member for the Girl Scouts.[33]

The Fort Des Moines facility allowed Black women to make up 10 percent of trainees at the base, a number equal to that of the overall Black population in the nation. Widespread and persistent racism kept most females of color from positions with serious responsibility, however. African American women with college degrees ended up cleaning floors and doing laundry. Black women served in segregated units, just as African American men did in the Army. Fort Des Moines maintained separate facilities for Black and white women, with two theaters and two service clubs, for example. Marjorie Randolph, an African American WAC from New Jersey noted, "So you were fighting these two wars at the same time"—one against racism and one against fascism. Such women regularly protested their treatment in Des Moines. For example, Black WACs were not allowed to roller skate in January 1943 and denied admittance to Riverview Park four months later. Local and national institutions, such as the NAACP and Black newspapers, fought against such discrimination, as did the servicewomen themselves.[34]

African Americans in Iowa fought for the right to be accepted as equals, appealing their inability to work in war jobs or their treatment off base. The Des Moines Ordnance Plant initially refused to hire Black workers. Pressure from the Negro Chamber of Commerce in Des Moines, the Black newspaper the *Iowa Bystander*, as well as the employment of Black workers in other ordnance factories, forced the plant eventually to employ African Americans. In April 1942 Elizabeth Shackelford sued the factory because it refused to hire Black workers. Her lawsuit was based on the plant's violation of Executive Order 8802, issued by Roosevelt the year before. The order required all defense plants to employ laborers regardless of race, color, or national origin. The ordnance factory eventually hired Black workers in a percentage equal to that of Des Moines's Black population—4 percent.[35]

Iowa farmers prospered during the conflict, as wartime demands for foodstuffs drove prices high. The state produced 20 percent of all the corn in the nation, as well as more chickens and eggs than any other state in 1943. Corn production increased by 25 percent from 1939 to 1944, with an average crop of just under 553 million bushels each year during the war. In 1945 farm income was higher than ever before. For the first time in almost twenty years, Iowa farms did not face a continued economic crisis that threatened their survival. They paid off debts, improved their homes, and bought new machinery. Home appliances proliferated and farm families enjoyed electric stoves, running water, and maybe even a vacuum cleaner. The gap in living standards between rural and urban life, which had been increasing for decades, narrowed. Still, while farmers benefited from increased prices, they faced a scarcity of laborers that threatened their ability to meet wartime production demands. Iowa lost seventy thousand farm workers during the war to military service or to better-paying jobs in urban areas. Many left farming permanently, their labor replaced by machinery. Farmers as old as eighty-three turned out to assist their neighbors harvest crops in 1943. Families relied upon their daughters to drive tractors and complete other chores. Thousands of girls did work normally done by males. Labor shortages accelerated the adoption of tractors during the war. By the middle of the war there was one tractor for every 218 acres of crops in Iowa.[36]

Faye Wookey and her husband Adrian farmed 240 acres in Montgomery County during the war. "We all worked really hard," she wrote. "We woke every morning at 5 a.m. and many nights didn't have supper until 10 p.m." Their children assisted them with farm work; Faye also helped in the fields. Everyone labored, all the time. "There is no gender discrimination in the farm business," she humbly recalled. In mid-1945 the REA reached them and electricity brightened their lives. It was "the greatest thing that ever happened for the farmers," she wrote. They spent the war years paying off debts, buying land and equipment, and enjoying their good fortune after years of struggle.[37]

An unusual labor force helped solve the increasingly dire labor shortage during the war. The towns of Algona and Clarinda had prisoner-of-war camps that housed captured Axis soldiers. Hundreds of thousands of Germans and Italians were taken prisoner during the war and sent to the United States. The first POW camps had been in southern and southwestern states, but large numbers of prisoners had overwhelmed them, leading to the construction of additional camps in the Midwest. POWs had been brought into Iowa in 1943 from Nebraska and Missouri to help harvest crops. An abundance of prisoners and a shortage of farm workers led to the building of POW camps in the state. Each could house three thousand prisoners and five hundred American guards. The first German and Italian prisoners arrived in early 1944. Japanese POWs came in 1945. Their captors, who did not trust the Japanese as they did the European prisoners, closely supervised them. American POWs captured by Japan had been brutally treated, with almost half of them dying because of mistreatment during the war, so Japanese prisoners were closely guarded. Barbed wire fences surrounded both camps and guard towers with machine gunners kept watch over all prisoners. Construction of the camps set off an economic boom in the area around Algona, as workers flooded in and bid up local rents.[38]

Prisoners were not idle. They grew their own gardens, cultivating peas, carrots, corn, potatoes, and cabbage. POWs enjoyed decent food, libraries, church facilities, and athletic competitions. Some studied the English language, while several guards took German lessons. Prisoners could earn ten cents an hour by working outside the camp, paid in scrip that could be used at the prison canteen. Farmers employed prisoners when workers could not be found, paying their full wage to the US Treasury. Some Iowa farms were desperate for workers, with only one-quarter of the necessary laborers available. Prisoners completed fieldwork, such as harvesting crops, cutting hay, building fences, and detasseling corn. Demand for such labor was high and smaller branch camps were established across the state to provide workers. In this sense Iowa reflected national trends, as POWs from camps across the central United States worked as lumberjacks in Minnesota or labored on farms in Kansas and Nebraska. Italian POWs helped build a levee with sandbags to control a Mississippi flood in April 1944, while Germans worked in plant nurseries in Shenandoah. Japanese POWs also worked on farms and in nurseries. Other prisoners assisted in digging holes for telephone poles for the REA.[39]

Iowa farmers also brought in Mexican workers during the war to meet the demand for agricultural laborers. During the Great Depression, the federal government had forcibly deported four hundred thousand Mexicans, many of them American citizens. But in World War II, agriculture was a war industry and labor shortages led to the recruitment of workers from Mexico. This guest worker system was known as the "bracero" program, from the Spanish word "brazos," or arms. Braceros worked in more than twenty American states, including Iowa, and harvested $432 million in crops nationwide in 1944. (This would be more than $6 billion in 2020.)

Most lived in western states, with about half living in California. Their pay was low and living conditions could be appalling. There were more than sixty thousand Mexican farm workers in the country in the last two years of World War II; in Iowa, more than one thousand braceros worked in the state each year from 1944 to 1946.[40]

Faculty from the State University of Iowa and Iowa State College were involved in two top-secret Allied programs in the war: the Manhattan Project, which produced the first atomic bomb, and Ultra, which deciphered high-level Nazi communications. Those at Iowa State College helped produce uranium, while a professor from Iowa City labored at Bletchley Park decoding German military orders.

Curt Zimansky spent about eighteen months at Ultra, the code name for a secret detachment in England that decoded intercepted Nazi communications. He was an English professor, who earned his PhD from Princeton University in 1937 and came to Iowa that same year. Mathematicians, linguists, and other scholars worked at a secret location, Bletchley Park, fifty miles northwest of London. Zimansky was fluent in several European languages and would focus much of his postwar academic career on codes and cryptology. The Ultra unit intercepted, deciphered, analyzed, and forwarded Nazi communications to Allied commanders. The Germans thought their Enigma machine, which encrypted their communications, was unbreakable. Ultra provided important information on the location of German submarines, as well as crucial intelligence on German army and air force plans that helped the Allies win the war. Zimansky also served in the US Army as an intelligence officer during the Korean War. He was an editor of *Philological Quarterly*, a literature journal, for twenty years. Zimansky retired in 1957 with the rank of major and died in 1973 at the age of fifty-nine.[41]

Researchers at Iowa State College played an important role in the Manhattan Project. Atomic weapons needed high-quality uranium, a rare substance, and ISC scientists decided to try and produce it. One of them was Harley Wilhelm, who had been born in 1900 near Ellston, Iowa. His parents were tenant farmers, and he attended a one-room school for the first years of his education. He was the only child in his family to finish high school. Wilhelm earned a degree in math from Drake University and completed a PhD in chemistry from Iowa State College in 1931. After years of teaching chemistry in Ames he was finally promoted to assistant professor. Wilhelm led a research group, headed by Frank Spedding, that found a way to produce uranium. They improvised a process using a spark plug to heat magnesium oxide, calcium, and uranium tetrafluoride in an iron pipe, producing two ounces of uranium. Soon, they were making larger amounts in the basement of the women's gym on campus. About one thousand tons of uranium were produced during the war. This important effort led to the establishment of the Ames Laboratory at ISC, a major federal center for energy research in the twenty-first century. Spedding became director of the Ames Lab after the war, while Wilhelm taught at the college until his retirement. Frank Spedding had a building named for him in 1974. ISU named the campus Metallurgy Building Wilhelm Hall in 1986. Harley Wilhelm died four years later.[42]

World War II had a profound impact upon Iowa. The war ended the agonies of the Great Depression and brought economic prosperity back to the state, even as it exacted a high cost, with 8,398 Iowans sacrificing their lives for their nation. The war accelerated the migration of people from farms to towns and cities, while also narrowing the living standards between the two. The conflict left Americans with healthy savings and high hopes for the future. It brought women and minority groups into well-paying industrial jobs, if only for a few years. The war also raised expectations for African Americans and helped lay the foundation for the postwar civil rights movement. World War II helped set the path for Iowa for the remainder of the century.

13
Postwar Iowa, 1945–1975

In the thirty years after the end of World War II, broad social and economic forces transformed Iowa. The state became increasingly urban and less agricultural as people left the countryside for better jobs. Local institutions, especially schools, suffered as small towns and the countryside lost population. A productivity revolution, thanks to new machinery, crops, and chemicals, led to tremendous growth in farm production. Iowa's economy continued to diversify after the war and the manufacturing sector became increasingly important. More factories came to the state, mostly tied to agriculture, and women increasingly worked outside the home. Minority groups fought for equality, protesting against their treatment as second-class citizens and the segregation and discrimination that limited their opportunities. While Iowa became more urban and less agricultural after the war—more like the rest of the country—its population continued to lack racial diversity and 97.4 percent of its people were white in 1980. At the same time, Iowa developed a competitive two-party system in the 1960s and 1970s and the Democratic Party successfully battled the dominant Republicans for political power.[1]

The end of World War II on August 14, 1945, brought celebrations to Iowa. Church bells rang and factory whistles blared across the country. Americans kissed strangers, lit bonfires, drank toasts, and danced in the streets. Across Iowa car horns honked and ticker tape streamed down from windows, littering streets. Cars and trucks, full of jubilant people, roamed cities, some dragging tin cans. People lit bonfires in Fayette and threw in firecrackers. A band played. Twenty-five thousand people thronged the streets of Des Moines; police estimated more than sixty thousand showed up in Waterloo. Fire trucks roared through Carroll with their sirens on. The celebration in Cedar Rapids "was pure bedlam," wrote the *Gazette*. "America flung off its wartime constraints," declared the *Council Bluffs Nonpareil*. Rationing of gas, fuel oil, and canned fruits and vegetables halted the day the war ended.[2]

Some survivors of the Holocaust came to Iowa. Jews in Europe had been targeted for extermination by the Nazi regime, which slaughtered six million Jews. By the end of World War II two-thirds of the Jewish population on the continent had been killed. Jacob Waizman and his family had lived near Krakow, Poland. His two older brothers, both in the Polish army, were killed during the war. His sister and parents were murdered at the Auschwitz death camp. He survived three years of slave labor and a three-week death march to Buchenwald in 1945, which killed nearly three thousand people. Jacob and a friend escaped murder in the gas chambers by hiding in a pile of dead bodies until liberated by the American army in April 1945. Waizman married Paula Oliwa after the war. They came to Des Moines with their daughter, Rosa, in 1950. Waizman was an engineer with the Des Moines Public Schools and regularly spoke to Iowa groups about the Holocaust. Paula Murawnik survived the brutal Riga ghetto that killed her husband, Abe, and a death march. After the war she ended up in a displaced persons camp in Germany, where she met Adam Murawnik, whom she married. They resettled in Sioux City in 1950, had a daughter, Esther, and eventually moved to Des Moines.[3]

After the celebrations died down, Americans worried about the effects that the end of the war would have on the economy, wondering if the conflict's end would bring a halt to wartime prosperity. Iowa newspapers predicted a sharp cut in jobs as government spending fell and military contracts were terminated. Millions of men would return home and need work. The *Council Bluffs Nonpareil* wrote that five million people would be discharged from their wartime employment. Seven million could be unemployed by Christmas. The US economy had been mired in depression before the war and Americans feared the return of such misery. Millions had found their first permanent jobs in the military or working in factories. Wartime restrictions and rationing ended quickly; companies began to produce civilian products again. Veterans returned home.[4]

Fears of a second Great Depression faded when a massive economic boom reshaped Iowa and the United States. The American economy grew strongly for almost three decades and most enjoyed a huge improvement in their living standards. Whereas in 1946, half of farm homes did not have electricity, by the 1970s phones, electricity, and flush toilets were widespread and most Americans graduated from high school. Supermarkets, fast-food restaurants, home air-conditioning, dishwashers, and four-lane highways became commonplace. The world that we know in the twenty-first century was created, in large part, in these three decades. But not everyone benefited. African Americans, Latinos, and other minority groups in Iowa were usually excluded from opportunities available to white Americans. Rural areas also often suffered as their populations shrank and farm incomes fell.[5]

The growing postwar economy improved American life by providing vaccines for diseases like polio, which terrified Americans in the mid-twentieth century. It was a virus that seemed to come out of nowhere and sicken children. Polio became widespread in the twentieth century, as improved sanitation reduced childhood exposure and any acquired immunity to it. The disease had left Franklin D. Roosevelt paralyzed below the waist. Polio sickened thousands of Iowans in the 1940s and 1950s, killing some and leaving others paralyzed. Many who were ill had to learn to walk again; others were confined to wheelchairs for life. Many endured multiple surgeries or walked with the help of canes and crutches. There were 3,564 cases of polio in Iowa in 1952. Parents kept their children away from schools and swimming pools for fear they would catch the disease. Vaccines in the 1950s quickly reduced caseloads. Iowa schoolchildren in Linn, Woodbury, and Scott Counties took part in successful vaccine trials. In 1957 there were only seventy-eight cases in the state. But there were three thousand polio survivors living in Iowa in 1997. One of those was Judy Hoit, who caught polio when she was four. Hoit spent the rest of her life getting around by wheelchair. She had two sons and was an entrepreneur, motivational speaker, and writer. Polio was eradicated in the United States in 1979, thanks to widespread vaccinations.[6]

The number of students in Iowa's colleges and universities increased after World War II and kept growing in the following decades. Families could afford to send students to school and an influx of high school graduates kept classrooms full. The GI Bill spurred college attendance by veterans. It included educational benefits and loans to start businesses or buy a home. Veterans made up half of all college students by 1947. John R. Ortega, whose family lived off scrap food from the Des Moines dump in the 1930s, used the GI Bill to attend Drake University. He had dropped out of high school but earned his GED in the Marine Corps and then finished law school. "A whole new middle class was about to emerge," he wrote in his memoir. In 1944 enrollment in Iowa colleges was at 15,277 students, down more than one-third from 1942. But by 1955 the number of students had reached 40,493. Iowa State Teachers College, later renamed the University of Northern Iowa, had only 1,233 students in 1945. This number grew to 6,419 students in 1965, when it cost only $156 a semester. This was about $1,300 in 2020 dollars. The number of students enrolled at the other public and private colleges also dramatically increased. By 1971 more than one hundred thousand Iowans were enrolled in college in the state, more than double the number of 1955.[7]

A housing shortage after the war led to a construction boom outside cities in Iowa, leading to the spread of suburbs. They grew up on the edges of urban areas where land was cheap, encouraged by federal tax breaks. These developments provided space and privacy for a population hungry for their own homes. In Iowa, suburbs grew around Des Moines and near towns such as Ames, Iowa City, and Waterloo. Ankeny was so small that it didn't even count as an urban area in 1950. It grew from 1,229 people in 1950 to 15,429 in 1980. By 2020 Ankeny had more than sixty-seven thousand residents. The city of Clive did not exist in 1950 but had more than six thousand residents by 1980. Urbandale grew from less than 2,000 in 1950 to 17,869 in 1980. Coralville, near Iowa City, grew sevenfold in these three decades to 7,687 people. At the same time, many towns stagnated or declined, as people and business were pulled away to larger cities or to new suburbs. Boone gained only 438 residents in thirty years, while Ottumwa lost almost 20 percent of its population between 1950 and 1980.[8]

The postwar construction of highways encouraged people to live in suburbs. Interstate highways provided Americans with affordable and efficient transportation. The interstate system tied the nation together, even as it doomed towns that it bypassed and destroyed urban neighborhoods that were razed for their construction. Iowa's 710 miles of interstate highways replaced 26,000 acres of productive farmland. By 1964 four-lane Interstate

80 ran from Des Moines to Davenport. Interstate 35 connected the capital to Osceola. North of Des Moines, I-35 was being built to Ames. Interstate 235 through Des Moines was also under construction, as was Interstate 29 along the Missouri River. By 1971 the interstate system in Iowa was complete, costing about 700 million dollars, or about $4.5 billion in 2020 dollars.[9]

In the 1940s Nikole Hannah-Jones's grandmother came to Waterloo with her three small children, fleeing Greenwood, Mississippi—"an apartheid state"—where lynching was common but Black opportunity was absent. In Mississippi, African Americans could not vote or use public libraries and labored in cotton fields or worked in white homes. But she still encountered Jim Crow in the north. Her father and his siblings grew up in a segregated Black neighborhood on Waterloo's east side. Jones's grandmother cleaned the homes of white Iowans—the only work she could find. Her dad joined the army at age seventeen, hoping that military service would help him escape poverty and earn him the right of equal treatment. But he was denied opportunities and discharged under murky conditions, laboring in low-paid service jobs for his whole life. "Like all black men and women in my family, he believed in hard work, but like all black men and women in my family, no matter how hard he worked, he never got ahead," she wrote. Hannah-Jones grew up in an area redlined by the federal government. This was a policy that had profoundly influenced the lives and opportunities of African Americans and lower-income people since the 1930s.[10]

In the postwar United States where one lived helped determine educational options, employment, and quality of life. Home ownership provided most people with their greatest financial asset, as real estate was the best way for most to accumulate wealth. Living in a good area also led to better schools and greater access to jobs and shopping. But Black families, such as that of Nikole Hannah-Jones, were not allowed to live in better neighborhoods and were pushed into segregated ones. The federal government created detailed maps of cities for the Home Owners' Loan Corporation, which was set up in 1933 to encourage home ownership. These maps graded neighborhoods on a scale from A to D. They evaluated the racial, ethnic, and class makeup of a place, as well as its housing. The best areas were colored green and blue. The worst areas were red and yellow. Those with old homes or even a tiny number of African Americans were rated D and outlined in red. Other minorities, including Jews, Asians, Italians, and Eastern Europeans, also suffered from discrimination.

Mortgages, federally backed or not, were rarely available in such areas, where a mix of racial and ethnic groups threatened neighborhood "stability." Some neighborhoods in Des Moines that were surrounded by redlined areas were labeled green. These places only allowed white people to buy homes in them. Redlining was finally outlawed by the Fair Housing Act of 1968. But it had devastating consequences.[11]

Large areas of Des Moines were redlined, as were parts of Waterloo, Davenport, Sioux City, Council Bluffs, and Dubuque, as well more than two hundred other cities in the United States. Most areas in Des Moines that were declared red or yellow were nonwhite and low-income. Black homeowners were five times more likely to live in redlined neighborhoods. Thirty-four percent of the city's neighborhoods, especially those in the south, east, and north, were redlined. Another 41 percent were colored yellow. Large areas of Des Moines were cut off from investment. It was difficult or impossible to get loans to buy or sell housing in these areas. Homes were not repaired, as owners found it hard to access financing. Wealthier families left, as did businesses. City services, such as fire and police, were reduced in declining areas. The schools were worse than those in better neighborhoods. The results were stark, wrote journalist Kim Norvell, with "lower property values, unsafe living conditions, crime, reduced access to insurance and health care." A majority of redlined areas in Des Moines had home values below the city median and these places still had primarily minority residents in 2020. Three neighborhoods had home values one-half of the median. This loss of home equity worsened inequality in Iowa and the United States. Areas in Des Moines that had been redlined in the 1930s had higher poverty, shorter life expectancies, and worse health conditions even in the 2010s. Many areas of Des Moines that had been redlined had fewer trees than other neighborhoods, due to poverty and a lack of investment. In 2016 the median income of African American households in Des Moines was less than half that of the median income of households in Polk County. Black unemployment was also more than four times higher than the county overall.[12]

Interstate construction devastated poorer neighborhoods, often those belonging to African Americans. Highways were usually routed through such areas, in cities from Baltimore to Los Angeles. Iowa was no different. The construction of Interstate 235 through Des Moines obliterated Black neighborhoods in the 1960s, including the vibrant Center Street area. Construction around the Methodist Hospital and a high school stadium also pushed out African Americans. Before the highway, Center Street was "the focal point of black economic, social, and cultural life," wrote Bruce Fehn and Robert Jefferson. It was full of Black-owned restaurants, nightclubs, and hotels. The community had a pharmacy, grocery stores, a record shop, a soda fountain, and Black churches. Jazz and blues musicians came to clubs on Center Street. The freeway and other urban renewal projects did not just destroy businesses—it eliminated affordable housing for Black families. The city of Des Moines gave low appraisals to homeowners and businesses, who could not afford to relocate. Kalanji Saadiq recalled that the city paid Black owners only 35 percent to 40 percent of a property's value. "If you didn't want to sell, they just condemned it," he said. White realtors and white residents kept displaced African Americans from moving into their neighborhoods. White landowners refused to sell property to Emery Jackson in 1963 so that she could build a home. African Americans were segregated into the deteriorating north side of the city. Black leaders protested that urban renewal was "Negro removal." At least one cross was burned in the front yard of a Black family that moved into a white neighborhood. Herbert DePatten, whose father had lost his Center Street business, expressed his outrage by saying "urban renewal was our 9/11."[13]

About the same time as Nikole Hannah-Jones's family came to Iowa, and about fifteen years before the Center Street neighborhood was razed, Edna Griffin and two other adults walked into Katz Drug Store in downtown Des Moines. Griffin and John Bibbs sat down at the lunch counter on July 7, 1948, and ordered dessert but were refused service because of their race. Griffin successfully sued Katz, eventually ending the store's discriminatory policies after a series of judicial battles over eighteen months. Iowa law supposedly forbade discrimination in public accommodations, such as lunch counters, but the Katz businesses had survived a long series of lawsuits over nearly twenty years. A 1944 letter to the national offices of the NAACP described Des Moines as "not badly prejudiced," but a place where discrimination was common. Katz Drug Store denied service to a Black WAC in her military uniform and two of her friends during World War II. The company was notorious for its treatment of African Americans. Edna Griffin was not easily dissuaded, though. A Fisk University graduate, married to a physician, she had been a WAC during the war. She had also joined the Communist Party and had a four-hundred-page FBI file. One of the agents who collected information on her wrote that she was "always fighting for some noble cause."[14]

The trial began October 6, 1948, and the jury quickly ruled in favor of Griffin. Katz Drug Stores appealed the ruling to the Iowa Supreme Court. In response, Griffin organized protests, sit-ins, and boycotts of the business. Protestors compared Katz's discriminatory policies to Nazi racial ideas to hurt the store's business. Griffin and her allies brought additional lawsuits against Katz on behalf of those denied service. An Iowa district court ruled in her favor. Facing further legal defeat the drug store settled out-of-court on December 2, 1949. The next day Black Iowans showed up to have lunch. Griffin and the Black community had won an important local civil rights victory and forced the Iowa legal system to begin to enforce laws that required equal treatment. Griffin died in 2000, having been a member of seemingly every civic organization in Des Moines.[15]

Their success did not resolve housing or employment discrimination in the state, issues that continued to harm African Americans and other nonwhites for decades. On paper, Iowa's Black population enjoyed some rights those in other states did not. Iowa had civil rights laws that were supposed to provide equal opportunities and equal protection. However, the state government did not enforce them. The struggle for equal rights gained momentum and influence in the state in the 1950s and 1960s. But whites in Des Moines and elsewhere were determined to keep Blacks out of their neighborhoods and to practice employment discrimination.[16]

While Iowa's racism was not as infamous as that of Southern states, it profoundly restricted the lives of the state's nonwhite population. African Americans were concentrated in two small areas of low-quality housing in Davenport in 1951. Schools were not officially segregated but the city had no Black teachers, police, or firefighters. Some doctors and dentists refused to treat Black patients; some cemeteries refused to accept African Americans or buried them in segregated plots. In the 1950s Waterloo employers refused to hire Blacks and discriminated against them in restaurants, theaters, and bars. African Americans could not rent or buy homes outside traditionally segregated areas of town, such as those Nikole Hannah-Jones's family lived in. Waterloo schools were segregated due to housing discrimination; desegregation of its schools only seriously began in the 1960s and 1970s. Only three of twenty factories in Keokuk employed African Americans in 1950, despite a Black population of fifteen hundred people. Neither Cedar Rapids nor Ottumwa employed any Black teachers in public schools in the mid-1950s. Des Moines employed no Black firefighters until 1967. Labor unions would not let Blacks enter apprenticeship programs. Police routinely mistreated African Americans as well. A 1957 report on employment discrimination issued a blunt assessment: "Negroes in Iowa are generally excluded from or given only limited opportunities for employment in professions, office and clerical work, retail trade, transportation, teaching, municipal employment, skilled crafts and trades, and in restaurants." Equal opportunities in education, housing, employment, or public accommodations did not exist in the state.[17]

Frustration with the glacial pace of change led to conflict in the late 1960s. Waterloo experienced a racial uprising in July 1967, part of a wave of unrest that hit the United States in the late 1960s. A sixty-eight-year-old Black man told a *New York Times* reporter that "things are a lot better here than they are in Mississippi." But housing segregation, a lack of good jobs for the young, and harsh policing sparked the confrontation. Tensions also boiled over on July 4, 1966, when young African Americans rioted against police mistreatment in Des Moines. Rioters hurled rocks and bottles at police. In 1968 African Americans in Iowa organized a Des Moines branch of the Black Panther Party for Self-Defense. While the organization became nationally famous for its militancy, in Iowa it focused upon Black self-reliance. It crusaded against police brutality and discrimination and fought for improved employment opportunities, high-quality education, and decent housing. The Des Moines chapter only survived two years and collapsed after its headquarters were suspiciously bombed and its leaders charged with crimes.[18]

Latinos and Latinas also struggled against discrimination and limited opportunities. Military service had improved prospects for those such as John Ortega. But life did not change for most. Saul Sanchez and his family were migrant workers who picked tomatoes near Muscatine, harvested sugar beets in Montana, and labored in California's fields. They first came to Iowa in 1958, living in housing converted from a pigsty. Men picked up to two hundred baskets of tomatoes each day. Sanchez graduated from high school, went to college, and became a teacher. Others in Iowa's Latino community, some from Cook's Point and Holy City, went on to advocate for migrant laborers in the state. Grassroots leaders, inspired by Cesar Chavez's struggle for farmworker rights in California, battled discrimination in housing, education, and employment. Some were former soldiers, such as Antonio Navarro, who said, "Our battle for eliminating social discrimination was less frightening when compared to the horrors of the war." Mexican American veterans were not allowed to join local

Iowans were shocked at the terrible living conditions and the exploitation of migrant workers in the 1960s. Legislation did little to curb abuses, though. Migrant workers harvesting cucumbers on Muscatine Island (Iowa) for Corinne and Clinton Zaehringer (*pictured in foreground*), July 1959. PH 13328, State Historical Society of Iowa, Des Moines.

Veterans of Foreign Wars posts. Whites did not sell homes to nonwhites and kept Mexican Americans out of their neighborhoods. The passage of the Civil Rights Act of 1964 did not end unofficial prejudice against Latinos, who were often refused service at stores and doctor's offices. The Davenport chapter of the League of United Latin American Citizens (LULAC) advocated for greater equality and emphasized the importance of education for Mexican Americans. This chapter was more militant than most, supporting a grape boycott to show solidarity with Chavez and pushing for legislation to protect migrant laborers in the state. The deplorable living conditions of such workers shocked many Iowans, who were unaware of such exploitation in their state. Weak bills, prohibiting labor for children under ten, passed the Republican-dominated legislature in the late 1960s. Such legislation did not do much to help farmworkers.[19]

Life in Iowa's overwhelmingly white countryside experienced profound change after World War II. While most of the US population had been urban since 1920, it took Iowa until the mid-1950s before more of its people lived in urban areas than rural ones. Migration to cities had been reducing the rural population of Iowa for many years. In southwest Iowa, counties reached their peak population in 1900 and suffered from steady outmigration throughout the century. In the 1940s and 1950s this movement accelerated. In the 1940s alone, two hundred thousand Iowans left the state, according to one research report. Much of this migration was away from agriculture. Between 1945 and 1974 the nation lost 60 percent of its farms. Iowa lost 40 percent of its farms in these three decades. A variety of factors, from low prices to the high cost to mechanize, pushed marginal producers out. As the farm economy shed workers, employment opportunities disappeared in the countryside. The loss of the farm population undermined the viability of small towns, which also lost people when residents and customers moved away. Workers migrated to find jobs, especially ones in manufacturing. Those in their twenties and thirties departed most often, leaving an aging rural population behind. Small towns only prospered if they were within easy commuting distance of new job opportunities. The tax base of rural communities also fell, with less revenue to provide services to those who were left behind.[20]

The shrinking rural population reduced the number of children in school. From 1930 to 1960, the percentage of school-aged children living on farms in the Midwest fell by half. Changing demographics led to the reorganization of schools in the region. Iowa's system of one-room country schoolhouses survived into the mid-twentieth century—they had provided a basic education to a dispersed rural population for many decades. But their limited resources and personnel handicapped their ability to prepare students for college or urban careers. Larger schools could provide a better education, with a greater variety of classes and better-trained teachers. In the 1954–1955 school year, Iowa had 4,417 school districts and 3,261 one-room schools. The state only had 525,000 students in public schools, though. The one-room school was romantic, but it was also highly inefficient. Teachers taught small numbers of students across a wide variety of grade levels. Buildings often needed repairs and transients sometimes lived in them during summer vacations.[21]

School consolidation was controversial but usually necessary, given outmigration. Many rural residents fought against the process. Natural resistance to change accounted for some opposition, as did a suspicion of cities. A fear of higher property taxes was a rational response, as farm owners often paid more taxes than city dwellers. Worry about a loss of local control over education also spurred resistance. However, the greater cost usually provided a superior education. Most of Iowa's school consolidation occurred from 1954 to 1961, with more than three thousand districts being absorbed into larger ones. Alice McMurry taught at a rural school in Benton Center in southern Iowa after World War II. So many families moved away that her school was closed after she had taught there for six years. The next school she taught at, in Bellflower, also shut down. She wrote in her memoir that enrollment in some rural schools fell from twenty to zero as families moved away. She retired after eighteen more years of elementary teaching in Promise City. Almost 90 percent of Iowa's one-room schoolhouses were closed by 1962. While the loss of one-room schools did not hurt the economic and social life of a small town, the closing of a high school could be a traumatic event. Towns lost their prized sports teams. They also lost the business that schools brought to small towns.[22]

Davis County, in southeast Iowa, voted in 1959 to combine the sixty-one school districts in the county into one large district. The reorganization eliminated fifty-five one-room schoolhouses as well as two small high schools in the towns of Troy and Pulaski. This was not unusual—90 percent of high schools in rural states, such as Iowa, Oklahoma, North Dakota, and Wyoming, had fewer than one hundred graduates each year. They could not provide an education equal to larger high schools. Each town had less than four hundred residents; Pulaski had forty-six students and Troy had twenty-five. The two high schools had a total of seven teachers. Students from the two closed schools went to Bloomfield High School, which had more than five hundred students. They could now take a fourth year of English or study a foreign language. Bloomfield High offered chemistry, physics, sociology, and driver's education—all subjects lacking at the smaller schools.[23]

In the mid-1950s Dennis Lindholm was in high school near Red Oak. School consolidation would have regularly made the news. But he faced greater struggles, as he was a gay man and American society would not accept him. Everything that he learned about homosexuality in high school was very negative, he recalled. Lindholm felt that he could not be himself and that his family did not accept him. He knew he was different in a way that he could not share; he didn't know anyone who was like him. "I spent so many years denying and subordinating and hiding the fact that I was gay. A lot of unhappiness and some severe depression." He told writer Will Fellows that society had robbed him of much of his life. Lindholm became a teacher, married, and had two children. "I didn't know that it was okay, that a normal person could be gay." When he came out, he said that a great weight had been lifted from his shoulders. By his mid-50s he lived on a farm in Wisconsin, enjoying the labor of farm life, and self-acceptance. Though the rural world of the mid-twentieth century did not accept him, he returned to the countryside and later found solace.[24]

American farmers enjoyed a productivity revolution after World War II, which contributed to the population decline in the countryside. More food was produced with less human labor. Herbicides, pesticides, improved seeds, tractors, and fertilizers led to increasingly larger crops from each acre. The yield for corn doubled from about forty bushels per acre in 1950 to eighty bushels per acre twenty years later. The agricultural workforce was cut in half by 1970 and farms became increasingly capital intensive. By 1970 combines harvested almost all corn in Iowa. New grain bins, combines, automated feedings systems, and other technologies showed that Iowa was an increasingly industrial landscape. Fertilizers allowed farmers to avoid exhausting their fields of vital nutrients, such as nitrogen. With these chemicals, farmers could grow crops in the same fields year after year. Herbicides killed nearly all weeds, eliminating the need to cultivate fields. This saved vast amounts of labor and allowed crops to be planted closer together, which increased yields. Hybrid seeds preserved desired traits, such as stronger corn stalks or disease resistance. Livestock breeding also greatly improved milk production. From the mid-1950s to the late 1960s farmers produced more than they could sell. Their costs also increased faster than the prices they earned from commodities. Farm prices did not begin to increase until 1969.[25]

In the 1950s Iowa's farmers struggled. Land prices were high. Expenses did not fall when prices did, however. Robert Anderson, a Korean War veteran who farmed two hundred acres near Roland, recalled that times were tough for young farmers. Farm profits fell 50 percent in 1955 alone, when he lost $338, about $3,300 in 2020 dollars. He hoped to earn a profit in 1956. Those who did not own land tried to save to buy it. Anderson took over his family farm after the death of his father, splitting income with his mother. He borrowed $6,000 for machinery, fuel, and livestock—almost $60,000 in 2020—but falling prices after the end of the Korean War undermined his income, leaving him with little to show for his work. One hundred dollars a month in assistance from the VA helped put food on the table. Anderson's wife, Jo Anne, helped with farm chores, cared for animals, and canned vegetables from their garden. Both worked fourteen-hour days. Despite serious challenges, he told a journalist that farming "gets in a man's blood. Somehow I just can't stand to work by the hour. I'd rather be my own boss." Despite such beliefs, many rural families left farms.[26]

Careful business management and frugality, as well as some luck, helped farmers survive the lean years of the 1950s and 1960s. Doyle Churchill began farming with 120 acres of rented land and some used equipment in 1950. His family prospered by specializing in growing corn—they did not own any cows or chickens and did not grow a vegetable garden. Instead, they purchased all their food at a supermarket. Churchill's wife, Louise, helped him with chores, but their two daughters had no eggs to gather or cows to milk. Louise Churchill was glad to work on their farm. Her father had been a farmer and she understood the importance and value of her work, she told a journalist in 1966. They lived near the town of Newton, about thirty miles east of Des Moines and enjoyed all the pleasures of modern life, cars having "done away with the remoteness of farm life," she said in 1966.[27]

Rural and small-town Iowans had left home during World War II for better paying jobs in urban areas. This continued after the war. Some farmers worked away from their property to supplement their agricultural income. Lonnie Shipley, who lived near Grimes, worked nearly full-time at a tool company in Des Moines. Shipley rented 160 acres of land and grew corn and soybeans. He also raised cattle and hogs. But he did not know if he would be able to continue to be a farmer, though he preferred it to factory work. One farmer's son made $400 a month working for IBM at the age of twenty-one, equal to about a monthly income of $3,500 in 2020. His father grimly noted that this income was a "damn sight more than I saw around here last year." Wilma Embres became a teacher to help support her family after agricultural prices fell in the mid-1950s. She earned $260 a month, about $2,500 a month in 2020 income. Others quit farming and moved to towns and cities to take jobs at factories and insurance companies.[28]

Manufacturing became an important employer in Iowa in the mid-twentieth century. Industrial work—especially in unionized factories—provided a good income. The postwar years were boom years for American industry. Productivity soared and workers benefited from economic growth. Labor unions gained higher wages and good benefits for their members. New

Deal reforms that protected collective bargaining and set minimum wages helped workers. By the early 1960s there were more union members in the state than farm operators. The state attracted an increasing number of agricultural-related factory jobs from the 1940s to the 1970s. In 1950 the value of manufactured products exceeded farm production by an estimated $500 million. Four years later manufacturing was worth $3.8 billion, nearly 40 percent more than farm production. (Manufacturing would have been worth about $37 billion in 2020 dollars). Most industry in the state was tied to agriculture, producing either machinery for farming or processing farm products. The meatpacking sector was an important industry—Iowa processed more livestock than any other state—as were John Deere factories. Manufacturing employed 148,000 workers in 1950, who earned an average weekly wage of $59.26, about $634 in 2020 income. In the early 1960s, continuing low agricultural prices pushed many rural people to work in towns and cities to supplement their farm incomes. Many took positions at the John Deere Tractor Works and other companies in Waterloo and eastern Iowa.[29]

Iowa's manufacturing sector grew in importance, adding factories and employees. In the 1950s, food processing and farm machinery were the leading industries. Eastern Iowa, especially the area around Cedar Falls and Waterloo, was a center of industry. Quaker Oats had a factory in Cedar Rapids in the 1950s. By the 1970s John Deere factories in these cities employed more than fourteen thousand workers. The Rath Packing Company produced Black Hawk brand sliced bacon and other ham products. John Deere also had major factories in Dubuque making tractors and construction equipment, employing more than eight thousand workers. A toy factory in Dubuque employed more than seven hundred people, most of them female. The Aluminum Company of America (Alcoa) had a large plant near Davenport. Major meatpacking facilities existed in Ottumwa and Dubuque. Newton and Hampton had important Maytag washing machine factories, with more than three thousand employees in the mid-1950s. Iowa led the nation in meat processing in 1954, producing nearly 2.7 billion pounds.[30]

Iowa women increasingly worked outside the home after World War II, with the number employed almost doubling between 1940 and 1960. Married women with children joined the workforce in increasing numbers. Close to nine hundred new industrial businesses moved to Iowa between 1950 and 1965 and many employed female laborers. Economic necessity drove them to work outside their homes, as the farm economy struggled. Pauline Fisher found work in a manufacturing plant in Oskaloosa, recalling, "I had to work." Her family rented land, hoping to save money to buy a farm, but low prices kept them from saving enough. "Our farm just wasn't paying at all," she said. The death or disability of a male wage earner, or a divorce, also led women to look for employment. Their income often helped farm families survive. Ilo Rhines had a job with the postal service, which she credited with helping to save her family farm. Mothers also did not want their children to suffer as they had during the war and Depression—they wanted them to have the comforts of life they had been deprived of. African American women had difficulty securing jobs in the manufacturing sector though, as some firms refused to hire them. Complaints to the federal government eventually forced meatpacking plants to hire some Black women.[31]

Most women worked in the clerical and service industries, but an increasing number found employment in manufacturing, which paid better. Some had previous work experience, such as Mary Speer, who had been a welder in shipyards during World War II. She returned to Iowa to work at a Firestone tire plant in Des Moines, working the night shift from eleven to seven in morning. Bev Clinton labored at an electrical factory in Cedar Rapids and Susan Rhum took a job at a spark plug plant in Burlington because their families needed two incomes to survive. Others were also employed at the Amana Refrigeration Company or at a pen company in Fort Madison. Many also worked in meatpacking plants, which had a long history of hiring women. This was an important industry, with plants scattered across the state from Fort Dodge to Ottumwa and Mason City. Women usually worked in lower-paid positions, stuffing sausages or making lunch meat. Meatpacking could be a very tough and dirty job. Velma Wetzel cleaned the large intestines of butchered hogs. "If you weren't careful, you could be completely covered in fecal matter by the end of the day," wrote historian Coreen Derifield.[32]

Fern Klopp was one of those women who took employment outside her home. She was from Cedar Rapids and began work for the Turner Microphone Company in 1943. She was thirty-six at the time and married with children. She began working when her daughter decided to train to be a nurse, thinking her family might need some extra income. Her husband Arthur was against his wife taking a job. She was at the company for a year before Arthur died of a heart attack. Klopp ended up with the business for thirty-five years, making walkie talkie radios. She only lived a couple blocks from the shop so she could go home and have lunch with her kids. Fern started cutting crystals with a diamond-edge saw, lubricated by oil. It was "kind of an oily, messy job," she recalled. Her sisters told her at the outset that she would never stay with the job. "It was the wrong thing for them to say, because I was determined that I was going to stick it out, and I did." She then moved to the machine shop, running a drill press. Her fellow employees were overwhelmingly female. She recalled that the people she worked with were like "one big family," and that they were well-treated by their employer. Their union negotiated pay and other benefits. She often worked ten hours a day, from five in the morning until 3:30 p.m. She also worked Saturdays. Klopp was a business manager for her company's union. The plant closed in 1979, a few years after she retired.[33]

Just a few years after Fern Klopp started her job in Cedar Rapids, the Cold War began. The end of World War II left the United States and the Soviet Union as the world's two superpowers. The rival nations fell into the long conflict known as the Cold War, which lasted until the early 1990s. In 1947 President Harry S. Truman adopted a policy of containment to halt the spread of Soviet communism, which would be the foundation for American foreign policy for more than forty years. The United States provided billions of dollars through the Marshall Plan to rebuild Western Europe and resist Soviet expansion, which helped keep it free from invasion. But the United States and its allies fought a bloody war in Korea from 1950 to 1953.[34]

In June 1950 North Korean troops invaded South Korea, overwhelming American and South Korean units. A daring amphibious invasion in September at Inchon turned the tide. Allied troops surged into North Korea, pursuing the crumbling North Korean army. The Chinese army then joined the war in late 1950 to aid their North Korean allies. The counterattack, in the middle of an awful winter, took the American army by surprise. Donald Noehren, a sergeant from Harlan, Iowa, was taken prisoner in the fighting when his unit was overrun by the Chinese. He died on January 22, 1951, in a North Korean camp. His remains were recovered more than fifty years later, and he was buried in Arlington National Cemetery in 2017. By the middle of 1951 the conflict had become a stalemate. It was "a horrible war," as Des Moines native Antonio Montognese recalled, in which Chinese and North Korean soldiers attacked in waves at night. Herbert Barger called the Battle of Heartbreak Ridge the toughest fighting he experienced.

"It was called Heartbreak, we took control of that mountain seven times and lost it seven times," he remembered. Most of the men in his platoon were killed in one night. Iowan Robert Gates, who served in the First Marine Division in 1951 and 1952, said that "the shelling and fighting went on as trench warfare." Vernon Becker, who grew up on a farm near Dyersville, recalled that men "lived like gophers or moles," fearing death every day on patrol. When the war ended with a cease fire in July 1953, Becker said that "we got to live like humans again."[35]

The United States also fought a long war in Vietnam in the 1960s and 1970s—Iowans fought in the conflict and struggled against it at home. In 1969 the United States Supreme Court decided *Tinker vs. Des Moines Independent Community School District*, an important case on the right to free speech in public schools. It was sparked by a 1965 antiwar protest by three teenaged students in Des Moines secondary schools. The court upheld their right to protest the war by wearing armbands to class. Des Moines school administrators had banned such protests because it might disturb the school day. The court ruled that the students presented no threat of disorder; its ruling protected the right to such protest. Protests against the war also occurred at universities and colleges in Iowa in the 1960s and early 1970s. They were mild compared to those in Berkeley and at Columbia University. Students burned draft cards at the University of Iowa and tried to block the Marine Corps from recruiting. Marches sometimes got unruly, resulting in broken windows for some businesses. After the killings of student protesters at Ohio's Kent State University in May 1970, thousands joined the antiwar demonstrations. Buildings were occupied and some were arrested. A National Guard unit was stationed at Iowa City's fairgrounds in case of violence. The university gave students the chance to end the semester early in spring 1970 and thousands left campus. Protests were smaller at ISU. Teach-ins gave way to antiwar rallies that reached their peak in spring 1970. Demonstrations declined quickly as the war wound down.[36]

Iowan James Seddon served in Southeast Asia in 1967 and 1968 and experienced the horrors of war. He grew up like many Iowa boys, completing chores for his family and playing with his brothers and friends. He joined the air force and became a mechanic. Seddon's idealism was quickly shattered. He had been raised to be a decent and moral human, but he found no honor or dignity in war. While riding in a helicopter, he grabbed a man's arm to steady himself as the chopper took incoming gunfire. The craft shuddered and Seddon found that all that remained of the man was the arm he was holding onto. In Cambodia a friend needlessly died, and he had to watch a farm family murdered on a reconnaissance mission. Staying alive became an obsession. "There is something about fear that scars deeply," he wrote. He killed a man while defending an airbase and watched him die. It haunted him, as did other horrors. The war came home with him. He lived in "two worlds. I had seen both sides and could live in neither. I had nightmares about one and no dreams of the other." He attempted college but quit. He became isolated from life, taking long walks until exhausted, plagued by guilt and wondering why he had survived. The love of his wife and children eventually redeemed him.[37]

One Iowa soldier, twenty-five-year-old Sergeant Michael Mullen, did not return from Vietnam. He was killed by American artillery fire on February 18, 1970. Mullen was from La Porte City, southeast of Waterloo, and had been a graduate student in animal nutrition at the University of Missouri when he was drafted. His parents, Peg and Gene, spent many months trying to figure out how their son died. The US government lied to them, covering up the fact that American shells had killed their son. The army claimed that Vietcong infiltrators had called down South Vietnamese artillery fire. The army was indifferent and uncaring; the Pentagon defensive and heartless. Elected representatives were unresponsive. Peg and Gene refused to accept Michael's medals after the army deducted money from his final paycheck for leave. They were convinced that their phone lines were tapped by the government. The Mullens' faith in their country was shattered by the sacrifice of their son. Michael Mullen was one of 3,731 men who were lost to noncombat deaths that were not classified as accidents, homicides, suicides, or drug abuse. He was listed as having died of other causes. A total of 869 Iowans died in the Vietnam War.[38]

Iowa's rural areas, like La Porte City where the Mullens lived, lost population after World War II. But they had outsized political power. As late as 1962, wrote journalist Lauren Soth, legislative districts were based on the population distribution of about 1900. Each county in Iowa had at least one member in the state house of representatives regardless of its population. Counties with major cities, such as Polk County with Des Moines, received only one additional house seat. A sparsely populated county, such as Adams County, with 7,468 people in 1960, had a house member. Polk County, with 266,315 people, only had two house members. As late as 1962, only 27 percent of voters could elect a house majority. It was almost as bad in the Iowa Senate, where 35 percent of voters could elect a majority. Attempts to reform this system in the early and mid-twentieth century were rejected by the state legislature, whose members benefited from the system of unfair apportionment.[39]

In 1964 the US Supreme Court ruled in the case *Reynolds v. Sims* that apportionment not based on population was unconstitutional. The court argued that malapportionment violated the Fourteenth Amendment's equal protection clause. This ruling redrew the political map of the United States. State legislatures and congressional districts could not be drawn to discriminate against urban areas. The ruling radically changed political boundaries across the country. In Iowa, the decision resulted in almost a decade of political battles, commissions, constitutional amendments, court cases, and legislation that pitted urban interests against rural ones. In 1972 the Iowa Supreme Court announced a plan that overruled partisan attempts to protect incumbents. New state house and senate districts helped break the rural and conservative control of Iowa politics and usher in a more competitive political landscape in the state.[40]

One of those who helped make Iowa more than a one-party state was Neal Smith, the boy who had pet raccoons in the 1930s. He survived the Great Depression and military service in World War II. Smith became a lawyer after the war, graduating from Drake University the same year as his wife, Bea, completed law school. When they both applied for a job at an insurance company, she was offered a little more than half of his salary. They declined the offer and opened their own thriving law firm. She discovered that female clients were happy to have a woman lawyer, even if an insurance company was not. Neal Smith served as a Democratic member of Congress from Iowa from 1959 to 1995, a humble political moderate who avoided publicity but was a successful legislator reelected for decades in a Republican leaning state.[41]

The Democratic Party in Iowa was successful in challenging the dominant Republicans in the 1960s and 1970s. The state elected a Democratic governor, Harold Hughes, in 1962 and then gave the Democrats control of both houses of the state legislature two years later. Hughes's leadership and popularity were crucial to Democratic gains. In the 1970s two Democratic US Senators were elected from Iowa, John C. Culver and Richard Clark. Democrats elected five new congressmen to the House of Representatives in 1974, after Nixon's Watergate scandals. Iowa had elected two Democrats as governor in the 1930s, when the crisis of the Great Depression turned the state's voters away from the Republican Party, as well as one more governor in the late 1950s. Still, the GOP normally dominated the state, often with incredible majorities in the state house and senate. In 1946 and 1952 the Republican Party controlled 105 of 108 seats in the state house. Within this context, Hughes was the most important Democratic governor of the twentieth century, leading the state for six years before being elected as US Senator from Iowa. He even briefly joined the Democratic race for the presidential nomination in 1972.[42]

Harold Hughes had a compelling personal story that influenced his remarkably successful political career. He was a reformed alcoholic, who credited his Christian faith with redeeming him from the evils of drink. In World War II, he served in the army, seeing combat in Africa and Italy. He was a tall, handsome, and charismatic speaker, who had been a truck driver after the war. Hughes's progressive platform was influenced by Lyndon Johnson's Great Society. He pushed a series of new laws that included tax reform, abolishing the death penalty, tripling state aid to schools, and authorizing more than a dozen new community colleges. These institutions helped rural and small-town Iowa with workforce development and vocational training and ensured that fifty thousand Iowans completed high school equivalency diplomas between 1965 and 1980. The Democrats made the state tax system more progressive, increasing taxes on higher earners but reducing them on the elderly and the poor. Most famously, Hughes legalized the sale of liquor by the drink statewide. He served as governor until 1968, when he broke with Lyndon Johnson and criticized the conduct of the Vietnam War. That year he ran for the US Senate in opposition to Johnson, winning his race by a narrow margin. Hughes served one term, declining to run for reelection. He briefly ran for the Democratic nomination for the presidency in 1971 before dropping out.[43]

Iowans elected Republican Robert D. Ray as governor in 1968. He was governor for fourteen years, a record only exceeded by his lieutenant governor, Terry Branstad, who was governor for more than twenty years. Ray was a moderate Republican, who significantly increased school funding and opposed the death penalty. He also signed a bipartisan collective bargaining law in 1974 for public employees—such as nurses, teachers, and firefighters—that improved their lives and working conditions. Unions gave up the right to strike in exchange for fair negotiations over benefits and wages. Personal income taxes were increased in 1971, with additional revenues dedicated to schools. State funding from income taxes replaced a reliance on property taxes for education, which often led to serious inequities between districts. This provided more funding and increased access to a high-quality education for lower-income students. In the 1970s the state economy boomed, providing growing revenues to fund spending. Expenditures grew quickly, from around $350 million in 1969 to almost $2 billion in 1983. Much of this budget growth was due to high inflation, which more than doubled nationally during Ray's fourteen years in office. Ray was criticized as too liberal by members of his own party. In the twenty-first century moderate Republicans like Robert Ray would be increasingly rare.[44]

Robert Ray is best remembered as a humanitarian. After the Vietnam War, he invited refugees from Southeast Asia to relocate to Iowa. They came in two waves, first in the mid-1970s and then at the end of the decade. About ten thousand people came to the state. The best-known of these refugee groups was the Tai Dam, the first of whom came to Iowa in late 1975. They fled communist China in the 1950s for Vietnam. The Tai Dam then left Vietnam for Laos, finally seeking shelter in Thailand. An employee of the federal government visited their refugee camp in Thailand and wrote to thirty American governors to explain their plight. Beginning in 1975, Ray welcomed them and thousands of other refugees from Southeast Asia. About thirteen hundred Tai Dam resettled in Iowa by 1979, mostly living in the Des Moines area. Despite an aversion to harsh winters, they were glad to live in the state because their community could remain together. Many worked in meatpacking plants but some started small businesses, including a contract sewing enterprise that operated out of a storefront.[45]

In the late 1970s hundreds of thousands of people fled Vietnam. The plight of these refugees, known as the "boat people," gained worldwide attention. Ray and staff members visited refugee camps in Thailand in October 1979 and saw people dying from malnutrition. Despite resistance from many Iowans, who believed that there were plenty of needy Iowans looking for work and that bringing in refugees would be unfair to them, Ray welcomed these newcomers. The state established a Refugee Service Center to assist new arrivals and Iowans donated more than $500,000 to provide food for those in Southeast Asia. Among the refugees were Thais, Laotians, Hmong, and Vietnamese. One man, thirty-one-year-old Tran Vinh Kiet, spoke English well, having worked in South Vietnam at an army base. Kiet was offered two industrial jobs within a week of his arrival in Iowa. His sister, Duong Muoi, worked at a tailor shop.[46]

Republican governor Robert Ray invited refugees from Southeast Asia to relocate to Iowa. Vietnamese refugees, woman smiling with child. From Pioneer Life–Immigration photo files, Special Collections, State Historical Society of Iowa, Iowa City.

When Ray left office in 1983, he visited Iowa's Refugee Service Center, where he met with some of the resettled refugees. One of them gave him a gift and told him, "We are giving you this present because if it weren't for you we would not be alive." Ray recalled, "That made me think I had done at least something worthwhile during all those years."[47]

Another Iowa humanitarian, Norman Borlaug, won the Nobel Peace Prize in 1970. Borlaug was the father of the "Green Revolution," credited with saving one billion human lives. He bred high-yield crops that helped feed much of the globe after World War II. Borlaug was born in 1914 near Cresco in northeast Iowa. He attended a one-room school for the first eight years of his education. He was a humble man, who called himself a "country-bred Iowa boy." Growing up on a farm and attending a modest school gave him empathy for those who struggled to achieve a better life. After his wife, Margaret, told him that he had won the Nobel

Prize he kept working in a farm field at an agricultural experiment station near Mexico City. He then went to a news conference with dirty hands and dust on his shoes. Borlaug earned all his degrees from the University of Minnesota, which he attended during the Great Depression. Hungry people in Minneapolis reminded him of the problem of food scarcity. He finished a PhD in plant pathology and moved to Mexico to help farmers improve their crops. Better sanitation reduced deaths, but birth rates grew after World War II; human populations in the developing world exploded but food supplies did not keep up. He traveled all over Mexico, battling illness, blazing sun, and floods, while tinkering with strains of wheat. After years of labor, Borlaug bred a compact, disease-resistant wheat plant that provided large amounts of grain. Wheat output tripled or quadrupled. He also helped breed better rice varieties—the staple crop for almost half of the world. Developing countries such as India, China, Brazil, and Mexico adopted improved crops. Pesticides and fertilizers helped with production. This led to great increases in the food supply. Between 1950 and 2006 global grain output more than tripled, while using about the same amount of land. Norman Borlaug died in 2009, having taught agronomy at Texas A&M University into his eighties.[48]

The great economic boom that began in the 1940s ran into difficulties in the 1970s. Gasoline prices spiked after Arab nations halted oil exports in late 1973. The country had its worst recession since the 1930s. In Iowa, things were not so bad, as strong farm prices helped to mute the burdens of high inflation and increasing unemployment. The small town of Forest City, in northern Iowa, suffered from severe job losses, though. Industries, such as Winnebago Motor Homes, laid off more than three thousand employees. Demand for its large vehicles had fallen as gas prices skyrocketed. But high farm prices buoyed the local agricultural economy and diluted the economic damage caused by the layoffs. Many had commuted to the town from their farms and now returned to full-time agriculture. The strong farm economy helped the state avoid the harsh realities most of the country faced during the decade.[49]

The three decades after World War II were prosperous ones for most Iowans, as the American economy grew at a fast rate. General prosperity and rural outmigration dominated these years, even as minority groups fought against housing and employment discrimination. Many were left out of the economic boom in the state, as farm families, African Americans, Mexican Americans, and the poor struggled. The GI Bill and growing incomes led more Iowans to attend college. People moved to suburbs, encouraged by expanding road networks and car ownership. Rural areas experienced increasing population loss, with people pushed out by low farm prices. Schools in the countryside closed as well. Iowa's politics became increasingly competitive. Iowa voters elected Harold Hughes as governor and choose other Democrats for the US Senate and the House of Representatives. In the late 1960s farm prices recovered and the 1970s were boom times for Iowa's farm families, even as the national economy struggled. However, the 1980s brought the state incredible difficulties that shattered the dreams of many. The farm crisis of that decade had its roots in the 1970s and is the subject of the next chapter.

14
Iowa and the Farm Crisis, 1975–2000

The agricultural boom of the 1970s ended in the early 1980s. Farm income fell dramatically, and the state experienced a brutal downturn that accelerated rural and small-town decline. The human cost was high, as bankruptcies, foreclosures, unemployment, and suicide destroyed lives. The farm crisis led to agricultural consolidation and poorer rural areas. It also hurt Iowa's industry, leaving lower-paying jobs, which were increasingly filled by immigrants. In the late 1980s and 1990s the state recovered, with urban areas benefiting the most. Two crops came to dominate Iowa's countryside—corn and soybeans—and diversified farm production declined. Iowa suffered from increasing environmental challenges in the late twentieth century, hammered by droughts and the Great Flood of 1993. Its politics were dominated by its longest-serving governor, Terry Branstad, and its two US Senators, Chuck Grassley and Tom Harkin. Iowa's presidential caucuses attracted huge amounts of attention every four years, as it was the first election in the presidential primary season. By 2000 the state's future seemed bright, the agony of the 1980s increasingly distant.

The 1970s saw a strong state economy, with a farm sector that was prospering better than any time since World War II. Agriculture thrived even as the national economy struggled with inflation and stagnant growth. "Agriculture was racing for the heavens in the late 1970s, and there seemed no end in the good things that would happen," wrote *Des Moines Register* reporter David Westphal. International demand for American farm goods grew in the 1970s, thanks to new grain exports to foreign markets. High food prices drove up the cost of farmland. The price of land in Iowa went up, nearly doubling between 1975 and 1981 in Pocahontas County, where some property sold for more than $3,500 an acre. (This would be about $10,000 in 2020 dollars.) Farmers put their equity to work, buying land and machinery and sending their children to college. Rural families finally seemed to be enjoying the lives of abundance found in postwar cities and suburbs. But farm debt grew, too. "Debt had not played such a large role in agricultural investments since 1915–1919," wrote historian Pamela Riney-Kehrberg. Business and governmental leaders thought that the state had become recession-proof, as tax revenues flooded into state accounts and money flowed into the pockets of farm families and workers.[1]

The prosperity did not last. Overproduction and falling demand led to an inevitable drop in farm prices. The bust of the 1980s led to the worst agricultural crisis in the United States since the Great Depression. It was known as a farm crisis, but it was also a rural community crisis, with small towns and businesses also hurting from a depressed agricultural economy. Urban areas suffered badly as well, when large employers like John Deere laid off thousands of employees.[2]

Iowa's growth was built, in large part, on high agricultural prices and low interest rates. The American farm economy became more integrated into the world economic system after World War II. This provided opportunities for new export markets but put American farmers in competition with those in other countries. A weakened dollar, which made American goods cheaper in other countries, made it easier for people in other nations to buy things produced in the United States. In the early 1970s US grain exports doubled. Farm income doubled as well, driven higher by increased overseas sales. The Nixon administration encouraged farmers to plant as many acres as possible, from "fencerow to fencerow." Responding to higher prices, and the best farm economy in decades, farmers produced as much as they could. They strove for maximum efficiency, buying more land and equipment and taking on new debts to grow as many bushels as possible on as many acres as they could buy. Some borrowed huge amounts of money to expand their operations, expecting prices would stay high. Others borrowed money to help their children start farming. Banks, the federal government, and other institutions told farmers to expand, advice which often led farmers to ruin in the following years. The United

States also began to sell millions of tons of grain to the Soviet Union, following crop failures in that nation. Droughts in many developing countries reduced grain reserves and led to further demand. A confluence of factors led to historically high prices for American farm goods in the 1970s.[3]

While Iowa enjoyed good times, the overall American economy was in trouble. High oil prices contributed to price inflation, which made almost everything more expensive. This hurt farm families but strong incomes reduced the burden. American unemployment also increased to 7.5 percent in 1975 and stayed high throughout the rest of the 1970s. Industries that had been the backbone of middle-class life, including the automotive and steel sectors, faced stiff competition from Japan or Germany. Factories closed across the country. Economic insecurity was widespread; wages fell for most workers. High inflation and high unemployment made life miserable for most Americans—a political crisis that forced the federal government to make major changes to economic policy which would help create the farm crisis of the 1980s.[4]

The prosperity of the 1970s slowed in the second half of the decade and collapsed in the early 1980s. Farm prices began to fall in the late 1970s as production, both in the United States and abroad, flooded the market. Some farmers struggled as income dipped, refinancing their loans periodically. If interest rates remained low, they could remain solvent. But the Federal Reserve chose to contract the money supply, beginning in October 1979, to reduce inflation, which exceeded 11 percent that year. This dramatically increased interest rates, which reached 18.9 percent in 1981. Higher domestic interest rates increased the strength of the American dollar on international markets. The US currency gained more than 70 percent against other major currencies from 1981 to 1985. This made everything produced in the United States more expensive for overseas consumers. President Jimmy Carter also halted grain shipments to the Soviet Union in response to their invasion of Afghanistan, eliminating a huge export market for American farmers. Agricultural prices began to fall. While agricultural expansion and overproduction was the result of high prices, the actions of the Federal Reserve and the collapse in overseas demand made what might have been a bad farm bust into a calamity.[5]

American farmers fell into an escalating crisis in the 1980s and Iowa suffered as much as any other midwestern state. High debts and steep interest rates left many farmers with large monthly payments that could not be met as prices fell. The average price of farmland in the state had increased from $419 in 1970 to $2,066 in 1980 (about $6,490 in 2020 dollars). But then land prices in Iowa plummeted, falling 63 percent in five years. Average net farm income in the state fell by more than half between 1981 and 1982, from $17,680 to $7,376. In 1982, respondents to a questionnaire from the *Cedar Rapids Gazette* compared the economic downturn to the tough times of the 1950s and to the Depression of the 1930s. The next year average net farm income fell to -$1,891, a loss equal to about $4,900 in 2020. Families gave up entertainment to conserve money. Then they cut spending on clothing and insurance. Prices stayed low in the mid-1980s, and the crisis got worse. By 1983 farm families made only one-quarter as much income as they had a decade earlier. They began to sell off their possessions to pay bills. The number of people in poverty in the state more than doubled from 1979 to 1986. In 1985 farm prices were lower "relative to the prices farmers paid than they had been at the depth of the Great Depression," wrote historian David B. Danbom. About one-third of Iowa farmers were in serious trouble in 1985, with debts exceeding forty percent of assets. This group held 73 percent of all farm debt in the state.[6]

David Pickhinke, who lived near the town of Early, added to his landholdings during the boom times. "We have two boys who wanted to farm so we'd bought land," he explained. Farming was all that he ever wanted to do and everyone in his family went into agriculture. "You're working next to the earth, you're growing things, you're raising livestock. You work 14 hours a day but there's nobody telling you you have to work the next day. A lot of this is just in your blood. It's a way of life." But his bank asked for loans to be paid back when it closed. He could not repay them and Pickhinke and his family lost all their property. He ended up renting the land he had once owned.[7]

Men and women desperately looked for new ways to bring in additional income, seeking work off-farm to supplement their meager earnings from agriculture. This began even before the crisis of the 1980s, with the income from outside jobs rising by 80 percent from 1975 to 1983. John Fischer, who farmed one thousand acres near Palmer, worked two jobs in addition to agriculture. "I'd go under if I tried to live just on farm income," he said. But few families lived near urban areas that had good-paying jobs. Worse, the entire state was suffering from the farm recession. Many existing jobs were disappearing, or hours were being cut. "I've never had so many farmers in my office," one manager of a job service in Pocahontas County said. "Some are getting out of farming, some would like to get out,

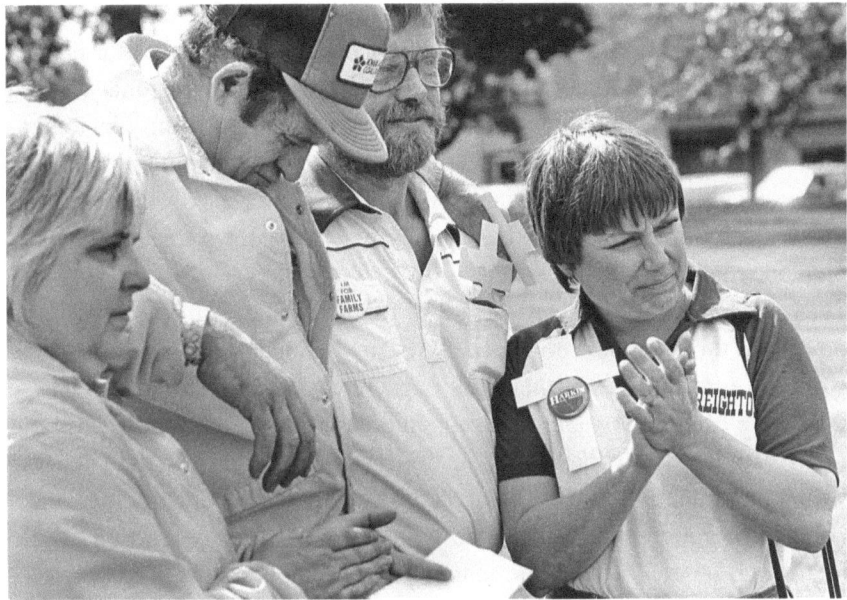

Iowans Elmer and Pat Steffes attending a rally at the Audubon County courthouse protesting their farm foreclosure, June 3, 1985. PH1988.15.18, Bill Gillette Collection, State Historical Society of Iowa, Des Moines.

but most would like something part time. And about the only time there's part-time work available is when they're out in the fields." The search for additional income became "almost frantic" by 1985, wrote David Westphal. Many had sold off their cattle to pay bills and relied on income from grain-farming.[8]

Depression was widespread, suicides spiked, and hunger became common in the nation's breadbasket. Farm families went on food stamps, as poverty rates in some counties approached 30 percent. The USDA gave surplus food to Iowa food banks to help feed the hungry. In the western Iowa town of Harlan, three farmers killed themselves in eighteen months. Five students at ISU committed suicide in 1984 and 1985. Child and spousal abuse, alcoholism, and the divorce rate increased. Medical care was neglected, as it was too expensive. Families even lacked money for soap or toilet paper. A reporter from the *Wall Street Journal* compared the state of Iowa to a Vietnam veteran with post-traumatic stress disorder. "Three generations—grandparents, parents, children—have been maimed by the Midwestern shakeout," wrote Dennis Farney in May 1988. People struggled to hold onto their homes and dreams, existing on the edge of despair. A grandmother in her seventies asked a social worker for help in finding a job. Teen-age kids managed farms while their parents worked jobs away from home. One farm wife worked three off-farm jobs to supplement her family's income, sleeping only four hours some nights. One farmer lost his land and lived in a house that was once his own, paying rent to a distant landlord. He cried as a new owner tore down trees that he had planted when he owned the land.[9]

Marriages were disrupted by years of upheaval. Farm women found their lives turned upside down, as they struggled to stave off failure. Many worked unfulfilling jobs that they expected would be temporary. These jobs were often low wage. Their income helped save the family farm but many wondered why they ended up doing jobs they didn't want to do. One woman told her college professor, "I am tired of supporting my husband's habit of farming." She doubted how long she would stay married, as did many who labored to save farms that never seemed to get ahead.[10]

Despair pushed Dale Burr to murder in December 1985. Burr was a sixty-three-year- old farmer who lived in the town of Lone Tree in Johnson County. He was a quiet man who found himself at least $500,000 in debt and without money to buy groceries. On December 9 he killed his wife, a bank president, and a fellow farmer before taking his own life. Burr shot his spouse, Emily, while she was baking cookies. Friends said that he probably didn't want her to live with his actions. He then went to Hills Bank and Trust Company, where he killed John Hughes, who was president. Burr owed the bank about $400,000. He then killed Richard Goody, a nearby farmer who had a land dispute with his son. Then he shot at Goody's wife, who escaped. On the way back to his farm, a sheriff pulled up behind Burr's old Chevy pickup. Burr parked by the side of the road and the officer waited for reinforcements. When they reached the vehicle, they found that Dale Burr had killed himself. The rampage shocked the country but did not surprise many in Iowa, who had seen the rising emotional toll that economic failure exacted. One mental health worker remarked that other farmers had threatened to shoot their bankers. In Minnesota a farmer killed two bank employees in 1983. Tragically, John Hughes was a popular man, a friend of farmers who had no intention of foreclosing on Burr. A memorial for Hughes had fifteen hundred mourners. Emily and Dale Burr were buried side by side in a cemetery a mile from their farm.[11]

The economic disaster cut deeply into the hearts of Iowans. Children suffered just as their parents did. One boy who watched his father's equipment hauled away hid his farm toys and tractors under his bed. He was afraid a banker might take them. One girl had to say goodbye to a dairy cow that she had raised and wept in a neighbor's lap. The family's dairy cattle were sold for slaughter to pay bank debts. A twenty-two-year-old man, facing failure and the loss of his family's land, hanged himself in a barn that his grandfather had helped build. When his parents returned from town, they found the body of their only child.[12]

Iowans organized to help each other and to battle the economic forces they faced. Farm families in Iowa had a highly effective rural advocacy group, the Iowa Farm Unity Coalition. It was made up of liberal churches, consumer groups, and leftist farm organizations that employed nonconfrontational, supportive tactics to aid beleaguered Iowans. It emphasized consensus building, mediation, and cooperation. Women played a major role. They counselled distraught farmers, led group therapy sessions, lobbied politicians, and were leaders in rural activism. Advocates, often female, sought to halt foreclosures by using financial regulations against agencies. They counseled farm families by phone to avoid tragedies. Workshops explained available options to those in financial peril. Community meetings provided morale boosts. Hotlines had counselors to provide information, advice, or support. Women confronted lenders, trying to delay foreclosures. They studied regulations and met with lawyers and accountants when their husbands lost their nerve or suffered a breakdown. One woman confronted a banker with a TV crew and saved her dairy farm for another year. Female social workers, mediators, counselors, and ministers helped families overcome a distrust of outsiders, accept help, resolve conflicts, and rebuild broken lives. They did everything from preventing male suicides to urging families to adopt food stamps to help feed themselves.[13]

One of those trying to aid Iowans was Joan Blundall, a social worker and therapist at the Northwest Iowa Mental Health Center in Spencer in the 1980s and 1990s. She came to Iowa in 1978 after a divorce, wanting to raise her son in place with "traditional values." Blundall lived in Fort Dodge and worked for ISU Extension before moving to Spencer in 1984. She was hired to help with the mental health crisis that accompanied the economic crisis in Iowa, responsible for a nine-county area in the state's northwest. Blundall trained community volunteers to visit farm families dealing with trauma and established support groups so people could help each other. She often went to see families on their farms to talk with them about anxiety and depression. She wrote a grant to fund her work and dedicated years to those struggling with mental health. A successful year was one when only four people committed suicide. Blundall eventually became director of the center, having refused to leave Spencer for jobs that paid twice as much.[14]

The crisis led to a wave of populist farm protest. Farmers lobbied state governments and went to Washington, DC, to ask for help. They pushed for moratoriums on foreclosures and more federal aid. They left crosses, symbolizing the "death" of farms, at county courthouses. Distressed farmers applied for food stamps in large groups on March 3, 1986, to protest their plight. Fifteen thousand went to Ames in February 1985 in the National Crisis Action Rally to demand help from the Reagan administration. Protestors tried to halt foreclosures and machinery sales. Farmers drove tractors to state capitals and Washington, DC, to publicize their cause. They staged protests at the USDA, timed to get positive news coverage on television. In 1985 singers Willie Nelson, John Mellencamp, and Neil Young organized concerts to raise funds and gain attention for threatened family farms. Money went to local groups in states like Iowa that supported farm families.[15]

The agricultural crash hurt Iowa's small towns, schools, and businesses. Forty-one percent of Iowans lived in rural areas in 1984, with 13 percent of the state's residents living on farms. The loss of farms led to fewer customers in towns and the failure of grocery stores and other shops. Businesses that had survived the Great Depression went under, such as a farm implement dealership in Laurens. Car dealers shut down when residents did not buy new vehicles. The closing of one business hurt others nearby. Restaurants, hotels, and banks closed. Feed stores and farm machinery dealers closed. Insurance agencies, plumbers, and electricians moved away. Doctors, nurses, and pharmacists left. Hospitals closed, forcing small town residents to travel long distances for health care. Between 1976 and 1986 Iowa's small towns lost 41 percent of their gas stations and 27 percent of their grocery stores. The town of Mechanicsville lost most of its main street shops, including clothing stores, hotels, a pharmacy, and a butcher shop. By 1990 most of its storefronts were empty. Fewer jobs also meant less tax revenue. In Marshall County, the sheriff laid off half of his eight deputies. Schools had fewer children and some closed, further undermining the economic and social life of towns. The number of students in the eight schools in Pocahontas County fell by one-third from 1975 to 1985.

Many who remained qualified for the free lunch program for low-income families. Few stayed after graduation. A boarded-up school sat at the highest point in the town of Pocahontas. Those who remained were older or poorer, often with homes that they could not sell.[16]

The arrival of the giant retailer Walmart provided additional challenges. The discount chain built large stores across the country that offered lower prices and a greater variety of goods than smaller shops. By 1989 it had nineteen stores in Iowa. They undermined local businesses, such as hardware stores and pharmacies. Each Walmart absorbed $200,000 in sales from small towns within twenty miles. The forty-five-thousand-square-foot store in Independence sold $10 million a year of goods. A mile to the east, businesses stood empty in the former commercial heart of the town. Walmart even damaged small-town newspapers, which were hurt by a decline in retail advertising. The giant chain did bring nearly one hundred jobs to Independence, as well as more customers to gas stations and restaurants. It paid taxes, too. But half of the new jobs were part-time and paid a little more than minimum wage. About a dozen local businesses closed in the four years after Walmart opened. While most consumers could travel to nearby stores, some elderly residents in small towns did not drive. When a grocer went out of business, it became harder for them to purchase necessities. Walmart stores provided efficient one-stop shopping but undermined the social and economic lives of small towns hurt by decades of rural population loss.[17]

More than 136,000 people left Iowa in the 1980s, almost 5 percent of the state's population. Iowa was one of only four states to lose population in the decade. Rural counties lost more than 227,000 residents, many of whom moved to urban areas in the state to find work. Richard and Sharon Thompson farmed three hundred acres near Boone. When they began farming in the 1950s, they had eleven family farms in their neighborhood. By the 1980s only four families lived nearby. Metro areas had usually increased in size, even as rural areas lost residents, in the twentieth century. But Waterloo lost 12.5 percent of its population. Almost 8 percent of Dubuque's residents departed; Ottumwa lost 10.6 percent of its people. Some lost everything and departed to try to start their lives again in states like Texas. Young people left the state in large numbers as economic opportunities vanished. The elderly stayed behind. Iowa had the fourth highest percentage of residents over sixty-five in the nation. Two of the other states in the top four, Florida and Arizona, were retirement destinations.

For example, three Iowans left the town of Dickens to find work in other states. One sold insurance, another worked in a meatpacking plant, and a third drove a truck. Those who lost their farms, or quit agriculture, did not usually leave Iowa. Most stayed within twenty miles of home and only 18 percent left the state. Those who were most likely to leave Iowa lived in urban areas.[18]

Businesses and corporations outside small towns and rural areas were badly hurt by the agricultural depression. Meatpacking and the manufacture of farm machinery were pillars of Iowa's agro-industrial economy. Iowa had 19 percent of the nation's farm machinery production in 1969, concentrated in eastern Iowa. Waterloo, Dubuque, Charles City, Davenport, and Ottumwa had important machinery factories. There were 29,039 workers in this industry in Iowa in 1980. But the demand for capital purchases, such as tractors, fell 60 percent from 1979 to 1986. Large corporations such as John Deere laid off thousands of workers in Iowa. Employment at Deere's Tractor Works in Waterloo dropped by almost ten thousand from 1980 to 1986. The plant in Dubuque also lost about half of its employees. An estimated 265 of Iowa's farm implement dealers went out of business. Dubuque County lost seventy-five hundred jobs from 1979 to 1982. Its unemployment rate reached 23 percent at the start of 1983, an extraordinary Great Depression-level of joblessness. The Quad City area, in Iowa and Illinois, lost eleven thousand jobs when John Deere and International Harvester shut down plants between 1979 and 1984. The nation's center of farm machinery manufacturing became an industrial wasteland by 1990. Only 12,555 employees in Iowa worked in the sector by 1990. Waterloo also lost the Rath meatpacking plant in 1984, leading to the loss of thousands of more jobs.[19]

Iowa suffered from economic distress not seen since the Great Depression. In the seven years from 1979 to 1986 Iowa lost eighty-four thousand middle-class jobs, which paid $20,000 a year or more. This was equal to about $52,000 in 2020 dollars. The state gained thirty-seven thousand lower-paying jobs, where employees earned $11,500 or less, about $29,900 in 2020. Fifty-nine thousand manufacturing jobs vanished between 1979 and 1987, equal to 23 percent of the state's industrial employment. Iowa also lost twenty-four thousand jobs in construction from 1979 to 1984, more than 40 percent of such jobs in the state. Average wages for workers fell by a little over 8 percent between 1979 and 1986. Approximately five thousand Iowa businesses also failed between 1981 and 1985. Nearly two hundred thousand more people left the state than moved into it from 1980 to 1987. The economic carnage helped reshape the state's economy, gutting its industry and leading to the growth of low wage employment in service sector jobs such as those at Walmart and in the meatpacking business.[20]

The weakening of unions in the mid- and late-twentieth century hurt the economic prospects of many workers. Labor encountered increasing political opposition from pro-business conservatives who sought to undermine the New Deal. A federal antiunion bill, the Taft-Hartley Act, became law in 1947 and limited the ability of unions to organize and allowed states to pass legislation that restricted their activity. Iowa passed a right-to-work law that same year. Things deteriorated further as the mining and manufacturing sectors nationwide declined in the late twentieth century, reducing union enrollment in labor's traditional fields. The number of workers in the service sector, a part of the economy that was harder to organize, also increased. The farm crisis badly hurt not only Iowa's industries but its unions. Membership fell nationwide as manufacturers in the state and elsewhere declined. Meatpacking and farm equipment unions in Iowa were especially hard hit. The wages of employees in meatpacking plants peaked in the 1970s and fell by almost half, adjusted for buying power, by 1997. In terms of worker's rights and protections, this was catastrophic, as from the 1930s to the 1980s, unions had "made the workplace less dangerous; they had won new rights and a measure of dignity on the shopfloor," and they helped unionized workers achieve economic prosperity, argued historian Shelton Stromquist.[21]

Meatpacking plants increasingly moved into rural areas in Iowa and nearby states in the 1980s and 1990s, lured by cheap labor and access to the region's livestock. While it had been the state's largest industry for many decades, the business fundamentally changed in the final decades of the twentieth century. Meatpackers abandoned their urban plants and dispersed into the countryside. The industry consolidated, battling unions by closing plants and forcing wage cuts. Mergers, buyouts, and tough competition left three major packing companies: ConAgra, Iowa Beef Packers, and Cargill. They moved into rural areas in Iowa in the wake of the farm crisis, setting up large plants that provided lots of low wage jobs to desperate small towns. Unionized workers had made good money, earning an average salary of $30,000 in 1981, equivalent to about $85,400 in 2020. "It was the best-paying job you could get, 100 percent, if you were unskilled," said Dan Smith, who retired from the Storm Lake pork processing plant in 2017 after thirty-seven years of employment. In the 1990s new employees were paid seven dollars an hour, less than $15,000 a year for a full-time worker. Starting pay more than doubled to $15 an hour in 2001—higher wages reduced worker turnover and costs. Pay increased little in the following years, though. By 1996, Iowa had nearly one-third of the nation's pork-processing plants.[22]

Meatpackers could not hire enough Americans to work in their plants, so they recruited immigrants, often undocumented. Businesses claimed that they did not knowingly hire such laborers. The jobs were grueling and dangerous, with packers regularly speeding up the rate of work. More than one-third of meatpacking workers suffered a serious injury each year. Workers stood in the same spot for eight hours or longer, cutting carcasses at a fast pace in near-freezing temperatures. In Iowa, most meatpacking employees came from the southwestern United States or Mexico, where unskilled farm workers might earn as little as four dollars a day. Packers also hired other Latin American immigrants, as well as those from countries such as Laos and Ethiopia. The influx of newcomers added a diverse mix of people from around the globe to Iowa. This provided many challenges to the state's towns and cities, but it reinvigorated declining rural areas whose native-born population had been leaving. Some encountered hostility and suspicion from those who did not think the newcomers assimilated quickly enough or learned English. Immigration opponents focused on rising crime and drug problems or the fear that new low-wage workers would pull down salaries in Iowa. The legislature even debated making English the state's official language in the late 1990s, a proposal that did not become law at the time.[23]

Immigration transformed Iowa towns. Storm Lake was dramatically altered by the arrival of a steady stream of immigrants from Mexico that started in 1982. By 2021 it was the most diverse city in the state and 85 percent of the students in its schools were nonwhite. Workers came to a pork-producing plant that killed, cut, and packaged up to thirteen thousand hogs a day. Their families followed. By 2017 less than half of the town's population was white, and students spoke thirty languages in local schools. Crime increased in the 1990s, but it was proportionate to the town's ethnic makeup, noted the police chief, Mark Prosser; the rate fell in the 2010s. The newcomers strained the local public school system, which had to provide costly English as a Second Language instruction. Schools added scores of teacher aides to help those who didn't know English. Racial tensions led to some fights. But schools fielded integrated soccer teams that attracted passionate local fans. Prosser was a coach. Residents came to realize that "their future is a shared one," wrote journalist Patricia Cohen. Uninsured employees taxed the local hospital, with unpaid hospital claims exceeding $2 million year in the mid-1990s. But Storm Lake did not have empty storefronts and did not close its schools. Some immigrants started businesses such as restaurants and grocery stores, which offered a kaleidoscope of produce from around the world. They also spent their money in town, bought homes, attended church, and learned English. Buena Vista University in Storm Lake recruited immigrants and their children, providing full-ride scholarships to first-generation college students. Immigrants saved the town, and its surrounding area, from the devastating population declines in most other rural areas. Storm Lake would have shrunk by 12 percent in the 2010s alone without nonwhite migrants.[24]

People came to Iowa for economic opportunities, like previous waves of Germans, Swedes, and Irish. Silvino Morelos came to Storm Lake after his business was looted and damaged during the 1992 riots in Los Angeles. He owned Valentina's Meat Market, which carried produce from Laos, Ecuador, and Nigeria. Morelos had always felt welcome in the town. His wife worked at the pork plant, as well as the market. He rarely had time off. But they owned a twenty-two-acre farm, where they raised lambs and goats. Refugees from Southeast Asia also lived in Storm Lake, including Abel Saengchanpheng, who came to the town at age sixteen. His family had fled Laos and he was born in a refugee camp in Thailand. He worked with his parents at the Tyson pork plant after he graduated from high school. "I was so blessed to get into Tyson," he told a reporter. Saengchanpheng became an American citizen and worked his way to be a foreman at the plant, supervising three hundred other employees. By 2017 he owned a home and two cars.[25]

But the American dream was elusive for some of these immigrants. Julio Barroso, an eight-year-old boy, and his parents, Antonio and Luisa, were deported from the United States in 1996. Julio was featured on the front page of the *Storm Lake Times* a month before deportation. Federal agents raided the IBP pork plant in the town, found his father working there, and sent the family and seventy-five others without documents back to their home countries. Julio returned illegally to work in Storm Lake at an egg facility at age seventeen, having learned English in his eight months as a student in the second grade. He became a supervisor at the factory. After four years in Iowa, he left to visit family in Mexico. He was not allowed to return and barred from legally returning to the United States for ten years. Barroso lived in Guadalajara, married, and had children. He earned $100 for working seventy-two hours a week as a truck driver, sometimes robbed by street gangs. Barroso wished to return to Storm Lake, which he remembered fondly. As a boy he had wanted to be a teacher. "Mexico is very beautiful but there is a lot of injustice," he told the *Storm Lake Times* in 2020.[26]

The economic crisis of the 1980s contributed to a devastating meth epidemic that gained national attention in the late 1990s and early 2000s. In 2004, 1,370 meth labs were seized in Iowa, about 10 percent of the estimated state total. Depressed economic conditions led to the spread of methamphetamine production and consumption in Iowa's countryside. "Across Iowa, meth had become one of the leading growth sectors of the economy," wrote journalist Nick Reding. Some farmers sold anhydrous ammonia, a fertilizer, to meth cooks to make money. A few went into meth manufacturing. The drug could be made from easy-to-obtain chemicals and cooked up in clandestine rural labs. It was cheaper than cocaine and provided a high that could last one or two days. It was easier, and much more lucrative, to sell meth than to work at a meatpacking plant for seven dollars an hour. Most of the supply came from Mexico. There was plenty of demand. Those who used meth found that it allowed them to work double shifts at meatpacking plants or dulled the tedium of construction work. Addiction to the drug brought paranoia and delusional violence. It also wrecked the human body, with long-term effects ranging from tooth rot to liver and kidney failure. One male meth addict had four heart attacks and lost almost all his teeth by age thirty-five. The crisis filled jails and ruined lives, until federal legislation greatly reduced the availability of drug components.[27]

The farm crisis eased in the late 1980s, but it did not end completely. Billions in aid from the federal government helped put money in the pockets of farmers, with agricultural subsidies in 1986 averaging about $13,000 per farm, about $30,000 in 2020 income. Federal farm subsidies, as well as non-farm jobs, allowed families to survive in the decades after the farm crisis. Interest rates also fell, and families refinanced their loans, reducing costs. Prices for corn and soybeans increased and many made more income or paid off some debt. Land prices stabilized and then increased.

Between 1978 and 1992 the total number of Iowa farms fell from 121,339 to 96,543—a loss of 20 percent of the state total. Most land lost to foreclosure or bankruptcy was bought by other family farms. Giant agricultural corporations did not dominate Iowa or Midwestern farming, as they did in California. Bankruptcies and foreclosures stayed high, with more than six thousand farms in Iowa still in default in 1990, only four hundred below the total for 1987–1988. Gary Barrett, a farmer in Stuart, Iowa, almost lost his farm in the late 1980s, spending three years in bankruptcy proceedings. "Guys that had it hard like me are just getting ready now to get back on their feet and walk again," he said in 1990.[28]

The weather complicated Iowa's recovery in 1988, when the worst drought in fifty years hit the state. Rain fell too late or too early, ending in May in northwestern Iowa. In some places only half of the usual rain came. Temperatures over one hundred degrees occurred near Iowa City. Livestock needed water every hour in such heat. Drought forced some farmers to sell entire herds because pastures were dead. Corn withered or did not grow. The state had the smallest corn crop since 1983, another drought year.[29]

Still, by the early 1990s the farm crisis looked to be mostly over. Farmers seemed to be prospering. Land values were increasing and income was improving across the Midwest. The agricultural economy was better off and more financially stable than it had been since the 1970s. The number of farmers in financial trouble in Iowa fell by almost half between 1985 and 1990. But profits were elusive. Parents told their children not to become farmers. A new federal land conservation program paid farmers to take land out of production, starting in 1986. Almost two million acres of land in Iowa were not planted in exchange for long-term cash payments. Such money helped but the mood among farmers was often grim.[30]

Iowa's largest city was flourishing, however. By 1993 Des Moines had a diversified and healthy economy, with a large service sector. The national recession of the early 1990s barely affected the city. Des Moines benefited from its status as the state capital, with plenty of government agencies that provided steady employment. It was also the third-largest insurance center in the world, employing about thirty-five thousand workers in the sector. Sixty insurance companies had headquarters in the city, as did Pioneer Hi-Bred, which provided 40 percent of the nation's seed corn. The housing market was buoyant. Home prices were recovering from the disaster of the 1980s and had increased by one-third in just five years. Bankers funded more than twenty-one thousand mortgages in Polk County in 1992, 50 percent more than the year before. Des Moines's industry and publishing sectors were strong. Unemployment was low. It had dropped to 3.3 percent in the city in December 1992. Overall, the state benefited from "a squeaky-clean Protestant ethic and tip-top schools," observed the *Economist*. Farm income across the state had also recovered by early 1993. Unemployment stayed low in Iowa throughout the 1990s, falling to 2 percent by 2000. In the late 1990s employers had trouble finding enough workers.[31]

The Great Flood of 1993, which hit the Midwest in the summer, interrupted what good times existed in the state. The year saw the worst flooding in Iowa's recorded history and was the wettest on record. It was worse than any predicted five-hundred-year flood event. Heavy winter snow and spring rain left soil saturated. More rain came in the summer—July was the wettest month in 121 years. Much of it came in a torrent, four or five inches at a time. The town of Jefferson received almost eight inches of rain on July 8 and 9. The water devastated the state, flooding twenty-one thousand homes and killing seven people. Cities and rural areas were swamped. Iowa State's basketball arena, Hilton Coliseum, was inundated with fourteen feet of water. Flooding wiped out the crops and income of one hundred thousand families across the Midwest. Farmers in Iowa had more than $1 billion in corn and soybean losses; Des Moines suffered almost as much in damage. The floods overwhelmed levees protecting the Des Moines water plant and left the city and its 250,000 inhabitants without water for more than two weeks. The Racoon River was a mile wide along Fleur Drive north of the airport. Iowa's small-town ethos was demonstrated daily, as people helped those they did not know. They aided each other, filling sandbags, and handing out water and food. The National Guard was deployed around the state, all of which was declared a disaster zone. The Great Flood killed thirty-eight people and inflicted more than $22 billion in damage across the Midwest. "Of all the states in the Mississippi and Missouri River basins, Iowa was worst hit by the year's flooding," wrote historian Pamela Riney-Kehrberg. The damage was another major setback for the state's farmers.[32]

In 1980 Curtis Harnack, an Iowa-born author, wrote of the agricultural recession and soil erosion that plagued Iowa. Some places lost ten tons of topsoil when heavy rains occurred. According to Harnack, crop rotation had disappeared and every possible row was planted to increase income. Corn and soybeans provided the highest returns and dominated the landscape. Fields of oats, barley, and alfalfa that had stopped water runoff and helped hold soil in place were gone. Tenants who rented land often sought immediate production and ignored long-term problems. Iowa's topsoil paid the price for this exploitation. The state had two to four feet of topsoil—some of the best in the world—in the late nineteenth century. A century later, sloping soils might only have six inches left. Iowa had probably lost half of its topsoil by the early twenty-first century. Major storms could erode a half-inch of it in a month. But it took from one hundred to five hundred years to create an inch of topsoil. Harnack, who came from a family of farmers, also lamented the pollution of Iowa's fields and waterways. Farmers used chemicals to control weeds and pests and improve yields. But chemical runoff left few surface wells in Plymouth County safe to drink. "In 100 years, the Iowa farmer has exploited and diminished his heritage of soil—a staggering spendthrift spree," Harnack wrote.[33]

Diversified family farms mostly disappeared in the second half of the twentieth century. Farmers of all backgrounds focused on the mass production of one or two commodities. "Farmers grew what was profitable, guided by economies of scale and governmental policies that promoted expanses of corn and soybeans," wrote ecologist Cornelia F. Mutel. By 2005 about two-thirds of Iowa was covered in these two crops. Farm size had grown even before the 1980s as farmers sold their land to neighbors. The number of farms in Fayette County, in northeast Iowa, fell by 30 percent from 1945 to 1969, as farm size grew by 37 percent. Fields merged and even marginal land was brought into production. "Parts of Iowa's flattest, most intensively cultivated landscape appear uninhabited," noted Mutel. By 2000 only 5.9 percent of the state's population lived on farms, about 15 percent of the rural population. Farmers also gave up livestock production, with the number of farms that had cattle dropping by over one-half. Land devoted to pasture fell. The number of farms raising hogs declined by about 80 percent between 1974 and 2002. Hog production moved away from smaller farms to large, automated feeding centers known as confined animal feeding operations (CAFOs) that could hold thousands of animals in buildings. CAFOs produced enormous amounts of manure, a serious threat to water and air quality that became a major problem in the state in the early twenty-first century. Hogs on farms provided manure to replenish soil. But thousands of hogs living in a CAFO were a threat to the natural environment and human health. The number of such facilities in Iowa rose steeply after 2000.[34]

Intensive agriculture degraded Iowa's environment in the late twentieth century, as Curtis Harnack observed. Iowa's rivers, streams, ponds, and wells were fouled by high concentrations of nitrates from fertilizer runoff, which was a threat to human health. It caused thyroid and colon cancer in adults and was linked to premature births and a "blue baby" condition caused by insufficient oxygen in the blood. From 1980 to 1996 the Raccoon River Basin in Iowa had the highest amounts of nitrate-nitrogen levels among the forty-two river systems reaching the Gulf of Mexico. Nitrogen boosted plant growth on land and in water. The 1993 midwestern floods sent so much down the Mississippi River that it created a giant algal bloom in the Gulf of Mexico. It was a "raft of gunk that turned out to be an ideal breeding ground for disease," wrote Richard Manning. The huge bloom then floated up the east coast of the United States, spreading a virus that killed whales, dolphins, and seals all the way to Canada. Such algae blooms happened regularly in the Gulf of Mexico and left an oxygen-deprived "dead zone" as large as New Jersey in some years. In 1999 it was 7,728 square miles; estimates in 2000 found that 25 percent of nitrates reaching the Gulf came from Iowa. Dead zones occurred when the algae died and sank into the ocean. As it decayed, it took oxygen from the water, choking marine ecosystems. Those who depended on the Gulf of Mexico for their living paid a high price. Eliminating giant algae blooms would require major changes to American farming, take billions of dollars, and decades to complete. This process has not yet really started.[35]

Republicans have dominated state politics since the Civil War, but divided government was the norm for most years from 1975 to 2000. The GOP controlled the governor's office almost all this period. Democrats controlled at least one house of the legislature about two-thirds of the time, holding a majority in both the state house and senate for fourteen of these twenty-five years. Republican Robert Ray served as governor from 1969 to 1983 and had much success working with Democratic legislators. He was succeeded by Terry Branstad, age thirty-six, his lieutenant governor, who was the youngest governor in Iowa history. Branstad served as governor from 1983 to 1999, as well as from 2011 to 2017, making him Iowa's—and the nation's—longest-serving executive. Branstad was a pro-business, anti-union, anti-abortion conservative who battled a Democratic-controlled state legislature and a depressed state economy in the 1980s. On October 1, 1985, Branstad declared an economic emergency in Iowa, triggering a

1933 law that allowed farmers to ask courts to halt foreclosures. This would have been a radical move five years earlier for a free-market Republican. Branstad was known as a tireless campaigner, visiting all ninety-nine counties in the state every year. "He is so aw-shucks and dull—and as honest as you will find" that Iowans happily reelected Branstad, argued liberal Democrat Art Cullen. In 1998 Democrat Tom Vilsack was elected governor after Branstad chose not to run for reelection. Vilsack was an orphan, raised in an abusive adoptive home. He married an Iowa girl and moved to Mount Pleasant. A state senator, he won a surprise victory and became the first Iowa Democratic Governor since 1969.[36]

Iowa was represented in the United States Senate by two long-serving men, Charles Grassley and Tom Harkin. Grassley had been first elected to the Iowa House of Representatives in 1959 and never lost a race. He was born in 1933 in a farmhouse without electricity or indoor plumbing. He was first elected to the US Senate in 1980, running an anti-Washington campaign that benefited from a Reagan landslide that year. Grassley ran as a candidate who was more conservative than the Republican governor at the time, Robert Ray. He had a folksy charm that reminded people of their grandfather. Iowans sent him back to the US Senate seven more times, re-electing him in 2022, rewarding his pragmatic conservatism and his fierce defense of small farmers. He supported Donald Trump's supreme court nominees, helping to ensure a conservative super-majority, while blocking Obama's supreme court nomination of Merrick Garland. Tom Harkin was the son of a coal miner who paid his way through ISU with the ROTC. He served as a congressman in Iowa for ten years before defeating incumbent Republican senator Roger Jepsen in 1984. Harkin was a senator until 2014, chairing the Senate Agricultural Committee, a plum post that endeared him to rural Iowa. Harkin was a progressive, known for writing the Americans with Disabilities Act, which became law in 1990. It was a major civil rights accomplishment, which prohibited discrimination against people with disabilities in areas such as employment, public accommodations, and transportation. Harkin's brother, Fred, had been deaf most of his life and the senator understood the challenges of those with disabilities. Tom Harkin ran for president in 1992, easily winning the Iowa caucuses, but he found little support outside his home state.[37]

The Iowa caucuses began the long American presidential primary season. "Iowa is not first because it is important; it is important because it is first," wrote Hugh Winebrenner and Dennis J. Goldford, two political scientists from Iowa. A caucus is an odd and problematic way to choose a candidate, as has been demonstrated by late and inconclusive results in 2012, 2016, and 2020. It is run by political parties, as opposed to primaries, which are run by individual states. A relatively small segment of Iowa voters, usually white and older, take part. Candidates who win in Iowa often do not win the nomination, though. About half of the victors earn their party's nominations, with three becoming president: Jimmy Carter, George W. Bush, and Barack Obama. In 2008, 2012, and 2016 the Republican who won Iowa did not go on to win the nomination. Iowa is more of a gatekeeper, winnowing the number of candidates, than a kingmaker. Normally the top three candidates have a chance to win each party's nomination. Candidates test messages, demonstrate their ability to organize, and fund-raise in the months of campaigning in Iowa. Some who win in the state, such as Republican George H. W. Bush in 1980 or Democrat Dick Gephardt in 1988, do not become the nominee that year. Many poor performers in Iowa, and those who do not meet expectations, quickly exit the race. Candidates who exceed expectations such as Carter in 1976 and Obama in 2008 often find their prospects have dramatically improved.[38]

The farm crisis of the 1980s battered Iowa, undermined its middle class, and devastated the state's rural areas. It left the state profoundly transformed, with fewer and larger farms and a smaller population in the countryside. "The agriculture-dependent Midwest would never be the same," wrote Pamela Riney-Kehrberg. Iowa lost one in five of its farms between 1978 and 1992. It also lost tens of thousands of industrial jobs. The state's population shrank by 4.7 percent in the eighties—nearly 137,000 people—even as the United States grew by more than ten percent. Its population recovered in the 1990s but barely exceeded that from twenty years earlier by 2000. Smaller towns lost businesses and residents, who often left for jobs in cities. Industry moved into rural areas, with meatpacking plants and CAFOs becoming widespread. The state grew more diverse, as larger numbers of immigrants moved to Iowa. Iowa remained almost 93 percent white in 2000, however. In the 1990s the urban economy recovered, even as farm families struggled. The state unemployment rate fell to 2 percent by 2000. Environmental challenges were more pronounced, with the Great Flood of 1993 attracting national attention, and regular droughts damaging farm production. From the 1970s to 2000, Iowa had a competitive two-party system but was governed mostly by Republicans. It attracted tremendous national attention during the presidential primaries, even if the state caucuses were less predictive of success than the New Hampshire primary. A new century brought new trials that continued to test the resilience of its people.[39]

15
Iowa in the Twenty-First Century

Iowa faced increasing economic and environmental challenges in the early twenty-first century. Rural areas continued to lose population, as residents left for jobs in cities. Larger cities enjoyed strong growth and benefited from population gains. The first few years of the twenty-first century saw low corn and soybean prices. But the agricultural sector benefited from higher prices from about 2007 to 2014. Farmers and the rural economy suffered when prices began to decline in the mid-2010s. Ethanol production and wind power provided some new opportunities to rural areas though. The state became more diverse as more immigrants and refugees moved in, but Iowa remained very white. Immigration was both a contested political issue and crucial to state economic development. The Great Recession of 2007–2009 helped lead to the first of a series of Democratic defeats in Iowa in the 2010s. Donald Trump mobilized conservatives in the second half of the decade. Democrats were routed and Republicans controlled the legislature and the governor's office by 2016. Additional Democratic defeats in 2020 left the party almost irrelevant in the state. Long-term environmental problems plagued Iowa, with increased flooding, alternating with drought, foreshadowing the consequences of a warming climate. In 2020 the coronavirus pandemic killed thousands and spread misery; a sharp, but brief, recession also hurt the state's people. Iowa had the third-highest per capita COVID-19 infection rate in the country at the end of 2020. By 2021 the state's economy was recovering, even as its poorest and nonwhite residents suffered from structural inequalities that limited their opportunities.[1]

The effects of the farm crisis lingered long after the 1980s. People continued to leave the agricultural countryside to find work in larger towns and cities, undermining the rural nature of the state. Proximity to larger metro areas allowed some towns to prosper. Counties near Cedar Rapids and Iowa City, close to Des Moines, or in western Iowa near Omaha gained population and thrived. Most other places lost people and jobs, though counties dominated by agriculture in northern Iowa did fairly well until farm prices fell in the mid- and late-2010s. Many Iowa counties away from larger cities continued to lose population—as they had for many decades—as deaths outnumbered births. Some of these counties had been losing residents since 1890. Few people moved to areas where populations fell since there were few job opportunities. Businesses also did not move into a place without a labor force. A lack of workers hindered economic development, increasing the gulf between growing urban and shrinking rural areas. This vicious cycle also occurred in nearby states such as Wisconsin and Illinois.[2]

Jobs and opportunities thus became concentrated in metropolitan areas with more than fifty thousand residents. Iowa's larger metros attracted newcomers because they offered employment opportunities, cultural attractions, and social life. Younger people especially moved to larger cities, leaving behind an increasingly older population in the countryside. Midsized cities such as Clinton, Mason City, and Keokuk lost population and had lower household incomes and higher poverty rates. Clinton was one of the worst hit of these midsize cities in the late twentieth and early twenty-first centuries. It lost more than one-third of its manufacturing jobs from 1978 to 2017 and 20 percent of its people from 1982 to 2017. Downtown buildings were vacant and a food bank saw increasing demand in the 2010s. Clinton tried to lure industry, but a declining work force made this a difficult proposition. Ashford University closed and even the large retailer Target shut down. Midsize cities like Clinton, with 10,000 to 49,999 people, were spread across Iowa and provided critical services, from college to health care. Their struggles made life more challenging for people who did not live near large metro areas. Towns near midsize cities relied on them for jobs and commerce, too.[3]

Smaller towns were hurt by outmigration from the countryside and by the struggles of midsize cities. From 2000 to 2013 metro areas with more than fifty thousand people grew by 13.3 percent while the population in outlying areas fell by 3.6 percent. This gap was larger than anywhere else in the Midwest. This trend continued through the 2010s, with Mason City and Fort Dodge both losing 5 percent of their population over the decade. Rural areas hemorrhaged younger residents, who were drawn to jobs in health care, insurance, and banking in Des Moines and other cities. Populations fell and public-school enrollment plummeted in places like Pocahontas, where the number of students declined by 32 percent from 2004 to 2014. As noted in the previous chapter, however, Latino immigration helped many small and midsize towns survive. Places such as Storm Lake, Marshalltown, and Muscatine benefited from such newcomers, who started businesses, filled school classrooms and churches, and helped towns prosper. The influx of Latinos into Marshalltown stabilized its population and helped revitalize its downtown. They opened more than forty businesses and worked in meatpacking, manufacturing, and construction.[4]

As already noted, the state's largest metro area, Des Moines, boomed in the early twenty-first century. Its suburbs, such as Waukee and Ankeny, expanded very quickly. Ankeny added twenty-four thousand people between 2010 and 2020, growing 54 percent. Waukee added thirteen thousand inhabitants, expanding by 90 percent. Enrollment in the largest school district in Dallas County, west of Des Moines, doubled from 2004 to 2014. The population of downtown Des Moines also doubled during this time, with new apartments and the first full-size supermarket arriving in the late 2010s. The city's downtown, usually empty after five p.m., began to come alive. Start-up tech companies moved into Des Moines and other major cities in the state. A lively cultural scene grew in the capital city and nationally known restaurants opened up. Clubs and breweries became common; theater, concerts and art exhibits added to its attractiveness. Politico, an influential political website, described the city as vibrant and hip, words not previously associated with Des Moines. In 2021 the magazine *U.S. News & World Report* ranked Iowa as the number one state for "opportunity." *Forbes* magazine named Des Moines the best place for businesses and careers.[5]

African Americans in Iowa's capital city would have not recognized it as a place that gave them opportunity, however. Blacks had a "marginalized existence in Des Moines and more generally in Iowa, with high unemployment, incarceration, and suspension rates," argued Charles E. Connerly, director of the University of Iowa School of Urban and Regional

Planning. The annual median income for Blacks in Des Moines was less than half that of all households in Polk County in 2016. Thirty-nine percent of African Americans in the county lived below the poverty line. Black unemployment was almost five times that of Polk County overall—16.7 percent compared to 3.5 percent. In Iowa City, Blacks were arrested at a rate six times their proportion of the population. The University of Iowa had few African American faculty, students, or staff. In Waterloo and Cedar Falls, Black household income was just a little more than half that of white families. More than twice as many white families owned their homes in the two cities. Iowa was third in the country, behind New Jersey and Wisconsin, in terms of the rate at which Blacks were imprisoned, compared to whites. They were incarcerated eleven times more than white Iowans. These long-term structural inequalities, from redlining to imprisonment, haunted Black communities in Iowa and "locked them out of equal access to the American dream," as journalist Rekha Basu wrote in December 2018. Seventeen months later such issues became unavoidable when a police officer in Minneapolis murdered African American George Floyd and racial justice protests spread across the country.[6]

Iowa weathered the Great Recession of 2007–2009 better than most places, but its recovery lagged adjacent states and the country overall. The recession gained its name because it was the worst economic downturn in the United States since the 1930s. The contraction left the country poorer, exacerbated income inequality, and left those without a college degree worse off. Birth rates fell, opioid use increased, and many areas, especially rural ones, did not fully recover. Uneven economic growth left many behind—people in distressed areas died younger and had higher suicide rates. Iowa escaped the worst consequences of the sharp worldwide downturn, as its housing market avoided the quick rise and devastating crash that hurt states like Florida. A strong agricultural sector and a more diversified economy of finance, insurance, and health care firms reduced the impact of the recession. Iowa had lower unemployment and greater income growth in the years afterward than most states. But smaller cities did not gain jobs and Iowa's employment grew slower than nearby states. Still, the unemployment rate fell to 2.5 percent in September 2018. Iowa farm income peaked in 2011, aided by high demand for corn and soybeans for food and biofuels. In August 2012 the average price for a bushel of corn reached $8.49. Land values rose over $8,500, far above the bottom of $787 an acre in 1986. Eighty percent of Iowa farmland had no mortgage by 2015, the result of decades of frugality. Sixty percent of it was owned by people over the age of sixty-five.[7]

But the mid- and late 2010s brought significant challenges to the state's economy. Farm prices declined steeply beginning in 2013. Agricultural production was strong, but exports slowed and a trade war with China and other countries reduced demand. By 2018 the real (inflation-adjusted) income of farmers was the lowest in twenty years. Prices for corn and soybeans were below the production cost and many farmers wanted to quit a business that seemed only to leave them in debt. Iowa's economy also consisted of sectors that grew slower than the nation overall. These included agriculture and manufacturing, which were stagnant or declining. One analysis concluded that if Iowa had the same economic mix as the rest of the country and had grown as fast as the nation overall, the state would have produced more than twice the jobs that it did from 2007 to 2018. Iowa's economy grew slower from 2010 to 2018 than any adjacent state and less than half the rate of the United States overall. In part this was because Iowa's economy had not contracted as severely as the rest of the country. Other states had lost more jobs than Iowa. But a slow-growing population was also a drag on economic growth. The state's midsize cities did not recover all of the jobs they lost after the Great Recession. Most job growth occurred in metro areas, with a population of 50,000 or more. Iowa had eleven of these larger metro areas, including Dubuque, Council Bluffs, Waterloo, Davenport, and Sioux City.[8]

Iowa's twenty-first century farms were a sophisticated, high-tech business operation. Combines equipped with computers and GPS allowed precision farming, which tracked planting, suggested fertilizer use, recorded field moisture levels, and estimated harvest. Genetically engineered seeds were planted with variable spacing, often within the same row. The combine's computers recorded information from previous harvests and used data to apply seed and fertilizer as needed. Precision created efficiencies for growers—chemical application has fallen, with insecticide use 80 percent below the 1972 peak. Fertilizer use had also declined since the 1980s, but nitrate runoff was still a serious problem for Iowa waterways. About one-third of the acres in Iowa in 2019 used no-till or reduced till methods, which planted seeds in unplowed fields, reducing erosion and the loss of soil moisture. Technology greatly increased agricultural production, but it required substantial capital investment, sometimes millions of dollars. Before World War II it took one hundred labor hours to produce one hundred bushels of corn. By the 2010s it took less than two hours. Iowa farmers averaged 182 bushels of corn an acre between 2011 and 2020, as well as 53.1 bushels of soybeans per acre over the same period. Average statewide soybean yields varied by 25 percent over the decade, while corn fluctuated by 32.5%. For both crops 2012 was the worst year because of drought and 2016 the best. Overseas export markets were important for Iowa producers. The state sold $10 billion in agricultural goods to countries such as Canada, Mexico, China, Japan, and Germany in 2019. Canada and Mexico were the top importers from Iowa, buying more than $5.5 billion in corn, soybeans, pork, and other farm goods.[9]

Iowa's farmers became more diverse, even as their numbers fell, as they had since the 1930s. Shrinking rural populations left fewer viable small towns. Those who lived in the countryside often had to drive long distances for groceries or health care. Schools consolidated, with twenty-one districts closing from 2010 to 2014. Many farm families could not afford the expensive equipment needed for maximum efficiency. About half of Iowa farmers considered agriculture their secondary occupation and worked full-time jobs off the farm. New and more diverse growers went into farming though. A married same-sex couple, Matt Russell and Patrick Standley, operated a 110-acre farm, growing chemical-free produce for the Des Moines Downtown Farmers' Market. A 1984 refugee from Laos, Phrakhounmany Philavanh, saved his money for years and bought eleven acres south of Des Moines to raise cattle. He had loved farming since he had helped on his grandfather's rice farm in Southeast Asia as a boy. Philavanh was the last of eight children to make it to the United States. Refugees from Bhutan, Burma, Burundi, and Rwanda grew crops on small plots of land around Des Moines, selling farm goods such as eggplant and radishes at a market. Nonwhite farmers in Iowa were rare though, numbering only one-half of one percent of the total number of producers in 2019. Thirty-four percent of growers were female. The state had 676 organic farms that year, with $95.2 million in sales.[10]

Iowa's rural areas and small towns benefited from the production of ethanol, which was mostly made from corn and then added to gasoline. About half of Iowa's corn production in 2020 was used to make 3.7 billion gallons of ethanol. Regular gasoline usually contains about 10 percent ethanol. Iowa was the nation's largest producer of ethanol and biodiesel and had about forty plants in the 2010s. They were scattered across Iowa and provided an important source of jobs, as well as a huge market for corn.

One economist calculated that the industry supported about eight thousand jobs in the state. The demand for ethanol increased greatly when a 2005 federal law mandated its use in gasoline. Supporters argued that ethanol was a renewable fuel source since it was made from plants. They also argued that it reduced pollution by helping gasoline burn cleaner. Huge amounts of corn went into ethanol—in 2020 one-third of the corn grown in the country was blended into fuel, reducing gas use by 7 percent. Critics argued that growing corn and making ethanol consumed more energy than it saved. But ethanol production increased the demand for grain and buoyed Iowa's economy. Its defense became part of political life in the state for its representatives, and those who competed in the Iowa caucuses.[11]

A second form of energy production in rural Iowa expanded with breathtaking speed in the early twenty-first century. Investment in wind energy dramatically increased thanks to federal tax credits—the industry grew sevenfold from 2007 to 2017. Wind energy produced nearly 60 percent of the state's electricity in 2020 and Iowa was second only to Texas in wind power capacity. It surpassed coal as an energy source in 2019, which had provided 71 percent of the state's energy needs just nine years earlier. Replacing coal with wind significantly reduced greenhouse gas emissions in the state. The industry had nearly fifty-nine hundred turbines in the state by the end of 2020. It was a major business in rural areas, employing more than nine thousand people and paying taxes that supported schools and maintained roads. A wind farm in O'Brien County had thirty permanent workers; the ethanol plant in the county had fifty. The state had the second largest number of wind energy jobs in the country, behind Texas. The wind industry also made $78.5 million in lease payments to landowners in 2016. Some who lived near the turbines opposed them, arguing that they were noisy and caused headaches and nausea. One farmer complained that his area had become a "windmill landfill," with six three-hundred-foot turbines near his home sounding like a tornado. But investment did not look to slow in the 2020s.[12]

The United States was engaged in two wars in Asia long before wind farms spread across the Iowa countryside. The September 11, 2001, terrorist attacks led to twenty years of warfare in Afghanistan, as well as a long war in Iraq. Less than a month after September 11, the United States struck the Taliban in Afghanistan. For twenty years the United States tried to subdue a Taliban-supported insurgency, its efforts undermined by a weak, corrupt Afghan government, difficult terrain, and Taliban sanctuaries in nearby Pakistan. Afghanistan was also a huge country, almost as big as Texas. About eight hundred thousand Americans served in Afghanistan, including thousands from Iowa. The defense department reported that 2,461 Americans died during the Afghanistan campaign and nearly 21,000 were wounded. In March 2003 the United States invaded Iraq, searching for weapons of mass destruction that were never found. The American invasion touched off a brutal war that lasted until US forces left in 2011. More than 1.1 million Americans served in the Iraq War. More than forty-five hundred were killed and more than thirty-two thousand were wounded. Thirty-one service members from Iowa died during the war in Afghanistan and sixty-four in the Iraq War.[13]

Iowan John Hintz served in both countries. After graduating from Wartburg College, he joined the army and spent four years in the Eighty-Second Airborne Division in the mid-1990s. After the September 11 attacks he rejoined the army. Hintz had just gotten married. In 2006 and early 2007 he commanded an infantry platoon east of Baghdad, battling improvised explosive devices (IEDs) and insurgents. Hintz was in eight vehicles hit by IEDs but survived every bombing. Eleven soldiers in his unit lost limbs from explosions. "So what we fought was the IEDs," he said in an interview. In 2010 Hintz was a captain, now in the 101st Airborne Division. He went to Afghanistan, commanding a company at an outpost in a high valley twelve miles from Pakistan. "And then when I went to Afghanistan, that was war." The Taliban were more numerous and better trained. Firefights could last two days. His company encountered hundreds of IEDs while clearing the village of Talukan in southern Afghanistan. "We stepped on a lot of them, lost a lot of soldiers there." Hintz returned safely to Iowa in 2011.[14]

More than ten thousand Iowa National Guard members were called up for active duty between September 2001 and the end of 2013. Most were mobilized by March 2004. The state was among the top five in terms of the percentage of Guard members who were on active duty. Constant deployment did not deplete its numbers though, and the Iowa National Guard enlisted more personnel than before the two wars. The first member of the guard killed in combat since Vietnam was Bruce Smith, age forty-one, from West Liberty. A missile hit the Chinook helicopter that he piloted in November 2003. He kept it airborne long enough to save the lives of some of his passengers. His wife, Olivia, recalled, "Those men on that copter needed my husband more in that split second than I needed him in a lifetime." Another guard member, Casey Byers, left behind a daughter, Hailey, whom he never met. Byers was killed in June 2005 and his daughter was raised by his parents. Twenty-two guard members from Iowa were killed and an estimated three hundred injured during deployments to Afghanistan or Iraq.[15]

A variety of immigrants came to Iowa from around the world. Some served in the Iowa National Guard, including Princy Mungedi, who had been born in the Democratic Republic of Congo. He served in a guard logistics unit and became a citizen in July 2021. Des Moines had a large foreign-born population, which was one of the fastest growing in the country in the 2010s. About sixty thousand immigrants lived in the metro area in 2019, from Myanmar, Mexico, Vietnam, and many other places. Some were refugees from regions plagued by conflict, while others came for economic opportunities. Immigrants chose to live in Iowa because of its low cost of living and because there were jobs, even for those who didn't speak English. A low crime rate or little traffic congestion attracted some. Migrants could find work at meatpacking plants in Perry or Marshalltown, often while living in Des Moines. About ten thousand immigrants from Mexico lived in the capital, the largest of any foreign-born group. Approximately four thousand people from Bosnia-Herzegovina also lived in the city. Vietnamese immigrants numbered about thirty-one hundred. Des Moines also had about twenty-five hundred immigrants from Myanmar in 2021, many coming as refugees from the Southeast Asian nation. They struggled with cold weather, isolation, and cultural differences. Min Tun arrived in 2007 with seven other refugees from Myanmar. He worked at a manufacturing company before opening his own grocery store in 2011. Tun's Golden Land Food Market provided products distinct to his home, such as fish paste noodles. Refugees like Tun were often entrepreneurial, starting businesses more often than other immigrants or native-born citizens.[16]

The increasing number of immigrants was an economic lifeline for the state. Iowa's population growth had been slower than the growth of the United States every decade since 1880. Almost half of its counties—forty-four—had peaked in population in 1900. Twenty-five more had reached their peak by 1950. Most of the state's college graduates, about 60 percent, left the state after graduation in the late 1990s, drawn to fast-growing cities with good jobs, often in the South or West. Iowa's population had declined significantly during the farm crisis and grew by only 9.5 percent from 1980 to 2020. In comparison, southern states grew by 17 percent and western states grew by 20 percent in the 1990s alone. Immigrants worked in low skill jobs, such as meatpacking, as well as high-skill jobs, such as finance. The wage distribution among such immigrants was like a barbell. About one third of immigrants worked in low and moderate wage industries. But a slightly larger number worked in high-paying fields, such as information technology, with employers like Wells Fargo or Principal Financial Group. Such employers had to bring workers from outside Iowa, or outside the United States, to fill these well-paying jobs.[17]

On May 12, 2008, Immigrations and Customs Enforcement (ICE) agents raided a kosher meatpacking plant in Postville, a small town in the northeast corner of the state that did not have a stoplight. ICE suspected that the plant employed undocumented workers and arrested almost four hundred people. It was one of the largest immigration raids in the nation's history, resulting in the arrest of almost one in six people in the town. Women and children—one girl sobbing because she could not find her mother—fled to a nearby church for safety. Volunteers provided food, clothing, and emotional support for weeks. Those who were arrested were shackled and charged with felonies, as opposed to lesser charges or deportation that undocumented employees usually received. About three hundred hastily pled guilty, seen more as criminals than victims. Most spent five months in prison and were deported. The raid also led to serious state and federal charges against the plant's management, including child labor and safety violations. Some employees were as young as thirteen. Others were forced to work more than one hundred hours a week in dangerous conditions. The town's economy was badly hurt when its largest employer shut down. Stores and restaurants closed, evictions increased, and homelessness became a problem. Postville gained national attention as an example of a broken immigration system that encouraged undocumented workers to come and allowed employers to exploit them.[18]

The small town of Storm Lake was deeply influenced by immigration, which helped save it from the economic decline experienced by much of Iowa outside the larger metro areas. One of these newcomers was Ofelia Rumbo Valdez, who lived in Storm Lake with her husband and two children. She came to the town at age fifteen from Durango, Mexico, following an aunt who worked in a meatpacking plant. She did not know much English, but Ofelia thrived at the local high school, earning a 3.98 GPA. After her aunt was deported, she raised two cousins and worked three jobs.

In college Valdez worked seventy hours a week to pay for her education and earned a business degree in 2008 from Buena Vista University. She found a job in human resources at a farm supply company and married. Her undocumented status put her at risk of deportation, but she finally received permanent residency. In 2021 she became an American citizen, one of thousands of immigrants who came to the state pursuing their dreams.[19]

Others in Iowa were also able to improve their lives significantly—the Meskwaki settlement near Tama thrived in the late twentieth and early twenty-first century. In the early 2000s the tribe had more than twelve hundred members, almost triple its population in the 1930s. They started high-stakes bingo in a tribal gym in the mid-1980s. Profits from the operation helped fund a modest casino with slot machines that opened in 1992. It evolved into a $135 million gambling business in the early twenty-first century. Revenues from gaming helped fund new homes, roads, water, and utility connections for the Meskwaki. More than three hundred new homes were built for tribal members, as well as new schools. Gaming profits also paid for a health clinic, youth recreation programs, a senior center, and financial aid for college. Most Meskwaki were employed by the tribe, but some worked in nearby schools, shops, or hospitals. Profits were also distributed to tribal members, reaching about $2,000 per person each month. Money was deposited in a trust fund for children. The casino's huge success also benefited the white citizens of Tama, as money flowed into the town and its businesses. Many whites worked for the casino, too. The tribe also built a travel plaza and hotel. In the 2010s the Meskwaki created new companies that sold tobacco, coffee, and other products. This allowed them to provide a variety of jobs for tribal members and diversify their income streams. The Meskwaki went "from a low-income community to an upper-middle-income one," wrote anthropologist Douglas Foley.[20]

Iowa attracted nationwide attention when it became the third state in the country to legalize same-sex marriage. The Iowa Supreme Court overturned a ban on same-sex marriage in a unanimous ruling on April 3, 2009. It was the first state outside New England to allow it. Six gay and lesbian couples sued the Polk County recorder, Timothy J. Brien, for denying them marriage licenses, in a case known as *Varnum v. Brien*. The lead plaintiffs were Kate Varnum and Patricia Hyde Varnum, members of an Episcopalian church in Cedar Rapids who worked as an insurance analyst and a business manager. The court ruled that same-sex couples had the right to marry because the state had a duty to ensure equal protection of the law.

Thus, a state law that defined marriage as an institution only for men and women was unconstitutional. In the next six years, thirty-six other states and Washington, DC, recognized same-sex marriages as a right. Many of these decisions were also made through court rulings. In 2015 the US Supreme Court approved it for the entire nation. More than nine thousand same-sex marriages occurred in Iowa from 2009 to 2013, including that of Chuck and Jason Swaggerty-Morgan, who adopted five children. The decision was controversial and only a small minority of Iowans supported it at the time. Conservatives defeated three justices in 2010 elections, the first defeats in a retention election in Iowa. Over time, opposition to marriage equality decreased as people learned that their gay and lesbian neighbors were pretty much just like them, with 67 percent of Americans supporting it by 2020.[21]

In 2020 the LGBTQ population of Iowa was estimated to be eighty-seven thousand, or about 3.6 percent of the state's adult inhabitants. While this percentage was about the same as Utah or Missouri, according to one study from 2017, Iowa's cities ranked better than the national average at protecting the rights of its gay, bisexual, and transgender citizens. The University of Iowa was the first public university to recognize a gay and lesbian student organization. Iowa City, a center of activism in the state, had one of the oldest pride parades in the Midwest. By the 2010s, its Pride Fest had become a major social and cultural event in the state. In Des Moines as many as thirty thousand people came to the 2019 Pride Fest celebration. Democratic presidential candidates also visited, seeking votes and declaring their support for LGBTQ rights. The Iowa City event began in 1970, one year after the 1969 Stonewall protests against the New York police that marked the start of the modern gay rights movement. Students from the University of Iowa formed the Gay Liberation Front and draped a "Gay Pride is Gay Power" banner across a car at the homecoming parade that year. Generally speaking, in the twenty-first century the United States became more accepting of those who were gay, lesbian, bisexual, transgender, or identified as not heterosexual. Younger adults who had grown up in a culture that increasingly allowed them to embrace their identity were most likely to identify as LGBTQ. But they faced many challenges, from discrimination to housing instability. Queer children were four times as likely to attempt suicide as their peers. They also became part of America's political culture wars in the early 2020s, with states enacting bans on transgender students who wanted to participate in sports matching their gender identity. Disputes over banning books, often those with LGBTQ themes, became common.[22]

Iowa began the century as a purple swing state and ended 2020 as a solidly red one. Northwest Iowa was the most conservative part of the state and was represented by Republican Steve King, a controversial, immigrant-bashing firebrand, for eighteen years, from 2003 to 2021. Much of the rest of the state was a battleground until 2016, when Republicans came to control all parts of state government, both US Senate seats, and three of four congressional seats after that year's November elections. Republicans' statehouse majorities expanded even more after the 2020 elections, another Democratic rout that benefited from the turnout of independents and conservatives who supported Donald Trump. In presidential elections from 1992 to 2012 Iowa always voted very close to the national results, never deviating by more than 1 percent from the outcome. Democrat Barack Obama won the state in 2008 and 2012. But Republicans won every gubernatorial and US senate race in the 2010s as well the presidential election in Iowa in 2016 and 2020. Hillary Clinton lost the state badly in 2016, as Iowa flipped from Democrat to Republican by a larger margin than any other state in the country. Donald Trump easily won Iowa in 2020, beating Joe Biden by a larger margin than he defeated Clinton, cementing the conservative hold on a state that was once highly competitive.[23]

Democrats had controlled the governor's mansion from 1998 to 2010, but a Republican wave of victories nationwide in 2010 began a decade of increasing GOP dominance in the state. Economic woes from the Great Recession, a well-known Republican challenger, and a backlash against the same-sex court ruling contributed to the defeat of Vilsack's successor, Chet Culver, in 2010. Former Republican governor Terry Branstad returned to office the next year. The Democrats lost control of the state house of representatives but held on to the state senate by one seat until they also lost the chamber in 2016. Clinton's decisive loss to Trump in 2016 highlighted Democratic weakness in rural areas beyond the larger, more diverse metros that had more college graduates. Art Cullen, a newspaper editor in Storm Lake, argued that Obama didn't deliver for average workers while in office, who suffered from low pay and expensive health care. Cullen also thought that Clinton lacked empathy and didn't try to win over the state's voters. Democratic defeats were part of a nationwide trend: states with more working-class white voters, smaller numbers of college graduates, and larger rural populations tilted more heavily toward Republicans. The Democratic party was less competitive in other midwestern states such as Ohio and Missouri for the same reasons.[24]

Even before Trump's victories cemented Republican control of state government, the GOP did well in Iowa. In 2014 Republican Joni Ernst won the US Senate seat vacated by liberal Democrat Tom Harkin. She became the first woman elected as a US senator from the state. The presidential campaign of Donald Trump helped make Iowa a solidly red state, mobilizing conservatives and independents with a populist anti-Washington message that targeted immigrants and promised to create jobs. Trump's ideas resonated with those who felt left behind in declining rural areas with limited job options and changing demographics. Chuck Grassley won reelection in 2016, with the help of a wave of Trump voters. A year later Kim Reynolds became the state's first female governor, succeeding Terry Branstad when he left office to become US ambassador to China. Republican control of the state legislature allowed Branstad to achieve conservative objectives before he left office, such as restricting abortion, expanding gun rights, and reducing union collective bargaining. The GOP also privatized the state's Medicaid system, a plan that attracted controversy and much criticism. Reynolds took over in May 2017 and was elected on her own in November 2018, pursuing a conservative agenda of tax cuts and pro-business legislation.[25]

Donald Trump's voters turned out to support him in the November 2020 elections, benefiting Republicans in Iowa, as Trump won by eight points and his party won big victories in the state. They took back two US congressional seats they lost in 2018 and won the hotly contested US Senate race, with the reelection of Joni Ernst. They also gained seats in the state legislature. After the elections, the GOP controlled both branches of the legislature with a majority greater than any time since the early 1970s. In 2020 Republicans tied Iowa Democrats to liberals in Washington, DC, in a relentless and highly effective campaign echoing Trump's claims that Democrats were radicals who would bring socialism to America. Republicans continued to stage rallies and gatherings, which helped motivate their voters. Democrats did not, avoiding most in-person events due to the coronavirus. Their caution contributed to their defeat.[26]

Iowa suffered from a more volatile climate in the twenty-first century, even as its political leanings became more predictable. Rain fell in greater amounts in the late twentieth and early twenty-first centuries than it had before. Eastern Iowa received one to two inches of increased spring rainfall between 1980 and 2010. Rain was also more likely to fall in larger amounts, with longer periods between storms. Flooding cost Iowa individuals, businesses, and farmers $17.6 billion from 1988 to 2018. Some counties were hit by floods seventeen times in three decades. Iowa suffered from 951 federal flood-related disaster declarations in these three decades and ranked fourth for floods among states. Every county had been hit by flooding, which was exacerbated by drainage tiles that moved water into rivers and streams faster. Extensive agriculture in the state reduced wetlands and limited the ability of the land to absorb water. Ambitious flood prevention and mitigation plans required as much as $10 billion over fifty years, a sum unlikely to be ever allocated.[27]

Rising greenhouse gases from human activity contributed to heavier rainfall, including a weather phenomenon known as the "Midwest water hose." Such a system, formed when moisture from the Gulf of Mexico meets cold dry air in the north, leading to heavy rainfall, has occurred more frequently in recent decades. Such dangerous events are expected to become more regular, as a warming climate leads to more extreme weather. This will likely bring more flooding and droughts. The 2019 floods in Iowa, which pushed the Missouri and Mississippi Rivers beyond their banks, were mostly caused by this "Midwest water hose."[28]

Iowa experienced severe flooding in 2008 and 2019. Both events resulted from very wet winters and springs, followed by a rainy summer. Iowa received 50.73 inches of precipitation from June 2018 to May 2019, almost 50 percent more than the normal. It was the wettest such period since official records began in 1895; six other midwestern states also set records for precipitation, as did the United States overall. There was no single cause for the record rainfall, but climate change and warming temperatures probably contributed to both the 2008 and 2019 floods. Above-average ocean temperatures in the Pacific Ocean, known as El Niño conditions, may have contributed to increased rainfall in 2019, as warmer air held more moisture and could release more rain. Flood waters carried fertilizers from farms and other sources south to the Gulf of Mexico. The "dead zone" in 2019 was predicted to be 8,717 square miles, or about the size of the state of New Hampshire.[29]

Tremendous amounts of water entered rivers and streams in both years. More than one million acres of farmland were flooded in Iowa in 2008, a year in which Iowa and Wisconsin were most affected. The worst flooding in the history of Cedar Rapids occurred in 2008. Most of its downtown flooded. Twenty-five thousand people were evacuated from their homes in Linn County. Coralville's business district flooded, and the University of Iowa sustained serious damage, with twenty-two major buildings swamped. The initial loss was $232 million. Six months later this number had more than tripled. The total cost of the 2008 flood was estimated at $10 billion, with the greatest losses in Linn and Johnson Counties. The 2008 floods were only rivaled by the 1993 floods and the 2020 derecho as the worst disasters in the state's recent history. In 2019 flooding in the Midwest began in March when heavy rain fell on frozen or saturated ground. More flooding occurred throughout the year. Levees failed along the Missouri River. Many communities were overwhelmed, with towns such as Hamburg along the Missouri inundated. Interstate highways in western Iowa were closed for months. Davenport was flooded, a broken barrier allowing water to pour into its downtown. The 2019 floods cost billions, damaging infrastructure, destroying towns, homes, and business, and harming agricultural production.[30]

Iowa also suffered from droughts, with a devastating 2012 dry period coming just four years after record flooding. Unstable weather patterns, probably influenced by climate change, were predicted to cause more frequent droughts. The 2012 drought affected two-thirds of the country, reducing crop yields from Indiana to South Dakota and leading to higher prices. It was the worst drought in Iowa since the 1930s. The corn harvest was reduced by about one-fourth nationwide; it was above seven dollars a bushel much of the year. Drought lingered until 2014, keeping the price for soybeans and corn high. Another drought in 2017 threatened about half of Iowa farmers, driving down yields. Corn prices were about $3.20 a bushel for fall delivery. The drought did not drive up prices, as it was not widespread. It simply punished those in the southeast and northwest who were unfortunate enough to be in its path. Dry weather returned in the summer of 2020 and continued into mid-2021. Almost 40 percent of Iowa was in a moderate or severe drought in May 2021.[31]

Iowa normally benefited from favorable temperatures and rainfall in the growing season, factors that long made it a great place for agriculture. A warming climate posed serious risks to farming in the state. Most of Iowa's spring rain came from evaporation from the Gulf of Mexico. A warmer climate would result in more evaporation and more rainfall. Increasing temperatures were predicted to bring more extreme rainfall events, often as shorter, but more intense, storms. The Cedar River basin in eastern Iowa is an example of this tendency. Floods that had been considered hundred-year events in the twentieth century were emerging as twenty-five-year events in the twenty-first. Heavy rain led to more erosion and to the loss of topsoil. In May 2017 a fierce storm hit southwest Iowa, eroding at least five tons of topsoil per acre from 4.2 million acres. Higher temperatures also increased the threat of pests and disease. Iowa's growing season had increased by nine days since 1901, as freezing temperatures came later in the fall and earlier in the spring. Another ten days would be added by the mid-twenty-first century. Longer growing seasons sound great. But hotter temperatures in the middle of summer reduced crop yields. The worst scenario might bring summer heat waves that could be eleven degrees hotter in the mid-twenty-first century. More droughts in between high rainfall years were predicted. All of this would substantially reduce crop yields in the state and endanger farmers and the parts of the Iowa economy that depended upon them.[32]

An immediate threat arrived with the coronavirus pandemic, which originated in China and reached Iowa in March 2020. The disease was new and highly transmissible, spreading quickly in crowded or enclosed spaces. Schools closed and classes were taught online. Government offices shut down; the state legislature suspended operations for more than two months. Many worked remotely from home. People who labored in retail or manufacturing jobs, often nonwhite, had to report to work and were at greater risk of catching COVID. Others, who lived in crowded housing or had to take public transportation, were also at higher risk. In May, Polk County was one of the ten counties with the fastest COVID spread in the country. Data from March, April, and May 2020 showed that Latinos in Polk County were more than twice as likely to become infected as whites, while African Americans were more than four times as likely to catch COVID as whites. Those of Asian descent were more than six times more likely to be sickened. In Linn County, home to a substantial Black community, African Americans were six times as likely to be infected as whites early in the pandemic. In Sioux County, incomplete data showed that Latinos were more than twenty-seven times as likely to get sick. Coronavirus was most dangerous to the elderly, killing many who were infected in Iowa nursing homes. Workers at meatpacking plants were vulnerable because employees labored close to each other. Many were Latino, Black,

Asian, or Pacific Islander and were forced to go back to work with limited safety measures. More than one thousand workers tested positive at one Tyson Foods plant in Waterloo. By October, the state had more than one hundred thousand confirmed cases. The number of cases may have been much higher, as millions of asymptomatic infections went undetected nationwide in mid-2020. Iowa was the only state in the country to allow high school sports to continue during the pandemic in 2020.[33]

The pandemic led to a fierce debate on the reopening of schools. Many school districts in big cities nationwide continued with online teaching. Governor Reynolds pushed schools to reopen in Iowa despite the surge in COVID cases in the late summer and fall of 2020. The Des Moines school district moved classes online for much of the fall, arguing that high caseloads and crowded classrooms endangered students and staff. COVID surges led some schools to teach courses remotely for a couple of weeks before returning to classrooms. Reynolds and most Republican governors fought to keep schools open during the 2020–2021 academic year, arguing that doing so would assist with economic recovery and was best for children. Iowa's five hundred thousand students endured a challenging year of illness, cancelled events, worry, and often isolation. Teachers and staff members suffered as well, with at least twenty Iowa educators dying from COVID in 2020. But schools did not end up being centers of COVID spread, as many people were not isolating at home anyway. Most Iowa students went to their regular classes in person, which turned out to be good policy as remote learning emerged as a failure. Students learned much less online. School closures hurt low-income students of color the most, who might not have had internet access or quiet places to work. In the end, an estimated 75 percent of K-12 students had contracted COVID by mid-2022, with unknown long-term health consequences.[34]

Iowa also suffered from a COVID-created economic recession. Unlike most states, Iowa never imposed a full stay-at-home order to try and control the spread of coronavirus. Governor Kim Reynolds emphasized the state economy over pandemic control, blocking mask mandates in cities or towns. Iowa reopened quickly and suffered less of an economic downturn than most states. But the spread of the coronavirus impeded the state's economic rebound. Businesses struggled as customers stayed home. Government mandated shutdowns of restaurants and other gathering places, as well as the closure of businesses, left the state with an unemployment rate that reached 11 percent in the spring of 2020. In late May, Reynolds began to lift restrictions on businesses such as bars and movie theaters, despite warnings that easing mitigation efforts might cause a second wave of infection. At the end of August, Iowa had the highest coronavirus rate in the country, spurred, in part, by the reopening of colleges. Its unemployment rate fell below 5 percent by September. A White House report urged the state to require mask-wearing to reduce the spread of COVID, but the governor refused, arguing that such a mandate was unenforceable and that Iowans could make their own choices about wearing masks. In October the state suffered from a virus level twice that of the nation overall, leading to what the federal government considered to be many preventable deaths. Governor Reynolds took part in an October election rally for President Trump, despite warnings that it could help spread COVID. Still, in November she issued a partial mask mandate as the virus spiraled out of control.[35]

On August 10 a devastating line of storms, known as a derecho, pummeled Iowa and other midwestern states. The event had the strength of a hurricane, with 140 mile-per-hour winds that shattered the power grid in Cedar Rapids and left many without electricity for weeks. This occurred only twelve years after the city had been battered by floods. Five hundred thousand people in Iowa lost power. The National Guard was sent to hard-hit Cedar Rapids to help clean up. Many in Des Moines and other places had no electricity for days. Downed power lines and debris blocked roads and made recovery more difficult; food pantries struggled to help feed those who had lost power. The storm damaged at least 14 million acres of crops in Iowa, as well as one-quarter of the state's forests. It killed three people in the state and cost at least $7.5 billion, the costliest windstorm in American history. Despite the pandemic and recession, Iowans turned out to help one another in the wake of this disaster, with restaurants providing food to the hungry and volunteers helping with neighborhood cleanups. The Meskwaki cut downed trees and gave wood to community members to use. Most of the homes on the Meskwaki settlement had been damaged by the derecho. The disaster did not receive much national attention but compounded the misery of 2020 for Iowans. By February 2021 dump trucks had hauled away 133,000 tons of debris in the state.[36]

The murder of George Floyd, a Black man, at the hands of a white police officer in Minneapolis on May 25, 2020, set off a wave of protests across the nation. A widely viewed video of his death made clear the terrible reality of police brutality against African Americans. The slogan "Black

Lives Matter" (BLM) became a rallying cry, morphing into the largest protest movement since the 1960s civil rights campaigns. Some protests demanding racial justice occurred in Iowa, helping to bring about legislation and an executive order that addressed some concerns of protestors. In June Governor Kim Reynolds signed a bill that banned the use of most chokeholds by police and allowed the state attorney general to investigate officer-involved deaths. The law also prevented police officers convicted of a felony or fired for misconduct from being hired in Iowa. It also required additional annual training on implicit bias and de-escalation techniques. In August Reynolds signed an executive order that restored voting rights to felons. Across the country Confederate monuments were removed and some states passed policing reform laws. After some success, progress stalled as racial justice protests became part of the presidential campaign and political culture wars. Property damage and looting in some cities hurt the cause. Republican victories in many states in November 2020 raised roadblocks to further reform, including in Iowa.[37]

The end of 2020 saw Iowa, and the United States, in the midst of a terrifying surge of the coronavirus. The state enjoyed one of the lowest unemployment rates in the country in January 2021—less than 4 percent. But it had one of the highest coronavirus infection rates in the nation, its hospitals flooded with COVID patients. Deaths spiked in the winter of 2020–2021. Exhausted hospital staff struggled to cope with months of seemingly endless crisis as the uncontrolled spread of the virus led to heartbreaking losses. Doctors were forced to ration intensive care beds. 4,564 Iowans died from the coronavirus in the year 2020 alone.[38]

The first two decades of the twenty-first century were challenging ones for Iowa and the United States. Larger metro areas in Iowa grew, while rural areas struggled, exacerbating an economic gap that had been growing for decades. Nonwhite populations were often left out of the economic gains in urban areas. An expanding immigrant population provided opportunities for economic growth and helped stabilize some smaller towns. But political battles over immigration divided the state. The Great Recession and the hard-edged politics of Donald Trump helped the Republican Party solidify its control of Iowa and ended the state's role as a battleground swing state. Meanwhile, growing environmental threats posed serious dangers to Iowa's agriculture. Floods and drought, as well as rising temperatures, became increasingly problematic. The coronavirus pandemic badly hurt the state, killing more than eighty-two hundred Iowans by January

2022. Persistent racial inequality limited the opportunities of Iowa's non-white population. The end of 2020 brought a close to one of the state's most difficult years. Some optimism arrived with 2021, as the arrival of vaccines and falling infection rates bred hope for a return to a more normal life in the state.[39]

Acknowledgments

I was a Fulbright Scholar in China in the spring semester of 2019. In April of that year, I visited Sichuan University to give several lectures on US history. One was about Iowa. A Chinese graduate student, who was writing a dissertation on populism in Wisconsin, asked me, "Why is Iowa important? What does it tell us about the United States?" I said something about agriculture and politics and realized that I needed to think a lot more about my book. (The American ambassador to China at the time was former Iowa governor Terry Branstad, so there was much curiosity about my home state and many questions that pushed me to think deeply about the manuscript that I was working on.) I hope that I have adequately answered that graduate student's question here.

This book took nine years to write. I began teaching Iowa history in 2014 and quickly realized that the state's history needed to be updated. Fortunately, Iowans have left behind a vast amount of published and unpublished material. This provided a wealth of information but required more time than expected to work through. I am indebted to the State Historical Society of Iowa (SHSI), a vital organization whose archives and publications are incredibly important for anyone who writes about Iowa. More than one thousand sources have been used in this book—one-third of these are articles in journals published by the SHSI. Most sources used here exist because they were preserved or published by the SHSI or a state university. They are found in the SHSI archives in Des Moines and Iowa City, as well as in archives at Iowa State University and the University of Iowa. The SHSI, the University of Iowa Press, and the now-defunct Iowa State University Press published almost one hundred books referenced in these pages. Many decades of manuscript conservation and historical publication have ensured that anyone writing about Iowa has a deep and broad base of historical information to draw upon. Research in the humanities can be criticized as overly specialized, impractical, or unnecessary. But *A New History of Iowa* would not exist without generations of scholars, writers, and editors who pursued topics that few considered important.

I am fortunate to teach at Iowa State University, a major research institution that supported years of research and writing. (Declining enrollments and challenging university finances will bring difficulties to the humanities in Iowa and elsewhere in the 2020s, though.) The history department at ISU is full of supportive colleagues and I am lucky to have an outstanding department chair in Simon Cordery. ISU's Parks Library sent material through the mail during the worst of the pandemic that helped me keep the project moving forward. At one point two hundred books and journals filled a spare room in my home. Two research grants from the Center for Excellence in Arts and the Humanities at Iowa State University supported this research, giving me many weeks of time to spend in archives. Additional small annual research grants from ISU's College of Liberal Arts and Sciences were important in sustaining this project as well. A research grant from the SHSI resulted in an article in the *Annals of Iowa*, parts of which have been incorporated into the manuscript.

Many people have helped me with this project, including historians, archivists, journal editors, and museum educators. Mary Bennett read the introduction and early chapters. Her ideas on framing the introduction are greatly appreciated, as were her answers to my questions every time I visited the SHSI center in Iowa City. Marvin Bergman, former editor of the *Annals of Iowa*, read three chapters in part 2 and gave me many helpful suggestions. Cynthia Sweet, from the Iowa Museum Association, read early drafts of the manuscript and caught embarrassing omissions and garbled writing. Janet Weaver from the Iowa Women's Archives at the University of Iowa was always helpful and patient even when I sent her too many email messages and asked her for yet another manuscript collection. (The IWA is a fantastic and underappreciated institution.) The staff at Special Collections and Archives at the University of Iowa were also always helpful, as were those at ISU's Special Collections and University Archives. Thanks to Hang Nguyen, Charles Scott, and Becki Plunkett at the State Historical Society for their generous and patient assistance with everything from photocopying to images. Andrew Klumpp, Marvin Bergman's successor at the *Annals of Iowa*, asked me to write a short article on immigration for the journal, which became part of chapter 6. He also provided permissions for material previously published in the *Annals*. Leo Landis, Mary Bennett, and Becki Plunkett answered questions about the CCC and other topics as well.

Parts of chapters 3 and 6 first appeared in two articles: "'Land Was the Main Basis for Business:' Merchants, Markets, and Communities in Frontier Iowa," *Annals of Iowa* 76, no. 3 (Summer 2017): 261–289 and "Immigration to Iowa: A Brief History and Historiography," *Annals of Iowa* 80, no. 4 (Fall 2021): 387–393.

Stacy Cordery, a colleague in ISU's history department, read the entire manuscript, catching mistakes and helping to clarify prose and ideas. Her help was invaluable, and she read my chapters even while finishing her own book and teaching in a different state. Pamela Riney-Kehrberg read most of part 3 and provided helpful suggestions and kind words about the challenges of writing state history. Kevin Hill read the introduction and the last chapter, reassuring me that this non-Iowan knew a bit about his adopted state.

Four historians read this manuscript and provided important feedback on it. Their ideas, suggestions, and corrections have greatly improved this book. Jon K. Lauck and an anonymous reviewer read parts of the volume when chapters were first submitted to the press. Jon's ideas helped me craft the introduction and influenced much of the overall book. The anonymous reviewer provided important assistance on how to better explain the lives of Iowa's nonwhite peoples. I am indebted to both. Terrence Lindell and Stephen Warren also provided great assistance. Warren's suggestions helped me clarify ideas and make sure that I avoided errors of fact and interpretation. His feedback also helped me to see the gaps in the story and provided useful ways to better explain key parts of Iowa's history. Terrence Lindell provided extraordinary assistance, reading the manuscript with the care of an editor and the deep knowledge of a historian who seemed to know everything about Iowa. The book is greatly improved thanks to these four individuals.

Many friends have provided help over the years. Thanks to Ramona

Ortega-Liston, who made sure that John R. Ortega's memoir became part of the SHSI collections. She read several chapters and met with me to discuss Iowa history only a few days after her husband passed away. Her fortitude was inspiring. Thanks also to Hal Chase for his support and to Bill Douglas, who provided suggestions on Iowa religious history. Brian and Laurie Peterson have been great neighbors and good friends, who have made living in the countryside a joy. I have learned a lot about Iowa and Iowans from the privilege of knowing them. I am very glad to have Allison and Nels Dovre nearby, too.

The Library of Congress's Veterans History Project is an extraordinary collection of oral history. Megan Harris at the Veterans History Project answered many questions and was always helpful. I could not reach all the individuals whose stories I include in chapters 13 and 15 but I would like to thank Antonio Montognese and Rita McClain, daughter of Vernon Becker, for allowing me to include their stories. I hope that their stories, as well as those of John Hintz, Robert Gates, and Herbert Barger, remind us of the courage and sacrifice of this nation's veterans.

Some of my students have also read parts of this manuscript. Daniel Sunne read a draft of every chapter but the last, which was not completed when he took a graduate level independent study class on Iowa history in 2021. The book is better because of his suggestions. Brad Edmondson, Thurston Gable, and Abra Nichol also read sections. They helped me to clarify my writing and arguments, especially Abra, who teaches LGBTQ history at Roosevelt High School in Des Moines and assisted me with a couple of important paragraphs in the last chapter.

Everyone mentioned above has helped make a sprawling, messy manuscript into a much better book. They noticed mistakes and improved ideas and arguments. Any errors in fact or interpretation are solely those of the author.

The staff at the University Press of Kansas were superb, with special thanks to Joyce Harrison. Her interest in the project and her assistance with its development are greatly appreciated. Kelly Chrisman Jacques helped with images; Erica Nicholson assisted with editing. Derek Helms and Karl Janssen helped with design and marketing. Bethany Mowry was a great acquisitions editor, who answered questions and supported this project despite the challenges of the pandemic. Erin Greb, of Erin Greb Cartography, created two excellent maps.

I have enjoyed the company of many dogs while working on this book, who need to be thanked for their companionship and loyalty, even if they do occasionally chase deer, bark at flocks of geese, and eat gross things. They include Dutch, Libby, Drew, Hannah, Gracie, Oliver, and Lily. Only the last two remain with us, but the others will always be treasured.

My grandfather, Henry Welcome, did not live to see me publish my first book, much less the second one. But he would have truly enjoyed the intellectual journey and his loss still hurts. Eugenia Morain has served as surrogate family for decades and I am fortunate to know someone as wonderful as her.

My wife, Yana, has been my greatest supporter, enduring the many challenges of being married to an academic. She has been the backbone of our family and has lovingly tolerated long research trips, which have left her to juggle work and home. She lived with my odd working schedule and a house full of books, journals, and newspapers. She survived a semester of living in China, enduring endless travel and culture shock with humor and grace. Most importantly, she always loved me and has always been my greatest ally and champion. I am so very grateful to have her in my life.

Finally, I must also thank Greg Olson. This book, in part, is dedicated to him. I have known Greg for more than forty years and he has been one of the most important people in my life. I grew up in California and spent much of my youth in the boy scouts. Greg was my scoutmaster—a model of honesty, compassion, and integrity. He grew up in Iowa and the state shaped his character. His values and ideals also deeply influenced me. If I have led a decent and honorable life, it is because of Greg Olson.

Notes

INTRODUCTION

1. Pam Belluck, "Short on People, Iowa Seeks to be Ellis Island of Midwest," *New York Times*, August 28, 2000, https://www.nytimes.com/2000/08/28/us/short-of-people-iowa-seeks-to-be-ellis-island-of-midwest.html; Cullom Davis, "Illinois: Crossroads and Cross Section," in *Heartland: Comparative Histories of Midwestern States*, ed. James H. Madison (Bloomington: Indiana University Press, 1988), 140; James H. Madison, "The States of the Midwest: An Introduction," in Madison, *Heartland*, 1–2, 5–6; Kenneth F. Millsap, "Town and Country," *Palimpsest* 32, no. 9 (September 1951): 361–363; World Bank, "Urban Population (% of Total Population)—United States," accessed February 10, 2023, data.worldbank.org/indicator; Edward E. Curtis IV, *Muslims of the Heartland: How Syrian Immigrants Made a Home in the American Midwest* (New York: New York University Press, 2022), 66–86, 132–162; Dorothy Schwieder, *Iowa: The Middle Land* (Ames: Iowa State University Press, 1996), 35–38, 109–118, 133, 201–209; William Edwards, "New Census of Agriculture Reveals Much about Iowa Farms," *AgDM Newsletter*, September 2019, www.extension.iastate.edu/agdm/articles/edwards/EdwSept19.html; "Quick Facts," www.iowadatacenter.org; "Farm Income and Wealth Statistics," https://www.ers.usda.gov/faqs/#Q1; Iman Ghosh, "Visualizing the U.S. Population by Race," Visual Capitalist, December 28, 2020, https://www.visualcapitalist.com/visualizing-u-s-population-by-race/; Elizabeth M. Grieco, "White Population for the United States, Regions, and States, and for Puerto Rico: 1990 and 2000," *The White Population: 2000, Census 2000 Brief*, https://www2.census.gov/library/publications/decennial/2000/briefs/c2kbr01-04.pdf; "Race and Hispanic Origin," https://www.census.gov/quickfacts/IA;

"New Analysis Measures Economic Impact of Iowa Industries," https://www.news.iastate.edu/news/2020/05/05/iowaecon. According to the 2020 census, the "white alone" population in Iowa has fallen to 84.5 percent. See Iowa's 2020 census information at: United States Census Bureau, "Iowa: 2020 Census," https://www.census.gov/library/stories/state-by-state/iowa-population-change-between-census-decade.html. Nonwhite is defined as "white alone, not Hispanic or Latino." All websites accessed May 1 and 2, 2021, except the 2020 census, viewed September 16, 2022. Most midwestern states are more rural than the nation overall. For an overview of the country and its rural population see Andrew Lisa, "States with the Biggest Rural Populations," Stacker, April 8, 2018, https://stacker.com/stories/2779/states-biggest-rural-populations. The July 1, 2021, Iowa Population estimates showed that Iowa was 84.1 percent white—see "Quick Facts: Iowa," accessed December 22, 2021, https://www.census.gov/quickfacts/IA.

2. Jon Gjerde, "Middleness and the Middle West," in *The Identity of the American Midwest: Essays on Regional History*, ed. Andrew R. L. Cayton and Susan E. Gray (Bloomington: University of Indiana Press, 2001), 180–187; R. Douglas Hurt, "Midwestern Distinctiveness," in Cayton and Gray, *Identity of the American Midwest*, 163–169; and Joseph Frazier Wall, *Iowa: A History* (New York: W. W. Norton, 1978), xvi. Ten of the top fourteen states in the USDA 2020 farm cash receipts rankings are in the Midwest. The Midwest overall earned 44.5 percent of all commodity income for that year, an imperfect accounting of production since this includes a wide diversity of items, such as fruit, nuts, coffee, cotton, honey, and trout. See US Department of Agriculture, Economic Research Service, "Cash Receipts by Commodity: State Ranking," accessed December 26, 2021, https://data.ers.usda.gov/reports.aspx?ID=17844. See https://www.nass.usda.gov/Statistics_by_State/index.php for production figures for each state. Also see US Department of Agriculture, Economic Research Service, "Crops," https://ers.usda.gov/topics/crops for national figures on crop production. The average midwestern state is about 80 percent white, with the exception of Illinois, whose demographics closely match those of the United States overall, see https://www.visualcapitalist.com/visualizing-u-s-population-by-race/. The nation overall is about 60 percent white, see "white alone" at United States Census, "Quick Facts," accessed February 10, 2023, https://www.census.gov/quickfacts/fact/table/US/IPE120219.

3. F. I. Herriot, "Is Iowa's History Worth While?" *Annals of Iowa* 6, no. 1 (April 1903): 70–73; Jon K. Lauck, *The Lost Region: Toward a Revival of Midwestern History* (Iowa City: University of Iowa Press, 2013), 1–2.

4. Schwieder, *Middle Land*, x–xiii; Leland L. Sage, *A History of Iowa* (Ames: Iowa State University Press, 1974); Grant Suneson, "These States Have the Highest—and Lowest—Percentage of Married People in the US," *USA Today*, March 7, 2019, https://www.usatoday.com/story/money/2019/03/07/marriage-us-states-highest-percent age-married-people/39043233/; "Voter Turnout Data," US Elections Project, accessed February 23, 2023, www.electproject.org/election-data/voter-turnout-data; Emma Kerr, "See High School Graduation Rates by State," *U.S. News & World Report*, April 28, 2021, https://www.usnews.com/education/best-high-schools/articles/see-high-school-graduation-rates-by-state; "Trends in High School Dropout and Completion Rates

in the United States," National Center for Education Statistics, accessed December 23, 2021, https://nces.ed.gov/programs/dropout/ind_04.asp; Kyle Munson, "Black-White Disparities Persist in Iowa," *Des Moines Register*, July 12, 2015, https://www.desmoinesregister.com/story/news/local/kyle-munson/2015/07/12/black-iowa-statistics-economics-incarceration/30059517/; Erika Frey, "Hawkeye Elegy: A collision of pandemic, disaster, and polarization in the heartland," *Fortune*, February/March 2021, https://fortune.com/longform/iowa-covid-derecho-thunderstorm-2020-election-trump-biden; Patricia Cohen, "Southerners, Facing Big Odds, Believe in a Path Out of Poverty," *New York Times*, July 4, 2019, https://www.nytimes.com/2019/07/04/business/economy/social-mobility-south.html. Economic mobility is defined as the ability to move from being a child in a family in the bottom fifth of pretax household income to be an adult in the top fifth. In Iowa, 12.3 percent of children were able to do this, ranked only behind Wyoming and North Dakota for states other than Alaska or Hawaii. Iowa's rate was almost double that of Missouri, for example. Most midwestern states ranked better than those in the Southeast. Even during the 1980s Farm Crisis, Iowa farm families raised successful children. Civic institutions, such as churches and schools, as well as engaged parents, allowed kids to achieve academic success, avoid problem behaviors, and become socially mature. See Glen H. Elder Jr. and Rand D. Conger, *Children of the Land: Adversity and Success in Rural America* (Chicago: University of Chicago Press, 2000), 8, 14–26, 244–249.

5. Jon K. Lauck, "Soft, Democratic, and Universalist: In Search of the Main Currents of Traditional Midwestern Identity and a Grand Historiographic Synthesis," *Middle West Review* 6, nos. 1–2 (Fall–Spring 2019–2020): 66–70, 75–77, 85; Paula M. Nelson, "Civic Life in a Midwestern Community," in *Finding a New Midwestern History*, ed. Jon K. Lauck, Gleaves Whitney, and Joseph Hogan (Lincoln: University of Nebraska Press, 2018), 97–99, 107–108. For more on this topic see Jon K. Lauck, *The Good Country: A History of the American Midwest, 1800–1900* (Norman: University of Oklahoma Press, 2022). Iowa's K-12 school system was close to average, when judged on nationwide reading and math scores in 2022. The 2022 "Nation's Report Card" showed that the reading scores for Iowa's eighth graders were below the national average, about the same as those of Kentucky. Reading scores for Iowa's fourth graders were about the national average, close to those of states such as Illinois. Iowa's students scored above the national average for math for both grades. The state did not rank in the top ten in any of these four categories. See Sarah Mervosh and Ashley Wu, "Math Scores Fell in Nearly Every State, and Reading Dipped on National Exam," *New York Times*, October 24, 2022, https://www.nytimes.com/2022/10/24/us/math-reading-scores.pandemic.html. Reading scores for these two grades have generally declined in Iowa in the twenty-first century. See https://www.nationsreportcard.gov/.

6. Bruce A. Rubenstein and Lawrence E. Ziewacz, *Michigan; A History of the Great Lakes State* (Chichester, West Sussex: John Wiley and Sons, 2014), vii–viii; James H. Madison, *Hoosiers: A New History of Indiana* (Bloomington: Indiana University Press, 2014), x–xi. Both state histories are excellent and quite accessible to general readers. Another outstanding state history is Craig Miner, *Kansas: A History of the*

Sunflower State, 1854–2000 (Lawrence: University Press of Kansas, 2002). The author's title is inspired by Madison's book, while the focus on primary sources is an idea borrowed from Miner.

7. Schwieder, *Middle Land*, xii; Phillip Sitter, "Last School Year Brought More Diversity among Fewer K-12 Students in Iowa, New Report Finds," *Des Moines Register*, December 3, 2021, https://www.desmoinesregister.com/story/news/education/2021/12/03/iowa-schools-annual-condition-education-fewer-students-more-diversity-2020-2021-report-finds/8852348002/; Mackenzie Ryan, "Where Does Iowa Stand When It Comes to Education Spending?" *Des Moines Register*, November 3, 2018, https://www.desmoinesregister.com/story/news/education/2018/11/03/iowa-public-school-funding-spending-state-legislature-education-costs-dollars-teacher-pay-salaries/1338535002/; and "Quick Facts: Iowa." Economic inequality in Iowa is often tied to geography, as well as race and class. See chapters 13 to 15.

8. Jill Lepore, *These Truths: A History of the United States* (New York: W. W. Norton, 2018), xix.

CHAPTER 1: NATIVE IOWA: IOWA TO 1833

1. Wayne I. Anderson, *Iowa's Geological Past: Three Billion Years of Change* (Iowa City: University of Iowa Press, 1998), 305, 350–352; Cornelia F. Mutel, *The Emerald Horizon: The History of Nature in Iowa* (Iowa City: University of Iowa Press, 2008), 3–5; William Cronon, *Nature's Metropolis: Chicago and the Great West* (New York: W. W. Norton, 1991), 24–25.

2. Mutel, *Emerald Horizon*, 4–5, 41–43, 64–65; Anderson, *Iowa's Geological Past*, 322–328, 333, 338, 344, 350; Leland L. Sage, *A History of Iowa* (Ames: Iowa State University Press, 1974), 8; Candace Savage, *Prairie: A Natural History* (Vancouver: Greystone Books, 2004), 74–75. Iowa and the Midwest are famous for tornadoes. See John L. Stanford, *Tornado: Accounts of Tornadoes in Iowa* (Ames: Iowa State University Press, 1987). For more on the Loess Hills see Cornelia F. Mutel, *Fragile Giants: A Natural History of the Loess Hills* (Iowa City: University of Iowa Press, 1989).

3. Janette R. Thompson, *Prairies, Forests and Wetlands: The Restoration of Natural Landscape Communities in Iowa* (Iowa City: University of Iowa Press, 1992), 3–4, 10; Savage, *Prairie*, 4, 23, 58, 63–68; Mutel, *Emerald Horizon*, 42–45; T. H. McBride, "The Landscapes of Early Iowa," *Iowa Historical Record* 11, no. 4 (October, 1895): 341–349; Kathleen Woida, *Iowa's Remarkable Soils: The Story of Our Most Vital Resource and How We Can Save It* (Iowa City: University of Iowa Press, 2021), 3–5, 30.

4. James J. Dinsmore, *A Country So Full of Game: The Story of Wildlife in Iowa* (Iowa City: University of Iowa Press, 1994), 1–16, 25, 46, 51, 91, 151–152.

5. "Neil Smith National Wildlife Refuge," US Fish & Wildlife Service, accessed July 14, 2020, https://www.fws.gov/refuge/Neal_Smith; Dinsmore, *So Full of Game*, 2–4, 7, 24–25, 34, 39–40, 50–51, 55–57, 62, 78, 82–83, 86, 91, 99, 117–119, 179–183.

6. Lynn M. Alex, *Iowa's Archaeological Past* (Iowa City: University of Iowa Press, 2000), 37–43, 54–61, 73, 87.

7. Alex, *Iowa's Archaeological Past*, 85, 100, 106–108, 124–125; David Mayer Gradwohl, "The Native American Experience in Iowa: An Archaeological Perspective," in *The World between Two Rivers: Perspectives on American Indians in Iowa*, ed. Gretchen M. Bataille, David Mayer Gradwohl, and Charles L. P. Silet (Iowa City: University of Iowa Press, 2000), 45–48.

8. Colin G. Calloway, *One Vast Winter Count: The Native American West before Lewis and Clark* (Lincoln: University of Nebraska Press, 2003), 70–72; Alex, *Iowa's Archaeological Past*, 85, 130.

9. Alex, *Iowa's Archaeological Past*, 85, 100, 106–110, 116, 130, 136; Gradwohl, "Native American Experience in Iowa," 47–54; Lance Foster, *The Indians of Iowa* (Iowa City: University of Iowa Press, 2009), 6–7; Mark Wyman, *The Wisconsin Frontier* (Bloomington: Indiana University Press, 1998), 31–32; Greg Olson, *Ioway Life: Reservation and Reform, 1836–1860* (Norman: University of Oklahoma Press, 2016), 3.

10. Martha Royce Blaine, *The Ioway Indians* (Norman: University of Oklahoma Press, 1979), 50; Colin G. Calloway, *New Worlds for All: Indians, Europeans, and the Remaking of Early America* (Baltimore: Johns Hopkins University Press, 1998), 6–7, 14–17, 21–23, 37–38; Richard White, *The Middle Ground: Indians, Empires, and Republics in the Great Lakes Region, 1650–1815* (Cambridge, UK: Cambridge University Press), 1–14, 131–132.

11. Benjamin F. Gue, *History of Iowa from the Earliest Times to the Beginning of the Twentieth Century*, vol. 1 (New York: Century History, 1903), 29–38; Jacob Van Der Zee, "French Discovery and Exploration of the Eastern Iowa Country before 1763," *Iowa Journal of History and Politics* 12, no. 3 (July 1914): 330–334.

12. Sage, *A History of Iowa*, 33–34; William J. Petersen, *The Story of Iowa: The Progress of an American State*, volume 1 (New York: Lewis Publishing, 1952), 195–196; William Salter, "Nicholas Perrot, the First Commercial Traveler on the Upper Mississippi," *Annals of Iowa* 4, no. 8 (1901): 610–613; Blaine, *Ioway Indians*, 17–21.

13. Blaine, *Ioway Indians*, 7–8, 16–17, 136; Greg Olson, *The Ioway in Missouri* (Columbia: University of Missouri Press, 2008), 6–8; Saul Schwartz and William Green, "Middle Ground or Native Ground? Material Culture at Iowaville" *Ethnohistory* 60, no. 4 (Fall 2013): 537; David Bernstein, "'We Are Not Now as We Once Were:' Iowa Indians' Political and Economic Adaptations during U.S. Incorporation," *Ethnohistory* 54, no. 4 (Fall 2007): 608–609; Richard White, "The Winning of the West: The Expansion of the Western Sioux in the Eighteenth and Nineteenth Centuries," *Journal of American History* 65, no. 2 (September 1978): 321–323; Olson, *Ioway Life*, 6; Pekka Hämäläinen, *Lakota America: A New History of Indigenous Power* (New Haven: Yale University Press, 2019), ix.

14. Olson, *Ioway in Missouri*, 9–11.

15. Foster, *Indians of Iowa*, 7–8; Olson, *Ioway in Missouri*, 11–14, 21; Blaine, *Ioway Indians*, 8–11.

16. Blaine, *Ioway Indians*, 37, 49, 60; Schwartz and Green, "Middle Ground or Native Ground?," 537–538, 547–549, 557–558; Bernstein, "'We Are Not Now," 610; Olson, *Ioway Life*, 7. The first quote is from Bernstein.

17. Schwartz and Green, "Middle Ground or Native Ground?," 547–559; Jacob Van Der Zee, "Fur Trade in the Iowa Country," *Iowa Journal of History and Politics* 12, no. 4 (October 1914): 487, 500–501, 505–506, 515.

18. Christina E. Pearce and William Green, "Plant Remains from Iowaville," *Journal of the Iowa Archeological Society* 61 (2014): 47–52.

19. Olson, *Ioway in Missouri*, 30; Bernstein, "'We Are Not Now,'" 610–612.

20. Bernstein, "'We Are Not Now,'" 606–608, 620, 624–626; Lance Foster, "A Closing Circle: Musings on the Ioway Indians in Iowa," in Battaile, Gradwohl, and Silet, *World between Two Rivers*, 145; Jeffrey Ostler, *Surviving Genocide: Native Nations and the United States from the American Revolution to Bleeding Kansas* (New Haven: Yale University Press, 2019), 235–237; Greg Olson, "Mahaska (White Cloud)," in *The Biographical Dictionary of Iowa*, ed. David Hudson, Marvin Bergman, and Loren Horton (Iowa City: University of Iowa Press, 2008), 334–335. The quote from White Cloud is from Bernstein.

21. Calloway, *One Vast Winter Count*, 322–324; Ostler, *Surviving Genocide*, 26–28; Foster, *Indians of Iowa*, 13. The Sauk and Meskwaki received more attention in Dorothy Schwieder's history of the state, for example. See chapters 1 and 2 in Dorothy Schwieder, *Iowa: The Middle Land* (Ames: Iowa State University Press, 1996).

22. John Ely Briggs, "The Sacs and Foxes," *Palimpsest* 50, no. 4 (April 1969): 222; Foster, *Indians of Iowa*, 13, 21; Alex, *Iowa's Archaeological Past*, 224; Anthony F. C. Wallace, "Prelude to Disaster: The Course of Indian-White Relations Which Led to the Black Hawk War of 1832," *Wisconsin Magazine of History* 65, no. 4 (Summer 1982): 255.

23. Wallace, "Prelude to Disaster," 256; Lucy Eldersveld Murphy, *A Gathering of Rivers: Indians, Metis, and Mining in the Western Great Lakes, 1737–1832* (Lincoln: University of Nebraska Press, 2000), 6–7, 41–42; Henry Schoolcraft, *Narrative Journal of Travels through the Northwestern Regions of the United States: Extending from Detroit through the Great Chain of American Lakes to the Sources of the Mississippi, Performed as a Member of the Expedition under Governor Cass in the Year 1820* (Albany: E. & E. Hosford, 1821), 317–318.

24. William T. Hagan, *The Sac and Fox Indians* (Norman: University of Oklahoma Press, 1958), 5–6, 12; Kerry A. Trask, *Black Hawk: The Battle for the Heart of America* (New York: Henry Holt and Company, 2006), 28–36; Jacob Van Der Zee, "Fur Trade Operations in the Eastern Iowa Country under the Spanish Regime," *Iowa Journal of History and Politics* 12, no. 3 (July 1914): 358–359. Quote is from Trask.

25. Kerry Trask, *Black Hawk*, 32–35; Hagan, *Sac and Fox Indians*, 6–8, 92; Thomas Forsyth, "Memoirs of the Sauk and Foxes: An Account of the Manners and Customs of the Sauk and Fox Nations of Indian Tradition," in *The Indian Tribes of the Upper Mississippi Valley and Region of the Great Lakes*, vol. 2, ed. Emma Helen Blair (Cleveland: Arthur H. Clark Company, 1911), 227. The Forsyth quote is from Trask.

26. Hagan, *Sac and Fox Indians*, 5–7; Foster, *Indians of Iowa*, 13–15, 19; Michael D. Green, "'We Dance in Opposite Directions:' Mesquakie (Fox) Separatism from the Sac and Fox Tribe," in *The Iowa History Reader*, ed. Marvin Bergman (Ames: Iowa

State University, 1996), 17–21; Forsyth, "Memoirs of the Sauk and Foxes," 233–234; Trask, *Black Hawk*, 40; Alex, *Iowa's Archaeological Past*, 226, 231.

27. Gue, *History of Iowa*, vol. 1, 109–110; Jacob Van Der Zee, "Early History of Lead Mining in the Iowa Country," *Iowa Journal of History and Politics* 13, no. 1 (January 1915): 8–10; Petersen, *Story of Iowa*, vol. 1, 200, 205–207; William Petersen, "Julien Dubuque," *Palimpsest* 47, no. 3 (March 1966): 107, 119; Murphy, *Gathering of Rivers*, 5; Michael D. Gibson, "Julien Dubuque," in *Biographical Dictionary of Iowa*, 139–140.

28. Petersen, *Story of Iowa*, vol. 1, 206–211; Sage, *History of Iowa*, 34–35; Gibson, "Julien Dubuque," 140.

29. Schoolcraft, *Narrative Journal of Travels*, 340–346.

30. Murphy, *Gathering of Rivers*, 79–80.

31. Kathryn E. M. Gourley, "Cementing American Control, 1816–1853," in *Frontier Forts of Iowa: Indians, Traders, and Soldiers, 1682–1862*, ed. William E. Whittaker (Iowa City: University of Iowa Press, 2009), 37–38; Foster, *Indians of Iowa*, 31–32, 40–41, 47–48, 61–62; "The Indians of Iowa in 1842," *Iowa Journal of History and Politics* 13, no. 2 (April 1915): 250–252.

32. Jeffrey Ostler, *The Plains Sioux and U.S. Colonialism from Lewis and Clark to Wounded Knee* (Cambridge, UK: Cambridge University Press, 2004), 21–22; Hämäläinen, *Lakota America*, 84; Kevin T. Mason, "Inkpaduta in Iowa: Dakota Decline, Dispossession, and Erasure," *Annals of Iowa* 80, no. 2 (Spring 2021): 128, 133–139.

33. Sage, *History of Iowa*, 35–40.

34. Hagan, *Sac and Fox Indians*, 14–25; Alvin M. Josephy Jr., *500 Nations: An Illustrated History of North American Indians* (New York: Alfred A. Knopf, 1994), 307; Ostler, *Surviving Genocide*, 220–221; James E. Davis, *Frontier Illinois* (Bloomington: Indiana University Press, 1998), 119; Gerald Kennedy, ed., *Life of Black Hawk, or Ma-ka-tai-me-she-kia-kiak: Dictated by Himself* (1833; reprint, New York: Penguin, 2008), 19; Wallace, "Prelude to Disaster," 261–263. Italics are original to the autobiography. Other treaties between the Sauk and Meskwaki and the United States followed, including the peace treaties after the War of 1812 and an 1825 settlement negotiated at Prairie du Chien. See Wallace, "Prelude to Disaster," 264, for a concise summary.

35. Gary E. Moulton, ed., *The Journals of the Lewis and Clark Expedition*, vol. 2 (Lincoln: University of Nebraska Press, 1986), 424–441, 471–474, 486; Stephen Ambrose, *Undaunted Courage: Meriwether Lewis, Thomas Jefferson, and the Opening of the American West* (New York: Simon and Schuster, 1997), 150–161.

36. Jared Orsi, *Citizen Explorer: The Life of Zebulon Pike* (Oxford: Oxford University Press, 2014), 7, 12, 81–83, 94–95; Sage, *History of Iowa*, 37–38.

37. Orsi, *Citizen Explorer*, 94–105, 116–120, 122–123; Elliott Coues, ed., *The Expeditions of Zebulon Montgomery Pike*, vol. 1 (New York: Francis P. Harper, 1895), 5, 10–16, 25–26, 42; Hagan, *Sac and Fox Indians*, 27–28; Sage, *History of Iowa*, 38.

38. Marshall B. McKusick, "Fort Madison, 1808–1813," in *Frontier Forts of Iowa*,

55–58; Schwieder, *Middle Land*, 13; "Fort Madison," *Annals of Iowa* 3, no. 2 (1897): 100–110. There were usually forty to eighty soldiers at the fort.

39. Jacob Van Der Zee, "Forts in the Iowa Country," *Iowa Journal of History and Politics* 12, no. 2 (April 1914): 174–178; McKusick, "Fort Madison," 58–59; Kennedy, *Life of Black Hawk*, 19–20.

40. McKusick, "Fort Madison," 59–63; Sage, *History of Iowa*, 42; "Fort Madison," *Annals of Iowa*, 105; Kennedy, *Life of Black Hawk*, 21–23; Patrick J. Jung, "Lonely Sentinel: A Military History of Fort Madison, 1808–1813," *Annals of Iowa* 75, no. 3 (Summer 2016): 230–232. Italics in the original autobiography.

41. William E. Whittaker, "Forts around Iowa," in *Frontier Forts of Iowa*, 1, 6–8; Ostler, *Surviving Genocide*, 156–160.

42. Ostler, *Surviving Genocide*, 232–234.

43. Ostler, *Surviving Genocide*, 2–5, 11–28; John P. Bowes, *Land Too Good for Indians: Northern Indian Removal* (Norman: University of Oklahoma Press, 2016), 4, 11–13.

44. J. W. Spencer, *Reminiscences of Pioneer Life in the Mississippi Valley* (Davenport, IA: Griggs, Watson & Day, 1872), 7, 11–12, 19–21, 32–34; John Carl Parish, "The Langworthys of Early Dubuque and Their Contributions to Local History," *Iowa Journal of History and Politics* 8, no. 3 (July 1910): 317–319; "Autobiographical Sketch of Lucius H. Langworthy," *Iowa Journal of History and Politics* 8, no. 3 (July 1910): 321; "Sketch of Edward Langworthy," *Iowa Journal of History and Politics* 8, no. 3 (July 1910): 341–342; Murphy, *Gathering of Rivers*, 162; Hagan, *Sac and Fox Indians*, 111–112; Davis, *Frontier Illinois*, 205–206; Trask, *Black Hawk*, 70–71. Spencer writes of an attack on the Sioux at Turkey River near Dubuque: see *Reminiscences of Pioneer Life*, 28. It is unlikely that the western Sioux would have been this far east, so the attack was probably by the Dakota.

45. Hagan, *Sac and Fox Indians*, 122–124; Ostler, *Surviving Genocide*, 298–299; Trask, *Black Hawk*, 74–77; Wallace, "Prelude to Disaster," 268–270.

46. Trask, *Black Hawk*, 77–79, 92, 102–105; Wallace, "Prelude to Disaster," 271–272; Ostler, *Surviving Genocide*, 299–301.

47. Davis, *Frontier Illinois*, 193–194.

48. Wallace, "Prelude to Disaster," 277–282; Ostler, *Surviving Genocide*, 301–302; Hagan, *Sac and Fox Indians*, 138–145.

49. Patrick J. Jung, *The Black Hawk War of 1832* (Norman: University of Oklahoma Press, 2007), 75–88; Davis, *Frontier Illinois*, 194–195; Frank Everett Stevens, ed., *Wakefield's History of the Black Hawk War* (1834; repr., Chicago: Caxton Club, 1908), 11, 131.

50. Jung, *Black Hawk War*, 88–90. Quote is Jung, 90. Italics are from Black Hawk.

51. Roger L. Nichols, *Black Hawk and the Warrior's Path* (Chichester: John Wiley & Sons, 2017), 134–138.

52. Nichols, *Black Hawk*, 138–142; Jung, *Black Hawk War*, 145–158, 209.

53. Nichols, *Black Hawk*, 142–145; Cecil Eby, *"That Disgraceful Affair:" The Black Hawk War* (New York: W. W. Norton, 1973), 247–261; Jung, *Black Hawk War*, 172.

54. Nichols, *Black Hawk*, 152–164; Joseph Frazier Wall, *Iowa: A History* (New

York: W. W. Norton, 1978), 12–13; Schwieder, *Middle Land*, 15–16, 19–20; Trask, *Black Hawk*, 304–305; F. R. Aumann, "Dispossession of the Tribes," *Palimpsest* 38, no. 2 (February 1957): 60–62. American army officers who had led troops in the Black Hawk war, such as Winfield Scott and Zachary Taylor, were transferred to Georgia and Florida to lead campaigns against other Indian tribes. Scott commanded a brutal war against the Seminole in Florida in the mid-1830s. He led troops against the Creek too. Taylor also led soldiers in the long, bloody war against the Seminole. See Claudio Saunt, *Unworthy Republic: The Dispossession of Native Americans and the Road to Indian Territory* (New York: W. W. Norton, 2020), 145–148, 241–251, 270–278, 297–301. Events at Spirit Lake are discussed in chapter 4.

CHAPTER 2: IOWA TERRITORY, 1833–1846

1. Ruth A. Gallaher, "Pioneers in Person," *Palimpsest* 14, no. 2 (February 1933): 87–88; Mel Prewitt, "George Davenport," in *The Biographical Dictionary of Iowa*, ed. David Hudson, Marvin Bergman, and Loren Horton (Iowa City: University of Iowa Press, 2008), 118–119; Loren N. Horton, "River Town: Davenport's Early Years," *Palimpsest* 60, no. 1 (January 1979): 23–24; Benjamin F. Gue, *History of Iowa from the Earliest Times to the Beginning of the Twentieth Century*, vol. 1 (New York: Century History, 1902), 331–350; State Data Center, "Iowa's Incorporated Places, 1850–1910," accessed January 28, 2022, https://www.iowadatacenter.org. The March 1934 issue of the *Palimpsest* is dedicated to Iowa's territorial period.

2. Gue, *History of Iowa*, vol. 1, 157; Cyrenus Cole, *Iowa through the Years* (Iowa City: State Historical Society of Iowa, 1940), 105; William J. Petersen, "Some Beginnings in Iowa," *Iowa Journal of History and Politics* 28, no. 1 (January 1930): 18–21; J. A. Swisher, "The Half-Breed Tract," *Palimpsest* 14, no. 2 (February 1933): 69–74; Jacob Van Der Zee, "The Half-Breed Tract," *Iowa Journal of History and Politics* 13, no. 2 (April 1915): 151–158, 162–163. B. L. Wick, "The Struggle for the Half-Breed Tract," *Annals of Iowa* 7, no. 1 (1905):16–29, is a good summary of the area's complex legal story and land fraud.

3. George C. Duffield, "Coming into Iowa in 1837," *Annals of Iowa* 6, no. 1 (1903): 1, 5–8; Duffield, "An Iowa Settler's Homestead," *Annals of Iowa* 6, no. 3 (1903): 211; "Kitturah Penton Belknap," in *Prairie Voices: Iowa's Pioneering Women*, ed. Glenda Riley (Ames: Iowa State University Press, 1996), 5–8; Claude W. Dutton, "Experiences of Francis Parker," *Annals of Iowa* 29, no. 2 (October 1947): 108, 125–128; Leland L. Sage, *A History of Iowa* (Ames: Iowa State University Press, 1974), 310.

4. Charles Augustus Murray, *Travels in North America during the Years 1834, 1835 and 1836. Including a Summer of Residence with the Pawnee Tribe of Indians, in the Remote Prairies of the Missouri, and a Visit to Cuba and the Azore Islands*, vol. 2 (London: Richard Bentley, 1841), 96–109, 151–157; William J. Petersen, "The El Dorado of Iowa," *Palimpsest* 21, no. 11 (November 1940): 348–352; William J. Petersen, "Crossroads of Empire," *Palimpsest* 32, no. 10 (October 1951): 377–379; "Iowa's Incorporated Places, 1850–1910."

5. William J. Petersen, "The Times in Review," *Palimpsest* 17, no. 3 (March 1936): 103–104; A. T. Andreas, *An Illustrated Historical Atlas of Louisa County, 1874* (Chicago: A. T. Andreas, 1874), 11–12; Lucius H. Longworthy, "Dubuque: Its History, Mines, Indian Legends, etc.," *Iowa Journal of History and Politics* 8, no. 3 (July 1910): 386–389; J. P. Walton, "Pioneer Life in Muscatine County," *Iowa Historical Record* 9, no. 1 (January 1893): 430. Sources differ on which Massey brother killed John Smith.

6. Gue, *History of Iowa*, vol. 1, 161–165; Kathryn M. Gourley, "Fort Des Moines no. 1, 1834–1837," in *Frontier Forts of Iowa: Indians, Traders, and Soldiers, 1682–1862*, ed. William E. Whittaker (Iowa City: University of Iowa Press, 2009), 135–144; Jacob Van Der Zee, "The Opening of the Des Moines Valley to Settlement," *Iowa Journal of History and Politics* 14, no. 4 (October 1916): 487–489, 519; William J. Petersen, "Iowa in 1835," *Palimpsest* 16, no. 3 (March 1935): 88; "Dragoon Soldier-Historical Background," National Park Service, accessed January 28, 2022, https://nps.gov/fosc/learn/education/dragoon5.htm.

7. Albert M. Lea, *Notes on Wisconsin Territory, with a Map* (Philadelphia: Henry S. Tanner, 1836), 7–14, 18; William J. Petersen, *The Story of Iowa: The Progress of an American State*, vol. 1 (New York: Lewis Historical, 1952), 273.

8. Petersen, "Some Beginnings in Iowa," 21–23; Sage, *History of Iowa*, 52–53; Joseph Frazier Wall, *Iowa: A History* (New York: W. W. Norton, 1978), 22–23. Sage and Wall disagree on the spelling of De Moine County, with Wall adding an *s* to De Moine. Quote is from Wall.

9. James E. Davis, *Frontier Illinois* (Bloomington: Indiana University Press, 1998), 94–95; Gue, *History of Iowa*, vol. 1, 173–176, 184–187; Todd E. Pettys, *The Iowa Constitution* (New York: Oxford University Press, 2018), 5–7; Wall, *Iowa*, 25.

10. William J. Petersen, "Robert Lucas," *Palimpsest* 44, no. 6 (June 1963): 241–252; Sage, *A History of Iowa*, 61–62; T. S. Parvin, "As Robert Lucas Became Iowa's Territorial Governor," *Annals of Iowa* 34, no. 2 (October 1957): 119; Richard Acton and Patricia Nassif Acton, "A Legal History of African-Americans from the Iowa Territory to the State Sesquicentennial, 1838–1996," in *Outside In: African-American History in Iowa, 1838–2000*, ed. Bill Silag, Susan Koch-Bridgford, and Hal Chase (Iowa City: State Historical Society of Iowa, 2001), 61–62; Robert R. Dykstra, *Bright Radical Star: Black Freedom and White Supremacy on the Hawkeye Frontier* (Ames: Iowa State University Press, 1993), 23; J. A. Swisher, "The First Territorial Assembly," *Palimpsest* 20, no. 2 (February 1939): 34–36; *The Statue Laws of the Territory of Iowa* (Dubuque: Russell and Reeves, 1839), 1–2. Quote by Parvin on drunkenness is from Petersen's article on Robert Lucas. The quote from Governor Lucas is from Parvin's article.

11. Louis Pelzer, "Iowa City: A Miniature Frontier of the Forties," *Iowa Journal of History and Politics* 29, no. 1 (January 1931): 3–5, 9–12, 19–23; Charles Negus, "The Early History of Iowa," *Annals of Iowa* 8, no. 2 (April 1870): 105–106; Petersen, *Story of Iowa*, vol. 1, 319–321; Benjamin F. Shambaugh, "This Town," *Palimpsest* 20, no. 5 (May 1939): 137–138; Emory H. English, "As Iowa Approached Statehood," *Annals of Iowa* 27, no. 3 (January 1946): 209.

12. Roscoe L. Lokken, *Iowa Public Land Disposal* (Iowa City: State Historical Society of Iowa, 1942), 22–23, 37–38, 46–48, 54–63; Ira Cook, "Government Surveying in Early Iowa," *Annals of Iowa* 2, no. 8 (January 1897): 603, 605–606, 610; Williard Barrows, "Willard Barrows' Defense," *Annals of Iowa* 18, no. 7 (January 1933): 544–546; Samuel W. Durham, "Another Chapter of Pioneer History," *Annals of Iowa* 3, no. 5 (Spring/Summer 1898): 439–444; "Original Field Notes of William Austin Burt of the Survey of the Fifth Principal Meridian (Now in) Iowa, November, 1836," *Annals of Iowa* 20, no. 2 (Fall 1935): 86. Burt's records seem to have been precise. See the whole article, pp. 83–122, for examples of surveying notes. See the Measuring Worth website at https://measuringworth.com/calculators/uscompare, to determine the real price (relative prices) of goods over time. Comparison dates here are 1840 and 2020.

13. Carroll J. Kraus, "A Study in Border Confrontation: The Iowa-Missouri Boundary Dispute," *Annals of Iowa* 40, no. 2 (Fall 1969): 81–83, 88–93, 95, 99, 101, 104–107; Wall, *Iowa*, 30–35; Mildred Throne, ed., "The Memories of Aristarchus Cone," *Iowa Journal of History* 49, no. 1 (January 1951): 69.

14. V. P. Van Antwerp, "Source Material of Iowa History: Reminiscences of Early Iowa," *Iowa Journal of History* 52, no. 4 (October 1954): 348–349; Duffield, "Iowa Settler's Homestead," 212; Suel Foster, "History of Muscatine," *Annals of Iowa* 10, no. 2 (April 1872): 98; Irving B. Richman, *Ioway to Iowa: The Genesis of a Corn and Bible Commonwealth* (Iowa City: Iowa State Historical Society, 1931), 166; Richard A. Bartlett, *The New Country: A Social History of the American Frontier, 1776–1890* (New York: Oxford University Press, 1974), 60; G. D. R. Boyd, "Sketches of History and Incidents Connected with the Settlement of Wapello County, from 1843 to 1859, Inclusive," *Annals of Iowa* 6, no. 2 (April 1868): 127.

15. Allan G. Bogue, *From Prairie to Corn Belt: Farming on the Illinois and Iowa Prairies in the Nineteenth Century* (Chicago: University of Chicago Press, 1963), 29–35; Hawkins Taylor, "Squatters and Speculators at the First Land Sales," *Annals of Iowa* 8, no. 3 (July 1870): 271; Earle D. Ross, *Iowa Agriculture: An Historical Survey* (Iowa City: State Historical Society of Iowa, 1951), 15–18; Benjamin F. Shambaugh, ed., *Constitution and Records of the Claim Association of Johnson County, Iowa, with Introduction and Notes* (Iowa City: State Historical Society of Iowa, 1894), 12–16, 44, 75, 82–83. Records of the Johnson County group include minutes from meetings from 1840–1843 and descriptions of the land claims. The names of three women are included: Olivia Currier, Rebecca Tyler, and Sarah Ann Abel.

16. John W. Wright and William A. Young, eds., *History of Marion County, Iowa, and Its People*, vol. 1 (Chicago: S. J. Clarke, 1915), 331–334; William Donnel, "Pioneers of Marion County: Chapter VI. Claim Law, And Club Laws," *Annals of Iowa* 8, no. 2 (April 1870): 121–128; J. D. Haworth, "Early Recollections of Keokuk County," *Annals of Iowa* 2, no. 1 (April 1895): 62–64.

17. Taylor, "Squatters and Speculators," 271–274; Malcolm J. Rohrbough, *The Land Office Business: The Settlement and Administration of American Public Land, 1789–1837* (New York: Oxford University Press, 1968), 75–77; Duffield, "An Iowa Settler's Homestead," 213–214; "The Diary of Kitturah Penton Belknap," in Riley, *Prairie Voices*, 8–10; Dutton, "Experiences of Francis Parker," 127–128; Charles A.

White, "The Early Homes and Home-Makers of Iowa," *Annals of Iowa* 4, no. 3 (1899): 189–190; Lokken, *Public Land*, 102. The Duffield family's property was northwest of the town of Keosauqua, on the west side of the Des Moines River; see Duffield, "Coming into Iowa," 5–6.

18. Van Antwerp, "Source Material of Iowa History," 349.

19. William T. Hagan, *The Sac and Fox Indians* (Norman: University of Oklahoma Press, 1958), 206–211; Sage, *History of Iowa*, 70–71; Dorothy Schwieder, *Iowa: The Middle Land* (Ames: Iowa State University Press, 1996), 16–17; Royce Kurtz, "Timber and Treaties: The Sauk and Mesquakie Decision to Sell Iowa Territory," *Forest and Conservation History* 35, no. 2 (April 1991): 57–59, 61–63.

20. Van Der Zee, "Des Moines Valley to Settlement," 512–516; Sage, *History of Iowa*, 70–72; "Sac and Fox Indian Council of 1841," *Annals of Iowa* 12, no. 5 (July 1920): 328–329; Hagan, *Sac and Fox Indians*, 221–224; Leo Landis and Jonathan L. Buffalo, "Iowa History Month: The Meskwaki Remain Dedicated to Land and Culture," March 21, 2021, *Des Moines Register*, https://www.desmoinesregister.com/story/life/2021/03/21/iowa-history-month-meskwaki-remain/4742238001/. Poweshiek quote is from Landis and Buffalo; Wapello quote is from "Sac and Fox Indian Council of 1841."

21. Van Der Zee, "Des Moines Valley to Settlement," 510–511, 518, 521–522, 525–526; Sage, *History of Iowa*, 310; Lokken, *Public Land*, 31–32; Cardinal Goodwin, "The American Occupation of Iowa, 1833 to 1860," *Iowa Journal of History and Politics* 17, no. 1 (January 1919): 91–92, 101; Erling A. Erickson, *Banking in Frontier Iowa* (Ames: Iowa State University Press, 1971), 36–37.

22. Vesta O. Robbins, *No Coward Soul* (Ames: Iowa State University Press, 1974), 3–11, 15, 22–33, 36–46, 60, 63–66, 83–86, 105, 114. Vesta Robbins was the granddaughter of Susan Wyatt.

23. Benjamin F. Shambaugh, *The Constitutions of Iowa* (Iowa City: State Historical Society of Iowa, 1934), 110–113; "Steps to Statehood," *Annals of Iowa* 27, no. 3 (January 1946): 217; English, "As Iowa Approached Statehood," 209–211; Alan Taylor, *American Republics: A Continental History of the United States, 1783–1850* (New York: W. W. Norton, 2021), 180–183.

24. "Steps to Statehood," 218; Shambaugh, *Constitutions of Iowa*, 123–126, 129, 144–149, 151–157; Pettys, *Iowa State Constitution*, 9–11; Sage, *History of Iowa*, 80–83; Schwieder, *Middle Land*, 32–33, 39; Taylor, *American Republics*, 108, 252, 276. Sage argues that the birthplace of delegates did not determine political beliefs. One could be born in the South but leave the region because they disliked slavery. See Sage, 82–83.

25. Shambaugh, *Constitutions of Iowa*, 140–144; Acton and Nassif Acton, "Legal History of African-Americans," 61–68; Willis Goudy, "Selected Demographics: Iowa's African-American Residents," in *Outside In*, 41; Dykstra, *Bright Radical Star*, 5–6, 23–27; Pettys, *Iowa State Constitution*, 12–14.

26. Dykstra, *Bright Radical Star*, 5–8; Ruth A. Gallaher, "Comment by the Editor: Slavery in Iowa," *Palimpsest* 28, no. 5 (May 1947): 158–160.

27. Robert Dykstra, "Dr. Emerson's Sam: Black Iowans before the Civil War,"

Iowa Heritage Illustrated 85, nos. 2–3 (Summer–Fall 2004): 55; Richard Acton and Patricia Nassif Acton, *To Go Free: A Treasury of Iowa's Legal Heritage* (Ames: Iowa State University Press, 1995), 40–46. Jordan Montgomery was a colonel in the Missouri state militia commanding two hundred men during the "Honey War" boundary dispute. See Acton and Nassif Acton, 47.

28. Dykstra, "Dr. Emerson's Sam," 55–57; Acton and Nassif Acton, *To Go Free*, 47; "Early Civil Rights Cases," accessed March 9, 2023, https://www.iowacourts.gov/for-the-public/educational-resources-and-services/iowa-courts-history/civil-rights. Ralph Montgomery seems to have married by 1845, as a miner mentions his wife in a diary. He also may have had a sister in Dubuque named Tilda. See Acton and Nassif Acton, 41.

29. Dykstra, *Bright Radical Star*, 10–13.

30. Dykstra, "Dr. Emerson's Sam," 56–59, 63.

31. Shambaugh, *Constitutions of Iowa*, 159–165, 171, 177, 181–197, 201–212; "Steps to Statehood," 218–219; Erickson, *Banking in Frontier Iowa*, 46–49; English, "As Iowa Approached Statehood," 212; Pettys, *Iowa State Constitution*, 15–19.

32. Claudia Lauper Bushman and Richard Lyman Bushman, *Building the Kingdom: A History of Mormons in America* (New York: Oxford University Press, 2001), 33–43; Wallace Stegner, *The Gathering of Zion: The Story of the Mormon Trail* (New York: Bison Books, 1992), 53–56, 61, 83, 85, 89, 100; Loren N. Horton, "'The Worst That I Had Yet Witnessed': Mormon Diarists Cross Iowa in 1846," *Iowa Heritage Illustrated* 77, no. 2 (Summer 1996): 70–73; Wall, *Iowa*, 57–59; William G. Hartley, "Mormons and Early Iowa History (1838 to 1858): Eight Distinct Connections," *Annals of Iowa* 59, no. 3 (Summer 2000): 252–259. Nine Mormon wagon trains also left from Iowa City in the late 1850s.

33. Shambaugh, *Constitutions*, 210–212; Cole, *Iowa through the Years*, 187–188; Pettys, *Iowa State Constitution*, 19–21.

34. Dykstra, *Bright Radical Star*, 12, 104–105; Kenneth W. Colgrove, "The Delegates to Congress from the Territory of Iowa," *Iowa Journal of History and Politics* 7, no. 2 (April 1909): 260–261; William J. Petersen, *Story of Iowa*, vol. 1, 328, 386–388; Rick L. Woten, "Augustus Caesar Dodge," *Biographical Dictionary of Iowa*, 131–132; Vernon L. Volpe, "George Wallace Jones," *Biographical Dictionary of Iowa*, 270–272; Joanne B. Freeman, *The Field of Blood: Violence in Congress and the Road to Civil War* (New York: Picador, 2018), 132. Quote about Jones, who claimed per diem and travel costs that he had not earned, from Freeman. Benjamin F. Gue, who lived in Iowa in the 1850s, wrote in *History of Iowa*, vol. 1, there was "no doubt that Senators Dodge and Jones truly represented a majority of the people of Iowa at this time," which was around 1850. See Gue, 262.

CHAPTER 3: FRONTIER IOWA, 1833–1870

1. Jeff Bremer, *A Store Almost in Sight: The Economic Transformation of Missouri from the Louisiana Purchase to the Civil War* (Iowa City: University of Iowa Press, 2014), 159–161; James Crawford to David Crawford, August 2, 1839, Crawford

Papers and Correspondence, Iowa State Historical Society, Des Moines (SHSI-DSM); Dorothy Schwieder, *Iowa: The Middle Land* (Ames: Iowa State University Press, 1996), 42–48; Harrison L. Waterman, ed., *History of Wapello County*, vol. 1 (Chicago: S. J. Clarke, 1914), 71.

2. Jeremy Atack and Fred Bateman, *To Their Own Soil: Agriculture in the Antebellum North* (Ames: Iowa State University Press, 1987), 76–80.

3. A. C. Sutliff to brother, November 23, 1838, A. C. Sutliff Letters, State Historical Society of Iowa, Iowa City (SHSI-IAC).

4. Susan Kuecker, ed., "'In Good Iowa Style:' The Kelsey Letters, 1848 to 1882," *Palimpsest* 72, no. 3 (Fall 1991): 114–117; Sarah Welch Nossaman, "Pioneering at Bonaparte and Near Pella," *Annals of Iowa* 13, no. 6 (October 1922): 441–448. Spelling and grammar errors are from Kelsey's letters.

5. C. J. A. Ericson, "Memories of a Swedish Immigrant of 1852," *Annals of Iowa* 8, no. 1 (April 1907): 1–7, 12; Ardith K. Melloh, "New Sweden, Iowa," *Palimpsest* 59, no. 1 (January–February 1978): 2–5, 8, 12, 17–19. Ericson's story of his family's trans-Atlantic journey, arrival in New York, and migration to the Midwest is a concise and enlightening one.

6. Robert P. Swierenga, ed., "A Dutch Immigrant's View of Frontier Iowa," *Annals of Iowa* 38, no. 2 (Fall 1965): 81–82; Ronald D. Rietveld, "Hendrick Peter Scholte and the Land of Promise," *Annals of Iowa* 48, nos. 3–4 (Winter–Spring 1986): 135–137, 141, 151–152.

7. Elmer Schwieder and Dorothy Schwieder, *A Peculiar People: Iowa's Old Order Amish* (Iowa City: University of Iowa Press, 2009), 4–5, 14–20, 23–24, 37–43, 51–52, 69; "The Amish," *Goldfinch* (Spring 1975): 1–4.

8. Peter Hoehnle, *The Amana People: The History of a Religious Community* (Iowa City: Penfield Press, 2003), 7, 11, 17, 22–24, 29–30, 33, 47; Barnett Richling, "The Amana Society: A History of Change," *Palimpsest* 58, no. 2 (March/April 1977): 34–39, 42; Millard Milburn Rice, "Eighty-Nine Years of Collective Living," *Palimpsest* 52, no. 4 (April 1971): 202; Barbara Selzer Yambura with Eunice W. Bodine, *A Change and a Parting: My Story of Amana* (Ames: Iowa State University Press, 1960), 28–32. Other utopian communities in Iowa included two socialist groups where members shared resources. See George Schulz-Behrend, "Communia, Iowa, a Nineteenth-Century German-American Utopia," *Iowa Journal of History* 48, no. 1 (January 1950): 27–54; Charles Gray, "The Icarian Community," *Annals of Iowa* 6, no. 2 (1903): 107–114; Lyman Tower Sargent, "The Icarians in Iowa," *Annals of Iowa* 41, no. 4 (Spring 1972): 957–968.

9. Hoehnle, *Amana People*, 28–43; Rice, "Eighty-Nine Years," 202–203; Yambura and Bodine, *A Change and a Parting*, 28–36; Richling, "The Amana Society," 41, 47; Charles Nordhoff, *The Communistic Societies of the United States: From Personal Visit and Observation* (New York: Harper & Brothers, 1875), 31, 34, 38. See the Measuring Worth website at https://measuringworth.com. Comparison dates here are 1874 and 2020.

10. Jeff Bremer, "'Land Was the Main Basis for Business:' Merchants, Markets, and Communities in Frontier Iowa," *Annals of Iowa*, 76, no. 3 (Summer 2017): 262–263;

Roscoe L. Lokken, *Iowa Public Land Disposal* (Iowa City: State Historical Society of Iowa, 1942), 135–142. Veterans could earn land warrants from service in conflicts beyond those listed here.

11. David B. Danbom, *Born in the Country: A History of Rural America* (Baltimore: John Hopkins University Press, 1995), 70–71; Atack and Bateman, *To Their Own Soil*, 111.

12. John Scott Garnavillo to Louis M. Trombly, December 19, 1849, Merle Davis Letters, SHSI-IAC. See Measuring Worth. Comparison dates here are 1849 and 2020.

13. Mary Jane Parsons, "The Patchwork Quilt: Memoirs of the Pioneer Life of Mary Jane Parsons, 1842–1938, as told to Myrtle Parsons, 1935," 79, 82, 85, Mary Jane Parsons Papers, Iowa Women's Archives, University of Iowa Libraries, Iowa City, Iowa (IWA); Robert Christie to Brother Lyman, January 31 and May 8, 1840, Robert Christie and Mary Christie Letters, SHSI-IAC. If a collection at the IWA or SHSI has more than one box it will be noted in these footnotes.

14. Bremer, *A Store Almost in Sight*, 55–56, 78–79, 160–161; Mildred Throne, "Southern Iowa Agriculture, 1833–1890: The Progress from Subsistence to Commercial Corn-Belt Farming," *Agricultural History* 23, no. 2 (April 1949): 124–125.

15. Glenda Riley, *Frontierswomen: The Iowa Experience* (Ames: Iowa State University Press, 1981), 83–87.

16. Danbom, *Born in the Country*, 87–88; George F. Parker, *Iowa Pioneer Foundations*, vol. 2 (Iowa City: State Historical Society of Iowa, 1940), 55; Glenda Riley, *Frontierswomen*, 53, 57–58; Etta May Lacey Crowder, "Pioneer Life in Palo Alto County: The Memories of E. May Lacey Crowder," *Iowa Journal of History and Politics* 46, no. 2 (April 1948), 176; John Mack Faragher, *Sugar Creek: Life on the Illinois Prairie* (New Haven: Yale University Press, 1986), 110–118; Eleanore Cammack, ed., "From Indiana to Iowa," *Annals of Iowa* 29, no. 5 (July 1948): 400–405.

17. Glenda Riley, "'Not Gainfully Employed': Women and the Iowa Frontier," *Pacific Historical Review* 49, no. 2 (May 1980): 241–243.

18. Florence Roe Wiggins, "Life on Grandfather's Iowa Farm," *Annals of Iowa* 37, no. 7 (Spring 1965): 582; Amelia Murdock Wing, "Early Days in Clayton County," *Annals of Iowa* 27, no. 4 (April 1946): 279–280; "The Memoirs of Matilda Peitzke Paul," in *Prairie Voices: Iowa's Pioneer Women*, ed. Glenda Riley (Ames: Iowa State University Press, 1996), 163; Harriet Connor Brown, *Grandmother Brown's Hundred Years, 1827–1927* (Boston: Little, Brown, 1929), 121–123; Riley, "'Not Gainfully Employed,'" 243–245.

19. Wiggins, "Life on Grandfather's Iowa Farm," 582; Cammack, "From Indiana to Iowa," 403; Mildred Throne, ed., "Iowa Farm Letters, 1856–1865," *Iowa Journal of History* 58, no. 1 (January 1960): 38, 45; Riley, *Prairie Voices*, 166; Riley, "'Not Gainfully Employed,'" 260.

20. "The Diary of Kitturah Penton Belknap," in Riley, *Prairie Voices*, 9; "The Memoir of Mary Archer Murray," in Riley, *Prairie Voices*, 130–131; Crowder, "Pioneer Life in Palo Alto County," 184–186; Kitturah P. Belknap, "History of the Life of My Grandmother," 3–6, SHSI-IAC.

21. Throne, "Iowa Farm Letters," 82–83; Crowder, "Pioneer Life in Palo Alto County," 76; Mary Ann Ferrin, "An Autobiography and a Reminiscence," *Annals of Iowa* 37, no. 4 (Spring 1964): 254; Riley, "'Not Gainfully Employed,'" 262.

22. Roger S. Galer, "Recollections of Busy Years," *Iowa Journal of History and Politics* 42, no. 1 (January 1944): 25; George W. Clarke, "Pages from Bygone Days in and about Drakeville, Iowa," *Annals of Iowa* 14, no. 5 (July 1924): 327, 336–337; William Porter Nutting, "Starting Life in Warren County," *Iowa Journal of History and Politics* 39, no. 2 (April 1941): 193–195.

23. Paul W. Gates, *The Farmer's Age: Agriculture, 1815–1860* (New York: Holt, Rinehart and Winston, 1960), 169–170, 217–218; R. Douglas Hurt, *American Agriculture: A Brief History* (West Lafayette, IN: Purdue University Press, 2002), 111, 120; John C. Hudson, *Making the Corn Belt: A Geographical History of Middle-Western Agriculture* (Bloomington: Indiana University Press, 1994), 74, 80–83, 96, 116; Clarke, "Pages from Bygone Days," 337.

24. William J. Petersen, *The Story of Iowa: The Progress of an American State*, vol. 1 (New York: Lewis Historical, 1952), 361–362; Allan G. Bogue, "Twenty Years of an Iowa Farm Business, 1860–1880," *Annals of Iowa* 35, no. 8 (Spring 1961): 563–564.

25. Steven Mintz, *Huck's Raft: A History of American Childhood* (Cambridge, MA: Harvard University Press, 2004), 134–135, 148–150; W. E. Sanders, "Cedar Brakes and Hamilton Prairie: A Century Ago in Iowa Pioneer Life," *Annals of Iowa* 34, no. 6 (October 1958): 437, 440–441.

26. Elliott West, *Growing Up with the Country: Childhood on the Far Western Frontier* (Albuquerque: University of New Mexico Press, 1989), 73–75, 97–98; Mintz, *Huck's Raft*, 135; Florence Call Cowles, *Early Algona: The Story of Our Pioneers, 1854–1876* (Des Moines: Register and Tribune, 1920), 174; Celia Gullixson Reminiscence, chapter 5, SHSI-IAC. Gullixson's memoir has no page numbers.

27. Faragher, *Sugar Creek*, 100; George C. Duffield, "Youthtime in Frontier Iowa," *Annals of Iowa* 7, no. 5 (1906): 349–351, 356; Tom Stempel, *Storytellers to the Nation: A History of American Television Writing* (Syracuse, NY: Syracuse University Press, 1996), 80. George C. Duffield's diaries are located at the State Historical Society of Iowa in Des Moines. See the collection description, SHSI-DSM, for biographical information. Also see "Driving Cattle from Texas to Iowa, 1866," *Annals of Iowa* 14, no. 4 (Spring 1924): 243–262, for Duffield's diary.

28. J. S. Clark, *Life in the Middle West: Reminiscence of J. S. Clark* (Chicago: Advance Publishing, 1916), 34–38, 40; O. J. Felton, "Pioneer Life in Jones County," *Iowa Journal of History and Politics* 29, no. 2 (April 1931): 248; Henry W. Wright, "Iowa—As I Knew It," *Annals of Iowa* 29, no. 5 (Summer 1948): 381–383.

29. West, *Growing Up with the Country*, 76–78, 82–88; Mintz, *Huck's Raft*, 151; Cowles, *Early Algona*, 174; C. Cruikshank, "Incidents of Pioneer Times," SHSI-IAC, 10; Ellison Orr, "Reminiscences of a Pioneer Boy," *Annals of Iowa* 40, no. 7 (Winter 1971): 556–557; Abbie Mott Benedict, "My Early Days in Iowa," *Annals of Iowa* 17, no. 5 (July 1930): 332. Garland quote is from Mintz.

30. John Mack Faragher, *Women and Men on the Overland Trail* (New Haven: Yale University Press, 1979), 51–53; Jack Larkin, *The Reshaping of Everyday Life,*

1790–1840 (New York: Harper Perennial, 1989), 17–18, 27–30; Emma Knowlton, "Knowlton Reminiscences," SHSI-IAC; Margaret E. Archer Murray, "Memoir of the William Archer Family," *Annals of Iowa* 39, no. 5 (July 1968): 358, 362–364.

31. James R. Howard, "Making an Iowa Farmer," SHSI-IAC.

32. A. T. DeGroot, ed., Benjamin H. Gavitt, *Eighty Years in Iowa* (Los Angeles: privately published, 1948), 38–39.

33. Daniel Walker Howe, *What Hath God Wrought: The Transformation of the United States, 1815–1848* (New York: Oxford University Press, 2007), 526, 565–569; Hurt, *American Agriculture*, 117, 127–128, 150–156; Danbom, *Born in the Country*, 88–90; Alan Taylor, *American Republics: A Continental History of the United States, 1783–1850* (New York: W. W. Norton, 2021), 232; Earle D. Ross, "An Overview," in *A Century of Farming in Iowa, 1846–1946, by Members of the Staff of the Iowa State College and the Iowa Experiment Station* (Ames: Iowa State College Press, 1946), vii; Gates, *Farmer's Age*, 176–178, 218–221; Jeremy Atack and Peter Passell, *A New Economic View of American History: From Colonial Times to 1940* (New York: W. W. Norton, 1994), 288–294, 403–406, 429–431.

34. Gerald Grob, *The Deadly Truth: A History of Disease in America* (Cambridge, MA: Harvard University Press, 2002), 65, 128–131; Ferrin, "An Autobiography and a Reminiscence," 249; Mildred Throne, ed., "The Memories of Aristarchus Cone," *Iowa Journal of History* 49, no. 1 (January 1951): 58, 68.

35. West, *Growing Up with the Country*, 217–218; Grob, *Deadly Truth*, 78–84, 104–106; Caleb Forbes Davis and James Cox Davis, "The Autobiographies of An Iowa Father and Son," *Annals of Iowa* 19, no. 7 (January 1935), 487; Benjamin F. Gue, *History of Iowa from the Earliest Times to the Beginning of the Twentieth Century*, vol. 1 (New York: Century History, 1902), 266.

36. Harriet Bonebright-Closz, *Reminiscences of Newcastle, Iowa: A History of the Founding of Webster City, Iowa* (Des Moines: Historical Department of Iowa, 1923), 155–160; Abbie Mott Benedict, "My Early Days in Iowa," 344–345; Brown, *Grandmother Brown's*, 144–145; Cammack, "From Indiana to Iowa," 404–405; Throne, "Iowa Farm Letters," 75–80; Elisha D. Ely, *The Ely and Weare Families: Pioneers of Michigan and Iowa* (Cedar Rapids: Torch Press, 1926), 80, 85–87.

37. Bonebright-Closz, *Reminiscences*, 147–148; Throne, "Iowa Farm Letters," 71; William Porter Nutting, "Starting Life in Warren County," *Iowa Journal of History and Politics* 39, no. 2 (April 1941): 193. A rod is equal to 16.5 feet, or 1/320th of a mile.

38. Throne, "Iowa Farm Letters," 60, 81; Cammack, "From Indiana to Iowa," 403; Ferrin, "An Autobiography and a Reminiscence," 250; Bonebright-Closz, *Reminiscences*, 215–216; Rev. John Todd, *Early Settlement and Growth of Western Iowa; or Reminiscences* (Des Moines: Historical Department of Iowa, 1906), 88, 97. Also see Charles Aldrich, "A Winter on the Open Prairie," *Iowa Historical Record* 12, no. 2 (April 1896): 450–458. Errors are present in Kenyon's letters.

39. Jno. M. Brainard, "The Great Blizzard of 1856," *Annals of Iowa* 1, no. 5 (1894): 391–395; N. Tjernagel, "Variable Iowa Weather," *Annals of Iowa* 31, no. 3 (Winter 1952): 208–209; Ira A. Williams, "Lost in an Iowa Blizzard," *Palimpsest* 2, no. 1 (January 1921): 1–12.

40. Belle Bailey, *Stories of the Beginning of Delaware County, Covering the Period of Slow Settlement from 1834 to 1850*, SHSI-IAC, 31; Bonebright-Closz, *Reminiscences*, 150–151; J. L. Ingalsbe, "Northwest Iowa in 1855," *Iowa Journal of History and Politics* 18, no. 2 (April 1920): 297–298; Throne, "Iowa Farm Letters, 1856–1865," 61.

41. Bremer, *Store Almost in Sight*, 129–132; Mildred Throne, "Southern Iowa Agriculture," 124–125.

42. "Source Material of Iowa History: Pioneer Reminiscences of Wapello County," *Iowa Journal of History* 57, no. 4 (October 1959): 331–340; Waterman, *History of Wapello County*, vol. 1, 61–65, 69, 102–103, 117–120, 137–138, 149, 161–162, 189.

43. Howard J. Nelson, "The Economic Development of Des Moines," *Iowa Journal of History* 48, no. 3 (July 1950): 193–206; F. Andrews, *Pioneers of Polk County, Iowa: And Reminiscences of Early Days*, vol. 1 (Des Moines: Baker-Trisler, 1908), 97; LeRoy G. Pratt, *From Cabin to Capital City* (n.p.: Heartland Area Educational Agency, 1990), 1–2, 13, 21; Frank M. Mills, "Early Commercial Travelling in Iowa," *Annals of Iowa* 11, no. 5 (April 1914): 328–329. The town of Fort Des Moines was incorporated on September 22, 1851.

44. Bill Silag, "Sioux City: An Iowa Boom Town," *Annals of Iowa* 44, no. 8 (Spring 1979): 587–592; Frank Harmon Garver, ed., "Reminiscences of John H. Charles," *Annals of Iowa* 8, no. 6 (July 1908): 416.

45. Garver, "Reminiscences of John H. Charles," 401–424.

46. Robert Leslie Jones, *History of Agriculture in Ohio to 1880* (Kent: Kent State University Press, 1983), 48; Crowder, "Pioneer Life in Palo Alto County," 182–183; Galer, "Recollections," 15, 20–21; Samuel Clough, "A Barefoot Sailor Becomes an Iowa Farmer, 1824–1905," *Annals of Iowa* 39, no. 8 (Spring 1969): 618–619; Albert Parks Butts, "A Calhoun County Pioneer," 6–7, SHSI-IAC.

CHAPTER 4: SLAVERY, POLITICS, AND TRANSPORTATION BEFORE THE CIVIL WAR

1. David M. Potter, *The Impending Crisis, 1848–1861* (New York: Harper and Row, 1976), 16–17, 42–43; James M. McPherson, *Battle Cry of Freedom: The Civil War Era* (New York: Oxford University Press, 1988), 8–9; Lowell J. Soike, *Busy in the Cause: Iowa, the Free State Struggle in the West, and the Prelude to Civil War* (Lincoln: University of Nebraska Press, 2014), xi, 27, 209, 212.

2. George S. May, ed., "An Iowan in the Mexican War," *Iowa Journal of History* 53, no. 2 (April 1955): 167–173; Ora Williams, "Forgetting Chapultepec," *Annals of Iowa* 28, no. 2 (October 1946): 83–90; John S. D. Eisenhower, *So Far from God: The U.S. War with Mexico, 1846–1848* (New York: Doubleday, 1989), 338–341; "Iowa in the War with Mexico," *Annals of Iowa* 4, no. 4 (1900): 313–315; Tom Savage, *A Dictionary of Iowa Place Names* (Iowa City: University of Iowa Press, 2007), 4–5, 8, 13–15; Ray Murray, "Lest We Forget," *Palimpsest* 29, no. 6 (June 1948): 179–180. Five hundred men from the Mormon battalion volunteered but saw no combat. George

May wrote that most Iowa troops in the Mexican War died from disease, while Ora Williams claims that most died in combat. Sources differ on how many men perished during the conflict.

3. Morton M. Rosenberg, *Iowa on the Eve of the Civil War: A Decade of Frontier Politics* (Norman: University of Oklahoma Press, 1972), 12–15; Joel H. Silbey, "Proslavery Sentiment in Iowa," *Iowa Journal of History* 55, no. 4 (October 1957): 289–292, 297–299, 318; John Connor, "The Antislavery Movement in Iowa," *Annals of Iowa* 40, no. 6 (Fall 1970): 475–478; Robert R. Dykstra, "The Issue Squarely Met: Toward an Explanation of Iowans' Racial Attitudes, 1865–1868," *Annals of Iowa* 47, no. 5 (Summer 1984): 430–432; Homer L. Calkin, "A Slaveowner in Iowa," *Palimpsest* 22, no. 11 (November 1941): 344–345.

4. Leslie A. Schwalm, *Emancipation's Diaspora: Race and Reconstruction in the Upper Midwest* (Chapel Hill: University of North Carolina Press, 2009), 26–32, 37–41; Brent M. S. Campney, *Hostile Heartland: Racism, Repression, and Resistance in the Midwest* (Urbana: University of Illinois Press, 2019), 14–25, 41, 188–190, 200; Eric Foner, *Free Soil, Free Labor, Free Men: The Ideology of the Republican Party before the Civil War* (New York: Oxford University Press, 1970), 262, 266–268, 297; Robert R. Dykstra, *Bright Radical Star: Black Freedom and White Supremacy on the Hawkeye Frontier* (Ames: Iowa State University Press, 1993), 24–27.

5. Richard Acton and Patricia Nassif Acton, "A Legal History of African-Americans from the Iowa Territory to the State Sesquicentennial, 1838–1996," in *Outside In: African-American History in Iowa, 1838–2000*, ed. Bill Silag, Susan Koch-Bridgford, and Hal Chase (Iowa City: State Historical Society of Iowa, 2001), 65–68; Dykstra, *Bright Radical Star*, 110–113; Dorothy Schwieder, *Iowa: The Middle Land* (Ames: Iowa State University Press, 1996), 86–87. Schwieder wrote that the law never went into effect because it was not published in the Mount Pleasant paper. Dykstra argued that it became law once the new volume of laws from the legislative session were printed. See Dykstra, 112. The draconian property confiscation section of the law does not seem to have ever been employed.

6. Leland L. Sage, *A History of Iowa* (Ames: Iowa State University Press, 1974), 310; Lowell J. Soike, *Necessary Courage: Iowa's Underground Railroad in the Struggle against Slavery* (Iowa City: University of Iowa Press, 2013), 24–32, 89–90; Dykstra, *Bright Radical Star*, 28–30; Lewis Thomas Jones, *The Quakers of Iowa* (Iowa City: State Historical Society of Iowa, 1914), 35–47.

7. Charles E. Payne, *Josiah Bushnell Grinnell* (Iowa City: State Historical Society of Iowa, 1938), 33–41, 49–51; L. F. Parker, "Josiah Bushnell Grinnell," *Annals of Iowa* 2, no. 4 (1896): 250–252; G. Galin Berrier, "Josiah Bushnell Grinnell," in *The Biographical Dictionary of Iowa*, ed. David Hudson, Marvin Bergman, and Loren Horton (Iowa City: University of Iowa Press, 2008), 199–200.

8. John Hope Franklin and Loren Schweninger, *Runaway Slaves: Rebels on the Plantation* (New York: Oxford University Press, 1999), 25–26, 116–117, 121, 150, 210–211, 228–231.

9. Soike, *Necessary Courage*, 1, 32–40; "An Iowa Fugitive Slave Case—1850," *Annals of Iowa* 6, no. 1 (1903): 9–15.

10. Soike, *Necessary Courage*, 38–46.

11. Potter, *Impending Crisis*, 130–131; Soike, *Necessary Courage*, 58–66; George Frazee, "The Iowa Fugitive Slave Case," *Annals of Iowa* 4, no. 2 (1899): 118–121, 130–134.

12. G. Galin Berrier, "The Underground Railroad in Iowa," in Silag, Koch-Bridgford, and Chase, *Outside In*, 47–48; Galin Berrier, "Charlotta Pyles," *Iowa Heritage Illustrated* 90, no. 2 (Summer 2009): 82–83; Mrs. Laurence C. Jones, "The Desire for Freedom," *Palimpsest* 8, no. 5 (May 1927): 153–158; Soike, *Necessary Courage*, 56. Jones, known as Grace Morris Allen before her marriage, was the granddaughter of Charlotta Pyles. She married Laurence C. Jones in 1912. Laurence was a University of Iowa graduate, who founded the Piney Woods School in Mississippi for Black students. See Laurence C. Jones, *Piney Woods and Its Story* (New York: Fleming H. Revell, 1922.)

13. Berrier, "Underground Railroad," 48; Jones, "Desire for Freedom," 158–163; Soike, *Necessary Courage*, 58–59.

14. McPherson, *Battle Cry of Freedom*, 121–125, 145–149, 152–153, 169.

15. Soike, *Busy in the Cause*, xi, 22, 56, 209; Kenneth M. Stampp, *America in 1857: A Nation on the Brink* (New York: Oxford University Press, 1990), 145–146.

16. Connor, "Antislavery Movement in Iowa," 464–467; Soike, *Necessary Courage*, 89–92, 137–138; Dykstra, *Bright Radical Star*, 143; Deacon Adams, "Tabor and Northern 'Excursion'" *Annals of Iowa* 33, no. 2 (Fall 1955): 129–131. Adams was a member of Iowa's underground railroad.

17. Rosenberg, *Iowa on the Eve of the Civil War*, 84–86, 105–106, 129–143; Soike, *Busy in the Cause*, 10–12; David S. Sparks, "The Birth of the Republican Party in Iowa, 1854–1856," *Iowa Journal of History* 54, no. 1 (January 1956): 2–3, 32–34; Potter, *Impending Crisis*, 246–259; Emory H. English, "Iowa Republicans Organized in 1856," *Annals of Iowa* 32, no. 1 (July 1953): 43–46. Quote is from Soike.

18. Joseph Frazier Wall, *Iowa: A History* (New York: W. W. Norton, 1978), 99–103; J. A. Swisher, "Constitution Making in 1857," *Palimpsest* 7, no. 3 (March 1926): 83–87; Benjamin F. Shambaugh, *The Constitutions of Iowa* (Iowa City: Iowa State Historical Society, 1934), 216–217, 235–236, 245–250, 262–266; "Nebraska 'Wild-Cat' Banks," *Annals of Iowa* 5, no. 1 (1901): 52–55; Todd E. Pettys, *The Iowa State Constitution* (New York: Oxford University Press, 2018), 24–25, 36–38.

19. Dykstra, *Bright Radical Star*, 136–144.

20. Soike, *Necessary Courage*, 137–158; Frederick Lloyd, "In the Name of Free Soil," *Palimpsest* 7, no. 3 (March 1926): 76–82; George Mills, "The Crusade of John Brown," *Annals of Iowa* 35, no. 2 (October 1959): 101–104; Benjamin F. Gue, "John Brown and His Iowa Friends," *Midland Monthly* 7 (February 1897): 103–106. The number of fugitives became twelve when a pregnant woman gave birth to a baby boy. See Mills, "Crusade of John Brown," 102.

21. McPherson, *Battle Cry of Freedom*, 202–206; Soike, *Busy in the Cause*, 108–110, 155–168; Wall, *Iowa*, 97–99.

22. Connor, "Antislavery Movement in Iowa," 471–474; Soike, *Busy in the Cause*,

165–168; Wall, *Iowa*, 104–105; "Hon. Samuel J. Kirkwood," *Annals of Iowa* 11, no. 4 (October 1873): 610–611; Benjamin F. Gue, "John Brown and His Iowa Friends," *Midland Monthly* 7 (March 1897), 273–276.

23. Rebecca Conard, "A Gamble for Freedom: Frances Overton and the Underground Railroad in Grinnell," *Iowa Heritage Illustrated* 85, no. 4 (Winter 2004): 156–159; Thomas A. Lucas, "Men Were Too Fiery for Much Talk: The Grinnell Anti-Abolitionist Riot of 1860," *Palimpsest* 68, no. 1 (Spring 1987): 12, 16–20.

24. Eric Steven Zimmer, "Settlement Sovereignty: The Meskwaki Fight for Self-Governance, 1856–1937," *Annals of Iowa* 73, no. 4 (Fall 2014): 314–318, 322, 346–347; L. Edward Purcell, "The Mesquakie Indian Settlement in 1905," *Iowa Heritage Illustrated* 85, nos. 2–3 (Summer– Fall 2004), 94; Ruth A. Gallaher, "The Tama Indians," *Palimpsest* 7, no. 2 (February 1926): 47–48.

25. Paul N. Beck, *Inkpaduta: Dakota Leader* (Norman: University of Oklahoma Press, 2008), xi–xx, 16, 52–55, 60–74, 140–142; Sage, *History of Iowa*, 107; Kevin T. Mason, "Inkpaduta in Iowa: Dakota Decline, Dispossession, and Erasure," *Annals of Iowa* 80, no. 2 (Spring 2021): 138–157. Though events occurred around the Okiboji Lakes, the episode is popularly known as the Spirit Lake Massacre. Spirit Lake is just north and northwest of West Okoboji Lake and East Okoboji Lake. One cabin on the southwest shore of Spirit Lake was attacked, but many casualties occurred around the other two lakes.

26. William H. Thompson, *Transportation in Iowa: A Historical Summary* (n.pl.: Iowa Department of Transportation, 1989), 9; George Rogers Taylor, *The Transportation Revolution, 1815–1860* (New York: Harper Torchbooks, 1951), 15–16, 56; Erik F. Haites, James Mak, and Gary M. Walton, *Western River Transportation: The Era of Early Internal Development, 1810–1860* (Baltimore: John Hopkins University Press, 1975), 11–15; Louis C. Hunter, *Steamboats on Western Rivers: An Economic and Technological History* (New York: Octagon Books, 1969), 12–13, 21, 38, 47; Charles A. White, "The Early Homes and Home-Makers of Iowa," *Annals of Iowa* 4, no. 3 (1899): 193.

27. George F. Parker, *Iowa Pioneer Foundations*, vol. 1 (Iowa City: State Historical Society of Iowa, 1940), 120, 216–221; C. L. Lucas, "Recollections of Early Times in Iowa," *Annals of Iowa* 6, no. 5 (1904): 382–383; Remley J. Glass, "Early Transport and the Plank Road," *Annals of Iowa* 21, no. 7 (January 1939): 505–510; Hoyt Sherman, "From Oskaloosa in a Wagon," *Annals of Iowa* 4, no. 3 (1899): 281–285.

28. Kenneth E. Colton, "Bringing the Stage Coach to Iowa, 1837–1842," *Annals of Iowa* 22, no. 1 (Summer 1939): 7–8, 13, 18–21, 38, 46; Kenneth E. Colton, "Stagecoach Travel in Iowa," *Annals of Iowa* 22, no. 3 (Winter 1939): 180–181, 187–188, 191–196; Dexter Bloomer, ed., *Life and Writings of Amelia Bloomer* (Boston: Arena, 1895), 202–203.

29. William J. Petersen, *The Story of Iowa: The Progress of An American State*, vol. 1 (New York: Lewis Historical, 1952), 511–520; Thompson, *Transportation in Iowa*, 9–10; H. W. Lathrop, "Early Steamboating on the Iowa River," *Iowa Historical Record* 13, no. 1 (January 1897): 44–46. For a good survey of unsuccessful attempts

to improve steamboat transportation see Dave Hubler, "Des Moines River Navigation: Expectations Unfulfilled," *Annals of Iowa* 39, no. 4 (Spring 1968): 287–306.

30. William J. Petersen, *Steamboating on the Upper Mississippi* (Iowa City: State Historical Society of Iowa, 1968), 328, 351–373, 381–383, 386, 405.

31. Donovan L. Hofsommer, *Steel Trails of Hawkeyeland: Iowa's Railroad Experience* (Bloomington: University of Indiana Press, 2005), 1–9; Thompson, *Transportation in Iowa*, 18–31; Cyrenus Cole, *Iowa through the Years* (Iowa City: State Historical Society of Iowa, 1940), 244; H. Roger Grant, ed., *Iowa Railroads: The Essays of Frank P. Donovan, Jr.* (Iowa City: University of Iowa Press, 2000), 170–173.

32. Dwight L. Agnew, "The Mississippi and Missouri Railroad, 1856–1860," *Iowa Journal of History* 51, no. 3 (July 1953): 213–215; Petersen, *Story of Iowa*, vol. 1, 585–586; Earl S. Beard, "Local Aid to Railroads in Iowa," *Iowa Journal of History* 50, no. 1 (January 1952): 8, 16, 18.

33. Dwight L. Agnew, "Iowa's First Railroad," *Iowa Journal of History* 48, no. 1 (January 1950): 12, 15–18, 21–23; Grant, *Iowa Railroads*, 170–171.

34. Grant, *Iowa Railroads*, 128; Thompson, *Transportation in Iowa*, 23–27; Agnew, "Iowa's First Railroad," 25–26.

35. Thomas R. Baker, *The Sacred Cause of Union: Iowa in the Civil War* (Iowa City: University of Iowa Press, 2016), 14, 31; Dykstra, *Bright Radical Star*, 195–196; William L. Barney, *Battleground for the Union: The Era of the Civil War and Reconstruction, 1848–1877* (Englewood Cliffs, NJ: Prentice Hall, 1990), 122, 135, 140–141; Sage, *History of Iowa*, 147. For an outstanding history of the Republican Party see Heather Cox Richardson, *To Make Men Free: A History of the Republican Party* (New York: Basic Books, 2021). The first four chapters explain the rise of the party, its role in the Civil War, and its drift away from its original ideals.

36. Wall, *Iowa*, 99. See Emory H. English, "Iowa Republicans Organized in 1856," 43–46, for a summary of the state's rapid embrace of the new Republican Party between 1854 and 1856.

CHAPTER 5: IOWA AND THE CIVIL WAR, 1861–1870

1. Leland L. Sage, *A History of Iowa* (Ames: Iowa State University Press, 1974), 153–154; Donald C. Elder III, ed., *A Damned Iowa Greyhound: The Civil War Letters of William Henry Harrison Clayton* (Iowa City: University of Iowa Press, 1998), vii. For the most comprehensive overview of units and their histories, see *Roster and Record of Iowa Soldiers in the War of the Rebellion Together with Historical Sketches of Volunteer Organizations, 1861–1866*, vols. 1–6 (Des Moines: Emery H. English, 1908–1911). Iowa provided forty-four regiments of white troops, including some regiments only employed for one hundred days in 1864, as well as nine regiments of cavalry, two of which served on the frontier. Two more units, border brigades, helped with state defense. One additional regiment of African American troops was organized in the state. Iowa also provided several smaller battalion size units. For a detailed political and military history of the conflict see Kenneth L. Lyftogt, *Iowa and the Civil War:*

Free Child of the Missouri Compromise, 1850–1862 (Iowa City: Camp Pope, 2018); Lyftogt, *Iowa and the Civil War: From Iuka to the Red River, 1862–1864* (Iowa City: Camp Pope, 2020); and Lyftogt, *Iowa and the Civil War: The Longest Year, 1864-1865* (Iowa City: Camp Pope, 2022).

2. Ted Hinckley, "Davenport in the Civil War," *Annals of Iowa* 34, no. 6 (October 1958): 402–403; Mildred Throne, ed., "The Civil War Diary of John Mackley," *Iowa Journal of History* 48, no. 2 (April 1950): 141–142; Kenneth L. Lyftogt, *From Blue Mills to Columbia: Cedar Falls and the Civil War* (Iowa City: University of Iowa Press, 1993), 18–21, 25; Thomas R. Baker, *The Sacred Cause of Union: Iowa in the Civil War* (Iowa City: University of Iowa Press, 2016), 63, 71; Cyrenus Cole, *Iowa through the Years* (Iowa City: State Historical Society of Iowa, 1940), 277–278; Luella M. Wright, "The Call to Arms," *Palimpsest* 22, no. 1 (January 1941): 3.

3. Seymour Dwight Thompson, *Recollections with the Third Iowa Regiment* (Cincinnati: Published for the author, 1864), 13–18. Thompson served with the regiment for two years, especially in Missouri and Tennessee. Henry H. Wright wrote another fine regimental history. He served throughout the war with the Sixth Regiment, fighting guerillas in Missouri and taking part in the battles of Shiloh and Chattanooga, as well as the Vicksburg campaign and Sherman's March to the Sea. See Henry H. Wright, *A History of the Sixth Iowa Infantry* (Iowa City: State Historical Society of Iowa, 1923).

4. Lyftogt, *From Blue Mills to Columbia*, 25–29; Throne, "Civil War Diary," 141–142, 151; William J. Petersen, *The Story of Iowa: The Progress of an American State*, vol. 1 (New York: Lewis Historical, 1952), 430; Baker, *Sacred Cause*, 84, 99; William L. Barney, *Battleground for the Union: The Era of the Civil War and Reconstruction, 1848–1877* (Englewood Cliffs, NJ: Prentice-Hall, 1990), 152–153; Michael Fellman, *Inside War: The Guerilla Conflict in Missouri during the Civil War* (New York: Oxford University Press, 1989), 127–128, 182.

5. S. H. M. Byers, *With Fire and Sword* (New York: Neale, 1911), 9–15, 23–24, 30–32, 40, 49; Ruth A. Gallaher, "With Sword," *Palimpsest* 13, no. 11 (November 1932): 489–490; "Civil War Army Organization," accessed January 25, 2022, https://www.battlefields.org/learn/articles/civil-war-army-organization.

6. Petersen, *Story of Iowa*, vol. 1, 430; Mildred Throne, ed., "Erastus B. Soper's History of Company D, 12th Iowa Infantry, 1861–1866—Part I," *Iowa Journal of History* 56, no. 2 (April 1958): 178–179; Baker, *Sacred Cause*, 107, 113–121; Mildred Throne, "Iowa and the Battle of Shiloh," *Iowa Journal of History* 55, no. 3 (July 1957): 211–224, 225. See Edwin C. Bates, "The Iowans at Fort Donelson: General C. F. Smith's Attack on the Confederate Right, February 12–16, 1862, Part II," *Annals of Iowa* 36, no. 5 (Summer 1962): 321–343, for more detail on the important role of Iowa troops in this battle.

7. Throne, "Erastus B. Soper's History," 179–181; Throne, "Battle of Shiloh," 234, 238, 242–245; Barney, *Battleground*, 172; George W. Crosley, "Some Reminiscences of an Iowa Soldier," *Annals of Iowa* 10, no. 2 (1911): 128–129. See the diary of Ira W. Gilbert, SHSI-IAC, for a detailed, sometimes gripping, account of Gilbert's experience in the 6th Iowa Infantry Regiment in 1861 and 1862.

8. James M. McPherson, *Battle Cry of Union: The Civil War Era* (New York: Oxford University Press, 1988), 414–421, 519–524, 586–590, 626–633; Mark Grimsley and Todd D. Miller, editors, *The Union Must Stand: The Civil War Diary of John Quincy Adams Campbell, Fifth Iowa Infantry* (Knoxville: University of Tennessee Press, 2000), 101–109; S. H. M. Byers, "How Men Feel in Battle: Recollections of a Private at Champion Hills," *Annals of Iowa* 2, no. 6 (1896): 438–439, 443–446; Cyrenus Cole, *Iowa through the Years*, 299.

9. McPherson, *Battle Cry of Union,* 635–637, 663–665; Edward G. Longacre, ed., "'Dear and Much Loved One:' An Iowan's Vicksburg Letters," *Annals of Iowa* 43, no. 1 (Summer 1975): 49–50, 53–60; Byers, "How Men Feel in Battle," 447–448; Cole, *Iowa through the Years*, 308. Errors are in Myers's letters.

10. J. L. Anderson, "The Vacant Chair on the Farm: Soldier Husbands, Farm Wives, and the Iowa Home Front, 1861–1865," *Annals of Iowa* 66, nos. 3–4 (Summer–Fall 2007): 241–265; Baker, *Sacred Cause*, 151; Glenda Riley, *Frontierswomen: The Iowa Experience* (Ames: Iowa State University Press, 1981), 114–115. Quote is from Baker.

11. Baker, *Sacred Cause*, 151–152; Riley, *Frontierswomen*, 119–123; George Mills, ed., "The Sharp Family Civil War Letters," *Annals of Iowa* 34, no. 7 (January 1959): 481–489, 494. John Sharp briefly reenlisted in 1865.

12. M. A. Rogers, "An Iowa Woman in Wartime, Part III," *Annals of Iowa* 36, no. 1 (Summer 1962): 42–43; Rogers, "An Iowa Woman in Wartime, Part I," *Annals of Iowa* 35, no. 7 (Winter 1961): 523, 525, 541–542; Rogers, "An Iowa Woman in Wartime, Part II," *Annals of Iowa* 35, no. 8 (Spring 1962): 597–599; Riley, *Frontierswomen*, 115–119.

13. McPherson, *Battle Cry of Freedom*, 816–818; Earle D. Ross, *Iowa Agriculture: An Historical Survey* (Iowa City: State Historical Society of Iowa, 1951), 52–57; Riley, *Frontierswomen*, 128; Emerson D. Fite, "The Agricultural Development of the West during the Civil War," *Quarterly Journal of Economics* 20, no. 2 (February 1906): 260–263, 267, 271–272, 276–278; R. Douglass Hurt, *Food and Agriculture during the Civil War* (Santa Barbara: Praeger, 2016), 39, 42, 77–82, 86, 90, 158.

14. Noah Zaring, "Competition in Benevolence: Civil War Soldiers' Aid in Iowa," *Iowa Heritage Illustrated* 77, no. 1 (Spring 1996): 10–13; Riley, *Frontierswomen*, 128–131.

15. Riley, *Frontierswomen*, 129; Susan Kuecker, "Reverberations of the War: Cedar Rapids in 1865," *Iowa Heritage Illustrated* 80, no. 3 (Fall 1999): 140–141; Zaring, "Competition in Benevolence," 13–14, 21; Rogers, "Iowa Woman in Wartime, Part II," 594–595.

16. Ruth A. Gallaher, "Annie Turner Wittenmyer," *Iowa Journal of History and Politics* 29, no. 4 (October 1931): 518–526; Elizabeth D. Leonard, *Yankee Women: Gender Battles in the Civil War* (New York: W. W. Norton, 1994), 51–56; Annie Wittenmyer, *Under the Guns: A Woman's Reminiscences of the Civil War* (Boston: E. B. Stillings, 1895), 72–75; Petersen, *Story of Iowa*, vol. 1, 401; Lisa Guinn, "Annie Wittenmyer and Nineteenth-Century Women's Usefulness," *Annals of Iowa* 74, no. 4 (Fall 2015): 351–352. For more on Civil War medical care, see Gerald Kennedy, "U.S. Army Hospital: Keokuk, 1862–1865," *Annals of Iowa* 40, no. 2 (Fall 1969): 118–136.

Records of the divorce between Annie and William Wittenmyer have been lost, but Lisa Guinn notes that William's second wife left him, and he owed Annie child support money in 1876. See footnote 4 in Guinn's article.

17. Gallaher, "Annie Turner Wittenmyer," 531, 538–543, 546, 552–553, 558–560; Wittenmyer, *Under the Guns*, 106–114, 259–267; Robert F. Martin, "Wittenmyer, Sarah Ann 'Annie' Turner," in *The Biographical Dictionary of Iowa*, ed. David Hudson, Marvin Bergman, and Loren Horton (Iowa City: University of Iowa Press, 2008), 565–566; Leonard, *Yankee Women*, 28–35, 59, 82–84; Guinn, "Annie Wittenmyer," 366.

18. Theresa R. McDevitt, "'A Melody before Unknown': The Civil War Experiences of Mary and Amanda Shelton," *Annals of Iowa* 63, no. 2 (Spring 2004): 105–113, 116–117, 121–124, 130–135. The emphasis can be found in the original letter.

19. Sage, *History of Iowa*, 141, 153–156, 162, 165–166; Cole, *Iowa through the Years*, 260–261, 269–270, 289, 302; Robert J. Cook, "Kirkwood, Samuel Jordan," *Biographical Dictionary of Iowa*, 286–288. Kirkwood also served the remainder of a US Senate term in 1865 and 1866, after James Harlan joined Andrew Johnson's cabinet.

20. Peter Irons, *A People's History of the Supreme Court* (New York: Penguin Books, 2006), 183, 211; David M. Silver, "Lincoln's Appointment of United States Justice Samuel F. Miller," *Annals of Iowa* 33, no. 7 (Winter 1957): 510, 514–519, 525; Michael A. Ross, *Justice of Shattered Dreams: Samuel Freeman Miller and the Supreme Court during the Civil War Era* (Baton Rouge: Louisiana State University Press, 2003), 1–21, 28–30, 242–243; Ross, "'Justice for Iowa' Samuel Freeman Miller's Appointment to the United States Supreme Court During the Civil War," *Annals of Iowa* 60, no. 2 (Spring 2001): 137–138.

21. Samuel Hawkins Marshall Byers, *Iowa in War Times* (Des Moines: W. D. Condit, 1888), 264–268, 474–476; Petersen, *Story of Iowa*, vol. 1, 439–440; S. A. Moore, "Hostile Raid into Davis County," *Annals of Iowa* 13, no. 5 (July 1922): 362–370.

22. Frank C. Arena, "Southern Sympathizers in Iowa during Civil War Period," *Annals of Iowa* 30, no. 7 (January 1951): 523–528, 535; McPherson, *Battle Cry of Freedom*, 493–494; Petersen, *Story of Iowa*, vol. 1, 439–441; Cole, *Iowa through the Years*, 300–301. For more on journalism during the conflict see David L. Lendt, *Demise of the Democracy: The Copperhead Press in Iowa, 1856–1870* (Ames: Iowa State University Press, 1973).

23. Arena, "Southern Sympathizers," 528–531; C. C. Stiles, "The Skunk River War (or Tally War), Keokuk County, August 1863," *Annals of Iowa* 19, no. 8 (April 1935): 615–622; J. L. Swift, "The Death of Cyphert Tally," *Annals of Iowa* 41, no. 3 (Winter 1972): 839–840. Most sources are pro-Union. Swift's article, for example, includes a statement by R. B. Sears, supposedly identifying the man who killed Tally.

24. Baker, *Sacred Cause*, 150; "Oldest Greybeard," *Annals of Iowa* 35, no. 6 (Fall 1960): 463; Petersen, *Story of Iowa*, vol. 1, 480; Edith Wasson McElroy, *The Undying Procession: Iowa's Civil War Regiments* (n.p.: Iowa Civil War Centennial Commission, n.d.), 70–71; Byers, *Iowa in War Times*, 558–559. Petersen and McElroy differ slightly in their numbers for dead and wounded from the Thirty-Seventh.

25. David Brodnax Sr., "'Will They Fight? Ask the Enemy:' Iowa's African-American

Regiment in the Civil War," *Annals of Iowa* 66, nos. 3–4 (Summer–Fall 2007): 266–278, 291; G. Galin Berrier, "The Underground Railroad in Iowa," in *Outside In: African-American History in Iowa, 1838–2000*, ed. Bill Silag, Susan Koch-Bridgford, and Hal Chase (Des Moines: State Historical Society of Iowa, 2001), 46.

26. Stephen J. Frese, "Clark, Alexander C.," *Biographical Dictionary of Iowa*, 83–85; Brodnax, "Will They Fight?'" 269–272; William S. Morris, "Black Iowans in Defense of Their Nation, 1863–1990," in Silag, Koch-Bridgford, and Chase, *Outside In*, 97.

27. Brodnax, "'Will They Fight?'" 278–288. An African American soldier, James Daniel, won the Medal of Honor at the Battle of New Market in Virginia. He settled in Ottumwa after the war. See Morris, "Iowans in Defense of Their Nation," 99–100.

28. Ted Genoways and Hugh H. Genoways, *A Perfect Picture of Hell: Eyewitness Accounts by Civil War Prisoners from the 12th Iowa* (Iowa City: University of Iowa Press, 2001), 4–5, 12–15, 33, 40–41, 46–50, 246–250, 262–270, 276–277; Brodnax, "'Will They Fight?'" 284–285, Baker, *Sacred Cause*, 118. Also see Amos W. Ames, "A Diary of Prison Life in Southern Prisons," *Annals of Iowa* 40, no. 1 (Summer 1969): 1–19. Ames was imprisoned at Andersonville.

29. McPherson, *Battle Cry of Freedom*, 677–681, 718–722, 743–753, 773–774, 805, 808–810; Baker, *Sacred Cause*, 210; Alonzo Abernethy, "Incidents of an Iowa Soldier's Life, or Four Years in Dixie," *Annals of Iowa* 12, no. 6 (October 1920): 401, 416–418; Byers, *With Fire and Sword*, 108–110.

30. Mildred Throne, ed., "A History of Company D, Eleventh Iowa Infantry, 1861–1865," *Iowa Journal of History* 55, no. 1 (January 1957): 71–78; Barney, *Battleground*, 219–220; Olynthus B. Clark, ed., *Downing's Civil War Diary* (Des Moines: Historical Department of Iowa, 1916), 229–235.

31. Byers, *With Fire and Sword*, 118–119, 122–138, 144–154, 164–167, 202–203; Kenneth L. Lyftogt, "Byers, Samuel Hawkins Marshall," *Biographical Dictionary of Iowa*, 68–70. Another excellent first-person account of the war is Mildred Throne, ed., *The Civil War Diary of Cyrus F. Boyd, Fifteenth Iowa Infantry, 1861–1863* (1953; repr., Baton Rouge: Louisiana State University Press, 1998).

32. Stephen E. Ambrose, *Nothing Like It in the World: The Men Who Built the Transcontinental Railroad, 1863–1869* (New York: Simon and Schuster, 2000), 31–35, 84–88, 130–135; Don L. Hofsommer, "Grenville Mellen Dodge," *Biographical Dictionary of Iowa*, 132–134; Ruth E. Dugan, "Greenville Mellen Dodge," *Palimpsest* 11, no. 4 (April 1920): 160–168.

33. Eric Foner, *A Short History of Reconstruction* (New York: Harper and Row, 1990), 204–205.

34. Robert R. Dykstra, *Bright Radical Star: Black Freedom and White Supremacy on the Hawkeye Frontier* (Ames: Iowa State University Press, 1993), 224–229, 240, 266–270; Richard Acton and Patricia Nassif Acton, "A Legal History of African-Americans: From the Iowa Territory to the State Sesquicentennial, 1838–1996," in Silag, Koch-Bridgford, and Chase, *Outside In*, 70–72.

35. Dykstra, *Bright Radical Star*, 229; Arnie Cooper, "A Stony Road: Black Education in Iowa, 1838–1860," *Annals of Iowa* 48, no. 3 (Winter 1986): 131–133; Leola

Nelson Bergmann, *The Negro in Iowa* (Iowa City: State Historical Society of Iowa, 1969), 50–51; Frese, "Clark, Alexander C.," 84–85; Acton and Nassif Acton, "Legal History of African-Americans," 72–73, 87; Jon K. Lauck, *The Good Country: A History of the American Midwest, 1800–1900* (Norman: University of Oklahoma Press, 2022), 140–141; Paul Finkelman, "Whose Midwest?" *Middle West Review* 9, no. 2 (Spring 2023): 120. Additional Iowa legislation, including the Iowa Civil Rights Act of 1884, protected African American access to public businesses and accommodations. It was not strongly enforced though in the following decades. See Acton and Nassif Acton, 74–75.

36. Dykstra, *Bright Radical Star*, 196; Frederick H. Dyer, *A Compendium of the War of the Rebellion*, vol. 3 (Des Moines: Dyer, 1908), 11–12; "The Mothers of Warriors," *Annals of Iowa* 30, no. 2 (Fall 1949): 146–147. Michigan troops' morality rate was 16.9 percent just slightly lower than the similar statistic for Iowa. The mortality rate for Arkansas's men was 20.6 percent, 18.05 percent for Louisiana troops, and 28.2 percent for Tennessee soldiers.

37. Byers, *Iowa in War Times*, 454. Byers overestimates the number of Iowa troops by two thousand.

CHAPTER 6: IMMIGRANTS, RAILROADS, AND FARM PROTEST

1. N. Levering, "Recollection of the Early Settlement of N. W. Iowa," *Annals of Iowa* 3 (1869): 300–303; William Silag, "Gateway to the Grasslands: Sioux City and the Missouri River Frontier," *Western Historical Quarterly* 14, no. 4 (October 1983): 398–400, 406–410.

2. Joseph C. Austin, "An Iowa Farm in the Making, 1867–1900," *Annals of Iowa* 40, no. 4 (Spring 1970): 308–309, 315; Thomas E. Fenton and Gerald Miller, "Soils," in *Iowa's Natural Heritage*, ed. Tom C. Cooper (Des Moines: Iowa Natural Heritage Foundation and the Iowa Academy of Science, 1982), 81; Frances Olsen Day, "Pioneering," 2, State Historical Society of Iowa, Iowa City (SHSI-IAC); Daryl Smith and Paul Chris Hansen, "Prairies," in Cooper, *Iowa's Natural Heritage*, 166; Hamlin Garland, *A Son of the Middle Border* (1917; repr., St. Paul: Minnesota Historical Society Press, 2007), 70; Cornelia F. Mutel, *The Emerald Horizon: The History of Nature in Iowa* (Iowa City: University of Iowa Press, 2008), 42, 48–50; Joseph B. McCullough, "Hamlin Hannibal Garland," in *The Biographical Dictionary of Iowa*, ed. David Hudson, Marvin Bergman, and Loren Horton (Iowa City: University of Iowa Press, 2008), 181–183.

3. Paul W. Gates, "The Homestead Law in Iowa," *Agricultural History* 38, no. 2 (April 1964): 67–70, 72, 74–78; James M. McPherson, *Battle Cry of Freedom: The Civil War Era* (New York: Oxford University Press, 1989), 450–451; Dennis Welland, "An Emigrant's Letter from Iowa, 1871," *Bulletin: British Association for American Studies* 12–13 (1966): 24. New research has shown how successful the Homestead Act was. A majority of claimants obtained their land and fraud was low. See Richard

Edwards, Jacob K. Friefeld, and Rebecca S. Wingo, *Homesteading the Plains: Toward a New History* (Lincoln: University of Nebraska Press, 2019), 197–203.

4. Frances Olsen Day, "More about Life on the Prairie," SHSI-IAC, 1–3; Abbie Mott Benedict, "My Early Days in Iowa," *Prairie Voices: Iowa's Pioneering Women*, ed. Glenda Riley (Ames: Iowa State University Press, 1996), 150–153; Riley, *Frontierswomen: The Iowa Experience* (Ames: Iowa State University Press, 1981), 39–40.

5. Mutel, *Emerald Horizon*, 76–92, 101, 105, 115; Kim Norvell, "Prairie Restoration Taking Root in Iowa: Conservation Groups Eye New Solutions," *Des Moines Register*, June 9, 2022, https://www.desmoinesregister.com/story/news/2022/06/09/iowa-prairie-restoration-efforts-underway-restore-land-once-covered-most-loess-hills/7473755001/; William Cronon, *Nature's Metropolis: Chicago and the Great West* (New York: W.W. Norton, 1991), 267–268. Iowa families in the late nineteenth-century lived in homes made of Wisconsin pine, wore clothes of Mississippi cotton made into fabric in Massachusetts, used plows produced from Pennsylvania steel, and drank coffee from Venezuela. See Cronon, 311–312, for an analysis of how railroads and Chicago tied Iowa to the world.

6. Mutel, *Emerald Horizon*, 51, 62–65, 126–130.

7. H.C. Webb Reminiscence, 1–3, SHSI-IAC; Day, "Pioneering," 1–4, SHSI-IAC. For a reminiscence of settlement in O'Brien County see Henry W. Wright, "Iowa—As I Knew It," *Annals of Iowa* 29, no. 5 (Summer 1948): 379–396.

8. Joyce Houser and Mildred Smith, "Settling Iowa's Last Frontier," *Iowan* 14, no. 1 (Fall 1965): 45–49.

9. Melinda Voss, "The Pioneer Diaries of Kate Martinson," *Iowan* 46, no. 1 (Fall 1997): 44–47, 65.

10. Gates, "Homestead Law," 76; Jacob Van der Zee, *The Hollanders of Iowa* (Iowa City: State Historical Society of Iowa, 1912), 123–132; Brian W. Beltman, "A Dutch Immigrant's Success Story: E. J. G. Bloemendaal's Sojourns and Settlement in Northwest Iowa," *Annals of Iowa* 62, no. 2 (Spring 2003): 205, 219–222; William Silag, "The Conquest of the Hinterland: Railroads and Capitalists in Northwest Iowa after the Civil War," *Annals of Iowa* 50, no. 5 (Summer 1990): 483–485.

11. Stephen E. Ambrose, *Nothing Like It in the World: The Men Who Built the Transcontinental Railroad, 1863–1869* (New York: Simon and Schuster, 2000), 63–64, 79–80; William H. Thompson, *Transportation in Iowa: A Historical Summary* (n.p.: Iowa Department of Transportation, 1989), 26–28; Don L. Hofsommer, *Steel Trails of Hawkeyeland: Iowa's Railroad Experience* (Bloomington: Indiana University Press, 2005), 13–18.

12. Thompson, *Transportation in Iowa*, 27–30; Hofsommer, *Steel Trails of Hawkeyeland*, 18–24; Dwight L. Agnew, "The Rock Island Railroad in Iowa," *Iowa Journal of History* 52, no. 3 (July 1954): 212, 218–222.

13. Joseph Frazier Wall, *Iowa: A History* (New York: W. W. Norton, 1978), 126–127; Thompson, *Transportation in Iowa*, 43–44; Hofsommer, *Steel Trails of Hawkeyeland*, 28–32, 37, 39–42; Leland L. Sage, *A History of Iowa* (Ames: Iowa State University Press, 1974), 310; Richard White, *"It's Your Misfortune and None of My Own:" A New History of the American West* (Norman: University of Oklahoma Press, 1991),

257–258; Mary K. Fredericksen, "The State of the State: Iowa in 1885," *Palimpsest* 65, no. 1 (January–February 1984): 5; William Silag, "A Mercantile History of Sioux City in the 1880s," *Palimpsest* 65, no. 1 (January–February 1984): 31.

14. A. T. DeGroot, ed., *Eighty Years in Iowa, Written by Benjamin H. Gavitt, in His 81st Year, at Des Moines* (Los Angeles: privately published, 1948), 62; Albert Butts, "A Calhoun County Pioneer," SHSI-IAC; W. E. Sanders, "Cedar Brakes and Hamilton Prairies: A Century of Change in Iowa Pioneer Life," *Annals of Iowa* 34, no. 6 (October 1958): 437, 453; Reuben Ellmaker to brother, February 18, 1859, Enos Ellmaker Papers, SHSI-IAC; Silag, "Conquest of the Hinterland," 495.

15. David B. Danbom, *Sodbusters: How Families Made Farms on the 19th-Century Plains* (Baltimore: Johns Hopkins University Press, 2014), 86; Myrtle Beinhauer, "Development of the Grange in Iowa, 1868–1930," *Annals of Iowa* 34, no. 8 (April 1959): 597–604, 609–612.

16. Julia Antoinette Losee Preston, "Washtub over the Sun," *Palimpsest* 68, no. 1 (Spring 1987): 3–10.

17. Glenda Riley, *Frontierswomen*, 100; *Compendium of the Eleventh Census*, part 3 (Washington, DC: Government Printing Office, 1897), 9.

18. *Iowa: The Home for Immigrants: Being a Treatise on the Resources of Iowa and Giving Useful Information with Regard to the State, for the Benefit of Immigrants and Others* (1870; repr., Iowa City: State Historical Society of Iowa, 1970), i–iv, 28–29, 38, 40, 46, 63, 67–70, 74, 84–89; Mary K. Frederickson, "The Grasshopper Wars," *Palimpsest* 62, no. 5 (September–October 1981): 151–152; Leola Nelson Bergmann, "Immigrants in Iowa," *Palimpsest* 37, no. 3 (March 1956): 140–144.

19. Mark Wyman, *Immigrants in the Valley: Irish, Germans, and Americans in the Upper Mississippi Country, 1830–1860* (Chicago: Nelson-Hall, 1984), 64–70; Thomas P. Christensen, "A German Forty-Eighter in Iowa," *Annals of Iowa* 26, no. 4 (Spring 1945): 248–249; *Census of Iowa for the Year 1895* (Des Moines: F. R. Conaway, State Printer, 1896), 306–307; Riley, *Frontierswomen*, 105. In 1895 the largest ethnic groups in Iowa were the Germans, Irish, Swedes, and Norwegians. Quote is from Riley.

20. Bela Vassady, "New Buda: A Colony of Hungarian Forty-Eighters in Iowa," *Annals of Iowa* 51, no. 1 (Summer 1991): 26–28, 34, 38–41, 48–52; *Census of Iowa*, 306–307. The 1895 Iowa census did not list Hungarians as a separate nationality. There were 4,195 people listed as "Other European."

21. Homer L. Calkin, "Settlers on the Iowa Frontier," *Palimpsest* 45, no. 2 (February 1964): 48–55; Homer L. Calkin, "Some Typical Irish Communities," *Palimpsest* 45, no. 2 (February 1964): 59–65, "Irish in Iowa, by County," *Palimpsest* 45, no. 2 (February 1964), maps following page 66; Homer L. Calkin, "Life among the Irish," *Palimpsest* 45, no. 2 (February 1964): 83–84; July 19, 1849, letter, William and Robert Mann to Joseph Brown, James McKee, copies from Record Office of Northern Iowa, SHSI-IAC; Wyman, *Immigrants in the Valley*, 42–46; *Census of Iowa*, 307; Timothy Walsh, *Irish Iowa* (Charleston, SC: History Press, 2019), 9, 15–16, 18, 43–44. Spelling errors are original in the Mann letter.

22. Homer L. Calkin, "Builders of the Hawkeye State," *Palimpsest* 45, no. 2

(February 1964): 90–91; Dwight G. McCarthy, *History of Palo Alto County Iowa* (Cedar Rapids: Torch Press, 1910), 22–23, 59, 62–65. For information on Soda Bar see: "Palo Alto County," Iowa Ghost Towns, accessed February 5, 2022, https://http://www.iowaghosttowns.com/palo_alto_county.htmlwww.iowaghosttowns.com/palo_alto_county.html.

23. Homer L. Calkin, "The Scandinavians," *Palimpsest* 43, no. 4 (April 1962): 161–164; Leola Nelson Bergmann, "They Came to Iowa," *Palimpsest* 40, no. 8 (August 1959): 289–303; Bergmann, "Their Occupations," *Palimpsest* 40, no. 8 (August 1959): 322–324; Bergmann, "Church and School," *Palimpsest* 40, no. 8 (August 1959): 346–350; *Census of Iowa*, 306. Quotes are from Calkin.

24. Dorothy Schwieder, *Iowa: The Middle Land* (Ames: Iowa State University, 1996), 101–102; Thomas Peter Christensen, *A History of the Danes in Iowa* (Solvang, CA: Dansk Folkesamfund, 1952), 22–30, 78–85.

25. Martha Eleanor Griffith, "The Czechs in Cedar Rapids," *Iowa Journal of History and Politics* 42, no. 2 (April 1944): 116–126; B. Shimek, "The Bohemians in Johnson County," 1–5, SHSI-IAC. Also see Pauline Skorunka Merrill, "Pioneer Iowa Bohemians," *Annals of Iowa* 26, no. 4 (Spring 1945): 261–274.

26. Maureen McCoy and William Silag, "The Italian Heritage in Des Moines," *Palimpsest* 64, no. 2 (March–April 1983): 60–67; Dorothy Schwieder, "Italian-Americans in Iowa's Coal Mining Industry," *Annals of Iowa* 46, no. 4 (Spring 1982): 267–278.

27. *Census of Iowa*, 306–308; Anthony J. Miller, "Pioneers, Sunday Schoolers, and Laundrymen: Chinese Immigrants in Iowa in the Chinese Exclusion Era, 1870–1890," *Annals of Iowa* 81, no. 2 (Spring 2022): 113–122, 127, 146; Beth Lew-Williams, *The Chinese Must Go: Violence, Exclusion, and the Making of the Alien in America* (Cambridge, MA: Harvard University Press, 2018), 8–9, 17, 117, 195–197, 247–251. Many states also prohibited Chinese and Japanese people from owning private property.

28. Miller, "Pioneers, Sunday Schoolers, and Laundrymen," 123–137, 141–143. Ar Shong, a US Navy veteran from the Civil War, was accused of larceny in 1893. He died the next year while under investigation. Dallas County took possession of his assets and liquidated them to be used for school construction. See Miller, 143–147.

29. Leslie A. Schwalm, *Emancipation's Diaspora: Race and Reconstruction in the Upper Midwest* (Chapel Hill: University of North Carolina Press, 2009), 35–37, 41–50, 67, 102–103, 135; Willis Goudy, "Selected Demographics: Iowa's African-American Residents, 1840–2000," in *Outside In: African-American History in Iowa, 1838–2000*, ed. Bill Silag, Susan Koch-Bridgford, and Hal Chase (Des Moines: State Historical Society of Iowa, 2001), 28; Ralph Scharnau, "African-American Wage Earners in Iowa, 1850–1950," in Silag, Koch-Bridgford, and Chase, *Outside In*, 218; James L. Hill, "Migration of Blacks to Iowa, 1820–1960," *Journal of Negro History* 66, no. 4 (Winter 1981–1982): 290–295; Glenda Elizabeth Gilmore and Thomas J. Sugrue, *These United States: A Nation in the Making, 1890 to the Present* (New York: W. W. Norton, 2015), 33–40, 97–98. Quotes are from Schwalm.

30. Orville Elder and Samuel Hall, *47 Years A Slave: A Brief Story of His Life before and after Freedom Came to Him* (Washington, IA: Journal Print Company, 1912). Hall's story has no page numbers. See Randall Bennett Woods, *A Black Odyssey: John*

Lewis Waller and the Promise of American Life, 1878–1900 (Lawrence: Regents Press of Kansas, 1981) for the story of John Lewis Waller, who became US consul to Madagascar in the 1890s after having fled enslavement and becoming a lawyer in Iowa.

31. Schwalm, *Emancipation's Diaspora*, 81–84, 92, 95, 99–106; Elder and Hall, *47 Years a Slave*.

32. Verlene McOllough, "The Orphan Train Comes to Clarinda," *Palimpsest* 69, no. 3 (Fall 1988): 145–150; Clark Kidder, "West by Orphan Train," *Wisconsin Magazine of History* 87, no. 2 (Winter 2003–2004): 32–33; Marilyn Irvin Holt, *The Orphan Trains: Placing Out in America* (Lincoln: University of Nebraska Press, 1992), 2–4, 48–50; Stephen O'Connor, *Orphan Trains: The Story of Charles Loring Brace and the Children He Saved and Failed* (Chicago: University of Chicago Press, 2001), xvii, 45.

33. "Paul Forch," *Orphan Train Riders: Their Own Stories*, vol. 1 (Springdale, AR: Orphan Train Historical Society of America, 2001), 33–37.

34. Frederickson, "Grasshopper Wars," 150–160; Frank C. Pellett, "Some Farm Pests of Pioneer Times," *Iowa Journal of History and Politics* 41, no. 2 (April 1943): 196, 199–201; Cyrus Carpenter, "The Grasshopper Invasion," *Annals of Iowa* 4, no. 6 (July 1900): 437–438, 441–445; H. C. Webb Reminiscence, 2–3, SHSI-IAC; Losee Preston, "Washtub over the Sun," 8–9.

35. Louis Bernard Schmidt, "Early Agricultural Societies," *Palimpsest* 31, no. 4 (April 1950): 120–125; Mildred Throne, "The Grange in Iowa, 1868–1875," *Iowa Journal of History* 47, no. 4 (October 1949): 289–293; W. A. Anderson, "The Granger Movement in the Middle West with Special Reference to Iowa," *Iowa Journal of History and Politics* 22, no. 1 (January 1924): 5–6.

36. Louis Bernard Schmidt, "The National Grange," *Palimpsest* 31, no. 4 (April 1950): 126–134; Throne, "Grange in Iowa," 298–299, 305–308, 312; E. Brownell, "History of the Grange," Madison County, SHSI-IAC; Richard White, *The Republic for Which It Stands: The United States During Reconstruction and the Gilded Age, 1865–1896* (New York: Oxford University Press, 2017), 257–258; Newton B. Ashby, *The Ashbys in Iowa: A Family History and Story of Pioneer Life* (Tucson: n.p, 1925), 42–43; Richard White, *Railroaded: The Transcontinentals and the Making of Modern America* (New York: W. W. Norton, 2011), 110–111; Earle D. Ross, *Iowa Agriculture: An Historical Survey* (Iowa City: State Historical Society of Iowa, 1951), 97–101. The quote is from White's *Railroaded*.

37. Mildred Throne, "The Anti-Monopoly Party in Iowa, 1873–1874," *Iowa Journal of History* 52, no. 4 (October 1954): 292–297, 308–313, 317, 323–326; Throne, "Grange in Iowa," 312–320; Fred A. Shannon, *The Farmer's Last Frontier: Agriculture, 1860–1897* (New York: Harper Torchbooks, 1945), 176–178; Wall, *Iowa*, 160–163; Ross, *Iowa Agriculture*, 100–103; White, *Railroaded*, 5; Charles Aldrich, "The Repeal of the Granger Law in Iowa," *Iowa Journal of History and Politics* 3, no. 2 (April 1905): 256–257, 260–261, 265. Aldrich's article explains the arrogant attitude of Iowa railroad companies. Sources provide different numbers of senate seats that the Anti-Monopolist forces won. The author is using Throne's here. She wrote the best article on the topic.

38. Ross, *Iowa Agriculture*, 102–106; H. W. Brands, *American Colossus: The*

Triumph of Capitalism, 1865–1900 (New York: Random House, 2010), 481–483; Myrtle Beinhauer, "Development of the Grange in Iowa, 1868–1930," *Annals of Iowa* 34, no. 8 (Spring 1959): 616–617.

39. Jeffrey Ostler, *Prairie Populism: The Fate of Agrarian Radicalism in Kansas, Nebraska, and Iowa, 1880–1892* (Lawrence: University Press of Kansas, 1993), 6–11, 132–135, 147–148, 152–153; Jonathan Levy, *Ages of American Capitalism: A History of the United States* (New York: Random House, 2021), 300–310; White, *Republic for Which It Stands*, 749–755.

40. Sage, *History of Iowa*, 310.

CHAPTER 7: RELIGION, EDUCATION, AND RURAL LIFE

1. Cyrenus Cole, *A History of the People of Iowa* (Cedar Rapids: Torch Press, 1921), 181–184; R. E. Harvey, "Faith and Works in the Black Hawk Purchase," *Annals of Iowa* 21, no. 4 (Spring 1938): 243–244.

2. Robert P. Swierenga, "The Little White Church: Religion in Rural America," *Agricultural History* 71, no. 4 (Autumn 1997): 417–419; Frederick J. Kuhns, "Religion on the Iowa Frontier in 1846," *Iowa Journal of History* 51, no. 1 (January 1953): 45. The first purpose-built mosque in Iowa, the "Mother Mosque," was built in Cedar Rapids in the 1930s. See chapter 10 for information on Muslim immigration to the state in the early twentieth century.

3. William J. Petersen, *The Story of Iowa: The Progress of an American State*, vol. 2 (New York: Lewis Historical, 1952), 661–667; Thomas Auge, "The Priest behind the Legends: Father John Alleman," *Palimpsest* 74, no. 2 (Summer 1993): 89; M. M. Hoffman, "Iowa's Early Catholic History," *Palimpsest* 34, no. 8 (August 1953): 342; B. E. Mahan, "The Abbey in Iowa," *Palimpsest* 42, no. 3 (March 1961): 116–120; B. E. Mahan, "The Life of the Trappists," *Palimpsest* 42, no. 3 (March 1961): 122–124; New Melleray Abbey website, accessed September 19, 2022, https://newmelleray.org.

4. Michael J. Pfeifer, "The Making of Midwestern Catholicism: Identities, Ethnicity, and Catholic Culture in Iowa City, 1840–1940," *Annals of Iowa* 76, no. 3 (Summer 2017): 291–293, 305; M. M. Hoffman, "The Diocesan Pattern in Iowa," *Palimpsest* 34, no. 8 (August 1953): 378, 382; Joseph Frazier Wall, *Iowa: A History* (New York: W. W. Norton, 1978), 137–138. Bishop Mathias Loras helped attract Catholic immigrants to Iowa. See Thomas E. Auge, "The Dream of Bishop Loras: A Catholic Iowa," *Palimpsest* 61, no. 6 (November–December 1980): 170–179. Iowa was not a majority Catholic state but Dubuque County, where Loras was bishop, had a Catholic majority population.

5. Ruth A. Gallaher, "Meet the Methodists," *Palimpsest* 32, no. 2 (February 1951): 59, 64; Wall, *Iowa*, 67–68; Ruth A. Gallaher, "The Circuit Riders," *Palimpsest* 32, no. 3 (February 1951): 75–76; Petersen, *Story of Iowa*, vol. 2, 668–671; Rev. W. Avery Richards, "Early Methodism in Northwest Iowa," *Iowa Historical Record*, 11, no. 3 (July 1895): 299–300, 304.

6. O. J. Felton, "Pioneer Life in Jones County," *Iowa Journal of History and Politics* 29, no. 2 (April 1931): 233–235, 255–259.

7. Ruth A. Gallaher, "Faith and Doctrine," *Palimpsest* 32, no. 3 (February 1951): 96–97; Henry A. Miller, "Methodist Revival Meeting: Remembering a Boyhood Experience in 1865," *Palimpsest* 71, no. 1 (Spring 1990): 12–15; Wall, *Iowa*, 72; Arleen Troester, "History of Colesburg, Iowa," *Annals of Iowa* 39, no. 6 (Fall 1968): 466.

8. Ruth A. Gallaher, "The Iowa Band," *Palimpsest* 11, no. 8 (August 1930): 355–364; Petersen, *Story of Iowa*, vol. 2, 679–683; Wall, *Iowa*, 68–69. Grinnell himself was not a member of the Iowa band that arrived in 1843.

9. Wall, *Iowa*, 70–71; Phillip D. Jordan, ed., "William Salter's Letters to Mary Ann Mackintire, 1845–1846," *Annals of Iowa* 24, no. 3 (Winter 1943): 116–119, 124, 128–130, 136, 140, 143–144, 179.

10. Ruth A. Gallaher, "The Inner Light," *Palimpsest* 9, no. 7 (July 1928): 235–237; J. A. Swisher, "Beginnings of Salem," *Palimpsest* 21, no. 5 (May 1940): 140–141; Louis T. Jones, *The Quakers of Iowa* (Iowa City: State Historical Society of Iowa, 1914), 38–41; Louis T. Jones, "The Coming of the Quakers," *Palimpsest* 9, no. 7 (July 1928): 228; https://quaker.org, accessed January 25, 2022; Thomas D. Hamm, *The Transformation of American Quakerism, Orthodox Friends, 1800–1907* (Bloomington: Indiana University Press, 1988), 2–10.

11. Jones, "Coming of the Quakers," 229–232; Jones, *Quakers*, 41–52, 57, 69, 74, 88.

12. Marie Haefner, "Called to Iowa," *Palimpsest* 15, no. 6 (June 1934): 193–195, 206; Frederick I. Kuhns, "Pitching Camp in Iowaland," *Palimpsest* 36, no. 9 (September 1955): 338–339, 343; Frederick I. Kuhns, "Baptist Numbers Climb," *Palimpsest* 36, no. 9 (September 1955): 346–349; Wall, *Iowa*, 72; Kuhns, "Religion on the Iowa Frontier," 43; Sarah Fisher Henderson et al., "Correspondence of the Reverend Ezra Fisher: Pioneer Missionary of the American Baptist Home Mission Society in Indiana, Illinois, Iowa and Oregon," *Quarterly of the Oregon Historical Society* 16, no. 1 (March 1915): 68–74, 90.

13. Dorothy Schwieder, *Iowa: The Middle Land* (Ames: Iowa State University, 1996), 115; Petersen, *Story of Iowa*, vol. 2, 701; Wall, *Iowa*, 72.

14. Kenneth W. Porter, ed., "A Little Girl on an Iowa Forty, 1873–1880—Catharine Wiggins Porter," *Iowa Journal of History* 51, no. 2 (April 1953): 133–137, 152–154; Petersen, *Story of Iowa*, vol. 2, 705; Frederick I. Kuhns, "Varieties in Iowa," *Palimpsest* 33, no. 4 (April 1952): 114; Kenneth W. Porter, ed., "School Days in Coin, Iowa, 1880–1885," *Iowa Journal of History* 51, no. 4 (October 1953): 324.

15. Lois A. McIntosh, "Biography of a Church," *Palimpsest* 29, no. 5 (May 1948): 129–137; L. C. Wuerffel, "Circuit Riders in Iowa," *Palimpsest* 29, no. 11 (November 1948): 325–330; Petersen, *Story of Iowa*, vol. 2, 718–719; A. B. Leamer, "The English Lutheran Church in Iowa," *Annals of Iowa* 11, no. 8 (January 1915): 586–589; N. G. Peterson, "The Danish and Lutherans in Iowa," *Annals of Iowa* 11, no. 8 (January 1915): 589. For more on the variety of Lutheran groups in the United States and Midwest, often divided by ethnicity or theological differences, see Mark Granquist, *Lutherans in America: A New History* (Minneapolis: Fortress Press, 2015).

16. Eva Jane Price, *China Journal, 1889–1900: An American Missionary Family*

during the Boxer Rebellion (New York: Charles Scribner's Sons, 1989), xx–xxi, 59, 67, 70–72, 90–95, 101, 147, 213, 239.

17. Sarah Pike Conger, *Letters from China with Particular Reference to the Empress Dowager and the Women of China* (Chicago: A. C. McClurg, 1909), 113, 124, 133; Grant Hayter-Menzies, *The Empress and Mrs. Conger: The Uncommon Friendship of Two Women and Two Worlds* (Hong Kong: Hong Kong University Press, 2011), 1–3, 9, 11–18, 173–174, 209–210, 224–225, 257–258, 264, 277.

18. Petersen, *Story of Iowa*, vol. 2, 745–746; Shari Rabin, "'A Nest to the Wandering Bird': Iowa and the Creation of American Judaism, 1855–1877," *Annals of Iowa* 73, no. 2 (Spring 2014): 101–108, 118; Michael J. Bell, "'True Israelites of America': The Story of the Jews of Iowa," *Annals of Iowa* 53, no. 2 (Spring 1994): 85–97, 105–109; Glenda Elizabeth Gilmore and Thomas J. Sugrue, *These United States: A Nation in the Making, 1890 to the Present* (New York: W. W. Norton, 2015), 17.

19. Frances E. Hawthorne, "The Church," in *Outside In: African American History in Iowa, 1838–2000*, ed. Bill Silag, Susan Koch-Bridgford, and Hal Chase (Des Moines: State Historical Society of Iowa, 2001), 387–394.

20. Clarence Ray Aurner, *History of Education in Iowa*, vol. 1 (Iowa City: State Historical Society of Iowa, 1914), 4–5, 281–284; Carl F. Kaestle, *Pillars of the Republic: Common Schools and American Society, 1780–1860* (New York: Hill and Wang, 1983), ix–x; Orville Francis Grahame, "The First Iowa School," *Palimpsest* 5, no. 11 (November 1924): 402–406.

21. Michael P. Harker, "Iowa's One-Room Schoolhouses," in Harker, *Harker's One-Room Schoolhouses: Visions of an Iowa Icon* (Iowa City: University of Iowa Press, 2008), 1; Aurner, *History of Education in Iowa*, vol. 1, 5, 27–28, 281–294; "The Sod-Covered Schoolhouse," *Annals of Iowa* 7, no. 8 (1907): 634–635.

22. Aurner, *History of Education*, vol. 1, 48–52; Keach Johnson, "Elementary and Secondary Education in Iowa, 1890–1900: A Time of Awakening," *Annals of Iowa* 45, no. 2 (Fall 1979): 90–94.

23. J. A. Swisher, "Public School Beginnings," *Palimpsest* 20, no. 9 (September 1939): 284; Johann N. Neem, *Democracy's Schools: The Rise of Public Education in America* (Baltimore: Johns Hopkins University Press, 2017), 172–175; Schwieder, *Middle Land*, 118; Wayne E. Fuller, *The Old Country School: The Story of Rural Education in the Middle West* (Chicago: University of Chicago Press, 1982), 32–33, 39, 226; Aurner, *History of Education*, vol. 1, 31–32.

24. Fuller, *Old Country School*, 26–29, 41, 129–131, 191; Aurner, *History of Education*, vol. 1, 43, 61, 73; Leland L. Sage, *A History of Iowa* (Ames: Iowa State University Press, 1974), 310; Keach Johnson, "Iowa's Industrial Roots, 1890–1910," *Annals of Iowa* 44, no. 3 (Winter 1978): 184.

25. Fuller, *Old Country School*, 47, 187–190; Elliott West, *Growing Up with the Country: Childhood on the Far Western Frontier* (Albuquerque: University of New Mexico Press, 1989), 189, 196; Hugh Orchard, *Old Orchard Farm* (Ames: Iowa State University Press, 1952), 48–49; Carl Hamilton, *In No Time at All* (Ames: Iowa State University Press, 1974), 134; Paul Theobald, *Call School: Rural Education in the*

Midwest to 1918 (Carbondale: Southern Illinois Press, 1995), 118–119. Orchard went to school in Iowa in the 1880s.

26. Theobald, *Call School*, 102–106; H. E. Wilkinson, *Memories of an Iowa Farm Boy* (Ames: Iowa State University Press, 1952), 32; Sarah Gillespie Huftalen, "School Days of the Seventies," *Palimpsest* 28, no. 4 (April 1947): 124; Amelia Murdock Wing, "Early Days in Clayton County," *Annals of Iowa* 27, no. 4 (April 1946): 276.

27. George W. Clarke, "Pages from Bygone Days in and about Drakeville, Iowa," *Annals of Iowa* 14, no. 5 (July 1924): 339; Eugene Hostic, "The Early History of Perry, Iowa," *Annals of Iowa* 40, no. 5 (July 1970): 384; Theobald, *Call School*, 106–117; Fuller, *Country School*, 72–73, 187–190; Carl E. Seashore, "The District School," *Palimpsest* 23, no. 3 (March 1942): 99–103; Rosa Schreurs Jennings, "The Country Teacher," *Annals of Iowa* 31, no. 1 (July 1951): 45; Rae McGrady Booth, "Memoirs of an Iowa Farm Girl," *Annals of Iowa* 38, no. 6 (Fall 1966): 469.

28. Seashore, "District School," 99–105; Carl E. Seashore, "Pioneering in Iowa," *Palimpsest* 22, no. 6 (June 1941): 180–183; Walter R. Miles, *Carl Emil Seashore, 1866–1949: A Biographical Memoir* (Washington, DC: National Academy of Sciences, 1956), 265–270.

29. Civil War Diary of Celestia Lee Barker, November 30, 1863, Iowa State University Special Collections and University Archives, Iowa State University, Ames, Iowa; Suzanne L. Bunkers, ed., *"All Will Yet Be Well: The Diary of Sarah Gillespie Huftalen, 1873–1952* (Iowa City: University of Iowa Press, 1993), 71; Mary Hurlbut Cordier, *Schoolwomen of the Prairies and Plains: Personal Narratives from Iowa, Kansas, and Nebraska, 1860s to 1920s* (Albuquerque: University of New Mexico Press, 1992), 78–82, 209–210, 229–232; Paul Theobald, *Call School*, 134–137; Cornelia Mallett Barnhart, "Phoebe W. Sudlow," *Palimpsest* 38, no. 4 (April 1957): 169–173.

30. Glenda Riley, *The Female Frontier: A Comparative View of Women on the Prairie and the Plains* (Lawrence: University Press of Kansas, 1988), 103–105; Jennings, "Country Teacher," 55; Thomas Morain, "The Departure of Males from the Teaching Profession in Nineteenth-Century Iowa," *Civil War History* 26, no. 2 (June 1980): 161–170; Cordier, *Schoolwomen*, 79; Agnes Briggs Olmstead, "Recollections of a Pioneer Teacher of Hamilton County," *Annals of Iowa* 28, no. 2 (Fall 1946): 93–97; B. F. Gue, "Early Iowa Reminiscences," *Iowa Historical Record* 16, no. 3 (July 1900): 110–111.

31. Floy Lawrence Emhoff, "A Pioneer School Teacher in Central Iowa," *Iowa Journal of History and Politics* 33, no. 4 (October 1935): 376–380, 384–385, 391. In 1909 Elizabeth Corey left Iowa to homestead in South Dakota. She worked as a teacher, living near Pierre, the state capital. Corey never married and taught for more than forty years, dying in 1954 in South Dakota. See Phillip L. Gerber, *Bachelor Bess: The Homesteading Letters of Elizabeth Corey, 1909–1919* (Iowa City: University of Iowa Press, 1990), xxxvi–li, lxviii, 390–391.

32. Emhoff, "Pioneer School Teacher," 392–395.

33. Richard M. Breaux, "'We Were All Mixed Together': Race, Schooling, and the Legacy of Black Teachers in Buxton, 1900–1920," *Annals of Iowa* 65, no. 4 (Fall 2006): 301–302, 308–311.

34. Breaux, "'We Were All Mixed Together,'" 309–311, 316, 319–328.

35. Harriet Connor Brown, "Schoolday Memories," *Palimpsest* 30, no. 4 (April 1949): 114; Harriet Connor Brown, "Harriet Connor Brown," *Palimpsest* 30, no. 4 (April 1949): 135–136; Clarke, "Bygone Days," 339, Theobald, *Call School*, 116; Cordier, *Schoolwomen*, 113; Huftalen, "School Days," 127–128; Porter, "Little Girl on an Iowa Forty," 149–151; Jennings, "Country Teacher," 48; Breaux, "'We Were All Mixed Together,'" 320.

36. Schwieder, *Middle Land*, 120–122; Sage, *History of Iowa*, 310.

37. Schwieder, *Middle Land*, 121–122; J. A. Swisher, "The High School," *Palimpsest* 16, no. 5 (May 1935): 158–164; Robert E. Belding, "Academies and Iowa's Frontier Life," *Annals of Iowa* 44, no. 5 (Summer 1978): 335–336, 355; Keach Johnson, "The State of Elementary and Secondary Education in Iowa in 1900," *Annals of Iowa* 49, no. 1 (Summer 1987): 29–30; Keach Johnson, "Elementary and Secondary Education in Iowa, 1890–1900: A Time of Awakening, Part II," *Annals of Iowa* 45, no. 3 (Winter 1980): 190; Elsie Boddicker Schallau, "My Life in the 20th Century: The Autobiography of Elsie Boddicker Schallau, 1913–1997," 16–17, Elsie Boddicker Schallau Papers, Iowa Women's Archives, University of Iowa Libraries, Iowa City (IWA).

38. Johnson, "State of Elementary and Secondary Education in Iowa," 28–36, 47–48; Schwieder, *Middle Land*, 121; Johnson, "Elementary and Secondary Education in Iowa, Part 2," 172–173. Johnson's 1980 article explains the limitations of rural schools.

39. Schwieder, *Middle Land*, 125–127; Stow Persons, *The University of Iowa in the Twentieth Century: An Institutional History* (Iowa City: University of Iowa Press, 1990), 3; Wall, *Iowa*, 192; Doris Malkmus, "Origins of Coeducation in Antebellum Iowa," *Annals of Iowa* 58, no. 2 (Spring 1999): 168–169, 175; "Once Upon a Cliff," Briar Cliff University, accessed January 21, 2022, https://www.briarcliff.edu/about/our-story/history.

40. R. Douglas Hurt, *American Agriculture: A Brief History* (West Lafayette, IN: Purdue University Press, 2002), 253–254; Hal S. Chase, "'You Live What Your Learn:' The African-American Presence in Iowa Education, 1839–2000," in *Outside In*, 140–141.

41. Sage, *History of Iowa*, 105–107; Petersen, *Story of Iowa*, vol. 2, 883–890. The Grinnell website states that the school's Board of Trustees was established in 1846. Two years later a one-room school opened in Davenport. College classes began in 1850. There are minor factual differences between Sage and the Grinnell College website, so most of this history comes from the school's brief online history. See "Grinnell College, a History," Grinnell College, accessed October 24, 2022, https://www.grinnell.edu/about/tradition/history. See Measuring Worth website at https://measuringworth.com. The starting date here for comparison is 1881.

42. Persons, *University of Iowa*, 1–12, 17; Wall, *Iowa*, 189–192; Robert E. Belding, "Iowa's Brave Model for Women's Education," *Annals of Iowa* 43, no. 5 (Summer 1976): 342–344. For a detailed history of the university in the 1800s, on everything from buildings to faculty, see J. L. Pickard, "Historical Sketch of the State University of Iowa," *Annals of Iowa* 4, no. 1 (1899): 1–66.

43. Persons, *University of Iowa*, 8–11. See Measuring Worth. The starting date here for comparison is 1890.

44. Pamela Riney-Kehrberg, "Foundations of the People's College: The Early Years of Iowa State," in *A Sesquicentennial History of Iowa State University: Tradition and Transformation*, ed. Dorothy Schwieder and Gretchen Van Houten (Ames: Iowa State University Press, 2007), xv, 11–14, 21–22.

45. Riney-Kehrberg, "Foundations of the People's College," 14–16.

46. Petersen, *Story of Iowa*, vol. 2, 909–910; D. Sands Wright, "Founding the Normal School," *Palimpsest* 13, no. 1 (January 1932): 1–5; D. Sands Wright, "The First Decade," *Palimpsest* 13, no. 1 (January 1932): 17–21; John Ely Briggs, "David Sands Wright," *Palimpsest* 13, no. 1 (January 1932): 36; Schwieder, *Middle Land*, 120, 130–131.

47. Wall, *Iowa*, 127, 137–139; Riney-Kehrberg, "Foundations of the People's College," 12; W. F. Main, "Mason City in Retrospect," *Palimpsest* 29, no. 12 (December 1948): 362–364, 367; State Data Center, "Iowa Quick Facts," accessed June 27, 2020, https://www.iowadatacenter.org/quickfacts.

48. Orchard, *Old Orchard Farm*, 226–229. For more on the lives of children in the late nineteenth and early twentieth centuries see Pamela Riney-Kehrberg, *Childhood on the Farm: Work, Play, and Coming of Age in the Midwest* (Lawrence: University Press of Kansas, 2005).

49. Allan G. Bogue, "Twenty Years of an Iowa Farm Business, 1860–1880," *Annals of Iowa* 35, no. 8 (Spring 1961): 577; Clifford Merrill Drury, "Growing Up on an Iowa Farm, 1897–1915," *Annals of Iowa* 42, no. 3 (Winter 1974): 162, 168–175, 182–185. Drury was a minister in China in the 1920s and earned a PhD in church history in Scotland.

50. Valerie Grim, "African-Americans in Iowa Agriculture," in *Outside In*, 169–177, 180. By the 1990s only thirty-three African American families owned farms in Iowa.

51. Ada Mae Brown Brinton, "In Sunshine and Rain in Iowa: Reminiscing through 86 Years," Ada Mae Brown Brinton Memoir, 19–23, IWA. Also see Glenda Riley, ed., "Eighty-Six Years in Iowa: The Memoir of Ada Mae Brown Brinton," *Annals of Iowa* 45, no. 7 (Winter 1981): 551–567.

52. Bruce E. Mahan, "Frontier Fun," *Palimpsest* 8, no. 1 (January 1927): 38–42.

53. Bessie C. Thompson, *I Remember, I Remember*, 1–3, SHSI-IAC. She wrote this memoir, which is a six-page pamphlet, in 1954. Thompson taught for more than thirty years, but when she had to give it up when she became sick in her fifties, it was "a blow." She started teaching in 1901 for $28 a month.

54. Mahan, "Frontier Fun," 39; H. Arnold Bennett, "The Great Snake Hunt," *Palimpsest* 9, no. 9 (September 1928): 334–337; Main, "Mason City," 365–366; Matilda Paul Memoir, 17, SHSI-IAC.

55. Mahan, "Frontier Fun," 38–41; Henry W. Wright, "Iowa—As I Knew It," *Annals of Iowa* 29, no. 5 (Summer 1948): 384–385.

56. Main, "Mason City," 366; Mahan, "Frontier Fun," 41–42; Charles Aldrich, "The Fourth at Webster City," *Palimpsest* 16, no. 7 (July 1935): 226–230; Bruce A.

Mahan, "Fourth of July in 1860," *Palimpsest* 7, no. 7 (July 1926): 209–212; July 4, 1889, Mary's Diary, 1888–1890, Van Zante and De Cook Family Papers, IWA.

57. William J. Petersen, "Christmas in Iowa," *Palimpsest* 16, no. 12 (December 1935): 373–385; Jennie Beck, tape 2, transcripts of 1984 interview, "Her Own Story," Ten Benton County Iowa Women, box 2, IWA.

58. Bruce E. Mahan, "At the Opera House," *Palimpsest* 5, no. 11 (May 1924): 408–423; Jill Norgren, *Belva Lockwood: The Woman Who Would Be President* (New York: New York University Press, 2007), xiii; Edith Harper Ekdale, "The Grand Opera House," *Palimpsest* 28, no. 6 (June 1947): 184–190. For more on Iowa opera houses see George D. Glenn and Richard L. Poole, *The Opera Houses of Iowa* (Ames: Iowa State University Press, 1993).

59. Chris Rasmussen, *Carnival in the Countryside: The History of the Iowa State Fair* (Iowa City: University of Iowa Press, 2015), 1–9, 19, 23–26, 37–39, 169; Rasmussen, "'Fairs Here Have Become a Sort of Holiday:' Agriculture and Amusements at Iowa's County Fairs, 1838–1925," *Annals of Iowa* 58, no. 1 (Winter 1999): 1–2; "Iowa State Fair Attendance Records Crushed in 2019," Iowa State Fair, August 19, 2019, https://www.iowastatefair.org/media/news-releases/iowa-state-fair-attendance-records-crushed-in-2019; Rasmussen, "Looking Forward and Backward: The Iowa State Fair at the Close of the 19th Century," *Iowa Heritage Illustrated* 80, no. 4 (Winter 1999): 149–152.

60. Sara Egge, *Woman Suffrage and Citizenship in the Midwest, 1870–1920* (Iowa City: University of Iowa Press, 2018), 70–73; Karen M. Mason, "Women's Clubs in Iowa: An Introduction," *Annals of Iowa* 56, no. 1–2 (Winter–Spring 1997): 2–5, 10–11; Christine Pawley, "'Not Wholly Self Culture': The Shakespearean Women's Club, Osage, Iowa, 1892–1920," *Annals of Iowa* 56, no. 1–2 (Winter-Spring 1997): 14–16, 30; "Women's Organizations in Iowa: Selected Holdings in Major Iowa Repositories," *Annals of Iowa* 56, no. 1–2 (Winter–Spring 1997): 128–129, 133–134. The State Historical Society of Iowa in Iowa City has more than one hundred manuscript collections on woman's clubs from Iowa. Also see Marian Wilson Kimber, "Musical Iowana: Iowa Women's Clubs and the Promotion of Iowa Composers," *Annals of Iowa* 78, no. 4 (Fall 2019): 331–360.

61. Ralph Spencer, "The Red Oak Chautauqua Pavilion," *Annals of Iowa* 41, no. 8 (Spring 1973): 1273–1277; Harrison John Thornton, "Chautauqua in Iowa," *Iowa Journal of History* 50, no. 2 (April 1952): 97–98, 116–120; Melvin Gingerich, "The Washington Chautauqua," *Palimpsest* 26, no. 12 (December 1945): 370–376. Thornton's article is the best brief overview of the Chautauqua movement.

62. Erik McKinley Eriksson, "Baseball Beginnings," *Palimpsest* 8, no. 10 (October 1927): 329–335; Carl B. Cone, "Baseball and Telephony," *Palimpsest* 24, no. 8 (August 1943): 248–252; David McMahon, "Adrian Constantine 'Cap' Anson," in *The Biographical Dictionary of Iowa*, ed. David Hudson, Marvin Bergman, and Loren Horton (Iowa City: University of Iowa Press, 2008), 19–20; John Liepa, "Baseball Mania Strikes Iowa," *Iowa Heritage Illustrated* 87, no. 1 (Spring 2006): 3–5; Ginalie Swaim, "Iowa Women in Baseball," *Iowa Heritage Illustrated* 87, no. 1 (Spring 2006): 8–10.

63. Jon K. Lauck, "Soft, Democratic, and Universalist: In Search of the Main Currents of Traditional Midwestern Identity and a Grand Historiographic Synthesis," *Middle West Review* 6, nos. 1–2 (Fall 2019–Spring 2020): 68–70.

CHAPTER 8: CITIES, INDUSTRY, AND TECHNOLOGY, 1833–1920

1. See "Total Population for Iowa's Incorporated Places: 1850–2000," Iowa Data Center, accessed February 27, 2023, https://www.iowadatacenter.org/datatables/PlacesAll/plpopulation18502000.pdf for information on the population of Iowa's incorporated places.

2. William Silag, "Gateway to the Grasslands: Sioux City and the Missouri River Frontier," *Western Historical Quarterly* 14, no. 4 (October 1983): 411–414; Dorothy Schwieder, *Black Diamonds: Life and Work in Iowa's Coal Mining Communities, 1895–1925* (Ames: Iowa State University Press, 1983), 67–68, 78; George Wesley Sieber, "Lumbermen at Clinton: Nineteenth Century Sawmill Center," *Annals of Iowa* 41, no. 2 (Fall 1971): 787–788; Wilson J. Warren, *Tied to the Great Packing Machine: The Midwest and Meatpacking* (Iowa City: University of Iowa Press, 2007), 3, 9, 17–19, 37, 39, 66–67; Sharon E. Wood, *The Freedom of the Streets: Work, Citizenship, and Sexuality in a Gilded Age City* (Chapel Hill: University of North Carolina Press, 2005), 10–13; Dorothy Schwieder, Joseph Hraba, and Elmer Schwieder, *Buxton: A Black Utopia in the Heartland* (Iowa City: University of Iowa Press, 2003), 22; Ralph Scharnau, "Workers, Unions, and Workplaces in Dubuque," *Annals of Iowa* 52, no. 1 (Winter 1993): 69–70.

3. "Early Manufacturing," *Goldfinch* 2, no. 2 (November 1980): 1–8; Lydia Belthuis, "The Lumber Industry in Eastern Iowa," *Iowa Journal of History and Politics* 46, no. 2 (April 1948): 117, 121, 124–126; Warren, *Great Packing Machine*, 9; William J. Petersen, "Business and Industry," *Palimpsest* 19, no. 4 (April 1938): 141.

4. "Early Manufacturing," 3–4; William J. Petersen, "Rafting on the Mississippi: Prologue to Prosperity," *Iowa Journal of History* 58, no. 4 (October 1960): 289–293, 298–301, 307; Belthuis, "Lumber Industry," 128–132, 136–137; George Bernhardt Hartman, "The Iowa Sawmill Industry," *Iowa Journal of History and Politics* 40, no. 1 (January 1942): 69–70, 73–75; Stewart H. Holbrook, *Holy Old Mackinaw: A Natural History of the American Lumberjack* (New York: Macmillan, 1938), 156–157.

5. Belthuis, "Lumber Industry," 140–146; Hartman, "Iowa Sawmill Industry," 54–56, 66–67, 71, 78–80. See Measuring Worth website, at https://measuringworth.com. Comparison start date is 1877.

6. Warren, *Great Packing Machine*, 1–3, 9–10, 18–20, 31; Lawrence O. Cheever, "Pork Packing Comes to Iowa," *Palimpsest* 47, no. 4 (April 1966): 146–149; *Semi-Centennial, 1871–1921* (n.p.: Cedar Rapids, 1921), source has no page numbers.

7. James H. Lees, "History of Coal Mining in Iowa," *Iowa Geological Survey*, vol. 19 (Des Moines: Iowa Geological Survey, 1909), 525–528, 531, 535; Morgan Thomas, "Pioneer Iowa Coal Operators," *Annals of Iowa* 33, no. 2 (Fall 1955): 118–119;

"History of Coal Mining in Iowa," *Annals of Iowa* 29, no. 1 (Summer 1947): 61; Iowa Writer's Program of the WPA, *Monroe County History, Iowa* (1940), SHSI-IAC, 58–59; Dorothy Schwieder, "Drawing the Personal Narrative into the Landscape of Iowa's Coal History," *Palimpsest* 74, no. 3 (Fall 1993): 127; Dorothy Schwieder, *Iowa: The Middle Land* (Ames: Iowa State University Press, 1996), 241. See Measuring Worth.

8. Thomas, "Pioneer Iowa Coal Operators," 120–126; J. P. Bushnell, *Iowa Resources and Industry* (Des Moines: J. P. Bushnell, 1885), 72–75; Lees, "History of Coal Mining in Iowa," 534, 551; Jacob Swisher, "Mining in Iowa," *Iowa Journal of History and Politics* 43, no. 4 (October 1945): 312–318.

9. Edith Gallo Widmer Blake, "An Italian-American Girlhood in Iowa's Coal Country," *Palimpsest* 74, no. 3 (Fall 1993): 119–126; Schwieder, "Personal Narrative," 127–128. See Measuring Worth. 1900 is the start date for comparison here.

10. Schwieder, "Iowa's Coal History," 129; Harry Booth, "'You Got to Go Ahead and Get Killed:' Lost Creek Remembered," *Palimpsest* 71, no. 3 (Fall 1990): 118–123; Merle Davis, "Horror at Lost Creek: A 1902 Coal Mine Disaster," *Palimpsest* 71, no. 3 (Fall 1990): 99–102, 109–113.

11. Schwieder, Hraba, and Schwieder, *Buxton*, vii–viii; 3–10, 42–45, 210–222.

12. Schwieder, *Black Diamonds*, 3–4, 159, 168–170.

13. Frances Schreurs Hurd, "The Pearl Button Industry of Muscatine, Iowa," *Annals of Iowa* 38, no. 6 (Fall 1966): 401–411; "Early Manufacturing," 11–13; O. D. Langstreth, *Pearl Button Industry in Iowa, 1906*, 4–7, 44–51, SHSI-IAC; Marie Haefner, "Argonauts of the Mississippi," *Palimpsest* 13, no. 12 (December 1932): 474–475. See Measuring Worth. 1890 is the starting date for the price comparison here.

14. Hurd, "Pearl Button Industry," 401–406, 410; Haefner, "Argonauts of the Mississippi," 474–480, 482–485; Kate Rousmaniere, "The Muscatine Button Workers' Strike of 1911–1912," *Annals of Iowa* 46, no. 4 (Spring 1982): 243–261. See Measuring Worth. The starting date here for the price comparison is 1900.

15. Iowa City Board of Trade, *Sketch of Johnson County, Iowa* (Iowa City: Republic Steam Printing, 1880), 15–17, 23; Silag, "Gateway to the Grasslands," 409–414.

16. Scharnau, "Workers, Unions, and Workplaces in Dubuque," 50–62.

17. Keach Johnson, "Iowa's Industrial Roots, 1890–1910," *Annals of Iowa* 44, no. 3 (Winter 1978): 165–182; Keach Johnson, "Iowa's Industrial Roots: Some Social and Political Problems," *Annals of Iowa* 44, no. 4 (Spring 1978): 248–249; Patrick Nunnally, "From Churns to 'Butter Factories:' The Industrialization of Iowa's Dairying," *Annals of Iowa* 49, no. 7 (Winter 1989): 555–569.

18. Johnson, "Iowa's Industrial Roots: Some Social and Political Problems," 262–271; E. H. Downey, *History of Work Accident Indemnity in Iowa* (Iowa City: State Historical Society of Iowa, 1912), 5–10. Brigham quoted in Johnson's article.

19. Shelton Stromquist, *Solidarity and Survival: An Oral History of Iowa Labor in the Twentieth Century* (Iowa City: University of Iowa Press, 1993), 4–8.

20. Schwieder, *Black Diamonds*, 130–156.

21. Roger Horowitz, "'It Wasn't a Time to Compromise:' The Unionization of Sioux City's Packinghouses, 1937–1942," *Annals of Iowa* 50, nos. 2–3 (Fall 1989–Winter 1990): 241–242; Stromquist, *Solidarity and Survival*, 5–9, 42–43, 81.

22. Jennie McCowen, "Women in Iowa," *Annals of Iowa* 3, no. 4 (October 1884): 97–103, 107–108; Sharon E. Wood, "Jennie C. McCowen," in *The Biographical Dictionary of Iowa*, ed. David Hudson, Marvin Bergman, and Loren Horton (Iowa City: University of Iowa Press, 2008), 351–352; Linda E. Speth, "The Married Women's Property Acts, 1839–1865, Reform, Reaction, or Revolution?" in *The Law of Sex Discrimination*, ed. J. Ralph Lindgren, Nadine Taub, Beth Anne Wolfson, and Carla M. Palumbo (Belmont, CA: Wadsworth, 2005), 15–17. See Measuring Worth. 1884 is the start date for the price comparison here.

23. Howard J. Nelson, "The Economic Development of Des Moines," *Iowa Journal of History* 48, no. 3 (July 1950): 206; William C. Page and Leah D. Rogers, *Walking to Work: Victorian Life in Des Moines*, SHSI-IAC; T. I. Stoner, *In My Time* (Des Moines: Advertiser's Press, 1948), 97–100; McCowen, "Women in Iowa," 98–99. See Measuring Worth. Starting date for comparison is 1890.

24. Robert J. Gordon, *The Rise and Fall of American Growth: The U.S. Standard of Living Since the Civil War* (Princeton: Princeton University Press, 2016), 68, 73–74, 81–84, 90–91; Thomas J. Schlereth, *Victorian America: Transformations in Everyday Life, 1876–1915* (New York: HarperPerrenial, 1991), 141–147, 149, 153, 163–164.

25. Lawrence H. Larsen, "Urban Iowa One Hundred Years Ago," *Annals of Iowa* 49, no. 6 (Fall 1988): 452–456, 461; Page and Rogers, *Walking to Work*; Heather Cox Richardson, *West from Appomattox: The Reconstruction of America after the Civil War* (New Haven: Yale University Press, 2007), 97–98; Gladys Trimble, "Stories Told by Gladys," Trimble Family Papers, Iowa Women's Archives, University of Iowa Libraries (IWA). Three of thirteen children in the Trimble family, who lived in rural northwest Iowa, likely much healthier than Iowa's cities, died from pneumonia or diphtheria in the early 1900s. The amount of horse manure and urine is for a city of twelve thousand. The amount of pollution would have increased as the city's population grew and the number of horses increased later in the nineteenth century. See Larsen, 453.

26. Larsen, "Urban Iowa," 456–457.

27. Larsen, "Urban Iowa," 458–461; Douglas Wertsch, "The Evolution of the Des Moines Police Department: Professionalization and the Decline of Public Disorder Arrests in the Twentieth Century," *Annals of Iowa* 48, no. 7 (Winter 1987): 437–442; Maureen Ogle, "Efficiency and System in Municipal Services: Fire Departments in Iowa, 1870–1890," *Annals of Iowa* 50, no. 8 (Spring 1991): 841, 845–848, 853–859.

28. Page and Rogers, *Walking to Work*; W. F. McGlothlen, "Des Moines Streetcars," *Annals of Iowa* 33, no. 2 (Fall 1955): 223–227; see "Total Population for Iowa's Incorporated Places" for information on the population of Iowa's cities and towns; Larsen, "Urban Iowa," 460–461.

29. William L. Hewitt, "Wicked Traffic in Girls: Prostitution and Reform in Sioux City, 1885–1910," *Annals of Iowa* 51, no. 2 (Fall 1991): 123–125, 128–133, 136, 138–142, 148; David Dary, *Seeking Pleasure in the Old West* (Lawrence: University Press of Kansas, 1995), 212–213; Anne M. Butler, *Daughters of Joy, Sisters of Misery: Prostitutes in the American West, 1865–1890* (Urbana: University of Illinois Press, 1987), 16, 51, 61, 67–68.

30. Wood, *Freedom of the Streets*, 7–12, 24–25, 34–39, 45, 79–87, 122–124, 138, 159, 166–168, 184–188, 203, 212–214. For a fine history of a neglected topic see Daniel Sunne, "Abortion in Iowa in the Nineteenth Century" (master's thesis, Iowa State University, 2022).

31. Jack Lufkin, "'Higher Expectations for Ourselves:' African-Americans in Iowa's Business World," in *Outside In: African-American History in Iowa, 1838–2000*, ed. Bill Silag, Susan Koch-Bridgford, and Hal Chase (Des Moines: State Historical Society of Iowa, 2001), 193–195.

32. Marjorie Levine, "'A Kind of Human Machine:' Women's Work at the Switchboard," *Palimpsest* 74, no. 1 (Spring 1993): 3; Carl B. Cone, "Hello Central," *Palimpsest* 24, no. 3 (March 1943): 73–80.

33. Levine, "'Kind of Human Machine,'" 2–13.

34. Vern Carpenter, "Making the Connection: The Story of a Small-Town Telephone Operator," *Palimpsest* 74, no. 1 (Spring 1993): 14–19; Levine, "'Kind of Human Machine,'" 2–5. See Measuring Worth. 1920 is the start date for this price comparison.

35. Alan Axelrod, "A Century of Light: The Development of Iowa's Electric Utilities," *Palimpsest* 60, no. 5 (September–October 1979): 130–139, 144; Mitchell Schmidt, "The Cost of Things: Why Energy Bills in Iowa Keep Growing," *Cedar Rapids Gazette*, July 14, 2019, https://www.thegazette.com/news/the-cost-of-things-why-energy-bills-in-iowa-keep-growing/. See Measuring Worth for price comparison.

36. Axelrod, "Century of Light," 144–146, 151–154; David E. Nye, *Electrifying America: Social Meanings of a New Technology* (Cambridge, MA: Massachusetts Institute of Technology Press, 1990), 381–391.

CHAPTER 9: SUFFRAGE, PROHIBITION, AND POLITICS, 1870–1920

1. Dorothy Schwieder, *Iowa: The Middle Land* (Ames: Iowa State University Press, 1996), 212–213.

2. Schwieder, *Middle Land*, 95–96, 214–215; Jerry Harrington, "Bottled Conflict: Keokuk and the Prohibition Question, 1888–1889," *Annals of Iowa* 46, no. 8 (April 1983): 594–595; Sharon E. Wood, *The Freedom of the Streets: Work, Citizenship, and Sexuality in a Gilded Age City* (Chapel Hill: University of North Carolina Press, 2005), 249; Frederick C. Luebke, *Bonds of Loyalty: German Americans and World War I* (Dekalb: Northern Illinois University Press, 1974), 59–61, 99.

3. George F. Parker, *Iowa Pioneer Foundations*, vol. 1 (Iowa City: State Historical Society of Iowa, 1940), 334–336; Daniel Okrent, *Last Call: The Rise and Fall of Prohibition* (New York: Scribner, 2010), 7–11; Jeff Bremer, *A Store Almost in Sight: The Economic Transformation of Missouri from the Louisiana Purchase to the Civil War* (Iowa City: University of Iowa Press, 2014), 85–86; Ruth A. Gallaher, "The Liquor Merry-Go-Round," *Palimpsest* 14, no. 6 (June 1933): 215.

4. Dan Elbert Clark, "The History of Liquor Legislation in Iowa, 1846–1861," *Iowa Journal of History and Politics* 6, no. 1 (January 1908): 55–82; Ballard C. Campbell,

"Did Democracy Work? Prohibition in Late Nineteenth-Century Iowa: a Test Case," *Journal of Interdisciplinary History* 8, no. 1 (Summer 1977): 88–89. An 1857 amendment to the 1855 law allowed for buying and selling intoxicating liquors for mechanical, medicinal, and other purposes, under certain circumstances.

5. M. M. Morris and E. E. Jack, "Early Handling of the Liquor Problem," *Annals of Iowa* 33, no. 4 (April 1956): 298.

6. Clark, "Liquor Legislation, 1846–1861," 82–87; Dan Elbert Clark, "The History of Liquor Legislation in Iowa, 1861–1878," *Iowa Journal of History and Politics* 6, no. 3 (July 1908): 339–344, 364, 372; Julie E. Nelson, "Liquor Legislation in Iowa," *Palimpsest* 62, no. 6 (November–December 1981): 190–191; Thomas S. Smith, "A Martyr for Prohibition: The Murder of Reverend George C. Haddock," *Palimpsest* 62, no. 6 (November-December 1981): 187–188; Ruth A. Gallaher, "The Liquor Merry-Go-Round," 221–222; Thomas G. Ryan, "Supporters and Opponents of Prohibition," *Annals of Iowa* 46, no. 7 (January 1983): 511; Campbell, "Did Democracy Work?," 89; Schwieder, *Middle Land*, 261.

7. Gallaher, "The Liquor Merry-Go-Round," 223–224.

8. Gallaher, "The Liquor Merry-Go-Round," 232; Campbell, "Did Democracy Work?," 89–90. Quote is from Campbell.

9. David C. Mott, "Judith Ellen Foster," *Annals of Iowa* 19, no. 2 (Fall 1933): 127–138.

10. Richard Jensen, "Iowa, Wet or Dry? Prohibition and the Fall of the GOP," in *Iowa History Reader*, ed. Marvin Bergman (Iowa City: University of Iowa Press, 2008), 271; Gallaher, "The Liquor Merry-Go-Round," 224–227; Adam Sullivan, "That Time a Drunken Mob of Iowans Threatened to Hang Prohibitionists," *Cedar Rapids Gazette*, March 9, 2020, https://www. thegazette.com/staff-columnists/that-time-a-drunken-mob-of-iowans-threatened-to-hang-prohibitionists/; Darcy Dougherty Maulsby, *A Culinary History of Iowa: Sweet Corn, Pork Tenderloins, Maid-Rites and More* (Charleston, SC: History Press, 2016), 137.

11. Harrington, "Bottled Conflict," 594; Leland L. Sage, *A History of Iowa* (Ames: Iowa State University Press, 1974), 209–213, 220; Thomas R. Ross, *Jonathan Prentiss Dolliver* (Iowa City: State Historical Society of Iowa, 1958), 65; Jensen, "Iowa, Wet or Dry?" 263.

12. Sara M. Evans, *Born for Liberty: A History of Women in America* (New York: Simon and Schuster, 1997), 126–131; Lisa Payne Ossian, "Iowa History Month: March toward Prohibition Paved Way for #MeToo," *Des Moines Register*, March 10, 2020, https://www.desmoinesregister. com/story/life/2020/ 03/10/iowa-history-month-march-toward-prohibition-paved-way-metoo/ 4933160002/.

13. Sara Egge, *Woman Suffrage and Citizenship in the Midwest, 1870–1920* (Iowa City: University of Iowa Press, 2018), 69–70, 85–89.

14. Smith, "Martyr for Prohibition," 187–193; Lynn Zerscling, "Sioux City's Prohibition Past Fascinates Historians," *Sioux City Journal*, October 2, 2011, https://siouxcityjournal.com/news/local/crime-and-courts/sioux-city-s-prohibition-past-fascinates-historians/article_f3c41279-0c0d-5c97-b98b-ffe9dde66e0a.html.

15. Gallaher, "Liquor Merry-Go-Round," 227–230; Campbell, "Did Democracy Work?" 90.

16. Gallaher, "Liquor Merry-Go-Round," 229–231; Daniel Okrent, *Last Call*, 1–2.

17. Evans, *Born for Liberty*, 94–95.

18. Cyrenus Cole, *A History of the People of Iowa* (Cedar Rapids: Torch Press, 1921), 456; Jean Florman, "Amelia Jenks Bloomer," in *The Biographical Dictionary of Iowa*, ed. David Hudson, Marvin Bergman, and Loren Horton (Iowa City: University of Iowa Press, 2008), 48; Ruth A. Gallaher, *Legal and Political Status of Women in Iowa: An Historical Account of the Rights of Women in Iowa from 1838 to 1918* (Iowa City: State Historical Society of Iowa, 1918), 176–179. Quote is from Gallaher.

19. Sara Egge, *Woman Suffrage*, 83–85; Cole, *History of the People of Iowa*, 456–457.

20. Gallaher, *Legal and Political Status of Women*, 179–181; Diana Pounds, "Suffragists, Free Love, and the Woman Question," *Palimpsest* 72, no. 1 (Spring 1991): 2–7.

21. Pounds, "Suffragists, Free Love, and the Woman Question," 4–10.

22. Gallaher, *Legal and Political Status*, 186–189, 198.

23. Gallaher, *Legal and Political Status*, 198–204; Louise R. Noun, *Strong-Minded Women: The Emergence of the Women-Suffrage Movement in Iowa* (Ames: Iowa State University Press, 1969), 231; John M. Witt, *The Carnegie Libraries of Iowa* (Washington, MO: Robidoux Books, 2003), x.

24. Evans, *Born for Liberty*, 165–166, Gallaher, *Legal and Political Status*, 212–220.

25. Florman, "Amelia Jenks Bloomer," *Biographical Dictionary of Iowa*, 47–49; Lorle Ann Porter, "Amelia Bloomer: An Early Iowa Feminist's Sojourn on the Way West," *Annals of Iowa* 41, no. 8 (Spring 1973): 1243–1246; D. C. Bloomer, ed., *Life and Writings of Amelia Bloomer* (Boston: Arena, 1895), 225–226, 229. Quote is from D. C. Bloomer's edited book.

26. Rachel Bohlmann, "Annie Nowlin Savery," *Biographical Dictionary of Iowa*, 438–440; "Annie N. Savery," *Annals of Iowa* 16, no. 6 (October 1928): 467–468; Louise Noun, "Annie Savery: A Voice for Women's Rights," *Annals of Iowa* 44, no. 1 (Summer 1977): 3–4, 9–11, 15–16, 28–30; Noun, *Strong-Minded Women*, 199–208.

27. Noun, *Strong-Minded Women*, 226–229; David McCartney, "Carrie Chapman Catt," in *The Biographical Dictionary of Iowa*, 79–80; Teresa Opheim, ed., "The Women's World: Carrie Lane Chapman in the Mason City Republican," *Palimpsest* 62, no. 5 (September-October 1981): 130–135.

28. Bohlmann, "Annie Nowlin Savery," 79–81; Noun, *Strong-Minded Women*, 227–244.

29. Egge, *Woman Suffrage*, 153–154, 158–165, 177–183; Evans, *Born for Liberty*, 170–172.

30. William L. Bowers, "The Fruits of Iowa Progressivism, 1900–1915," *Iowa Journal of History* 57, no. 1 (January 1959): 34–59; Sage, *History of Iowa*, 230–238; John D. Buenker, "Albert Baird Cummins," in *Biographical Dictionary of Iowa*, 111–113.

31. Loren N. Horton, "A Place in the Sun: Iowa Politics at the Turn of the Century," *Palimpsest* 64, no. 6 (November/December 1983): 188–199; Sage, *History of Iowa*, 219–222; Buenker, "Dolliver," 134–137; Nancy Lee, "James 'Tama Jim' Wilson," in *Biographical Dictionary of Iowa*, 561–563.

32. Rebecca Conard, "John Fletcher Lacey," in *Biographical Dictionary of Iowa*,

297–298; Rebecca Conard, "A Brief History of Iowa's State Park System," in Conard, *Iowa State Parks: A Century of Stewardship, 1920–2020* (Des Moines: Iowa Parks Foundation, 2020), 1–5; Conard, *Places of Quiet Beauty: Parks, Preserves, and Environmentalism* (Iowa City: University of Iowa Press, 1997), 26–27, 78–80. More than 150 natural, cultural, and historical sites have been preserved using this law. Herbert Hoover used it to help create Arches, Death Valley, and Saguaro National Parks, as well as add sections to Grand Canyon National Park. For a list of areas protected by the 1906 Antiquities Act see "Monuments Protected under the Antiquities Act," National Parks Conservation Association, accessed February 13, 2023, https://www.npca.org/resources/2658-monuments-protected-under-the-antiquities-act.

33. Paul Nienkamp, "Seaman Asahel Knapp," in *Biographical Dictionary of Iowa*, 290–291; Dorothy Schwieder, *75 Years of Service: Cooperative Extension in Iowa* (Ames: Iowa State University Press, 1993), 14–18, 30–31, 65, 75–78, 124; David B. Danbom, *Born in the Country: A History of Rural America* (Baltimore: Johns Hopkins University Press, 1995), 173–174. For more on extension see: "Quick Facts," Iowa State University Extension and Outreach, accessed April 19, 2023, https://www.extension.iastate.edu/our-story/content/quick-facts. See *Biographical Dictionary of Iowa*, page x–xi, for the complicated history of public college names.

34. Glenda Elizabeth Gilmore and Thomas J. Sugrue, *These United States: A Nation in the Making, 1890 to the Present* (New York: W. W. Norton, 2015), 62; Flora Dunlap, "Roadside Settlement of Des Moines," *Annals of Iowa* 21, no. 3 (January 1938): 161–164, 176; Karen M. Mason, "Flora Dunlap," in *Biographical Dictionary of Iowa*, 143–145.

35. "Jewish Community Center," *Annals of Iowa* 21, no. 3 (January 1938): 182–185; "Negro Community Center," *Annals of Iowa* 21, no. 3 (January 1938): 186–188; Mabel F. Hoyt, "History of Community House Sioux City, Iowa," *Annals of Iowa* 21, no. 3 (January 1938): 190–208; Schwieder, *Middle Land*, 181–182. See Suzanne O'Dea Schenken, "The Immigrants' Advocate: Mary Treglia and the Sioux City Community House, 1921–1959," *Annals of Iowa* 50, nos. 2–3 (Fall 1989–Winter 1990): 180–213, for a biography of the leader of the community house in Sioux City for almost forty years.

36. Wayne A. Wiegand, *Main Street Public Library: Community Places and Reading Spaces in the Rural Heartland, 1876–1956* (Iowa City: University of Iowa Press, 2011), 8–9, 54–57; Witt, *Carnegie Libraries of Iowa*, v–x, 3–7, 95–96; Paul Kruty, "Patton and Miller: Designers of Carnegie Libraries," *Palimpsest* 64, no. 4 (July 1983): 110–116; H. E. Wilkinson, *Memories of an Iowa Farm Boy* (Ames: Iowa State University Press, 1952), 186–189; Abigail Weaver, "Establishing an Institution: The Public Library Movement in Iowa, 1900–1920," *Iowa Historical Review* 7, no. 1 (2017): 7–8, 14–15. For more information on Carnegie Libraries in Iowa see: Carnegie Libraries in Iowa Project, accessed September 16, 2020, https://www.carnegielibrariesiowa.org. The UI website provides a comprehensive list of towns and their libraries. Indiana, Illinois, and Ohio also built more than one hundred libraries with Carnegie grants. Carnegie was a ruthless tycoon who gave 90 percent of his fortune to charity. See Richard White, *The Republic for Which It Stands: The United States*

during Reconstruction and the Gilded Age, 1865–1896 (New York: Oxford University Press, 2017), 655–657, 670–674 on Carnegie.

37. Cole, *History of the People of Iowa*, 487–490; Jack London, "Tramping with Kelly through Iowa," *Palimpsest* 7, no. 5 (May 1926): 145–154; Carlos A. Schwantes, "Soldiers of Misfortune," *Iowa Heritage Illustrated* 88, no. 2 (Summer 2007): 91–92; Nell Irvin Painter, *Standing at Armageddon: The United States, 1877–1919* (New York: W. W. Norton, 1987), 116–121; Annie Braniff, "Historic Events I've Lived Through: Kelly's Army on the March," *Iowa Heritage Illustrated* 88, no. 2 (Summer 2007): 93–95; William J. Petersen, "Kelly and His Men," *Palimpsest* 52, no. 6 (June 1971): 303.

38. Cole, *People of Iowa*, 487–493; Dennis S. Nordin and Roy V. Scott, *From Prairie Farmer to Entrepreneur: The Transformation of Midwestern Agriculture* (Bloomington: Indiana University Press, 2005), 9; Painter, *Standing at Armageddon*, 116; Benjamin F. Gue, *History of Iowa: From the Earliest Times to the Beginning of the Twentieth Century*, vol. 3 (New York: Century History 1903), 174–181.

39. Danbom, *Born in the Country*, 162–166; Bruce L. Gardner, *American Agriculture in the Twentieth Century: How It Flourished and What It Cost* (Cambridge, MA: Harvard University Press, 2002), 1; Earle D. Ross, "The New Agriculture," *Iowa Journal of History* 47, no. 2 (April 1949): 119, 124–125; Merrill E. Jarchow, "Life on a Jones County Farm, 1873–1912," *Iowa Journal of History* 49, no. 4 (October 1951): 337.

40. Roy Alden Atwood, "Routes of Rural Discontent: Cultural Contradictions of Rural Free Delivery in Southeastern Iowa, 1899–1917," *Annals of Iowa* 48, nos. 5–6 (Summer–Fall 1986): 264–267, 273; Jarchow, "Life on a Jones County Farm," 127–128; Wilkinson, *Memories of an Iowa Farm Boy*, 85–86.

41. Atwood, "Routes of Rural Discontent," 265–273.

CHAPTER 10: IOWA IN WORLD WAR I AND THE 1920S

1. John Keegan, *The First World War* (New York: Alfred A. Knopf, 1999), 49–61, 66–69, 124, 131–137; Jennifer D. Keene, *The United States and the First World War* (Harlow, UK: Pearson Education, 2000), 12–17; Michael S. Nieberg, *The Path to War: How the First World War Created Modern America* (New York: Oxford University Press, 2016), 153, 178, 215–221; Leland L. Sage, *A History of Iowa* (Ames: Iowa State University Press, 1974), 251.

2. Keene, *First World War*, 23–27, 35–37; Hendrick A. Clements, *The Presidency of Woodrow Wilson* (Lawrence: University Press of Kansas, 1992), 144–155. World War I collections at the State Historical Society in Iowa City provide insight on the federal government's new responsibilities. See boxes 3 and 4, World War I Materials, SHSI-IAC, for information on the Interior, Treasury, and Labor Departments.

3. Earl Stanfield Fullbrook, *The Red Cross in Iowa*, vol. 1 (Iowa City: State Historical Society of Iowa, 1922), 93, 99, 121; Earl Stanfield Fullbrook, *The Red Cross in Iowa*, vol. 2 (Iowa City: State Historical Society of Iowa, 1922), 1, 5, 8–9, 12, 18–19,

23, 27, 29; Sara Egge, *Woman Suffrage and Citizenship in the Midwest, 1870–1920* (Iowa City: University of Iowa Press, 2018), 158–159.

4. Lynn Dumenil, *The Second Line of Defense: American Women and World War One* (Chapel Hill: University of North Carolina Press, 2015), 112–113, 136–137; Fullbrook, *Red Cross in Iowa*, vol. 2, 152, 157, 160, 161, 169; Robert H. Zieger, *America's Great War: World War One and the American Experience* (Lanham, MD: Rowman and Littlefield, 2000), 142; Ralph W. Cram, ed., *History of the War Activities of Scott County Iowa, 1917–1918* (Davenport, IA: Scott County Council of National Defense, n.d.), 119–120, 143–145; Merle Wright Carter and Dean Gabbert, "Hospital Unit R in World War One: Fairfield to France," *Palimpsest* 67, no. 5 (September 1986): 145, 150–152, 155, 157; Lois Orr Preach, "The Army Nurse—World War 1," 1–4, Lois Orr Preach Autobiographical and Genealogical Notes, SHSI.

5. Fullbrook, *Red Cross in Iowa*, vol. 1, 144–152, 162, 169; Dumenil, *Second Line of Defense*, 94.

6. Fullbrook, *Red Cross in Iowa*, vol. 2, 40–54. Many men assisted with Red Cross activities, but women dominated canteen service.

7. Ivan I. Pollock, *The Food Administration in Iowa*, vol. 2 (Iowa City: State Historical Society of Iowa, 1923), 1–8, 36, 52, 69–73, 92–93, 118–119.

8. Deemer Lee, *Esther's Town* (Ames: Iowa State University Press, 1980), 122–126.

9. Nathaniel R. Whitney, *The Sale of War Bonds in Iowa* (Iowa City: State Historical Society of Iowa, 1923), 2–6, 14–19, 52, 95; Keene, *First World War*, 32–33; Newspaper Ads, Liberty Loan Papers, box 1, SHSI-IAC. Smaller amounts could be bought like stamps, which could be combined to buy larger amounts.

10. Whitney, *War Bonds in Iowa,* 14–28, 30–35, 129–130, 134–138, 144–157; Cram, *History of War Activities*, 60; Lee, *Esther's Town*, 124; Nathaniel R. Whitney, "The First Three Liberty Loans in Iowa," *Iowa and the War* 15 (September 1918): 6–8. See the editor's note in the September 1918 issue on Whitney's article for more information on the third and fourth bond drives.

11. Keene, *First World War*, 35; Cram, *History of War Activities*, 66–67; Zieger, *America's Great War*, 80; Committee on Public Information, *Purpose and Plan of the Four Minute Men: A National Organization of Volunteer Speakers for Government Presentation of Topics of National Importance to the Nation—Picture Their Audience* (Washington, DC: Government Printing Office, 1918), 3–7, 13–14; World War I Materials, box 6, SHSI-IAC.

12. Leola Allen, "Anti-German Sentiment in Iowa during World War I," *Annals of Iowa* 42, no. 6 (Fall 1974): 418, 421, 426–427; Christopher Capozzola, *Uncle Sam Wants You: World War I and the Making of the Modern American Citizen* (New York: Oxford University Press, 2010), 122; David W. Jordan, "Edward A. Steiner and the Struggle for Toleration during World War I," *Annals of Iowa* 46, no. 7 (January 1983): 523; Sage, *History of Iowa*, 251–252; Keene, *First World War*, 29; Cram, *History of War Activities*, 66; Nancy Derr, "William Lloyd Harding," in *The Biographical Dictionary of Iowa*, ed. David Hudson, Marvin Bergman, and Loren Horton (Iowa City: University of Iowa Press, 2008), 210–211; Steven Wrede, "The Americanization of

Scott County, 1914–1918," *Annals of Iowa* 44, no. 8 (Spring 1979): 630–636. See Measuring Worth website at https://measuringworth.com for price comparisons.

13. Schwieder, *Middle Land*, 186–187; Frederick C. Luebke, *Bonds of Loyalty: German Americans and World War I* (Dekalb: Northern Illinois University Press, 1974), 267–282; Wrede, "Americanization of Scott County," 635–636.

14. Zieger, *America's Great War*, 85–89, 108.

15. Bill Douglas, "Wartime Illusions and Disillusionment: Camp Dodge and Racial Stereotyping, 1917–1918," *Annals of Iowa* 57, no. 2 (April 1998): 114–116, 119; William S. Morris, "Black Iowans in Defense of the Nation, 1863–1991," in *Outside In: African-American History in Iowa, 1838–2000*, ed. Bill Silag, Susan Koch-Bridgford, and Hal Chase (Iowa City: State Historical Society of Iowa, 2001), 106–110, 114; Robert V. Morris, *Tradition and Valor: A Family Journey* (Manhattan, KS: Sunflower University Press, 1999), 3–4, 7–9, 36–37, 40, 46–60; Henry G. LaBrie III, "James B. Morris, Sr., and the Iowa Bystander," *Annals of Iowa* 42, no. 4 (Spring 1974): 314, 321. William S. Morris is the grandson of Robert B. Morris Sr.

16. Jack Lufkin, "The Founding and Early Years of the National Association for the Advancement of Colored People in Des Moines, 1915–1930," *Annals of Iowa* 45, no. 6 (Fall 1980): 439–449, 452–460.

17. Douglas, "Wartime Illusions," 111–116, 119–121, 126–128; Zieger, *America's Great War*, 104–105; Morris, "Black Iowans in Defense of the Nation," 108.

18. Keegan, *First World War*, 340–343; Keene, *First World War*, 17, 53–56.

19. Bryon Farwell, *Over There: The United States in the Great War* (New York: W. W. Norton, 1995), 11–13, 297; Joan Muyskens, "Merle Hay and His Town," *Annals of Iowa* 39, no. 1 (July 1967): 27–31; Sage, *History of Iowa*, 251.

20. John H. Taber, *The Story of the 168th Infantry*, vol. 1 (Iowa City: State Historical Society of Iowa, 1923), 73–74, 86–92, 276, 283–284; James H. Hallas, *Doughboy War: The American Expeditionary Force in World War One* (Boulder, CO: Lynne Rienner, 2000), 61, 184. For another fine account of the war, by a lieutenant from Mount Vernon, see Nathan R. Mannheimer, "'The Old War Still Continues:' Roe Howard's Letters from France, 1917–1918," *Iowa Heritage Illustrated* 93, no. 2 (Summer 2014): 97–106.

21. Taber, *The Story of the 168th Infantry*, vol. 1, 280–284, 379; Taber, *The Story of the 168th Infantry*, vol. 2 (Iowa City: State Historical Society of Iowa, 1923), 178, 188, 207, 218–219, 229; Arthur Zelle, *Diary and Letters of an Infantry Soldier in France* (Waverly, IA: G & R Publishing, 2003), 93–95; Fred H. Takes Diary, November 3 and 11, Fred H. Takes Papers, SHSI-IAC; Collection Description and Certification of Military Service, Ernest F. Merkles and Rita M. Spooner Correspondence, 1917–1918, SHSI-IAC.

22. Gerald N. Grob, *The Deadly Truth: A History of Disease in America* (Cambridge, MA: Harvard University Press, 2002), 224–225; Fullbrook, *Red Cross in Iowa*, vol. 2, 93–94; John M. Barry, *The Great Influenza: The Epic Story of the Deadliest Plague in History* (New York: Viking, 2004), 4, 91, 97, 176, 238–239, 407–408, 446; Thomas Morain, *Prairie Grass Roots: An Iowa Small Town in the Early Twentieth Century* (Ames: Iowa State University Press, 1988), 206–208; William H. Cumberland, "Epidemic: Iowa Fights the Spanish Influenza," *Palimpsest* 62, no. 1 (January

1981): 27–28, 31–32; Dorothy Pearl Unmack Dix Memoir, Dorothy Pearl Unmack Dix Papers, Iowa Women's Archives, University of Iowa Libraries, Iowa City (IWA), 3; Ida Hammer, *Book of Des Moines* (Des Moines: Board of Education, 1947), 99; Diary of Beulah Marie Lucas, December 1 and 22, 1918, Jerry Yocum Papers, IWA; John M. Barry, "What We Can Learn From How the 1918 Pandemic Ended," *New York Times*, January 31, 2022, https://www.nytimes.com/2022/01/31/opinion/covid-pandemic-end.html.

23. Fullbrook, *Red Cross in Iowa*, vol. 2, 36–38.

24. William E. Leuchtenburg, *Herbert Hoover* (New York: Henry Holt, 2009), 1–21, 30–42, 51, 80–81, 87. See Measuring Worth. Starting date for this comparison is 1914.

25. Geoffrey Perrett, *America in the Twenties: A History* (New York: Simon and Schuster, 1982), 117–118; Lonzo Jones, *Roots in Mid-America: My Family, My Pride, 1890–1954* (Southport, CT: Ergo Publications, 1981), 70–76; Nathan Miller, *New World Coming: The 1920s and the Making of Modern America* (New York: DaCapo Press, 2003), 87.

26. Perrett, *America in the Twenties*, 118–121; Miller, *New World Coming*, 87; Allen Gregory, *The Boy and the Meadowlark* (New York: Vantage Press, 1977), 163–164, 167.

27. William H. Cumberland, "The Davenport Socialists of 1920," *Annals of Iowa* 47, no. 5 (Summer 1984): 451, 456, 463–470, 473.

28. Lynn Dumenil, *The Modern Temper: American Culture and Society in the 1920s* (New York: Hill and Wang, 1995), 200, 203.

29. Randall Balmer, "The Tragedy of Billy Sunday: The Allure of Populism and the Peril of Anachronism," *Annals of Iowa* 55, no. 4 (Fall 1996): 369–371; Robert F. Martin, "Billy Sunday and the Mystique of the Middle West," *Annals of Iowa* 55, no. 4 (Fall 1996): 345–353, 356–360; Robert F. Martin, "William Ashley 'Billy' Sunday," *Biographical Dictionary of Iowa*, 503–504.

30. Eric Burns, *1920: The Year That Made the Decade Roar* (New York: Pegasus Books, 2016), 39–41, 47–52, 126, 135–137; Bryce T. Bauer, *Gentlemen Bootleggers: The True Story of Templeton Rye, Prohibition, and a Small Town in Cahoots* (Chicago: Chicago Review Press, 2016), 61, 69, 77; Nathan Miller, *New World Coming*, 102, 296–297; Lee, *Esther's Town*, 164; Virgil Lagomarcino, *Window on Main Street: Life above Corner Drug* (Ames: Iowa State University Press, 1994), 60; Gerald and Fay Goodwin, Oral History Interview Transcript, July 13, 1978, Correctionville, Iowa, Oral History Project, Earthwatch, SHSI-IAC, 29–30.

31. Dorothy Schwieder, "A Farmer and the Ku Klux Klan in Northwest Iowa," *Annals of Iowa* 61, no. 3 (July 2002): 287, 291, 294–298, 317–320; Dorothy Schwieder, *Iowa: The Middle Land* (Ames: Iowa State University Press, 1996), 163–166; David J. Goldberg, *Discontented America: The United States in the 1920s* (Baltimore: Johns Hopkins University Press, 1999), 137–139; Leanore Goodenow, "My Encounters with the Ku Klux Klan," *Palimpsest* 76, no. 2 (Summer 1995): 53; Robert J. Neymeyer, "In the Full Light of Day: The Ku Klux Klan in 1920s Iowa," *Palimpsest* 76, no. 2 (Summer 1995): 58–63; Morris, *Tradition and Valor*, 61; Deborah Fink, *Cutting into*

the Meatpacking Line: Workers and Change in the Rural Midwest* (Chapel Hill: University of North Carolina Press, 1998), 127–128; George Mills, "When the Ku Klux Klan Was (Briefly) a Power in Iowa GOP Politics," December 12, 1987, *Des Moines Register*, https://www.newspapers.com/image/legacy/127633101/?terms=KKK%20power%20GOP%20politics%20Iowa&match=1.

32. Ralph Scharnau, "African-American Wage Earners in Iowa, 1850–1950," in *Outside In*, 217, 223–230, 233, 235; Willis Goudy, "Selected Demographics: Iowa's African-American Residents, 1840–2000," in *Outside In*, 28.

33. Omar Valerio-Jimenez, "Racializing Mexican Immigrants in Iowa's Early Mexican Communities," *Annals of Iowa* 75, no. 1 (Winter 2016): 1–8, 12; Janet Weaver, "From Barrio to !'Boicoteo'!: The Emergence of Mexican American Activism in Davenport, 1917–1970," *Annals of Iowa* 68, no. 3 (Summer 2009): 217; "David Macias" and "Manuel Macias," Ernest Rodriquez Papers, IWA.

34. "Leno and Maria: A Success Story," by Vincent Cano, 42–48, Maria Cano Martinez Papers, IWA; Valerio-Jimenez, "Racializing Mexican Immigrants," 13–16, 32.

35. Valerio-Jimenez, "Racializing Mexican Immigrants," 11–14, 16–19, 23, 32; Bill Vogrin, "Celebration of 'American Dream' Is Yearly Event," August 5, 1987, *Rock Island Argus*, Cook's Point, Davenport, "Migration Is Beautiful," http://migration.lib.uiowa.edu, Iowa Women's Archives (IWA); Jim Arpy, "Remembering Cook's Point," August 22, 1974, *Davenport Quad City Times-Democrat*, Adella Martinez Papers, IWA; Weaver, "From Barrio to '!Boicoteo'!," 220–223; "The Story Continues," Ernest Rodriquez Papers, IWA.

36. Salom Rizk, *Syrian Yankee* (Garden City, NY: Doubleday, 1952), vii–viii, 13–26, 46–48, 69–71, 99–104, 120–126, 162–165, 170–177, 193, 204, 302–306, 316. His book was originally published in 1943, in the middle of World War II.

37. Grace King, "How Did the Oldest Mosque in the U.S. End up in Cedar Rapids?" *Cedar Rapids Gazette*, April 12, 2021, https://www.thegazette.com/kids-articles/how-did-the-oldest-mosque-in-the-u-s-end-up-in-cedar-rapids/; "Early American Mosques," the Pluralism Project, accessed January 4, 2022, https://pluralism.org/early-american-mosques; Peter Rugg, "Will America's Oldest Muslim Community Survive President Trump?" *Rolling Stone*, February 22, 2017, https://www.rollingstone.com/culture/culture-news/will-americas-oldest-muslim-community-survive-president-trump-123405/; P. J. Huffstutter, "Salvaging Hope at Iowa Mosque," *Los Angeles Times*, July 1, 2008, https://www.latimes.com/nation/la-na-rebuild1-2008jul01-story.html; "History of Mother Mosque," Mother Mosque of America, accessed February 13, 2023, https://mothermosque.org/history/. Thanks to Bill Douglas, who is writing a religious history of Iowa, for his assistance on the Cedar Rapids Muslim community. See Edward E. Curtis IV, *Muslims of the Heartland: How Syrian Immigrants Made a Home in the American Midwest* (New York: New York University Press, 2022), 115–118, 147–152, on the construction of the first mosques in the United States. The *Rolling Stone* article states that the first Muslims immigrants to Iowa arrived in 1885, but it is much more likely they arrived at the start of the twentieth century. See Curtis for more on this topic.

38. Morain, *Prairie Grass Roots*, 110–113, 116–117; John Zug, "Early Iowa

Automobiles," *Annals of Iowa* 36, no. 4 (Spring 1962): 276; Kenneth Hassebrock, *Rural Reminiscences: The Agony of Survival* (Ames: Iowa State University Press, 1990), 4, 17–19; H. E. Wilkinson, *Memories of an Iowa Farm Boy* (1952; repr., Ames: Iowa State University Press, 1994), 113; Keith W. Graham, "My Father's First Model T Ford," 3, SHSI-IAC; G. B. Hippee, "A 1905 Auto Trip to Spirit Lake," *Iowa Heritage Illustrated* 80, nos. 1–2 (Spring–Summer 1999): 22–27.

39. Hassebrock, *Rural Reminiscences*, 19–20; Floyd A. Robinson, *This Is Home Now* (Ames: Iowa State University Press, 1983), 65, 84, 171–172; Robert J. Gordon, *The Rise and Fall of American Economic Growth: The U.S. Standard of Living since the Civil War* (Princeton: Princeton University Press, 2016), 163; Morain, *Prairie Grass Roots*, 110–111, 117, 125, 131–136; Miller, *New World Coming*, 173; Ruth M. Wenger, *My Dear Grandchildren* (Minneapolis: Dillon Press, 1982), 124–125; Autobiographical Sketch, 2–3, Elizabeth R. Miller Papers, IWA. See the Elizabeth R. Miller Papers collection description for a summary of her life. Miller was a teacher, raised four children, and an active clubwoman. She was also elected to the Iowa House and Senate in the 1960s and 1970s, where she served for twelve years.

40. Gordon, *Rise and Fall*, 152–156, 164; Nathan Miller, *New World Coming*, 173–174; Graham, "First Model T," 1–3, SHSI-IAC. See Measuring Worth for price comparisons.

41. Joanne Wilke, *Eight Women, Two Model Ts, and the American West* (Lincoln: University of Nebraska Press, 2007), 8–14, 21–27, 46, 65, 81–86, 99, 102, 113–117, 122, 145, 166–168. Marie's last name is not given in Wilke's book. For more on automobiles in the state in the early 1900s, see Ginalie Swaim, ed., "Car Culture, Iowa Style," *Iowa Heritage Illustrated* 87, no. 4 (Winter 2006): 168–185.

42. Gordon, *Rise and Fall*, 161–164; Hammer, *Book of Des Moines*, 100–101. For more on how daily life changed in the early twentieth century, see "History of the Harris Family From 1898 to Approximately 1930," by Marie H. Giddings, IWA.

43. Rodney O. Davis, "Iowa Farm Opinion and the Good Roads Movement, 1903–1904," *Annals of Iowa* 37, no. 5 (Summer 1964): 321–322, 327; Miller, *New World Coming*, 189–190; Leo Landis, *Building Better Roads: Iowa's Contribution to Highway Engineering, 1904–1974* (Ames: Center for Transportation Research and Education, 1998), 1–4; Morain, *Prairie Grass Roots*, 119; George Mills, *Rogues and Heroes from Iowa's Amazing Past* (Ames: Iowa State University Press, 1994), 58; Wenger, *My Dear Grandchildren*, 123; George S. May, "The Old Roads," *Palimpsest* 46, no. 2 (February 1965): 66; Eula Van Meter, "Courage and American Brandeur—1915," 1–2, SHSI-IAC. Quote is from Mills.

44. Miller, *New World Coming*, 190–192; Landis, *Building Better Roads*, 17, 21; Maury Klein, *Rainbow's End: The Crash of 1929* (New York: Oxford University Press, 2001), 30–31; George S. May, "Getting Out of the Mud," *Palimpsest* 46, no. 2 (February 1965): 103–104, 115; Peter T. Harstad and Diana J. Fox, "Dusty Doughboys on the Lincoln Highway: The 1919 Army Convoy in Iowa," *Palimpsest* 56, no. 3 (March 1975): 71–82. May writes that Iowa only paved 3,272 miles of road by 1930, but the present author relies on Landis's higher number due to the more recent research on this topic.

45. Rebecca Conard, "The Lincoln Highway in Greene County: Highway Politics, Local Initiative, and the Emerging Federal Highway System," *Annals of Iowa* 52, no. 4 (Fall 1993): 351, 363; Morain, *Prairie Grass Roots,* 121–125; Earl Swift, *Big Roads: The Untold Story of the Engineers, Visionaries, and Trailblazers Who Created the American Superhighways* (New York: Mariner Books, 2011), 1, 31–32, 35–36, 47.

46. Margaret Ott Onerheim, *Threads of Memory: A Memoir of the 1920s* (Ames: Iowa State University Press, 1993), 16, 37; Robert Stech, *Along the Way: Farm Life during the 1920s—1930s—1940s* (Williamson, IA: Robert Stech, 1976), 65; Klein, *Rainbow's End,* 115–117; Burns, *1920,* 197–198; US Bureau of the Census, *Statistical Abstract of the United States* (Washington, DC: Government Printing Office, 1941), 45.

47. Miller, *New World Coming,* 192–197; Lagomarcino, *Window on Main Street,* 49–50; Memoirs of John R. Ortega, 58, SHSI-IAC; Everett Ludley, "It Always Has," 49–50, SHSI-IAC.

48. Ruth Perkins Messenger Memoir, IWA. Also see the collection guide to Ruth Perkins Messenger Memoir. There are no page numbers for her reminiscence, which was written in 1978.

CHAPTER 11: THE GREAT DEPRESSION AND IOWA

1. David M. Kennedy, *Freedom from Fear: The American People in Depression and War, 1929–1945* (New York: Oxford University Press, 1999), 34–41, 58; Anthony J. Badger, *The New Deal: The Depression Years, 1933–1940* (New York: Hill and Wang, 1989), 30; Jeffry A. Frieden, *Global Capitalism: Its Fall and Rise in the Twentieth Century* (New York: W. W. Norton, 2006), 174–175.

2. Badger, *New Deal,* 18, 30–31; Kennedy, *Freedom from Fear,* 65–68, 76–78, 105; Eric Rauchway, *The Great Depression and the New Deal: A Very Short Introduction* (New York: Oxford University Press, 2008), 31, 40; Michael E. Parrish, *Anxious Decades: America in Prosperity and Depression, 1920–1941* (New York: W. W. Norton, 1992), 217–218, 235.

3. Badger, *New Deal,* 41–53; William E. Leuchtenburg, *Herbert Hoover* (New York: Henry Holt, 2009), 130–135.

4. Shelton Stromquist, *Solidarity and Survival: An Oral History of Iowa Labor in the Twentieth Century* (Iowa City: University of Iowa Press, 1993), 57–58, 68, 70; Studs Terkel, *Hard Times: An Oral History of the Great Depression* (New York: Pantheon Books, 1970), 95–98; Memoir of John R. Ortega, 31–32, 44, State Historical Society of Iowa, Iowa City (SHSI-IAC); Kennedy, *Freedom from Fear,* 168.

5. Neal Smith, *Mr. Smith Went to Washington: from Eisenhower to Clinton* (Ames: Iowa State University Press, 1995), xiv–xv, 3–17; William Morris, "Former US Rep. Neal Smith, Dead at 101, Recalled as 'Epitome' of a Good Public Servant, 'A True Iowa Treasure,'" *Des Moines Register,* November 3, 2021, https://www.desmoines register.com/story/news/politics/2021/11/03/neal-smith-iowa-longest-serving-mem ber-house-congressman-dies-101-obituary/ 6249942001/. He died at age 101 in 2021.

6. Terkel, *Hard Times,* 217–218; H. Roger Grant and L. Edward Purcell, eds., *Years of Struggle: The Farm Diary of Elmer G. Powers* (Dekalb: Northern Illinois University Press, 1995), 10; Frank Yoder, "Staying on the Farm: Surviving the Great Depression in An Iowa Township, 1920–1950," *Annals of Iowa* 51, no. 1 (Summer 1991): 53–56; VaDonna Jean Leaf, "'Sure Hope Things Go Better Tomorrow:' Letters from a Travelling Salesman, 1928–1935," *Palimpsest* 71, no. 4 (Winter 1990): 186–192.

7. Patrick B. Bauer, "Farm Mortgagor Relief Legislation in Iowa during the Great Depression," *Annals of Iowa* 50, no. 1 (Summer 1989): 24–25; Calvin W. Coquillette, "The Struggle to Preserve Iowa's State Banking System, 1920–1933," *Annals of Iowa* 60, no. 1 (Winter 2001): 36–38, 52–54.

8. Coquillette, "Struggle to Preserve," 46–53, 58; J. H. Redman, "Restored Confidence in Iowa Banks," *Annals of Iowa* 30, no. 1 (Summer 1949): 56–62; James Hearst, "We All Worked Together: A Memory of Drought and Depression," *Palimpsest* 59, no. 3 (May–June 1978): 72. See Measuring Worth, at https://measuringworth.com. The starting date here for comparison is 1925, the midpoint of the 1920s.

9. Faye Elsie Tomilinson Wookey, "Life on a Montgomery County Farm," Faye T. Wookey Papers, Iowa Women's Archives (IWA); Irma J. Long Memoranda Concerning July 1936, SHSI-IAC; Otto W. Knauth, "The Winter of 1935–36," *Annals of Iowa* 35, no. 4 (Spring 1960): 291. For more on Iowa farm life in the 1930s see Horace Miner, *Culture and Agriculture: An Anthropological Study of a Corn Belt County* (Ann Arbor: University of Michigan Press, 1949). Miner's book is full of useful information, on topics from newspaper circulation to crime, work, and education. It is a study of Hardin County.

10. Grant and Purcell, *Years of Struggle,* 31–32; James Hearst, *Time Like a Furrow* (Iowa City: Iowa State Historical Department, 1981), 134.

11. Mary Huber, "James Schell Hearst," in *The Biographical Dictionary of Iowa,* ed. David Hudson, Marvin Bergman, and Loren Horton (Iowa City: University of Iowa Press, 2008), 224–226. See Scott Cawelti, ed., *The Complete Poetry of James Hearst* (Iowa City: University of Iowa Press, 2001), for a collection of Hearst's work.

12. December 21, 1930, Martie Ward to Rev. Leo R. Ward, Leo R. Ward Letters, SHSI-IAC; December 14, 1932, Clara Ackerman Diaries, SHSI-IAC; James and Ruby Howorth Interview Transcript, Tape 18, SHSI-IAC; Grant and Purcell, *Years of Struggle,* 29–32; Gladys Moeller Lage Memoir, IWA; Ruth Mumford oral history interview conducted by Ann Harrison, 1984 (no exact date provided), tape 2, 26, Ruth Mumford Transcripts, Her Own Story: Ten Benton County Women, IWA. See Measuring Worth. The starting date here for comparison is 1930, the year of Martie Ward's diary entry. For an entertaining and popular account of Iowa in the 1930s, see Mildred Armstrong Kalish, *Little Heathens: Hard Times and High Spirits on an Iowa Farm during the Great Depression* (New York: Bantam Press, 2007).

13. Hearst, *Time Like a Furrow,* 238–240; Deborah Fink and Dorothy Schwieder, "Iowa Farm Women in the 1930s," *Annals of Iowa* 49, no. 7 (Winter 1989): 572–577; Deborah Fink, *Open Country, Iowa: Rural Women, Tradition, and Change* (Albany: State University of New York Press, 1986), 35, 48, 60–61; Gerald and Fay Goodwin, Oral History Interview, July 13, 1978 (transcript), Correctionville, Iowa, Oral History

Project, Earthworks, SHSI-IAC, 17; Inez Frick Henze Badger, "Historic Events I've Lived Through," Iowa Commission on the Aging, Box 1, SHSI-IAC.

14. Priscilla Wayne, "Feeding the Multitudes: How One City Served 350,000 Meals at One Cent Apiece," *Saturday Evening Post*, August 27, 1932, 12–13, 70–71.

15. Valerie Grim, "African-Americans in Iowa Agriculture: A Portrait, 1830–2000," in *Outside In: African- American History in Iowa, 1838–2000*, ed. Bill Silag, Susan Koch-Bridgford, and Hal Chase (Des Moines: State Historical Society of Iowa, 2001), 179; Ralph Scharnau, "African-American Wage Earners in Iowa, 1850–1950," in *Outside In*, 230, 236.

16. Badger, *New Deal*, 33; Kennedy, *Freedom from Fear*, 163, 168, 173, 189, 191; Hearst, "We All Worked Together," 70.

17. Grant and Purcell, Y*ears of Struggle*, 47–49; January 29, 1933, Diary of Clara Ackerman, SHSI-IAC; John M. Wilkinson, *Rock Bottom: An American Heartland Farm-Town and Family from Settlement through the Great Depression* (Lexington, MA: John M. Wilkinson, 1993), 144, 152; George Mills, *Looking in Windows: Surprising Stories of Old Des Moines* (Ames: Iowa State University Press, 1991), 187–190; Ian M. Koontz, ed., *Hometown Heroes: Dubuque Remembers World War II* (n.p.: Woodward Communications, 2001), 198. See Measuring Worth. The starting date here for comparison is 1935.

18. Joseph Frazier Wall, *Iowa: A History* (New York: W. W. Norton, 1978), 176–177; John L. Shover, *Cornbelt Rebellion: The Farmers' Holiday Association* (Urbana: University of Illinois Press, 1965), 29–30.

19. Shover, *Cornbelt Rebellion*, 30–33; Wall, *Iowa: A History*, 174–177.

20. Rodney D. Karr, "Farm Rebels in Plymouth County, Iowa, 1932–1933," *Annals of Iowa* 47, no. 7 (Winter 1985): 637–638; William C. Pratt, "Rethinking the Farm Revolt of the 1930s," *Great Plains Quarterly* 8, no. 3 (Summer 1988): 131–136; Leland L. Sage, *A History of Iowa* (Ames: Iowa State University Press, 1976), 275–278, 281–282, 297–298; "Milo Reno," *Annals of Iowa* 20, no. 5 (Summer 1936): 392–393.

21. Karr, "Farm Rebels," 637–644; Pratt, "Rethinking the Farm Revolt," 134, 139–140; Shover, *Cornbelt Rebellion*, 116–118.

22. Rauchway, *Great Depression*, 56–69.

23. Parrish, *Anxious Decades*, 289–293.

24. Frank J. Rader, "Harry L. Hopkins, the Ambitious Crusader: An Historical Analysis of the Major Influences on His Career, 1912–1940," *Annals of Iowa* 44, no. 2 (Fall 1977): 83–86, 90, 96–97; David L. Roll, *The Hopkins Touch: Harry Hopkins and the Forging of the Alliance to Defeat Hitler* (New York: Oxford University Press, 2015), 6–11, 405, 409; Kennedy, *Freedom from Fear*, 94–96, 161. Roll's biography is focused on World War II but is recent and very readable. See the first chapter for background on Hopkins' life in Iowa. Roll wrote that Hopkins was FDR's "gaunt, chain-smoking shadow." Also see Marilyn Brookwood, *The Orphans of Davenport: Eugenics, the Great Depression, and the War Over Children's Intelligence* (New York: Liveright Publishing, 2021) for an important history of the Iowa Child Welfare Research Station and the development of neuroscience in the late twentieth century.

25. David L. Lendt, "Jay Norwood 'Ding' Darling," in *Biographical Dictionary of*

Iowa, 116–118; David L. Lendt, *Ding: The Life of Jay Norwood Darling* (Mt. Pleasant, SC: Maecenas Press, 2001), 61–62, 67, 75–77, 85. Another Iowan who was important for American conservation was Aldo Leopold, who grew up in Burlington. Leopold's *A Sand County Almanac* is a classic of environmental writing. See Aldo Leopold, *A Sand County Almanac and Sketches Here and There* (New York: Oxford University Press, 1949).

26. Lauren Soth, "Henry Wallace and the Farm Crisis of the 1920s and 1930s," *Annals of Iowa* 47, no. 2 (Fall 1983): 196–198, 202–206, 213–214; John C. Culver and John Hyde, *American Dreamer: A Life of Henry A. Wallace* (New York: W. W. Norton, 2000), 82–84.

27. Rauchway, *Great Depression*, 77–80; Terkel, *Hard Times*, 219–220, Soth, "Henry Wallace," 207–209; Culver and Hyde, *American Dreamer*, 123–125; William J. Petersen, "Agriculture and the AAA," *Palimpsest* 17, no. 8 (August 1936): 256–257; Richard H. Roberts, "The Administration of the 1934 Corn-Hog Program in Iowa: A Study in Contemporary History," *Iowa Journal of History and Politics* 33, no. 4 (October 1935): 331–332. See Measuring Worth. The starting date here for comparison is 1935.

28. Parrish, *Anxious Decades,* 294; Gregg R. Narber, *The Impact of the New Deal on Iowa: Changing the Culture of a Rural State* (Lewiston, NY: Edwin Mellen Press, 2008), 187–189, 194, 209–216; Rebecca Conard, "The Legacy of Hope from an Era of Despair: The CCC and Iowa State Parks," *Books at Iowa* 64 (April 1996), accessed at https://www.lib.uiowa.edu/scua/bai/conard.htm; Jessie A. Bloodworth and Elizabeth J. Greenwood, *The Personal Side* (Washington, DC: Works Progress Administration, Division of Research, 1939), 302. Quote is from Conard. See Measuring Worth. The starting date here for comparison is 1935.

29. C. N. Alleger and C. A. Alleger, eds., *Civilian Conservation Corps: Iowa District History* (Rapid City, SD: Johnson and Bordewyk, 1935), 12–13, 44–45, 62–63, 68, 79; Narber, *Impact of the New Deal*, 190; Conard, "Legacy of Hope." The CCC played an important role in helping to launch the postwar conservation movement. See Neil M. Maher, *Nature's New Deal: The Civilian Conservation Corps and the Roots of the American Environmental Movement* (New York: Oxford University Press, 2008). African Americans served in segregated CCC camps nationwide, see Maher, 106. Several of these camps were in Minnesota, see https://www.mnopedia.org/civilian-conservation-corps-minnesota-1933-1942. Thanks to Leo Landis, Mary Bennett, and Becki Plunkett of the State Historical Society of Iowa for their help with questions on the CCC.

30. Judith M. Daubenier, *The Meskwaki and Anthropologists: Action Anthropology Reconsidered* (Lincoln: University of Nebraska Press, 2008), 29–38; Eric Zimmer, "Settlement and Sovereignty: Land and Meskwaki Self-Governance, 1856–1937," 40–41, SHSI-IAC; Eric Zimmer, "The 'Busy Meskwaki:' Tribal Autonomy, Social Transformation, and the Indian Reorganization Act, 1900–1937," 34–35, SHSI-IAC.

31. Interview with Sebastian Alvarez, May 12, 1994, by Deborah Fink, 1–10, 13, 19–21, 27–30, SHSI-IAC.

32. Alleger and Alleger, *Civilian Conservation Corps*, 45–46, 62–63, 79.

33. Badger, *New Deal*, 200–207; "History of Community House Sioux City, Iowa," *Annals of Iowa* 21, no. 3 (Winter 1938): 204; Bloodworth and Greenwood, *Personal Side*, 288, 313, 322; Narber, *Impact of the New Deal*, 124–125, 176–179; John R. Ortega Memoir, SHSI-IAC, 7.

34. Louise Rosenfield Noun, *Iowa Women in the WPA* (Ames: Iowa State University Press, 1999), 7–10, 16, 24, 38–45, 54–55, 91.

35. Parrish, *Anxious Decades*, 347–350; "History of Community House Sioux City, Iowa," 205; Noun, *Iowa Women in the WPA*, 67–70, 72, 76–79. The original 1938 WPA guide has been reprinted as *The WPA Guide to 1930s Iowa* (Ames: Iowa State University Press, 1986).

36. R. Tripp Evans, *Grant Wood: A Life* (New York: Alfred A Knopf, 2010), 4–5, 14–25, 31–33, 38, 44–49, 54–55, 104–107, 119, 165–167, 195–198, 282, 291–292.

37. "History of Community House," 205; National Youth Administration for Iowa, Final Report, October 30, 1943, SHSI-IAC, 1–4, 28, 67, 101–106.

38. Kennedy, *Freedom from Fear*, 290–291, 344–345, 365–375, 379; Melvyn Dubofsky and Foster Rhea Dulles, *Labor in America: A History* (Wheeling, IL: Harlan Davidson, 2010), 252–253. One of the great union leaders of the mid-twentieth century was John L. Lewis, who was born in Iowa and worked in the state's coal mines as a young man. He was president of the United Mine Workers for decades. See Dubofsky and Dulles, 227–235 and 291–302.

39. D. Clayton Brown, *Electricity for Rural America: The Fight for the REA* (Westport, Connecticut: Greenwood Press, 1980), xii–xv, 3–5; Ronald R. Kline, *Consumers in the Countryside: Technology and Society in Rural America* (Baltimore: Johns Hopkins University Press, 2000), 132; David E. Nye, *Electrifying America: Social Meanings of a New Technology* (Cambridge, MA: MIT Press, 1997), 261, 299. See Measuring Worth. The starting date here for comparison is 1930.

40. Brown, *Electricity for Rural America*, 40–43, 68–70, 75; Harold Severson, *Rural Iowa Turns on the Lights: The Story of the Electric Power Revolution in the Hawkeye State* (n.p.: Midwest Historical Features, 1965), 46–50; Nye, *Electrifying America*, 321.

41. History of Clara P. Saride Winkie, Autobiographical Sketches of Rural Iowa Women, IWA.

42. Robert Seltz, *Between the Corn Rows: Stories of an Iowa Farm Family's Survival in the Great Depression* (Bloomington, Indiana: iUniverse, 2012), 42; Hearst, *Time Like a Furrow*, 9, 242, 245; Kline, *Consumers in the Countryside*, 265–267; Mary Hagen Memoir, 10–11, IWA. Hagen was born in 1922 and grew up in Manly, Iowa. She married Orville Hagen at age nineteen and they raised eight children. See the collection description of her memoir for biographical information.

43. William J. Petersen, "Economics and the Alphabeticals," *Palimpsest* 17, no. 8 (August 1936): 263–270; Petersen, "Agriculture and Industry," *Palimpsest* 18, no. 8 (August 1937): 262–269; Jeremy Atack and Peter Passell, *A New Economic View of American History from Colonial Times to 1940* (New York: W. W. Norton, 1994), 643. See Measuring Worth. Comparison dates here are 1935 and 1940 for total statewide expenditures and per capita spending. Prices changed little between these two years.

44. Hearst, "We All Worked Together," 76; Leaf, "Sure Hope Things Go Better Tomorrow," 192.

CHAPTER 12: IOWA IN WORLD WAR II

1. David M. Kennedy, *Freedom from Fear: The American People in Depression and War, 1929–1945* (New York: Oxford University Press, 1999), 381–385, 401, 408–409, 421–425.

2. Kennedy, *Freedom from Fear*, 438–440, 460–461, 467–470, 476, 482, 495; George Gallup, "What We, the People, Think about Europe," April 30, 1939, *New York Times*, https://www.nytimes.com/1939/04/30/archives/what-we-the-people-think-about-europe-a-crosssection-of-opinion-on.html?search ResultPosition=1. George Gallup was born in Jefferson, Iowa, and educated at the State University of Iowa (now the University of Iowa). See Becky Wilson Hawbaker, "Gallup, George Horace," in *The Biographical Dictionary of Iowa*, ed. David Hudson, Marvin Bergman, and Loren Horton (Iowa City: University of Iowa Press, 2008), 177–178. Elena Skrjabina survived the siege of Leningrad and a German labor camp and emigrated to the United States in 1950. She earned a PhD from Syracuse University and became a professor of the Russian language at the University of Iowa in 1960. See Elena Skrjabina, *Siege and Survival: The Odyssey of a Leningrader* (Carbondale: Southern Illinois University Press, 1971), vii–xi, 157.

3. *Des Moines Register*, June 2, 2002, article clipping, Birdie Matthews Diaries, SHSI-IAC; Shelby Myers-Verhage, "Postmarked from Amsterdam—Anne Frank and Her Iowa Pen Pals," *Palimpsest* 76, no. 4 (Winter 1995): 152–154, 158–159. Birdie Matthews was a teacher for decades and had used her salary during the 1930s to keep her school open and heated. Her diaries are at the State Historical Society in Iowa City. Matthews retired in 1945, after nearly fifty years of teaching. She died in 1974 at age ninety-four.

4. Susan Marks Conner, ed., *I Remember When . . . Personal Recollections and Vignettes of the Sioux City Jewish Community, 1869–1984, Based on Oscar Littlefield's History* (Sioux City, IA: Jewish Federation of Sioux City, 1985), 42–43, 58–60, 67–70, 92–93.

5. Michael Luick-Thrams, *Out of Hitler's Reach: Scattergood Hostel for European Refugees, 1939–1943* (n.p.: Iowa Community Action Coalition, 1996), vi–viii, 22–23, 40–51, 304; Peter H. Curtis, "A Place of Peace in a World at War: The Scattergood Refugee Hostel, 1939–1940," *Palimpsest* 65, no. 2 (March–April 1989), 42–52; Scattergood Friends School, accessed September 21, 2018, https//:scattergood.org/history/.

6. Kenneth W. Huck, ed., *A Log of World War II: A Pacific Naval Diary, as Recorded by Vincent Evo DeCook, Yeoman Second Class U.S.S. Minneapolis* (n.p.: Xlibirs, 2010), 9, 13–20; John Patrick Diggins, *The Proud Decades: America in War and in Peace, 1941–1960* (New York: W. W. Norton, 1988), 4–5; George A. Freund, *Hometown Heroes: Dubuque Remembers World War Two* (n.p.: Telegraph Herald, 2001), 198–200.

7. Lisa Ossian, *The Home Fronts of Iowa, 1939–1945* (Columbia: University of Missouri Press, 2009), 19–20; Ronald Takaki, *Double Victory: A Multicultural History of America in World War Two* (New York: Little, Brown, 2000), 137, 152–154; Chad W. Timm, "Working with the Enemy: Axis Prisoners of War in Iowa during World War Two," *Annals of Iowa* 70, no. 3 (Summer 2011): 247; Jerry L. Twedt, *Growing Up in the '40s: Rural Reminiscence* (Tampa, FL: Mancorp, 1994), 42; William J. Petersen, "Remember Pearl Harbor," *Palimpsest* 23, no. 2 (February 1942): 37. Quote is from Petersen.

8. John Morton Blum, *V Was for Victory: Politics and American Culture during World War Two* (New York: Harcourt, Brace, 1976), 91; Geoffrey Perrett, *Days of Sadness, Years of Triumph: The American People, 1939–1945* (New York: Coward, McCann and Geoghegan, 1973), 257; Alan M. Winkler, *Home Front, U.S.A.: America during World War Two* (Wheeling, IL: Harlan-Davidson, 1986), 1, 9, 14, 21; Kennedy, *Freedom from Fear*, 626.

9. Winkler, *Home Front, U.S.A.*, 31–32; Perrett, *Days of Sadness*, 233; Ossian, *The Home Fronts of Iowa*, 101–104, 147–150; Mrs. Alexander George, "How to Stretch Your Weekly Meat Ration," *Sioux City Sunday Journal*, January 3, 1943, World War Two Iowa Press Clippings, University of Iowa Digital Library, https://digital.lib.uiowa.edu; Twedt, *Growing Up in the '40s*, 45.

10. Doris Kearns Goodwin, *No Ordinary Time: Franklin and Eleanor Roosevelt: The Home Front in World War Two* (New York: Simon and Schuster, 1994), 355–356; Winkler, *Home Front, U.S.A*, 37–39; William L. O'Neill, *A Democracy at War: America's Fight at Home and Abroad in World War Two* (Cambridge, MA: Harvard University Press, 1993), 137; Memoirs of John R. Ortega, 39, SHSI-IAC.

11. Goodwin, *No Ordinary Time*, 355–359; Blum, *V Was for Victory*, 95–96; Perrett, *Days of Sadness*, 238–239; Mark Jonathan Harris, Franklin D. Mitchell and Steven J. Schechter, *The Homefront: America during World War Two* (New York: G. P. Putnam's Sons, 1984), 76–77.

12. Winkler, *Home Front, U.S.A*, 32, Ossian, *Home Fronts of Iowa*, 134–137; O'Neill, *Democracy at War*, 137; "Victory Garden Project," "Lots Wanted," and untitled pages, folder 17, box 2, Johnson County Civilian Defense Council Papers, SHSI-IAC.

13. Ossian, *Home Fronts of Iowa*, 92–100; Twedt, *Growing Up in the '40s*, 44–45. See Measuring Worth, at https://measuringworth.com. Comparison dates here are 1943 and 1944. For a useful background on World War II war bonds see James J. Kimble, *Mobilizing the Home Front: War Bonds and Domestic Propaganda* (College Station: Texas A&M University Press, 2006).

14. "Jeeps! And with WAACs Too; $18.75," *Mason City Globe Gazette*, April 20, 1943; "10 Million Daily Needed in Bond Drive," *Des Moines Morning Register*, September 23, 1943; "What Your Money Bought," *Des Moines Morning Register*, November 19, 1943 (all articles from WWII Clippings, UI Library); Ossian, *Home Fronts of Iowa*, 95–97, 100.

15. Deemer Lee, *Esther's Town* (Ames: Iowa State University Press, 1980), 198–201.

16. Jim Davis, *Lest We Forget: World War Two Veterans of North Des Moines County* (n.p.: unknown publisher, 2002), 49–50; Associated Press, "Last Meskwaki Code Talker Remembers," July 4, 2002, *USA Today*, http://usatoday30.usatoday.com/news/nation/2002/07/06/codetalkers.htm; Tim Gallagher, "Former Odebolt Resident Remembers 6 Brothers Who Survived Pearl Harbor," *Sioux City Journal*, December 7, 2011, https://siouxcityjournal.com/news/local/gallagher-former-odebolt-resident-remembers-6-brothers-who-survived-pearl-harbor/article_776ea1ee-2979-5d5f-ab8f-1a2df3cd9d97.html; Ossian, *Home Fronts of Iowa*, 112–113, 160. No one from Iowa with the surname Reyes died in either the army or navy during World War II, so it is likely that all lived to see the end of the conflict. See "State Summary of War Casualties, Iowa, U.S. Navy, 1946," at https://www.archives.gov/research/military/ww2/navy-casualties/iowa.html and "World War II Honor List of Dead and Missing, State of Iowa," War Department, June 1946, at https://www.archives.gov/research/military/ww2/army-casualties/iowa.html. Other first-person accounts from World War II Iowa include the letters of Richard Robinson, who wrote more than five hundred letters to his family. See Richard Robinson Collection, SHSI-IAC, especially July–August 1944 and May–June 1945, on the Pacific theater. For maps and intelligence materials on D-Day, some marked "top secret," see the Herbert H. Hauge Papers, box one, SHSI-IAC. Norman A. Erbe, governor of Iowa from 1961 to 1963, left a riveting account of bombing raids over Europe in "Bomber '44: A War Memoir and Diary," SHSI-IAC. Also see his autobiography, Norman A. Erbe, *Ringside at the Fireworks: The Air Battle of World War II as Experienced by a Lead Pilot in a B-17 Bomber, Governor of Iowa, and Federal Executive* (Des Moines: Toreador Press, 1997).

17. James Q. Lynch, "Meskwaki Code Talkers' Receive Congressional Gold Medal," *Cedar Rapids Gazette*, November 20, 2013, https://www.thegazette.com/2013/11/20/meskwaki-code-talkers-receive-congressional-gold-medal/; AP, "Last Meskwaki Code Talker Remembers"; Mary Bennett, "Meskwaki Code Talkers," *Iowa Heritage Illustrated* 84, no. 4 (Winter 2003): 154–156. Jonas M. Poweshiek, grandson of the man who led the Meskwaki in the 1840s, wrote that forty-eight Sauk and Meskwaki had served in the American military during the war by early 1945. See Jonas M. Poweshiek, "Indians Again on the Warpath," *Annals of Iowa* 26, no. 4 (Spring 1945): 291–299. Poweshiek was a veteran of World War I who worked for the State Historical Society of Iowa from 1925 to 1956. See Jonas M. Poweshiek, "An Autobiography," *Annals of Iowa* 20, no. 6 (Fall 1936): 435–443. For more on Poweshiek see the May 21, 1958, article "An Indian Problem in Iowa" in the *Des Moines Register*. Written by the paper's editors, it is both an obituary of Poweshiek and a brief sketch of Meskwaki history in the state.

18. Henry Langrehr and Jim DeFelice, *Whatever It Took: An American Paratrooper's Extraordinary Memoir of Escape, Survival, and Heroism in the Last Days of World War Two* (New York: HarperCollins, 2020), 5–7, 21, 33, 57, 60, 80–81, 91, 133, 140–157, 173–183, 190–193, 199–201, 217–219.

19. October 18, 27, 28, 29, November 6 and 11, December 25 and 26, 1944, Quinones Family Correspondence, SHSI-IAC; January 9, 1945, *Mason City Globe Gazette*, clipping in Quinones Family Correspondence.

20. Edward C. Kramer, *We Salute You: World War Two Veterans from Central Iowa Share Their Experiences* (n.p.: Xlibris, 2010), 78, 86–88; Joseph Caver, Jerome Ennels and Daniel Haulman, *The Tuskegee Airmen: An Illustrated History, 1939–1949* (Louisville, KY: New South Books, 2011), 175, 182–183; William S. Morris, "Black Iowans in Defense of the Nation, 1863–1991," in *Outside In: African-American History in Iowa, 1838–2000*, ed. Bill Silag, Susan Koch-Bridgford, and Hal Chase (Des Moines: State Historical Society of Iowa, 2001), 119–121; Maureen Harmon, "The Flight of a Red-Tailed Angel," *Iowa Magazine*, February 2006, https://magazine.for iowa.org/archive/archive-story.php.

21. Robert D. McFadden, "Harold Hayes, Survivor of Secret World War II Odyssey, Dies at 94," January 24, 2017, *New York Times*, https://www.nytimes.com/2017/01/24/world/europe/harold-hayes-dead-world-war-ii-albania-crash.html; Darlene Diebler Rose, *Evidence Not Seen: A Woman's Miraculous Faith in the Jungles of World War Two* (New York: Harper Collins, 2001), ix–x, 14–21, 153–160, 223–224; "Darlene Rose," February 29, 2004, https://www.chattanoogan.com/2004/2/29/47410/Rose-Darlene. aspx. For more on Hayes's extraordinary story, see Cate Lineberry, *The Secret Rescue: An Untold Story of American Nurses and Medics behind Nazi Lines* (New York: Little, Brown, 2013). George Stout, who grew up in Winterset, helped lead the famed "Monuments Men" during World War II. He was a World War I veteran, who went to the State University of Iowa before going to Harvard for graduate school. He pushed the military and the arts community to create a group to protect and preserve European art, popularly known as the "Monuments Men." See Robert M. Edsel with Bret Witter, *The Monuments Men: Allied Heroes, Nazi Thieves, and the Greatest Treasure Hunt in History* (New York: Center Street, 2009), xiv, 25–30 for biographical information on Stout.

22. Studs Terkel, *"The Good War:" An Oral History of World War Two* (New York: Pantheon Books, 1984), 178–185.

23. Bruce Kuklick, *The Fighting Sullivans: How Hollywood and the Military Make Heroes* (Lawrence, KS: University Press of Kansas, 2016), 7–9, 36, 65–70, 171–174.

24. Goodwin, *No Ordinary Time*, 436; Rick Atkinson, *An Army at Dawn: The War in North Africa, 1942–1943* (New York: Henry Holt, 2002), 395–397; Milton Lehman, "Red Oak Hasn't Forgotten," *Saturday Evening Post*, August 17, 1946, 12–13, 71–72. Powell quote is from Lehman's article.

25. Winkler, *Home Front, U.S.A*, 49–55; Perrett, *Days of Sadness*, 344; Jacqueline Smetak, "Women on the Home Front: The Iowa WIPEs," *Palimpsest* 76, no. 4 (Winter 1995): 174–180. See Measuring Worth. The starting date here for comparison is 1943.

26. Emily Yellin, *Our Mother's War: American Women at Home and at the Front during World War Two* (New York: Free Press, 2004), 62–63; Ossian, *Home Fronts of Iowa*, 70–71.

27. Shelton Stromquist, *Solidarity and Survival: An Oral History of Iowa Labor in the Twentieth Century* (Iowa City: University of Iowa Press, 1993), 130–131; Ossian, *Home Fronts of Iowa*, 56–61.

28. Shelton Stromquist, *Solidarity and Survival*, 127–128.

29. Emily Yellin, *Our Mother's War*, 114–117; 137–148, 159–161. The best history of the WASPs is Katherine Sharp Landdeck, *The Women with Silver Wings: The*

Inspiring True Story of the Women Airforce Service Pilots of World War II (New York: Crown, 2020).

30. Yellin, *Our Mother's War*, 116–117; "A West Point for Women," *Des Moines Evening Tribune*, May 15, 1942; "Liberty No Catchword for These 2 WAACs," *Des Moines Evening Tribune*, April 21, 1943, WWII Clippings, UI Libraries; William S. Morris, "Black Iowans in Defense of the Nation," in *Outside In*, 123.

31. Lynn Ethan Nielsen and Mary Taylor Nielsen, *I'll Be Seeing You: World War II Diary and Correspondence, Cpl. Mary Elizabeth Osen, February 1943–September 1945* (Parkersburg, IA: Mid-Prairie Books, 1994), 5–7, 15, 20–21, 55–56, 109, 136.

32. Rosemary Tharp, "Spring of Our Lives," Rosemary Tharp Papers, Iowa Women's Archives, University of Iowa Libraries, Iowa City (IWA), 4–19, 22, 26, 30. See collection description for biographical information on Tharp. Iowa State Teachers College (now UNI) had a Naval Training School on its campus, which trained WAVES (Women Appointed for Voluntary Emergency Services). It was the first one in the nation. The first class graduated in January 1943 and training continued until 1945. See Gladys Whitley Hearst, "The WAVES at Cedar Falls," *Palimpsest* 28, no. 12 (December 1947): 367–376.

33. Ortha Neff Memoirs, Ortha Neff Papers, IWA.

34. Yellin, *Our Mother's War*, 210–212; Freddie D. Hawkins, "Discrimination against WAACs Is Charged," *Des Moines Evening Tribune*, January 11, 1943, WWII Clippings, UI Libraries.

35. Ossian, *Home Fronts of Iowa*, 68–69.

36. Timm, "Working with the Enemy," 228; Kennedy, *Freedom from Fear*, 645–647; Ossian, *Home Fronts of Iowa*, 25, 29, 33–37, 41–43.

37. "Work and Sacrifice for Farm Ownership," Life on a Montgomery County Farm, Faye Wookey Papers, IWA.

38. Timm, "Working with the Enemy," 225–232, 246–251; "Algona's 'Boom' Due to War Camp Work," October 15, 1943, *Des Moines Morning Register*, WWII Clippings, UI Libraries.

39. Timm, "Working with the Enemy," 236–239; "POW Camp Will Plant 120 acres for Victory Garden," *Clarinda Herald Journal*, February 21, 1944; "Prisoners Help in Labor Shortage," *Clarinda Herald Journal*, July 22, 1943; "Italian POWs Work on Iowa Levee," *Des Moines Evening Tribune*, April 15, 1944; "War Prisoners to Aid in Iowa's Nursing Work," *Des Moines Morning Register*, April 20, 1944; C. C. Clifton, "Iowa Nazi 'Guests' Well Fed and Guarded," *Des Moines Morning Register*, April 23, 1944; "War Prisoners Dig Postholes for REA," *Des Moines Morning Register*, October 11, 1944; "Tells Change in Prisoners since Defeat," *Des Moines Morning Register*, June 17, 1945; "Prisoner of War Camp Impresses," and "Prisoner Demand Exceeds Supply," *Council Bluffs Nonpareil*, both June 15, 1944; "Wide Variety in German Prisoners at Algona Camp," *Fort Dodge Messenger*, November 18, 1944, all WWII Clippings, UI Libraries. Most of these articles can also be found through https://www.newspapers.com.

40. Takaki, *Double Victory*, 90–97; Ossian, *Home Fronts of Iowa*, 32; Daniel Martinez, "The Impact of the Bracero Programs on a Southern California Mexican-American

Community: A Field Study of Cucamonga, California" (MA thesis, Claremont Graduate School, 1958), 18; Andrea Kay Tucker, "Together: They Lived, Worked and Learned, The History of Latinos in Valley Junction, Iowa" (MA thesis, Iowa State University, 2008), 12–14. Iowa farmers employed 1,178 braceros in 1944, 1,467 in 1945 and 1,378 in 1946. This number fell to 188 in 1947. See Measuring Worth.

41. Collection description, Curt A. Zimansky Collection of Prints, Special Collections and University Archives, University of Iowa Libraries, University of Iowa, Iowa City; Kennedy, *Freedom from Fear*, 453; Landis Gores, "Princetonians in the Ultra Service," *Princeton Alumni Weekly*, May 27, 1975, 10–13; Alan Cowell, "Overlooked No More: Alan Turing, Condemned Code Breaker and Computer Visionary," *New York Times*, June 5, 2019, https://www.nytimes.com/2019/06/05/obituaries/alan-turing-overlooked.html. Ultra may have helped win the Battle of Britain and the Battle of the Atlantic, aided in the defeat Rommel in North Africa, and hastened Allied victory in Normandy. See Frederick William Winterbotham, *The Ultra Secret* (New York: Harper & Row, 1974).

42. Teresa Wilhelm Waldof, *Wilhelm's Way: The Inspiring Story of the Iowa Chemist Who Saved the Manhattan Project* (Rochester, MN: Third Generation Publishing, 2022), 19, 73–77, 87–103, 119, 127–129, 145–152, 168, 184–188, 289–291; Dorothy Schwieder, *Iowa: The Middle Land* (Ames: Iowa State University Press, 1996), 285. For more on the Manhattan Project in Iowa see Susan Futrell, "Atoms amidst the Cornfields: Pride, Patriotism, and Secret Atomic Research at Ames, Iowa," *Iowa Heritage Illustrated* 93, no. 2 (Summer 2014): 66–74. Uranium production left slag behind. A thousand whiskey barrels were ordered to store it, which led to questions from the college's purchasing office. Once they arrived, eager volunteers offered to unload a freight car, enjoying whiskey that remained in barrels. Liquor was rationed during the war. See Futrell, 72–73.

CHAPTER 13: POSTWAR IOWA, 1945–1975

1. *1980 Census of Population, Volume 1, Characteristics of the Population, Chapter B, General Population Characteristics, Part 1, United States Summary* (Washington, DC: US Government Printing Office, 1983), 1–125.

2. Geoffrey Perrett, *A Dream of Greatness: The American People, 1945–1963* (New York: Coward, McCann and Geoghegan, 1979), 19; H. W. Brands, *American Dreams: The United States Since 1945* (New York: Penguin Books, 2010), 10; James T. Patterson, *Grand Expectations: The United States, 1945–1974* (New York: Oxford University Press, 1996), 3; John Patrick Diggins, *The Proud Decades: America in War and Peace, 1941–1960* (New York: W. W. Norton, 1988), 51; "Pure Bedlam Sweeps C.R. at News—'It's Wonderful,'" *Cedar Rapids Gazette*, August 15, 1945, https://www.newspapers.com/image/legacy/550924896/; "World War Is Ended," *Fayette County Leader*, August 16, 1945, https://www.newspapers.com/image/868741; "War Ends, Big Job Ahead," *Des Moines Register*, August 15, 1945, https://www.newspapers.com/image/legacy/129314892/; Howard R. Wilson, "Carroll Hails End

of War with Whoopee, Closing of Stores and Church Services," *Carroll Daily Times Herald*, August 15, 1945, https://www.newspapers.com/image/legacy/4906161/; "Mt. Pleasant Greeted News with Thanks," *Mount Pleasant News*, August 15, 1945, https://www.newspapers.com/image/30095850; "Waterloo Stages Riotous V-J Show," *Waterloo Courier*, August 15, 1945, https://www.newspapers.com/image/legacy/35604352 0/; "Tears, Laughter Greet War's End," and "Rationing of Gas, Canned Goods, Fuel Oil Is Terminated," *Council Bluffs Nonpareil*, August 15, 1945, https://www.newspapers.com/image/ legacy/37660285/. September 2, 1945, was the date of the official Japanese surrender.

3. "Jewish Population of Europe," Holocaust Museum, accessed February 7, 2022, https://encyclopedia.ushmm.org/content/en/gallery/jewish-population-of-europe; Adele Anolik, *The Liberation of the Concentration Camps 1945, the Des Moines, Iowa Survivors* (North Liberty, IA: Ice Cube Press, 2008), 48–49, 64–65.

4. Brands, *American Dreams*, 11, 27–28; Perrett, *Dream of Greatness*, 20–22, 25, 36–37, 52; "What War's End Means to U.S.," *Council Bluffs Nonpareil*, August 15, 1945, https://www.newspapers.com/image/legacy/37660285/; "Nine Million to Be Out of Jobs by Next June," *Carroll Daily Times Herald*, August 15, 1945, https://www.newspapers.com/image/4906161.

5. Patterson, *Grand Expectations*, 10, 61–63, 67.

6. Ginalie Swaim, "The Polio Epidemics," *Goldfinch* 19, no. 1 (Fall 1997): 25–26; David M. Oshinsky, *Polio: An American Story* (New York: Oxford University Press, 2005), 1–6, 255, 282–285; Gerald N. Grob, *The Deadly Truth: A History of Disease in America* (Cambridge, MA: Harvard University Press, 1992), 189–192; Judy Hoit, "Living with Polio," *Goldfinch* 19, no. 1 (Fall 1997): 27; Joe Coffey, "History Happenings: Before Covid-19 Came Polio and, Finally, a Vaccine," *Cedar Rapids Gazette*, April 20, 2021, https://www.thegazette.com/history/history-happenings-before-covid-19-came-polio-and-finally-a-vaccine/; Judy Hoit, *Wheels of Dreams* (Iowa City: Access Now, 2016), 3–11, back cover; "Polio Elimination in the United States," Center for Disease Control and Prevention, accessed February 13, 2023, https://www.cdc.gov/polio/what-is-polio/polio-us.html. Polio was found in New York in the summer of 2022. For more see Apoorva Mandavilli, "Polio Was Almost Eradicated. This Year It Staged a Comeback," *New York Times*, August 18, 2022, https://www.nytimes.com/2022/08/18/health/polio-new-york-malawi.html.

7. "Iowa Statistics," *Palimpsest* 36, no. 7 (July 1955), inside back cover of magazine; "Iowa Statistics," *Palimpsest* 34, no. 7 (July 1953), inside back cover; "Iowa Statistics," *Palimpsest* 37, no. 7 (July 1956), inside back cover; Perrett, *Dream of Greatness*, 68–69; Robert Wuthnow, *Remaking the Heartland: Rural America since the 1950s* (Princeton: Princeton University Press, 2011), 115, 121; Douglas Biggs, "The 1940s: Iowa State and a World at War," *Visions* (Summer 2014): 15–17; Memoir of John R. Ortega, 15, 21–22, SHSI-IAC; UNI Factbook information online at: https://scua.library.uni.edu/university-archives/articles/uni-fact-sheet. See Measuring Worth, at https://measuringworth.com for price comparisons. The *Palimpsest* published a useful summary of Iowa's weather, politics, agriculture, and industry in its July issue in the mid- and late 1950s.

8. Roger Biles, *Illinois: A History of the Land and Its People* (DeKalb: Northern Illinois University Press, 2005), 252–255; "Total Population for Iowa's Incorporated Places," State Data Center, accessed October 2, 2021, https://www.iowadatacenter.org; Shelby Fleig, "Growth in Des Moines Metro Accounts for Half of Iowa's Recent Population Increase," *Des Moines Register*, May 22, 2020, https://www.desmoinesregister.com/story/news/2020/05/22/des-moines-suburbs-booming-while-iowa-towns-lose-population-ankeny-waukee-bondurant-grimes-johnston/5247715002/.

9. Patterson, *Grand Expectations*, 274, 316; Robert J. Gordon, *The Rise and Fall of American Growth: The U.S. Standard of Living since the Civil War* (Princeton: Princeton University Press, 2016), 389–392; William H. Thompson, *Transportation in Iowa: A Historical Summary* (n.p: Iowa Department of Transportation, 1989), 245–250; Earl Swift, *The Big Roads: The Untold Story of the Engineers, Visionaries, and Trailblazers Who Created the American Superhighways* (New York: Mariner Books, 2011), 255. See Measuring Worth. The $4.5 billion dollar figure is based on 1971 as a comparison year. If an earlier year is used, such as 1965, the cost would be $5.7 billion in 2020 dollars. Most of the Iowa interstate system was built in the 1960s. See Thompson for more information.

10. Nikole Hannah-Jones, "Our Democracy's Founding Ideas Were False When They Were Written. Black Americans Fought to Make Them True," *New York Times Magazine*, August 14, 2019, https://www.nytimes.com/interactive/2019/08/14/magazine/black-history-american-democracy.html. Iowan Nikole Hannah-Jones won a Pulitzer Prize for Commentary in 2020 for the 1619 magazine special edition published by the *New York Times* on August 14, 2019. Some historians have argued that Hannah-Jones, and the *Times*, made avoidable errors. This minor criticism aside, the 1619 project is one of the most important reinterpretations of American history in decades. For an example of historical criticism, see Leslie M. Harris, "I Helped Fact-Check the 1619 Project. The Times Ignored Me," *Politico*, March 6, 2020, https://www.politico.com/news/magazine/2020/03/06/1619-project-new-york-times-mistake-122248. See https://pulitzercenter.org for more on Hannah-Jones.

11. Thomas J. Sugre, *Sweet Land of Liberty: The Forgotten Struggle for Civil Rights in the North* (New York: Random House, 2008), 201–205; Brenda Richardson, "Redlining's Legacy of Inequality: Low Home Ownership Rates, Less Equity for Black Households," *Forbes*, June 11, 2020, https://www.forbes.com/sites/brendarichardson/2020/06/11/redlinings-legacy-of-inequality-low-homeownership-rates-less-equity-for-black-households/?sh=d518ae62a7c9; Kim Norvell, "Redlining: How Racist Policy from a 1930s Program Has Left Scars Still Visible in Today's Des Moines," *Des Moines Register*, June 25, 2020, https://www.desmoinesregister.com/story/news/2020/06/25/how-redlining-legacy-persists-des-moines-iowa-lowering-home-values-systemic-racism/3216594001/.

12. Norvell, "Redlining"; Richardson, "Redlining's Legacy of Inequality"; Charles E. Connerly, *Green, Fair, and Prosperous: Paths to a Sustainable Iowa* (Iowa City: University of Iowa Press, 2020), 119–120; Shelby Fleig, "From Redlining to the Ash Borer, Des Moines' City Forester Has Put the Finishing Touches on a Master Plan. Now He Can Retire," *Des Moines Register*, May 3, 2021; https://www.desmoinesregister.com

/story/news/local/des-moines/2021/05/03/retiring-des-moines-forester-created-citys-first-urban-forestry-plan-environment-government-policy/7356359002/. The "Mapping Inequality: Redlining in New Deal America," at https://dsl.richmond.edu, has digitized maps for Iowa, as well as major cities around the country, with data on poverty, life expectancy, and disease.

13. Swift, *Big Roads*, 265–267; Bruce Fehn and Robert Jefferson, "North Side Revolutionaries in the Civil Rights Struggle: The African American Community in Des Moines and the Black Panther Party for Self-Defense, 1948–1970," *Annals of Iowa* 69, no. 1 (Winter 2010): 55–57, 60; Ashley Halsey III, "A Crusade to Defeat the Legacy of Highways Rammed through Poor Neighborhoods," *Washington Post*, March 29, 2016, https://www.washingtonpost.com/local/trafficandcommuting/defeating-the-legacy-of-highways-rammed-through-poor-neighborhoods/2016/03/28/ffcfb5ae-f2a1-11e5-a61f-e9c95c06edca_story.html; Gaynelle Narcisse, *They Took Our Piece of the Pie: Center Street Revisited* (Des Moines: Iowa Bystander Company, 1996), 3–4, 10–11, 16–17, 21–25, 32; Jack Lufkin, "Patten's Neighborhood: The Center Street Community and the African-American Printer Who Preserved It," *Iowa Heritage Illustrated* 77, no. 3 (Fall 1996): 122–124, 139–142; Norvell, "Redlining,"; James Beaumont, "Evicted Negroes Relocate Nearby," *Des Moines Register*, March 24, 1967, https://www.newspapers.com/image/338920494; Dean Fischer and Jerry Szomski, "500 Hear Clash on Housing," *Des Moines Register*, October 24, 1963, https://www.newspapers.com/image/legacy/129202070/?terms=.

14. Noah Lawrence, "'Since It Is My Right, I would Like to Have It': Edna Griffin and the Katz Drug Store Desegregation Movement," *Annals of Iowa* 67, no. 4 (Fall 2008): 298–305, 311, 316–317, 328. A copy of Griffin's FBI file can be found at the Iowa Women's Archives at the University of Iowa Libraries.

15. Lawrence, "'Since It Is My Right,'" 308, 315–319, 321, 324–329.

16. Fehn and Jefferson, "North Side Revolutionaries," 53–54, 61–62.

17. Glenda Riley, *Cities on the Cedar: A Portrait of Cedar Falls, Waterloo, and Black Hawk County* (Parkersburg, IA: Mid-Prairie Books, 1994), 72–74; Dorothy Schwieder, *Iowa: The Middle Land* (Ames: Iowa State University Press, 1996), 308; Fehn and Jefferson, "North Side Revolutionaries," 52–53, 61; Connerly, *Green, Fair, and Prosperous*, 112–113. Quote is from Schwieder. Cecil Reed was a Black businessman from Cedar Rapids who spent decades in a white world that did not see him as an equal. He was elected to the Iowa House of Representatives in 1966 as a Republican and served in a variety of state and federal positions for twenty years. See Cecil A. Reed with Priscilla Donovan, *Fly in the Buttermilk: The Life Story of Cecil Reed* (Iowa City: University of Iowa Press, 1993), 24–29, 77, 117.

18. Fehn and Jefferson, "North Side Revolutionaries," 51–52, 64–68, 77; Gene Roberts, "Waterloo Iowa, Puzzled by Riots," *New York Times*, July 14, 1967, https://www.nytimes.com/1967/07/14/archives/waterloo-iowa-puzzled-by-riots-negro-youth-hostile-despite.html.

19. Saul Sanchez, *Rows of Memory: Journeys of a Migrant Sugar-Beet Worker* (Iowa City: University of Iowa Press, 2014), xi, xviii, xxii, 31, 52, 73, 103–110, 129, 165, 183–184; Janet Weaver, "From Barrio to "¡Boicoteo!": The Emergence of

Mexican-American Activism in Davenport, 1917–1970," *Annals of Iowa* 68, no. 3 (Summer 2009): 215–216, 224–225, 230, 234, 240–248. Ramona Ortega-Liston's memoir is a moving account of the Mexican American experience in mid-twentieth century Iowa. See Ramona Ortega-Liston, *Betrayal and Conquer: An American Story of Courage and Resilience* (Dublin, OH: Telemachus Press, 2016).

20. Ronald C. Powers, *The Population Change of Eight Southern Iowa Counties* (Ames: Iowa State University of Science and Technology Cooperative Extension Service, 1965), 3–11; Thomas G. Johnson and James K. Scott, "Population Trends and Impact on Viability," in *The American Midwest: Managing Change in Rural Transition*, ed. Norman Walker (Armonk, NY: M. E. Sharpe, 2003), 70–71; *1978 Census of Agriculture—U.S. Data, Part 51* (Washington, DC: Bureau of the Census, 1981), 1; *Iowa: A State in Social and Economic Transition* (Iowa City: Iowa College-Community Research Center, 1958), 3–8, 16–17. For a fine overview of postwar female activism see Jenny Barker Devine, *On Behalf of the Family Farm: Iowa Farm Women's Activism since 1945* (Iowa City: University of Iowa Press, 2013).

21. Wuthnow, *Remaking the Heartland*, 107–109; George S. May, "Religion and Education," *Palimpsest* 37, no. 7 (July 1956): 382; "Iowa Statistics," *Palimpsest* 36, no. 7 (July 1955), inside back cover of magazine; Associated Press, "Big High Schools Gaining in Iowa," *New York Times*, October 29, 1961, https://www.nytimes.com/1961/10/29/archives/big-high-schools-gaining-in-iowa-students-said-to-get-more.html; George S. May, "The Rural School Problem," *Palimpsest* 37, no. 1 (January 1956): 5–10; David R. Reynolds, "The Making of Buck Creek: Country Life Reform, Religion, and Rural School Consolidation," *Annals of Iowa* 58, no. 4 (Fall 1999): 386–387.

22. George S. May, "Overcoming Opposition," *Palimpsest* 37, no. 1 (January 1956): 36–43; AP, "Big High Schools Gaining in Iowa"; Alice C. McMurry, "Eight Decades on the Prairie," 65–66, Alice C. McMurry Papers, Iowa Women's Archives, University of Iowa Libraries, University of Iowa, Iowa City (IWA).

23. AP, "Big High Schools Gaining in Iowa."

24. Will Fellows, ed., *Farm Boys: Lives of Gay Men from the Rural Midwest* (Madison: University of Wisconsin Press, 1996), 84–89.

25. Kenneth F. Millsap, "Town and Country," *Palimpsest* 32, no. 9 (September 1951): 363–365; Paul K. Conkin, *A Revolution Down on the Farm: The Transformation of American Agriculture since 1929* (Lexington: University Press of Kentucky, 2008), 87, 95–112, 115–124, 131; J. L. Anderson, *Industrializing the Corn Belt: Agriculture, Technology, and Environment, 1945–1972* (Dekalb: Northern Illinois Press, 2009), 5–9, 193–195; *Iowa: A State in Social and Economic Transition*, 4. Also see Derek S. Oden, *Harvest of Hazards: Family Farming, Accidents, and Expertise in the Corn Belt, 1940–1975* (Iowa City: University of Iowa Press, 2017) for an overview of the perils that new technology presented to farm families.

26. Seth S. King, "A Young Farmer Faces the Farm Problem," *New York Times Magazine*, April 29, 1956, 9–10, 68–70, 76; William Barry Furlong, "The Farmer's Winter of Discontent," *New York Times Magazine*, February 28, 1960, 23, 80, 81; David B. Danbom, *Born in the Country: A History of Rural America* (Baltimore: Johns Hopkins University Press, 1995), 240–241. See Measuring Worth. Comparison year here is 1955.

27. "The New American Family Farmer," *Newsweek*, May 2, 1966, 21–22.

28. Furlong, "Farmer's Winter of Discontent," 23; Lauren Soth, "Iowa, or What's Happening to Farming," *New York Times Magazine*, December 2, 1962, 79, 82; Wilma Embres, Oral History Interview, September 18, 2001, conducted by Doris Malkmus, Voices from the Land: An Oral History Project in Iowa, 9–10, IWA. See Measuring Worth. The comparison year for the IBM employee is 1960 and 1955 for Embres.

29. Kenneth F. Millsap, "Town and Country," *Palimpsest* 32, no. 9 (September 1951): 361–363; Riley, *Cities on the Cedar*, 65–67; Lauren Soth, "Report from the American 'Heartland,'" *New York Times Magazine*, June 3, 1962; Ralph Scharnau, "Workers, Unions, and Workplaces in Dubuque," *Annals of Iowa* 52, no. 1 (Winter 1993): 67–79; George S. May, "Industry and Agriculture," *Palimpsest* 36, no. 7 (July 1955): 265–266. In 1954 Iowa had the nation's largest number of hogs and was second, behind Texas, in the size of its beef herds. It was, of course, the leading producer of corn. See May, 266. See Measuring Worth for price comparisons.

30. Riley, *Cities on the Cedar*, 65–69; George S. May, "Industry and Agriculture," 262–265; Robert Rutland, "Agriculture and Industry," *Palimpsest* 33, no. 11 (November 1952): 348; George S. May, "Agriculture and Industry," *Palimpsest* 37, no. 7 (July 1956): 366–367; Scharnau, "Workers, Unions, and Workplaces," 70–72.

31. Coreen Derifield, "'I Thought of the Money That We Could Use': Iowa Women and Industrial Wage Work, 1950–1970," *Annals of Iowa* 73, no. 1 (Fall 2014): 28–31, 35–37, 39–44, 58–59.

32. Derifield, "'I Thought of the Money,'" 38–42, 45, 49–51, 55–56.

33. Fern Klopp, Oral History Interview transcript, September 12, 1980, Iowa Labor History Oral Project, State Historical Society of Iowa, 1–13, 25–29, Iowa Digital Library, University of Iowa Libraries, https://digital.lib.uiowa.edu/islandora/object/ui%3Ailhop.

34. Patterson, *Grand Expectations*, 126–131, 207–210.

35. Clay Blair Jr., *The Forgotten War: America in Korea, 1950–1953* (New York: Times Books, 1987), x; Hampton Sides, *On Desperate Ground: The Epic Story of Chosin Reservoir—The Greatest Battle of the Korean War* (New York: Anchor Books, 2019), 14, 19, 51, 116–117; Joseph Morton, "Kin of Captured Korean War Soldier from Iowa Gather for Long Overdue Burial," *Omaha World-Herald*, April 3, 2017, https://omaha.com/local/kin-of-captured-korean-war-soldier-from-iowa-gather-for-long-overdue-burial/article_03264c0c-64c6-5a88-9cc6-a78e6a6f72d6.html; Robert Lee Gates Collection (AFC/2001/001/115920), Veterans History Project, American Folklife Center, Library of Congress (VHP-LOC); Antonio Montognese Collection (AFC/2001/001/115920), VHP-LOC; Herbert Bill Barger Collection, (AFC/2001/001/73740), VHP-LOC; Vernon Joseph Becker Collection (AFC/2001/001/73740), VHP-LOC.

36. Stow Persons, *The University of Iowa in the Twentieth Century: An Institutional History* (Iowa City: University of Iowa Press, 1990), 194–201; John C. Gerber, *A Pictorial History of the University of Iowa* (Iowa City: University of Iowa Press, 1988), 214–219; John W. Johnson, *The Struggle for Student Rights: Tinker v. Des Moines and the 1960s* (Lawrence: University Press of Kansas, 1997), ix–x, 4–9, 173, 217; David

Hamilton, "Science with Humanity: The Parks Years," in *Tradition and Transformation: A Sesquicentennial History of Iowa State University*, ed. Dorothy Schwieder and Gretchen Van Houten (Ames: Iowa State University Press, 2007), 92–96.

37. James D. Seddon, *Morning Glories among the Peas: A Vietnam Veteran's Story* (Ames: Iowa State University Press, 1990), 4, 7, 17, 23–27, 35–36, 103–104, 107, 128–133.

38. C. D. B. Bryant, *Friendly Fire* (New York: G. P. Putnam, 1976), 1, 15, 36–49, 107, 110, 145, 185, 210, 221–223, 247, 259, 434–436; Rod Boshart, "Iowans Who Died, Served in Vietnam War Honored," *Cedar Rapids Gazette*, May 7, 2014, https://www.thegazette.com/state-government/iowans-who-died-served-in-vietnam-war-honored/. Also see Peg Mullen, *Unfriendly Fire: A Mother's Memoir* (Iowa City: University of Iowa Press, 1995).

39. Leland L. Sage, *A History of Iowa* (Ames: Iowa State University, 1974), 322–323; Lauren Soth, *An Embarrassment of Plenty: Agriculture in Affluent America* (New York: Thomas Y. Crowell, 1965), 170–171.

40. Peter Irons, *A People's History of the Supreme Court* (New York: Penguin Books, 1999), 416–417; Sage, *History of Iowa*, 326–329.

41. Neal Smith, *Mr. Smith Went to Washington: From Eisenhower to Clinton* (Ames: Iowa State University Press, 1995), xiv–xxiii, 11, 17–19, 50–52; William Morris, "Former US Rep. Neal Smith, Dead at 101, Recalled as 'Epitome' of a Good Public Servant, 'A True Iowa Treasure,'" *Des Moines Register*, November 3, 2021, https://www.desmoinesregister.com/story/news/politics/2021/11/03/neal-smith-iowa-longest-serving-member-house-congressman-dies-101-obituary/6249942001/. He died at age 101 in 2021.

42. James C. Larew, *A Party Reborn: The Democrats of Iowa, 1950–1974* (Iowa City: Iowa State Historical Department, 1980), 1–2, 7–9, 74–77, 127–128, 133–134; Sage, *History of Iowa*, 318–321; Neal Smith, *Twentieth Century Politics in Iowa and the Emergence of the Democratic Party* (N.p.: Iowa Democratic Party, 1998), 47–50. Also see Jerry Harrington, *Thunder from the Prairie: The Life of Harold E. Hughes* (Lawrence: University Press of Kansas, forthcoming).

43. Larew, *Party Reborn*, 73, 77–87, 95, 117–124; Janice Nahra Friedel, "Engines of Economic Development: The Origins and Evolution of Iowa's Comprehensive Community Colleges," *American Educational Historical Journal* 37, nos. 1–2 (2010): 207–220; Bart Barnes, "Harold Hughes Dies at 74," *Washington Post*, October 25, 1996, https://www.washingtonpost.com/archive/local/1996/10/25/harold-hughes-dies-at-74/5c2e1ca8-ce34-4d3f-93f4-d684ba9f1e5b/; Harold E. Hughes and Dick Schreider, *The Man from Ida Grove: A Senator's Personal Story* (Lincoln, Virginia: Chosen Books, 1979), 298–300. Hughes's autobiography is the best source on his early life. Harrington's *Thunder from the Prairie* is the sole biography of Hughes.

44. Daniel P. Finney, "Branstad vs. Ray: Defining Heroes and Villains," *Des Moines Register*, March 9, 2017, https://www.desmoinesregister.com/story/news/local/columnists/daniel-finney/2017/03/08/branstad-vs-ray-defining-heroes-and-villains/98855476/; Schwieder, *Middle Land*, 309–311; Jon Bowermaster, *Governor: An Oral History of Robert D. Ray* (Ames: Iowa State University Press, 1987), 87, 103, 106,

135–139, 224, 253–54; Wuthnow, *Remaking the Heartland*, 113; John W. McKerley, "Collective Bargaining: Why Dismantle Landmark Law?," *Des Moines Register*, February 10, 2017, https://www.desmoinesregister.com/story/opinion/columnists/iowa-view/2017/02/10/collective-bargaining-why-dismantle-landmark-law/97732230/. Ray served three two-year terms and two four-year terms as governor, after the gubernatorial term was extended to four years, starting in 1974.

45. Schwieder, *Middle Land*, 311–312; Douglas E. Icneeland, "'Boat People' Find Jobs, Fellow Asians in Iowa," *New York Times*, May 8, 1979, https://www.nytimes.com/1979/05/08/archives/boat-people-find-jobs-and-fellow-asians-in-iowa-easier-than.html; Bowermaster, *Governor*, 237–241; Siang Bacthi, InNgeun Baccam, Saul Inahauong and Jack Lufkin, "'So We Stayed Together:' The Tai Dam Immigrate to Iowa," *Palimpsest* 69, no. 4 (Winter 1988): 163–164.

46. Icneeland, "Boat People"; Bowermaster, *Governor*, 241.

47. Bowermaster, *Governor*, 241.

48. Justin Gillis, "Norman Borlaug, Plant Scientist Who Fought Famine, Dies at 95," *New York Times*, September 13, 2009, https://www.nytimes.com/2009/09/14/business/energy-environment/14borlaug.html; Greg Easterbrook, "The Man Who Defused the 'Population Bomb,'" *Wall Street Journal*, September 16, 2009, https://www.wsj.com/articles/SB10001424052970203917304574411382676924044; Jerry Perkins and Tom Longden, "From the Archives: September 12 Marks Anniversary of Nobel Laureate, Iowa Native Norman Borlaug's Death," *Des Moines Register*, September 12, 2017, https://www.desmoinesregister.com/story/news/2017/09/12/nobel-laureate-iowa-native-norman-borlaug-world-food-prize/658320001/; Leon Hesser, *The Man Who Fed the World: Nobel Peace Prize Laureate Norman Borlaug and His Battle to End World Hunger* (Princeton: Righter's Mill Press, 2009), 1–4, 201; Norman Borlaug Institute, " Dr. Norman Borlaug," accessed April 19, 2023, https://Borlaug.tamu.edu/home/dr-norman-borlaug/. For a fine overview of Borlaug and his importance, see Charles C. Mann, *The Wizard and the Prophet: Two Remarkable Scientists and Their Dueling Visions to Shape Tomorrow's World* (New York: Vintage Books, 2019.)

49. Seth S. King, "Iowa Town, Aided by Farm Prosperity, Weathering Fuel Shortages," *New York Times*, March 9, 1974, https://www.nytimes.com/1974/03/09/archives/iowa-town-aided-by-farm-prosperity-weathering-the-fuel-shortage.html; Brands, *American Dreams*, 195–198; Joshua B. Freeman, *American Empire: The Rise of a Global Power, the Democratic Revolution at Home, 1945–2000* (New York: Penguin Books, 2013), 296–297.

CHAPTER 14: IOWA AND THE FARM CRISIS, 1975–2000

1. Dorothy Schwieder, *Iowa: The Middle Land* (Ames: Iowa State University, 1996), 313–314; David Westphal, "Riches to Rags: Iowa's Economic Upheaval: Flat, Fertile Iowa's Promised Land Is Now a Land of Broken Promises," *Des Moines Register*, June 16, 1985, https://www.newspapers.com/image/legacy/131190361/?terms=; Pamela Riney-Kehrberg, *When A Dream Dies: Agriculture, Iowa, and the Farm Crisis*

of the 1980s (Lawrence: University Press of Kansas, 2022), 20–25. See Measuring Worth, at https://measuringworth.com. Comparison dates here are 1980 and 2020.

2. Osha Davidson, "The Rise of the Rural Ghetto," *Nation*, June 14, 1986: 820–822; Barry J. Barnett, "The U.S. Farm Financial Crisis of the 1980s," *Agricultural History* 74, no. 2 (Spring 2000): 366.

3. Barnett, "U.S. Farm Financial Crisis," 366–375; Kathryn Marie Dudley, *Debt and Dispossession: Farm Loss in America's Heartland* (Chicago: University of Chicago Press, 2000), 12–13, 32–35; "Early, Crossroads of the Nation," *People*, November 3, 1986, 124–134; Curtis Hartman, "On the Road: Johnson County, Iowa," *Inc.*, May 1, 1986, https://www.inc.com/magazine/19860501/839.html.

4. Barnett, "U.S. Farm Financial Crisis," 367–368; Kevin M. Kruse and Julian E. Zelizer, *Fault Lines: A History of the United States Since 1974* (New York: W. W. Norton, 2019), 28–33.

5. Barnett, "U.S. Farm Financial Crisis," 366, 373–375; John J. McLaughlin, "Farm Blues," *National Review* (March 1985): 24; Riney-Kehrberg, *When a Dream Dies*, 25–28, 37–38.

6. Osha Gray Davidson, *Broken Heartland: The Rise of America's Rural Ghetto* (New York: Free Press, 1990), 9–10, 14–21, 75; Westphal, "Fertile Iowa's Promised Land"; Michael D. Boehlje, Brent A. Gloy, and Jason R. Henderson, "U.S. Farm Prosperity: The New Normal or Reversion to the Mean," *American Journal of Agricultural Economics* 95, no. 2 (January 2013): 312; Mark Friedberger, "Women Advocates in the Iowa Farm Crisis of the 1980s," *Agricultural History* 67, no. 2 (Spring 1993): 224; David B. Danbom, *Born in the Country: A History of Rural America* (Baltimore: Johns Hopkins University Press, 1995), 263; Paul Lasley, "The Crisis in Iowa," in *Is There A Moral Obligation to Save the Family Farm?* ed. Gary Comstock (Ames: Iowa State University Press, 1987), 105; Al Swegle, "Economic Tough Times Topped Farm Stories of 1982," *Cedar Rapids Gazette* December 27, 1982, https://www.newspapers.com/image/legacy/550848157/?terms=economic%20tough%20times&match=1. See Measuring Worth for price comparisons.

7. "Early, Crossroads of the Nation."

8. Westphal, "Fertile Iowa's Promised Land;" David Westphal, "Riches to Rags, Iowa's Economic Upheaval: Farmers Find Need to Supplement Income," *Des Moines Register*, June 19, 1985, https://www.newspapers.com/image/legacy/131192408/.

9. Dennis Farney, "In Iowa, Mental Anguish Still Racks Families, Taxes Social Workers, Even as Farm Crisis Abates," *Wall Street Journal*, May 18, 1988; Davidson, *Broken Heartland*, 9; James A. Rubin, "Farmers in Crisis," *New York Times*, February 26, 1987, https://www.nytimes.com/1987/02/26/opinion/farmers-in-crisis.html; Paul Hendrickson, "Those Who Are No Longer With Us," in *Is There A Moral Obligation*, 47–50; "CAA, Farm Crises Units to Bring Food to Hungry," *Sioux City Journal*, December 29, 1985, https://www.newspapers.com/image/legacy/337030498/?terms=CAA%20farm%20crises%20units&match=1; Mark Friedberger, *Shake-Out: Iowa Farm Families in the 1980s* (Lexington: University Press of Kentucky, 1989), 73.

10. Riney-Kehrberg, *When a Dream Dies*, 184–185.

11. Jacob V. Lamar Jr. and Lee Griggs, "'He Couldn't Manage Any More:' A

Shooting Spree in Iowa Underscores the Farmers' Plight," *Time Magazine*, December 23, 1985, 26; Ann Marie Lipinski, "A Farming Legacy Wiped Out," *Chicago Tribune* December 11, 1985, https://www.chicagotribune.com/news/ct-xpm-1985-12-11-8503250563-story.html; Hartman, "On the Road: Johnson County, Iowa." Burr's brother-in-law, Keith Forbes, estimated that Dale Burr's debts could have totaled $1 million.

12. Jim Schwab, *Raising Less Corn and More Hell: Midwestern Farmers Speak Out* (Urbana: University of Illinois Press, 1988), 80–81.

13. Friedberger, "Women Advocates," 224–234.

14. Claudia Dreifus, "Families Who Needed Someone to Care," *Redbook*, December 1988, 108–109, 174, Joan Blundall Papers, Iowa Women's Archives, University of Iowa Libraries, Iowa City, Iowa (IWA); Phil Brown, "Joan Blundall: A Woman for All Seasons," *Dickinson County News*, June 3, 2000, Joan Blundall Papers, IWA; Joan Blundall, oral history interview, October 24, 2001, conducted by Doris Malkmus, Voices from the Land: An Oral History Project in Iowa, IWA.

15. Denise O'Brien, "We Who Are Hanging on the Edge," in *Moral Obligation*, 61; Jim Schwab, "Farm Protests Hit the Statehouses," *Nation*, January 19, 1985: 42–43; William C. Pratt, "Using History to Make History? Progressive Farm Organizing During the Farm Revolt of the 1980s," *Annals of Iowa* 55, no. 1 (Winter 1996): 24–29, 34, 40–41; "About Us," accessed October 1, 2022, https://www.farmaid.org/about-us/; Harrison Weber, "Mass Food Stamp Drive Set to Show Farmers Not Alone," *Cedar Rapids Gazette*, February 19, 1986, https://www.newspapers.com/image/legacy/551774474; Don Muhm, "Tractor Duo Doesn't Regret Protest," *Des Moines Register*, June 9, 1985, https://www.newspapers.com/image/131920228; Associated Press, "Farmers Reaping Bitter Harvest," *Waterloo Courier*, January 27, 1985, https://www.newspapers.com/image/356557313.

16. Roger G. Ginder, Kenneth E. Stone, and Daniel Otto, "Impact of the Farm Financial Crisis on Agribusiness Firms and Rural Communities," *Journal of Agricultural Economics* 67, no. 5 (December 1985): 1184–1190; Davidson, "Rural Ghetto"; William Robbins, "Farms' Crisis Endangering Rural Towns," *New York Times*, October 14, 1985, https://www.nytimes.com/1985/10/14/us/farms-crisis-endangering-rural-towns.html; Davidson, *Broken Heartland*, 10, 55–56; Westphal, "Fertile Iowa's Promised Land;" Westphal, "Riches to Rags: Iowa's Economic Upheaval: High School Students Wrestle with Emotional Strife of Farming Crisis," *Des Moines Register*, June 17, 1985, https://www.newspapers.com/image/legacy/131192019/; Westphal, "Riches to Rags: Iowa's Economic Upheaval: Livestock Seen as Cause and Cure in Rural Troubles," *Des Moines Register*, June 21, 1985, https://www.newspapers.com/image/legacy/131194302/; Associated Press, "Is the Mid-Sized Family Farm a Thing of the Past?" *Sioux City Journal Farm Weekly*, July 23, 1984, https://www.newspapers.com/image/336790430. The small town of Waucoma has lost almost half of its population since 1900, as had the surrounding township. See Dona Schwartz, *Waucoma Twilight: Generations on the Farm* (Washington, DC: Smithsonian Institution Press, 1992), 26–27.

17. Davidson, *Broken Heartland*, 49–51; Jon Bowermaster, "When Wal-Mart

Comes to Town," *New York Times Magazine*, April 2, 1989, https://timesmachine.nytimes.com/timesmachine/1989/04/02/issue.html.

18. Rubin, "Farmers in Crisis"; Ginder, Stone, and Otto, "Farm Financial Crisis," 1189; Jake Hansen, "Population Trends in Rural Iowa: Decline and Recovery," *Major Themes in Economics* 2 (Spring 2000), 21–24; Charles E. Connerly, *Green, Fair, and Prosperous: Paths to a Sustainable Iowa* (Iowa City: University of Iowa Press, 2020), 29; Davidson, *Broken Heartland*, 63; Patrick Slattery, *Caretakers of Creation: Farmers Reflect on Their Faith and Work* (Minneapolis: Augsburg Fortress, 1991), 57, 64.

19. Connerly, *Green, Fair, and Prosperous*, 9–22; Greg Hanson, "Beyond the Farm Debt Crisis," *Choices* 5, no. 4 (1990): 33–35.

20. Ginder, Stone, and Otto, "Farm Financial Crisis," 1187; Davidson, *Broken Heartland*, 58–59. See Measuring Worth. Comparison starting date here is 1983.

21. Melvyn Dubofsky and Foster Rhea Dulles, *Labor in America: A History* (Wheeling, WV: Harlan Davidson, 2010), 325–327, 345–348; "Adding Right to Work Law to Iowa Constitution Advances," *Ames Tribune*, January 24, 2013, https://www.amestrib.com/story/news/politics/2013/01/24/adding-right-to-work-law/27301905007/; Thomas B. Edsall, "Republicans Sure Love to Hate Unions," *New York Times*, November 18, 2014, https://www.nytimes.com/2014/11/19/opinion/republicans-sure-love-to-hate-unions.html; Glenda Elizabeth Gilmore and Thomas J. Sugrue, *These United States: A Nation in the Making, 1890 to the Present* (New York: W.W. Norton, 2015), 303–304; Shelton Stromquist, *Solidarity and Survival: An Oral History of Iowa Labor in the Twentieth Century* (Iowa City: University of Iowa Press, 1993), 301–302; Wilson J. Warren, *Tied to the Great Packing Machine: The Midwest and Meatpacking* (Iowa City: University of Iowa Press, 2007), 39–43. Warren would agree with Stromquist, writing that unions helped improve workers' material lives. See Warren (39). Conservatives also disliked unions because their members and money usually supported Democrats.

22. Deborah Fink, *Cutting into the Meatpacking Line: Workers and Change in the Rural Midwest* (Chapel Hill: University of North Carolina Press, 1998), 1–3, 57–60, 194–197; Stephen J. Hedges and Dana Hawkins, "The New Jungle," *U.S. News & World Report*, September 23, 1996; Patricia Cohen, "Immigrants Keep an Iowa Meatpacking Town Alive and Growing," *New York Times* May 29, 2017, https://www.nytimes.com/2017/05/29/business/economy/storm-lake-iowa-immigrant-workers.html; Art Cullen, *Storm Lake: Change, Resilience, and Hope in America's Heartland* (New York: Penguin Books, 2018), 160. See Measuring Worth.

23. Hedges and Hawkins, "New Jungle;" Fink, *Meatpacking Line*, 192, 196–197; Cohen, "Iowa Meatpacking Town"; Pam Belluck, "Short of People, Iowa Seeks to Be Ellis Island of Midwest," *New York Times*, August 28, 2000, https://www.nytimes.com/2000/08/28/us/short-of-people-iowa-seeks-to-be-ellis-island-of-midwest.html. See Art Cullen, "Vilsack Delivers for Workers," *Storm Lake Times*, June 2, 2021, for a brief history of meatpacking in the state.

24. Cullen, *Storm Lake*, 157–167; Hedges and Hawkins, "New Jungle"; Cohen, "Iowa Meatpacking Town"; Art Cullen, "My Iowa Town, We Need Immigrants," *New York Times*, July 30, 2018, https://www.nytimes.com/2018/07/30/opinion/trump

-immigrants-iowa-farmers-workers.html; Tom Cullen, "Census Count: SL Up 6.3%, BV Up 2.7," *Storm Lake Times*, August 18, 2021.

25. Cohen, "Immigrants."

26. Tom Cullen and Karina Guerrero, "Julio Barroso Hopes Biden Will Let Him Come Home to Storm Lake," *Storm Lake Times*, December 18, 2020.

27. Nick Reding, *Methland: The Death and Life of an American Small Town* (New York: Bloomsbury, 2009), 6, 25–34, 42–45, 84, 201–202; Dan McGraw and Gordon Witkin, "The Iowan Connection," *U.S. News & World Report*, March 2, 1998.

28. Jon Gertner, "Fields and Dreams," *Money* 29, no. 13 (December 2000): 126–135; Greg Hanson, "Beyond the Farm Debt Crisis," 35; Danbom, *Born in the Country*, 266; Bruce L. Gardner, *American Agriculture in the Twentieth Century: How It Flourished and What It Cost* (Cambridge, MA: Harvard University Press, 2002), 84; Michael Pollan, *The Omnivore's Dilemma: A Natural History of Four Meals* (New York: Penguin Books, 2006), 34; James Risen, "After Crisis, Farm Economy Growing Again," *Los Angeles Times*, August 12, 1990, https://www.latimes.com/archives/la-xpm-1990-08-12-mn-1021-story.html; Riney-Kehrberg, *When a Dream Dies*, 4–8; *1992 Agricultural Census, Part 15, Iowa* (Washington, DC: Bureau of the Census, 1992), 8. See Measuring Worth.

29. Riney-Kehrberg, *When a Dream Dies*, 177–178.

30. Risen, "After Crisis"; Riney-Kehrberg, *When a Dream Dies*, 163–169, 180, 189–192. Taking land out of production meant farmers spent less money in local stores, which did not help the rural economy improve. See Riney-Kehrberg, 180.

31. "No Mud on Their Boots: Iowa," *Economist*, February 27, 1993, 34–35; Belluck, "Short of People."

32. Alan Mairson, "The Great Flood of '93," *National Geographic* 185, no. 1 (January 1994): 51–59, https://archive.nationalgeographic.com/national-geographic/1994-jan/flipbook/42/; Larry Fruhling, "Iowa," in *The Flood of 1993: Stories from a Midwestern Disaster*, ed. Betty Burnett, (Tucson: Patrice Press, 1994), 19–23, 31–33, 37–40; Bill Bryson, "Riding Out the Worst of Times," *National Geographic* 185, no. 1 (January 1994): 82–85, https://archive.nationalgeographic.com/national-geographic/1994-jan/flipbook/82/; Willie Nelson, "A Thanksgiving for Our Farmers," *Newsweek*, November 29, 1993, 22–24; Gerald E. Galloway, "The Great Flood of 1993: Did We Learn Any Lessons?" in *A Watershed Year: Anatomy of the Iowa Floods of 2008*, ed. Cornelia F. Mutel (Iowa City: University of Iowa Press, 2010), 228; Riney-Kehrberg, *When a Dream Dies*, 192–195. Riney-Kehrberg calls the floods of 1993 "relentless and breathtaking," possibly only rivaled by those in 1851. Flood measurement in 1851 was crude, so it is impossible to make direct comparisons. See Riney-Kehrberg, 192.

33. Curtis Harnack, "In Plymouth County, Iowa, the Rich Topsoil's Going Fast. Alas," *New York Times*, July 11, 1980, https://www.nytimes.com/1980/07/11/archives/in-plymouth-county-iowa-the-rich-topsoils-going-fast-alas.html?searchResultPosition=1; Pollan, *Omnivore's Dilemma*, 33. Decaying prairie grasses could build an inch of topsoil every ten to twenty years, wrote Pollan. But prairies were almost extinct in Iowa in the early twenty-first century.

34. Cornelia F. Mutel, *The Emerald Horizon: The History of Nature in Iowa* (Iowa

City: University of Iowa Press, 2008), 30–32; Ted Genoways, *The Chain: Farm, Factory, and the Fate of Our Food* (New York: HarperCollins, 2014), 102, 107–110; Schwartz, *Waucoma Twilight*, 27.

35. Richard Manning, *Against the Grain: How Agriculture Has Hijacked Civilization* (New York: North Point Press, 2004), 137–138; Pollan, *Omnivore's Dilemma*, 46–47; Peter Annin, "Down in the Dead Zone," *Newsweek*, October 18, 1999, 60–61; Connerly, *Green, Fair, and Prosperous*, 58–59, 63, 68.

36. Daniel P. Finney, "Robert Ray, Beloved 5-Term Governor, Dies at 89," *Des Moines Register*, July 8, 2018, https://www.desmoinesregister.com/story/news/2018/07/08/bob-ray-obituary-iowa-governor-robert-ray-dies/998099001/; Cory Haala, "'There Exists a Conservative Veneer:' Terry Branstad, Chuck Grassley, and the New Right's Capture of Republican Politics in Iowa, 1976–1986," in *The Conservative Heartland: A Political History of the Postwar American Midwest*, ed. Jon K. Lauck and Catherine McNicol Stock (Lawrence: University Press of Kansas, 2020), 216–221; Christopher W. Larimer, *Gubernatorial Stability in Iowa: A Stranglehold on Power* (New York: Palgrave Macmillan, 2015), 1–5, 28–31, 87–88; Jerry Perkins, "Branstad Triggers Law Delaying Foreclosures," *Des Moines Register*, October 2, 1985, https://www.newspapers.com/image/legacy/128325097/; Cullen, *Storm Lake*, 109–110.

37. Haala, "'Conservative Veneer,'" 213–215; Cullen, *Storm Lake*, 106–110; Elaine Godfrey, "What Does Chuck Grassley Fear?" *Atlantic*, April 13, 2016, https://www.theatlantic.com/politics/archive/2016/04/chuck-grassley-scotus-garland/478038/; US Department of Labor, "Americans with Disabilities Act," accessed April 19, 2023, www.dol.gov/general/topic/disability/ada; Lyz Lenz, "Chuck Grassley's Last Act," *Vanity Fair*, June 16, 2022, https://www.vanityfair.com/news/2022/06/chuck-grassley-last-act; Brianne Pfannenstiel, "The Republican Red Wave Foundered Nationally, but in Iowa It Swept Away Democrats," *Des Moines Register*, November 11, 2022, https://www.desmoinesregister.com/story/news/politics/elections/2022/11/11/republican-red-wave-election-results-2022-iowa-kim-reynolds-mixed-nationally/69632525007/.

38. Hugh Winebrenner and Dennis J. Goldford, *The Iowa Precinct Caucuses: The Making of a Media Event* (Iowa City: University of Iowa Press, 2010), 337–343; Christopher C. Hull, *Grassroots Rules: How the Iowa Caucus Helps Elect American Presidents* (Stanford: Stanford University Press, 2008), 51–60; Katie Akin, "Historically, Do Winners of the Iowa Caucus Go on to Earn Their Party's Nomination, Become President?" *Des Moines Register*, January 5, 2020, https://www.desmoinesregister.com/story/news/elections/presidential/caucus/2020/01/05/do-iowa-caucus-winners-win-presidency-party-nomination-general-election/4410195002/.

39. Connerly, *Green, Fair, and Prosperous*, 29; Belluck, "Short of People"; Riney-Kehrberg, *When a Dream Dies*, 11–13. The census definition of white does not include Latinos. In 2022 the Democratic Party reordered its presidential primary calendar, stripping Iowa of its first-in-the-nation caucus status. Iowa was replaced by South Carolina as the first state in the party's primary calendar, followed by Nevada, New Hampshire, Georgia, and Michigan. The new primary calendar emphasized states with a more diverse electorate. Meanwhile, the Republican Party kept Iowa as the first state in their primary contest. See Brianne Pfannenstiel and Francesca Chambers, "Iowa No

Longer First; Democrats Reorder the Presidential Primary Calendar for 2024," *Des Moines Register*, December 2, 2002, https://www.desmoinesregister.com/story/news/politics/2022/12/02/dnc-democrats-primary-calendar-south-carolina-first-over-iowa-caucus/69695090007/.

CHAPTER 15: IOWA IN THE TWENTY-FIRST CENTURY

1. "Coronavirus in the US: Latest Map and Case Count," *New York Times*, January 1, 2021, https://www.nytimes.com/interactive/2021/us/covid-cases.html. By January 1, 2021, Iowa had 282,662 cases, with an 8.96 percent infection rate, or 8,959 people per 100,000 population. North Dakota had 12,174 and South Dakota had 11,209 per 100,000 people, ranking ahead of Iowa. For an overview of crop prices since 1925 see "Iowa Cash Corn and Soybean Prices (USDA NASS)," accessed March 5, 2023, http://www.extension.iastate.edu/agdm/crops/pdf/a2-11.pdf.

2. Iowa State University Extension and Outreach, "A Snapshot of Rural Iowa," http://www.rwhc.com/mediasite/7App%20%20Tim%20Borich%20Plenary%20am_Iowa_Snapshot.pdf; Mike Kilen, "How Iowa's Midsize Cities Have Been Left Behind," *Des Moines Register*, March 30, 2017, https://www.desmoinesregister.com/story/news/2017/03/30/how-iowas-midsize-cities-have-been-left-behind/99423726/; Michael Barbaro, "With Farms Fading and Urban Might Rising, Power Shifts in Iowa," *New York Times*, October 20, 2014, https://www.nytimes.com/2014/10/21/us/politics/iowa-senate-election.html.

3. Dionne Searcey et al., "The Graying of the American Economy Is On Display in Iowa," *New York Times*, February 2, 2020, https://www.nytimes.com/2020/02/02/us/politics/iowa-economy-2020.html; Kilen, "Iowa's Midsize Cities."

4. Barbaro, "With Farms Fading"; Dave Swenson, "Iowa Employment since the Great Recession," Department of Economics, Iowa State University, January 2020, https://www.icip.iastate.edu/sites/default/files/uploads/reports/Iowa%20Emploment%20Trends%202010s.pdf, 4–5; Maribel Hastings, "Future Arrives to Diversify Small-Town USA," *Atlantic*, May 18, 2012, https://www.theatlantic.com/politics/archive/2012/05/future-arrives-to-diversify-small-town-usa/427470/; Editorial Board, "One Way to Increase Iowa's Work Force," *Des Moines Register*, November 12, 2006; Marshalltown Swift Raids, 2005–2013, West Liberty Latino History Collection, Iowa Women's Archives, University of Iowa Libraries, University of Iowa, Iowa City (IWA); Tyler Jett, "Des Moines Metro's Waukee, Grimes, Ankeny Lead Iowa Population Growth, Latest Census Estimates Show," *Des Moines Register*, May 27, 2021, https://www.desmoinesregister.com/story/money/business/2021/05/27/2020-census-estimates-iowa-des-moines-suburbs-growth-waukee-ankeny-grimes-norwalk-johnston/7470183002/.

5. Lissandra Villa, "4 Takeaways from Politico's Story on How Des Moines Got Cool," *Des Moines Register*, January 22, 2016, https://www.desmoinesregister.com/story/news/local/des-moines/2016/01/22/4-takeaways-politicos-story-how-des-moines-got-cool/79184070/; Barbaro, "With Farms Fading"; Robin Opsahl, "Best

Place to Get Ahead? New Study Ranks Iowa no. 1 in 'Opportunity' Nationally," *Des Moines Register*, March 11, 2021, https://www.desmoinesregister.com/story/money/business/2021/03/11/us-news-world-report-study-ranks-iowa-1-opportunity-nationally/6938495002/; Jett, "Des Moines Metro's."

6. Charles E. Connerly, *Green, Fair, and Prosperous: Paths to a Sustainable Iowa* (Iowa City: University of Iowa Press, 2020), 118–120; Rekha Basu, "Black Job Seekers in Waterloo-Cedar Falls Understand Its Ranking for Racial Disparity," *Des Moines Register*, December 13, 2018, https://www.desmoinesregister.com/story/opinion/columnists/rekha-basu/2018/12/13/highest-racial-disparities-u-s-whats-going-waterloo-iowa/2279606002/.

7. Jeffrey Sparshott, "U.S. Economic Expansion Is Unevenly Spread, Study Says," *Wall Street Journal*, September 25, 2017, https://www.wsj.com/articles/study-says-u-s-economic-expansion-is-unevenly-spread-1506344400; Annie Lowrey, "The Great Recession Is Still 3with Us," *Atlantic*, December 1, 2017, https://www.theatlantic.com/business/archive/2017/12/great-recession-still-with-us/547268/; A. G. Sulzberger, "Economic Health in Iowa Conflicts with a G.O.P. Theme," *New York Times*, December 17, 2011, https://www.nytimes.com/2011/12/18/us/politics/economy-rules-gop-message-but-iowa-differs.html; Donnelle Eller, "Despite Low Price, Trade Wars, This Ag Downturn Is 'Piece of Cake' Compared to 1980s," *Des Moines Register*, October 28, 2018, https://www.desmoinesregister.com/story/money/agriculture/2018/10/28/iowa-agriculture-trump-trade-wars-tariffs-commodity-prices-1980-s-farm-crisis-worries-corn-soybeans/1733030002/; "Fields of Gold," *Economist*, February 23, 2013, https://www.economist.com/united-states/2013/02/23/fields-of-gold; Swenson, "Iowa Employment," 4–6; Beth Hoffman, *Bet the Farm: The Dollars and Sense of Growing Food in America* (Washington, DC: Island Press, 2021), 137, 167. The percentage of farmers over sixty-five is for 2018, see Hoffman.

8. Swenson, "Iowa Employment," 6–9, 12–13, 15–16; Tyler Jett, "Iowa Fell Behind Most States in Job Growth after Great Recession, New Paper Asserts," *Des Moines Register*, January 19, 2020, https://www.desmoinesregister.com/story/money/business/2020/01/19/iowas-job-growth-after-great-recession-lags-behind-nation-new-paper-finds/4495538002/; Eller, "Despite Low Prices"; USDA National Agricultural Statistics Service, "Prices Received for Corn by Month—United States," accessed April 19, 2023, https://www.nass.usda.gov/Charts_and_Maps/Agricultural_Prices/pricecn.php; USDA, NASS, "Prices Received for Soybeans by Month—United States," accessed April 19, 2023, https://www.nass.usda.gov/Charts_and_Maps/Agricultural_Prices/pricesb.php; Donnelle Eller, "ISU Report: Iowa Farm Finances Continue to Erode with 44% of Growers Struggling to Cover Costs," *Des Moines Register*, November 14, 2019, https://www.desmoinesregister.com/story/money/agriculture/ 2019/11/14/iowa-farmers-struggling-financially-ag-economy-downturn-trade-war/4115343002/; "Iowa Cities by Population," accessed January 16, 2022, https://www.iowa-demographics.com/cities_by_population.

9. Robert Paarlberg, *Resetting the Table: Straight Talk about the Food We Grow and Eat* (New York: Alfred A. Knopf, 2021), 31–37; Paarlberg, "The Environmental Upside of Modern Farming," *Wall Street Journal*, February 5, 2021, https://www.wsj

.com/articles/the-environmental-upside-of-modern-farming-11612534962?mod=searchresults_pos2&page=1; Chrystia Freeland, "The Triumph of the Family Farm," *Atlantic*, July–August 2012, https://www.theatlantic.com/magazine/archive/2012/07/the-triumph-of-the-family-farm/308998/; Donnelle Eller, "Iowa Follows US, Losing About 3% of Its Farms over 5 Years, Ag Census Shows," *Des Moines Register*, April 15, 2019, https://www.desmoinesregister.com/story/money/agriculture/2019/04/15/iowa-agriculture-ag-census-consolidation-continues-losing-farms-women-farming-conservation-crops-pig/3471596002/; ISU Extension, "Iowa Corn and Soybean County Yields," accessed January 17, 2022, https://www.extension.iastate.edu/agdm/crops/pdf/a1-14.pdf; "Agriculture Export Highlights," accessed March 6, 2023, https://www.iowaeda.com/UserDocs/2021Q3AgExportHighlights.pdf; "Iowa: Facts and Figures," accessed January 17, 2022, https://www.usglc.org/state-facts/iowa/.

10. Sharyn Jackson and Christopher Gannon, "Harvest of Change, Part 2, Towns Gray, Shrink," *Des Moines Register*, September 4, 2014, https://www.desmoinesregister.com/story/money/agriculture/2014/09/04/harvest-of-change-virtual-farm-day-2/15109889/; Sharyn Jackson and Christopher Gannon, "Harvest of Change, Part 3, Ag's New Faces," *Des Moines Register*, September 4, 2014, https://www.desmoinesregister.com/story/money/agriculture/2014/09/04/harvest-of-change-virtual-farm-day-3/15110421/; Eller, "Iowa Follows US."

11. Swenson, "Iowa Employment," 3; Jim Spencer, "Why Ethanol Endures as Important Market for Midwestern Farmers," *Minneapolis Star Tribune*, January, 18, 2020, https://www.startribune.com/ethanol-didn-t-work-out-as-planned-but-that-doesn-t-mean-it-s-going-away-anytime-soon/567084142/?refresh=true; Donnelle Eller, "Iowa's Ethanol Production Falls by 500 Million Gallons as American Drive Less Due to Covid-19," *Des Moines Register*, January 22, 2021, https://www.desmoinesregister.com/story/money/agriculture/2021/01/22/renewal-fuels-iowa-ethanol-production-fell-2020-covid-travel-down/4244237001/; Unmesh Kher and Betsy Rubiner, "The Men Who Turned Corn into Gold," *Time*, December 25, 2006, 146–147; David Swenson, "The Economic Impact of Ethanol Production in Iowa," Department of Economics, Iowa State University, accessed March 6, 2023, http://www2.econ.iastate.edu/papers/p11222-2008-01-01.pdf, 1, 4–5, 8–9. Nebraska, Illinois, and Minnesota were the next three largest producers of ethanol, see Spencer's article for this information. See "Biofuels Explained: Ethanol and the environment," at eia.gov/energyexplained/biofuels/ethanol-and-the-environment.php, accessed January 16, 2022, for a summary of ethanol's effects.

12. Donnelle Eller, "More Than Half of Iowa's Power Now Comes from Wind, as State Nears 6,000 Turbines," *Des Moines Register*, April 9, 2021, https://www.desmoinesregister.com/story/money/agriculture/2021/04/09/iowa-electricity-generation-wind-energy-surges-2020-540-turbines-added-nears-6000/7107580002/; Tim Webber, "Wind Blows by Coal to Become Iowa's Largest Source of Electricity," *Des Moines Register*, April 16, 2020, https://www.desmoinesregister.com/story/tech/science/environment/2020/04/16/wind-energy-iowa-largest-source-electricity/5146483002/; Donnelle Eller, "Is Wind Power Saving Rural Iowa or Wrecking It?" *Des Moines Register*, April 20, 2017, https://www.desmoinesregister.com/story/tech/science/en

vironment/2017/04/20/wind-power-saving-rural-iowa-wrecking/99789758/. Coal produced 22 percent of Iowa's energy in 2020, see Eller's 2021 article.

13. Andrew J. Bacevich, *America's War for the Greater Middle East: A Military History* (New York: Random House, 2016), 224–225, 293–294, 297–300, 307, 312; Adela Suliman, "Nearly 20 Years of War, 10 Days to Fall: Afghanistan, by the Numbers," *Washington Post*, August 20, 2021, https://www.washingtonpost.com/world/2021/08/20/afghanistan-war-key-numbers/; Mike Kilen, "12 Years of Valor," *Des Moines Register*, December 21, 2013, https://www.desmoinesregister.com/story/news/2013/12/22/12-years-of-valor/4155311/; Dan Solomon, "How Big Is Texas, Compared with Other Land Masses?," *Texas Monthly*, January 14, 2015, https://www.texasmonthly.com/the-daily-post/how-big-is-texas-compared-to-other-land-masses/. The Department of Defense divides casualties from these campaigns into different geographic regions and time periods. The casualty numbers for Afghanistan are for October 7, 2001–June 27, 2022 (Operation Enduring Freedom and Operation Freedom's Sentinel). Numbers for Iraq are from Operation Iraqi Freedom and Operation New Dawn (March 19, 2003, to December 31, 2011). See https://www.defense.gov/casualty.pdf. The number of Iowa dead is from the Department of Veterans Affairs. See "Iowa's Fallen: Iraq," accessed March 6, 2023, https://va.iowa.gov/media/e83e3737-f130-4f4b-b881-40c41ecceb6c.

14. John Phillip Hintz Collection, (AFC/2001/001/82377), Veterans History Project, American Folklife Center, Library of Congress. The Veterans History Project can be found at www.loc.gov/vets/. For more on Talukan see Peter Beaumont, "Afghanistan's Three Parallel Wars," *Guardian*, November 13, 2010, https://www.theguardian.com/world/2010/nov/14/afghanistan-kandahar-taliban-coalition. Hintz's interview is unclear about the unit that he was in when he served in Iraq, but it was probably the Fourth Infantry Division. See biographical information on Hintz at the Veterans History Project. Also see Scott A. Huesing, *Echo in Ramadi: The Firsthand Story of U.S. Marines in Iraq's Deadliest City* (Washington, DC: Regnery History, 2018), chapter 10, for the story of Iowa's Downing family. Kimberly Downing's husband, Jeff, and her two sons, Ryan and Justen, served with the Marines in Iraq. For the story of Iowan Salvatore A. Giunta, who won a Medal of Honor in Afghanistan, see Salvatore A. Giunta and Joe Layden, *Living with Honor* (New York: Threshold Editions, 2012).

15. Todd Dorman, "War Hits Home for Soldiers, Relatives Who Worry Wait and Fight for Freedom," *Sioux City Journal*, March 14, 2004, https://siouxcityjournal.com/news/war-hits-home-for-soldiers-relatives-who-worry-wait-and-fight-for-freedom/article_e418b782-0db0-5c5f-9836-446c5add7081.html; "List: Iowa Soldiers Killed in Iraq, Afghanistan," *Cedar Rapids Gazette*, August 13, 2021, https://www.thegazette.com/news/list-iowa-soldiers-killed-in-iraq-afghanistan/; Kilen, "12 Years of Valor." See Miyoko Hikiji, *All I Could Be: My Story as a Woman Warrior in Iraq* (New York: Chronology Books, 2013), an enlightening memoir by an Iowa National Guard veteran. More than sixty-eight hundred Iowa National Guard members were called to active duty by March 2004. See Dorman's article for additional information. Hailey Byers was raised by her grandparents after her mother went to prison, see Mike Kilen, "A 13-Year-Old Iowa Girl Becomes the Face of Iraq War Sacrifice,"

Des Moines Register, May 24, 2018, https://www.desmoinesregister.com/story/news/2018/05/24/iraq-war-sacrifice-iowa-fallen-casey-byers-hailey-byers-endures-iowa-guard/620993002/.

16. Tyler Jett, "Study: Des Moines' Immigrant Population among Fastest-Growing in the U.S." *Des Moines Register*, May 26, 2021, https://www.desmoinesregister.com/story/money/business/2021/05/26/des-moines-iowa-immigrant-population-growth-ranked-among-united-states-fastest-heartland-forward/7437283002/; Tyler Jett, "Why Is the Des Moines Metro among National Leaders in Immigrant Growth," *Des Moines Register*, June 1, 2021, https://www.desmoinesregister.com/story/news/2021/06/01/des-moines-iowa-immigrant-population-growth-ranked-among-united-states-fastest-heartland-forward/7478976002/; Anita R. Kellogg, "Why Do Some U.S. Mayors Want More Refugees?" *Washington Post*, June 28, 2021, https://www.washingtonpost.com/politics/2021/06/28/why-do-us-mayors-want-more-refugees/. Princy Mungedi was awarded a visa through the US Diversity Visa Lottery. His name is a variant of the French name Prince. See "Iowa National Guard Soldier Becomes a Citizen," Defense Visual Information Distribution Service, https://www.dvidshub.net/news/401236/iowa-national-guard-soldier-becomes-citizen.

17. "Iowa Census Data Tables: Decennial Census," https://www.iowadatacenter.org/; "Fare Thee Well, Iowa: A Fading State," *Economist*, August 16, 2001, https://www.economist.com/united-states/2001/08/16/fare-thee-well-iowa; Jett, "Why Is the Des Metro."

18. Mark Grey, Michele Devlin, and Aaron Goldsmith, *Postville, U.S.A.: Surviving Diversity in Small-Town America* (Boston: Gemma Media, 2009), 12, 57–58, 62–63, 73–87; Betsy Ribiner, "Postcard: Postville," *Time Magazine*, June 16, 2008, 6; Julia Preston, "After Iowa Raid, Immigrants Fuel Labor Inquiries," *New York Times*, July 27, 2008, https://www.nytimes.com/2008/07/27/us/27immig.html; Stephen G. Bloom, *Postville: A Clash of Cultures in Heartland America* (New York: Harcourt, 2000) is a wonderful portrayal of the clash between the world of rural Iowa and the Orthodox Jewish company that ran the meatpacking plant. Also see Kristy Nabhan-Warren, *Meatpacking America: How Migration, Work, and Faith Unite and Divide the Heartland* (Chapel Hill: University of North Carolina Press, 2021).

19. Art Cullen, *Storm Lake: Change, Resilience, and Hope in America's Heartland* (New York: Penguin, 2018), 160–165; Dolores Cullen, "Citizen Ofelia," *Storm Lake Times*, February 24, 2021.

20. Douglas E. Foley, *The Heartland Chronicles* (Philadelphia: University of Pennsylvania Press, 1995), 222–226; Judith M. Daubenmier, *The Meskwaki and Anthropologists: Action Anthropology Reconsidered* (Lincoln: University of Nebraska Press, 2008), 278–279; Kevin Hardy, "With Future Generations in Mind, Iowa's Meskwaki Tribe Looks to Diversify Business Profile," *Des Moines Register*, October 12, 2017, https://www.desmoinesregister.com/story/money/business/2017/10/12/future-generations-mind-iowas-meskwaki-tribe-looks-diversify-business-profile/719558001/; Meskwaki, accessed October 2, 2022, https://meskwaki.com.

21. Mike Kilen, "Iowa's Gay Marriage Plaintiffs Are Proud 6 Years Later," *Des Moines Register*, May 1, 2015, https://www.desmoinesregister.com/story/life/2015/05

/01/iowa-gay-marriage-couples/26734823/; Tom Witosky and Marc Hansen, *Equal before the Law: How Iowa Led Americans to Marriage Equality* (Iowa City: University of Iowa Press, 2015), 65, 86–88, 91–92, 100–101, 135, 138–139, 147, 159, 174–175, 204; Amy Merrick and Phillip Shishkin, "Iowa Supreme Court Overturns Gay-Marriage Ban," *Wall Street Journal*, April 4, 2009, https://www.wsj.com/articles/SB123876672206286609; Adam Liptak, "Supreme Court Ruling Makes Same-Sex Marriage a Right Nationwide," *New York Times*, June 26, 2015, https://www.nytimes.com/2015/06/27/us/supreme-court-same-sex-marriage.html; Summer Lin, "Gay Marriage Support Rises to New High in Poll—With Half of Republicans Now in Favor," *Miami Herald*, October 21, 2020, https://www.miamiherald.com/news/nation-world/national/article246616638.html.

22. Hristina Byrnes, John Harrington, and Grant Suneson, "Supreme Court Decision Aside, Some States Are Better—and Some Worse—for LGBTQ Community," *USA Today*, June 19, 2020, https://www.usatoday.com/story/money/2020/06/19/the-best-and-worst-states-for-lgbtq-people/111968524/; Julianne McShane, "A Record Number of U.S. Adults Identify as LGTBQ. Gen Z Is Driving the Increase," *Washington Post*, February 17, 2022, https://www.washingtonpost.com/lifestyle/2022/02/17/adults-identifying-lgbt-gen-z/; MacKenzie Elmer, Andy Davis, and Kim Norvell, "How LGBTQ-Friendly Are Iowa Cities?," *Des Moines Register*, October 23, 2017, https://www.desmoinesregister.com/story/news/crime-and-courts/2017/10/23/how-lgbtq-friendly-iowa-cities/779573001/; Paris Barraza, "'A Great Respect for Iowa City:' Pride Celebration Returns with Community March, 50-Year Milestone," *Iowa City Press-Citizen*, September 29, 2021, https://www.press-citizen.com/story/entertainment/2021/09/29/iowa-city-pride-2021-festival-kicks-off-friday-celebrating-50th-anniversary-lgbtq-things-to-do/5804924001/; Josh O'Leary, "How Iowa City Became a Focal Point for LGBTQ+ Activism," *Iowa Magazine*, September 26, 2022, https://magazine.foriowa.org/story.php?ed=true&storyid=2244; Tony Leys and Barbara Rodriguez, "Presidential Candidates Flock to Des Moines' Pride Fest, Touting Their Support for LGBTQ Rights," *Des Moines Register*, June 8, 2019, https://www.desmoinesregister.com/story/news/2019/06/08/presidential-candidates-flock-des-moines-pride-iowa-caucus-lgbtq-rights-buttigieg-sanders-gillibrand/1385858001/; Marissa Payne, "Iowa City Pride Throws Biggest Festival in Its 48-Year History," *Cedar Rapids Gazette*, June 17, 2018, https://www.thegazette.com/community/iowa-city-pride-throws-biggest-festival-in-its-48-year-history/; Elijah Decious, "As Anti-LGBTQ Legislation Proliferates, Some Iowans Depart," *Cedar Rapids Gazette*, August 31, 2022, https://www.thegazette.com/iowa-ideas/as-anti-lgbtq-legislation-proliferates-some-iowans-depart/. Iowa was one of the states to pass legislation to ban transgender girls from taking part in female sports. See Stephen Gruber-Miller and Ian Richardson, "Kim Reynolds Bans Transgender Girls from Female Sports, Signing Republican-Backed Law," *Des Moines Register*, March 3, 2022, https://www.desmoinesregister.com/story/news/politics/2022/03/03/trans-transgender-girls-banned-womens-sports-kim-reynolds-lgbtq-iowa-signs-bill/9349887002/. For background on book bans, see Samantha Hernandez, "Iowa Library, Roiled by Book Banning Debate, Temporarily Closes with No Director," *Des Moines Register*, July 15, 2022, https://

www.desmoinesregister.com/story/news/politics/2022/07/15/vinton-iowa-library-embroiled-banned-book-debate-temporarily-closes-director/10012526002/. For information on how Iowa's cities ranked according to the Human Rights Campaign's index of municipal nondiscrimination legislation, see https://www.hrc.org/resources/municipalities/search?q=iowa. The transgender population faced some of the greatest difficulties, from violence to higher poverty rates. Health care was often a challenge, too, as many faced hostility, or a lack of understanding, from health care providers. See Liam Stack, "The Challenges That Remain for L.G.B.T. People after Marriage Ruling," *New York Times*, June 30, 2016, https://www.nytimes.com/2016/07/01/us/the-challenges-that-remain-for-lgbt-people-after-marriage-ruling.html. For attendance for the 2019 Des Moines event see https://www.capitalcitypride.org/single-post/2019/06/10/2019-pride-fest-breaks-record-and-puts-iowa-on-the-national-stage. For a summary of each state's LGBT population see UCLA School of Law, Williams Institute, "Adult LGBT Population in the United States," July 2020, https://williamsinstitute.law.ucla.edu/wp-content/uploads/LGBT-Adult-US-Pop-Jul-2020.pdf. In March 2023 the *Des Moines Register* published an article asking if transgender children and their families would need to leave Iowa for more accepting states, such as Minnesota. A ban on gender-affirming care for transgender children had passed the Iowa legislature in March 2023. Minnesota was considering a Trans Refuge Bill at the same time. See Grace Deng, "Families with Transgender Children Seek Refuge in Minnesota. Will Iowa Trans Kids Follow?" *Des Moines Register*, March 14, 2023, https://www.desmoinesregister.com/story/news/politics/2023/03/14/families-with-transgender-children-seek-refuge-in-minnesota-iowa-lgbtq-laws/70007232007/.

23. Brianne Pfannenstiel, "Donald Trump Drives Voter Turnout in Iowa, Lifting Republicans Down the Ballot," *Des Moines, November Register* 4, 2020, https://www.desmoinesregister.com/story/news/politics/2020/11/04/2020-election-donald-trump-surge-iowa-republicans-down-ballot/6160672002/; Thomas Beaumont, "'Past the Point of No Return?' Iowa Democrats Feel Hopes Fading, Party Receding in the State," *Des Moines Register*, June 2, 2021, https://www.desmoinesregister.com/story/news/politics/2021/06/02/iowa-democrats-president-joe-biden-republican-donald-trump-election-farmers-factory-towns/7493701002/; Trip Gabriel, "Why Iowa Has Become Such a Heartbreaker for Democrats," *New York Times*, April 27, 2021, https://www.nytimes.com/2021/04/27/us/politics/iowa-democrats-republicans.html; Richard C. Longworth, *Caught in the Middle: America's Heartland in the Age of Globalism* (New York: Bloomsbury, 2008), 119–120; Brett Hayworth, "Steve King, Conservative Icon and Progressive Antagonist, Exits Iowa Seat after 18 Years," *Sioux City Journal*, December 25, 2020, https://siouxcityjournal.com/news/local/govt-and-politics/steve-king-conservative-icon-and-progressive-antagonist-exits-iowa-seat-after-18-years/article_7073ff45-6715-55d5-9a83-e3bbc52888b3.html.

24. "In the Red: The Governor's Races," *Economist*, November 4, 2010, https://www.economist.com/united-states/2010/11/04/in-the-red; Cullen, *Storm Lake*, 135–138; Christopher W. Larimer, *Gubernatorial Stability in Iowa: A Stranglehold on Power* (New York: Palgrave Macmillan, 2015), 13, 29–30, 34–35; Lisa Lerer, "Joe from Scranton Didn't Win Back the Working Class," *New York Times*, December

5, 2020, https://www.nytimes.com/2020/12/05/us/politics/biden-blue-collar-voters.html.

25. Larimer, *Gubernatorial Stability*, 29–30; Janet Adamy and Paul Overberg, "Places Most Unsettled by Rapid Demographic Change Are Drawn to Donald Trump," *Wall Street Journal*, November 1, 2016, https://www.wsj.com/articles/places-most-unsettled-by-rapid-demographic-change-go-for-donald-trump-1478010940; Pfannenstiel, "Donald Trump Drives Voter Turnout;" Cullen, *Storm Lake*, 140; Brianne Pfannenstiel, "Branstad Resigns Governorship, Takes Office as U.S. Ambassador to China," *Des Moines Register*, May 24, 2017, https://www.desmoinesregister.com/story/news/2017/05/24/gov-terry-branstad-no-more-nations-longest-serving-governor-becomes-u-s-ambassador-china/341852001/; Kim Norvell, Kevin Hardy, and Brianne Pfannenstiel, "Iowa Election 2018: Kim Reynolds Wins Full Term, a Validation of the Republican Policies She Has Led," *Des Moines Register*, November 5, 2018, https://www.desmoinesregister.com/story/news/politics/elections/2018/11/05/iowa-election-2018-results-governor-republican-kim-reynolds-democrat-fred-hubbell-jake-porter-vote/1732343002/. For more on the 2017 legislation on Iowa public unions, see Emmett Rensin and Lucy Schiller, "Republicans Are Set to Destroy Iowa's Labor Unions," *New Republic*, February 7, 2017, https://newrepublic.com/article/140485/republicans-set-destroy-iowas-labor-unions. Most of Iowa's public employees were female and many lived in rural areas. Lower pay and more costly benefits did not help Iowa's struggling rural areas. Reynolds was reelected in 2022 by a huge margin, dealing the state Democrats another crushing blow. Only one Democrat retained their statewide office, Auditor Rob Sand. See Brianne Pfannenstiel, "Republican Red Wave Foundered Nationally, But in Iowa It Swept Away Democrats," *Des Moines Register*, November 11, 2022, https://www.desmoinesregister.com/story/news/politics/elections/2022/11/11/republican-red-wave-election-results-2022-iowa-kim-reynolds-mixed-nationally/69632525007/.

26. Pfannenstiel, "Trump Drives Voter Turnout;" Ian Richardson and Stephen Gruber-Miller, "Iowa Republicans Expanded Their Statehouse Majority. Here's How They Did It and What That Could Mean," *Des Moines Register*, November 8, 2020, https://www.desmoinesregister.com/story/news/politics/2020/11/08/iowa-legislature-republican-house-senate-victory-what-are-2021-priorities/6166154002/; Peter Slevin, "The Power of Political Disinformation in Iowa," *New Yorker*, March 24, 2021, https://www.newyorker.com/news/campaign-chronicles/the-power-of-political-disinformation-in-iowa; Larimer, *Gubernatorial Stability*, 28–30. For the historical makeup of the Iowa legislature see "Historical Tables of the Iowa Legislature," Iowa Legislature, accessed April 19, 2023, https://www.legis.iowa.gov/legislators/legisInfo/historicalLegislatureTables.

27. Donnelle Eller, "Flooding Has Slammed Every Iowa County since 1988, Some as Many as 17 Times," *Des Moines Register*, April 29, 2018, https://www.desmoinesregister.com/story/money/agriculture/2018/04/29/iowa-flood-center-ranks-disaste-damages-billions-wapsipinicon-river/422336002/; Eugene S. Takle, "Was Climate Change Involved?" in *A Watershed Year: Anatomy of the Iowa Floods of 2008*, ed. Cornelia F. Mutel (Iowa City: University of Iowa Press, 2010), 112–113.

28. Donnelle Eller, "Climate Change-Driven 'Midwest Water Hose' Caused Massive 2019 Flooding in Iowa, Elsewhere, UI Researchers Find," *Des Moines Register*, March 2, 2021, https://www.desmoinesregister.com/story/money/agriculture/2021/03/02/ui-study-climate-change-midwest-water-hose-dumping-rain-university-iowa/6884486002/.

29. Sarah Almukhtar, Blacki Migliozzi, John Schwartz and Josh Williams, "The Great Flood of 2019: A Complete Picture of a Slow-Motion Disaster," *New York Times*, September 11, 2019, https://www.nytimes.com/interactive/2019/09/11/us/midwest-flooding.html; Gage Miskimen, "It's a Record: Iowa Has Wettest 12-Month Period since Official Records Began in 1895," *Des Moines Register*, June 14, 2019, https://www.desmoinesregister.com/story/news/2019/06/14/iowa-climate-change-agriculture-flood-rain-farming-environment-weather-precipitation-temperature/1433128001/.

30. A. Allen Bradley Jr., "What Causes Floods in Iowa?" in Mutel, *Watershed Year*, 11–14; Witold F. Krajewski and Ricardo Mantilla, "Why Were the 2008 Floods So Large?" in Mutel, 19, 26, 29; Barbara Eckstein and Rodney Lehnertz, "The University of Iowa and the Flood," in Mutel, 41–44; Linda Langston, "Linn County and the Flood," in Mutel, 49; Daniel Otto, "Economic Losses from the Floods," in Mutel, 141–144; Connerly, *Green, Fair, and Prosperous*, 83–84; Kim Norvell, "'On Pins and Needles:' Flooded-Out Iowans Brace for a Third Round in Six Months," *Des Moines Register*, September 17, 2019, https://www.desmoinesregister.com/story/news/2019/09/17/iowa-flooding-2019-missouri-river-levee-breaches-mills-fremont-county-pacific-junction-hamburg/2355669001/; "Eight Years after the Flood," *Cedar Rapids Gazette*, June 12, 2016, www.thegazette.com/news/eight-years-after-the-flood/.

31. Donnelle Eller, "Punishing Drought Threatens Yields, Income for Thousands of Iowa Farmers," *Des Moines Register*, August 11, 2017, https://www.desmoinesregister.com/story/money/agriculture/2017/08/11/drought-hits-parts-iowa/554320001/; David Pitt, "Iowa Scientists: Drought a Sign of Climate Change," *USA Today*, November 20, 2012, https://www.usatoday.com/story/weather/2012/11/20/drought-climate-change-iowa/1717505/; Pitt, "Final 2012 Drought Report Shows Corn Harvest Took Hardest Hit," *Washington Post*, January 14, 2013, https://www.washingtonpost.com/politics/final-2012-drought-report-shows-corn-harvest-took-hardest-hit/2013/01/13/a66113d2-5c45-11e2-88d0-c4cf65c3ad15_story.html; Donnelle Eller, "Iowa Farmers Are Cautious about Taking Advantage of Rising Crop Prices as Drought Concerns Deepen during Planting," *Des Moines Register*, May 7, 2021, https://www.desmoinesregister.com/story/money/agriculture/2021/05/07/corn-soybean-prices-rising-but-iowa-farmers-wary-drought-deepens/4879594001/; Orlan Love, "2012 Iowa Drought Now Worse Than '88," *Cedar Rapids Gazette*, August 1, 2012, https://www.thegazette.com/news/2012-iowa-drought-now-worse-than-88/. See US Drought Monitor, accessed April 19, 2023, https://droughtmonitor.unl.edu for drought information for the twenty-first century.

32. Eugene Takle and William Gutowski, "Iowa's Agriculture Is Losing Its Goldilocks Climate," *Physics Today* 73, no. 2 (February 2020): 26–33; Tom Philpott, *Perilous Bounty: The Looming Collapse of American Farming and How We Can Prevent*

It (New York: Bloomsbury, 2020), 130–134. A sobering October 2022 report argued that climate change would significantly reduce corn production in Iowa by 2050. The state's southern counties would be hit the hardest by higher temperatures. Davis County might lose up to sixty bushels per acre in output by 2050, reducing productivity gains that were expected in the mid-twenty-first century. Iowa farmers in Tama County might produce about 260 bushels of corn per acre, rather than almost 300 bushels per acre by 2050. See Environmental Defense Fund, "How Climate Change Will Impact U.S. Corn, Soybean, and Wheat Yields," accessed April 19, 2023, https://www.edf.org/sites/default/files/2022-10/climate-impacts-midwest-crop-yields.pdf. Pages 11–16 and 27–28 are most useful.

33. Tim Webber, "How Did We Get Here? A Look at the Pandemic Events That Led Iowa to Where It Is Today," *Des Moines Register*, January 25, 2021, https://www.desmoinesregister.com/in-depth/news/health/2021/01/25/coronavirus-iowa-how-state-has-weathered-covid-19-month-month/6556282002/; Tom Cullen, "CDC Reports Latinos Have Highest Rate of Covid Infection in Agriculture, Food Processing," *Storm Lake Times*, October 23, 2020; Art Cullen, "Reynolds Comes Around," *Storm Lake Times*, November 13, 2020; Neil Vigdor, "Months into the Pandemic, the U.S. Had Six Times as Many Cases as Reported, an N.I.H. Study Finds," *New York Times*, June 24, 2021, https://www.nytimes.com/2021/06/24/world/us-covid-cases-nih.html; Richard A. Oppel Jr. et al., "The Fullest Look Yet at the Racial Inequity of Coronavirus," *New York Times*, July 5, 2020, https://www.nytimes.com/interactive/2020/07/05/us/coronavirus-latinos-african-americans-cdc-data.html; Lyz Lenz, "Welcome to Iowa, a State That Doesn't Care If You Live or Die," *Washington Post*, February 10, 2021, https://www.washingtonpost.com/outlook/2021/02/10/iowa-lift-all-restrictions/; Donnelle Eller, "Number of Workers with Coronavirus at Waterloo Tyson Plant More Than Double Earlier Figures," *Des Moines Register*, May 7, 2020, https://www.desmoinesregister.com/story/money/agriculture/2020/05/07/infected-workers-waterloo-plant-more-than-double-earlier-figure/3092376001/. Data on infection numbers is incomplete for Iowa but COVID information for March 2020 to March 2021 from the *Atlantic* shows that Native Hawaiian and Pacific Islanders had an infection rates three times that of whites. Infection rates for Latinos were more than 50 percent higher than whites and 23 percent higher for Blacks. See Covid Tracking Project, "Iowa," accessed April 19, 2023, covidtracking.com/data/state/iowa. The information on March, April, and May is from the July 5 *New York Times* article, which provides county-level data. This information is also incomplete, with 87 percent of cases in Polk County disclosing race but only 62 percent of cases in Sioux County doing so.

34. Emily Oster, "Schools Aren't Super-Spreaders," *Atlantic*, October 9, 2020, https://www.theatlantic.com/ideas/archive/2020/10/schools-arent-superspreaders/616669/; Dan Levin and Kate Taylor, "'Science versus Politics': School District Defies Governor's Reopening Order," *New York Times*, September 10, 2020, https://www.nytimes.com/2020/09/10/us/des-moines-school-opening-coronavirus.html; David Leonhardt, "'Not Good for Learning,'" *New York Times*, May 5, 2022, https://www.nytimes.com/2022/05/05/briefing/school-closures-covid-learning-loss.html; Robin Opsahl, "The Latest: Iowa School Districts Prepare to Start Classes in

COVID-19 Pandemic," *Des Moines Register*, July 28, 2020, https://www.desmoines register.com/story/news/education/2020/07/28/what-we-know-iowa-school-districts-plans-reopen-fall/5528239002/; Register Staff Report, "After Finishing 2020 Online, Here's How Des Moines Area School Districts Are Reopening in 2021," *Des Moines Register*, January 5, 2021, https://www.desmoinesregister.com/story/news/education/2021/01/05/des-moines-schools-reopening-plans-2021-covid-19-coronavirus-pandemic/4125841001/; Lena H. Sun, Dan Keating, and Joel Achenbach, "Coronavirus Has Infected Majority of Americans, Blood Tests Indicate," *Washington Post*, April 26, 2022, https://www.washingtonpost.com/health/2022/04/26/majority-americans-coronavirus-infections/. For more on the debate on opening schools see chapter 11 in Emily Mendenhall, *Unmasked: COVID, Community, and the Case of Okoboji* (Nashville: Vanderbilt University Press, 2022). See Iowa COVID-19 Tracker, "COVID-19 Deaths in Our Schools," accessed April 19, 2023, https://iowacovid19tracker.org/covid-19-deaths-in-our-schools/ for a list of adult COVD deaths in Iowa schools. This list includes some who taught at community colleges, as well as private K-12 institutions.

35. Tyler Jett, "With Another 17,500 Initial Claims Filed Last Week, the Number of Iowans on Unemployment Tops 220,000," *Des Moines Register*, May 21, 2020, https://www.desmoinesregister.com/story/money/business/2020/05/21/iowa-unemployment-initial-claims-reopening/5233389002/; Barbara Rodriguez, "University of Iowa Researchers Warn 'A Second Wave of Infections Is Likely' if Covid19 Prevention Efforts Are Lifted," *Des Moines Register*, April 29, 2020, https://www.desmoinesregister.com/story/news/health/2020/04/28/university-iowa-researchers-warn-kim-reynolds-administration-second-coronavirus-wave/3040849001/; Tony Leys, "White House Says Iowa Has the Highest Coronavirus Rate in the Country, Should Close More Bars," *Des Moines Register*, August 31, 2020, https://www.desmoinesregister.com/story/news/health/2020/08/31/white-house-coronavirus-taskforce-says-iowa-has-highest-rate-country/3449153001/; Tony Leys, "White House: Iowa's Coronavirus Outbreak Is Causing 'Many Preventable Deaths,'" *Des Moines Register*, October 8, 2020, https://www.desmoinesregister.com/story/news/health/2020/10/08/white-house-coronavirus-experts-say-iowa-is-suffering-many-preventable-deaths-from-covid-19/5923607002/; Ben Casselman and Jim Tankersley, "Iowa Never Locked Down. Its Economy Is Struggling Anyway," *New York Times*, October 22, 2020, https://www.nytimes.com/2020/10/22/business/economy/economy-coronavirus-lockdown-iowa.html?referringSource=articleShare; Ian Richardson, "Iowa Gov. Kim Reynolds Defends Wednesday's Crowded Trump Rally, Says Many Wore Face Masks," *Des Moines Register*, October 15, 2020, https://www.desmoinesregister.com/story/news/politics/2020/10/15/iowa-gov-kim-reynolds-defends-trump-rally-citing-first-amendment-rights/3664414001/; Cullen, "Reynolds Comes Around."

36. Andrea May Sahouri, "$7.5 Billion and Counting: August Derecho That Slammed Iowa Was Most Costly Thunderstorm in US History, Data Shows," *Des Moines Register*, October 17, 2020, https://www.desmoinesregister.com/story/news/2020/10/17/iowas-august-derecho-most-costly-thunderstorm-us-history-7-5-billion-damages/3695053001/; Perry Beeman, "State: Derecho Flattened a Quarter of Iowa's Forest,"

Des Moines Register, November 14, 2020, https://www.desmoinesregister.com/story/news/2020/11/14/state-derecho-flattened-quarter-iowas-forest/6271797002/; "Photos: Meskwaki Community Members Finding New Use for Derecho Damaged Trees," *Des Moines Register*, March 20, 2021, https://www.desmoinesregister.com/picture-gallery/life/2021/03/20/meskwaki-community-members-finding-new-use-derecho-damaged-trees/4784011001/; Tyler Jett, "Derecho Recovery: Why Was Outside Help for the Power Company Serving Iowa's Hardest-Hit Area So Slow?" *Des Moines Register*, October 12, 2020, https://www.desmoinesregister.com/story/money/business/2020/10/12/utility-aid-lagged-hardest-hit-part-iowa-after-derecho-why/5939435002/; Andrea May Sahouri, "Derecho Storm Aftermath: Here Are Ways the Des Moines Community Can Help with Disaster Relief Efforts," *Des Moines Register*, August 15, 2020, https://www.desmoinesregister.com/story/news/2020/08/15/derecho-storm-ways-des-moines-community-can-help-disaster-relief-efforts/5584812002/; Erika Frey, "Hawkeye Elegy: A Collision of Pandemic, Disaster, and Polarization in the Heartland," *Fortune*, February/March 2021, https://fortune.com/longform/iowa-covid-derecho-thunderstorm-2020-election-trump-biden.

37. Audra D. S. Burch et al., "The Death of George Floyd Reignited a Movement. What Happens Now?" *New York Times*, April 20, 2021, https://www.nytimes.com/2021/04/20/us/george-floyd-protests-police-reform.html; Stephen Gruber-Miller and Ian Richardson, "'We Are Ready and Willing to Act': Gov. Kim Reynolds Signs Law Banning Most Chokeholds, Addressing Police Misconduct," *Des Moines Register*, June 12, 2020, https://www.desmoinesregister.com/story/news/politics/2020/06/12/police-misconduct-chokehold-law-governor-kim-reynolds-sign-black-lives-matter-george-floyd/5347514002/; Ian Richardson and Stephen Gruber-Miller, "A Year Ago, Iowa Lawmakers United on a Police Accountability Law. Then They Moved Backward, Racial Justice Advocates Say," *Des Moines Register*, June 12, 2021, https://www.desmoinesregister.com/story/news/politics/2021/06/12/iowa-kim-reynolds-most-racist-or-successful-racial-profiling-police-accountability-law-george-floyd/7616383002/; Stephen Gruber-Miller and Ian Richardson, "Gov. Kim Reynolds Signs Executive Order Restoring Felon Voting Rights, Removing Iowa's Last-In-The-Nation Status," *Des Moines Register*, August 5, 2020, https://www.desmoinesregister.com/story/news/politics/2020/08/05/iowa-governor-kim-reynolds-signs-felon-voting-rights-executive-order-before-november-election/5573994002/.

38. "South Dakota's Economy Defies Conventional Wisdom about Covid-19," *Economist*, March 18, 2021, https://www.economist.com/united-states/2021/03/18/south-dakotas-economy-defies-conventional-wisdom-about-covid-19; Elaine Godfrey, "Iowa Is What Happens When Government Does Nothing," *Atlantic*, December 3, 2020, https://www.theatlantic.com/politics/archive/2020/12/how-iowa-mishandled-coronavirus-pandemic/617252/; Webber, "How Did We Get Here." By late September 2022 Iowa had reached ten thousand deaths from COVID. See Michaela Ramm, "10,000 COVID Deaths in Iowa: 'The Numbers Do Not Tell You about a Human Life,'" *Des Moines Register*, September 19, 2022, https://www.desmoinesregister.com/story/news/health/2022/09/19/10000-iowa-covid-deaths-broderick-daye-bryce-wilson/8024135001/.

39. Tim Webber and Tony Leys, "Iowa Has the Most New Covid Cases since November 2020, Nearing a Weekly Record, Latest Update Shows," *Des Moines Register*, January 12, 2022, https://www.desmoinesregister.com/story/news/health/2022/01/12/iowa-covid-cases-near-record-number-omicron-vaccine-deaths-report/9174894002/; Associated Press, "Reynolds: Iowa Vaccinations Will Rise as More Doses Arrive," *Marshalltown Times-Republican*, February 26, 2021, https://www.timesrepublican.com/news/todays-news/2021/02/reynolds-iowa-vaccinations-will-rise-as-more-doses-arrive/.

Bibliographic Essay

This overview is a starting point for those interested in learning more about the state. It includes sources that are easily accessible through libraries or are available online and focuses on books and articles directly tied to Iowa. For additional information on various topics, see the footnotes for each chapter. At the end of this essay is a list of twelve important books—on subjects such as the Civil War, small towns, rural life, and the Farm Crisis—that the author believes will help readers better understand the state.

Three one-volume state histories were published in the late twentieth century. The first of these was Leland L. Sage's *A History of Iowa* (Ames: Iowa State University Press, 1974), a book mostly focused on politics. Joseph Frazier Wall wrote *Iowa, A Bicentennial History* (New York: W. W. Norton, 1978), a series of topical essays that is accessible and easy-to-read, even if it is an incomplete history of the state. Dorothy Schwieder, the most important historian of the state, often called the dean of Iowa historians, wrote the standard survey, *Iowa: The Middle Land* (Ames: Iowa State University Press, 1996). It is a comprehensive history, covering topics such as women, immigrant groups, and African Americans, who had been left out of previous state histories.

Older histories of the state contain much useful information but are products of their time and are mostly focused upon the experiences of white men and politics. William J. Petersen, *The Story of Iowa: The Progress of An American State* (New York: Lewis Historical, 1952), two volumes, is a narrative encyclopedia of Iowa, spanning more than eleven hundred pages and covering topics from climate and geology to transportation, education, and religion. Cyrenus Cole, *A History of the People of Iowa* (Cedar Rapids: Torch Press, 1921), emphasizes the frontier experience, the Civil War, politics, and railroads. Benjamin F. Gue, *History of Iowa from the Earliest Times to the*

Beginning of the Twentieth Century (New York: Century History, 1903), four volumes, focuses on the same themes as Cole.

Outside In: African-American History in Iowa, 1838–2000, edited by Bill Silag, Susan Koch-Bridgford, and Hal Chase (Des Moines: State Historical Society of Iowa, 2001) is a crucial resource. This wonderfully illustrated and clearly written history is a comprehensive account of Black life, with chapters on legal history, agriculture, education, civil rights, demographics, politics, religion, and more. Almost every chapter in this book cites some part of *Outside In*. Specific chapters are not identified in this essay, since many of them are topical (i.e., African American military service) and do not easily match the chronological format here. Anyone studying Iowa should have this invaluable resource in their library.

Iowa's historical journals are incredibly important for the history of the state—they contain much of its history. The *Annals of Iowa*, published almost continuously since 1863, is the one Iowa journal still being produced by the State Historical Society of Iowa. (There are three different "series" of the journal. The first ran from 1863 to 1874. It was not published again until 1882. The second series ran from 1882 to 1884. In 1893 it began publication again, with the third series published into the twenty-first century.) Older issues contain much local history and plenty of memoirs and reminiscences, while the past few decades have focused on topics ranging from labor history and women's history to immigration and Iowa's nonwhite population. The *Iowa Journal of History and Politics*, published from 1903 to 1949, and its successor, the *Iowa Journal of History* (1949–1960), are especially good on Iowa's nineteenth-century history. They contain many outstanding primary sources, especially on the Civil War and white settlement. The *Palimpsest*, a slim popular history magazine, published from 1920 to 1995, and its successor, *Iowa Heritage Illustrated* (1996–2014), cover a vast range of topics. Both are well-written and accessible to nonspecialists. The *Annals of Iowa* and the *Palimpsest* are available online—thousands of articles in the two journals are available, thanks to digitization by the State Historical Society of Iowa.

Wayne I. Anderson, *Iowa's Geological Past: Three Billion Years of Change* (Iowa City: University of Iowa Press, 1998), Lynn M. Alex, *Iowa's Archaeological Past* (Iowa City: University of Iowa Press, 2000), and Cornelia F. Mutel, *The Emerald Horizon: The History of Nature in Iowa* (Iowa City: University of Iowa Press, 2008) provide excellent overviews of their topics. Mutel will be the most readable and useful of these books for general readers, while Anderson and Alex are written for a more academic audience.

The Native history of Iowa is badly outdated, but Martha Royce Blaine's *The Ioway Indians* (Norman: University of Oklahoma Press, 1979) and William T. Hagan's *The Sac and Fox Indians* (Norman: University of Oklahoma Press, 1958) are still the best surveys of these tribes. Lance Foster, *The Indians of Iowa* (Iowa City: University of Iowa Press, 2009), is a very brief but useful overview. Gretchen M. Bataille, David Mayer Gradwohl, and Charles L. P. Silet, eds., *The World between Two Rivers: Perspectives on American Indians in Iowa* (Iowa City: University of Iowa Press, 2000); Saul Schwartz and William Green, "Middle Ground or Native Ground? Material Culture at Iowaville," *Ethnohistory* 60, no. 4 (Fall 2013): 537–565, and David Bernstein,

"'We Are Not Now as We Once Were:' Iowa Indians' Political and Economic Adaptations during U. S. Incorporation," *Ethnohistory* 54, no. 4 (Fall 2007): 605–637, update our knowledge of Native peoples in the state. Kevin T. Mason, "Inkpaduta in Iowa: Dakota Decline, Dispossession, and Erasure," *Annals of Iowa* 80, no. 2 (Spring 2021): 123–157, is a valuable article that highlights the long history of the Dakota in the state.

Iowa was a borderland between Native and European nations in the 1700s and early 1800s. William E. Whittaker, ed., *Frontier Forts of Iowa: Indians, Traders, and Soldiers, 1682–1862* (Iowa City: University of Iowa Press, 2009) and Lucy Eldersveld Murphy, *A Gathering of Rivers: Indians, Metis, and Mining in the Western Great Lakes, 1737–1832* (Lincoln: University of Nebraska Press, 2004) tell the story of the variety of people in and around Iowa very well. Patrick J. Jung has a fine article that surveys early Iowa, titled "Iowa without Borders: Iowa History from European Contact to Statehood," *Annals of Iowa* 80, no. 4 (Fall 2021): 365–371.

The Black Hawk War has received lots of attention. The best overview is Kerry Trask *Black Hawk: The Battle for the Heart of America* (New York: Henry Holt, 2006). Patrick J. Jung, *The Black Hawk War of 1832* (Norman: University of Oklahoma Press, 2007) is a superb military history of the conflict. Roger L. Nichols's *Black Hawk and the Warrior's Path* (Wheeling, IL: Harlan Davidson, 1992) is an essential biography. *Life of Black Hawk* (Cincinnati: J. B. Patterson, 1833) is critical to understanding the man and Sauk life, though it has been edited and interpreted by those who helped him write it.

There is no book focusing on territorial Iowa or articles that adequately survey the period. William Petersen has a chapter on the subject in volume 1 of *The Story of Iowa*, mostly focusing on politics. George C. Duffield has two excellent reminiscences of early Iowa. See "Coming into Iowa in 1837," *Annals of Iowa* 6, no. 1 (1903): 1–8, and "An Iowa Settler's Homestead," *Annals of Iowa* 6, no. 3 (1903): 206–215. The most recent survey of Iowa settlement is George F. Parker, *Iowa Pioneer Foundations* (Iowa City: State Historical Society of Iowa, 1940), two volumes, which is an incomplete and outdated history. However, more recent historians have broadened our understanding of the state. Glenda Riley's *Frontierswomen: The Iowa Experience* (Ames: Iowa State University Press, 1981) is important for its emphasis on the role of women. Riley's edited collection of first-person accounts, *Prairie Voices: Iowa's Pioneering Women* (Ames: Iowa State University Press, 1996), is a wonderful assembly of autobiographies and reminiscences, most originally published in Iowa historical journals. Vesta O. Robbins, *No Coward Soul* (Ames: Iowa State University Press, 1974), is the remarkable story of Susan Wyatt. Harriet Bonebright-Closz, *Reminiscences of Newcastle, Iowa: A History of the Founding of Webster City, Iowa* (Des Moines: Historical Department of Iowa, 1921), is a detailed and important account of daily life on the Iowa frontier. It is available online.

Two books on political history and three on Iowa's agriculture are important. Robert R. Dykstra, *Bright Radical Star: Black Freedom and White Supremacy on the Hawkeye Frontier* (Ames: Iowa State University Press, 1993) is crucial to understanding race in Iowa history. Todd E. Pettys, *The Iowa Constitution* (New York: Oxford University Press, 2018) has much historical background and excellent analysis.

Iowa's agricultural history is quite outdated. The most recent book on the subject is Allan G. Bogue, *From Prairie to Corn Belt: Farming on the Illinois and Iowa Prairies in the Nineteenth Century* (Chicago: University of Chicago Press, 1963). Earle D. Ross, *Iowa Agriculture: An Historical Survey* (Iowa City: State Historical Society of Iowa, 1951), reviews Iowa farming into the twentieth century. Kathleen Woida, *Iowa's Remarkable Soils: The Story of Our Most Vital Resource and How We Can Save It* (Iowa City: University of Iowa Press, 2021) is an important new addition to the literature. J. L. Anderson has an excellent survey of Iowa farming. See J. L. Anderson, "Iowa Agricultural History: Old Perspectives and New Directions," *Annals of Iowa* 80, no. 4 (Fall 2021): 371–377.

Many have written about Iowa and the Civil War. The most recent book is Thomas R. Baker, *The Sacred Cause of Union: Iowa in the Civil War* (Iowa City: University of Iowa Press, 2016), an effective introduction to the topic. Kenneth L. Lyftogt has written a three-volume history: *Iowa and the Civil War, Volume 1: Free Child of the Missouri Compromise, 1850–1862* (Iowa City: Camp Pope Publishing, 2018), *Iowa and the Civil War, Volume 2: From Iuka to the Red River, 1862–1864* (Iowa City: Camp Pope Publishing, 2020) and *Iowa and the Civil War, Volume 3: The Longest Year, 1864–1865* (Iowa City: Camp Pope Publishing, 2022). Lowell J. Soike, *Busy in the Cause: Iowa, the Free State Struggle in the West, and the Prelude to Civil War* (Lincoln: University of Nebraska Press, 2014) and Soike, *Necessary Courage: Iowa's Underground Railroad in the Struggle against Slavery* (Iowa City: University of Iowa Press, 2013) provide useful historical context. Also see Dykstra, cited above and Riley's *Frontierswomen*. Excellent first-person accounts include Annie Wittenmyer, *Under the Guns: A Women's Reminiscences of the Civil War* (Boston: E. B. Stillings, 1895) and S. H. M. Byers, *With Fire and Sword* (New York: Neale Publishing, 1911). Both are available online. David Brodnax Sr., "'Will they Fight? Ask the Enemy:' Iowa's African-American Regiment in the Civil War," *Annals of Iowa* 66, nos. 3–4 (Summer–Fall 2007): 266–292, is the most important history of this unit. Leslie A. Schwalm's *Emancipation's Diaspora: Race and Reconstruction in the Upper Midwest* (Chapel Hill: University of North Carolina, 2009), tells the neglected story of slavery, race, and freedom in the region after the Civil War. Dwain Coleman's "Iowa, the Bright Radical Star of the Civil War Era," *Annals of Iowa* 80, no. 4 (Fall 2021): 383–387, is a brief overview of the literature.

Don L. Hofsommer, *Steel Trails of Hawkeyeland: Iowa's Railroad Experience* (Bloomington: University of Indiana Press, 2005) is a detailed history of Iowa railroads. William H. Thompson's *Transportation in Iowa: A Historical Summary* (n.p.: Iowa Department of Transportation, 1989) is a clearly written and comprehensive overview. William J. Petersen, *Steamboating on the Upper Mississippi* (Iowa City: State Historical Society of Iowa, 1968), has much material on Iowa. Petersen also dedicates five chapters in volume 1 of *The Story of Iowa* to steamboats, stagecoaches, railroads, and other forms of transport.

The literature on immigration to Iowa is vast. For an overview of the topic see Jeff Bremer, "Immigration in Iowa: A Brief History and Historiography," *Annals of Iowa* 80, no. 4 (Fall 2021): 387–393. An older, but still useful, history of Dutch migration is Jacob Van der Zee, *The Hollanders of Iowa* (Iowa City: State Historical Society of Iowa, 1912). Mark Wyman, *Immigrants in the Valley: Irish, Germans, and Americans in the Upper Mississippi Country, 1830–1860* (Chicago: Nelson-Hall, 1984) is a good survey. Timothy Walch's *Irish Iowa* (Charleston, SC: History Press, 2019) is a concise and useful addition to the state's history. Elmer Schwieder and Dorothy Schwieder, *A Peculiar People: Iowa's Old Order Amish* (Iowa City: University of Iowa Press, 2009) is the standard account. Barbara Selzer Yambura and Eunice W. Bodine, *A Change and a Parting: My Story of Amana* (Ames: Iowa State University Press, 1960), discusses Iowa's famous Amana colonies. For Black immigrants to Iowa see Schwalm, cited above, as well as *Outside In*. The *Palimpsest* dedicated its May 1966 issue to Swedish immigration and its August 1959 issue to Norwegian immigrants. Shari Rabin, "'A Nest to the Wandering Bird': Iowa and the Creation of American Judaism, 1855–1877," *Annals of Iowa* 73, no. 2 (Spring 2014): 101–127, is an important history of Jewish immigration to the state. Omar Valerio-Jimenez, "Racializing Mexican Immigrants in Iowa's Early Mexican Communities," *Annals of Iowa* 75, no. 1 (Winter 2016), 1–46, is the essential introduction to an immigrant group whose history is mostly unexplored. Anthony J. Miller's "'Pioneers, Sunday Schoolers, and Laundrymen:' Chinese Immigrants in Iowa in the Chinese Exclusion Era, 1870–1890," *Annals of Iowa* 81, no. 2 (Spring 2022): 113–148, is a significant addition to the state's immigration history.

Iowa does not have a recent history of its education or any book-length survey of its religious history. Clarence Ray Aurner, *History of Education in Iowa* (Iowa City: State Historical Society of Iowa, 1914–1920), five volumes, is a century old but full of useful information. Wayne E. Fuller, *The Old Country School: The Story of Rural Education in the Middle West* (Chicago: University of Chicago Press, 1982) has much on Iowa. For the state's two main universities see Stow Persons, *The University of Iowa in the Twentieth Century: An Institutional History* (Iowa City: University of Iowa Press, 1990), which also reviews the nineteenth century, and Dorothy Schwieder and Gretchen Van Houten, eds., *A Sesquicentennial History of Iowa State University: Tradition and Transformation* (Ames: Iowa State University Press, 2007). Petersen has several useful chapters on elementary and secondary education, as well as on colleges and universities in volume 2 of *The Story of Iowa*. He also has a long chapter on religion in the same volume. Louis T. Jones, *The Quakers of Iowa* (Iowa City: State Historical Society of Iowa, 1914) is a dated, but solid, history. Andrew Klumpp has an excellent overview of the state's religious history, "Everywhere and Nowhere: Histories of Religion in Iowa," *Annals of Iowa* 80, no. 4 (Fall 2021): 394–400.

Iowa's urban history has been neglected—there is no good historical survey of the city of Des Moines, for example. The history of industry, especially meatpacking, has received adequate attention. Sharon E. Wood, *The Freedom of the Streets: Work, Citizenship, and Sexuality in a Gilded Age City* (Chapel Hill: University of North Carolina Press, 2005), is an important history of women, work, and urban life. Warren J. Wilson, *Tied to the Great Packing Machine: The Midwest and Meatpacking* (Iowa City: University of Iowa Press, 2007), and Dorothy Schwieder, *Black Diamonds: Life and Work in Iowa's Coal Mines* (Ames: Iowa State University Press, 1983), tell the story of these two important state industries. Dorothy Schwieder, Joseph Hraba, and Elmer Schwieder, *Buxton: A Black Utopia in the Heartland* (Iowa City: University of Iowa Press, 2003) recounts Buxton's unique experience.

The best history of the struggle for female suffrage in Iowa is Sara Egge, *Woman Suffrage and Citizenship in the Midwest, 1870–1920* (Iowa City: University of Iowa Press, 2018). Also see Louise R. Noun, *Strong-Minded Women: The Emergence of the Women-Suffrage Movement in Iowa* (Ames: Iowa State University Press, 1969). An older but valuable source is Ruth A. Gallaher, *Legal and Political Status of Women in Iowa: An Historical Account of the Rights of Women in Iowa from 1838 to 1918* (Iowa City: State Historical Society of Iowa, 1918). There is no book-length survey of the prohibition struggle in Iowa but Ruth A. Gallaher, "The Liquor Merry-Go-Round," *Palimpsest* 14, no. 6 (June 1933): 213–222, is a good summary. Egge also has a good overview of women's history in the state. See Sara Egge, "Iowa's History of Gender at 175: A Brief Survey," *Annals of Iowa* 80, no. 4 (Fall 2021): 400–405.

There are no book-length histories of Iowa in World War I or the 1920s. The State Historical Society of Iowa published *Chronicles of the World War*, a seven-volume history of the home front. None of the books make for riveting reading but they are all important histories of the state's role in the conflict. Earl S. Fullbrook, *The Red Cross in Iowa* (Iowa City: State Historical Society of Iowa, 1922), two volumes, Ivan L. Pollock, *The Food Administration in Iowa* (Iowa City: State Historical Society of Iowa, 1923), two volumes, and Nathaniel R. Whitney, *The Sale of War Bonds in Iowa* (Iowa City: State Historical Society of Iowa, 1923) provide plenty of details and statistics. Thomas J. Morain, *Prairie Grass Roots: An Iowa Small Town in the Early Twentieth Century* (Ames: Iowa State University Press, 1988) is a fine examination of social and economic change in the town of Jefferson. John H. Taber, *The Story of the 168th Infantry* (Iowa City: State Historical Society of Iowa, 1923), two volumes, is an excellent history of the unit and its role in the war. Stephen H. Taber, ed., *A Rainbow Division Lieutenant in France: The World War One Diary of John H. Taber* (Jefferson: McFarland, 2015), is a valuable firsthand account of the conflict.

A number of first-person accounts of late nineteenth- and early twentieth-century Iowa are worth reading. Deemer Lee, *Esther's Town* (Ames: Iowa State University Press, 1980), is a charming history of Estherville, written by the editor of the town's newspaper. Carl Hamilton, *In No Time at All* (Ames: Iowa State University Press, 1974), H. E. Wilkinson, *Memories of an Iowa Farm Boy* (Ames: Iowa State University Press, 1952), and Margaret Ott Onerheim, *Threads of Memory: A Memoir of the 1920s* (Ames: Iowa State University, 1993) are all lively accounts of the period. Wilkinson's memoir is an especially informative and entertaining reminiscence of rural life in the 1890s and early 1900s.

A good history of Iowa during the Depression remains to be written. The story of Elmer Powers, a farmer in Boone County, is a helpful starting point. See H. Roger Grant and L. Edward Purcell, eds., *Years of Struggle: The Farm Diary of Elmer G. Powers* (Dekalb: Northern Illinois University Press, 1995). VaDonna Jean Leaf, "'Sure Hope Things Go Better Tomorrow:' Letters from a Travelling Salesman, 1928–1935," *Palimpsest* 71, no. 4 (Winter 1990): 186–192, is an excellent article that explains the challenges and despair of the depression. Lisa L. Ossian, *The Depression Dilemmas of Rural Iowa, 1929–1933* (Columbia: University of Missouri Press, 2012), is a useful survey of the first years of the Depression, while John L. Stover, *Cornbelt Rebellion: The Farmer's Holiday Association* (Urbana: University of Illinois Press, 1965) is the best history of the subject. Mildred Armstrong Kalish, *Little Heathens: Hard Times and High Spirits on an Iowa Farm during the Great Depression* (New York: Random House, 2007) is a highly readable and popular memoir of the Depression, but the author's experience does not fully illuminate how awful the 1930s were for many in the state. John C. Culver and John Hyde, *American Dreamer: A Life of Henry A. Wallace* (New York: W. W. Norton, 2000), is a big, admiring biography. Gregg R. Narber, *The Impact of the New Deal on Iowa: Changing the Culture of a Rural State* (Lewiston, NY: Edwin Mellen Press, 2008), describes the impact of the New Deal on the state's infrastructure and culture. Louise Rosenfield Noun, *Iowa Women in the WPA* (Ames: Iowa State University Press, 1999), is a concise and informative overview of the topic. The best brief biography of Iowa's only president is William E. Leuchtenburg, *Herbert Hoover* (New York: Henry Holt, 2009). R. Tripp Evans, *Grant Wood: A Life* (New York: Alfred A. Knopf, 2010), is a thorough and readable biography of the state's most famous artist.

Iowa's role in World War II has received less attention than you would think. Lisa Ossian, *The Home Fronts of Iowa, 1939–1945* (Columbia: University of Missouri Press, 2009), is the best book on the war in the state. Ossian's book is comprehensive and well-written. Mary Bennett, "Meskwaki Code Talkers," *Iowa Heritage Illustrated* 84, no. 4 (Winter 2003): 154–156, is a fine summary of this important topic. Henry Langrehr and Jim DeFelice, *Whatever It Took: An American Paratrooper's Extraordinary Memoir of Escape, Survival, and Heroism in the Last Days of World War Two* (New York: HarperCollins, 2020), and Darlene Diebler Rose, *Evidence Not Seen: A Woman's Miraculous Faith in the Jungles of World War Two* (New York: Harper Collins, 2001), are incredible stories of survival. Langrehr's book is an inspiring and gripping memoir. Iowa's published histories of the conflict are surprisingly few.

Iowa after World War II changed greatly, and the historical literature on many topics, such as race and gender, is unfortunately limited. J. L. Anderson, *Industrializing the Corn Belt: Agriculture, Technology, and Environment, 1945–1972* (De Kalb: Northern Illinois University Press, 2009), is an important history of the postwar transformation of Iowa farming. Charles E. Connerly, *Green, Fair, and Prosperous: Paths to A Sustainable Iowa* (Iowa City: University of Iowa, 2020), has sections on race and agriculture for this period. Deborah Fink, *Open Country, Iowa: Rural Women, Tradition, and Change* (Albany: State University of New York Press, 1986), is a valuable examination of women in rural Iowa, especially during World War II and the following decades. On politics see James C. Larew, *A Party Reborn: The Democrats of Iowa, 1950–1974* (Iowa City: Iowa State Historical Department, 1980). Several outstanding articles provide important context, including Noah Lawrence, "'Since It Is My Right, I Would Like to Have It': Edna Griffin and the Katz Drug Store Desegregation Movement," *Annals of Iowa* 67, no. 4 (October 2008): 298–330, and Coreen Derifield, "'I Thought of the Money That We Could Use': Iowa Women and Industrial Wage Work,

1950–1970," *Annals of Iowa* 73, no. 1 (January 2014): 28–59. Shelton Stromquist, *Solidarity and Survival: An Oral History of Iowa Labor in the Twentieth Century* (Iowa City: University of Iowa Press, 1993) is a thorough and informative survey of the topic, full of firsthand accounts of the state's labor history, especially from the 1930s until the end of the century. Neal Smith's memoir of his thirty-six years as a congressman, *Mr. Smith Went to Washington: From Eisenhower to Clinton* (Ames: Iowa State University Press, 1996), is a folksy memoir of politics, legislation, and presidents in the late twentieth century.

C. D. B Bryant, *Friendly Fire* (New York: G. P. Putnam, 1976), and James D. Seddon, *Morning Glories among the Peas: A Vietnam Veteran's Story* (Ames: Iowa State University Press, 1990), are devastating indictments of the conflict and heartbreaking stories of loss and survival. Matthew R. Walsh, *The Good Governor: Robert Ray and the Indochinese Refugees of Iowa* (Jefferson: McFarland, 2017), is the best biography of one of the state's most important and admired governors. It also has much material on refugees from Southeast Asia. The best article on the Tai Dam is Siang Bacthi, inNgeun Baccam Soulinthavong, and Jack Lufkin, "'So We Stayed Together:' The Tai Dam Immigrate to Iowa," *Palimpsest* 69, no. 4 (Winter 1988): 163–172. Anthropologist Douglas E. Foley, an Iowan whose hometown is Tama, has a perceptive study of the Meskwaki in the late twentieth century. See Douglas E. Foley, *The Heartland Chronicles* (Philadelphia: University of Pennsylvania Press, 1995).

The late twentieth century, especially Iowa's farm crisis, is understudied. Pamela Riney-Kehrberg's *When A Dream Dies: Agriculture, Iowa, and the Farm Crisis of the 1980s* (Lawrence: University Press of Kansas, 2022) is an important new history. Osha Gray Davidson, *Broken Heartland: The Rise of America's Rural Ghetto* (New York: Free Press, 1990), is a valuable account. Connerly, cited above, puts the 1980s in economic and political context. Deborah Fink, *Cutting into the Meatpacking Line: Workers and Change in the Rural Midwest* (Chapel Hill: University of North Carolina, 1998), is a useful introduction to meatpacking and the late twentieth-century Iowa economy, as well as issues of race and gender in the industry. Nick Reding, *Methland: The Death and Life of an American Small Town* (New York: Bloomsbury, 2009), focuses on the town of Oelwein and the many challenges of rural America after the Farm Crisis. Hugh Winebrenner and Dennis J. Goldford, *The Iowa Precinct Caucuses: The Making of a Media Event* (Iowa City: University of Iowa Press, 2010), is full of good history and analysis.

The history of Iowa in the early twenty-first century is often told by journalists. Richard C. Longworth, *Caught in the Middle: America's Heartland in the Age of Globalism* (New York: Bloomsbury, 2008), written by a Boone native, is a fine survey of the pre–Great Recession Midwest, with plenty on Iowa. Art Cullen, *Storm Lake: Change, Resilience, and Hope in America's Heartland* (New York: Penguin Books, 2018) recounts how immigration has transformed the town and provides an overview of the state's recent history. Stephen G. Bloom, *Postville: A Clash of Cultures in Heartland America* (New York: Harcourt, 2000), also focuses on immigration. Salvatore A. Giunta grew up in Cedar Rapids, joined the army, and won a Medal of Honor in Afghanistan. His beautifully written memoir, full of dark humor, heroism, and tragedy, details the savage reality of war. See Salvatore A. Giunta and Joe Layden, *Living With Honor* (New York: Threshold, 2012). Cornelia F. Mutel, *A Sugar Creek Chronicle: Observing Climate Change from a Midwestern Woodland* (Iowa City: University of Iowa Press, 2018), is a keen observation of Iowa's environment and how it is changing. Tom Witosky and Marc Hansen, *Equal before the Law: How Iowa Led Americans to Marriage Equality* (Iowa City: University of Iowa Press, 2015), details the recent story of gay and lesbian rights in the state and their struggle for equality. Tom Philpott, *Perilous Bounty: The Looming Collapse of American Farming and How We Can Prevent It* (New York: Bloomsbury, 2020), has much on Iowa farming and environmental challenges, as does Connerly, cited above. Beth Hoffman's *Bet the Farm: The Dollars and Sense of Growing Food in America* (Washington, DC: Island Press, 2021), is a humorous and effective overview of the challenges of farming in the twenty-first century. Emily Mendenhall's *Unmasked: COVID, Community, and the Case of Okoboji* (Nashville: Vanderbilt University Press, 2022), is a vital, if sobering, firsthand account of the conflict between public health, individual rights, and economic gain in the first year of the pandemic emergency.

For those who want to further explore Iowa history, here are a dozen books that will allow you to better understand the state. They are all readable and important. Readers should begin with Cornelia F. Mutel's *The Emerald Horizon: The History of Nature in Iowa*. You could then read the first-person accounts in Glenda Riley's *Prairie Voices: Iowa's Pioneering Women*, a collection of diaries and autobiographies from farmwomen and teachers. For the Civil War, start with Thomas R. Baker's *The Sacred Cause of Union: Iowa in the Civil War* and S. H. M. Byers's gripping memoir *With Fire and Sword*. Then read *Buxton: A Black Utopia in the Heartland*, by Dorothy Schwieder, Joseph Hraba, and Elmer Schwieder, an important story that all Iowans should know. See H. E. Wilkinson, *Memories of an Iowa Farm Boy*, for an entertaining introduction to rural life in the late nineteenth century. The best account of small-town life in the first part of the twentieth century is Thomas J. Morain's *Prairie Grass Roots: An Iowa Small Town in the Early Twentieth Century*. Mildred Armstrong Kalish's *Little Heathens: Hard Times and High Spirits on an Iowa Farm during the Great Depression* is a wonderful, often humorous, autobiography. Shelton Stromquist's *Solidarity and Survival: An Oral History of Iowa Labor in the Twentieth Century* is the moving story of Iowa's industrial workers. Lisa Ossian's *The Home Fronts of Iowa, 1939–1945* is a thorough history of the state in World War II. Pamela Riney-Kehrberg's *When A Dream Dies: Agriculture, Iowa, and the Farm Crisis* is crucial to understanding recent Iowa. For more on the state since the Farm Crisis see the gritty but essential *Methland: The Death and Life of an American Small Town* by Nick Reding.

Index

Abernethy, Alonzo, 105
Ackerman, Clara, 240
Acton, Patricia Nassif, 75
Acton, Richard, 75
Addams, Jane, 163, 200
Afghanistan War, 328–329
African Americans
  agriculture, 157
  businesses of, 157, 181
  churches of, 143
  in Civil War, 103–104, 127
  in Des Moines, 324–325
  discrimination against, 45–46, 74, 82–83, 280, 282, 283, 325
  emancipation of, 126–127, 128
  employment opportunities, 153, 174, 222, 241, 283–284
  during Great Depression, 241
  household income, 281, 325
  immigration to Iowa, 128
  incarceration rate, 325
  in Iowa, compared to in the South, 157
  male suffrage, 107
  newspapers of, 214, 215
  police mistreatment of, 284, 340
  population of, 102, 107, 126, 150, 164, 222
  regulation of lives of, 37, 45
  resistance to slavery, 46–47, 76–78, 102
  in rural areas, 157
  schools for, 107–108, 149–150, 157
  segregation of, 280, 282
  settlements of, 181
  struggle for equal rights, 74, 75, 81, 102, 283
  unemployment of, 281
  urban renewal and, 282
  in US Army, 213–214, *214*
  violence against, 47
  white Iowans and, 127–128
  in World War I, 213–214
  in World War II, 264–265, 271
African Methodist Episcopal Church, 102, 143
Agricultural Adjustment Act (AAA), 247
agriculture
  diversity of, 119
  exhibits, 161
  export market, 326, 327
  growth of, 203–204, 219, 300, 326
  new opportunities for, 322
  period of decline, 203, 302, 310, 322
  productivity revolution, 276
  railroads and, 119–120
  social life and, 158
  Westward migration and, 64
Alex, Lynn M., 12
Allen, L. P., 74
Allenby, Ted, 263, 265–266
Allison, William Boyd, 198
Aluminum Company of America (Alcoa), 290
Alvarez, Sebastian, 249
Amana community, 51, 54, *55*, 56
Ambrose, Stephen, 23
American Gothic (painting), 251, 252
Ames Laboratory at ISC, 275
Amherst College, 139
Amish
  communal life of, 55–56
  occupations of, 56
  settlements of, 51, 54–55
Anderson, Jo Anne, 288
Anderson, Kate Emily, 117
Anderson, Robert, 288
Andersonville prison, 104
Ankeny, Iowa, 279
Anson, Adrian, 220
Anthony, Susan B., 78, 193, 196
anti-Chinese riots, 125

448 INDEX

anti-Communist hysteria, 219
Anti-Monopoly Party, 131, 132
Antiquities Act, 199
anti-Semitism, 257–258
anti-slavery movement, 79–80
Ashby, Newton, 130
Atack, Jeremy, 52
Atlanta, Battle of, 105, 106
Atwood, Roy Alden, 204
Auschwitz death camp, 277
Austro-Hungarian Empire, 124
automobiles
   affordability of, 226
   Ford Model T, 226–227
   impact on daily life, 220, 227–228, 231
   reliability of, 225
   spread of ownership, 226
   travel by, 225–226, 228

Backbone State Park, 199
Bad Axe, Battle of, 30
Badger, Inez Frick Henze, 241
Baeck, Grete, 258
Baptists
   churches, 136, 139, 140, 143
   colleges, 153
Barger, Herbert, 292
Barker, Celestia Lee, 148
barn-raising, 159
Barrett, Gary, 315
Barroso, Julio, 313–314
Barrow, Willard, 38
Barry, John M., 218
baseball, 163
Basu, Rekha, 325
Beaman, Gamaliel Carter, 140
Beason, Murda, 150
Beck, Jennie, 160
Beck, Paul N., 84
Becker, Vernon, 293
Belknap, George, 33, 41
Belknap, Kitturah Penton, 33, 41, 60
Bell, Michael J., 142
Benedict, Abbie Mott, 63, 115
Bennett, Carey, 46
Bennett, telephone service, 182
Bettendorf Company, 223
birth rates, 325
Black Hawk (Sauk warrior)
   abandonment of Saukenuk, 27, 28
   attack on Fort Madison, 24
   Battle of Bad Axe, 30
   Battle of Stillman's Run, 29
   childhood of, 19
   death of, 30
   in Illinois, 28–29
   imprisonment of, 30
   portrait of, *25*
Black Hawk Purchase, 30, 41, *43*
Black Hawk War, 9, 22, 27–30, 31, 33
Black Lives Matter (BLM) movement, 340–341
Black Panther Party for Self-Defense, 284
Blake, Edith Gallo Widmer, 170
Bland, Austin A., 181
Bleeding Kansas, 79
blizzards, 64, 66–67, 71, 116
Bloom, Moses, 142
Bloomer, Amelia, 86, 192, 195
Bloomer, Dexter, 195
Bloomfield High School, 287
Blundall, Joan, 307
Boepple, John, 172
Bogue, Allan G., 39
Boies, Horace, 132, 189
Boland, Robert, 243, 259
Boone, Daniel, 35
Boone, Iowa
   fire protection, 179
   population of, 279
Boone, Nathan, 35
Booth, Harry, 171
bootlegging, 187
Borlaug, Margaret, 298
Borlaug, Norman, 298, 299
Boxer Rebellion, 141, 142
bracero program, 273–274
Bradley, Charles C., 244
Branstad, Terry
   economic policy of, 318–319
   governorship of, 296, 301, 318, 335
   personality of, 319
Brewer-Bonebright, Sarah, 65
Briar Cliff College, 152
Brickley, William, 127
Brien, Timothy J., 332
Briggs, Ansel, 49
Brigham, Edward D., 175
Brinton, Ada Mae Brown, 158
Brodnax, David, Sr., 102
Brown, Daniel, 65
Brown, Harriet Connor, 150
Brown, John
   allies of, 81, 82
   attack on Harper's Ferry, 73, 79, 82
   raid into Missouri, 81
   war on slavery, 79
Brown, Joseph, 122
Brown, Maria, 59
Brown, William, 65
Brownell, E., 131
Brown vs. Board of Education, 108
Bryan, William Jennings, 163

INDEX 449

Brydolf, Fabian, 73
Buchenwald concentration camp, 277
Buena Vista University, 152, 313
buffalo hunting, 15–16
burial mounds, 13
Burlington, Iowa, 33, 40–41, 186
Burlington ordnance plant, 268–269
Burr, Dale, 306
Burt, William, 38
Busey, James, 127
Busey, Matilda, 127
Bush, George W., 320
businesses
    closure of, 308–309, 310–311
    fire hazards, 175
Butler, Ann Binnall, 49
Butler, Lorenzo, 49
button-making business, 172–173
Butts, Albert, 71, 119
Buxton, Iowa
    African American population, 171–172
    Black schools, 150
    coal mining industry, 165, 171
    decline of, 172
    view of, *171*
Byers, Casey, 330
Byers, Samuel H. M., 92, 93, 105–106, 108
    Iowa in War Times, 100, 108

Calloway, Colin G., 13, 18
Cammack, Elizabeth, 58, 59, 66
Cammack, James, 66
Camp Dodge, 213, 214, 215, 217, 218
Cano, Magdaleno, 223
Cano, Maria, 223
Cargill company, 311
Carnegie, Andrew, 202
Carnegie libraries, 194, 202
Carpenter, Cyrus C., 129, 130
Carpenter, Nellie Knight, 182
Carpenter, Vern, 182
Carter, Edward, 150
Carter, Jimmy, 303, 320
Carver, George Washington, 152, 153
Catholic church, 135–136, 152
Catt, Carrie Chapman, 4, 185, 195, 196, *197*
Catt, George, 196
Cedar Rapids, Iowa
    baseball team, 163
    Black Methodist churches, 143
    celebration of the end of World War II, 277
    community center, 201, 202
    electricity in, 184
    first power plant, 183
    lighting, 183
    population of, 122, 165
    pork processing plant, 168
    weather, 340
Cedar Rapids Ladies Soldiers' Aid Society, 97
Cedar River, 178, 338
Center Street (Des Moines neighborhood), 281–282
Central College in Pella, 153
Chambers, John, 44, 46
Champion's Hill, Battle of, 93–94
Chapman, Leo, 196
Charles, John H., 70
Chattanooga, Battle of, 105
Chautauqua movement, 134, 158, *162,* 162–163, 164
Chavez, Cesar, 284
Chicago fire of 1871, 121
Chicago's Hull House, 200
Chiesa, Marco, 125
child labor, 61–63, 175, 198
Children's Aid Society, 128
Chinese immigrants, 125–126
cholera, 65
Christian missionaries, 141–142
Christie, Robert, 57
Christmas celebrations, 160
churches, 134–135, 225. *See also individual congregations*
Churchill, Doyle, 289
Churchill, Louise, 289
cities
    crime, 179
    diseases, 165, 178
    economic development, 165
    fires, 179
    growth of, 67–68, 322
    job opportunities, 323
    migration, 286, 323–324
    policing, 179
    pollution, 165
    population, 165, 323
    public health, 178–179
    sewer system, 178
    sex work, 180–181
    streetcars, 179–180
    transportation, 184
    water delivery, 179
    See also specific cities
Civilian Conservation Corps (CCC), 248, 249, 254
Civil Rights Act of 1964, 285
Civil War
    agricultural production during, 96
    Black troops, 90, 103–104
    care for wounded and sick soldiers, 99
    casualties, 92
    charity and aid societies, 97, 98

Civil War, *continued*
  diseases, 94, 96
  end of, 106–107
  fall of Atlanta, 105
  German immigrants in, 122
  Iowa contribution to, 4, 90, 91–92, 93, 94, 96, 101–102, 108
  Missouri in, 92
  Northern economy during, 96
  prisoners, 104
  suspension of habeas corpus, 100–101
  train attacks, 102
  women during, 94–97
  See also individual battles
Cixi (Chinese empress dowager), 142
claims clubs, 39–40
Clarinda, Iowa
  Black residents, 127
  farming, 157
  orphans in, 129
  prisoner-of-war camps, 272
Clark, Alexander, Jr., 108
Clark, Alexander, Sr.
  diplomatic service, 108
  life of, 102–103
  portrait of, *103*
  recruitment of Black soldiers, 103
  struggle for civil rights, 90, 107
Clark, J. S., 62
Clark, Richard, 295
Clark, Susan, 107
Clark, William, 22
Clarke, George W., 60, 61, 147
Clarke College, 152
climate change, 335–336, 337–338
Clinton, Bev, 291
Clinton, Hillary, 334
Clinton, Iowa
  economic development of, 168, 323
  population of, 181, 323
Clive, Iowa
  population of, 279
Clough, Samuel, 71
coal mining, 119, 165, 169–171, 172, 328
Coates, J. Warren, 104
Coe College, 152
Cohen, Patricia, 313
Cold War, 292
Cole, Cyrenus, 203
collective bargaining law, 296
colleges
  acceptance of women, 164
  agricultural, 153
  establishment of, 134
  public and private, 152
  religious, 152, 153

Collier, Slim, 237, 247
Committee on Public Information (CPI), 212
Compromise of 1850, 73
ConAgra, 311
Cone, Aristarchus, 39, 64
confined animal feeding operations (CAFOs), 317
Conger, Edwin, 141–142
Conger, Sarah Pike, 141
  Letters from China, 142
Congregationalists, 138, 140
Connerly, Charles E., 324
conservation movement, 199
Consolidation Coal Company, 172
Cook, H. J., 177
Cook, Ira, 38
Copperheads, 100
Coppoc, Barclay, 82
Coppoc, Edwin, 82
Coquillette, Calvin W., 239
Coralville, Iowa, 279
corn
  consumption of, 59, 60–61
  cultivation of, 13, 19, 301, 316, 326–327
  ethanol production from, 327–328
  harvesting of, 60
  hybrid strains of, 13
  prices of, 130, 314, 326, 337
Cornell College, 152
corn husking, 159
corporations, 165–166
Council Bluffs, Iowa, 118, 261
county agents, 200
county fairs, 161
COVID-19
  among K-12 students, 339
  deaths from, 341–342
  economic impact, 339–340
  infection rates, 322, 338–339, 340, 341, 342
Cowles, Florence Call, 62
Cow War, 243–244
Crawford, James, 52
crime, 34–35
Crowder, Etta May Lacey, 58, 60, 70
Crowder, Mary Lacey, 60
Crowhurst, Seth, 104
Cruikshank, C., 63
Cullen, Art, 319, 334
Culver, Chet, 334
Culver, John C., 295
Cummins, Albert Baird, 197–198
Curran, Celia, 127
Czech immigrants, 124

Daggs, Ruel, 76, 77
dairy industry, 174

INDEX 451

Dakota, 15, 21, 83–84
Danbom, David B., 120, 304
Danish immigrants, 124
D'Appolonia, Peter, 125
Darling, Jay Norwood "Ding," 246
Davenport, George, 32–33
Davenport, Iowa
  Cook's Point neighborhood, 223–224
  establishment, 33
  mayoral elections, 219–220
  population, 33, 181
  power plant, 183
  steamboat traffic and railroads, 180
  water delivery, 179
Davis, Caleb Forbes, 65
Davis, Jefferson, 33, 101
Day, Frances Olsen, 114, 115
Debs, Eugene V., 220
DeCook, Vincent, 258
Deere's Tractor Works, 310
Democrats. *See* Iowa Democratic party
Denmark, Iowa, 77
DePatten, Herbert, 282
derecho, 340
Derifield, Coreen, 291
Desart, Catherine, 108
Des Moines, Iowa
  Black community, 282, 324–325
  buildings, 177
  businesses, 178, 315
  canteen station, 210
  capital status, 315
  celebration of the end of World War II, 277
  community centers, 201
  downtown area, *227,* 324
  drinking establishments, 191
  economic development, 315, 324
  electricity, 183
  entertainment, 324
  Farmers' Market, 327
  fire protection, 179
  floods, 316
  food drive in, 241
  housing market, 315–316
  industries, 173, 316
  Jews in, 201, 277
  Ku Klux Klan march in, 221
  library, 195
  location of, 69
  manufacturing sector, 177
  police, 179
  population of, 165, 227, 324, 330
  Pride Fest celebrations, 333
  public health, 178–179
  racial uprising in, 284
  railroad service, 69, 118
  sanitation, 177–178
  stagecoach routes, 69
  streetcars, 179–180
  suburbs, 324
Des Moines Ordnance Plant, 267, 271
Des Moines River, 35
Des Moines Women's Relief Association, 241
Dinsmore, James J., 11
diseases, 64, 65
Dodge, Augustus C., 49, 70
Dodge, Caesar, 99
Dodge, Grenville, 106
Dolliver, Jonathan, 189, 198
Douglass, Frederick, 78
Douglass, Stephen, 79
Downey, Ezekiel, 175
Downing, Alexander G., 105
Drake, Francis M., 153
Drake University, 153
droughts, 203, 315, 337
Drury, Clifford Merrill, 157
Dubuque, Iowa
  airport, 250
  churches in, 134–135
  Jewish population, 142
  Methodist service in, 136
  mining area, 34
  population of, 309
  suffrage associations, 192
  transportation, 33
Dubuque, Julien, 9, 20, 21, 23
Dubuque and Pacific Railroad, 87
Duffield, George, 39, 62
Duffield, James, 40
Dunlap, Flora
  portrait of, *201*
  school named after, 201
  social activism, 200
Dutch migrants, 53–54, 117–118
Dutton, Celinda, 34
Dykstra, Robert R., 47, 108

Eastwood, Clint, 62
education
  development of, 134
  expenditures on, 297
  funding of, 297
  languages, 151
  legislation on, 145, 198
  secondary system, 164
  success of, 145–146
Egge, Sara, 162, 192
Eighteenth Amendment, 191
Eisenhower, Dwight D., 228
Ekdale, Edith Harper, 160

452 INDEX

electricity
  cost of, 184, 253
  impact on rural life, 165, 253–254, 278
  introduction of, 183–184
Elk Horn settlement, 124
Ellen, Mary, 78
Ellmaker, Reuben, 119
Emancipation Proclamation, 107
Embres, Wilma, 289
Emergency Banking Act, 245
Emerson, George, 117
Emmet, Robert, 123
environmental problems, 116, 159–162, 177, 318, 320
Ericson, Charles J. A., 53
Erie Canal, 64
Ernst, Joni, 335
Espionage Act, 208, 213
Estherville, Iowa
  volunteers from, 210
  war efforts, 262
ethanol production, 327–328
exclusion law of 1851, 75
extralegal organizations. *See* claims clubs

factories, 175
Fairchild, Ephraim, 59
Fairfield's public library, 202
Fair Housing Act of 1968, 281
fairs, 161, 164
farm crisis
  children and, 306–307
  crime and, 306
  evolution of, 301, 303–304, 314, 315
  mental health crisis and, 307–308
  roots of, 300, 302–303
  social impact of, 305–306, 320, 323
Farmers' Alliance, 130, 132, 133
Farmer's Holiday movement, *242,* 244–245
farms
  AAA programs, 247
  advocacy group, 307
  bankruptcies and foreclosures, 286, *305,* 308, 315, 320
  childcare, 59
  child labor, 61–63
  cut of agricultural workforce, 288
  daily life on, 120–121, 230, 278
  debts, 302, 304, 306, 307
  drought and, 315
  economic challenges, 52, 57, 248, 306
  efficiency, 304–305, 326–327
  electricity, 278
  employment of POWs, 273
  exports to foreign markets, 302
  falling agricultural prices and, 130, 219

  fertilizer use, 326
  freight rates, 131
  fundraising campaigns, 308
  Great Depression and, 237–238
  hazards, 65
  insect invasions, 129–130
  labor shortage, 273
  land ownership, 325–326
  male labor, 57–58, 60, 61
  manufacturing equipment for, 175–176, 310
  Mexican workers, 273–274
  oil prices and, 303
  ownership, 327
  period of prosperity, 203–204, 206, 301–302
  in postwar period, 288–289
  poverty, 305, 308
  productivity of, 58–59, 130, 288, 302, 303
  profitability of, 288, 289, 304
  property taxes, 287
  protests, 131–132, 243–234
  size of, 317
  spread of, 2, 51
  statistics of, 315, 317, 320
  subsidies for, 308, 314
  suicides on, 305
  technology and, 326
  women's role at, 58, 59–60, 63
  during WWII, 272
Farney, Dennis, 305
Federal Deposit Insurance Corporation (FDIC), 245
Federal Highway Act of 1916, 228
Federal Writer's Project, 250
Fehn, Bruce, 282
Felton, O. J., 62, 136
female labor, 51
ferries, 87
Ferrin, Mary Ann, 60, 64, 66
Fifteenth Amendment, 90
Fifteenth Regiment, 73
Fifth Iowa Infantry Regiment, 92
Fink, Deborah, 240
Finkelman, Paul, 108
First Iowa Volunteers (African Descent), 103–104
Fischer, John, 304
Fisher, Ezra, 139–140
Fisher, Pauline, 291
floods, 69, 301, 316, 336–337, 338
Florida, 48
Floyd, Charles, 23
Foley, Douglas, 332
Foner, Eric, 107
food production, 58–59
Forch, Paul, 129
Ford Motor Company, 226

INDEX

Forest City, Iowa, 299
Forsyth, Thomas, 19
Fort Armstrong, 32
Fort Des Moines, 35, 85, 213
    women training facilities at, 269–270, 271
Fort Des Moines Number Two, 69
Fort Dodge, 120, 324
Fort Dodge Railroad, 123
Fort Madison, 9, 24, 26
Fort Sumter, 88, 90–91
Foster, E. C., 188
Foster, Judith Ellen, 188
Four Minute Men organization, 212
Fourth Iowa Infantry regiment, 106
Fourth of July celebrations, 159–160
Frank, Anne, 257
freedom suits, 47
French settlers, 9
Fugitive Slave Act, 49, 77, 80
Fulcher, Dorcas, 76
Fulcher, Sam, 76, 77
Fulz, William S., 105
Fun, Wong, 126
fur trade, 14, 16, 26

Gage, Frances Dana, 192
Galer, Roger S., 71
Gallaher, Ruth A., 139, 188, 191
Galland, Isaac, 143
Gallo, Frank, 170
gambling business, 180, 332
Gardner, Abbie, 84
Garland, Hamlin, 63, 114
Garnavillo, John, 56, 57
gasoline taxes, 229
Gates, Paul W., 114
Gates, Robert, 293
Gavitt, Benjamin, 63, 64, 120
gay rights movement, 333
Gellhorn Boylan, Louisa Sophia H., 121
Gephardt, Dick, 320
German immigrants, 91, 121–122, 212
Gettysburg, Battle of, 94
GI Bill, 279
Gjerde, Jon, 1
glaciers, 9–10
Goldford, Dennis J., 320
Goldstein, Joseph, 258
Goodman, Fay, 241
Gordon, Frances, 78
Gordon, Hugh, 78
Graham, Keith, 225, 226
grain production, 299, 302
Grange program, 130, 131, 132
Grant, Ulysses S., 92, 99, 105
grassland, 11

Grassley, Chuck, 301, 319, 335
Gray, John Henry, 128
Great Depression
    African Americans during, 241
    banking crisis, 236, 238–239, 245
    barter economy, 243
    causes, 235, 236
    Congress emergency session, 245
    economic impact of, 207, 235–236, 237–238
    farm life during, 237–238, 239, 240–241, *242*
    hunger, 241, 248
    martial law, 244–245
    poverty, 237
    rural insurgencies, 244
    social impact of, 242, 254–255
    unemployment, 236, 241, 248, 254
    violence and, 244
    women during, 243
    WPA programs, 249, 250
Great Flood of 1993, 301, 316
Great Recession of 2007–2009, 322, 325
Greeley, Horace, 76
Green, Jason, 102
Green, Michael D., 20
Green, William, 16
Greenback Party, 132
"Green Revolution," 298
Gregory, Allen, 219
Gregory, Uriah, 38
Griffin, Catherine, 102
Griffin, Edna
    lawsuit against Katz Drug Stores, 282–283
    social activism of, 283
Grim, Valerie, 157, 241
Grimes, James W., 80, 81
Grinnell, Iowa, 75–76
Grinnell, Josiah, 76, 81, 138
Grinnell College, 138, 153, 195
Grinnell schools, 82–83
Grob, Gerald N., 217
Gue, Benjamin F., 203
Gulf of Mexico, 318
Gullixson, Celia, 62
Guter, Joe, 205

Haddock, George, 190, 191
Hagan, William T., 19
Hagen, Mary, 254
Hall, Samuel, 127, 128
Hamilton, Carl, 146
Hannah-Jones, Nikole, 280, 282
Harding, William L.
    "Babel Proclamation" of, 212
    ban of use of foreign languages, 212–213
Harkin, Tom, 301, 319, 335
Harnack, Curtis, 316, 317, 318

454 INDEX

Harpers Ferry, 73, 82
Harrison, William Henry, 22
Hassebrock, Kenneth, 225
Hawkins, Samuel, 106
Hay, Merle, 215, *216*
Hayes, Harold, 263, 265
H. B. Glover Company, 174
Hearst, James, 238, 239–240, 254
Heartbreak Ridge, Battle of, 292–293
Heline, Oscar, 238, 247
Henderson, David B., 198
Henn, Bernhardt, 70
Hepburn, William, 198, 199
Herriott, Frank I., 2
high schools, 151, 287
highways, 229, 279–280, 281–282, 288
Hilton Coliseum, 316
Hinkley, Myron, 116
Hintz, John, 329
Hippee, George B., 226
Hitler, Adolf, 256, 257
Ho-chunk (Winnebago), 21, 30–31
Hoehnle, Peter, 55
Hofsommer, Don L., 118
hog production, 61, 168, 174, 317
Hoit, Judy, 278
Holbrook, Stewart H., 166
Holden, Perry G., 200
Holocaust survivors, 277
Holy City (Bettendorf neighborhood), 223–224
homelessness, 203
Home Owners' Loan Corporation, 280
homes
 construction of, 159, 279
 prices of, 56–57
Homestead, Iowa, 54, 55
Homestead Act, 56, 113, 114, 117
homestead claims, 114–115
"Honey War," 32, 38–39
Hoover, Herbert
 birthplace of, 218
 federal construction programs, 236–237
 political career of, 4, 210, 218–219
Hopkins, Harry, 246
Horton, Loren N., 199
Howard, James R., 63
Howard, Milton, 102
Howe, Ethel, 183
Howorth, James, 240
Howorth, Ruby, 240
Hraba, Joseph, 171
Huftalen, Sarah Gillespie, 146, 148
Hughes, Harold
 political career of, 295, 296, 300
 progressive reforms of, 296
Hughes, John, 306

Hungarian immigrants, 122
hunting and foraging, 13, 15–16, 158
Hurt, R. Douglas, 2

Illinois volunteers, 29
immigrants
 Civil War and, 96
 countries of origin, 51, 52, 53–54, 71, 75, 170, 222–224
 crime and, 312
 deportations of, 313, 331
 diversity of, 113, 121, 225
 economic, 313
 employment of, 51–52, 222, 223, 331–332
 hardship of, 331–332
 impact on towns, 312
 motivations for settling in Iowa, 52
 naturalization of, 332
 politics and, 340
 racial tensions and, 313
 railroads and, 113, 120–121
 recruitment of, 313
 statistics of, 124, 125, 133, 322
 stories of, 52–53
 in the twenty-first century, 330
 undocumented, 331, 332
Immigrations and Customs Enforcement (ICE), 331
improvised explosive devices (IEDs), 329
industrial sector, 165–166, 178, 252–253
influenza outbreak, 217–218
Ingalsbe, J. L., 67
Inkpaduta (Dakota leader), 84
insect invasions, 129–130
International Harvester, 310
Iowa
 capital city, 80–81
 civic society, 3
 communication, 207
 conservation movement, 199
 constitution, 80–81
 daily life, 70–71
 demographics, 286
 economic development, 1, 2, 3, 33, 202–203, 277–228, 308–309, 310, 314, 322–323, 326
 ethnic and racial diversity, 4
 European expeditions to, 14–15, 16
 food export, 64
 governance, 74, 197–198, 296
 histories of, 3, 4–5
 homestead claims, 114–115
 House of Representatives, 319
 hydrology, 116
 labor participation, 3, 326
 landscape, 9–12
 languages, 4, 312

law code, 75
legislative districts, 294–295
literacy rate, 3, 146
map of, *6*
national political figures from, 198
Native people of, 12–15, 26
New Deal programs, 247–254
outmigration, 309–310
political life, 131, 132–133, 189, 295, 334–335
population, 71, 75, 88–89, 108, 113, 119, 121, 133, 146, 165, 276, 308, 320, 323, 330–331
post-war years, 276–300
poverty, 304
presidential primaries in, 319–320, 321
progressive reforms, 90, 341
prohibition law, 187, 189
promotion of, 121
prosperity of, 299–300
racism, 249, 283
ranking, 324
religions, 1, 163–164
right-to-work law, 311
school districts, 286
state extension program, 200
student population, 278–279
suffrage, 107, 192–193
support of the Union, 101–102
Tally War, 101
territory, 36
topsoil erosion, 317
transportation, 207
in the twenty-first century, 321–342
urban development, 276, 286
as white state, 1–2
Iowa: A Guide to the Hawkeye State, 250
Iowa: Home for Immigrants, 121
Iowa Agricultural College, 153, 154, 156
"Iowa Band, The," 138
Iowa Beef Packers, 311
Iowa City
  Beer Riots, 189
  as capital city, 80
  constitutional convention in, 45
  fire protection, 179
  industry in, 183
  location of, 37
  population of, 38, 325
  telephone in, 181
Iowa counties, 73
Iowa Democratic party, 80, 186, 276, 295, 318, 334, 335
Iowa Extension Service, 200
Iowa Farmers' Alliance (IFA), 132
Iowa Farm Unity Coalition, 307
Iowa Federal Theater Project, 251

Iowa Infantry Regiments, 91
Iowa League of Women Voters, 200
Iowa National Guard, 263, 266, 329–330
Iowa Red Cross, 209
Iowa River, 116
Iowa's Refugee Service Center, 297, 298
Iowa State College of Agriculture and Mechanic Arts. *See* Iowa State University
Iowa State Fair, 161
Iowa State Normal School. *See* University of Northern Iowa
Iowa State Teachers College. *See* University of Northern Iowa
Iowa State University, 134, 154, 155, 199, 256, 274–275
Iowa Supreme Court, 188
Iowa Territory
  admission to the US, 44, 48, 49
  African Americans, 45–46
  border modification, 48
  constitution, 45
  creation of, 36
  governance of, 36–37
  Indian cessions in, 42, *43*
  land sales, 39, 40–41
  legislature, 37, 49
  mapping to, 35–36
  migration into, 31, 32, 33–34, 42, 44
  population of, 36, 41, 45–46, 50
  statehood bill, 48
  surveys of, 38, 50
  towns, 34
Iowaville (Ioway village), 16
Iowa Wesleyan University, 99, 152
Iowa Woman Suffrage Association (IWSA), 192, 193
Ioway
  agriculture, 15–16
  Americans and, 17–18
  conflict with other tribes, 17
  diseases, 16, 17
  forced migration, 16, 18
  lifestyle, 15–16, 17
  origin of, 9, 15
  trade of, 16–17
Iraq War, 329
Irish immigrants, 91, 122–123
Italian immigrants, 124–125

Jack, E. E., 187
Jackson, Andrew, 17, 36, 45
Jackson, Emery, 282
Janes, Martha, 190
Japan, 256–257
Japanese internees, 258, 259
Jarred, Ethel, 269

Jefferson, Robert, 282
Jefferson, Thomas, 22
Jennings, Berryman, 143
Jennings, Rosa Schreurs, 148, 150
Jews
  in Civil War, 142
  extermination by the Nazis, 277
  Holocaust survivors, 277
  in Iowa, 165, 257–258
  refugees from Russia, 142
  settlements, 142
  in World War II, 258
J. M. Sinclair, 166
job market, 165–166
John Deere factories, 290, 302, 310
John Morrell and Company, 168–169
Johnson, J. P., 157
Johnson, Keach, 144
Johnson County Claim Association, 39
Jolliet, Louis, 9, 14
Jones, George W., 49, 70, 101
Jones, Lonzo, 219

Kansas, 72, 79, 81
Kansas-Nebraska Act, 79, 80
Katz Drug Store, 282–283
Kearny, Stephen, 35, 46
Kee, Sam, 126
Kelly, Oliver H., 130
Kelly's Army, 203
Kelsey, John, 52
Kendricks, Joseph, 78
Kennedy, David M., 246, 252
Kent State shootings, 293
Kenyon, John, 60, 65, 66
Kenyon, Sarah, 60, 66
Keokuk (Sauk leader), 27–28, 30, 42
Keokuk, Iowa
  Black residents, 126, 181, 283
  cholera outbreak, 65
  coal import, 169
  Jewish population, 142
  liquor sales, 186
  location of, 33
  schools in, 143
  slavery in, 74, 75
  telephone service in, 181
  trade, 34
Keokuk Reserve, 30
Keokuk Soldiers' Aid Society, 98
Ketchum, Minnie, 129
Kiet, Tran Vinh, 297
Kimball, Sarah Jane, 204
King, Charles, 101
King, Steve, 334
Kingsley, Alpha, 24

Kirkwood, Samuel, 82, 91, 99–100
Klopp, Fern, 291, 292
Knapp, Seaman, 199
Knauth, Otto W., 239
Knowlton, Emma, 63
Koenemann, Howard, 267
Korean War, 292–293
Ku Klux Klan, 207, 214, 231, 258
  second Klan, 221, 222

labor shortage, 323
Lacey, John F., 199
LaFollette, Robert, 163
Lage, Gladys Moeller, 240
Lagomarcino, Virgil, 230
Lakota, 15, 21
land
  competition for, 42
  price of, 57, 188, 238, 302, 304, 314
  speculation, 70, 117
  value of, 203, 219, 240, 325
  wealth and, 52
Land Grant College Act of 1862 (Morrill Act), 154
Landolt, Lillie Cordes, 267
Langrehr, Henry, 263–264
La Porte City, 294
Larsen, Lawrence, 179
Laskowski, Melvin, 263
Latinos
  businesses of, 313
  COVID-19, effect on, 338–339
  discrimination against, 223, 249, 274, 284–285
  during Great Depression, 249, 279
  employment, 223, 249, 273–274, 284, 312–314, 330, 331, 338
  immigration to Iowa, 222–223, 249, 264, 312–313, 330, 331
  in Storm Lake, 312–313, 314, 331–332
  struggle for equal rights, 284
  in World War II, 224, 249, 264, 284
Lawrence, Alice Money, 149
Lawrence, Elmer, 149
Lea, Albert M., 35–36
lead production, 34
Leaf, Arthur, 238, 254
Leaf, Marie, 238
League of United Latin American Citizens (LULAC), 285
Leamer, A. B., 141
Lee, Deemer, 262
Lee, Hang, 126
Lee, Robert E., 94
legislative districts, 294–295
Le Mars, Iowa, 163

Lenin, Vladimir, 215
Lepore, Jill, 5
LeSueur, Pierre Charles, 15
Levi, Alexander, 142
Lewis and Clark expedition, 9, 22–23
Lew-Williams, Beth, 125
LGBTQ+ population, 252, 265–266, 287–278, 332–334
Liberty Loans (war bonds), 210–211
Lincoln, Abraham, 28–29, 88, 100–101, 105
Lincoln Highway, 229
Lindholm, Dennis, 287
liquor licenses, 186–187
"Little Switzerland" region, 10
Lockwood, Belva, 161
Loess Hills, 10
Logan, Jeff, 102
London, Jack, 203
Long, Irma J., 239
Loras College, 152
Lost Creek mine explosion, 171
Louisiana
  discovery of, 14
  US purchase of, 9, 22, 36, 48, 71
Louis XIV (king of France), 14
Lucas, Beulah Marie, 218
Lucas, C. L., 85
Lucas, Robert, 37, 39, 44, 45, 186
Ludley, Everett, 230
lumber industry, 57, *167*, 167–168, 174
Lutheran church, 141, 160
Luther College, 123–124, 153
Lyons, Iowa, 168

Macias, David, 222, 223
Macias, Manuel, 222
Mackley, John, 92
Madison, James, 24
Mahan, Bruce, 158, 160
Mahony, D. A., 101
mail delivery, 204–205, *205,* 206
Main, W. F., 158, 159
Majors, Jacob, 40
"Majors' War, The," 40
malaria, 64–65, 71
Manhattan Project, 274–275
Mann, Robert, 122
Mann, William, 122
Manning, Richard, 318
Mansfield, Arabella Babb, 152
manufacturing sector
  agricultural sector and, 166, 290
  businesses in, 174
  decline of, 311
  in postwar Iowa, 289–290
  wages, 290
  workers, 290
  working conditions in, 175
Maquoketa, Iowa
  CCC camp, 249
  first school in, 143
  newspapers, 212
Marquette, Jacques, 9, 14
marriage, state law on, 332–333
Marshall Plan, 292
Marshalltown, Iowa
  baseball team, 163
  Blue Ribbon celebration, 187
  fire protection, 179
  Latino immigrants, 324
  store, *68*
Martin, Robert F., 98, 220
Martinson, Andrew, 117
Martinson, Kate, 117
Mason, Charles, 186
Mason City, Iowa, 156, 324
  public library, 202
Massey, Louisa, 34–35
Massey, Woodbury, 34
Matthews, Birdie, 257
Mazzuchelli, Samuel Charles, 135
McCarthy, Fern, 268–269
McCowen, Jennie, 176
McElroy, Edith Wasson, 102
McKinley, William, 141, 198
McMurry, Alice, 287
meatpacking industry, 166, 168, 174, 176, 290, 311–312
Mellencamp, John, 308
Merkles, Ernest F., 217
Meskwaki
  casino, 332
  during Great Depression, 248–249
  encounter with Europeans, 20–21
  forced migration, 9, 14, 27, 29–30, 41, 42
  hunting, 20
  land dispossession, 22, 31, 83
  mining, 20–21
  origin story, 18
  relations with other tribes, 17, 26, 248
  settlements, 16, 20, 248–249, 332
  Tama, land purchase, 83
  territory, 21
  in World War II, 263
Messenger, Franklin, 230
Messenger, Ruth Perkins, 230
methamphetamine production, 314
Methodists, 136, 137–138, 143, 152, 164
Mexican-American War, 48, 56, 72, 73
Mexican immigrants, 222–224, 249, 273–274, 284, 285, 330
Michigan Territory, 32, 36, 64

Middle Eastern immigrants, 224–225
migrant workers, 285
Miller, Anthony J., 125
Miller, Elizabeth R., 226
Miller, Samuel Freeman, 100
Miller, Henry A., 137, 138
Miller, John Ross, 102
Miller, Mary, 160
Mills, Frank M., 69
Milwaukee Railroad, 166, 169
Miner's Bank of Dubuque, 45
mining industry, 21, 34, 176
minority groups, 2–3, 278, 280–281
Mississippi & Missouri Railroad, 87–88
Mississippi River, 32, 33, 34, 87
Missouri
   Civil War in, 91–92
   "Honey War" with, 38–39
Missouri Compromise, 44, 47, 73, 80
Montgomery, Jordan, 46
Montgomery, Ralph, 46, 47
Montgomery, William, 46
Montognese, Antonio, 292
Moon Law of 1909, 191
Morelos, Silvino, 313
Morgan, Charlotte, 47
Morgan, Nathaniel, 47
Mormons, 48–49, 138
Morningside College, 152
Morris, James, 78
Morris, James B., Sr., 213–214, 221
Morris, Mary, 78
Morris, M. M., 187
Mosques, 225
Mother Mosque, 225
Mott, Lucretia, 78
movie theaters, 230
Mulct law, 191
Mullen, Michael, 294
Mulroney, John, 123
Muoi, Duong, 297
Murawnik, Adam, 277
Murawnik, Paula, 277
Murphy, Lucy Eldersveld, 18, 21
Murray, Charles Augustus, 34
Murray, Margaret Archer, 59, 63
Muscatine, Iowa, 102
   African Methodist Episcopal church in, 143
   Black residents, 126
   industry, 172–173
   segregated schools, 107
Muslim communities, 224–225
Mutel, Cornelia F., 10, 116, 317
Myers, John, 94

National Association for the Advancement of Colored People (NAACP), 214, 215
National Cordage Company, 202–203
National Crisis Action Rally, 308
National Labor Relations Act of 1935, 252
National Parks, 199
National Wildlife Refuge system, 246
National Woman Suffrage Association, 196
National Youth Administration (NYA), 252
Native Americans
   agriculture, 13
   diseases, 14, 16
   Europeans and, 13–14
   exchange network, 12–13
   forced migration of, 14
   land dispossession, 22, 26, 30–31, 41–42
   paternalistic policies toward, 83
   resistance to United States, 22, 24, 26, 27, 30, 41–42, 83–84
   rivalry between, 18–19, 26, 41
   War of 1812 and, 26
   See also specific tribes
Navarro, Antonio, 284
Neal Smith National Wildlife Refuge, 12
Nebraska, 72, 79
Neem, Johann N., 144
Neff, Ortha, 270–271
Negro Community Center of Des Moines, 201
Neiberg, Michael S., 208
Nelson, Julie E., 187
Nelson, Willie, 308
Neutral Ground, 21
New Buda colony, 122
New Deal, 245, 247, 248–249, 250, 252–253, 254
New Purchase, The, 42, 43
newspapers, 195
New Sweden, Iowa, 53
Newton, Iowa, 187, 289
Nielsen, Ole, 123
Nineteenth Amendment, 196, 197
Ninety-Second Division, 213, 215
Ninety-Ninth Pursuit Squadron ("Tuskegee Airmen"), 264–265
Noehren, Donald, 292
Nordhoff, Charles, 56
Norvell, Kim, 281
Norwegian Evangelical Lutheran church, 153
Norwegian immigrants, 122–124
Nossaman, Sarah Welch, 53
Noun, Louise R., 196
Nutting, William Porter, 60, 66

Obama, Barack, 320, 334
O'Connor, Patrick, 36
oil crisis of 1973, 299

INDEX

O'Keaf, George, 36
Oliwa, Paula, 277
Olmstead, Agnes Briggs, 148
168th Infantry Regiment, 215, 216–217
Oneota cultural tradition, 13
Onerheim, Margaret Ott, 229
one-room schoolhouses, *145*, 146–147, 164, 286, 287
opera houses, 160
Orchard, Hugh, 146, 156
orphan train migrants, 128–129
Orr, Ellison, 63
Orsi, Jared, 23
Ortega, John, 237, 250, 279, 284
Osen, Mary Elizabeth, 270
Oskaloosa College, 153
Oskaloosa manufacturing plant, 291
Oster, Helena, 257
Oster, Richard, 257
Ottumwa, Iowa
    mail service, 68–69
    meatpacking plant, 169, 269
    population of, 279, 309
    railroad, 88

Pacific Railroad Act, 118
Page, William C., 177
Parker, George F., 58
Parrish, Michael E., 245
Parsons, Mary Jane, 57
Parvin, Theodore, 37
Passel, Peter, 52
Patrons of Husbandry. *See* Grange
Paul, Matilda, 59, 159
Pea Ridge, Battle of, 106
Pearl Harbor attack, 258–259
Pella colony, 53, 117, 122
Perrot, Nicholas, 14, 16
Persons, Stow, 154
Petersen, Christian, 252
Petersen, William J., 36, 155
Philavanh, Phrakhounmany, 327
Pickhinke, David, 304
Pidgeon, Isaac, 139
Pike, Zebulon, 22, 23–24
Pocahontas County, 122
polio, 278
Polk County, 195
Populist Party, 133
pork consumption, 60–61
Porter, Catharine Wiggins, 140
post offices, 205
Pounds, Diana, 193
POW camps, 272–273
Powell, Clifford, 267

power plants, 183
Powers, Elmer, 239, 240
Poweshiek (Meskwaki chief), 42
Prager, Rachel, 270
prairie fires, 63, 64, 65–66, 71
prairies, 11, 12, 114, 116
Preach, Lois Orr, 209
precipitation, 10, 336
Presbyterian church, 140, 152
presidential elections, 334
Preston, Julia Antoinette Losee, 120, 129
Preston, Peter, 120
Price, Charles, 141
Price, Eva, 141
progressive movement, 185, 188–189, 190–191, 198, 199
Prohibition
    introduction of, 221
    legislation, 187, 188, 189, 191, 206
    politics and, 185–186
    riots against, 189
    women's role in, 187, 188
prostitution, 180, 181
Protestant faith, 136, 163–164
public education, 143–144
public health, 178–179, 195
public libraries, 185, 202, 206
Pure Food and Drug Act, 198
Pyles, Barney, 78
Pyles, Charlotta, 78
Pyles, Harry, 78

Quakers, 75, 76, 78, 82, 139
Quinones, William, 263, 264

Raccoon River, 35, 316, 318
racial inequality, 74, 342
radio, 229–230
railroads
    advantages of, 86–87
    coal transportation, 169
    construction of, 69, 72, 73, 84, 87–88, 89, 118
    economic impact, 119–120, 174, 175
    freight cost, 130, 131
    immigration and, 120–121
    impact on daily life, 119–120
    regulation of, 131–132
Rainbow Division, 215, 216
Rasmussen, Chris, 161
Rath meatpacking plant, 310
Rath Packing Company, 166, 290
rattlesnakes, 67, 158–159
Rawhide (television series), 62
Ray, Robert, 296, 297, 298, 318, 319
Reconstruction Finance Corporation, 237

460 INDEX

Red Cross, 207, 208–209, 210, 218
Reding, Nick, 314
redlining, 280–281
refugees, 297, *298,* 313
Reno, Milo, 244
reptiles, 67
Republican Party of Iowa
  establishment of, 99
  leadership of, 76
  political domination, 186, 276, 295–296, 318, 321, 334, 335, 341
  position on slavery, 74, 80
  stance on prohibition, 194
  support of Black male suffrage, 107
Reyes, Virginia, 262
Reynolds, Kim, 335, 339, 340, 341
Reynolds v. Sims, 295
Rhines, Ilo, 291
Rhum, Susan, 291
Riley, Glenda, 58, 95, 96
Riney-Kehrberg, Pamela, 154, 302, 316, 320
Rizk, Salom, 224
roads, 84, 85, 225–226, 228, 229
Roadside Settlement of Des Moines, 200, 201
Rock Island, 118
Rocky Mountain Locust, 129
Rodriquez, Ernest, 223
Rodriquez, Patricia, 223
Rogers, Harriet Jane, 53
Rogers, Leah D., 177
Rogers, Marjorie Ann, 95, 96
Rogers, Samuel C., 95
Romano, Egidio, 125
Roosevelt, Franklin D.
  1932 election, 242
  advisors, 246
  illness, 246, 278
  inauguration, 239, 245
  New Deal, 235, 245
Roosevelt, Theodore, 198
Rose, Darlene Diebler, 263, 265
Rose, Russell, 265
Rosenberg, Morton M., 73
Ross, Earle, 131
Ross, Michael A., 100
runaway slaves, 46–47, 76–77, 78, 102
Rural Electrification Administration (REA), 253
rural life
  agriculture, late nineteenth century, 156–157, 158
  decline of population, 286, 300
  entertainment, 159
  mail delivery, 204–205, 206

  telephones, 204, 206
Russell, Matt, 327
Rutherford, Thomas, 77

Saadiq, Kalanji, 282
Saengchanpheng, Abel, 313
Sage, Leland, 99, 189
  A History of Iowa, 3, 4
Salem, Iowa, 77, 139
Salem, Massachusetts, 75
Salle, Rene Robert, Cavelier de la, 14
Salter, William, 138–139
same-sex marriages, 332–333
Sanache, Frank, 263
Sanache, Willard, 263
Sanchez, Saul, 284
Sanders, W. E., 119
Santa Fe Railroad, 249
Sauk
  agriculture, 19
  forced migration, 9, 14, 19, 27, 28–29, 41, 42
  hunting, 19, 26
  land dispossession, 22, 31
  language, 15
  military power, 19
  Pike's exploration and, 23
  relations with the Meskwaki, 17, 18, 26
  settlements, 16, 19
  territory, 21
Saukenuk, 19, 20, 27–28
Savage, Candace, 11
Savery, Annie, 195
sawmill business, 166–167, 168
Scattergood Hostel in West Branch, 258
Schallau, Elsie Boddicker, 151
Scharnau, Ralph, 174
Scherer, Jacob, 141
Scholte, Dominee Hendrik Peter, 53
Schoolcraft, Henry, 20–21
schools
  absenteeism, 146
  Black students, 149–150, 157
  Black teachers, 150
  consolidation of, 286–287, 327
  construction of, 145
  daily life in, 146, 147
  desegregation of, 108
  discipline, 147–148
  districts and subdistricts, 144
  dropouts, 146, 152
  early, 134, 143
  economic crisis and, 308
  hazards in, 146
  layout, 146–147

INDEX 461

lessons, 147
libraries, 152
online learning, 339
physical punishment in, 148
private, 143, 144–145
reform of, 151
rural, 151–152
salaries at, 148
schedules, 146
semipublic, 144–145
student population, 308–309
urban, 152
See also high schools; one-room schoolhouses
Schumann, William, 213
Schwartz, Saul, 16
Schwieder, Dorothy, 52, 54, 125, 152, 171, 176, 186, 200
Iowa: The Middle Land, 3, 4
Schwieder, Elmer, 54, 171
Searle, Martha Turner, 94
Seashore, Carl, 147
Seddon, James, 293–294
Seed Corn Gospel Train, 200
Seltz, Robert, 254
Seneca Falls, 192
September 11 terrorist attacks, 328
service sector, 311
sewer system, 178–179
sex work, 180–181
Shackelford, Elizabeth, 271
Shakespearean Club in Osage, 162
Sharp, Helen Maria, 95
Sharp, John, 95
Shaw, Leslie, 198
Shellady, Stephen, 101
Shelton, Amanda, 99
Shelton, Mary, 99
Sherman, Hoyt, 85, 105
Sherman, William T., 92
Shiloh, Battle of, 90, 92–93, 104, 108
Shipley, Lonnie, 289
Shong, Ar, 126
Sietmann, Vernon, 261
Simpson College, 152, 153
Sinclair Company, 168
Sioux, 15, 21–22
  uprising in Minnesota, 84
Sioux City, Iowa
  canteen station, 210
  Charles Floyd monument, 23
  community center, 201–202
  establishment of, 70, 114
  industries, 169, 173
  Jews in, 257, 277

labor force in, 166
location of, 70
population of, 119, 165, 222
prohibition in, 191
racial segregation, 180
saloons and gambling halls, 180
trade center, 173–174
Sioux City Journal, 246
Sixtieth Colored Regiment, 4
Skunk River War, 101, 109
slavery, 32, 72, 73–74, 75, 76, 79, 80, 88. *See also* runaway slaves
smallpox epidemic, 16, 17, 43
Smith, Bruce, 329
Smith, Dan, 312
Smith, John, 34
Smith, Joseph, 48
Smith, Luther, Jr., 263–265
Smith, Neal, 237, 295
Smith, William, 34–35
snakes, 67, 158–159
Snyder, Seymour, 136
Socialist Party, 219–220
Social Security, 252
sod homes, 115
Solon, Iowa, *137*
Soper, Erastus B., 93
Soth, Lauren, 294
Soviet Union
  Nazi invasion of, 257
  war in Afghanistan, 303
soybeans, 301, 314, 316, 326, 327
Spedding, Frank, 274
Speer, Mary, 291
spelling bee competitions, 159
Spencer, John, 27
Spencer, Ralph, 163
Spencer Woman's Club, 162
Spirit Lake Massacre, 30, 83–84
sports, 13, 163
squatters, 39, 40
stagecoach service, 85, 86, 87
Standley, Patrick, 327
Stanton, Elizabeth Cady, 193
Stanton, Iowa, 141
state parks, 199
State University of Iowa (University of Iowa), 147, 153–154, 163
steamboats, 84, 86
Stech, Robert, 229
Stibbs, John, 104
Stillman, Isaiah, 29
Stillman's Run, Battle of, 29
Stone, William, 99, 107
Stoner, T. I., 177

Storm Lake, Iowa
  immigration to, 312, 331
  pork processing plant, 312
  public school system, 312–313
  racial tensions, 313
  refugees, 313
storms, 340
Story, Dorothy, 262
Street, Aaron, Jr., 139
Street, Joseph, 11
Stromquist, Shelton, 311
Stuart, Iowa, 158
suburbs, 279
Sudlow, Phoebe, 148
suffrage associations, 192
Sullivan, Alleta, 266
Sullivan, Thomas, 266
Sumbardo, Charles, 104
Sunday, William Ashley "Billy," 220–221
Sunday schools, 140
surveying, 38
Sutliff, A. C., 52
Swaggerty-Morgan, Chuck, 333
Swaggerty-Morgan, Jason, 333
Swedish immigrants, 53, 141
Swierenga, Robert P., 134
synagogues, 134

Taber, John, 216, 217
Tabor, Iowa, 72, 75, 79–80, 138
Taft-Hartley Act, 311
Tai Dam refugees, 297
Takes, Fred H., 217
Tally, George C., 101
Tally War, 101, 109
taxation, 229, 296–297
Taylor, Zachary, 27
teachers
  Black, 150
  certification, 151
  COVID-19 pandemic and, 339
  education of, 149, 150
  female, 148, 177
  income, 152, 289
  male, 151
  replacement, 152
technology, 165, 178
telephone service, 165, 181–182, *183*
temperance movement, 185, 186, 187–188, 190–191
Templeton, Iowa, 221
Terkel, Studs, 237, 266
Tharp, Rosemary, 270
theaters, 160–161
Third Iowa Regiment, 91
Thirty-Fourth Infantry Division, 266

Thirty-Seventh Iowa Infantry Regiment, 101–102
Thomas Sinclair Company, 168
Thompson, Bessie C., 158
Thompson, Richard, 309
Thompson, Seymour Dwight, 91
Thompson, Sharon, 309
Thompson, William, 113–114
Throne, Mildred, 68, 131
timber industry, 168
Tinker vs. Des Moines Independent Community School District, 293
Todd, John, 66
topsoil erosion, 317
toy factory, 290
transportation, 69, 72–73, 84–85
Trappist Abbey of New Melleray, 135
traveling shows, 160, 163
Trombly, Louis, 56
Truman, Harry S., 292
Trump, Donald, 322, 334, 335, 341
Tun, Min, 330
Turner, Asa, 138
Turner, Dan, 243
Turner, David, 98
Turner, Mary, 177
Twain, Mark, 161
Twedt, Jerry, 259, 260, 262
Twelfth Iowa Infantry Regiment, 104
Tyson Foods plant, 339

Ultra project, 274
underground railroad, 79, 81
unemployment, 203, 303, 310, 316, 325, 341
Union Pacific Railroad, 106, 118, 170
unions, 176, 296
United Mine Workers (UMW), 176
United States
  declaration of war to Japan, 258–259
  economic development, 303
  isolationism, 257
United States Dragoons, 35
universities
  establishment of, 153–154, 155
  female students, 155
  in postwar period, 279
  students, 154, 279
  tuition fees, 154
University of Dubuque, 152
University of Iowa, 134, 333, 337
University of Northern Iowa (Iowa State Normal School, Iowa State Teachers College), 155, 240, 279
Unmack, Dorothy, 217
Upper Iowa University, 152
Upper Mississippi River, 18, 23–24, 31

urban economy, 320
US Congress, Iowans in, 295, 319

vaccination, 278
Valdez, Ofelia Rumbo, 331–332
Van Buren, Martin, 37
Vandever, William, 91
Van Meter, Eula, 228
Van Zante, Mary, 159
Varnum, Kate, 332
Varnum, Patricia Hyde, 332
Varnum v. Brien, 332
Vermilion, Mary Alice, 94
Vicksburg, siege of, 90, 92, 94
Vietnamese boat people, 297
Vietnam War, 293–294
Vilsack, Tom, 319
voting rights for felons, 341

Wagner, Betty, 257
Wagner, Juanita, 257
Wah, Ah, 126
Waizman, Jacob, 277
Wakefield, John A., 29
Walker, Catiline, 78
Walker, John, 76, 77
Walker, Mary, 77
Wall, Joseph Frazier, 119, 136, 156
Wallace, Henry A., 153, 246–247
Wallace, Henry C., 247
Wallace, William, 127
Wallace's Farmer, 246
Wallace's Ferry, Battle of, 104
Walmart stores, 309
Wapello (leader of the Meskwaki), 42
Ward, Martie, 240
War of 1812, 26
Warren, Wilson J., 169
Wartburg College, 153
water delivery, 179
Waterloo, Iowa
  population decline, 309
  racial uprising in, 284
  segregation, 280
weather, 66–67, 116, 239, 335–336
Weaver, James B., 132, 133
Webb, Archie, 127, 128
Webb, Horace, 116, 129
Webster City, Iowa, 120, 159
Webster County, 122
West, Elliott, 146
Westphal, David, 302, 305
Wetzel, Velma, 291
wheat production, 299
Whig Party, 80
White, Charles A., 41, 84

White Cloud (Mahaska), 17
Whited, Alice, 155
Wiggins, Florence Roe, 59
wildlife, 11, 12, 23, 199
Wilhelm, Harley, 274
Wilkinson, H. E., 202, 204, 225
Wilkinson, John M., 243
Willard, Frances, 190
Williams, David, 67
Williams, Reuben, 67
Wilson, James G., 153, 198, 199
Wilson, T. S., 46, 47
Wilson, William E., 208
Wilson, Woodrow, 210–211
wind industry, 328
Winebrenner, Hugh, 320
Winkie, Clara Saride, 253
Wirz, Henry, 104
Wisconsin Territory, 32
Wittenmyer, Annie Turner
  care for the orphans, 99
  charity work, 97–98
  as Iowa sanitary agent, 98–99, 109
  portrait of, *97*
  WCTU President, 190
Wittenmyer, William, 98
Woida, Kathleen, 11
women
  during Civil War, 94–98
  control of sexuality, 181
  daily life, 55, 58–60
  during farm crisis, 306–308
  farm work, 94–95
  food drives, 241
  during Great Depression, 243
  humanitarian work, 97–98
  meal preparation, 58–59
  occupations, 58, 59–60, 177, 291
  patriotism, 196–197
  postwar employment, 290–292
  right to vote, 192–197
  in teaching profession, 148
  as telephone operators, 182, *183*
  temperance movement, 188, 190
  wages, 291
  during World War I, 208–210
  during World War II, 267, 268, *268*, 269, 270–271
Women Airforce Service Pilots (WASPs), 269
Women's Army Auxiliary Corps (WAAC), 269–271
Women's Army Corps (WAC), 256
Women's Christian Temperance Union (WCTU), 188, 190
women's clubs, 134, 157, 164
women's suffrage, 185, 191–193, 194, 195, 205

Wood, Grant, 251–252, *251*
Woodhull, Victoria, 193–194
Woodland Tradition, 12–13
Woods, Mehitable, 97
Wookey, Faye Elsie Tomilinson, 239, 272
Works Progress Administration (WPA), 249, 250, 251
World War I
   African Americans in, 213–215
   American troops in, 207, 208, 213, 215
   ban of foreign languages, 212–213
   canteen stations, 209–210
   civil liberties during, 212
   economic impact of, 207, 208
   end of progressive reforms, 206
   equipment shortages, 213
   fatalities, 207, 215, 216–217
   financing of, 210–211
   food conservation campaign, 210
   German Americans and, 212
   hospital trains, 209
   Iowans in, 209, 215–217
   Liberty Loans (war bonds), 210–211
   outcome of, 256
   propaganda, 212
   recovery from, 219
   recruits, 213
   Red Cross activities, 208–209
   renaming of cities and banks during, 213
   Russia's peace treaty, 215
   social impact of, 207
   submarine warfare, 208
   suffrage and, 196–197
   training camps, 213, 214, 215
   volunteers, 210
World War II
   African Americans in, 264–265
   bond drives, 261–262
   casualties, 261, 266–267
   celebration of the end of, 276–277
   collection of scrap materials, 260
   corn production, 271–272
   economic impact of, 256, 271–272, 275
   entertainment during, 261
   food rationing, 260
   industrial production, 259–260
   Iowans in, 259–260, 262–266
   labor force, 267, 272
   Native Americans in, 263
   outbreak of, 256–257
   Pearl Harbor attack, 258–259
   persecution of Jews, 257
   prisoner-of-war camps, 272–273
   refugees, 258
   salvage committees, 260
   tires and gasoline rationing, 260–261
   training centers, 256
   victory gardens, 261
   women during, 267–271
Wright, David Sands, 155–156
Wright, Henry W., 62
Wright, Merle, 209
Wyatt, Jabe, 43
Wyatt, Susan, 43–44, 58

Yambura, Barbara S., 55
Yarmouth, Iowa, 156
Yosemite National Park, 227
Young, Neil, 308
Youngbear, Dewey, 263
Younker Brothers firm, 142

Zaehringer, Clinton, 285
Zaehringer, Corinne, 285
Zaring, Noah, 96
Zelle, Arthur, 217
Zimansky, Curt, 274
Zimmer, Eric, 83

www.ingramcontent.com/pod-product-compliance
Lightning Source LLC
Chambersburg PA
CBHW031721230426
43669CB00007B/196